LABOR LAW IN CONTRACTORS' LANGUAGE

Engineering News-Record Series

Stokes International Construction Contracts

Guttman The International Consultant

Stokes Construction Law in Contractors' Language

Stokes Labor Law in Contractors' Language

LABOR LAW IN CONTRACTORS' LANGUAGE

McNEILL STOKES

McGRAW-HILL BOOK COMPANY

New York   St. Louis   San Francisco
Auckland   Bogotá   Düsseldorf   Johannesburg
London   Madrid   Mexico   Montreal   New Delhi
Panama   Paris   São Paulo   Singapore   Sydney
Tokyo   Toronto

Library of Congress Cataloging in Publication Data

Stokes, McNeill.
    Labor law in contractors' language.

    Includes index.
    1. Construction workers—Legal status, laws, etc.—
United States. 2. Collective labor agreements—Con-
struction industry—United States. I. Title.
KF3580.C6S78   344′.73′01769   79-15883
ISBN 0-07-061650-7

1234567890   KPKP   89876543210

The editors for this book were Jeremy Robinson and Tobia L. Worth,
the designer was Bill Frost, and the production supervisor
was Sally L. Fliess. It was set in Century Schoolbook
by KBC/Rocappi.

Printed and bound by The Kingsport Press.

DEDICATION

I acknowledge the great help and guidance that I have received over the years from my father, Jordan Stokes, III, who kicked me out of the nest early to deal with unions and labor law. I could not have learned from a better teacher. He has had more than 50 years of experience in the practice of law, and he filed one of the first cases under the National Labor Relations Act in 1936.

CONTENTS

109974

PREFACE

Legal problems are inherent in every stage of general contractors' and subcontractors' daily business. No matter how conscientious contractors may be about referring legal matters to their attorneys, natural limitations of expense and time make it neither feasible nor desirable to submit every-day business to an attorney's scrutiny. Many of these daily legal problems arise within the context of labor relations. Everyone associated with the building industry must have some basic acquaintance with the legal problems involved in the context of labor relations. It is therefore important that general contractors and subcontractors be aware of their legal rights and liabilities in dealing with their employees or the union representing their employees, or both.

One of the purposes of this book is to make those associated with the construction industry more deeply conscious of the facets of labor law that affect their day-to-day business. Contractors must be aware of situations in which they can benefit from the law and must also recognize legal pitfalls in time to safeguard their interests. In many instances, their knowledge of labor law helps them to avoid problems that might otherwise arise. When legal questions of immediate or potential importance arise, however, a lawyer should be consulted.

The national labor law had its genesis in 1932, during the Depression, when the Norris-LaGuardia Act set a public policy giving employees freedom of association, self-organization, and designation of representatives of their own choosing, as well as the rights of collective bargaining to negotiate the terms and conditions of their employment, and guaranteeing these rights free from interference. The act also prohibited federal courts from issuing injunctions in most labor disputes.

The National Labor Relations Act (NLRA), popularly known as the Wagner Act, was originally enacted in 1935 and paralleled the earlier Railway Labor Act. It covered employers whose activities involved interstate commerce, provided machinery for election by secret ballot of a representative of the employees for the purposes of collective bargaining, and prohibited as unfair labor practices an employer's interference with the rights of employees or discrimination against employees with regard to union activity. The employer was required to bargain collectively with a duly authorized representative of the employees.

In 1947 the Labor-Management Relations Act (LMRA), commonly called the Taft-Hartley Act, amended the NLRA to cover union unfair labor practices and to prohibit unions from interfering with the rights of employees. It also outlawed secondary boycotts and jurisdictional disputes in most instances.

In 1959 the NLRA was again amended by the Labor-Management Reporting and Disclosure Act, commonly called the Landrum-Griffin Act, which was aimed at prohibiting certain corrupt practices and added provisions applicable to subcontract clauses and prehire contracts in the construction industry. It also vested the federal courts with jurisdiction over suits under collective bargaining agreements and damage suits against labor organizations.

The NLRA established the National Labor Relations Board (NLRB), an administrative agency composed of five members sitting in Washington and having jurisdiction throughout the United States. In practice, the Board operates through regional offices headed by regional directors who have authority to hold elections in the representative process and to investigate and prosecute unfair labor practices. A complaining party typically initiates a complaint of unfair labor practice by filing with a regional office a charge which is then investigated by an NLRB agent or attorney. If probable cause that the company or union has committed an unfair labor practice is found to exist, a complaint is issued by the NLRB, which prosecutes the complaint as an advocate before an administrative law judge from another division of the Board. The administrative law judge holds hearings and then makes findings of facts and conclusions of law as to whether an unfair labor practice has been committed. The judge's findings are reviewable by a panel of members of the NLRB.

The Board typically orders the offending party to cease and desist from continuing to violate the act and requires posting appropriate notices or remedial back pay when appropriate, or both. NLRB orders are not self-executing but must be enforced in a court of appeals located where the employer or union committed the unfair labor practice.

Labor law is a constantly expanding field. The development of a national labor law policy has brought a burgeoning of case laws and rulings that provide a long list of contractors' "do's and don'ts" vis-à-vis their employees or the union, or both. Similarly, employees and unions are prohibited from taking certain actions, and contractors may avail themselves of the labor laws to protect their business in such situations. Aside from these laws, collective bargaining agreements may be tailored, within limits, to further define contractors', employees', and unions' respective rights and duties.

Gone are the days when contractors were free to conduct labor relations without interference. At present, they must carry on their business within the limitations imposed by various laws. Federal labor laws set wage and hour standards, prohibit employment discrimination, and regulate occupational safety and health and employee retirement income and security. The development of labor law has largely been an attempt to accommodate contractors' interests in being able to run their own business with employees' and unions' interests in being protected against particular actions by employers. Labor law has further defined limitations on particular types of agreements between contractors and unions. Contractors are well advised to know what they can and cannot do under the law so that they may avoid problems that might cripple their business.

This book is organized to reflect chronologically the process of labor relations for contractors or subcontractors in the construction industry. Chapter 1 discusses the hiring of employees; the peculiarities of the construction industry are reflected in the special laws applicable to hiring within it. Because jobs in the industry are of short duration and contractors often must get skilled labor on short notice, many contractors have hiring-hall agreements with the particular union. Sometimes these agreements may lawfully provide that an employee must become a union member within a certain time. Contractors should be aware of employers' and unions' rights and liabilities under such agreements.

Once employees have been hired, contractors must know what types of discharge and disciplinary policies they may lawfully implement. If contractors run afoul of the law, they may be required to reinstate employees with back pay. Under the law, employees have various protected rights, and contractors act unlawfully where they take certain actions that infringe upon these rights. Moreover, a contractor's discharge policies may conflict with the applicable collective bargaining agreement. A knowledge of the law in this area will enable construction contractors to run their business more effectively while abiding by the spirit of the law.

Contractors encounter special problems when employees strike or honor another union's picket line. They should know under what conditions work stoppages are unlawful and when strikes and picketing are unlawful. This book seeks to inform contractors what relief they may lawfully pursue against unlawful strikes and picketing. A prevalent union tactic in the construction industry involves attempts to coerce a contractor in the selection or retention of representatives for collective bargaining or the adjustment of grievances. Often a union attempts to have an employer fire a supervisor who is also a union member or threatens to strike if the contractor does not take certain actions against the supervisor-member. Sometimes the union threatens to strike to force a contractor either to join or to withdraw from a contractors' bargaining association. In these areas, contractors must know when the union violates the law and what their remedies are.

Another area of concern for construction contractors involves agreements with unions on the contracting or subcontracting of work to be done at the jobsite. A union has an incentive to press for these types of agreements, which preserve work for its members. Contractors should know the circumstances under which they would act unlawfully in agreeing to this type of provision and the impact it would have on their ability to compete. Furthermore, contractors should be aware of their remedies against a union that seeks to enforce unlawful restrictions.

A recurring problem in the construction industry is work assignment or jurisdictional disputes, in which a union strikes or pickets to force a contractor to assign work to its members rather than to those of another union. Jurisdictional strikes and picketing, or even threats by a union to strike or picket, are unlawful, and contractors should know what remedies are available to combat the union's unlawful act.

Also of special concern are secondary boycotts, in which a union strikes or pickets a neutral contractor to force it to cease doing business with a contractor with whom the union has a dispute or to force the latter contractor to recognize it. Because many contractors normally work alongside each other on a common jobsite (common situs), it is often difficult to determine whether an illegal secondary boycott exists. Contractors caught in this type of dispute have available unfair-labor-practice, injunction, and damage suit remedies which they should not hesitate to utilize.

Once a union has been recognized as the exclusive bargaining agent for the employees, a contractor has the obligation to bargain in good faith over the terms and conditions of employment. This book will examine when the duty to bargain arises and what subjects are mandatory. It will also outline some of the tactics and contract clauses that may be used by contractors and their bargaining agents to obtain favorable collective bargaining agreements.

Another area of concern involves various types of fringe benefit funds for employees, under which union and contractor may have various duties and liabilities. The duties of a contractor in administering such funds will be examined.

There is a growing movement among contractors in the construction industry to go "dual shop." Under particular circumstances, contractors may establish and maintain independent parts of their business and be union in one operation and nonunion in another. This book will also touch upon the factors which an open-shop contractor must know to avoid being organized by a union, and how to mix union and nonunion contractors on the same jobsite.

Federal laws regulate the pay and hours of work for contractors' employees, employment discrimination, and occupational safety and health. Much of the construction contracting business involves work under contract with the federal government. One requirement for contractors who bid on a government project is that they pay "prevailing wages" as determined by the Secretary of Labor.

The chapters of this book are designed to point out some of the many realities concerning labor law and labor relations on a construction project. The book attempts to treat the subject in a practical manner and in plain language so that it may readily be understood by general contractors, subcontractors, owners, and design professionals as well as attorneys. The text is based on actual cases decided by courts, the NLRB, and various administrative agencies. Included are illustrative cases so that the reader may obtain a general understanding of the fundamental principles of labor law in the construction industry. The statements made herein are not intended as a substitute for legal advice from an experienced attorney in a specific factual setting.

MCNEILL STOKES

ACKNOWLEDGMENTS

I would like to acknowledge with gratitude the assistance and inspiration of the late William Dunn, formerly executive vice president of the Associated General Contractors of America, who convinced me of the need of the construction industry for a comprehensive book on construction labor law.

I would also like to acknowledge the invaluable contributions of the many association and individual clients who helped me gain an insight into the specialized field of construction labor law. Particularly, I wish to thank Joe F. Canterbury, Jr., attorney at law; Peter A. Cockshaw, editor, *Construction Labor News + Opinion*; Joe Baker and Tom McGlone of the Association of Wall and Ceiling Industries International; George Peterson of the Atlanta chapter, National Electrical Contractors Association; Donald D. Clark and James Ray of the Sheet Metal and Air-Conditioning Contractors of America; Debby Imle Miller, director of labor relations, National Association of Home Builders; Harry Taylor, formerly president of the Council of Construction Employers; and representatives of the American Subcontractors Association and the National Roofing Contractors Association, without whose help and guidance this book would not have been as practical and comprehensive.

I am particularly grateful to John P. Trimmer and Joseph C. Fagan of the Associated Builders and Contractors, Inc., for their assistance in writing Chapter 12, "Merit Shop," and to the Special Agreements Task Force of the Business Roundtable Construction Committee and E. D. Hoekstra and Maurice L. Mosier of the National Constructors Association for their assistance in writing Chapter 7, "Special Agreements."

I would like to express my gratitude for the assistance of Ira J. Smotherman, Jr., Herman L. Fussell, Lloyd A. Fox, Peter R. Spanos, Sally A. Blackmun, and Neil C. Schemm of Stokes & Shapiro, and I would like to show my appreciation for the many hours of legal research by David Ness and James Richter while they were students at Emory University Law School. I would like to acknowledge the assistance of Betty S. Murphy, member and former chairman of the National Labor Relations Board; D. Quinn Mills, former assistant to the Secretary of Labor and professor of business at Harvard University; Charles Harding, senior editor, *Engineering News-Record*; Henry A. Huettner, attorney at law, Fischer & Phillips; and Molly Warner, attorney at law, Seward & Kissel.

I am extremely grateful for the support and understanding of my wife, Judy, and my children, Ford and Ashley Stokes, which have been invaluable during the long periods of time that I have necessarily spent in writing this book.

LABOR LAW IN CONTRACTORS' LANGUAGE

1 HIRING

A construction project cannot proceed in a timely and efficient manner unless the contractor is able to hire a sufficient number of skilled workers. Because of the peculiar nature of the construction industry, special hiring laws and practices have evolved among contractors. Since many construction projects are intermittent, a contractor need hire a workforce for only a limited time. To be assured of sufficient qualified workers, many contractors have agreed with the building trades unions to hire through what are known as "hiring halls." In the construction industry the parties to a hiring-hall arrangement may agree to require employees to become union members after 7 days from the commencement of their employment, as opposed to the 30-day period in effect in other industries. (These agreements, which are known as "union security provisions," are not permitted in right-to-work states.) Contractors often work in different localities and are concerned with having a ready supply of labor as they begin projects in each area; therefore, they are permitted to contract with the unions concerning hiring, union security, and any other terms and conditions of employment before a single employee has been hired. Such prehire agreements are unlawful in other industries. Finally, collective bargaining in the construction industry is normally handled on the local level by associations on behalf of groups of employers. Such multiemployer bargaining counterbalances the trade unions' great bargaining leverage.

Hiring halls, union security provisions, and prehire agreements each have a great impact upon contractors' relations with their employees. This chapter discusses each of these three topics so that contractors may be better informed on how to conduct hiring policies.

HIRING HALLS

Over the years the hiring hall has been considered by many contractors to be the most convenient means for meeting their fluctuating labor force requirements. Taken as a whole, the hiring hall has relieved contractors of the difficulty and expense of maintaining their own personnel functions. However, that benefit has been gained at the costly expense of creating a major base of union power and of badly handicapping the contractors' ability to manage their workforces.

Hiring-hall procedures vary considerably. Like so many aspects of the construction industry, the work referral systems in practice are complex and varied. They may be exclusive or nonexclusive, formal or informal, and they may be established by long-standing practice or by contract.

A few agreements permit a contractor to hire new employees without going through the union's referral procedure. This method obviously has the advantage of permitting the contractor to select employees upon the basis of qualifications while giving the contractor the option of obtaining employees from the union hall. Most contracts require the exclusive use of hiring halls or, in actual practice, a method approaching the exclusive hiring-hall procedure. Section 8(f)(3) of the National Labor Relations Act (NLRA) permits a construction contractor and a building trades union to make an agreement which requires the contractor "to notify such labor organization of opportunities for employment with such employer, or to give the labor organization an opportunity to refer qualified applicants for employment." A pure hiring-hall agreement would obligate management to hire only workers referred by the union. This procedure tends to relieve the contractor of the problems and costs of operating a personnel department. At the same time, however, it creates a base of union power and severely curtails the ability of the contractor to control the quality of the workforce.

Through hard bargaining with unions, contractors may obtain a hiring procedure which best fulfills their needs. Contractors should examine the effectiveness and possible disadvantages of the various procedures in their locality and particular trade. They should seek a provision which will both assure a sufficient labor supply and permit control of the quality of the workforce. A hiring clause which might achieve these dual goals would permit a union to refer applicants and effectively reserve the contractors' right to reject unqualified applicants without fear of reprisal by the union. The clause should also provide that if the union fails to provide qualified applicants within a certain time after a referral request has been made, contractors may hire whomever they please or allow contractors to utilize either the hiring hall or any other source which will enable them readily to acquire a skilled labor force.

These management rights are rarely exercised by management. Contractors have generally been much too willing to let unions administer referral systems on their own in an arbitrary and discriminatory manner so as to deny contractors a sufficient supply of capable workers. Union officials are often biased against nonunion applicants, members of sister locals, and union members opposed to the union leadership. Some skilled craftsmen have even been denied referrals for refusing to limit their output to a predetermined amount of work fixed by a union local. Applicants have been forced to make illegal promises or payments as a condition of referral.

Contractors with hiring-hall agreements who want to regain some control over their labor force must insist to the union that the referral system be administered in a lawful manner and in the way in which the union has agreed with the contractors to operate it. The union's administration of the hiring hall must be monitored, and contractors should insist that the union promptly reform its procedures if the hall is not being operated properly.

A hiring-hall clause is unlawful if it discriminates among job applicants according to whether they are members of the union local administering the hall. This is true because Sections 8(a)(3) and 8(b)(1)(A) of the NLRA make it an unfair labor practice for contractor or union to discriminate in regard to conditions of employment in order to encourage union membership. A contractor who agrees to and enforces such a clause against an applicant commits an unfair labor practice and may be jointly and severally liable with the union in an award of back pay to the applicant. If the union insists that an illegal hiring clause be included in a contract as a condition to further bargaining or to final agreement or threatens to or actually strikes or pickets for its inclusion, the contractor may file charges of unfair labor practice with the National Labor Relations Board (NLRB) against the union.

Even discrimination in hiring directed against members of sister locals of a union may be an unfair labor practice. For example, a contractor who agrees to restrict referrals under the hiring hall to members of the union local acts unlawfully. Similarly, a provision which places applicants who are not members of the union local but might be members of a sister local on a lower-priority list may be illegal. However, these nonmember applicants may properly be excluded or given a lower priority for job referrals when the standards for referral are based upon other considerations which are lawful. Under Section 8(f)(4) of the NLRA, the contractor and a building trades union may specify "minimum training or experience qualifications for employment or provide for priority in opportunities for employment based upon length of service with such employer, in the industry, or in the particular geographical area."

It is often unclear whether a hiring-hall provision or its application discriminates according to local-union membership. An agreement that gave priority in referrals to one group over another might be lawful if the contractor could demonstrate that this decision was motivated by legitimate considerations. The contractor might show that there was no unlawful motivation to encourage union membership by the fact that not all members of the favored group were necessarily local-union members. Or the contracts could justify the agreement by proof that many members of the disfavored group were members of the union local. However, it is no defense to claim that the nonunion employees could easily join the union, because such discriminatory treatment nonetheless would operate unlawfully to encourage union membership.

Hiring hall agreements which grant priority in job referrals to employees who previously worked for employers subject to collective bargaining agreements with the union may be illegal under the NLRA. Section 8(f)(4) allows a hiring hall to grant priority to a worker "based upon length of service with *such* employer, in the industry or in the particular geographical area." The issue arises whether "such employer" includes a single employer only or whether "such employer" includes any employer for which the employee has worked under union-negotiated collective bargaining agreements in the union's geographical area.

The NLRB has ruled that construction unions may lawfully maintain and enforce an exclusive hiring-hall contract which grants priority in job referrals based on an applicant's length of service with contractors who have collective bargaining contracts with the union. Also, the NLRB held that this group of contractors need not be limited to those who either bargained on an individual basis with the unions or were members of contractor associations but may also include contractors who came into the area and agreed to be bound by the agreement's terms.

However, the Court of Appeals for the Tenth Circuit has recently overruled the NLRB's interpretation of Section 8(f)(4) and has held that hiring-hall arrangements linking job referral preferences to prior work experience with employers signatory to multiemployer bargaining agreements are illegal under the NLRA. The court found that Section 8(f)(4) only permits preferences limited to prior service for the particular employer to whom the employee is referred, and that general preferences linked to service with the unionized employers in a given area unlawfully encourages union membership.

Illustrative Case

The Wyoming Chapter of the National Electrical Contractors Association (NECA) entered into a series of collective bargaining agreements with Local 322 of the Electrical Workers which covered both members of the NECA chapter and other contractors who would come into the area and agree to be bound by their terms. The most recent contract contained an exclusive hiring-hall agreement which granted the highest priority in job referrals and retention to employees who had worked 1 out of the last 4 years for a contractor who was either a member of the NECA chapter or had agreed to be bound by the collective bargaining agreement. Individual employee Paul H. Robertson charged the employer, Bechtel Power Company, with violating Section 8(a)(1) and (3) and Local 322 of the Electrical Workers with violating Section 8(b)(1)(a) of the National Labor Relations Act. The Court of Appeals ruled that the hiring-hall arrangement giving priority to employees who had been employed under a collective bargaining agreement was discriminatory on its face. The court stated that the plain meaning of Section 8(f)(4) referred to a single employer only and that any other construction would have the foreseeable consequence of illegal discrimination in favor of applicants who had worked for unionized employers and who were very likely to be union members. In a companion case involving the same hiring hall, the court found that in practice the union did not permit referrals of nonunion workers from its hiring hall, and ordered the employer to reinstate Robertson with back pay to be paid by the employer and the union.[1]

One reason why contractors agree to use the hiring halls of different union locals is that they have done little work in the particular area before and consider such a hiring hall necessary to provide a ready supply of skilled workers. Another, not so legitimate reason is that many contractors

[1] Robertson v. NLRB, ___ F.2d ___ (10th Cir. 1979).

erroneously believe that when they begin work in an area, they are required to accede to the area agreement between the union local and the contractors' association, including its provision for an exclusive hiring-hall arrangement. The contractor has a lawful right to bargain on whether or not to use a union's hiring hall.

A negative effect of agreeing to use a union local's exclusive referral system may be that the contractor will have to discharge an entire crew and replace it with workers referred by the union when the contractor commences work in the local's jurisdiction. If the agreement is based on lawful considerations as to applicants' length of service in the area and is not used to discriminate against some employees because they are not members of the local, the local may strike or picket to enforce the lawful contract and require the contractor to terminate the employment of the original crew.

Illustrative Case

Marino was awarded a subcontract for the installation of sewer and water lines. Prior to commencing work Marino agreed to abide by the terms of the general contractor's agreement with Operating Engineers Local 542, which provided that the union was the exclusive source of referrals unless it could not supply workers within a 24-hour period after notice to do so. Marino already had a four-man crew who were members of a different local of the Operating Engineers and sought to use that crew on its work in Local 54's jurisdiction. Local 542's business manager threatened to shut down the project if Marino's crew were not terminated and replaced by individuals referred by the local. Marino complied and terminated the regular crew, substituting referrals from Local 542. Two of the discharged employees filed Section 8(b)(1)(A) and Section 8(b)(2) unfair-labor-practice charges against Local 542 for attempting to cause and causing an employer to discriminate against them for not being members of Local 542. The NLRB held the Local 542 did not violate the NLRA and was entitled to enforce the hiring-hall provision by threats against Marino since the provision was based on considerations of employees' length of service in the area, permitted under Section 8(f)(4). Since members of the original crew were not denied employment because of lack of membership in Local 542 but rather because they had not utilized the lawful referral system mandated in the contract, Local 542 could properly enforce the contract by threatening to halt work unless Marino discharged the employees who had bypassed the referral system.[2]

Even though the hiring-hall agreement on its face is limited to lawful considerations permitted under Section 8(f)(4) and states that the referral procedure will not be used to discriminate because of membership or nonmembership in the union local, the union will have committed Section 8(b)(1)(A) and Section 8(B)(2) unfair labor practices if the system has in fact been administered to discriminate against travelers (members of sister locals who are not members of the local). If the contractor is threatened with a strike or picketing or other coercive action unless the contractor terminates the work crew and if the contractor can show that the union has operated the hiring hall in a discriminatory manner, then the contractor

[2]Local 542, Operating Engineers (Marino), 151 NLRB No. 55 (1965).

need not yield to the union's demands and should file unfair-labor-practice charges against the union.

A contract clause making competence a basis for hiring is not illegal even if the test is administered solely by union members. This is true because the NLRA allows an agreement to specify "minimum training or experience qualifications for employment." Such an agreement would be illegal if it were applied so that either membership in the union local were a prerequisite for taking the test or test results were disregarded in favor of local-union members.

Illustrative Case

Local 592 of the Electrical Workers refused to refer an applicant from another union local. There was a provision in the hiring-hall agreement that a prerequisite to referral was an applicant's passage of journeymen's test. The applicant failed this test. Since these test standards were "essential to the union's representation of its employees" and since they were enforced in a nondiscriminatory manner, the NLRB held that the union had not committed an unfair labor practice.[3]

When the union administering the hiring hall has a union security clause in the agreement, it may lawfully deny use of the hiring hall to employees who have failed to tender their initiation fees and periodic dues after 7 days (or a longer period if provided by the contract) from the commencement of employment. Employees who fall into union disfavor for any other reason may not be discriminated against by the union through its use of the hiring hall. This is true because Section 8(b)(2) prohibits a union from causing or attempting to cause a contractor to discriminate "against an employee with respect to whom membership has been denied or terminated on some grounds other than the failure to tender the periodic dues and the initiation fees uniformly required as a condition of acquiring or retaining membership." Under some conditions a union may lawfully impose and collect a fine or impose other discipline against a member for failure to participate in a legitimate union activity, but the union violates the NLRA if it retaliates either by denying the member a place on the job referral or retention lists or by placing the number on a lower-priority list than the member would otherwise occupy.

A union may not operate a hiring hall so as to penalize employees for engaging in a protected concerted activity. For example, a union operates a hiring hall unlawfully if it either denies referral or places on a lower-priority list an employee who files unfair-labor-practice charges against the union. An unlawful motivation may be found by first determining the position the applicant would have held on the list if the established procedure had been followed and then comparing that position with the position the applicant actually did occupy on the list.

[3] *IBEW Local 592*, 223 NLRB No. 139 (1976).

Illustrative Case

An applicant had filed charges with the NLRB against Local 25 of the Electrical Workers. The employee contended that the local had operated an exclusive hiring hall in an improper manner, and thereby had breached its duty of impartial representation of employees, by giving referrals to some employees even though they had signed up on the list after the complaining employee. The local could offer no justification for deviating from the referral procedure which gave priority to those who signed up earliest. Since its motive for refusing to refer this applicant was that he had filed charges with NLRB against the union, the NLRB held that the local violated the NLRA in its operation of the hiring hall.[4]

The union may not condition its agreement to refer a nonmember applicant upon a promise by the applicant that is not also requested from union-member applicants. By imposing this condition only on nonmembers, the union commits an unfair labor practice of discriminating in regard to a condition of employment in order to encourage union membership unlawfully.

Illustrative Case

Local 630 of the Plumbers, which operated an exclusive hiring hall, refused to permit nonmembers to sign an out-of-work list. Also, the union conditioned an agreement to refer nonmembers upon their promise to quit their jobs on request to make room for members to their take jobs. According to the NLRB, the Plumbers local operated the hiring hall in an unlawful manner by imposing conditions for referral on nonmembers which were not also imposed on union members.[5]

A union administering an exclusive hiring hall has a duty to conduct it in a manner that is fair to all applicants. Therefore, when a union agent deviates from the established referral procedure and refers applicants according to irrelevant grounds or personal preference, the union acts unlawfully whether or not the applicants denied referral are union members. Arbitrary action by the union in its administration of the hiring hall harms contractors since they are deprived of the hiring procedure which they have bargained for with the union, and they will sometimes be denied capable and experienced workers. In addition, employee morale may be harmed by the union's unfair and unregulated referral practices, and this will in turn injure the contractors.

Illustrative Case

Local 433 of the Ironworkers repeatedly violated the terms of the hiring-hall agreement by dispatching individuals not eligible for dispatch since their names were not on the out-of-work list and by giving some of them referral slips at places outside the hiring hall without notifying other applicants at the hiring hall of these jobs. The union violated the NLRA by breaching its duty of fair representation in the operation of the hiring hall. The NLRB reasoned that "instances of 'backdooring' were so pervasive as to substantially undermine the hiring hall procedure and replace objective procedures in the hiring hall contract with the union agent's own 'clandestine desires.' "[6]

[4] *IBEW Local 25 (S. & M. Electric Co.)*, 223 NLRB No. 223 (1976).

[5] *Plumbers Local 630 (Ebasco Services, Inc.)*, 222 NLRB No. 82 (1976).

[6] *Ironworkers Local 433 (AGC of California)*, 228 NLRB No. 181 (1977).

A union's duty of fair representation also encompasses an obligation to deal fairly with an applicant's request for information concerning the applicant's status on a job referral or retenion list.

Illustrative Case

Local 324 of the Operating Engineers denied an unemployed applicant's request for information concerning his position on a job referral list of an exclusive hiring hall. The NLRB held that the union breached its duty of fair representation by denying the applicant's request for the names, addresses, and telephone numbers of employees above and below him on the out-of-work list.[7]

A union may lawfully threaten to or actually picket or strike a contractor who has hired employees outside the agreed-upon hiring-hall procedure. Sometimes, however, the union has the mistaken albeit good-faith belief that the employee is required to go through the hiring hall. If this is the case, the union commits an unfair labor practice by wrongfully attempting to cause the contractor to discriminate against the employee. In such cases, the contractor may file an unfair-labor-practice charge against the union so that the Board may seek to enjoin the unlawful strike or picketing.

Illustrative Case

Bricklayers Local 7 walked off the job in an effort to have the contractor discharge an employee on the ground that this employee had not gone through the hiring hall. However, the employee had merely gone on vacation and was not required to go through the hiring hall since he was not a new hire. The union violated the NLRA since it had no legitimate reason to seek the employee's discharge. The NLRB stated had there was no legitimate reason to enforce the hiring-hall procedure.[8]

Use of the hiring hall exists by virtue of the contractor's and union's agreement, yet in normal operation the system of referring applicants for work is administered largely by the union. Union business agents are often susceptible to internal union pressures to refer union members for work over travelers even though the agreement on its face specifies that the hiring hall will be operated in a nondiscriminatory fashion. Contractors should try to remain aware of how the referral system is being operated, since its improper administration may often deny the contractor the use of capable workers. Furthermore, in some instances the contractor might be liable in a back-pay award for the union's unfair labor practice even though the contractor actually had no improper motivation for refusing to hire the job applicant. When the contractor knows or has reason to know that an applicant was denied referral or placed on a lower-priority list for an unlawful reason, the contractor commits a Section 8(a)(3) unfair labor practice and might be required to pay at least part of the back-pay that the applicant would have received but for the union's illegal action. If the contractor discovers that the union had administered the hiring hall illegally, the

[7] Operating Engineers Local 324, 226 NLRB No. 91 (1976).

[8] Bricklayers Local 7, 224 NLRB No. 19 (1976).

contractor should insist that union promptly correct its procedures. The contractor should emphasize to the union that otherwise both of them might incur monetary damages. It is no defense for the contractor to claim compliance with the union's unlawful demands solely to avert the threat of a crippling work stoppage. When this situation arises, the contractor should refrain from giving in to the union's illegal demand. Instead, the contractor may file unfair-labor-practice charges with the Board. And if there is reason to believe that the union will engage in the illegal work stoppage, an injunction prohibiting it might be obtainable by the Board.

Illustrative Case

Utility & Industrial Construction Co., which was involved in pipeline construction work, and Laborers Local 1076 entered into an exclusive hiring-hall agreement. The agreement did not contain a union security provision. Subsequently, the contractor desired to lay off two union members who had been referred by the union because of their "lack of performance." However, the union steward informed the contractor that it should first lay off two nonunion employees whom the contractor had originally brought to the project. So the company laid off these two nonunion employees first, even though under its prior layoff policy it made layoffs according to competence to perform the work. When the nonunion employees were laid off first, the contractor told them that they were laid off because of the union's request and that the union's demand was due to the employees' membership in a sister local. The contractor and Laborers Local 1076 both committed unfair labor practices. The NLRB stated that a union with an exclusive hiring-hall system acts unlawfully when it causes a contractor to discharge an employee on the ground that the employer is a member of a sister local and there is no union security provision, and the contractor violates the NLRA by discharging this employee when it knows that to be the reason.[9]

UNION SECURITY AGREEMENTS

Often a union negotiating for a prehire contract will seek a union security agreement. This type of clause requires an employee to become a union member 7 days after the commencement of employment or after the execution date of the agreement, whichever is later. The 7-day period is merely the minimum period that must be available to the employee to become a union member; a longer period may be agreed upon. The contractor and the union both act unlawfully if they set the execution date of the contract prior to the time of execution.

Although the NLRA permits union security agreements, it also allows individual states to pass right-to-work laws prohibiting them. When a union seeks to bargain for a union security agreement, the contractor is well advised first to determine if the state in which the agreement is to be executed or in which a major portion of the work is to be done has a right-to-work law. If the state has a right-to-work law, the contractor should not even consider agreeing to a union security provision. If the contractor agrees to and maintains a union security clause in a right-to-work state, the contractor may be in violation of the state law and may be required to offer

[9]*Utility & Indus. Constr. Co.*, 214 NLRB No.152 (1974).

reinstatement to an employee with back pay from the time of wrongful discharge or denial of employment. On the other hand, if there is no applicable right-to-work law, the contractor must bargain in good faith concerning a proposed union security provision, since such a provision is a mandatory subject of bargaining. Still, the duty to bargain in good faith does not mean that the contractor must agree to inclusion of the provision in the contract.

Twenty states now have right-to-work laws, all of which prohibit union security agreements. Some, but not all, of these laws also prohibit agency shop contracts. Under an agency shop clause, employees are required either to become union members or to pay to the union a service fee equal to the dues and fees paid by the union members. Of the twenty states with right-to-work laws, thirteen by their terms have also outlawed the agency shop, five states by court interpretation have outlawed it, and one state has indicated that while the agency shop agreement itself is lawful, enforcement by discharge is outlawed.

When a lawful union security agreement has been entered into, the contractor should make sure that employees have been notified of their consequent obligations. Discharge for failure to abide by the terms of a union security clause is unlawful unless employees knew or had reason to know that they had to be union members to keep their jobs. The contract should spell out the precise terms of the union security provision (dues requirements, amounts owed, time when tender of payment must be made). If the contractor and the union agree to extend the term of the provision beyond the expiration period of the collective bargaining contract, appropriate notices should be given to the employees.

Any requirement that an applicant for employment become a union member on or before the seventh day from the beginning of employment is illegal. A contractor commits an unfair labor practice merely by agreeing to this provision even if the contractor does not attempt to enforce it. Even if the agreement is more than 7 days old when an applicant is hired, the applicant must be given at least 7 days from the commencement of employment to tender initiation fees and periodic dues. If the contractor enforces a union security clause by improperly discharging an employee for failing to become a member within that 7-day period (or a longer period set by the agreement), the contractor may be required to reinstate the employee with back-pay from the date of discharge.

Reinstatement fees may be charged against a former union member who is reemployed by a contractor with a union shop agreement. Such amounts may be larger than the initiation fees required of new employees as long as they are not excessive or discriminatory. If there is a question as to whether an employee is a new hire so that a reinstatement fee may be imposed, the terms of the union's bylaws or the collective bargaining agreement itself might provide the answer. A former union member who is treated as a new employee under a union shop provision must be given at least 7 days from the commencement of employment (or a longer period if specified in the contract) to tender the reinstatement fees before the former members may be discharged.

Illustrative Case

T. J. Butters, a construction subcontractor, employed a member of an Operating Engineers local until December 31, 1968, when he was suspended from membership for nonpayment of dues. From the date of his suspension until he began working for Butters in June 1971, the employee did not work for any employers with a contract with the Operating Engineers local. The employee was hired by Butters on June 9 under an agreement whereby all employees who are not members of the Operating Engineers local shall become members within 8 days after their hire. On June 14, the local notified Butters that the employee should not be working until he got his back dues straightened out. The local told the employee he had to pay the entire reinstatement fee immediately and then caused him to be discharged, on the ground that he was 3 years delinquent in dues payments. The NLRB held that the union violated the NLRA: "It is well settled that a union's demand for payment of back dues which arose during a period when there was no obligation to maintain membership cannot lawfully be imposed as a condition of employment, even under a valid union security agreement. The employee was a new employee of the employer and although a suspended union member, he was like any other new employee entitled to the [7-day] statutory or [longer] contractual grace period before being required to join or to be reinstated into the union." The employee was entitled to at least an 8-day grace period, and he was given only 6 days.[10]

An employee's only obligation under a valid union security clause is to tender the initiation fees and periodic dues uniformly required as a condition of membership. A union that causes or attempts to cause a contractor to discriminate against an employee for any reason "other than his failure to tender the periodic dues and the initiation fees uniformly required as a condition" of membership commits an unfair labor practice. This provision has a direct impact in the area of union-imposed discipline against members. A union's fine against a member may be lawful unless it is imposed for the members's refusal to engage in an unlawful activity. Thus, a union's bylaws may impose a fine against a union member who fails to attend a union meeting, but the union cannot seek to cause the employer to discharge the member for failure to pay the fine, since fines are not periodic dues.

When a contractor knows or has reason to know that a union is seeking to cause an employee's discharge or denial of employment for a reason other than failure to tender initiation fees and periodic dues uniformly required as a condition of union membership, the employer acts unlawfully by complying with the union's demand. The employer's claim to have complied under the threat of a work stoppage if the employer refused is no defense to an unfair-labor-practice charge. An employer who gives in to the union in this situation may be liable for up to the entire amount of wages and other benefits that this employee would have received but for the wrongful discharge or denial of employment. Employers faced with what

[10] *Operating Engineers Local 139 (T.J. Butters Constr.)*, 198 NLRB No. 167 (1972).

they know are unlawful union demands may file unfair-labor-practice charges with the NLRB against the union.

Illustrative Case

The union requested the employer, Alcoa Construction System, to discharge an employee for allegedly being delinquent in his membership dues. The contract contained a union security agreement as well as a dues-checkoff provision. This employee had authorized a dues checkoff from his wages. The NLRB ruled that Alcoa committed an unfair labor practice by complying with the union's demand that the employee be discharged for nonmembership in the union, since Alcoa had reason to believe from the fact that the employee had authorized a dues checkoff that the employee could not have been delinquent in rendering his dues payments to the union.[11]

PREHIRE AGREEMENTS

Under Section 8(f) of the NLRA, an employer engaged primarily in the construction industry may lawfully, but is not required to, enter into a prehire agreement with a building and construction trades union. This agreement in the construction industry will be valid even if the union has not achieved majority status and even if no employees have been hired at the time when the agreement is made.

The Section 8(f) provision for the construction industry is an exception to the general rule in other industries that an employer may not lawfully recognize the union until both a representative complement of employees have been hired and a majority of them have designated the union as their exclusive bargaining agent. This exception reflects the peculiar needs of the construction industry. Many construction projects are short-term, so that agreements with unions will often apply to jobs that have not even started. The importance of prehire agreements is emphasized in the peculiar need of construction contractors to know their labor costs before they bid on construction projects and in the need to have a ready supply of skilled labor that they feel the union can supply.

A recent U.S. Supreme Court decision involving a prehire agreement indicates that a union may lack the ability to enforce a prehire agreement by striking or picketing. In *NLRB v. Local 103, Ironworkers,*[12] the Supreme Court considered the situation of the Higdon Construction Company under its prehire collective bargaining agreement with Local 103. In 1973 Higdon signed an agreement to abide by the terms of a multiemployer Ironworkers contract with the Tri-State Ironworkers Employers Association, Inc. At about the same time, a sister company, Higdon Contracting, was formed for the express purpose of carrying on construction work with nonunion labor. When Local 103 picketed two of Higdon Construction's projects, the company filed a charge with the NLRB alleging that Local 103 was engaging in illegal recognitional picketing in viola-

[11] *Alcoa Constr. Sys., Inc.,* 212 NLRB No. 62 (1974).
[12] 434 U.S. 335 (1978).

tion of Section 8(b)(7) of the NLRA by continuing the picketing for more than 30 days without requesting an election. The picketing was for the purpose of enforcing Local 103's agreement with Higdon Construction, and the NLRB expressly found that Higdon Construction and Higdon Contracting were the same employer (and therefore no secondary boycott was involved); the NLRB held that Local 103's picketing was unlawful. The Board noted that Higdon Construction's collective bargaining contract was a prehire agreement entered into before the union achieved majority status. The contract contained no union security clause which would ensure that Higdon's employees would all become union members, and Local 103 had not been certified as the bargaining representative of Higdon's employees or filed a petition for an election to gain certification. Speaking for the majority, Justice White summarized:

Under the Board's view of Section 8(f), a pre-hire agreement does not entitle a majority union to be treated as a majority representative of the employees until and unless it attains majority support in the relevant unit. Until that time the pre-hire agreement is voidable and does not have the same stature as the collective bargaining contract entered into where the union actually representing a majority of the employees and recognized as such by the employer. Accordingly, the Board holds, as it did here, that picketing by a minority union to enforce a pre-hire agreement that the employer refuses to honor, effectively has the object of attaining recognition as a bargaining representative with majority support among the employees, and is consequently violative of Section 8(b)(7)(C).

The Supreme Court upheld the Board's decision and decided that although Section 8(f) does permit a union which does not represent a majority of a construction contractor's employees to enter into a collective bargaining agreement before any workers are hired, the existence of a prehire agreement does not imply that the union enjoys majority status and the right to enforce the prehire agreement by strikes, picketing, or unfair-labor-practice charges.

The Court's decision in *Local 103, Ironworkers* has far-reaching consequences for the future of construction industry bargaining. First, as expressly stated by the Court, a construction contractor does not commit an unfair labor practice when the contractor refuses to honor a prehire agreement or engage in further bargaining with the union if the union has never demonstrated its majority support among the employees. Thus, to enforce a prehire agreement by strikes, picketing, or unfair-labor-practice charges, the union must either petition for an election and be designated by a majority of the contractor's employees as their choice of bargaining representative or achieve majority status by the operation of a valid union security clause. The Supreme Court stated: "The employers' duty to bargain and honor the contract is contingent on the union attaining majority support at the various construction sites."

The decision in *Local 103, Ironworkers* also has broader and more significant implications regarding the conduct of the bargaining relationship in the construction industry. Since the Court held that Section 8(f), which authorizes prehire agreements, does not "expand the duty of an employer under Section 8(a)(5), which is to bargain [in good faith] with a *majority* representative," the decision indicates that there may be no duty to bargain in good faith concerning the terms and conditions of prehire agreements in the construction industry. Thus, this recent case may signal a broad-based change in the bargaining rights and duties of construction industry employers and unions.

Contractors in the construction industry often perform work in areas that are within the jurisdiction of different union locals. These unions will already have contracts with the area contractors, and they will seek also to bind a contractor who is commencing work in the area to the terms of the area agreement. The contractor is not legally required to sign a prehire agreement. If the standard agreement would require the nonmember contractor to designate the area contractors' association as the contractor's representative for bargaining or grievance adjustment, union pressure to force agreement to that proposal is an unfair labor practice under Section 8(b)(1)(B) of the NLRA. Sometimes the union seeks to have the nonmember contractor appoint the association as its representative for a limited purpose, such as to settle jurisdictional dispute or to help administer employee benefits under a pension plan. Union pressure for even that limited purpose is also unlawful. (See Chapter 5, section "Nonmandatory Bargaining Subjects.")

A prehire agreement will not be valid if the union is established, maintained, or assisted by the employer in violation of Section 8(a)(2) of the NLRA, which makes unlawful certain forms of support or domination of a union. Thus, the contractor or the contractor's supervisors should refrain from soliciting employees either by promising them benefits if they do join the union or by threatening them with adverse treatment if they refuse to join.

Illustrative Case

Precision Carpet, Inc., threatened some employees with discharge if they failed to join the Carpenters local, which it favored, and the company solicited other employees to join the union. The company entered into a contract with that union. The NLRB held that the company violated Section 8(a)(2) of the NLRA when it executed and maintained the contract with the Carpenters local, since the union did not represent an uncoerced majority of employees when the contract was executed.[13]

A union security clause entered into in the context of a prehire agreement will be valid whether or not there is a representative complement of employees and whether or not the union has achieved majority status at the time that an agreement on the union's security clause is reached.

Illustrative Case

Pursuant to a prehire agreement, the contractor, Progressive Construction Corp., agreed to a 7-day union security clause. At the time that Progressive signed the agreement, a repre-

[13]*La Ron Corp. and Carpenters Local 484,* 223 NLRB No. 63 (1976).

sentative complement of employees had already been hired. The General Counsel of the NLRB contended that a prehire agreement with a union security clause is unlawful when the employees have already been hired unless a majority of the employees also have authorized the union security provision. The NLRB ruled that the provision in the NLRA allowing a 7-day union security agreement in the construction industry applies whether or not, at the time the agreement is made, the contractor has a representative complement of employees and whether or not the union represents a majority of the employees.[14]

Still, the employees may petition the Board to deauthorize a union security provision, and the Board will order a deauthorization election if the petition is signed by at least 30 percent of the employees within the bargaining unit. The contractor commits an unfair labor practice by continuing to enforce the union's security agreement once it has been deauthorized even if the contract has not yet expired.

A valid prehire agreement which is executed before a substantial workforce has been hired will not bar an election to decertify the union, and once the election results have been certified by the Board, the contractor is not permitted to give further effect to the prehire agreement even if it has not yet expired. Therefore, since the prehire agreement will not necessarily serve as a contract bar to a representation election for another union, the contractor should execute another agreement with the union at a time when the union does have majority status.

A contractor acts unlawfully by entering into a prehire agreement after a decertification election has been ordered but before the results are certified, since the contractor has an affirmative duty to remain neutral while there are conflicting claims of representation. In this case, the Board will order the contractor to refrain from bargaining with and entering into a collective bargaining agreement with the union until the election results are certified.

Conversely, once a valid prehire agreement has been reached, the contractor acts unlawfully by entering into an agreement with another union covering the same unit of employees. The union also commits an unfair labor practice by entering into or coercing a contractor into signing a union security contract with it when the contractor already has a valid prehire agreement with another union. It is no defense for the contractor to claim that this agreement was entered into under the threat of reprisal from the union if the contractor refused.

A contractor who no longer desires to be bound by a prehire agreement may petition for a representation election at any time after the agreement has been entered into, provided the contractor can show reasonable grounds to believe that the union has not and will not attain majority status. So when a contractor desires not to bargain any further with the union that it has recognized under a prehire agreement the contractor may petition for a decertification election.

A union that pickets for more than a reasonable period of time not to exceed 30 days, without filing a petition for a representation election, in

---

[14] *Progressive Constr. Corp.*, 218 NLRB No. 209 (1975).

order to extract a prehire agreement from a contractor commits an unfair labor practice. The contractor should file unfair-labor-practice charges so that the Board may seek an injunction in federal district court against the union. (See Chapter 4 for a discussion of the limits and restriction on recognitional picketing.)

A union also may not picket a contractor to enforce a validly executed prehire agreement when there has been a representation election resulting from the contractor's union or employees' petition and the union has lost the election. These exceptions are based on the rationale that continued picketing is intended to force the contractor's accession to a new agreement, which is unlawful, and the contractor may file charges with the Board so that the Board may seek an injunction in federal district court against the picketing. If the union pickets in this situation, the contractor should by no means feel compelled to agree to a prehire agreement with the union.

Illustrative Case

Carpet Control, Inc., and Painters Local 86 voluntarily entered into a prehire agreement. Subsequently, the local attempted to compel recognition under a new agreement, and the Board ordered an expedited election, which the local lost. The local continued to picket, however, after certification of the expedited election which it had lost. The NLRB held that the local's continued picketing after certification of the results of a properly held expedited election which it lost violated the NLRA.[15]

---

[15] *Painters Local 86 (Carpet Control, Inc.)*, 216 NLRB No. 190 (1975).

2 DISCHARGE AND DISCIPLINE

Construction contractors have a legitimate interest in being allowed to run their own businesses and to control their workforces. Yet there are several limitations on an employer's right to discharge or otherwise discipline employees that contractors should always be aware of. One is the National Labor Relations Act (NLRA), under which particular acts by an employer in disciplining and discharging employees may be unfair labor practices. Another limitation is the collective bargaining agreement itself, which may contain a "just-cause" or analogous requirement for the discharge or discipline of an employee. Additionally, the Equal Employment Opportunity Act (EEOA) prohibits discrimination in discharges or discipline "on the basis of race, color, religion, sex or national origin." The Occupational Safety and Health Act (OSHA) makes discriminatory treatment against an employee for filing charges or giving testimony against an employer for alleged unsafe working conditions unlawful. So a contractor who plans to act against an employee should first determine whether any of these limitations are operative.

Under Section 8(a)(1) of the NLRA, it is an unfair labor practice for an employer to "interfere with, restrain, or coerce employees in the exercise of the rights engaged in Section 7 [of the NLRA]." Employees' protected rights called "Section 7 rights" include the right to self-organization and the right to form, join, or assist labor organizations, to bargain collectively through representatives of their own choosing, to engage in other concerted activities for the purposes of collective bargaining or other mutual aid or protection, and to refrain from any and all such activities. Along the same lines, Section 8(a)(3) of the NLRA makes it unlawful for an employer by "discrimination in regard to hire or tenure of employment or any term or condition of employment to . . . discourage membership in any labor organization."

Although a collective bargaining agreement provides that an employer "has the sole right, in his absolute discretion, to discharge or discipline employees," this is not the end of the matter for the employer. Even with such a protective clause, the employer still commits an unfair labor practice if the employer's actions against employees operate to "interfere with, restrain, or coerce" them in the exercise of their protected Section 7 rights. As a consequence, an employer might be required to reinstate an employee with back pay, post notices stating that the employer refrain from prohibited acts, and possibly incur other costs as well. A contractor who decides to discharge or otherwise discipline an employee should *first* (1) examine the terms of the applicable collective bargaining agreement and (2) check to see if the proposed action might be an unfair labor practice.

The fact that an employee is engaged in a protected concerted activity does not mean that the employer may not discharge or discipline the employee for legitimate business reasons. But if the employee's protected concerted activity was one factor, even if not the primary one, in motivating the discharge or discipline, the employer might be guilty of an unfair labor practice. Therefore, the employer should justify treatment of the employee solely on the basis of legitimate business reasons and avoid taking any acts or making any statements inconsistent with this justification.

Some obvious forms of protected concerted activity are union activities, such as joining a union, soliciting other employees to join a union, going on strike, honoring a picket line, and attending union meetings. But employees who either strike or refuse to cross a picket line may be discriminated against if they are under a contractual obligation not to engage in either of those activities. If the strike is illegal, either because it is conducted for an illegal purpose or because notice requirements under Section 8(d) of the NLRA are not satisfied, the strikers may be discharged or disciplined. Similarly, employees who honor a picket line that is itself illegal may be validly subject to discharge or discipline by the employer. Finally, the employer may retaliate against strikers who engage in serious acts of misconduct, such as violence. (For a fuller discussion of employer and employee rights in picketing situations see Chapter 4.)

Employees may be engaged in protected concerted activity even when there is no union activity and no union activity is contemplated. And employees are engaged in protected concerted activity even if it is not preparatory to collective bargaining, as long as the activity is for their mutual aid or protection. Thus, when there is no union and two employees join together to present a complaint concerning working conditions to their employer, the employer might be violating the NLRA if he disciplined them in reprisal for presenting the grievances.

Actions short of discharge, such as layoffs, downgrading of seniority status, and transfer of or restrictions on job assignments, also are prohibited interference if they are premised upon employees' protected activities. In addition, threats to take any of the above actions violate the act. Moreover, offers of benefits to employees if they will refrain from engaging in a protected concerted activity will support an unfair-labor-practice charge against the employer. Certain veiled forms of discharge are also prohibited. For example, a statement to employees that the employer will consider the employees to have "voluntarily quit" if they do not resume work despite a lawful strike is a prohibited threat of discharge, in that in puts the employees on notice that they will no longer be employed if they do not refrain from their protected activity.

In addition, to provide a violation it need not be shown that employees were actually restrained or coerced if such acts or statements had a "reasonable tendency" to restrain or coerce them. Thus, if the employer threatens to discharge employees for their union activities, a violation can be found, even though their protected activity was not actually deterred, because the threats had a reasonable tendency to restrain them from engaging in the protected activity.

Even if there is no actual intent to interfere with employees' protected rights, the employer commits an unfair labor practice by creating an impression among employees that they will somehow be discriminated against for engaging in the protected activity. An employer should avoid even in jest telling an employee "you'd better watch out if you join the union," because the National Labor Relations Board (NLRB) will look at the possible *effect* of this statement on the employee, not the *intent* of the employer, to determine if the statement constitutes an unfair labor practice. Only if the employer takes sufficient steps to assure employees that their impression is mistaken will be employer avoid committing an unfair labor practice.

An employer may discipline or discharge employees for many reasons which are arguably unfair but which nonetheless do not constitute an unfair labor practice because the employees are not engaged in a protected concerted activity. For example, an employer commits no unfair labor practice by discharging employees merely because the employer dislikes them, since the employees are not being discharged for engaging in a protected concerted activity. Still, in many instances an employer is not well advised to do this, especially if the collective bargaining agreement has a just-cause provision, since the employer may then be required to reinstate the employees with back pay. Even if there is no express just-cause provision, one may sometimes be implied in the agreement by the arbitrator.

In other instances, the presence of a union may preclude a finding that employees' concerted activities are protected against discharge or discipline by the employer. For example, a small group of employees that seek to negotiate with their employer over terms of employment that are contrary to an existing collective bargaining agreement are not engaged in a protected activity. In fact, an employer who complies with this unlawful demand, even under the threat of a costly work stoppage, may violate the NLRA because of bargaining in bad faith. This rule is based upon the national labor policy of favoring the promotion of collective bargaining and upon the fact that this policy is significantly thwarted if employees are free to bypass their representative to force an employer to bargain with them individually or on basis that covers less than the entire bargaining unit.

On the basic of this rule, a group of employees that threaten to or engage in a work stoppage over a dispute that is arguably covered by the grievance procedure in the union's contract with the employer, without first exhausting all possible means of settlement under the grievance process, may be discharged. By striking so as to bypass the grievance process, the employees are unlawfully attempting to force the employer to bargain with them in derogation of the union's status as the bargaining representative. Even if the striking employees are protesting an employer's alleged racially discriminatory employment practices, they may not strike without first exhausting the contract's grievance procedures.

Illustrative Case

Emporium Capwell Company's agreement with the union recognized the union as the exclusive bargaining agent for the employees. The agreement prohibited employment discrimination based on race, and it contained a no-strike clause along with grievance and arbitration machinery for processing a claimed violation of the contract, including a violation of the antidiscrimination clause. Even though the union was attempting to press the employees' grievances, four employees walked out and picketed in an effort to get the employer to bargain directly with them over the race discrimination issue. The employees were subsequently discharged. The U.S. Supreme Court held that the company did not violate the NLRA by discharging a minority group of employees for striking to force the company to bargain with them instead of with the union. Additionally, the Court held that the NLRA is itself a part of the broad national policy of nondiscrimination which is expressed explicitly in Title VII of the Civil Rights Act of 1964. In spite of this, the employees of Emporium Capwell Company could not rely on that fact to protect the racial protest that they made in derogation of their union. The reason that they could not be protected was that their concerns regarding racial discrimination were already protected by the union's duty under the act not to discriminate or bargain for the establishment or continuation of discrimination. Although Title VII also protects employees' efforts to oppose race discrimination, that does not allow employees to bypass their union representative.[1]

Employees are protected only in their concerted, not their individual, activities. Nevertheless, an employee acting alone may still be engaged in concerted activity. In many situations, a group of employees talk among themselves and appoint one employee to act as their spokesman. In that situation, the individual employee clearly is representing the views of the other employees and therefore may not be discharged for presenting their views.

An employee who acts alone and without prior discussion with any other employees may be protected against discharge or discipline if the action might arguably benefit both this employer and the other employees. For example, an employee who seeks to enforce particular terms of a collective bargaining agreement, even though solely for personal benefit and without any showing that any other employees share this employee's interest, may not be discriminated against for that reason.

Illustrative Case

An employee made complaints to the employer, Hughes Sheet Metal Inc., about certain work practices that were contrary to the terms of the collective bargaining agreement. The employee objected to the use of personal tools on the job contrary to the contract and to

---

[1] *Emporium Capwell Co. v. Western Community Addition Organ.*, 420 U.S. 50 (1975).

the use of apprentices when the contract required journeymen to be employed. No other employees expressed an interest in joining the employee in presenting these complaints. The employee was subsequently discharged. Although no other employees joined the employee in complaints to the employer concerning deviations from the terms of the contract, the NLRB held that these solo complaints were still protected concerted activity since they were an attempt to enforce the contract, thus constituting "grievances within the framework of a contract that affects the rights of all the employees." Also, the Board rejected the employer's excuse that the employee was laid off because of lack of work, since the employer's practice was to lay off according to seniority, and this employee was laid off prior to other employees with less seniority, and the employer failed to justify this deviation from an established layoff policy.[2]

Thus, the lesson for the employer is this: although an employee presents a grievance alone and there has been no prior discussion with other employees, do not retaliate against that employee if the claim arguably involves an attempt to enforce the contract. If the employer does have a legitimate reason for adverse treatment of the employee, that reason should be given in writing to the employee and the union at the time of the discharge. The employer should never give a reason that would be unlawful.

A contractor acts unlawfully by taking action designed to induce an employee to abandon the terms or conditions of a collective bargaining agreement. Thus, the contractor commits an unfair labor practice by threatening to retaliate against an employee unless the employee agrees to sign an individual contract at variance with the terms of a collective bargaining agreement.

Illustrative Case

The employee was told that he was being transferred to a truck that paid a lower rate than that specified in the contract. The employee refused, filed a grievance, threatened to go to the Wage and Hour Division, and was subsequently denied further employment. The Board ruled that the employer violated the NLRA by bargaining individually with the employee and by threats of and actual discharge of the employee for refusal to sign an individual contract at variance with the terms of a collective bargaining agreement.[3]

An employee also is engaged in protected concerted activity when the employee threatens to or does file charges with OSHA alleging unsafe working conditions, even though there has been no preliminary discussion with other employees, and it therefore is unlawful for the contractor to threaten to or actually to discharge or discipline the employee for that reason.

Illustrative Case

The employee, without talking to any other employees, filed charges with the local OSHA office alleging numerous safety hazards which the employer, Alleluia Cushion Company,

[2] *James T. Hughes Sheet Metal, Inc.*, 224 NLRB No. 111 (1976).

[3] *John M. Lastooka, Trading as Ram Constr.*, 228 NLRB 94 (1977).

had failed to remedy. After an OSHA inspection, the employee, who was earlier reprimanded for getting in touch with OSHA, was discharged. The NLRB held: "Where an employee speaks out and seeks to enforce statutory provisions relating to occupational safety designed for the benefit of all employees in the absence of any evidence that the employees have disavowed such representation," such activity is concerted and protected.[4]

Section 8(a)(4) of the NLRA makes it an unfair labor practice for an employer "to discharge or otherwise discriminate against an employee because he has filed charges or given testimony" pursuant to either an unfair-labor-practice proceeding or a representation hearing. Thus, an employer should avoid either threatening or actually retaliating against an employee in this area. A violation will be found when such threats would have a reasonable tendency to intimidate the employee even if the employee has nonetheless filed charges or given testimony. Also, it is an unfair labor practice to condition the reinstatement of an employee who was originally laid off for just cause upon a promise either to withdraw unfair-labor-practice charges or not to testify. Finally, an employer acts unlawfully by threatening or actually discharging or disciplining an employee for giving sworn statements to a Board field examiner making an investigation to decide whether to file unfair-labor-practice charges.

Although employees who strike to protest an alleged Title VII violation without first exhausting a contractual grievance procedure may be discharged, employees may not be discharged or otherwise disciplined or discriminated against for filing a complaint with the EEOC against their employer alleging racially discriminatory employment practices. This is true because Section 704(a) of Title VII, 42 U.S.C. Section 200 (e)(3)(a) provides:

It shall be an unlawful employment practice for an employer to discriminate against any of his employees or applicants for employment . . . because he has opposed any practice made an unlawful employment practice by this subchapter, or because he has made a charge, testified, assisted, or participated in any manner in an investigation, proceeding, or hearing under this subchapter.

Even if the dispute is submitted to grievance and arbitration under the no-discrimination clause of a collective bargaining agreement and the employee's complaint of racial discrimination is denied there, the employee may nonetheless continue to pursue the complaint with a state or federal EEOC or in federal court under Title VII and may not be discharged or otherwise discriminated against for that reason.

Illustrative Case

Following his discharge by Gardner-Denver Company, a black employee filed a grievance under the collective bargaining contract, which included a broad arbitration provision, claiming that his discharge had resulted from race discrimination. Upon rejection of his

[4]*Alleluia Cushion Co.*, 221 NLRB 162 (1976).

claim by the arbitrator, the employee filed his complaint with the state civil rights commission, which in turn referred the complaint to the EEOC. Upon rejection of the claim by the EEOC, the employee then filed his suit in federal district court. Ultimately, a United States appeals courts held that an employee who has submitted a claim of racially discriminatory employment practices under the no-discrimination clause of a collective bargaining agreement is not precluded from maintaining his Title VII action and may not be retaliated against by the company for that reason.[5]

Sometimes what might be concerted activity because it involves more than one employee is not protected because the activity is not for the purpose of protecting or improving the employees' working conditions or terms of employment, so that these employees may be discharged or otherwise disciplined. Rather, the employees may merely be loitering or refusing to obey a lawful work order, both of which are lawful grounds for discharge. Circulation of handbills that attack the quality of an employer's work product without referring to any labor dispute or to collective bargaining is not protected activity since it does not refer to a labor dispute with the employer. Instead, it constitutes disloyalty to the employer, for which employees may be discharged or disciplined.

Illustrative Case

Employees engaged in a strike and picketing in a dispute over the terms of the new collective bargaining agreement between the Electrical Workers of the Jefferson Standard Broadcasting Company. The picketers distributed handbills which made no reference to a union, to a labor dispute, or to collective bargaining. Instead, the handbills attacked the quality of the company's work product. The picketers were discharged for engaging in this distribution of handbills. The Supreme Court held that the company could lawfully discharge the employees for distributing the handbills which attacked the quality of the employer's product and "which made no reference to a union, to a labor controversy, or to collective bargaining, in a manner reasonably calculated to harm the employer's reputation and reduce his income . . . though at the time of the distribution of handbills a labor dispute existed . . . The LMRA seeks to strengthen, rather than to weaken, that cooperation, continuity of service . . . between the employer and the employee that is born of loyalty to their common enterprise."[6]

On the other hand, if these employees had circulated handbills protesting working conditions, this probably would be protected activity even if it might also harm the employer. Even if employees' activities are contrary to their best business interest, an employer may not discharge them if their complaints refer to a labor controversy.

An employer should examine the purpose of group activity before taking any action against employees. If the employer has a legitimate justification for discharging or otherwise discriminating against the employees, it should be given in writing to them at the time of the discharge. The notice of discharge or discipline should be given as soon as possible after the employer learns of employees' unprotected activities.

[5] *Alexander v. Gardner-Denver Co.*, F.2d 503 (10th Cir. 1975), *cert. denied*, 823 U.S. 1058 (1976).

[6] *NLRB v. IBEW Local 1229*, 346 U.S. 414 (1953).

Often a union will seek to press an employer to discharge, discipline, or otherwise discriminate against an employee for refusal either to join the union or to participate in a protected union activity. The employer acts unlawfully by threatening to discriminate or actually discriminating against the employee for refusal to engage in union activity. It is no defense to an unfair-labor-practice charge against the employer to claim that the employer was merely giving in to the union's pressure to protect the business. An employer who does comply with the union's unlawful demands may be jointly and severally liable with the union in a back-pay award to the employee. This means that the employer might have to pay the entire amount of the back-pay, even though the union is also liable. Therefore, if the employer is faced, for example, with the threat of a work stoppage, the employer should file unfair-labor-practice charges with the NLRB for the union's unlawful attempt to cause the employer discriminate unlawfully against an employee.

Illustrative Case

The supervisor for Stearns-Roger, Inc., a contractor involved in engineering and construction work, threatened to lay off employees who would not sign a petition asking for the day off from work. Stearns-Roger committed an unfair labor practice by threatening to retaliate against employees for refusing to participate in a protected concerted activity.[7]

When a valid union security clause is in effect, an employer may lawfully discharge an employee who has failed to tender the initiation fees and the periodic dues uniformly required as a condition of membership in the union. Yet if the employer knows or has reason to know that the union is seeking the employee's discharge for any reason other than the failure to render these payments, the employer violates the NLRA by discharging the employee.

Illustrative Case

The NLRB has ruled: "The employer's compliance with the union's demands that the employee be discharged for nonmembership in the union is unlawful, since the employer had reason to believe that the employee was suspended wrongly for nonpayment of dues that were not delinquent under the agreement of the parties."[8]

An employer faced with a union's demand to discharge or otherwise take disciplinary action against an employee should check to see (1) if there is a valid union security agreement and, if so, (2) whether the union is seeking the employee's discharge for any reason other than failure to pay initiation fees or periodic dues uniformly required as a condition of membership. If the union's demand for the employee's discharge is based on

[7] Stearns-Roger, Inc., 222 NLRB No. 165 (1976).
[8] Alcoa Constr. Sys., Inc., 212 NLRB No. 62 (1974).

any other reason, the employer should not give in to the union pressure to discharge the employee. Instead, the employer should consider filing unfair-labor-practice charges with the Board for the union's unlawful attempt to cause the employer to discriminate unlawfully against the employee.

As previously discussed, an employer has the right to discharge or otherwise discipline an employee on the ground that the employee was not engaged in a protected activity. However, the mere fact that an employee is engaged in a protected concerted activity is not a bar to discharge or discipline. If the employer can show that the employee's protected concerted activity is not a factor at all in motivating the discharge, there is no violation of the NLRA. If the employer or the supervisor can show that neither of them had any knowledge of the employee's activities at the time that decision to discharge or discipline was made, no unfair labor practice is committed. Even if there is knowledge of the employee's union activity, any unlawful motivation may be completely negated by offering legitimate business reasons for the discriminatory treatment of the employee. Of course, these legitimate reasons should be given in writing to the employee at the time that the employee is discharged or disciplined.

Illustrative Case

Oneglia and Gervasini Construction Corporation discharged a union steward who left his post without notifying the supervisor in order to investigate an employee's alleged grievance. At the time of the discharge, the employer did not know that the steward was leaving his post to engage in a union activity. The NLRB ruled that the discharge was lawful since at the time of the discharge the company did not know the steward's reason for leaving his post. The company had a legitimate business reason for requiring the steward to give notice that he was leaving his job because of its interest in the public's and fellow employees' safety.[9]

The Board will often examine the employer's offer of legitimate business reasons to determine whether it was a mere pretext to hide the actual unlawful motivation, especially when the employer has a prior history of poor labor relations or antiunion animus. If an employer has recently been cited for unfair labor practices, the employer should be very careful to document legitimate reasons to justify the discharge.

When an employee is laid off after the employer learns of the employee's union activity, a justification for the layoff because of lack of available jobs will be ignored either if the employer has hired other employees to do the same work or if there is contrary proof of an expanding demand for the employer's work. The discharge will be unlawful if it can be shown that the employer's established practice, when there is a reduction in the workload, is to transfer employees to other tasks, rather than to lay them off, and when a transfer could have been arranged for this employee.

[9]*Oneglia and Gervasini: Constr. Corp.*, 222 NLRB No. 96 (1976).

> A construction industry employer, Odell Mitchell, discharged two employees. Mitchell contended that the discharges were justified, despite his knowledge that the employees were attempting to enforce the terms of a collective bargaining contract, on the ground that the layoffs were required because of a reduced demand for work. The NLRB ruled that Odell Mitchell violated the NLRA by discharging two employees who protested the failure to give them the benefits set forth in the collective bargaining contract. Mitchell's contention that the discharges were justified because of a lack of materials and reduced production was mere pretext because task flexibility would have permitted the employees' continued employment beyond the date of the discharge and their duties actually increased during the last month of employment.[10]

Another common justification for discharge or discipline, despite knowledge of employees' protected activity, is that the employer is merely enforcing legitimate company rules against an employee who has concededly violated the rules. If the rules have been applied evenhandedly to all employees, this justification is likely to absolve the employer. But if the rule has been applied only sporadically, this reason is more likely to be insufficient. Thus, a union activist who is always late for work may not lawfully be discharged if the employer's tardiness rule has not been enforced before against other employees. If the rule has been uniformly applied in the past but the penalty against this employee is greater than the normal penalty for the same violation, an unlawful discharge is more likely to be found. Also, the Board may look at the gravity of the alleged offense and the question of whether the punishment fits the offense. On the other hand, if many employees have broken the same rule, the employer need not discharge all of them but is entitled to set an example by discharging only some of them. To be safe, the number of employees discharged who are also simultaneously engaged in protected activity should not be disproportionately high.

When an employer seeks to justify a discharge on the ground of an employee's inability to perform the work, the Board will scrutinize the truthfulness of this justification. Of course, any statements of the employer indicating antiunion animus or saying or inferring that the discharge is motivated by the employee's protected activity will be given great weight, so the employer and the supervisor should always refrain from making such statements. An employer should never state or imply antiunion feelings because they will surely be used against the employer later in unfairlabor-practice proceedings. Here are a few of the other factors that the NLRB may consider in determining whether the employer's motive for the discharge is lawful or not:

1. What is the employee's actual work record?

2. When did the employer learn of the employee's poor work performance, and were any attempts made at that time to correct the inefficiency?

[10] *Odell Mitchell*, 222 NLRB No. 171 (1976).

3. Was the employee given any wage increases or bonuses prior to engaging in the protected activity?

4. Was this reason for the discharge given at the time of the discharge or later at the unfair-labor-practice hearing?

5. Has the employer given contrary explanations for the discharge?

6. How active was the discharged employee in the protected activity?

3 SUPERVISION

A primary concern of construction contractors is to maintain control over the supervision of job operations. Control over supervision is the major means by which contractors can realistically enforce work rules and run a job in an efficient manner. Over the years, contractors have perhaps been too willing to relinquish a degree of control over supervision to unions. They should realize that many types of union control over supervision and supervisory personnel may be unlawful and that they may resist these union efforts. Contractors can and should recapture control over the critical right of supervision of the workforce by individuals responsible solely to management.

A union often attempts to control a contractor's supervisors by including them in the bargaining unit for the purpose of negotiating their wages, hours, and terms and conditions of employment. By bargaining on behalf of supervisors, the union hopes to make supervisors believe that all they have gained is due to the union's efforts. In this manner, the union hopes to have the supervisors act on behalf of the union instead of the contractor when these two interests conflict.

Supervisors are excluded from the coverage of the National Labor Relations Act (NLRA) and do not possess the organizational, collective bargaining, and other rights granted to other employees by the act. Contractors must bear in mind that supervisors are management's representatives under management control. A contractor may, but is never required to, bargain with the union over the wages, hours, and terms and conditions of employment of supervisors. Therefore, a contractor may lawfully refuse even to consider proposals that for example, supervisors be union members or be hired only through a hiring hall. Contractors are free to insist that they retain sole power to hire and control supervisors and to set their wages and other terms of employment. A contractor should file unfair-labor-practice charges with the National Labor Relations Board (NLRB) for a union's failure to bargain in good faith if the union insists that supervisors' terms of employment be included in a contract as a condition either to further bargaining or to final agreement.

The union, Southern California Pipe Trades District Council No. 16, submitted a standard areawide agreement to the contractor, Aero Plumbing Co. Aero refused to sign the agreement on the ground that it applied to supervisors. The union refused to bargain further unless Aero agreed to the entire contract, including its application to supervisors. Since the wages, hours, and terms and conditions of employment of supervisors are not a mandatory bargaining subject, the union did not bargain in good faith when it refused to meet further with Aero because Aero refused to apply the terms of the contract to supervisors.[1]

Of course, a contractor should make sure that the persons over whose conditions of employment a union seeks to bargain are actually supervisors within the meaning of the act. If they are not in fact supervisors, the contractor fails to bargain in good faith by refusing to negotiate concerning their conditions of employment. The act in Section 2(11) defines a "supervisor" as any individual having authority, in the interest of the employer, to hire, transfer, suspend, lay off, recall, promote, discharge, assign, reward, or discipline other employees, or responsibility to direct them, or to adjust their grievances, or effectively to recommend such action, if the exercise of such authority is not of a merely routine or clerical nature but requires the use of independent judgment. If the individual has the authority to perform any one of such acts or effectively to recommend such acts, the individual is probably a supervisor, provided the individual must use independent judgment to perform or recommend any such act. The individual's job title as a supervisor is meaningless if the above requirement is not satisfied. Conversely, an employee can be a supervisor despite the lack of supervisory job title or despite the fact of union membership.

If it is unclear whether the employee is in fact a supervisor under the above-described test, the NLRB often looks at secondary indicators, such as whether the employed is regarded by employer or other employees as a supervisor; is paid on a weekly or monthly, rather than an hourly, basis; receives substantially greater pay than other employees; participates in regular production work to a lesser extent than other employees; and is directly answerable to top management officials, not to other supervisors.

On a recent case, the Board relied upon some of these factors in determining that a union member was also a supervisor.

A member of an Operating Engineers local who at various times served as the general manager and assistant general manager for the employer, Redi-Mix Products, had the following duties and possessed the following attributes:

1. He was in charge of purchasing materials and dispatching drivers to the job site.

2. He responsibly directed the work of employees, assigned work to them, gave them time off, and recommended hiring and firing.

---

[1] *Southern California Pipe Trades Dist. Council (Aero Plumbing Co.)*, 167 NLRB No. 143 (1967).

3. All orders concerning daily operations either emanated from him or were relayed directly from the company president to the employees through him.

4. He had attributes of a management representative and was regarded as such by union officials with whom he dealt in adjusting grievances.

On the basis of those factors, the NLRB held that the union member was a supervisor.[2]

Often a union seeks to control the selection or retention of supervisors by means other than bargaining over their conditions of employment. For example, a union might threaten to or actually strike or picket the contractor for such purposes. This action will constitute an unfair labor practice by the union under Section 8(b)(1)(B) of the act, which makes it unlawful for a union to "restrain or coerce an employer in the selection of his representatives for the purposes of collective bargaining or the adjustment of grievances." This section protects employers' freedom to deal with their supervisors without union interference.

Although threatened actions by the union to influence the selection or retention of a supervisor are not an unfair labor practice under Section 8(b)(1)(B) unless the supervisor is also the contractor's "representative for the purposes of collective bargaining or the adjustment of grievances," the Board and most courts (except the federal Court of Appeals for the Second Circuit) have ruled that once an individual can be defined as a supervisor, that individual automatically is considered to be an employer representative for these purposes. This view is known as the "reservoir doctrine," under which supervisors are viewed as a reservoir of persons who are available and are likely to be chosen as grievance adjusters or collective bargaining agents at some future date. Since union discipline might adversely affect a supervisor's loyalty to the employer, the employer is unlawfully restricted in the choice of future representatives if the supervisor cannot be hired or fired at the employer's desire. Under this rule the supervisor is the contractor's representative for the purpose of collective bargaining or grievance adjustment even in the absence of proof that the supervisor actually has the authority to handle grievances or to bargain with the employees.

Section 8(b)(1)(B)'s prohibition is important for two reasons. First, when there is a possible violation, unfair-labor-practice charges should be filed so that the Board will order the union to cease its conduct if a violation is found. Second, activities which violate Section 8(b)(1)(B) are unprotected, so that a contractor may lawfully threaten to or actually discharge or otherwise discriminate against employees who participate in such activities.

A union acts unlawfully if it threatens to or actually strikes or pickets in support of a demand that the proposed contract include a provision requiring supervisors to be union members. This result follows even if the contract specifically disclaims any union power to discipline a supervisor.

---

[2] *Operating Engineers Local 3 (Redi-Mix Products, Inc.)*, 219 NLRB No. 100 (1975).

Illustrative Case

The Roofers local threatened to and actually struck Midwest Roofing & Insulation Co. because the supervisor was not a member of the local. The NLRB held that the union local's action protesting the supervisor's retention on the ground that he was not a member of the local unlawfully operated to restrain the contractor in the retention of his representative for handling grievances.[3]

Similarly, threats of retaliation or actual retaliation against a contractor for failure to discharge a supervisor because the union disagrees with the supervisor's conduct in representing the contractor's interests is unlawful. Likewise, if such threats of retaliation are made to protest a contractor's decision to fire a supervisor who is also a union member, the union acts unlawfully, since these actions operate to restrain or coerce the contractor in the selection or retention of a representative.

Illustrative Case

The Plumbing and Pipefitters local attempted to cause a supervisor's discharge and to restrict his being hired by other contractors by threats of work stoppages and picketing and thereby violated Section 8(b)(1)(B). The local had disagreed with the supervisor's conduct on behalf of the contractor by whom he was employed. The NLRB held: "The Act is designed to preclude the union from bringing pressure upon the employer to remove a supervisor or from disciplining a supervisor because of his conduct as supervisor, regardless of the merit of the union's reasons for its dissatisfaction with the supervisor's conduct."[4]

Too often contractors acquiesce to a union's demand that supervisors must be union members. When this has occurred, the union is often able to influence supervisors' conduct by threatening them with fines or other discipline. By taking action directly against a supervisor-member however, a union may unlawfully restain or coerce the contractor. This type of violation will frequently occur when a union threatens to discipline or actually disciplines the supervisor-member for conduct as the contractor's representative, since these actions by the union are likely to deprive the contractor of the supervisor's services and undivided loyalty.

A union may lawfully fine or discipline supervisor-members for purely internal union activity. For example, a union may normally impose a fine for failure to pay union dues or to attend union meetings. However, the fine becomes unlawful when it is imposed for supervisors' failure to attend a union meeting during working hours, because the fine in that case operates to restrict employers' use of their representatives. If the union's motive for threatening supervisor-members with disciplinary action if they fail to attend a union meeting is to assure their presence in order to influ-

[3] *Roofers Local 106 (Midwest Roofing Insulation Co.)*, 202 NLRB No. 127 (1973).

[4] *United Ass'n of Journeymen and Apprentices of Plumbing and Pipefitting Indus*, 220 NLRB No. 181 (1975).

ence them in their conduct as employer representatives, the union's conduct also is unlawful. In that event, the contractor is justified in discharging union employees who made such threats, because these concerted activities were unlawful and therefore unprotected.

Illustrative Case

Several union employees sent to a supervisor-member a letter threatening him with disciplinary action if he failed to attend a union meeting whose stated purpose was to "discuss ways and means of having a more harmonious job." The true purpose of having the supervisor-member at the meeting was to convince him to represent the union's viewpoint concerning certain grievances involving overtime work. He was directed to attend under the threat of discipline if he failed to do so, because the union believed him to be high enough in management to influence the employer to change his decision. The NLRB held that the union's conduct was clearly calculated to interfere with control over the employer's own representative: "Employees who engage in intraunion activity are protected from reprisal or discrimination by their employer. However, where such activity transcends purely union internal affairs and interferes with a supervisor-member's conduct in the course of representing the interest of the employer, the activity may be violative of Section 8(b)(1)(B) of the NLRA and therefore lose its protection."[5]

Discipline of supervisor-members likewise becomes unlawful when it is imposed because a union disagrees with the way in which they act in their role as the contractor's management force. For example, a union commits an unfair labor practice when it threatens to or does discipline a supervisor-member for being too strict in enforcing rules against tardiness or absenteeism or, in the exercise of his management duties, for either laying off union employees because of declining business conditions or refusing to reinstate a former union employee. Finally, union attempts to cause a supervisor's discharge for "the good of the union," as in retaliation for the supervisor's layoff of a union steward instead of another employee because the latter was a better worker, are unfair labor practices. The union's interest in preserving work for its members is not a valid defense.

Illustrative Case

The supervisor was a member of a Bricklayers local. Because of a declining supply of bricks the supervisor determined that he needed to lay off some of the employees. After he laid off at least five bricklayers, intraunion charges were preferred against him for violating the union's bylaw prohibiting foremen from laying off union members unless this was warranted by job conditions. The supervisor-member was found guilty of the violation and fined $50. The NLRB held that the union violated Section 8(b)(1)(b) when it imposed a fine on the supervisor-member for allegedly violating the hiring-and-firing provision of the union's bylaws because the fine was not imposed for an intraunion activity; rather, it was illegally imposed as a protest for his conduct on behalf of the contractor.[6]

[5] Bovee & Crail Constr. Co., 224 NLRB No. 71 (1976).

[6] Bricklayers Union No. 18 (Lonie and Son, Inc.), 185 No. 119 (1970).

Another unfair labor practice occurs when a union fines a supervisor-member whose interpretation of a collective bargaining agreement differs from the union's. For example, a supervisor who assigns work to one group of employees instead of to the union of which the supervisor is a member may not be threatened or actually disciplined by the union, since the employer is entitled to the supervisor's undivided loyalty in performing supervisory tasks.

Illustrative Case

A Laborers local brought intraunion charges and fined a supervisor member for his alleged deviation from the terms of the collective bargaining agreement relating to work assignments by assigning work to members of a union other than the Laborers. The NLRB held that the supervisor-member was exercising judgment and authority in furtherance of the employer's interest consistent with his interpretation of the collective bargaining agreement. By preferring intraunion charges against the supervisor, the union unlawfully attempted to impose its own interpretation of the contract upon the supervisor-member.[7]

A union also violates the act by threatening a union member with a fine or discipline unless the member resigns as supervisor for a nonunion employer, because the effect of the union's threat would be to deprive the nonunion employer unlawfully of the services of the supervisor.

The question often arises as to whether a union commits a Section 8(b)(1)(B) violation if it disciplines a supervisor-member for crossing a lawful picket line during a lawful strike. On the one hand, the union seeks to assure that all its members act as one to further their common interest; on the other hand, the employer expects to have the supervisor available to act on the employer's behalf. The U.S. Supreme Court held in a 5–4 vote in a 1978 decision that the union may not discipline or threaten with discipline supervisor-members who cross a picket line to perform their usual supervisory duties.[8] On the other hand, the Supreme Court has also ruled that disciplinary action may be legal if the supervisor-member crosses the picket line to perform more than a minimal amount of rank-and-file struck work which the supervisor-member would not have done but for the strike.[9]

If the supervisor-member has performed some rank-and-file work before the strike which is incidental to management tasks, then whether union discipline is lawful may depend upon whether the supervisor-member a substantially greater amount of rank-and-file work after the strike commences. The test is, did the supervisor-member perform a greater amount of rank-and-file struck work or continue to perform duties as the

[7] Construction, Product, & Maintenance Laborers Local 383 (Chanen Constr. Co., Inc.), 221 NLRB No. 211 (1975).

[8] NLRB v. Writers Guild of America, 437 U.S. 411 (1978).

[9] Florida Power & Light Co. v. Electrical Workers Local 641, 417 U.S. 790 (1974).

contractor's representative during the period of time when the supervisor-member continued to work over the union's objections?

Illustrative Case

When the contractor, Skippy Enterprises, refused to sign a new collective bargaining agreement negotiated by a contractors' association with the Carpenters district council, the council issued a no-contract, no-work order to its members. The supervisor, who was a member of the Carpenters, spent about 30 percent of his time performing manual work as a carpenter in addition to his largely supervisory duties. He ignored the union's no-work order, and during the strike his duties and work performance (30 percent rank-and-file work) remained the same. Then the Carpenters local imposed a fine on the supervisor for violation of the union's no-work rule and sought to collect the fine by legal action. The NLRB held that the union committed an unfair labor practice. Although a union may lawfully impose a fine on a supervisor-member who performs rank-and-file struck work normally performed by the striking employees, the supervisor-member normally spent 30 percent of his time on rank-and-file work, and that amount did not increase with the strike. Rather, his duties and performance did not change; he continued to spend 70 percent of his time in supervisory functions, which is not a minimal amount of time. Thus, compliance by the supervisor-member with the union's demands would have meant quitting his job and thus depriving the employer of his usual services.[10]

Thus, if supervisor-members continue to perform their principally supervisory tasks during a lawful strike, union discipline is unlawful. But if they cross a picket line to perform more than the minimal amount of rank-and-file struck work which they performed prior to the strike, they may be subject to union discipline, since they are not being punished for exercising any duties as employer representatives. Union discipline of supervisor-members who cross lawful picket lines to perform work of which 50 percent is rank-and-file struck work and who performed no rank-and-file struck work prior to the strike is probably lawful.

Illustrative Case

The Carpenters local levied a fine against a supervisor-member who crossed the union's picket line to work. Fifty percent of his work during the strike consisted of rank-and-file struck work. Prior to the strike, all his work was supervisory in nature. The NLRB held that the union did not violate the NLRA by fining the supervisor-member for working during the strike, since he performed more than a minimal amount of struck work during the strike.[11]

The union violates the NLRA by fining a supervisor for working for less money than the standards provided in the union's work rules and the collective bargaining contract with the contractor. Such a fine is unlawful even if it is imposed after the supervisor no longer works for the contractor if it resulted from events occurring during employment as a supervisor.

---

[10] *Carpenters Dist. Council (Skippy Enterprises, Inc.)*, 218 NLRB No. 157 (1975).

[11] *Carpenters Local 1959 (Aurora Modular Indus.)*, 217 NLRB No. 82 (1975).

Similarly, threats of striking or picketing or an actual work stoppage or picketing for the purpose of enforcing the contract as it applies to the terms or conditions of employment of a supervisor are unlawful, because the contractor is entitled under the act to be free from union coercion in setting the terms of the contractor's representative's employment.

Illustrative Case

A Sheet Metal Workers local fined a supervisor-member who allegedly violated the collective bargaining agreement by working for less than the area wage scale provided in the contract, being paid for 40 hours' work per week while working more than 40 hours, and having no health and welfare pension contribution for hours worked. The fine was imposed when the supervisor no longer worked for the employer, but it related to events occurring while he was a supervisor. Also, the union went out on strike to force the employer to accede to its demands to comply with the collective bargaining contract in regard to the supervisor's terms and conditions of employment. The NLRB held: "If an employer is to be free from union coercion in the selection of its employer representative, then surely the employer must be free from union coercion in the matter of setting the terms of such representative's employment. Thus, to find one who agrees to serve as the employer's representative solely because he and the employer agreed on terms and conditions of employment which the union may find objectionable must necessarily have a coercive effect on the employer in the future selection of his representatives. And this is true no matter at what point in time fine itself may have been imposed. The message to the employer will be clear for the future—don't select a supervisor unless the union approves of the terms and conditions of his employment."[12]

It is important to emphasize at this point that contractors may be held to unfair-labor-practice liability for the acts or statements of their supervisors, even if the supervisors are also union members, since the law presently treats supervisors as contractors' agents and representatives. Since it is supervisors who most frequently come in contact with the employees, contractors are well advised to tell supervisors about the things they should and should not do or say vis-á-vis the employees. Contractor's should always keep in mind that what is unlawful for them is also unlawful if supervisors do it. Of course, if supervisors are actually ordered by contractors to commit unfair labor practices, then the latter are guilty. Yet contractors might also be guilty of supervisors' unauthorized acts if the employees may reasonably believe that the supervisors have the authority to carry out their unlawful threats even if the contractors themselves are neutral. Thus, contractors should always be aware of what their supervisors are doing. If an unlawful act comes to their attention, contractors should be prepared to take swift and effective measures to demonstrate that the supervisors are without any power to carry out their illegal threats or acts.

What constitutes an effective means of removing a contractor's guilt for a supervisor's unauthorized acts will depend upon the circumstances. A mere statement of neutrality may not be enough, especially if there is a history of poor labor relations or if there have been repeated instances of

---

[12] Sheet Metal Workers Local 17 (George Koch Sons, Inc.), 199 NLRB No. 26 (1972).

supervisory misconduct. The contractor should also cite the specific instances of the supervisor's misconduct and state to the employees that those acts were without the contractor's authority and that any future acts will also be without that authority. The contractor should also warn the supervisor not to repeat such conduct and notify the employees that the supervisor has been so forewarned.

In summary, contractors cannot and should not give up control over supervisory personnel even if they are union members. Supervisors are the agents and representatives of management and are subject to the discretion of management in hiring, firing, and job performance. One way for contractors to regain control of their economic future is to take back responsibility for supervision.

4 STRIKES, PICKETING, AND BOYCOTTS

The right to strike is an important means by which employees are able to exert pressure upon employers to achieve various ends. It is an important right, but because it is susceptible to abuse, it is not an unlimited or an unqualified right.[1] Indeed, the Supreme Court has never completely resolved the question of the extent to which strikes are constitutionally protected. Because of this, most of the legal basis for the right to strike remains statutory.

The earliest statutory protections for striking workers are to be found in the Clayton Act, 15 U.S.C. Sections 12-27, and in the Norris–La Guardia Act, 29 U.S.C. Sections 101-115. However, for the purposes of most employers, the most significant statutory basis for the right of employees to strike is contained in the National Labor Relations Act (NLRA). Section 13 of the act states:

Nothing in this subchapter, except as specifically provided for herein, shall be construed so as to either interfere with or impede or diminish in any way the right to strike, or to affect the limitations or qualifications on that right. . . .

In addition, Section 7 of the act gives employees "the right to self-organization, to form, join, or assist labor organizations . . ., and to engage in other concerted activities for the purpose of collective bargaining or other mutual aid or protection. . . ." Thus, the right to strike, though subject to limitations, is protected, and it is deemed to be encompassed by Section 7's term "other concerted activities." An additional protection of the right to strike, appears in Section 2(3) of the NLRA, which states that "[t]he term 'employee' shall include any employee, . . . and shall include any individual whose work has ceased as a consequence of, or in connection with, any current labor dispute or because of any unfair labor practice, and who has not obtained any other regular and substantially equivalent employment. . . ." From the language of the section, it is clear that employees who go out on protected strikes do not lose their status as employees, which is one of the most important protections of the right to strike.

Generally speaking, two main types of strikes are protected by the act: unfair-labor-practice strikes and economic strikes. An "unfair-labor-prac-

---

[1]*Dorchy v. Kan.*, 272 U.S. 306 (1926).

tice strike" is a strike in response to an unfair labor practice on the part of an employer. Unfair labor practices by employers are set forth at Section 8(a) of the act. Under Section 2(3), striking employees do not lose their employee status, and employees who go out on strike in response to an unfair labor practice are protected against losing their jobs to replacements. They have the right to return to their jobs, and if they wish to return, the employer must make room for them by discharging any employees hired as replacements during the strike. An "economic strike" is generally directed at forcing an employer to agree to economic or other terms sought by the striking employees. Thus, employee strikes directed at obtaining more favorable wages, benefits, or working conditions are examples of an economic strike. In contradistinction to unfair-labor-practice strikers, who are protected against replacement while on strike, an economic striker may be replaced while on strike. Thus, while an employer may not fire economic strikers, the employer may replace them with other permanent workers (see Chapter 6, section "Strikes," for a discussion of economic strikes and the right to hire replacements).

The right to strike is not unqualified. The NLRA proscribes certain illegal types of strikes such as sit-down and wildcat strikes. Strikers who are guilty of violence or other serious misconduct while on strike are likewise unprotected. The act also forbids certain forms of secondary-boycott activities, and it places severe limits upon picketing for recognition or in instances in which jurisdictional disputes are involved. The presence of a no-strike clause in a collective bargaining agreement and the breach of such a clause by employees constitute yet another set of circumstances in which a strike may be unprotected under the act. These exceptions to the general rule that the right to strike is protected by the act will be treated more fully in the sections which follow.

NO-STRIKE AGREEMENTS

Normally, employees are free to strike. However, the right to strike may be significantly curtailed by an express agreement not to strike in the collective bargaining agreement. When a mandatory grievance and arbitration procedure is specified in the contract and a strike occurs over an issue subject to this procedure, there is often an implied obligation not to strike. Whether the strike violates either an express or an implied no-strike clause will have several important consequences to the contractor. When employees strike despite a contractual obligation not to strike, the strikers may be able to be discharged lawfully. In some cases the contractor may also be justified in refusing to bargain with the union and may institute unilateral changes in the employees' working conditions until the unlawful strike is terminated. Furthermore, the contractor may be able to obtain an injunction enforcing a no-strike agreement and requiring the union to arbitrate the dispute over which the employees have struck. The contractor may also recover in a suit for damages against the union.

What remedies are available to the contractor will depend on the scope of the no-strike clause. In the construction industry, there are basically two types of no-strike clauses. One limits strikes, while the other totally prohibits strikes. Under the limited no-strike clause, strikes are prohibited in a dispute in regard to the terms of the agreement. If the strike concerns terms or conditions of employment not specified in the contract, the strikers cannot be discharged, the strike will not be enjoinable, and damages will not be recoverable against the striking union. If at all possible, the contractor should refrain from agreeing to a provision which will allow a strike for a limited purpose. This type of agreement will be of little value in preventing strikes, since the union will simply attempt to cause disputes in the excepted area in order to avoid the prohibition against strikes and to press the contractor to accede to its demands.

The unconditional no-strike clause prohibits strikes during the term of the contract both for disputes arising under the agreement and for disputes not covered by the agreement. If this type of agreement is violated, the strikers may be discharged and the contractor will probably be able to recover damages against the union. In addition, the strike will be enjoinable if there is also a provision requiring the parties to arbitrate any disputes that may arise during the period of the contract and if the dispute resulting in the strike is arguably covered by the arbitration clause.

Even if there is no express no-strike provision, a promise not to strike will often be implied by the presence in the contract of a mandatory grievance and arbitration procedure that covers the dispute over which the strike arose. This implication may result unless the parties have expressly provided that a strike may occur despite the presence of the arbitration mechanism. The contractor should press for the inclusion of an express no-strike pledge which applies to all matters and disputes that may arise during the contract term even if the matter is not covered by the contract. The union may resist such a provision; however, as far as possible it is to the contractor's advantage to approach a tight no-strike clause.

For the contractor to obtain an injunction in federal district court to prohibit a strike pending arbitration, the contract must provide that the union is required to arbitrate the dispute, and the dispute over which the strike arose must arguably be covered by the arbitration clause. This type of injunction is called a *Boys Market* injunction after a case in the U.S. Supreme Court which held that the existence of a mandatory grievance and arbitration provision is a prerequisite for enforcing a no-strike clause by injunction. For the strike to be enjoined the contractor must allege that:

(1) The collective bargaining agreement contains a mandatory grievance or arbitration procedure;
(2) The agreement gives rise to an obligation on the part of the union to refrain from a strike or other concerted activity over a grievance subject to the grievance or arbitration procedure;

(3) The strike or concerted activity sought to be enjoined arises out of a grievance subject to the grievance or arbitration procedure;

(4) Breaches of the agreement are occurring and will continue to occur, or have been threatened and will be committed;

(5) The breaches have caused or will cause irreparable injury to the contractor; and

(6) The employer will suffer more from the denial of an injunction than will the union from its issuance.[2]

Therefore, the grievance and arbitration machinery should be mandatory, it should cover all disputes that might arise during the term of the collective bargaining agreement, and it should also expressly apply to any secondary boycotts or sympathy strikes. If a strike arises, the contractor should be willing to arbitrate the dispute.

The Supreme Court has also held that employers may file suit in state courts, as well as in federal district courts, to enjoin unions from violating no-strike clauses contained in collective bargaining agreements. This is applicable even in cases in which the work stoppage in question is arguably an unfair labor practice under Section 8(b)(4)(i)(D) of the NLRA. The usual rules of federal preemption, which in federal jurisdiction is exclusive, will not be applicable.[3]

A contractor may bring in an appropriate federal district court against the union for damages resulting from the breach of its promise, express or implied, not to strike, under Section 301(a) of the NLRA, which provides:

Suits for violation of contracts between an employer and a labor organization representing employees in an industry affecting commerce as defined in this Act, or between any such labor organizations, may be brought in any district court of the United States having jurisdiction of the parties without respect to the amount in controversy or without regard to the citizenship of the parties.

The contractor may also bring an action for damages in a state court. The union may attempt to remove the case to a federal district court when the more stringent *Boys Market* requirements for obtaining prearbitration injunctive relief against the strike must be satisfied.[4]

The court may not proceed in the breach-of-contract action if the dispute is over a matter subject to the grievance and arbitration procedure which has not yet been exhausted. The contractor will first be required to arbitrate the dispute over which the strike arose, and damages may be recovered in court only if the arbitrator rules in favor of the contractor. Generally the courts favor a strong presumption that a particular dispute is arbitrable.[5] Only when the contract expressly excludes the dispute over which the work stoppage arose from the arbitration procedure may the contractor bring a Section 301 suit for violation of a no-strike obligation without first processing the claim through arbitration.[6]

[2] *Boys Market v. Retail Clerks.*, 398 U.S. 235 (1970).

[3] *William E. Arnold Co. v. Carpenters Dist. Council*, 417 U.S. 12 (1974).

[4] *Avco Corp. v. Aero Lodge No. 735*, 390 U.S. 557 (1968).

[5] *United Steelworkers of America v. Warrior & Gulf Navigation Co.*, 363 U.S. 574 (1960).

[6] *Atkinson v. Sinclair Refining Co.*, 370 U.S. 195 (1962).

Under Section 301(b), if the union is liable for the strike, damages can be recovered only from the union and not from its individual members. If the international union is involved, the international union may also be liable for damages.

The union may be liable even if the strike is not specifically authorized by union officials. Many courts have relied on what is known as the "mass action" theory to support a union's liability. Under this theory a union is responsible for the mass action of its members. For the union to be absolved from liability, it may be required to use "every reasonable means" to end the strike. The absence of a provision in the collective bargaining agreement requiring the union to employ every reasonable means will not negate the union's duty to take all reasonable steps necessary to end the illegal work stoppage. Still, it is a good idea for a contractor to seek such a provision in the agreement in order to impress upon union leaders the need for them to ensure that union members are aware of their no-strike obligations.

Whether the union has taken all reasonable steps to end an illegal strike will depend upon all the circumstances. A mere disavowal of the strike by union officers will probably not be sufficient. Neither might a request for employees to return to work or a statement to them that the strike is illegal be sufficient in some circumstances.

Illustrative Case

Eazor Express and Daniels Motor Freight both had no-strike agreements with the Teamsters International and two of its locals. Members of the two locals engaged in a strike that was unauthorized by the locals (wildcat strike). The contract with the companies provided that only strikes authorized by the union officials should be deemed to be authorized by the union and that the employer should "not hold the union liable for any unauthorized acts." The agreement made it mandatory upon the union to "undertake every reasonable means to induce [striking] employees to return to their jobs during an [unauthorized] strike." The court held that even though the strikes were unauthorized, the locals were liable for the actions of their members because they failed to take "every reasonable means to put an end to the unauthorized strike." The locals were obligated to take every reasonable means to end the strike, although they had not contracted to do so, since "implied in a no-strike provision of a collective bargaining agreement is the duty of a union to undertake every reasonable means to end the unauthorized strike; such obligation . . . is mandatory." In regard to what would constitute "every reasonable means," the court said that "where the mood of wildcat strikers is ugly, officials of the union local should have used politics of power rather than merely policies of persuasion . . .[;]the duty of the union went beyond merely beckoning strikers back to work; it made it mandatory for the union to undertake every reasonable means available to terminate . . . the unauthorized strike; the union should have taken additional measures such as threatening to or removing stewards who were leading and organizing the strike and insuring that no strikers were elsewhere employed or imposing daily fines, etc."[7]

Since the international union is generally more affluent than its local, it is often to a contractor's advantage to show that the international is

[7] Eazor Express, Inc. v. IBT, 357 F. Supp. 158 (W.D. Pa. 1973).

liable in a Section 301 damage suit for breach of a no-strike agreement. For the same reason the contractor will want to implicate the international in an unfair-labor-practice proceeding involving illegal secondary activities, or jurisdictional disputes, since damages resulting from those unlawful acts may be recovered in a Section 303 suit.

To prove the international's liability for the local's illegal strike the contractor must prove that the international or one of its representatives has authorized, ratified, or participated in the local's illegal act. The mere fact that the local is affiliated with the international union or that the international has approved the local's bylaws may not be enough to implicate the international. Advice or support given by the international to the local during an illegal strike is evidence that will help a damages suit against the international succeed. Payment of strike benefits to the local may make the international liable on the ground that it has ratified the local's action.

The international may also be liable for its affiliate's breach of a no-strike obligation if it knew that the local was planning or had engaged in an illegal strike and failed to take reasonable steps to terminate it. If no officer of the international knew that the local would engage in the strike, liability might not be imputed to the international. But if an officer of the international union was present at a meeting when the local decided to strike but failed to utilize reasonable means to dissuade the local, the international might be liable. A simple notice to the local's members that the strike was illegal might not be sufficient to shield the international if stronger measures, such as fines, denial of strike benefits, or even a trusteeship over the local, could have been threatened or taken.

Sometimes the illegal relationship between the international and the local union will cause the international to be liable for the local's breach of a no-strike promise. The parent union may be liable if the local is under its trusteeship and violates a no-strike agreement or if the terms of its constitution give it substantial control over the local's affairs.

Illustrative Case

W. L. Crow Construction Co. was a general contractor engaged in the construction of an addition to a General Motors plant. UAW Local 422 had gone on strike against GM and picketed at a gate reserved for Crow's employees. The National Labor Relations Board held that Local 422 and the UAW international committed a Section 8(b)(4)(B) unfair labor practice for engaging in a secondary boycott by picketing at the reserved gate of Crow when its dispute was with GM. The international was liable together with the local since its constitution gave it strong control over its local unions and since international representatives were involved to a considerable extent in the local's affairs.[8]

Nearly all the case law to date has ruled that individual strikers may not be liable for damages when neither the local nor the international

---

[8] Auto Workers Local 422 (Crow Constr. Co.), 192 NLRB No. 127 (1971).

union can be found liable. However, a recent federal district court decision has been the first to hold that when a union is not liable, an individual union member may be personally liable for damages incurred by a contractor for an unauthorized strike in violation of a no-strike provision.[9] Nonetheless, it is questionable whether other courts will follow this court's lead in permitting recovery of damages against individual strikers. And even if this remedy were allowed, it would not be very effective for a contractor since not much could be recovered from individual strikers.

Sometimes a union strikes in violation of a no-strike provision to protest a contractor's unfair labor practice. This circumstance raises the question of whether the strikers have the status of unfair-labor-practice strikers, entitled to automatic reinstatement upon termination of the strike, or whether they may be lawfully discharged for violating the no-strike agreement. If a union has expressly waived the right to strike to protest a contractor's unfair labor practice, the strike is unlawful, and the strikers may be discharged. The union will also be liable for damages in a suit under Section 301 of the NLRA. If there is no express waiver, then according to a recent United States of court of appeals ruling, the question of whether a contractor may lawfully terminate a collective bargaining agreement and unilaterally change the terms and conditions of employment and discharge strikers may depend on whether the contractor has first exhausted all attempts at peaceful resolution of the dispute. When a strike is held to protest an alleged unfair labor practice by the contractor and the contract has a mandatory arbitration provision covering this dispute, the contractor must be willing to arbitrate the dispute. If the union refuses to arbitrate, the contractor must at least seek an injunction to compel arbitration before the contractor may terminate the agreement and discharge the strikers. If there is no mandatory arbitration procedure but there is an agreement not to strike until all the steps of the grievance process have been satisfied, then the contractor must attempt to follow all the grievance steps before repudiating the contract and firing the strikers. If the contractor shows willingness to comply with the grievance machinery but the union does not, then discharge of the strikers and repudiation of the contract will probably be justified.

Illustrative Case

District 50 of the Allied and Technical Workers Union went on strike at a Dow Chemical plant to protest Dow's unilateral change in working conditions when it altered the work schedule from a 7-days-on-the-job–2-days-off shift to a regular 5-day workweek. Dow contended that it was permitted to do this under the agreement's management rights clause. The contract provided that the union would not strike until a four-step grievance procedure had been exhausted and arbitration had either been completed or been requested by the union and refused by the company. The strike began after the fourth step of the grievance procedure failed to resolve the dispute. Neither the company nor the union ever requested

9 *Alloy Cast Steel Co. v. Steelworkers*, 429 F. Supp. 445 (N.D. Ohio 1977).

from each other that the dispute be submitted to arbitration. The company wrote several letters beseeching the employees to discontinue the "unlawful strike." Eventually the company discharged the strikers, hired replacements, rescinded the contract, and informed District 50 that it would no longer recognize it as the bargaining agent. The company argued that it had the right under the management rights clause to alter the work schedule and that even if it did not have the right the strike was unprotected since it violated the no-strike clause. The union argued that the strike was to protest the company's unfair labor practice and was therefore a protected activity despite the no-strike clause. The court of appeals held that the National Labor Relations Board was warranted in finding that the company had committed a Section 8(a)(5) unfair labor practice when it made a unilateral change in a mandatory subject of bargaining that was not within the management rights clause. The court, however, disapproved of the Board's rationale that a strike in breach of a no-strike agreement automatically may give an employer the right to terminate a contract and discharge strikers. Nor did the right to strike, according to the court, necessarily depend upon the seriousness of the employer's unfair labor practice which the strikers were protesting. The court held that "in evaluating the company's post-strike actions, the Board should have considered as a factor the company's failure to seek peaceful resolution through the grievance procedure and in the arbitral forum, even if the contract did not make arbitration mandatory upon the company, because the national labor policy favors the peaceful settlement of disputes, rather than resort by the parties to self-help.[10]

Another situation may arise when a group of minority employees engage in a strike to protest the employer's racially discriminatory employment policies which violate Title VII of the Civil Right Act of 1964 despite the presence of a no-strike obligation and a mandatory grievance and arbitration mechanism. In the case of a strike in violation of a no-strike clause, these employees may be discharged, and an injunction may be obtained to prohibit the strike to require the union to arbitrate the dispute, provided the employer has shown willingness to submit the dispute to arbitration.

Illustrative Case

The Emporium Capwell Co. had a collective bargaining agreement with the Department Store Employees Union which recognized the union as the exclusive bargaining agent for the company's employees. The agreement had a no-strike clause and prohibited employment discrimination based on race. It also had a grievance and arbitration mechanism for processing any claimed violation of the agreement, including a violation of the no-discrimination clause. A group of employees met with the secretary-treasurer of the union to present a list of grievances involving race discrimination, and the union concluded that the company was discriminating and that it would process every such grievance through to arbitration if necessary. Hollins, Hawkins, and two other employees whose testimony the union intended to use in the grievance procedure refused to participate and instead sought to discuss the issue of discrimination with the company president. When the president refused to discuss the matter, they picketed the company's store and distributed handbills urging customers not to patronize the store. The four employees were fired when they continued to picket after the company's warning that continued picketing would lead to their discharge. Section 8(a)(1) unfair-labor-practice charges were filed with the National Labor Relations Board on the ground that the company had unlawfully discharged the employees for engaging in a protected concerted activity. The Board held that the employees were not engaged in a protected activity since the NLRA does not protect employees who attempt to bypass their representative and bargain directly with their employer. The Supreme Court, reversing the court of appeals, held that the Board properly concluded that

[10] *Steelworkers v. NLRB (Dow Chemical Co.)*, 530 F.2d 266 (3d Cir. 1976).

the company had committed no unfair labor practice. The Court held that the employees went against the NLRA's principle of exclusive representation by striking the company to force it to bargain directly with them rather than through the union and therefore that they were engaged in an unprotected activity. Although Title VII of the 1964 Civil Rights Act protects employees' efforts to oppose race discrimination, that does not permit employees to bypass their union representative.[11]

Another involves a walkout of employees to protest alleged unsafe working conditions despite the presence of a no-strike clause and a mandatory arbitration procedure. Section 502 of the NLRA provides:

Nor shall the quitting of labor by an employee or employees in good faith because of abnormally dangerous conditions for work at the place of employment of such employee or employees be deemed a strike.

For the walkout not to be a strike, so that there is no violation of a no-strike agreement, the employees' belief that working conditions pose an immediate hazard to their physical safety is not alone sufficient. Rather, there must be objective data to support that belief to justify a walkout without going through arbitration.

Illustrative Case

Fruin-Colnon Construction Co. was engaged in a project to construct a shaft, 450 feet deep and 27 feet in diameter which would commence from the basin of a reservoir atop a mountain and connect with a tunnel bored along the mountainside and linked to a second reservoir. Four miners plus a foreman, Fitzgerald, comprised one of three 8-hour shifts assigned to work in the shaft. The miners complained to Fitzgerald about abnormally unsafe working conditions and requested work elsewhere. They contended that the surface on the ledge where they were working was slippery, there was a danger of falling rocks which might hit them and cause them to fall down the shaft, and cold weather which caused a mist in the shaft hindered their vision. Fitzgerald agreed to present their complaints to Superintendent Finlay, who denied the miners' request for a work transfer and ordered them back to work. The four miners refused to resume their shift work the next day and were subsequently discharged. The miners were members of Hod Carriers Local 916, which had a contract and a no-strike agreement with the company. The National Labor Relation Board (NLRB) held that the company committed a Section 8(a)(1) unfair labor practice by discharging the miners, since by walking out in protest of abnormally unsafe working conditions they were engaged in a protected concerted activity and were not on strike. The court of appeals, refusing to enforce the NLRB's order, held that the NLRB trial examiner erred in relying on the four miners' testimony concerning the unsafe working conditions and that other findings that conditions were abnormally unsafe were not supported by substantial evidence. The court held that if "employees acting concertedly leave their jobs believing in good faith abnormally dangerous working conditions prevail, they run the risk of discharge for engaging in a strike in contravention of a no-strike clause should proof later of physical facts fail to support their prior belief."[12]

A recent U.S. Supreme Court decision has declared that the national labor policy favoring a presumption of arbitrability also applies to alleged

[11] *Emporium Capwell Co. v. Western Community Addition Organ.*, 420 U.S. 50 (1975).

[12] *NLRB v. Fruin Colnon Constr. Co.*, 330 F.2d 885 (8th Cir. 1964).

unsafe working conditions. If there is a question as to whether safety disputes are subject to arbitration, that is for the arbitrator to determine, and a *Boys Market* injunction to prohibit a strike and to require the parties to arbitrate a safety dispute may be obtained.

Illustrative Case

Some employees walked out because of the presence of two foremen who the employees contended were responsible for unsafe working conditions. The collective bargaining agreement between the Mineworkers and Gateway Wall Co. contained a mandatory arbitration clause to cover "local trouble of any kind." The company sought a *Boys Market* injunction to prohibit the walkout and to require the union to arbitrate the safety dispute. The U.S. Supreme Court held that despite Section 502 a presumption of arbitrability also applies to safety disputes and that relegating safety disputes to the arena of economic combat offers no greater assurance that the ultimate resolution will ensure employee safety. The safety of the workshop would then depend on the relative economic strength of the parties rather than on an informed and impartial assessment of the facts. Only if the union had presented objective data that showed an immediate danger to the employees' physical safety (the employees' subjective estimate was insufficient) would an injunction not have been issued and damages not be recoverable.[13]

HONORING PICKET LINES OF OTHER UNIONS

A traditional strategy of unions engaged in primary strikes against their employers is to set up a picket line in the hope that other employees will not cross the line. If these employees honor the picket line, their employer's work must be halted. The picketing union hopes that by achieving that result the employer of the employees who honor the picket line will press the employer of the picketing employees to accede to their demands. Contractors whose employees honor a lawful picket line should be aware of what their rights and obligations are in that situation and of the steps that they may take in the future to avoid the problem.

Employees who refuse to cross another union's lawful picket line are known as sympathy strikers. The National Labor Relations Board (NLRB) and appellate courts have held that sympathy strikers may be engaged in a protected concerted activity. Section 7 of the NLRA gives employees the right to "engage in concerted activities for the purpose of . . . mutual aid or protection," and this section has generally been held to protect employees who honor the lawful picket line of another union. In addition, an exception to the Section 8(b)(4)(B) prohibition on secondary boycotts specifies that "a refusal by any person to enter upon the premise of any employer (other than his own employer), if the employees of such employer are engaged in a strike ratified or approved by a representative of such employees whom such employer is required to recognize," is not unlawful. The right to refuse to cross another union's lawful picket line is viewed as a personal right of individual employees. Even if the union of which the employees are

---

[13] *Gateway Coal Co. v. Mineworkers*, 414 U.S. 368 (1974).

members orders them to cross the picket line or their fellow employees cross the picket line, contractors commit an unfair labor practice they either threaten to or actually discharge or otherwise discriminate against employees who honor another union's lawful picket line.

Employees who lawfully refuse to cross another union's picket line are treated by the NLRB and most courts in the same manner as are economic strikers. Permanent replacements may be hired if contractors can establish a "legitimate and substantial business justification." Contractors should never tell sympathy strikers that they have been "discharged" for honoring a lawful picket line, even if they intend immediately to hire replacements since that statement will suggest to the NLRB that the employees are being discriminated against for participating in a protected activity, which is a Section 8(a)(1) unfair labor practice.

For contractors to provide sufficient justification for replacing sympathy strikers is often difficult. The NLRB has held that contractors may legally hire permanent replacements for employees as long as they act solely to preserve efficient job operations. If replacements have not been hired or are not immediately available to work when the sympathy strikers are terminated, that alone will suggest that they have been discharged for honoring another union's lawful picket line, which is an unfair labor practice and which may entitle the strikers to back pay and reinstatement.[14] Even the contractors' rationale that replacements were necessary to complete the job on schedule may be insufficient if no urgency is attached to completion of the task.

Illustrative Case

Newberry Energy Corp. was employed as an electrical subcontractor by the general contractor, Mountain States Engineering, to provide services at a mine. Newberry's employees were represented by Local 570 of the Electrical Workers. Several employees of Newberry who were informed that the Teamsters had erected a picket line at the mine in a dispute against another contractor refused to cross the picket line. These employees were discharged, and replacements were hired on the ground that a full crew was necessary to complete the project on time. The NLRB held that the company was guilty of an unfair labor practice because "the practical effect of the company's contention would be the virtual abolition of sympathy strikes, since employees would be reluctant to engage in such strikes where an employer could lawfully terminate them merely by establishing necessity to complete a job with a certain time frame.[15]

A contractor should refrain from terminating employees when other employees or supervisors could easily have been reassigned to perform the necessary vacant jobs. If the contractor tells these employees that they are being replaced, the contractor should be certain that replacements are available and will be hired immediately. A contractor should never tell

[14] *Redwing Carriers, Inc.*, 137 NLRB No. 1545 (1962).

[15] *Newberry Energy Corp.*, 227 NLRB No. 58 (1976).

sympathy strikers that they are being discharged for honoring a lawful picket line, but only that they are being replaced since the job needs to be completed on time.

Illustrative Case

Two employees were discharged for refusing to cross a picket line at a customer's premises to which they were assigned to make an electrical installation. At the time of their refusal no replacements were immediately available in the job market. Reassignment of the work to existing employees was not feasible. Upon the termination of the two employees no immediate replacements were hired. The NLRB, with the Ninth Circuit affirming, held that the discharge of the two employees was an unfair labor practice because there was no legitimate business justification. There was no justification because the contractor knew that he could not hire replacements within a short time since there was a shortage of skilled labor to fill these positions and because in fact no replacements were immediately made.[16]

Employees have no protected right to honor the illegal picket line of another union. If another union's picketing constitutes a secondary boycott or other unfair labor practice, the employees should be told that their refusal to work because of the picketing may be just cause for discharge or other discipline. Employees' protected right to honor another union's lawful picket line may be waived by contract. If this right has been effectively waived, the contractor may justifiably discharge or discipline and need not reinstate the honoring employees. In addition, damages may be recovered against the breaching union in a Section 301 breach-of-contract action if the union fails to utilize all reasonable steps to get its members to cross the picket line.

Illustrative Case

Three employees who worked for Daniel Construction Company refused to cross a primary line established by the Ironworkers at the Kansas Power Plant construction project in Kansas. The dispute was a primary labor dispute between Daniel Construction Company and the Ironworkers on the expiration of the collective bargaining agreement. Daniel discharged the three employees (a carpenter, a laborer, and an operating engineer), relying on the project agreement no-strike clause, which stated: "During the existence of this Agreement, the union shall not permit any strike, slow-down, or other work stoppage and there shall be no lock-out by the employer; provided, however, this shall not apply to any union signator to this agreement which calls a strike arising out of the termination of the union's local working agreement. . . ." The NLRB ruled that in the absence of a specific provision against honoring a picket line against the union, the clause could not be construed so broadly as to prohibit the honoring of picket lines, pointing out: "Contractual waiver of the right to honor such picket lines will only be found if such intent is embodied expressly in the party's agreement or clearly evident from the relevant bargaining history."[17]

[16] *NLRB v. Swain & Morris Constr. Co.*, 168 NLRB No. 1064 (1967), *aff'd*, 431 F.2d 861 (9th Cir. 1970).
[17] *Daniel Constr. Co.*, 239 NLRB No. 160 (1979).

A contractor's safest course is to be precise in setting out the written terms of the stranger-picket-line clause in the collective bargaining agreement. The NLRB and courts have ruled that the waiver of the right to cross another union's picket line must be shown by "clear and unmistakable language" in the contract. The contractor should bargain for the inclusion in the contract of a clause expressly prohibiting both primary strikes and sympathy strikes. Or, a provision in the general-purposes section of the agreement "to eliminate work stoppage of all kinds and causes" is likely to waive the union's right to honor stranger picket lines. The Board and the courts will also examine the parties' bargaining history to determine whether a general-purposes provision to eliminate work stoppages was intended to prohibit sympathy strikes.

The contractor should by all means refuse to agree to a picket-line clause which recognizes the right of union members to honor picket lines of specified unions. It will probably be determined that such a clause does not waive the employees' right not to cross the picket line of an unspecified union.[18]

The importance of an unambiguous stranger-picket-line clause is stressed in the need of a contractor to take prompt action to dissuade employees from engaging in a sympathy strike. The threat of discharge or discipline is one disincentive to honoring another union's picket line. The inclusion in the contract of a general no-strike clause or a stranger-picket-line clause, or both, along with a broad arbitration provision, will permit the arbitrator to interpret the terms of the agreement to determine whether the employees' right to honor another union's picket line has been waived. A contractor should be certain that the contract clearly prohibits sympathy strikes before discharging or disciplining employees. If the arbitrator decides against the contractor, then the contractor might be required to reinstate the employees with back pay despite a good-faith belief that the contract prohibits sympathy strikes. On the other hand, if the arbitrator finds that a sympathy strike is not permitted, then under the *Spielberg* doctrine[19] the NLRB will ordinarily defer to the arbitrator's decision and not determine whether the discharges constitute an unfair labor practice.

A recent U.S. Supreme Court ruling has held that a contractor cannot obtain an injunction in federal district court to prohibit a sympathy strike pending the outcome of arbitration. The contractor may still obtain a federal court injunction to require the union to arbitrate the issue as to whether sympathy strikes are banned by the contract if the contract has a mandatory-arbitration provision. If the arbitrator decides that sympathy strikes are prohibited under the contract, an injunction may be available to enforce the arbitrator's decision. Also, the contractor will be able to recover damages from the union in a Section 301 suit for breach of contract.

[18] *Mosler (Keller Crescent Co.)*, 217 NLRB No. 100 (1975).

[19] 112 NLRB No. 1080 (1955).

Buffalo Forge employed both office clerical-technical employees and production and maintenance employees at three locations. These employees were represented by the Steelworkers. The clerical employees went on strike and set up picket lines at all three locations to enforce their bargaining demands. Consequently, the production and maintenance employees honored the picket lines and refused to work solely in sympathy with the striking clerical employees. The contract provided that "there shall be no strikes, work stoppages or interruption or impeding of work . . . should differences arise between the employer and any employee covered by this agreement as to the meaning and application of the provisions of this agreement"; then there would be work stoppages, "but an earnest effort shall be made to settle such differences immediately [under the grievance and arbitration procedure]. . . ." Buffalo Forge sought a *Boys Market* injunction in federal district court against the sympathy strike and to compel arbitration. The company contended that since the contract contained a no-strike clause and a broad arbitration provision, the issue concerning whether the sympathy strike violated the terms of the agreement was arbitrable, so that a *Boys Market* injunction was appropriate. The district court denied injunctive relief against the sympathy strike on the ground that the sympathy strike was not over an arbitrable dispute. The Supreme Court affirmed the denial of a *Boys Market* injunction in a situation involving a sympathy strike. Justice White held that since the sympathy strike itself was not over a dispute that was subject to mandatory arbitration, a *Boys Market* injunction to prohibit the strike pending arbitration could not be obtained. It was deemed irrelevant that the arbitrator could decide whether the no-strike clause also applied to prohibit sympathy strikes. The majority permitted an injunction to require the parties to submit the issue to arbitration.[20]

A contractor might still obtain an injunction against a sympathy strike pending arbitration in state court, where the *Buffalo Forge* restriction on the issuance of this type of injunction does not apply. However, at the union's option the suit might be removed to an appropriate federal district court, where federal law and the *Buffalo Forge* rule do apply.[21] Once the suit has been removed to federal court, a state court temporary restraining order against the strike pending arbitration may remain effective for no longer than 10 days.[22]

SECONDARY BOYCOTTS

Sometimes a union which has its primary dispute with an employer will put pressure on neutral (secondary) employers in order to attempt to have them cease doing business with the primary employer. For example, a union which seeks recognition from an employer might threaten to or actually strike or picket other employers if they continued to do business with the primary employer. Or the union might picket at the secondary employer's premises with the objective to induce that employer's employees to stop working, so that the secondary employer would have no choice but to stop dealing with the primary employer. In both of these cases, the union's aim is to require a neutral employer to refuse to deal with another employer in order to place pressure on that employer to acquiesce to the

---

[20] *Buffalo Forge Co. v. Steelworkers,* 422 U.S. 397 (1976).

[21] *Avco Corp. v. Aero Lodge No. 735,* 390 U.S. 557 (1968).

[22] *Granny Goose Foods, Inc. v. Teamsters,* 415 U.S. 423 (1974).

union's demands. Section 8(b)(4)(B) of the NLRA makes it an unfair labor practice for a union to exert pressure against neutral employers or their employees with the intent of causing the neutrals to cease doing business with the employer with whom the union has its dispute or to force the neutral employer to cause the primary employer to recognize and bargain with the union. Primary and neutral employers who fall prey to an illegal secondary boycott may file unfair-labor-practice charges under Section 8(b)(4)(B) with the NLRB and request the NLRB to obtain an injunction against the unlawful union pressure. Damages may also be recovered from a union for an illegal secondary boycott in a suit in federal district court.

It is essential that contractors realize the difference between lawful primary and illegal secondary activity. One of the purposes of the NLRA is to protect a union's right to picket the employer with which it has a primary dispute while preserving the interest of neutral employers and their employees to be insulated from the strikes and turmoil of labor disputes between other empoyers and their employees. To this end, a proviso to Section 8(b)(4)(B) permits a union to picket the primary employer at its premises and protects employees of other employers from employer retaliation for refusing to cross the picket line if the picketing is a lawful primary activity. But when the picketing is directed against a neutral employer or when a neutral employer's premises are picketed, the picketing is no longer a protected primary activity and is instead an illegal secondary boycott, so that the union which pickets is guilty of a Section 8(b)(4)(B) unfair labor practice.

A union threatening or engaging in a strike or picketing must have the intent to require a neutral employer to cease doing business with the primary employer or to force the primary employer to recognize and bargain with the union for it to be guilty of a Section 8(b)(4)(B) unfair labor practice. If this proscribed object is absent, it is irrelevant that the picketing actually causes neutral employers to cease doing business with the primary employer or causes neutral employees to halt work. Conversely, if the intent is present, an unfair labor practice has been committed even if the threatened or actual picketing or strike does not achieve its purpose. The illegal intent may be shown if the picket signs are directed against a neutral employer or if the picketing occurs at premises or times when the primary employer's employees are not working. Threatened strikes and picketing against neutral employers or against neutral employees may reveal a union's unlawful purpose to cause a neutral employer to cease doing business with the employer with which the union has its primary dispute. Statements by union agents are particularly useful in proving the illegal object of secondary-boycott activity.

Common-Situs Picketing

The secondary-boycott problem frequently arises in the construction industry as a result of what is known as "common-situs picketing." On the typical construction jobsite there are frequently a general contractor and many subcontractors whose employees are usually represented by different building trades unions and work alongside each other. A union may have a dispute with a union contractor because, for example, the contractor has employed workers outside the union's hiring hall, used prefabricated materials, or allegedly violated other requirements in their bargaining agreement. Or the union's dispute with the employer may be that the employer is nonunion and does not have a collective bargaining agreement with the union. To publicize its dispute, the union will set up a picket line, and the result may be that members of the other unions will refuse to work, and part of the project or even the entire project will be shut down. The dispute could be resolved quickly and work could proceed if the primary contractor either complied with the union's demands or were removed from the project. The general contractor may be either unable or unwilling to terminate the subcontractor because the subcontract does not permit termination or because the general contractor may reason that it will cost more to replace the subcontractor than it will cost to resist union pressure. There are various practical and legal remedies that the general contractor and subcontractors should be aware of to eliminate the costly work stoppages associated with common-situs picketing.

It is often unclear whether common-situs picketing is a lawful primary or an illegal secondary activity prohibited by Section 8(b)(4)(B). The *Moore Dry Dock* test has been utilized to determine whether common-situs picketing has an illegal objective. The test evolved in a dispute in which a nonunion employer contracted with a company to perform alterations on the nonunion employer's ship at the company shipyard. A union picketed with signs directed against the nonunion employer at the entrance to the shipyard since the company would not allow the pickets any closer to the ship on which some of the nonunion employer's crew were working. The NLRB held that the picketing was a lawful primary activity since it complied with all the following conditions: (1) the picketing was limited to times when employees of the primary employer were on the site that was picketed, (2) the primary employer was engaged in normal business at the site that was picketed, (3) the picketing was limited to places reasonably closed to the location of the situs, and (4) the picketing disclosed clearly that the dispute was with the primary employer.[23] In 1951 the U.S. Supreme Court held that the general contractor and various subcontractors on a construction project were separate employers over the union's contention that because their operations were interrelated, they must be a single employer. Therefore, the union committed a Section 8(b)(4)(B) unfair labor practice by attempting to coerce a neutral employer to cease doing business with the primary employer when it picketed the entire jobsite to force a general contractor to terminate the contract of a nonunion subcontractor.[24]

[23] *Sailors Union of the Pacific (Moore Dry Dock Co.)*, 92 NLRB No. 93 (1950).

[24] *NLRB v. Denver Bldg. & Constr. Trades Council*, 341 U.S. 675 (1951).

The NLRB and the courts have utilized the *Moore Dry Dock* test and *Denver Building Trades* decision to determine whether common-situs picketing constitutes a secondary boycott. If the picketing fails to comply with any of the four conditions in the test, there is normally a strong presumption that the union's purpose is to attempt to require a neutral contractor to cease doing business with the primary contractor. In the event, contractor should file a Section 8(b)(4)(B) unfair-labor-practice charge with the NLRB so that the Board may seek an injunction against the illegal picketing.

Illustrative Case

The New Orleans Building and Construction Trades Council had a dispute with Markwell & Hartz, Inc., a nonunion general contractor. Markwell & Hartz set up two gates for the exclusive use of the employees of two subcontractors, Binnings Construction Co. and Bernes Electrical Co., and a third for its employees. Although the council had notice of the separate gates, picketing continued at all the gates. The picketing continued even after the council was notified that Markwell & Hartz's employees had left the jobsite. The NLRB ruled that the council committed a Section 8(b)(4)(B) unfair labor practice. By failing to locate its pickets at the gate reserved for Markwell & Hartz, with the council had its dispute, the council failed to satisfy the *Moore Dry Dock* requirement that the picketing be confined to an area reasonably close to the situs of the dispute. This decision endorsed the use of separate gates to determine whether common-situs picketing is an illegal boycott.[25]

Over the years the building trades unions have sought without success legislation which would drastically alter the present law concerning common-situs picketing. The common-situs–picketing bill, vetoed by President Ford in 1976 and subsequently rejected by Congress in 1977, in effect would have overruled the *Denver Building Trades* decision and treated the various contractors on a construction project as a single employer. If common-situs picketing ever becomes law, it would permit a union to picket an entire jobsite and shut down a project over a dispute with one of the contractors, which would put enormous pressure on all the contractors to force the dispute to the resolved in the union's favor. It would allow many of the types of secondary union pressures which were the original impetus for Congress in 1947 to enact the law prohibiting secondary boycotts.

Separate Gates and Separate Hours

When it is learned that a union intends to picket either the general contractor or one of the subcontractors, setting up a "reserved-gate system" should be considered. Under this system a separate gate for the exclusive use of the employees and suppliers of the contractor with whom the union has a dispute is clearly marked and located away from another gate reserved for the neutrals' employees and suppliers. Around the project should be posted signs which unambiguously state that employees and

[25] *Building Trades Council (Markwell & Hartz, Inc.),* 155 NLRB No. 42 (1965).

suppliers of the contractor with whom the union is disputing may pass *only* through the reserved gate. Only one separate gate for neutral contractors need be provided. The union and the pickets should be notified as soon as possible of the existence of the separate gates. Proper wording on the gates might state, for example: "This entrance is for the exclusive use of [name of primary employer], its employees, agents, and suppliers only. No others use this entrance." Other signs should be posted for neutral contractors with similar instructions, and the following should be added: "No employees of [primary employer] use this entrance."

If the general contractor properly sets up a reserved-gate system which is rigidly adhered to, then to comply with the *Moore Dry Dock* conditions which determine whether picketing has a lawful primary or unlawful secondary purpose the union muct picket in close proximity to the gate of the contractor with whom it has the dispute. The job is then more likely to proceed because the other union members may be more likely to work since they will not have to cross picket lines at the gates where they must enter. If the union does not comply with a reserved-gate system that is properly set up, that will be a strong indication that the union is guilty of a Section 8(b)(4)(B) unfair labor practice for attempting to force a neutral contractor to stop doing business with the contractor with whom the union has its dispute. The union may be guilty of the unfair labor practice even if the picketing fails to cause the neutral's employees to cease work.

Letters or telegrams should be sent promptly to the unions to advise them of the establishment of separate gates, since a union's obligation to abide by the reserved-gate system does not arise at least until it is notified that such a system has been set up. A dated copy of the telegram should be retained by the contractor to support the contention in a subsequent unfair-labor-practice proceeding or damages suit that the union received notice of the reserved-gate system and did not adhere to it.

Contractors must make certain that the primary employer's employees and suppliers at all times pass only through the gate reserved for them. A result of mixed use of the neutral's gates by the primary employer's employees or suppliers may be that the union will be allowed to picket at those gates too, since the union is entitled under the NLRA to put pressure on primary employers by notifying their employees of the dispute. If possible, a fence or similar barriers and signs should be placed around the entire jobsite instructing employees and suppliers as to the entrances to which they are restricted. Otherwise, the reserved-gate system might break down because of mixed use of the neutral's gates. In that event, the union might be able to picket the entire jobsite, and the project might be shut down because union workers would refuse to cross the picket lines.

Illustrative Case

In furtherance of its dispute with O'Brien Electric Co., an electrical contractor, IBEW Local 441 picketed an entire construction project and not just at a gate reserved for O'Brien's employees, which was labeled "O'Brien Electric Employees Entrance Only." Prior to that time, O'Brien's employees had entered through an unmarked and unenclosed area, and after this reserved gate was set up, that area remained unenclosed and unmarked. The NLRB ruled that the IBEW local did not violate the NLRA by picketing away from the reserved gate for O'Brien's employees, since that gate was not marked in such a clear manner as to give the local reasonable assurance that its message would reach O'Brien's employees. The sign did not negate the possibility that O'Brien's employees might also enter through other gates or through the unenclosed area which did not have any instructions to employees to enter only through their reserved gate.[26]

To remove the situs of the dispute from most of the construction activity so that the job is more likely to proceed, the gate for the primary contractor should be located as far as possible from the other gates. At the same time the reserved gate for the primary contractor must not be located unreasonably far from the primary contractor's construction activities.

Illustrative Case

Laborers Local 1290 was given notice that the gate reserved for employees of the contractor with whom the union had the dispute, Walters Foundation, Inc., would be switched from the southwest to the north gate. Upon receiving notice of the change the pickets were removed to the north gate. Walters's business activity could not be seen from the north gate, and it was apparent from construction work near that gate that it would soon be inaccessible to Walters's employees. The Laborers switched the pickets back to the southwest gate. The NLRB held that Local 1290 did not engage in an illegal secondary boycott, even though the picketing was not at all times confined to the reserved gate, since the "situs of the dispute was not defined with sufficient degree of permanence to the circumscribed area of lawful primary picketing."[27]

Separate gates will sometimes appear to be ineffective to keep the job running because union employees of neutral contractors may refuse to enter their neutral gate if there is picketing anywhere on the project. If the picketing union properly limits its picketing to the primary contractor's gate and in all other respects does not engage in an illegal secondary activity, then the fact that union employees refuse to work may not make the picketing union guilty of an illegal secondary boycott. But the neutral employees who refuse to pass through their reserved gate may be lawfully discharged or disciplined since the NLRA does not protect employees who honor illegal picket lines, and their refusal to enter a neutral gate is equivalent to honoring an illegal picket line. Union contracts often contain clauses which protect employees who honor certain picket lines. Such provisions may be illegal and unenforceable if they purport to protect employees who refuse to cross illegal secondary picket lines. The District of Columbia Court of Appeals has held that a picket-line provision which is interpreted to protect employees who refuse to pass through their neutral gate because of picketing at other gates is the same as a clause which attempts to protect employees for honoring an illegal secondary picket line,

---

[26] IBEW Local 441 (Jones & Jones, Inc.), 158 NLRB No. 57 (1976).

[27] Laborers Local 1290 (Walters Foundation), 195 NLRB No. 71 (1972).

so that it is unenforceable and does not protect neutral employees who refuse to work from discharge or discipline. This decision, then, may be used by neutral contractors as a device to get their employees back to work during lawful union picketing at separate gates for the primary contractor's employees and suppliers.

Illustrative Case

Gunnar Johnson & Son, Inc., general contractor on a project to build a school, employed members of the Bricklayers, Laborer, and Operating Engineers. Gorham Construction Co., the prime mechanical contractor, employed members of the Plumbers; and Design Electric, Inc., the prime electrical contractor, employed members of Christian Labor Association, which unlike the other unions was not affiliated with the AFL-CIO. Local 110 of the Electrical Workers posted at the construction site a sign which read: "Electrical Work Being Performed on This Job Is at Substandard Wages and Benefits by Design Electric—This Notice Is for Information of the Public and Is Not Intended to Cause any Person to Refuse to Pick Up or Deliver or to Perform Any Service–IBEW L.U. 10." Employees of Johnson and Gorham refused to work when they saw this sign. Subsequently, Johnson designated an east gate as being reserved for employees and suppliers of Johnson and Gorham (neutral contractors) and a west gate for employees and suppliers of Design (primary contractor). Local 110 properly restricted its picketing to the west gate; yet Johnson's and Gorham's employees continued to refuse to enter through the neutral gate reserved for them. The Bricklayers, Laborers, and Operating Engineers contended that the picketing clause in their agreements justified their refusal to enter through the reserved gate. That clause read: "The employers may not request or instruct any employees except watchmen or supervisory personnel to go through a picket line except to protect life or property." The Plumbers defended themselves on the ground that their picket clause provided that "refusal to pass through a lawfully permitted picket line will not constitute a violation of the agreement." In interpreting these clauses, the arbitrator held that they "were broad enough to protect employee refusals to work on the project," so that the decision not to pass through the reserved gate was protected by the picket-line clauses. The NLRB ruled that the clauses were illegal since they were "broad enough to permit employee refusals to cross not only lawful picket lines but also secondary picket lines at the employer's place of business." The District of Columbia Circuit Court of Appeals upheld the NLRB's order, stating that the picket-line clauses were illegal and that the members of the four unions who refused to pass through the neutral reserved gate because a lawful primary picket line had been set up elsewhere on the jobsite were not protected against discharge since the NLRA affords no protection to employees who honor illegal picket lines, and the refusal to pass through a neutral gate that has been properly complied with is the same as refusing to cross a secondary picket line.[28]

It is sometimes difficult to ascertain the reason why employees of neutral employers refuse to work during picketing. These employees should be asked what their union business agents have told them concerning working while picketing is in effect. They should be advised that the picketers have no dispute with the neutral employers, and their union should be told that its members' refusal to pass through a gate properly reserved for neutral employees because of another union's dispute with another contractor may

[28] *Bricklayers and Stone Masons Local 2 et al. v. NLRB*, 562 F.2d 775 (D.C. Cir. 1977).

constitute an unfair labor practice. The union should also be advised of possible breaches of and liability for violations of a no-strike clause. If the union does have a no-strike obligation which applies to prohibit the honoring of another union's picket line, its members may be notified that they may be discharged or otherwise disciplined if they refuse to work.

Another method by which a job may progress despite a threat of picketing is to institute separate hours of work for the contractor with whom the union has its dispute. The picketing must be limited to the contractor's scheduled working hours to satisfy the *Moore Dry Dock* condition that picketing be reasonably limited to times when the primary contractor's employees are on the jobsite. Sometimes a separate-hours system or weekend schedules might be necessary to complete the job because other union members might refuse not only to cross another union's picket line but to work behind a picket line.

Illustrative Case

Local 519 of the Plumbing and Pipefitters Union had a dispute with H. C. Robertson, a nonunion plumbing contractor whom it was trying to organize. Both to keep Robertson on the job and to prevent picketing against Robertson to shut down the entire job, Babcock, the general contractor, and Robertson agreed that Robertson's employees would no longer work during the day and would instead work after hours and on weekends. The union received notice of the revised work schedule but continued to picket during the day when Robertson's employees were not working. The District of Columbia Circuit, affirming the NLRB, ruled that separate hours are equivalent to separate gates. The union committed a Section 8(b)(4)(B) unfair labor practice by continuing to picket for substantial periods of time when the employees of Robertson, with whom the union had its dispute, were not working and the union had notice that they would not be working at those times.[29]

It is essential that unambiguous and timely notice of the institution of a separate-hours system be given to the picketing union. It has been held that the union may picket during the primary contractor's absence when the primary contractor had work remaining to do on the project and the contractor's return could not reasonably be predicted by the union.

Illustrative Case

Electrical Workers Local 697 picketed Home Electric Co., which had a contract to install electrical panels and socket boxes, to protest what it contended was the payment of substandard area wages. At the time of the picketing none of Home Electric's employees were working. There was work left to do, and the local could not predict when the employees would return to work since such installation work had been performed sporadically in the past. The court of appeals held that the union could lawfully picket Home Electric even during its employees' absence from work, since it could reasonably assume that they would return at some time because there was work left to do and since it could not reasonably predict when they would return to work.[30]

[29] *Local 519, Journeymen v. NLRB (H.C. Robertson)*, 416 F.2d 1120 (D.C. Cir. 1969).

[30] *Kolodziej v. IBEW Local 697*, 535 F.2 1257 (7th Cir. 1976).

Even if the union has received notice of the change in working hours, the contractor should make sure that none of the primary contractor's employees and none of its supervisors are present except during the revised hours. Measures should also be taken to assure that the primary contractor's suppliers do not enter the jobsite except during the revised hours. This is necessary because it may be lawful for the union to picket whenever the primary contractor's supervisors, employees, or suppliers are present.

Illustrative Case

After Linbeck Construction Corp., the general contractor, received notice that Local 450 of the Operating Engineers intended to picket Luckie Construction Co., an excavation and storm sewer subcontractor, Linbeck notified Local 450 of a reserved gate for the employees and suppliers of Luckie. Nevertheless, electricians, plumbers, and pipefitters on the job refused to work when the pickets appeared, so that Linbeck sent a telegram to the local that Luckie's employees would no longer perform any daytime work. Although none of Luckie's employees worked during the day, Luckie's supervisor occasionally appeared during the day to inspect the previous evening's work, and supplies destined for Luckie's use continued to be delivered during the day. The local continued the daytime picketing after receiving notice of the revised work schedule. The NLRB held that since Luckie had failed to honor the revised time schedule by having its supplies delivered at other times and by itself arriving at the jobsite at these other times, Local 450 was not required to limit its picketing to the revised hours.[31]

Once a separate-gate or separate-hours system has broken down, the contractor is still permitted to reestablish it. The contractor who reestablishes the system should promptly notify the union of its revision and make sure that the new system is being properly complied with by the primary contractor's employees and suppliers. Once the union receives notice of the revision and the system is actually reestablished, the union will probably act unlawfully if it pickets away from the gate reserved for the primary contractor. It is unclear whether the union violates the NLRA when it pickets elsewhere after receiving notice of the revision but before actual reestablishment.

Illustrative Case

Local 470 of the Carpenters picketed Mueller-Anderson, Inc., the general Contractor, to protest its payment of substandard area wages. Anderson had set up one gate for its employees and suppliers and another gate for subcontractors' employees and suppliers. The Carpenters picketed both gates when Anderson's employees began entering through the gate reserved for the subcontractors. After Anderson received notice that the separate-gate system had broken down, it notified the Carpenters that the separate gates would be reinstituted and revised to accommodate new subcontractors. Anderson's employees and suppliers thereafter entered only through the gate clearly labeled for them, yet the Carpenters continued to picket at both gates. The court of appeals affirmed the NLRB's ruling that the Carpenters had engaged in a secondary boycott by continuing to picket at locations

---

[31] *Operating Engineers Local 450 (Linbeck Constr. Corp.)*, 219 NLRB No. 133 (1975).

other than the gate reserved for Anderson's employees and suppliers after the union received notice of the system's intended and actual reestablishment.[32]

One of the advantages of establishing a reserved-gate system is that neutral employees will sometimes continue to work despite limited picketing, so that the union may feel pressure to use other, illegal tactics to close down a project. Besides complying with a separate-gate or separate-hours system, the contractor should become aware of all facets of the union's conduct to determine whether to file unfair-labor-practice charges against the union for engaging in a secondary boycott.

Ally Doctrine

When a subcontractor agrees to perform struck work for a general contractor that the subcontractor would not otherwise have performed and has not customarily performed in the past, the union may picket the subcontractor. A subcontractor who does this ceases to remain a neutral employer and instead becomes what is known as an "ally" of the general contractor, so that the union whose dispute is with the general contractor may picket the ally subcontractor. A contractor who contemplates filing a Section 8(b)(4) charge with the NLRB against a picketing union should make sure that no ally situation exists.

A general contractor who arranges to have the struck work of a subcontractor performed by another employer is not an ally and therefore may not be picketed by a union whose dispute is with the subcontractor. An employer who performs the subcontractor's struck work is an ally and may be picketed.

Illustrative Case

McDonald Cast Stone Co., a stone supplier, was struck by Laborers Local 859. Byrne, Citadel, and Brown, all of whom were building contractors, arranged to have the stones delivered to the jobsite by a group of independent truckers. The Laborers threatened to and did picket with signs stating "This Picketing Is Directed Only at Employees of McDonald Stone Products" at times other than when the independent truckers were at the jobsite. The District of Columbia Court of Appeals held that the independent truckers were allies of McDonald since the independent truckers' employees were performing work which would normally be performed by McDonald's employees. Therefore, the Laborers could lawfully picket the independents whenever their employees were performing the struck work, including the jobsite. However, the Laborers could not lawfully take or threaten any action to induce Byrne, Citadel and Brown to cease doing business with the independents, since they were not allies because their employees were not performing the struck work. Therefore, a reserved-gate system could be instituted for the independents' employees, and the Laborers would be required to comply with the *Moore Dry Dock* test by limiting their picketing to that gate.[33]

[32] *Carpenters Local 470 v. NLRB (Mueller-Anderson, Inc.)*, 564 F.2d 1360 (9th Cir. 1978).

[33] *Laborers Local 859 v. NLRB*, 446 F.2d 1319 (D.C. Cir. 1971).

Publicity by the Union

The act may permit a union to engage in some activities which are aimed at a neutral secondary employer with the goal of influencing a primary employer with whom the union has a dispute. A proviso to Section 8(b)(4) allows a union to use publicity, "other than picketing, for the purpose of truthfully advising the public . . . that a product [is] produced by an employer with whom the labor organization has a primary dispute and [is] distributed by another employer, as long as such publicity does not have an effect of inducing any individual employed by any person other than the primary employer in the course of his employment to refuse to pick up, deliver, or transport any goods, or not to perform any services, at the establishment of the employer engaged in such distribution.[34] This means that a union may, at the premises of a neutral employer, publicize and inform the public of its dispute with a primary employer as long as this does not have the effect of halting deliveries and services at the premises of the neutral secondary employer. Although the proviso states that means other than picketing must be used, the Supreme Court has interpreted this statement as allowing union picketing of a secondary employer when the picketing is truly informational and is directed at a primary employer.

The proviso to Section 8(b)(4) is applicable mainly to the picketing of retail establishments which carry for sale the products of employers with whom a union has a dispute. Picketing in the retail context is readily seen as directed to informing the public, while picketing of a nonretail contractor usually is not directed to the public or informational in nature. Thus, when a union pickets a construction contractor's establishment to protest the mere use or purchase of products of another employer with whom it has a dispute, this form of protest will usually be found unlawful, particularly when it causes work stoppages or halts deliveries.

Illustrative Case

Glaziers and Glassworkers Local No. 558 objected to what it felt were substandard wage rates paid by Cupples Products Corporation, a manufacturer of preglazed windows. Learning that Sharp Bros., a construction contractor, was using windows made by Cupples in its construction project, the union decided to picket the construction site. Soon thereafter, Sharp Bros. experienced a work stoppage. In reviewing the case, the court of appeals found that the windows made by Cupples were not being sold on Sharp Bros. premises, nor did any potential buyers come to the construction site for the purpose of purchasing windows. Thus, the picketing was not truly directed to the public, for it was intended to make Sharp Bros. stop purchasing Cupples windows for use in its building project. Because of this and the fact that the picketing resulted in a work stoppage, the union was held to have violated Section 8(b)(4). It was unable to avail itself of the protection of the provision.[35]

An exception to the publicity proviso principle has been created for "merged" products; it prohibits a union from a publicity appeal when the

---

[34] *NLRB v. Fruit and Vegetable Packers and Warehousemen Local 760,* 377 U.S. 58 (1974).

[35] *Glaziers Local 558 v. NLRB,* 408 F.2d 197 (1969).

primary employer's product is merged into the goods of a neutral employer so that the primary goods are not clearly identifiable from those of the secondary employer. Since the construction craft work of a subcontractor is merged into the final construction product, this defense may be available for the general contractor or the developer if the union attempts publicity distributing handbills or picketing the general contractor or developer.

Illustrative Case

Area standards picketing and handbill distribution by Local 399 of the Carpenters union was directed against the developer of a housing project, Panther Valley, Ltd., because a nonunion construction subcontractor, K & K Construction Company, Inc., had performed carpentry work in framing the houses. The Third Circuit Court of Appeals reversed the NLRB and found that the union had violated the secondary-boycott provisions of the NLRA; specifically, it pointed out that the publicity proviso does not apply when the primary product or service merged with the secondaries and the union cannot limit its appeal for a boycott without enmeshing the neutral in its dispute.[36]

Legal Remedies

A contractor who is faced with a secondary boycott has legal remedies both through the NLRB and in the federal courts. The contractor is wise to gather evidence to support the case in either forum. Evidence should be collected to determine whether *Moore Dry Dock* conditions for the picketing of a primary employer have been violated. The exact wording of picket signs should be written down, and photographs of the picketing should be taken. A schedule of the primary contractor's working hours should be kept, and a record of the times that the pickets arrive at and leave the jobsite should be retained to determine whether the picketing has been lawfully limited to times when the primary contract's employees are working or illegally extended to other times when they are not on the jobsite. If separate gates are established, photographs should be taken of each separate gate and of the picketing to determine whether the pickets have been lawfully restricted to the gate reserved for the primary contractor or have unlawfully also included the gates set aside for neutral contractors.

One of the most useful sources of proof of a union's secondary objective consists of statements made by union agents. The primary employer and secondary employers should make notes of conversations and meetings with union business agents, job stewards and members of the union. Often these statements will diclose that picketing which otherwise is legally conducted by following *Moore Dry Dock* standards has an illegal secondary-boycott object and therefore is an enjoinable unfair labor practice.

Illustrative Case

Local 441 of the Electrical Workers picketed a subcontractor, Robbins communications, to protest its failure to pay prevailing area wages and benefits. The picketing clearly dis-

---

[36]*K & K Constr. Co. v. NLRB——F.2d——(3d Cir. 1979).*

closed that the dispute was with Robbins. The local informed Carter, the general contractor, that it would cease the picketing if Carter would give written assurance to Local 441 that Robbins would not be allowed back on the jobsite unless it agreed to pay prevailing wages and benefits. The NLRB ruled that the local's statement to Carter was in effect an attempt to enmesh it in the union's dispute with Robbins, because Carter was the only party with the power to remove the subcontractor from the job. The union committed an illegal secondary boycott even though it complied with the *Moore Dry Dock* test.[37]

A union might attempt to use pressure tactics against a neutral contractor which might include a threat to withhold job referrals from the general contractor unless the latter agreed to remove a nonunion or substandard contractor from the job. A union's threat to terminate any or all of its obligations under its contract with a neutral contractor is unlawful. Besides threats or inducements against neutral contractors, the contractor should be aware of any union threats or inducements directed toward neutral employees. Threats to fine or discharge from union membership neutral employees who work despite a picket line will support an unfair-labor-practice charge against the union even if the *Moore Dry Dock* test is satisfied.

Illustrative Case

The Carpenters district council picketed Pace Construction Co. with signs stating that Pace had no labor agreement with the council. The council fined one of its members who was employed by another subcontractor on the jobsite for working despite the picket line. The NLRB held that even though the council satisfied *Moore Dry Dock* standards, it nonetheless acted unlawfully since its purpose for fining the union member for crossing the picket line was unlawfully to coerce neutral employees to cease working so as to cause a neutral subcontractor to cease doing business with the contractor with whom the union was at odds.[38]

Conversations with union business agents and picketers may also disclose a proscribed secondary objective of the union. Employees of secondary employers should be asked what their union business agents have told them concerning working while the picketing is in effect. Threats of fines or other union discipline by the union to these employees constitute an unfair labor practice. Any conversations with employees and union business agents should be promptly recorded in writing. It is wise to hold any conversations with picketers or union agents in the presence of at least one witness other than the parties to the conversation.

Once picketing begins, local law enforcement agencies should be notified, and extra patrols should be requested if trouble is anticipated. On some occasions picketing may either prevent or discourage neutral employees and suppliers from working, and the presence of police officers may be necessary to allow access by these employees to the jobsite. A record of

[37] *IBEW Local 441 (Robbins Communications)*, 222 NLRB No. 24 (1976).

[38] *Carpenters Dist. Council (Pace Constr. Co.)*, 222 NLRB No. 104 (1976).

damages and monetary costs as a result of the picketing should be kept as evidence in a subsequent damage action against the union.

A contractor who is confronted with a secondary boycott should file a Section 8(b)(4)(B) unfair-labor-practice charge against the union in the appropriate NLRB regional office. Evidence to support the charge, including affidavits and photographs, should be presented by the contractor and the contractor's attorney. If the Board office finds that there is reasonable cause to believe that an unfair labor practice has been committed, it will file a complaint and is required under Section 10(1) of the NLRA to petition a federal district court for an injunction to prohibit the illegal secondary activity. Issuance of the complaint will usually cause the union to cease its picketing. If the picketing does not end at that point, an unfair-labor-practice hearing will be held, and the complaint will be prosecuted by the regional office before an administrative law judge of the NLRB. The administrative judge's decision may be appealed to the Board members of the NLRB, and if they uphold the judge's decision, then under Section 10(e) the General Counsel of the NLRB will petition the appropriate United States circuit court of appeals for a cease-and-desist order.

In some cases the contractor may diligently obtain an injunction in federal district court to prohibit an unlawful strike or picketing. If the strike or picketing is over a dispute that is arguably covered by a mandatory-arbitration provision, the contractor may obtain a *Boys Market* injunction to prohibit those activities pending arbitration. Neutral contractors whose employees refuse to work because of common-situs picketing may have bargaining agreements with their unions containing a mandatory-arbitration provision and a clause forbidding sympathy strikes. These contractors are entitled under Section 301 of the NLRA to bring a suit in federal district court to enforce the agreement by an injunction to require the union to arbitrate the issue as to whether the work stoppage violates the prohibiting of sympathy strikes. However, under the U.S. Supreme Court's *Buffalo Forge* decision[39] the injunction may not prohibit the sympathy strike pending the outcome of arbitration if the work stoppage is not over a grievance subject to arbitration. An injunction may be obtained in federal district court to require the neutral contractors' employees to resume work if the arbitration determines that the contract barred the work stoppage. (See Chapter 4, section "No-Strike Agreements.")

If the union has a no-strike agreement with a contractor, that contractor may recover damages in federal district court under Section 301 of the NLRA for the union's breach of its no-strike promise. In addition, Section 303 of the NLRA permits any contractor injured as a result of a union's illegal secondary activity to bring a damage suit in federal district court against the union. Even if the union eventually decides to comply with the NLRB's cease-and-desist order, damages caused by its unlawful action prior to compliance may be recovered. A contractor is wise to file charges

[39]428 U.S. 397 (1976).

with the NLRB if the contractor is also contemplating bringing a damage action under either Section 301 or Section 303, since the rules of evidence in an NLRB hearing are more lenient than in a federal court proceeding, and a favorable decision by the NLRB may, by collateral estoppel, establish the union's guilt in the damage suit.

Both Section 301 and Section 303 permit a contractor to recover damages that will compensate for the actual losses that the contractor has sustained as a result of a union's unlawful action. Even if an unlawful work stoppage lasts a shorter time than the delay in construction, damages may be recovered for the entire period of the construction delay that was a result of the work stoppage.[40] A subcontractor who was removed from a construction job because of a union's illegal secondary pressures against the general contractor has been permitted to recover the unpaid contract price less the costs the subcontractor would have incurred to complete the job. If this measure of damages cannot be proved with reasonable certainty, the subcontractor has been permitted to prove the profit margin on similar projects as the measure of damages.[41]

A contractor is permitted to recover for the actual expenses incurred between the period when a job would have been completed and when it was actually completed because of an unlawful work stoppage. Recovery has been permitted for overhead, rental, and depreciation expenses for the period of the job delay and also for excess administrative costs, wages, and overtime premiums. Compensation has also been allowed for equipment and supplies that were damaged as a consequence of the union's unlawful acts. Section 303 does not permit a contractor to recover punitive damages in federal court for a union's unfair labor practice.

The courts in a Section 303 proceeding have permitted a contractor to recover expenses incurred to terminate an illegal work stoppage. The Supreme Court has held that attorney's fees that were directly related to ending illegal picketing may be awarded in a Section 303 suit, including the prosecution of the unfair-labor-practice charge before the NLRB when union members resumed work after the charge had been filed.[42] Legal fees expended in the prosecution of the Section 303 suit itself are not compensable.[43]

Generally, attorneys' fees have not been recoverable by a successful contractor in a Section 301 suit for a union's violation of a no-strike promise. When a losing union refused to submit to arbitration a dispute that was plainly covered by the contract's grievance and arbitration procedure and went on strike instead, the court might be more willing to allow the contractor to recover legal expenses.

---

[40] *Lawhon Constr. Co. v. Carpet Local 1179*, 513 F.2d 733 (8th Cir. 1975).

[41] *Refrigeration Contractors v. Plumbers Local 211*, 501 F.2d 668 (5th Cir. 1974).

[42] *Ironworkers Local 597 v. Linbeck Constr. Co.*, 434 U.S. 955 (1977).

[43] *Bryant Air Conditioning & Heating Co. v. Sheet Metal Workers Local 541*, 472 F.2d 969 (9th Cir. 1973).

Another way to terminate a secondary boycott and to get union employees back to work is for the general contractor to capitulate to the union and either to force the nonunion subcontractor to accept the union's demands or to remove the subcontractor from the job and substitute a subcontractor who is willing to recognize the union.

The easiest way to stop union picketing and to get a job running again may be for the contractor to give in to the union's demands and terminate the nonunion subcontractor. However, what might save the contractor costs in the short run may impose much larger costs in the long run on a contractor who desires to work with nonunion contractors. A contractor who gives in to a union once without a fight is more likely to be faced with similar illegal tactics by the union in the future. The contractor should generally not give in to the union's unlawful action without first exhausting all practical and legal remedies. Damage suits against unions help to deter illegal secondary pressures, and a contractor should never give up a good damages action without obtaining concessions from the union. If the contractor does decide to remove a nonunion contractor from a job, the union should be promptly notified.

RESTRICTIVE AGREEMENTS

The Building trades unions often seek to include in their collective bargaining agreements with contractors various types of restrictions on the contractors' right to subcontract work. Some of these agreements may be illegal and unenforceable if they have the proscribed affect of requiring one contractor to "cease doing business' with another contractor. But other agreements will be lawful even if they have this cease-doing-business effect because they are also intended to achieve certain permissible objectives.

If a clause is illegal, a union that insists upon its inclusion in a contract should be told that the clause would be illegal and unenforceable and that the contractor therefore would not even consider it. The union should be reminded that agreement to some illegal provisions might expose both parties to antitrust liability of millions of dollars. If the union continues to insist upon an illegal restrictive clause, the contractor should file an unfair-labor-practice charge with the NLRB for the union's failure to bargain in good faith. A threatened or actual work stoppage or picketing to force the contractor to accede to such a provision may also be a secondary boycott, which is an unfair labor practice in violation of Section 8(b)(4)(B). Sometimes the language of the agreement is lawful, but the union acts unlawfully by taking certain coercive actions against the signatory contractor in an attempt to enforce the agreement. In that event, the union may have committed an illegal secondary boycott, and an unfair-labor-practice charge can be filed. The contractor should request the NLRB to seek an injunction in federal district court. Contractors may also be able to recover in federal court for damages caused by a union's unfair labor practice.

Section 8(e) of the NLRA permits a union and an employer in the construction industry to enter into an agreement "relating to the contracting or subcontracting of work to be done at the site of the construction, alteration, painting or repair of a building, structure, or other work." The effect of this proviso is that a union may lawfully seek from contractors who traditionally work in construction agreements restricting the subcontracting of jobsite work to contractors who recognize or have a contract with a union. If the subcontracting clause is lawful, the contractor is not required to agree to its inclusion in the contract but must at least bargain in good faith over the proposal.

Subcontracting Clauses

Construction unions traditionally sought restrictive subcontracting clauses under which a contractor agreed essentially not to subcontract to other nonunion firms or to firms which had other unions. Construction unions also legally and practically sought to expand these restrictive clauses to restrict the use of prefabricated products. Called "hot-cargo agreements," these restrictive clauses resulted in 1959 in amendments to the NLRA which, under Section 8(e), outlaw hot-cargo agreements, except to a limited extent, in the construction industry and the garment industry. Section 8(e) provides:

It shall be an unfair labor practice for any labor organization and any employer to enter into any contract or agreement, express or implied, whereby such employer ceases or refrains or agrees to cease or refrain from handling, using, selling, transporting or otherwise dealing in any of the products of any other employer, or to cease doing business with any person, any contract or agreement entered heretofore or hereafter containing such an agreement shall be to such extent unenforceable and void: PROVIDED, That nothing in this subsection (e) shall apply to an agreement between a labor organization and an employer in the construction industry relating to the contracting or subcontracting of work to be done at the site of the construction, alteration, painting, or repair of a building, structure, or other work. . . .

A common union bargaining demand is to have a contractor agree not to enter into any subcontracts with a nonunion employer. The Supreme Court has held that for such an agreement to be lawful the restriction on subcontracting must be limited to jobsite work and the union must seek to or actually represent the contractor's employees. If either of these conditions is not satisfied, the clause is probably illegal and the union may be subject to antitrust liability.

Illustrative Case

Connell Construction Company, a general contractor, employed no plumbers but regularly subcontracted its plumbing and mechanical work to both union and nonunion employers on a competitive-bidding basis. Plumbers Local 100 in Dallas picketed the general contractor to induce the company to agree to subcontract the plumbing work only to employers that had collective bargaining agreements with the union. The U.S. Supreme Court held that a collective bargaining agreement limiting subcontracting to firms under contract with the union was not within the Section 8(e) construction industry proviso and would subject the union to antitrust liability if it was "outside the context of a collective bargaining relationship and not restricted to a particular jobsite."[44]

While the language of *Connell* might lead one to believe that a collective bargaining relationship is a prerequisite for the validity of a subcontracting restriction agreement, the NLRB recently held otherwise. The Board stated that it read *Connell* to mean that a subcontracting clause sought outside a collective bargaining relation might be lawful if it was addressed to common-situs relationships on a particular jobsite.[45]

A limitation on the subcontracting of work to union employers that is valid under the Section 8(e) construction industry proviso must concern work which is to be done and traditionally has been done directly on the jobsite. If the limitation concerns work which is not to be or cannot be done directly on the jobsite, it is illegal. A provision requiring off-site prefabrication work to be subcontracted only to contractors who employ the union's members is illegal since the work is not to be done on the jobsite.[46] The NLRB has long held that the unloading and delivery of materials at the jobsite is not "work to be done on the site," and a proposed clause restricting such work to union employees therefore is illegal.[47] Also illegal is a provision that restricts to union employees of a contractor the work of loading and unloading materials at a storage facility which serves the construction project, since such work is not on-site work. A union commits an unfair labor practice if it threatens to or actually strikes or pickets a contractor to force the contractor either to accept such a provision or to enforce it.

Illustrative Case

Macias-Farwell Co., a contractor engaged in heavy steel construction, contracted to furnish and install penstocks at a hydroelectric generating plant under construction in California. Macias contracted with Bigge Drayage Co. to transport the penstocks and other materials to the Bigge terminal for storage and from there to the project site. The Macias employees were represented by Boilermakers Local 92, and Bigge's employees by various Teamsters locals. There was no construction at the Bigge storage facility, and all loading and unloading of material there was done by Bigge's employees. Macias had with the Boilermakers a collective bargaining agreement which stated that it would not subcontract any work covered by the agreement to an employer who did not have an agreement with the Boilermakers. Another provision applied this restriction on subcontracting to the loading and unloading of materials to and from a "secondary field construction site established for the specific purpose of servicing the primary field construction site." The Boilermakers con-

---

[44] *Connell Constr. Co. v. Plumbers and Steamfitters Local 100,* 421 U.S. 616 (1975).

[45] *Woelke and Romero Framing, Inc.,* 239 NLRB No. 40 (1978) and companion cases in which appeals are pending.

[46] *Ohio Valley Carpenters Dist. Council (Hankins & Hankins Constr. Co.),* 144 NLRB No. 16 (1963).

[47] *Teamsters Local 294 (Rexford Sand & Gravel Co.),* 195 NLRB No. 75 (1972).

tended that this clause restricted the work at the Bigge storage facility to its members, and it threatened to strike and picket Macias to force it to assign the work to its members. The NLRB held that the provision was an illegal hot-cargo clause prohibited by Section 8(e). The Board found that the Bigge storage facility was not set up specifically to service the project site since it was also used to store materials for other contractors. Even if it were so set up, however, the area was not on-site within the meaning of the construction industry proviso since the loading and unloading of materials there was not directly on the site of construction. The Board held that the Section 8(e) exception for the construction industry did not apply to work done away from the actual site of construction, even though such work might be viewed as part of the actual construction process and was of a kind which could feasibly have been done at the project site.[48]

An agreement which seeks to restrict the task of mixing, delivering, and pouring concrete at the construction site to union members is an illegal hot-cargo clause because that is not on-site work. Since by the nature of the concrete-mixing process work cannot be performed until the concrete has been poured, the agreement relates to the delivery of materials to the jobsite, which is not on-site work. If the union attempts to induce a contractor to agree to or enforce this provision under the threat of a work stoppage or picketing, a Section 8(b)(4)B) unfair-labor practice charge may be filed against it.

Illustrative Case

Inland Concrete Enterprises contracted with a nonunion supplier to deliver ready-mixed concrete to a site where Inland was engaged in the construction of a sewer and drainage system. Teamsters Local 982 had a contract with Inland which limited the subcontracting of on-site construction work to companies whose employees were covered by an appropriate union contract. It sought to enforce this clause by interfering with deliveries of the concrete to the jobsite. The local contended that because the concrete mobile mixer used by the supplier actually mixed the concrete at the project site, the supplier performed on-site work that was restricted by its agreement with Inland to union employees. The NLRB held that the local violated Section 8(e) when it contended that its contract with Inland applied to such work, since the mixing and delivery of ready mixed concrete at a construction site was not construction work but the delivery of a material to the site, which was not protected by the Section 8(e) construction industry proviso.[49]

Repair work which is to be done on the jobsite only infrequently or for short periods of time cannot be restricted to certain employers with a union contract. Repair work is not on-site work within the meaning of the Section 8(e) construction industry exception since the need to avoid jobsite friction between union and nonunion workers is not found to exist if nonunion repairers appear only sporadically at the construction site. A union which attempts to obtain or enforce a repair work provision by economic reprisal commits an unfair labor practice.

[48]Boilermakers Union (Bigge Drayage Co.), 197 NLRB No. 34 (1972).

[49]Teamsters Local 982 (Inland Concrete Enterprises), 225 NLRB No. 32 (1976).

Local 12 of the Operating Engineers had with several associations representing building contractors in the San Diego and Los Angeles areas an agreement which required all repairs and servicing done on certain equipment on or near the jobsite to be performed by members of the Operating Engineers. Traditionally, the seller of the equipment had been called upon for servicing and repair. When repair work was minor, it was normally performed on the site but away from most of the construction activity and usually after the construction laborers had quit for the day. This was done to minimize disruption of the project by the presence of nonunion repairmen. Major repair work was done at the dealer's shop. Coincident with Local 12's drive to organize the dealers, it sought to enforce the repair work clause by assessing fines under its grievance procedure against contractors who used nonunion suppliers to do repair work. The court of appeals affirmed the NLRB's ruling that the clause was an illegal hot-cargo clause since the on-site equipment repair was not such an integral part of the construction process as to be within the Section 8(6) construction industry proviso. As in the case of the delivery of supplies to the jobsite, the danger of jobsite friction from the occasional appearance of nonunion repairmen was slight, so the repair work could not lawfully by restricted to members of the Operating Engineers.[50]

Although a union may lawfully threaten to or actually strike or picket a contractor to force the contractor to accede to a subcontracting restriction protected by Section 8(e), it acts illegally if it seeks to enforce such a provision against a nonunion subcontractor by a threatened or actual work stoppage or by picketing or other economic reprisal against the contractor with whom the union has its agreement. The union's pressure is an illegal secondary boycott since its purpose is to force the neutral contractor to cease doing business with the nonunion subcontractor, who is the primary employer with whom the union has its dispute. A Section 8(b)(4)(B) unfair-labor-practice charge may be filed so that the NLRB may seek an injunction in federal court against the union's illegal pressure. Damages may be recovered in federal court under Section 303 by any contractor injured by the union's unfair labor practice.

Walsh Construction Co. was the general contractor in charge of erection of a multimillion-dollar power plant. It had with the Carpenters International an agreement not to subcontract jobsite work except to a subcontractor who had an agreement with the international or with one of its affiliates or who had agreed in writing to be bound by the terms of such an agreement. Walsh let a subcontract to Kinnear Corp. for the fabrication off site and the erection on site of roll-up steel doors. Kinnear arrived at the site to install the doors with members of the Ironworkers, the union with which Kinnear had an agreement entitling its members to that work. Local 644 of the Carpenters went on strike and picketed Walsh. Walsh filed an unfair-labor-practice charge against Local 644 under Section 8(b)(4)(B) for engaging in an illegal secondary boycott. Local 644 defended itself on the ground that its purpose was to preserve lawfully bargaining-unit work for its members. The NLRB held, with the District of Columbia Court of Appeals affirming, that Local 644's purpose in picketing Walsh was aimed not only at lawfully preserving traditional bargaining-unit work for

[50]*Operating Engineers Local 12 v. NLRB (Acco Constr. Equipment, Inc.),* 511 F.2d 848 (9th Cir. 1975).

its members but also at unlawfully forcing the subcontractor Kinnear to recognize Local 644 as the bargaining representative instead of the Ironworkers. A union with a legitimate subcontracting clause cannot enforce it by a strike against a signatory contractor in order to force the contractor either to require the nonunion subcontractor to recognize the union or to remove the subcontractor from the project.[51]

It is illegal for a union to enforce a valid subcontracting clause against an identifiable subcontractor by a strike or picketing against the signatory contractor who breaches the agreement, and any provision which will permit the union to take strike or picketing action against a contractor in the event of a breach will also be illegal. A provision which would allow a union freely to disregard any or all of its obligations under its collective bargaining agreement with a contractor who breached a subcontracting restriction would be illegal. A clause that would permit the contractor's employees to stop work without being subject to discipline if the contractor violated the subcontracting provision would also be unlawful.[52] If the contractor is faced with a demand by the union that such a provision be included in a collective bargaining agreement, the contractor should respond that the clause is illegal and should not consider it. The contractor may file a Section 8(b)(3) charge with the Board for the union's failure to bargain in good faith if the union threatens to or does strike or picket or otherwise retaliate against the contractor to force its inclusion in a contract.

Work Preservation

The U.S. Supreme Court has recognized that a union has a legitimate interest in preserving traditional bargaining-unit work for members of the unit. When a contractor uses materials that have been prefabricated away from the jobsite, union pressure against the contractor not to use these materials may be lawful if work on these materials has customarily been done by the employees at the jobsite. Even though the effect of the union pressure may be to force the contractor to cease doing business with the manufacturer of the materials, the union's tactics are still primary and lawful in nature if the union's purpose is to protect and preserve for the bargaining unit work customarily done by it. A threatened or actual work stoppage or other coercive action to obtain or to enforce a provision limiting the contractor's right to use these materials may then be lawful.

Illustrative Case

The Carpenters International and the General Building Contractors Association included in their contract a provision that no member "handle . . . any doors . . . which have been fitted prior to being furnished on the job." In the past these doors had customarily been fitted by carpenters. Frouge Corp., a member of the association, ordered prefitted doors which the carpenters refused to install. Frouge contended that the agreement itself was an illegal hot-

[51] *Local 644, Carpenters v. NLRB (Walsh Constr. Co.)*, 533 F.2d 1136 (D.C. Cir. 1975).

[52] *NLRB v. Bricklayers Local 5 (Greater Muskegon Contractors Ass'n)*, 378 F.2d 859 (6th Cir. 1967).

cargo clause since it unlawfully required Frouge to cease handling the products of another employer, so that the carpenters' refusal to work on the doors was necessarily a secondary boycott and a Section 8(b)(4)(B) unfair labor practice. The U.S. Supreme Court agreed with the NLRB that the clause and union pressure to enforce it were legal. The Court held that in determining whether an agreement is lawful "the touchstone is whether the agreement is addressed to the labor relations of the contractor vis-á-vis his own employees . . . or whether the agreement was tactically calculated to satisfy union objectives elsewhere." Since the union's purpose was to preserve work traditionally performed by the unit employees, the agreement and its enforcement by the unit's refusal to install the doors were lawful. If the work in fitting the doors customarily had not been done by the unit in the past, the agreement would have been illegal and the union's pressure would have been an illegal secondary activity since it would not have had the primary purpose of preserving and protecting the bargaining-unit work.[53]

If a proposed restriction on the use of prefabricated materials is lawful, a contractor must bargain in good faith over this proposal, since the issue of subcontracting bargaining-unit work is a mandatory subject of bargaining. Also, if the proposal is legal, the union may threaten to or actually strike or picket to obtain the contractor's agreement to it. The mere fact that the restriction will drastically limit the contractor's use of equipment at a lower cost will not negate the contractor's duty to bargain in good faith. Still, the fact that the restriction will result in higher costs may be used as a legitimate reason by the contractor for refusing to agree to it, provided the contractor otherwise bargains in good faith. The contractor should point out to the union that even though this provision will preserve this particular work for its members, in the long run it may cost its members jobs, since the restriction on the use of prefabricated materials will increase the contractor's costs and make it harder for the contractor to compete for construction jobs.

If the union bargaining unit has not actually worked on the materials in the past, the fact that it is capable of performing the work is irrelevant. The union will have the unlawful purpose of expanding work for its members and not the lawful purpose of work preservation. A union which threatens to or does strike or picket a contractor to obtain such work acts illegally.

Illustrative Case

Overaa, a general contractor with a collective bargaining agreement with Local 342 of the Steamfitters, was awarded the job of constructing a pumping plant in the San Francisco area. Overaa was required to install cement-lined pipe in the plant, and the specifications required the pipe to be tested hydrostatically and stress-relieved upon the completion of certain stages of the fabrication. Overaa subcontracted the fabrication of the pipe to Conduit Fabricators, Inc. Conduit's employees were represented by Teamsters Local 490; thus, no members of the Steamfitters worked on the pipe. Conduit delivered the completed pipe to the construction site, but the Steamfitters refused to handle and install it. The NLRB held that the Steamfitters committed a Section 8(b)(4)(B) unfair labor practice by refusing to work on the pipe since the union had no lawful work preservation purpose. The Board held

---

[53] *National Woodwork Ass'n v. NLRB,* 386 U.S. 612 (1967).

that it was not enough that the Steamfitters were capable of fabricating the pipe if they had not customarily done such work in the past.[54]

When a new material is to be installed on a jobsite for the first time, there may be a question whether a union's refusal to handle it has a legitimate work preservation purpose. If this work is found to be a "substitute" for work which customarily has been done by the unit in the past, the union's refusal to handle it may be lawful.

Illustrative Case

Local 433 of the Carpenters had with the Southerm Illinois Builders Association, of which Bauer Brothers Construction Co. was a member, an agreement which contained a provision requiring that the "erecting, fastening or dismantling of all materials of work, plastic, metal . . . and all substituting materials" be performed only by Local 433. Bauer subcontracted the work of erecting certain blocks which had never before been used on the project to Lippert Brick Contracting. Lippert did not recognize Local 433. The Carpenters struck to protest what it claimed was a violation of Bauer's agreement with it. The District of Columbia Court of Appeals reversed the NLRB's finding that Local 433 had engaged in an illegal secondary boycott. The Court held that the new work was merely a substitute for work traditionally performed by Local 433, so that the union had a valid work preservation purpose and not an illegal secondary purpose to require Bauer to cease doing business with Lippert.[55]

Often a contractor will be bound by a collective bargaining agreement with a union that preserves specific work for its members. The contractor will then enter into a contract for a job knowing that the contract with the general contractor or project owner will require it to install prefabricated materials. When the contract specifications require the prefabricated work, the contractor may have lost the legal "right to control" concerning assignment of the disputed work. Threats of or an actual work stoppage or picketing against a contractor who has lost the right to control the work may be a secondary boycott even if the union's purpose is to preserve work traditionally done by its members. Express orders by the union to its members that they not install the prefabricated materials may support an unfair-labor-practice charge against the union. Other forms of inducement, such as threats of discipline or union fines if the numbers perform this work, might also be unlawful. The union's pressure against the contractor without the right to control the disputed work may be an illegal secondary boycott since the contractor may become a neutral employer when it loses the right to control. The NLRB has reasoned, with the U.S. Supreme Court's approval in the 1977 *Enterprise* decision, that the picketing is illegal since its purpose must be to force the neutral to cease doing business with the general contractor or project owner, who is the primary employer with whom the union really has its dispute since it has the right to control the work.

[54] *Plumbers Local 342 (Conduit Fabricators, Inc.)*, 225 NLRB No. 195 (1976).

[55] *Carpenters Local 433 v. NLRB (Lippert Brick Contracting, Inc.)*, 509 F.2d 447 (D.C. Cir. 1974).

Illustrative Case

A plumbing and pipe-fitting union had a collective bargaining agreement with Hudik, a mechanical subcontractor, which required that "the cutting and threading of internal piping," such as that found in climate control units, was to be performed on the jobsite by Hudik's employees. These employees had traditionally performed such work. Subsequently, Hudik signed a contract with Alston, the general contractor, under which Hudik would be required to install units whose internal piping had been cut and threaded elsewhere. At the time that Hudik signed this agreement it was aware that these requirements would conflict with its collective bargaining agreement with the union. When the union members refused to install these units, an unfair-labor-practice charge was filed against the union on the ground that it engaged in a secondary boycott. The Supreme Court affirmed its holding in *National Woodwork* that the Board must look at all the circumstances in determining whether the union's purpose was lawful work preservation or the unlawful accomplishment of objectives elsewhere. Nonetheless, the Court appeared to permit the Board to place almost exclusive reliance on the right-to-control test. The Court held that even if the union's purpose in refusing to handle prefabricated materials was to protect and preserve unit work, the conduct was unlawful when the employer had assigned away the right to control the work in question.[56]

For the union pressure against a contractor who has lost the right to control to be unlawful secondary activity, the contractor must be a neutral "unoffending" employer. The courts have indicated that the right-to-control test will not be applied mechanically. A contractor who bids on a contract knowing in advance that the job specifications concerning the work in question will conflict with the work preservation clause in its collective bargaining agreement with the union may still be an unoffending employer, according to a United States courts of appeals decision. The contractor will remain a true neutral even if the contractor fails to try to get the general contractor or project owner to change the requirements. But if it is the contractor who suggests making the specification which will conflict with the union's interest in preserving the bargaining-unit work, the contractor may cease to remain a neutral unoffending employer and lawfully be picketed by the union. The demand must be made by an independent third party, such as the general contractor or the project owner, for the subcontractor to be a neutral unoffending employer and union pressure against it to be an illegal secondary boycott.

Illustrative Case

Atlas Construction Co. was the general contractor for two projects in Connecticut, a processing plant for the Stamford Pressed Beef Co. and an office building for Hilti, Inc. Atlas awarded the permanent electrical work on the Hilti project to Rice Electrical Contracting Co. and subcontracted with Santella, Inc., to install the permanent wiring and fixtures at the Stamford project. Atlas retained control over the operation of temporary electrical power at both sites in its contracts with Santella and Rice. Santella and Rice were both members of the National Electrical Contractors Association and were bound by an agreement with Electrical Workers Local 501. The agreement contained a work preservation clause that Local 501 contended assigned the right to operate temporary power to its members. Members of Local 501 refused to work at both projects since Atlas employees

---

[56] *NLRB v. Pipefitters Local 638 (Enterprise Ass'n)*, 429 U.S. 507 (1977).

had manned the temporary-power equipment. The District of Columbia Court of Appeals enforced the NLRB's order that Local 501 was guilty of a Section 8(b)(4)(B) secondary-boycott violation for walkouts against subcontractors Rice and Santella. The Court reasoned that since the subcontractors had lost the right to control the operation of temporary power in their contracts with Atlas, then Local 501's purpose must have been to force the neutral employers, Rice and Santella, to cease doing business with Atlas, the primary employer with whom the union's dispute actually existed. The Court adopted the NLRB's ruling that a contractor remains a neutral and, therefore, a secondary unoffending employer, unless the contractor engages in "some *affirmative* conduct which the employer could reasonably conclude would conflict with his collective bargaining obligations, coupled with the *absence* of any demand for such conduct by an independent third party such as a general contractor or project owner." The Court held that a contractor may remain neutral even if the contractor knows when bidding for the job that its requirements will conflict with a contractural obligation to the union concerning the disputed work. Also, the Court will not consider whether the subcontractor made a good-faith effort to get the general contractor or project owner to alter the job specification.[57]

Union Standards

Another subcontracting restriction, known as the union standards clause, may require a contractor to subcontract bargaining-unit work only to employers who meet the equivalent of the union-negotiated area wages and economic conditions. As in the work preservation clause in *National Woodwork,* the work to which the area standards provision refers must be claimable fairly by the bargaining unit. The union may be permitted to strike or picket a contractor to force the contractor to agree to such a clause since it has a legitimate interest in preventing bargaining-unit work from being assigned to substandard employers. The contractor must bargain in good faith over such a proposal, but that does not mean that the contractor must agree to include it in the contract. If the type of work which the provision preserves from being assigned out has not traditionally been performed by the bargaining unit and is not within the Section 8(e) proviso relating to on-site work, the provision is an illegal hot-cargo clause that has no lawful primary purpose to protect bargaining-unit work but instead has an illegal purpose to require a neutral contractor not to do business with another contractor. The contractor should not consider such a proposal since agreement to it may subject it to antitrust liability. If the union attempts to coerce the contractor to agree to the proposal under threat of a strike or similar action, a Section 8(b)(b)(3) unfair-labor-practice charge should be filed for the union's failure to bargain in good faith.

A union standards provision may require a contractor to assign unit work only to employers who will pay union wages and the cost of economic benefits under the union contract and who have a grievance procedure for adjusting disputes over those matters. Sometimes a union will threaten to strike or picket a contractor to force the contractor to assign bargaining-unit work only to employers who comply with the "terms of the union agreement." If the terms include, for example, a union recognition clause, a

---

[57] *Electrical Workers Local 501 v. NLRB,* 566 F.2d 348 (D.C. Cir. 1977).

union security agreement, or a provision requiring employees to be hired though the union hiring hall and if the subcontracting restriction does not refer only to traditional jobsite work protected by the Section 8(e) construction industry proviso, then agreement to such a provision may be illegal and subject contractor and union to antitrust liability.[58] All a union standards provision may lawfully provide is that a potential subcontractor meet the economic costs of the union contract. It may not require the subcontractor to make payments into a union fringe-benefits plan as long as the subcontractor incurs costs equivalent to those that union contractors face in making their contributions to the union plan.

Illustrative Case

Arrowhead, the general contractor for the construction of a health center in Montana, was a member of the Flathead Contractors Association which had a contract with the Carpenters district council. The company subcontracted the thermal-insulation work to Lilienthal Insulation Co., which did not have an agreement with and did not employ members of the Carpenters Union. The Carpenters protested to Arrowhead that by using Lilienthal on the project it violated its agreement with the Carpenters, which stated that "in order to preserve the standards established by this Agreement," the company will not "subcontract any work falling within the scope of this Agreement to any firm which does not protect those of its employees performing such work by providing working terms, conditions and rates of pay inferior to those herein provided. . . ." Lilienthal wrote to Arrowhead a letter in which it agreed to pay union wages and to furnish health insurance by direct cash payments to its employees instead of payments into the Carpenters' fringe-benefits program. The Carpenters picketed the jobsite to protest Arrowhead's refusal to comply with the area standards. The NLRB held that the Carpenters had an illegal secondary objective in insisting that Lilienthal provide its employees benefits equivalent to those enjoyed by its members rather than permitting it merely to pay the same amount that it was costing employers who contributed to the Carpenters' benefit plan. The Carpenters were interested in forcing the subcontractor to sign a union contract by secondary pressure against a general contractor and were not interested in lawfully protecting the terms and conditions of employment that it had negotiated.[59]

A proposal that a contractor will not handle any equipment of a supplier who does not have an agreement with the union is clearly illegal if there is no valid work preservation purpose and if the proposal is not limited to the performance of jobsite work. A contractor who agrees to such a provision in the contract might violate the antitrust laws. If the union insists that such a clause be included in the contract or threatens to or does strike or picket for that purpose, the contractor should file unfair-practice charges with the Board.

Illustrative Case

Operating Engineers Local 542 sought to have York County Bridge, Inc, enter into a collective bargaining agreement with a provision that "no operator be required to operate equip-

58 *IBEW Local 437 (National Electrical Contractors Ass'n)*, 180 NLRB No. 32 (1969).

59 *Carpenters (Lilienthal Insulation Co.)*, 220 NLRB No. 183 (1975).

ment belonging to a contractor or supplier with whom this Local Union is not in signed relations." Local 542 threatened to and actually stopped referring workers from its hiring hall until York acceded to the provision. The NLRB held that Local 542 committed an illegal secondary boycott by using economic coercion against York to force it to agree to an illegal hot-cargo clause. It reasoned that the agreement had a proscribed cease-doing-business purpose and did not seek lawfully to prevent loss of work to its members. The provision was not saved by the Section 8(e) proviso, whose purpose is to eliminate friction between union and nonunion workers at the same site, since a separate section in the contract was addressed to the problem of union and nonunion employees. Its purpose was to force the supplier illegally to recognize Local 542 by pressure against York, a neutral employer.[60]

Breach of Contract

Although a union may not utilize economic pressure against a contractor to enforce a lawful subcontracting clause, it may still seek to enforce it against the contractor who signs it in a breach-of-contract action if the suit is filed in good faith to enforce a colorable claim.[61]

A collective bargaining agreement often contains a grievance and arbitration procedure which applies to disputes under the contract, including the interpretation and application of a legal subcontracting clause. The Board and some circuit courts have expressed contrary views on whether a union that files a grievance and recovers a fine against a contractor pursuant to the arbitration procedure in the contract engages in a prohibited form of pressure against the contractor to have the contractor cease doing business with another employer. This situation may occur when a union files a grievance against a contractor with whom it has an agreement because either (1) the contractor has subcontracted jobsite work to a nonunion employer, (2) the contractor has subcontracted bargaining-unit work to a substandard employer, or (3) the contractor has agreed not to use prefabricated materials.

RECOGNITIONAL PICKETING

Building trades unions will often picket to induce a nonunion contractor to sign a collective bargaining agreement. Picketing for that purpose has a recognitional objective. Frequently lawful picketing to preserve area standards of employee benefits is a disguise for picketing which has a recognitional objective and which might be an unfair labor practice under Section 8(b)(7) of the NLRA. If a union pickets allegedly to protest a contractor's substandard wages and also attempts to have the contractor sign a contract with the union, the picketing has a recognitional objective and might be unlawful.

Threats of or actual picketing with a recognitional objective may constitute an unfair labor practice under Section 8(b)(7) in the following circumstances:

[60] *Operating Engineers (York County Bridge, Inc.)*, 216 NLRB No. 67 (1975).

[61] *Building and Constr. Trades Council (Noble Elec.)*, 217 NLRB No. 139 (1975).

(*A*) Where the employer has lawfully recognized in accordance with this Act [NLRA] any other labor organization and a question concerning representation may not appropriately be raised under Section 9(C);

(*B*) Where within the preceding 12 months a valid election has been conducted; or

(*C*) Where such picketing has been conducted without a petition for an election being filed within a reasonable period of time not to exceed 30 days from the commencement of such picketing.

A contractor who is faced with recognitional picketing that violates any of the above provisions may file an unfair-labor-practice charge with the NLRB. The Board will normally conduct an expedited investigation within 72 hours after charges have been filed. If the investigation reveals reasonable cause to believe that an unfair labor practice under Section 8(b)(7) has been committed, then the NLRB will normally, but is not required to, petition the appropriate federal district court for an injunction against the picketing pending a decision on the unfair-labor-practice charge. If the NLRB finds that the union committed the unfair labor practice and the contractor reasonably fears that recognitional picketing will recur at other area jobsites, then the contractor should try to convince the Board that a broader order against the union to apply to all the contractor's area projects is justified.

A contractor who is faced with recognitional picketing should collect evidence for use later in an unfair-labor-practice proceeding if Section 8(b)(7) is violated. Statements of union agents, letters from union officials, and the wording on picket signs should be preserved. Since picketing for recognition beyond a 30-day period is sometimes an unfair labor practice, a record of the duration of the picketing should also be kept.

Because of the short-term nature of the employment relationship in the construction industry, Section 8(f) of the NLRA permits the contractor and the building trades union to execute a prehire agreement. Such an agreement may be entered into validly before the union has achieved majority support and even before any employees have been hired. In some instances, threats of or actual picketing to induce a contractor to execute a prehire contract will be illegal (see also Chapter 1, section "Prehire Agreements").

If another union is currently certified by the NLRB as the exclusive bargaining representative, recognitional picketing by a second union is a Section 8(b)(7)(A) unfair labor practice. A contractor is not required to bargain with the picketing union; one who does so has failed to bargain in good faith with the certified union, which is an unfair labor practice by the contractor under Section 8(a)(5).

A union that pickets to have a contractor bargain with it or to recognize it as the employees' bargaining representative also commits an unfair labor practice under Section 8(b)(7)(A) if the contractor has already lawfully recognized another union. A union may be lawfully recognized as an exclusive bargaining agent even though it has never been certified as such by the NLRB. For an incumbent union to be lawfully recognized it must have with the contractor a current valid contract which was executed when a representative and substantial workforce was already employed and a majority of those employees favored representation by that union. The union's majority status may be shown by authorization cards signed by a majority of the employees, which are counted by an impartial third party. The cards state on their face that their only purpose is to demonstrate that the signers of the cards desire that union to represent them. When the agreement is executed, at least 30 percent of the contractor's total workforce must already be employed and 50 percent of the job classifications must be in existence.

Illustrative Case

Gessin Electrical Contractors had entered into a collective bargaining agreement with Teamsters Local 363 on February 26, 1973, for a term ending on November 14, 1973. On February 1, 1974, the company executed with Local 363 an agreement extending the term of the earlier agreement until November 14, 1976. During the first week of October 1975, IBEW Local 3 began recognitional picketing at a construction site where the company was engaged as a subcontractor. The NLRB held that IBEW Local 3 committed a Section 8(b)(7)(A) unfair labor practice when it picketed the company with the object of gaining recognition as the bargaining representative, since the extension agreement with Local 363 barred the picketing union's raising the representation question.[62]

The mere fact that a contractor has executed a valid and current prehire agreement may not necessarily protect the contractor from recognitional picketing and an election petition by another union. A contractor who wants to continue the relationship with the union with which the contractor already has a valid prehire agreement and avoid the inconvenience of a representation election on behalf of another union should execute another agreement with the incumbent union when it enjoys majority status and 30 percent of the total workforce has been hired and 50 percent of the job classifications are in existence. An agreement of 3 years or less from the date on which it is executed will make unlawful under Section 8(b)(7)(A) recognitional picketing for that length of time from the execution date. If the agreement is to last more than 3 years, under Section 8(b)(7)(A) recognitional picketing may be illegal for the 3-year period only.

A union commits a Section 8(b)(7)(B) unfair labor practice if it pickets for recognitional purposes within 12 months after a representation election has been held by the NLRB. Picketing within that period is illegal if either another union or no union had won representation rights. Recognitional picketing can continue after the election is held but must terminate once the results have been certified. The 12-month period in which picketing is prohibited commences either from the date of the election or from the date in which picketing is discontinued, whichever is later.

If a union pickets to induce a contractor to bargain with it or to sign a contract for more than a reasonable time, not to exceed 30 days, without

---

[62] *IBEW Local 3 (Gessin Electrical Contractors)*, 224 NLRB No. 195 (1976).

petitioning the NLRB for an election, the union commits a Section 8(b)(7)(C) unfair labor practice. If the contractor has no existing contract with another union and is not required by the NLRB to recognize another union, a building trades union may picket the contractor to induce the contractor to sign a prehire contract, but picketing for that purpose may last no longer than 30 days. The period may be less than 30 days if there is mass picketing or violence or significant interference with the contractor's operations. If recognitional picketing lasts longer than a reasonable time not in excess of 30 days, the contractor should file a Section 8(b)(7)(C) unfair-labor-practice charge. The employer can petition for an expedited election if the union pickets for recognition. The NLRB will then conduct an expedited election to determine whether the picketing union should be certified as the bargaining-unit representative. Picketing may continue after the election is held, but once the results are certified against the union, the picketing must cease. If the union continues to picket after it has lost the expedited election, the contractor may file charges with the Board so that it may seek an injunction in federal district court to prohibit the picketing.[63]

The building trades unions traditionally have sought to enforce the terms of a prehire agreement by strikes or pickets against the contractor. An important U.S. Supreme Court decision has held that a union may sometimes commit an unfair labor practice under Section 8(b)(7)(C) in this manner if it fails to petition for a representation election within 30 days or less after the picketing commences. In *NLRB v. Local 103, Ironworkers*,[64] the Supreme Court ruled that a union without majority status may not picket for more than 30 days to enforce a valid prehire agreement. Unless the union has demonstrated its majority support either by its designation by the NLRB as the certified bargaining representative or by the operation of a valid union security clause in the prehire agreement, picketing for 30 days or less to enforce the agreement without seeking a representation election will be an unfair labor practice. The Court's decision also indicates that until a union has demonstrated its majority support, a contractor is not required to bargain over the terms of a proposed prehire contract and may refuse to honor the terms of an existing contract without committing an unfair labor practice.

Informational picketing has an immediate purpose of informing the public that a particular employer is a nonunion employer. Section 8(b)(7)(C) of the NLRA permits informational picketing "unless an effect is to induce any individual employed by any other person in the course of his employment not to pick up, deliver, or transport any goods or not to perform any services." In other words, informational picketing is permitted unless it disrupts the picketed employer by keeping suppliers from completing deliveries and performing services or causes work stoppages.

[63] *Painters Local 86 (Carpet Control, Inc.)*, 216 NLRB No. 190 (1975).
[64] 434 U.S. 335 (1978).

An inherent difficulty in determining whether picketing is informational is that a case of purely informational picketing is unlikely. Usually, a union involved in informational picketing has the additional objective of obtaining recognition. Although Section 8(b)(7)(C) contains a broad prohibition against recognitional picketing unless certain conditions are met, this prohibition does not apply if the recognitional picketing is informational as well. Thus, recognitional picketing which is informative (that is, informs the public that the employer is nonunion) is lawful if it does not violate the proviso of Section 8(b)(7)(C) of the act that it not disrupt the business of the employer.[65] However, if the picketing disrupts deliveries or causes work stoppages, the union cannot avail itself of the informational defense for otherwise illegal recognitional picketing.

Illustrative Case

Local 239 of the International Brotherhood of Teamsters began picketing a nonunion employer. At first the picketing was clearly intended to have the result of organizing the employees of Stan-Jay. Later, attempting to make its picketing informational, the union changed its picket-sign message from clearly recognitional language to the following: "To the public. Please be advised Stan-Jay . . . does not employ members of, nor has a contract with, any labor union including Local 239, I. B. of T." In spite of this change, deliveries to the employer ceased. The Second Circuit held that the recognitional picketing violated Section 8(b)(7)(C) of the NLRA because the union had failed to file an election petition within 30 days from the commencement of picketing. Even if the picketing were assumed to have been informational at all times, it was not protected because it caused the stoppage of deliveries to the employer.[66]

Even when informational and recognitional picketing interferes with the operations of an employer, it will not always constitute a violation of the proviso to Section 8(b)(7)(C) of the act. The Ninth Circuit has held that a quantitative test concerned solely with the number of deliveries not made or services not performed is an inadequate method of determining whether to remove informational picketing from the protection of the act. Rather, the presence or absence of a violation will depend upon the degree to which the picketing has truly disrupted, interfered with, or curtailed the employer's business.[67] Thus, even if there are delivery stoppages and delays or work delays because of the picketing, as in the *Barker* case, it is possible that a court might hold that no violation had occurred. Generally, however, the rule remains that informational and recognitional picketing loses its protection when it disrupts or interferes with the business of the picketed employer.

AREA STANDARDS PICKETING

A union is permitted to advise the public truthfully that a contractor is paying substandard area union wages and employee benefits. This type of

[65] *Smitley, d/b/a Crown Cafeteria v. NLRB*, 327 F.2d 351 (9th Cir. 1964).

[66] *NLRB v. Local 239, Int'l Bhd. of Teamsters, Chauffeurs, Warehousemen, & Helpers of America*, 289 F.2d 41 (2d Cir. 1961), *cert. denied*, 368 U.S. 832 (1961).

[67] *Barker Bros. Corp. v. NLRB*, 328 F.2d 431 (9th Cir. 1964).

picketing is allowed because of the NLRA's policy that the union has a legitimate interest in assuring that the wages and benefits which it has negotiated will not become depressed by the assignment of work to contractors who pay lower wages and that, without this right to picket, contractors may have an incentive to subcontract the bargaining-unit work to substandard employers.

Area standards picketing may lawfully require a substandard contractor to meet the total economic costs of a contract. Economic costs include, for example, wages, vacation benefits, and employer contributions to pension, health and welfare, and disability plans. Picketing for that purpose is lawful because these costs are incurred by contractors to pay employee benefits, and if contractors were freely permitted not to meet these costs, there would be an incentive to assign work to substandard contractors, so that the area union standards would be depressed. A union is probably no longer engaged in area standards picketing if it tries to specify how these costs should be allocated or if it insists on comparable benefits.[68] A contractor is required only to incur the same costs for the economic terms that the union has negotiated in the area. Once the contractor agrees to meet the total economic costs of the union contract, continued picketing may suggest a recognitional or bargaining objective of the union which might be an unfair labor practice under Section 8(b)(7).

If a union is engaged in lawful area standards picketing, the fact that a contractor already has a contract with or is required to recognize another union is irrelevant. The contractor may meet the picketing union's demands without having to bargain with or recognize the union in derogation of another union's status as the exclusive bargaining representative; so the picketing is lawful.

Illustrative Cases

Trumbo Welding & Fabricating Co. in Memphis had a collective bargaining agreement with District 50 of the Allied and Technical Workers. The company recognized District 50 after it had obtained valid authorization cards from a majority of the employees in the bargaining unit. A representative of District 50 admitted that no employee under the agreement would receive "as much as $7, $6 or even $5 an hour." After the company commenced a construction job in Memphis, Steamfitters Local 614 picketed the site with signs stating that the company "does not meet the standard of wages, fringe benefits and working conditions as established in the Memphis area." At the time the prevailing wage and benefits standards in the Memphis area totaled $7.82 per hour, which was the same as Local 614's rate. Local 614's business manager testified that his belief that the company was substandard was based upon surveys and reports made by other companies and the Department of Labor and on common knowledge in the industry that District 50 did not meet the prevailing wage rate. The business manager notified the company president that the company was substandard and that the picketing would stop when the company paid the area wage rate. The NLRB held that Local 614 did not violate Section 8(b)(7)(A) by picketing the company which had lawfully recognized District 50 as the exclusive bargaining agent, since the picketing had no recognitional objective. Local 614 was engaged in lawful area standards picketing since it had reason to believe that the company was not meeting area standards

---

[68] *Centralia Bldg. Trades Council v. NLRB (Pacific Sign & Steel Bldg. Co.),* 363 F.2d 699 (D.C. Cir. 1966).

and since at no time did the union request the company to give its employees specific benefits.[69]

Local 12 of the Christian Building Trades was certified by the NLRB as the exclusive bargaining representative for employees of De Jong, a member of the Calumet Contractors Association. De Jong commenced work under a contract to build a church. Local 41 of the Hod Carriers picketed the church site and distributed handbills which read: "NOTICE TO PUBLIC—The work being performed by the following contractor is not being done by qualified BUILDING TRADES CRAFTSMEN. The prevailing rate of pay and conditions are not being met. This notice is addressed only to the general public and not to the employers or employees on the job GEO DE JONG & EMPLOYER MEMBERS OF THE CALUMET CONTRACTORS ASS'N. LABOR UNION #41 AFL-CIO." Local 41's president testified that there would have been no picketing had De Jong met the prevailing rates of pay and conditions and that the local's purpose was to obtain these prevailing rates. The local did not request recognition or demand bargaining as the employees' representative. The NLRB held that Local 41's purpose in picketing De Jong was lawfully to protest subnormal working conditions and not unlawfully to force the company to recognize or bargain with it in the face of another union's certification as the bargaining representative. The Board recognized that a union may legitimately be concerned that an employer has undermined area standards of employment by maintaining lower standards and that a union may protect that concern by picketing the substandard employer. Since De Jong could meet Local 41's demands without bargaining with or recognizing the union and since the local president disclaimed a recognitional objective, Local 41 was engaged in lawful area standards picketing.[70]

It is important to distinguish between area standards picketing and recognitional picketing under Section 8(b)(7)(C) of the act. Area standards picketing seeks to advise the public that an employer is not adhering to area union standards in paying employees. Recognitional picketing informs the public that an employer is nonunion and also seeks to organize the employer. Both types might be termed "informational" in nature, but they are treated differently. Proper area standards picketing may be upheld even if it results in work stoppages or interferes with deliveries to an employer. On the other hand, picketing for recognitional or organizational purposes is lawful for a reasonable period, not to exceed 30 days, if it is informational in nature, *unless* it has the effect of stopping deliveries.

Illustrative Case

Carpenters Local 480 picketed the construction site of National Mill Designs, Inc., with signs protesting the company's failure to meet the area wage and benefits standards. The union representative never requested that the company sign a contract with Local 480 and he stated that the picketing would cease if the company complied with the area standards. This picketing continued after Local 480 had lost a representation election. The administrative law judge reasoned that since Local 480 knew that the picketing had effectively halted deliveries to the jobsite, the picketing necessarily had a recognitional objective which was an unfair labor practice under Section 8(b)(7)(B) since the picketing was conducted within

[69] Steamfitters Local No. 614 (Trumbo Welding & Fabricating Co.), 199 NLRB No. 57 (1972).

[70] Hod Carriers Union (Calumet Contractors Ass'n), 133 NLRB No. 57 (1961).

12 months after the union had lost an election. The NLRB dismissed the complaint. The Board held that the fact that the picketing to protest substandard conditions succeeded in halting deliveries or in stopping the picketed company's operations and that the union intended that result did not mean that the union had a prohibited recognitional objective.[71]

As a practical matter, area standards picketing is often a disguise for secondary-boycott picketing or recognitional picketing, and its real objective can be enjoinable under the secondary-boycott prohibitions or the 30-day limit for recognitional picketing.

Picketing to protest a substandard contractor which would otherwise be lawful may still violate the NLRB's ban on a secondary activity. A union whose dispute is with the substandard contractor violates Section 8(b)(4)(B) if it attempts to exert pressure on another contractor to cease doing business for not meeting the area wage and benefits standards. The fact the union has a lawful subcontracting clause with the general contractor to assign work only to subcontractors who will meet the area union standards does not permit the union to exert economic pressure against the general contractor to enforce the agreement. Pressures exerted against neutral contractors and their employees to stop working will constitute an unfair-labor-practice secondary-boycott violation against the union.

Proper area standards picketing should be distinguished from picketing which has a recognitional or bargaining objective and which will constitute an unfair labor practice under Section 8(b)(7) in particular circumstances. A contractor who is faced with area standards picketing may have no legal remedy to halt the picketing and may even face an interruption in operations until the contractor complies with the union's demands. On the other hand, the contractor may obtain an injunction against and recover damages for recognitional picketing in excess of the prescribed time limits.

Often alleged area standards picketing is a disguise for recognitional picketing. A contractor should not be misled to believe that picketing is lawful merely because the picket signs protest the contractor's substandard wages and benefits. Solicitation of employees that they join the union during picketing which protests the substandard contractor may suggest that the union's purpose is to organize the employees, which might be an unfair labor practice under Section 8(b)(7). Conversations with union officials will often reveal an underlying proscribed purpose. If the union representative not only protests the substandard wages but also requests that the contractor sign a contract, become a union contractor, or accede to noneconomic terms, such as a union security clause or a hiring-hall provision, then the union is no longer engaged in area standards picketing. Submission of an entire union contract to a contractor with the condition that the contractor agree to sign it before picketing will cease shows a recognitional objective.

---

[71] *Carpenters Local 480 (National Mill Designs, Inc.)*, 209 NLRB No. 162 (1974).

Illustrative Case

James N. Wilson was a general contractor engaged in the construction of an apartment building. Carpenters Local 1570, which was affiliated with the Yuba, Sutter & Colusa Counties Building and Construction Trades Council, picketed the project with signs stating that the employer "employs carpenters at wages and conditions below standards as established by Carpenters Local 1570." At a meeting with Wilson, Local 1570's business agent described the benefits of unionization to him. The agent tried to persuade Wilson that it was more desirable for him to pay fringe benefits into the Carpenters trust fund than to pay them directly to his employees. In addition, one of the union representatives stated that the pickets had been removed temporarily because the local had erroneously believed that Wilson had agreed to sign a union contract. Another union representative had told Wilson that a nonunion company could not be permitted to work in the area and urged him to sign a contract. Wilson filed a Section 8(b)(7)(C) unfair-labor-practice charge against the council and Local 1570 on the ground that the picketing had a recognitional purpose which unlawfully continued for more than 30 days without an election petition's being filed by the union. The council and local contended that the picketing was lawful since its sole purpose was to protest Wilson's failure to meet the area wage standards. The NLRB ruled that the council and Local 1570 violated Section 8(b)(7)(C), holding that picketing which had a dual objective of protecting area standards and of obtaining recognition was illegal since the union did not file a petition for an election within a reasonable time not to exceed 30 days.[72]

If a union has not even investigated, or refuses a contractor's offer to examine, its payroll records in order to determine whether the contractor's wages are substandard, a recognitional objective is more likely. The contractor should request from the union a detailed list of the alleged substandard conditions to determine the union's real purpose. If a comparison of the contractor's wage rates and employee benefits with the union's allegations reveal that the contractor is not substandard, the union is probably engaged in picketing for recognition.

Illustrative Case

Several days prior to June 26 the business agent for Carpenters Local 745 advised the local's financial secretary that James W. Glover, Ltd., a general contractor involved in a freeway construction project, was paying substandard wages. The local secretary accepted the business agent's report as true without even questioning him as to the source of his information. On June 26 the secretary wrote Glover a letter requesting information concerning his employees' wages so that the local could determine whether the company's scale was substandard. The letter expressly stated that the union's request was not made for any recognitional or organizational purpose. The next day the secretary, without waiting for a reply to the June 26 letter, wrote Glover to protest the substandard wages of his employees. The letter warned that picketing solely to protest the substandard conditions and not to obtain recognition would ensue "unless prevailing wages, hours, and working conditions are established for the employees." The secretary also received from the business agent what the agent called a "payroll paper" and which contained "a lot of names on one side and the wages on it." At the time that the union sent the letters, Glover was paying his carpenters the prevailing union base wage rate plus the cost of fringe benefits fixed by the state department of labor for persons employed on construction jobs in the area. On

---

[72] Yuba, Sutter & Colusa Counties Bldg. & Constr. Trades Council (James N. Wilson), 189 NLRB No. 70 (1971).

July 1, without waiting for a reply to either of the two letters, picketing commenced at the freeway project with signs protesting Glover's substandard wages and working conditions. On August 20, Glover wrote the local a letter in which it compared his employees' wages and fringe benefits with those provided in the local's agreements with area contractors. Seven days later the union sent a reply letter describing in detail specific items which it contended were substandard. All these detailed objections were erroneous. The court of appeals enforced the NLRB's order that the local had committed an unfair labor practice under Section 8(b)(7)(C) by picketing for recognition without filing an election petition within 30 days. The NLRB had rejected the local's contentions that it was engaged in lawful area standards picketing, because the local's allegation that Glover's wages and working conditions were substandard was false and because it neither investigated Glover's wages and working conditions nor waited for the reply letters when it began picketing. The local's reliance on both the union business agent's statement that conditions at Glover were substandard and the perfunctory examination of the "payroll paper" without further examination and without waiting for Glover's reply revealed that the local was not really concerned with preserving area union standards and that the picketing had an unlawful recognitional objective.[73]

JURISDICTIONAL DISPUTES

A jurisdictional dispute is a dispute between two or more rival unions competing for the same work. Construction delays due to such disputes often involve substantial costs for the contractor. A contractor who is faced with threats of or actual strikes or picketing to compel a work assignment must be aware of the various forms of relief which the law provides.

Section 8(b)(4)(D) of the NLRA prohibits strikes, picketing, boycotts, threats, or other coercive action designed to force a contractor to assign work to one group of employees rather than to another. The contractor should be informed of the union's conduct and whether it has included the threat of work stoppages to compel a job assignment. A mere claim to the work without implied threats of a work stoppage or a threat to file a lawsuit to support a good-faith claim is not unlawful.

For a jurisdictional dispute to exist there must be competing claims for the same work. Such dispute ordinarily arises when one union is assigned particular work by a contractor, another union claims the work for its members, and one of the unions threatens to or does halt work or pickets to compel the contractor to assign the work to its members. The fact that work has not begun is irrelevant if one group has already been assigned the work. A work assignment dispute also exists when the union that threatens to strike has already been assigned or commenced the work if its purpose is to compel the contractor not to reassign the work away from it. The rival claimants need not both be unions: a dispute will be present between a union and a group of unorganized employees.

A contractor who has reason to believe that a jurisdictional dispute exists can file unfair-labor-practice charges with the NLRB. Once charges have been filed, Section 10(k) authorizes the NLRB to hold a hearing to determine which group of employees is entitled to the work. The contractor

---

[73] *NLRB v. Carpenters Local 745 (James W. Glover, Ltd.)*, 450 F.2d 1255 (9th Cir. 1971).

and the rival claimants for the work are allowed to participated in this hearing. However, relief under this procedure can be a slow process, since a Section 10(k) hearing cannot be held for a minimum of 10 days after the charges have been filed, and the delay is often considerably longer. If the Board receives proof during this period that the parties have resolved the dispute, the hearing will not be conducted and the unfair-labor-practice charges will be dismissed. If within the period all the parties agree to a voluntary method for settlement of the dispute, the hearing will not be held at that time, but the unfair-labor-practice charges will be kept alive in the event that the agreed-upon method for settlement fails to resolve the dispute.

When both the contractor and *all* the unions contesting the work assignment have agreed to settle the dispute on their own by a private settlement procedure, the NLRB will not resolve the work assignment. If either the contractor or one of the unions has not agreed to submit the dispute for private settlement within 10 days after an unfair labor charge has been filed, however, the NLRB will conduct a Section 10(k) hearing and make the job assignment.

Illustrative Case

Texas State Tile & Terrazzo Co. and Martini Tile & Terrazzo Co. were contractors engaged in the installation of tile and terrazzo. Texas State and Martini both had agreements with Tile Setters Local 20 that assigned to its members the task of laying the float coat of mortar for tile. Plasterers Local 9 picketed the jobsites of Texas State and Martini, claiming that the work of applying mortar to receive tile belonged to its members and not to workers represented by the Tile Setters. Neither Texas State nor Martini had agreements with the Plasterers. Before the Texas State picketing began, the Plasterers submitted the work assignment dispute to the National Joint Board for Settlement of Jurisdictional Disputes, which had been established by agreement of the Building Trades Department of the AFL-CIO and certain employer groups. The Plasterers and Tile Setters locals were both bound by this procedure, since the international unions with which they were affiliated were members of the department. However, neither Texas State nor Martini had agreed to be bound by the joint board's settlement procedure. The joint board awarded the work to the Plasterers. When Texas State and Martini refused to reassign the work, the Plasterers began to picket both jobsites. In response, Martini and Southwestern Construction Co., which had hired Texas State, filed a Section 8(b)(4)(D) unfair-labor-practice charge against the Plasterers. The NLRB conducted a Section 10(k) hearing and awarded the work to the Tile Setters. When the Plasterers refused to halt the picketing, a Section 8(b)(4)(D) complaint was issued, and the Plasterers were found to have committed the unfair labor practice. The NLRB rejected the Plasterers' argument that Section 10(k) precluded a job assignment by the NLRB because the competing unions had agreed to a voluntary method for settlement. On appeal, the District of Columbia Court of Appeals ruled that the NLRB was without authority to make a Section 10(k) job assignment, since the contractors were not parties to the disputes; only the competing unions were parties and they had both agreed to a private procedure for settlement. The Supreme Court reversed the decision and held that the NLRB was required to make the job determination under Section 10(k). The Court held that contractors who are picketed to force a reassignment of the work are necessarily parties to the dispute since they have a financial stake in its outcome. When the competing unions but not the contractor have agreed upon a method of settlement, the NLRB may not dismiss the Section 10(k) proceeding but must instead determine the dispute, with the contractor being given a chance to participate in the hearing.[74]

Under this rule, if the dispute concerns a contractor's work assignment and rival unions are parties to the Impartial Jurisdictional Disputes Board (IJDB) settlement procedure but the contractor is not, there is no agreed-upon method of private settlement, since one of the interested parties, the contractor, has not consented to submit the dispute to the IJDB, and the NLRB will make the Section 10(k) job assignment.[75]

If a contractor and competing unions have already agreed upon a private method for settling such a dispute in their collective bargaining agreements, the Board will permit this procedure to resolve the dispute. The Plan for Settlement of Jurisdictional Disputes in the Construction Industry created the Impartial Jurisdictional Disputes Board, to which practically all international unions and their locals are stipulated as parties. Contractors may become stipulated as parties by individual contractors' signing stipulations agreeing to be bound by IJDB procedures, by their associations having authority to stipulate them to the board, or by negotiating a collective bargaining agreement which provides that they are bound by IJDB procedures.

Time is usually important when strikes and picketing force a cessation of the work because of a work assignment dispute. A work stoppage of even a few days will impose large costs upon a contractor. The Plan for Settlement of Jurisdictional Disputes in the Construction Industry contains a no-strike clause in which the unions agree not to strike or picket pending a decision by the IJDB. When the rival unions are contractually bound to submit a work assignment dispute to this settlement procedure, the contractor should obtain in federal district court a *Boys Market* injunction to prohibit a strike and picketing pending the IJDB's decision. The procedure to obtain this type of injunction takes only a few days because the contractor may proceed directly to federal court and need not go through the NLRB to obtain an injunction.

If a union continues to strike or picket after a Section 8(b)(4)(D) unfair-labor-practice charge has been filed, the NLRB may seek a Section 10(1) injunction in federal district court if it has reasonable cause to believe that the unfair labor practice has been committed. The contractor should try to persuade the Board's regional director to seek a Section 10(1) injunction if the work stoppage continues. In addition, the Board may seek a temporary restraining order under Section 10(1) to prohibit the work stoppage or picketing. A temporary restraining order usually may grant relief from a work stoppage within a few days, and the order usually lasts for 10 days from its issuance. To obtain a temporary restraining order or injunction irreparable injury must be shown; the mere fact of monetary loss

[74] *NLRB v. Plasterers Local 79 (Texas State Tile & Terrazzo Co.)*, 404 U.S. 116 (1971).

[75] *Ironworkers Local 21 (Weder Constr. Co.)*, 233 NLRB No. 158 (1978).

alone may not be sufficient, since such losses are usually recoverable in a damages suit against the union.

A Section 10(1) injunction usually takes considerably more time to obtain than a *Boys Market* injunction, which the contractor may obtain directly to enforce a no-strike agreement in federal court if the agreement provides for mandatory arbitration of the grievance over which the strike arose. Only the NLRB and not the contractor may petition a federal court for a Section 10(1) injunction, and the Board has discretionary authority on whether to seek the injunction at all. Work stoppages of even a short duration may do much damage to a contractor. Therefore, a Section 10(1) injunction may not be as effective as a *Boys Market* injunction to terminate a work stoppage, since it may take the Board several days even to decide whether to seek the injunction.

In some instances voluntary settlement of a work assignment dispute between the contractor and the competing unions may be preferred to litigation in any form. Such disputes are often resolved at a jobsite meeting between representative of the rival unions, which sometimes will agree to a composite crew consisting of members of both unions to perform the particular job. Unless a dispute over the same work assignment is likely to recur, so that the contractor will want a decision of either the NLRB or the IJDB with legal force, the contractor may prefer to pursue a voluntary settlement.

If all the parties have neither settled the dispute nor agreed to settle it on their own within 10 days after an unfair-labor-practice charge has been filed, the NLRB will conduct a Section 10(k) hearing and make the job assignment. The Board will decide each case on its merits, but traditionally it has relied on several factors in assigning the disputed work. These factors include the contractor's assignment; economy and efficiency; prior Board certifications; special skills necessary for performance of the work; company, industry, and area practice; agreements between unions or between the contractor and the unions; and awards of arbitrators and joint boards in the same or similar cases. The NLRB has usually placed primary reliance on the contractor's preference in assigning the disputed work, especially if this preference is consistent with the considerations of economy, skill, and efficiency.

The IJDB normally considers several factors, such as trade practice, union agreements, and, unfortunately many times, union politics, in making its decision. Historically, it has not seriously considered contractor's assignments or economic realities when deciding which craft union is entitled to the work. However, since in recent years the IJDB has been composed of contractors, some building trades unions have complained that the board has been dominated by employer politics.

If a contractor has encountered union coercion at other jobsites to force an assignment of the same work to its members, the contractor should try to persuade the NLRB at the Section 10(k) hearing to make the job award applicable to other jobsites in the area. The Board has sometimes been willing to issue such a broader award when it has determined that there is a likelihood of similar disputes at other jobsites.

If the union that loses at the Section 10(k) hearing continues to threaten to or actually to strike or picket or fails to give sufficient assurances to the NLRB that it will cease its illegal acts, the Board will issue a complaint alleging a Section 8(b)(4)(D) unfair labor practice. After another hearing, if the charge has merit, the Board will issue a cease-and-desist order against the union. If the union refuses to comply, the Board will petition the appropriate circuit court of appeals to enforce its order.

The NLRB will also determine the Section 8(b)(4)(D) charge and make the job assignment if one of the unions fails to abide by an IJDB award and continues to strike or picket. Work stoppages or picketing for more then 48 hours after the union receives notice of the IJDB decision will normally cause the NLRB to decide the dispute. The NLRB will not necessarily defer to the IJDB assignment, especially if the assignment does not promote considerations of economy and efficient operations or is inconsistent with area practice.[76]

In addition to seeking injunctive relief either directly in a *Boys Market* injunction in federal district court or indirectly through the NLRB under Section 10(1), a contractor may be able to recover for damages incurred because of the jurisdictional dispute. Section 303 of the NLRA enables any contractor damaged by a work assignment dispute to sue in federal district court to recover damages from the union. Contractors should not hesitate to file damage suits against unions which carry their jurisdictional disputes to the jobsite. The threat of a damage suit often deters illegal union activity more than the threat of an injunction. Unions reason that they can picket or strike until an injunction has been obtained and can cease the picketing or striking with impunity. However, damage suits cannot be turned off so easily. Even if the union has ceased its coercive acts by the time that the unfair labor charge against it is decided, damages may be recovered for the union's prior illegal acts.

Illustrative Case

Harnischfeger Corp. was engaged through outside contractors in the construction of several new buildings. The company decided to utilize its own employees, members of UAW Local 632, to construct a spray paint booth to be housed in one of the buildings. Sheet Metal Workers Local 94 picketed to compel the company to contract out the disputed work to a contractor that employed Local 94 members. The NLRB conducted a Section 10(k) hearing and ruled that the company's employees were entitled to the disputed work. At that point Local 94 ceased its picketing. The company brought a suit in federal district court under Section 303 of the NLRA to recover for damages caused by the illegal picketing. The court awarded the company $500,000 compensatory damages but held that punitive damages could not be recovered in the Section 303 suit. The court states that "union compliance with a jurisdictional award of the NLRB is not a defense against a damage suit based on an unfair labor practice charge.[77]

[76] *Carpenters Union (Pacific Coast Fireproofing)*, 223 NLRB No. 7 (1976).

[77] *Harnischfeger Corp. v. Sheet Metal Workers Int'l Ass'n & Local 94*, 436 F.2d 351 (6th Cir. 1970).

Section 8(b)(4)(D) states that no unfair labor practice is committed by a striking or picketing union if the contractor "is failing to conform to an order or certification of the Board determining the bargaining representative for its performing such work." Section 303 does not permit recovery for damages against a striking union which the NLRB had determined was entitled to the work. So if the NLRB awards the job to the striking or picketing union, the contractor should *immediately* readjust the job assignment in accord with that determination; otherwise the contractor will be faced with a strike or picketing against which it will have no remedy.

In a Section 303 suit the court may defer to the job award of the IJDB when contractor and rival unions have voluntarily agreed to submit the dispute to the IJDB. At least one federal district court has held that an award of disputed work to a striking union by the IJDB to which all the parties have agreed to be bound is a defense to a Section 303 suit against the union for damages from a work stoppage.

Illustrative Case

ACMAT Corp. was the subcontractor for all the mechanical work to be done in the construction of the Hartford Fire Insurance office building. Part of the work required ACMAT to assemble a large crane, and ACMAT arranged to have the crane assembled by a composite crew of steamfitters and ironworkers. The Ironworkers and Steamfitters acquiesced to this assignment, but the Operating Engineers were not a party to the arrangement. There arose among the members of the locals a dispute which prevented the assembly work from being done. The Operating Engineers contended that the assembly work should be done by its members and members of the Ironworkers. The dispute was submitted to the IJDB, to which ACMAT and the three locals had agreed to be bound. The IJDB awarded the assembly work to a composite crew of ironworkers and operating engineers on the basis of trade practice. ACMAT sued the Operating Engineers and Ironworkers in federal district court and obtained an injunction to enforce the no-strike clause in the IJDB procedured which was agreed to by the unions. ACMAT also sued under Section 303 for damages resulting from the work stoppage. The two unions argued that the decision of the IJDB assigning the disputed work to them constituted a finding that they had committed no unfair labor practice, so that the Section 303 suit was barred. ACMAT argued that only an award of the NLRB, and not one of a private settlement procedure such as the IJDB, in favor of the striking unions could bar a Section 303 suit. The United States district court held that an award by a private settlement procedure to which the contractor and all the rival unions had voluntarily agreed to be bound and in favor of a union may be a defense to a Section 303 suit against that union. The court ruled that entitlement to the disputed work is a defense to a Section 303 action and that entitlement may be established either by the NLRB in a Section 10(k) hearing or by a private tribunal chosen by the parties.[78]

When the IJDB makes a job award but one of the unions resumes a work stoppage or picketing, the NLRB will make its own job assignment, which sometimes will differ from the IJDB award. Some federal courts have expressed conflicting views concerning whether a union initially denied the work that is awarded the job by the IDJB but is subsequently denied it by the NLRB may recover damages against the contractor. One

[78] *ACMAT Corp. v. Operating Engineers Local 478*, 442 F. Supp. (D. Conn. 1977).

court has ruled that a union that is denied the work by the NLRB may nonetheless recover against the contractor in a breach-of-contract suit if the IJDB had awarded the work to that union,[79] but another court has declared that damages may be recovered by the union only if the NLRB had awarded it the work.

Illustrative Case

The UAW and Rockwell had signed a contract assigning certain work to the UAW's members. After Rockwell allowed the same work to be performed by the Teamsters, the UAW filed a grievance under its collective bargaining agreement with Rockwell which resulted in an arbitration award in its favor. The Teamsters struck despite the adverse arbitration, and the NLRB gave the work to the Teamsters. The UAW sought enforcement of the arbitration award in a Section 301 breach-of-contract action in federal district court against Rockwell. The federal district court ruled that the NLRB's determination that the Teamsters were entitled to the disputed work barred recovery of damages by the UAW in its breach-of-contract suit against Rockwell even though Rockwell had expressly assigned the work under the contract to the UAW. Otherwise, "enforcement of the arbitration award would undermine the Board's stationary authority to hear and determine work assignment disputes."[80]

Many work assignment disputes which result in strikes or picketing may also constitute a secondary boycott, which is a Section 8(b)(4)(B) unfair labor practice. For example, a union that seeks a reassignment by a subcontractor of work to its members might picket the general contractor to remove the subcontractor from the project unless the reassignment is made. The U.S. Supreme Court has ruled that the same activity can violate both Section 8(b)(4)(B) and Section 8(b)(4)(D). The General Counsel of the NLRB is required to seek a Section 10(1) injunction against a secondary boycott, whereas the General Counsel may exercise discretion as to whether to pursue an injunction against a jurisdictional dispute. So if illegal union conduct to compel a work assignment also violates the ban on secondary boycotts, the contractor should also allege a Section 8(b)(4)(B) unfair labor practice in the complaint to the NLRB regional office.

Illustrative Case

White, a subcontractor, installed an electric welding machine and assigned the job of pushing the buttons to operate the machine to members of the Ironworkers. The members of the Operating Engineers Local 825 struck after Burns & Roe, the general contractor, refused to sign a contract, binding on all subcontractors and Burns & Roe, which would give Local 825 jurisdiction over all power equipment operated on the jobsite, including electric welding machines. The NLRB found that Local 825 had committed unfair labor practices under section 8(b)(4)(B) and Section 8(b)(4)(D). The court of appeals held that Local 825 violated Section 8(b)(4)(D) but not Section 8(b)(4)(B). The U.S. Supreme Court reversed the court of appeals and held that by striking Burns & Roe and implying in its demands that Burns & Roe must either force a change in White's work assignment or

[79] AGC v. Operating Engineers, 529 F.2d 1395 (9th Cir. 1976).

[80] UAW v. Rockwell, 94 LRRM 2721 (E.D. Mich. 1977).

terminate White before the strike would cease, Local 825 violated both 8(b)(4)(B) and Section 8(b)(4)(D). The Court ruled that Section 8(b)(4)(D) "is not an exclusive remedy for secondary pressure aimed at involving a neutral employer in a jurisdictional dispute over work assignments made by the primary employer."[81]

VIOLENCE AND MASS PICKETING

Peaceful stikes may be lawful as long as they are not prohibited by a no-strike or no-picketing agreement in a contract and do not constitute an unfair labor practice under NLRA. However, not all work stoppages and picketing are peaceful. Contractors sometimes are faced with union violence and mass picketing which prevents the free access of suppliers and workers to a construction site. An open-shop contractor commencing work in a union stronghold is more likely to face a violent union response. Some unions may attempt to engage in strong-arm tactics to halt or delay the project work so that the contractor will be more willing to accede to its demands for a union contract containing the terms it dictates to the contractor. The law has condemned threats or actual union violence and picket-line misconduct. There are remedies that a contractor may utilize to get the law to work in the contractor's favor. Since a work stoppage of even a few days may cost many thousands of dollars, the contractor must know the remedies that are available to halt strike violence and picket-line misconduct as quickly as possible.

Contractors faced with union violence and mass picketing involving imminent threats of violence can promptly seek an injunction in state court. Under the doctrine of preemption, state courts may be foreclosed from issuing injunctions against peaceful picketing, which is an area in which the NLRB alone has jurisdiction. However, the U.S. Supreme Court has recognized that union violence which threatens personal safety and damage to property is a threat to the public order and is a legitimate matter for local concern, so that a state court may issue an injunction against union violence and mass picketing which threatens violence. Normally the injunction may prohibit only the picket-line misconduct but not the picketing itself because of the preemption doctrine. But if the contractor can prove that there is a pattern of violence which inevitably accompanies picketing once it is resumed, peaceful picketing might also be enjoined. This type of injunction is usually limited in time and location to prohibit only peaceful picketing which in the past has led inevitably to violence or imminent threats of violence.

Illustrative Case

Altemose Construction Co. was a nonunion builder engaged in the construction of a Sheraton hotel and office building. Members of the Philadelphia Building and Construction Trades Council, in protest against Altemose's presence on the job, engaged in what the

---

[81] NLRB v. Operating Engineers Local 825 (Burns & Roe, Inc.), 400 U.S. 297 (1971).

state trial court found to be a "virtual military assault" on the project which resulted in over $300,000 damages. Altemose sought an injunction in state court to prohibit further acts of violence and destruction. The court determined that the building trades had in the past either been unwilling or unable to comply with court orders which permitted peaceful picketing and enjoined only the violence. It concluded that the "peaceful picketing was so inextricably interwoven with acts of violence as to render impossible the maintenance of domestic order and peace in the community." Consequently, the court issued an injunction to prohibit all picketing within 1 mile of the construction site. The construction trades council appealed to the Pennsylvania Supreme Court that the lower court had jurisdiction to enjoin only the violence but not the peaceful picketing because of the preemption doctrine and that the prohibition on picketing within 1 mile was overly broad. The court upheld the injunction as it applied against peaceful picketing but agreed that the 1-mile restriction was too broad, so that the injunction was limited to restrict peaceful picketing within 125 yards of the jobsite. The court reasoned that despite the preemption rule the lower court still could enjoin peaceful picketing that was accompanied by violence, mass picketing, and other imminent threats of violence, since the state has a compelling interest in preserving peace and public order. A state court may prohibit peaceful picketing within reasonable limits when there has been "a pattern of picketing coupled with intimidation, harassment and fear that would inevitably turn even peaceful picketing to violence."[82]

Even though the doctrine of preemption might not disallow the injunction against the violence and mass picketing, some states have what are known as "little Norris–La Guardia statutes" which prohibit injunctions against strikes and picketing arising from a labor dispute. Still, these statutes either expressly or by court interpretation usually do not apply to prevent injunctions against illegal union acts which constitute a breach of the peace.

A contractor who is faced with strike violence and picket-line misconduct should file a complaint in state court and request a temporary restraining order. In many states such a temporary restraining order may be immediately granted *ex parte* if the contractor shows irreparable harm from the union's conduct. Along with the complaint, the contractor should submit affidavits for all the instances of misconduct. The affidavits should, if possible, identify the participants in the misconduct and give all the details, including number of participants, location, and time. The contractor should also give details as to the number of pickets, the wording on the picket signs, and any threatening words or gestures. If there is mass picketing, a record should be kept of the manner in which the picketing has been conducted and of which suppliers or employees have been prevented from entering the jobsite. If weapons have been used, that should be noted in an affidavit. It is important to have affidavits from as many witnesses as possible, and it is even better to get the testimony of a neutral bystander, such as a passerby who has been threatened with violence or denied access to the project by the picketers. The fact that the local police have been unable to curb the union misconduct should also be contained in an affidavit. Sometimes a union will halt the misconduct when the police arrive and resume it when they leave, so that fact and the times when the police

---

[82]*Altemose Constr. Co. v. Trades Council,* 296 A.2d 504 (E.D. Pa. Sup. Ct. 1972).

arrive and leave and when the misconduct halts and resumes should be recorded. Photographs and motion pictures which show the specific incidents of violence, such as a striker waving a weapon or scenes of mass picketing which prevent free access through a gate at the worksite, should be taken. Tape recorders with shotgun microphones to record threatening remarks of strikers might also be useful.

A contractor who is faced with union violence should immediately request the assistance of the local police. There are various criminal statutes, such as those directed against assault and battery, breach of the peace, disorderly conduct, resisting arrest, and malicious mischief, which might be invoked against union misconduct. The police are often reluctant to enforce these statutes in some urban areas where building trades unions are strong and local police sympathize with the unions. In addition, conviction under these statutes requires a high standard of proof, and prosecutors in many areas are often influenced by local politics and will refuse to conduct a vigorous enforcement of the penal statutes. Still, when where is violence, an appeal should be made for police protection and a state court injunction sought at the same time. Sometimes appeals to the general public through the news media will spur local officials to move against union violence.

A wise contractor plans ahead for violence and gets to know the local police before violence occurs. Getting to know the local authorities and supporting local police events will go a long way toward getting a fast reaction from the police if violence occurs. Of course, this relationship is also useful for common thefts. Contractors should also have a plan of security of the jobsite, and if violence is expected, private guards may be in order. Guard dogs are particularly useful in preventing violence. Without an advance plan of action there is usually great confusion when violence occurs. But if there is an advance plan, violence and mass picketing can be dealt with very coolly, perhaps with only a call to local authorities for extra police presence in the area. Often, off-duty police officers can be privately hired to maintain the constant presence of uniformed police to have a definite cooling effect. (See Chapter 12, section "Jobsite Management.")

The U.S. Supreme Court has held that the preemption doctrine does not prevent a state court from enjoining a union that trespasses on a contractor's property in violation of the state's trepass laws if it rejects the contractor's request to leave. According to the Court, an injunction against the trespass may be issued even though the picketing is peaceful.

Illustrative Case

Business agents of the Carpenters visited a Sears department store in California and determined that certain carpentry work was being performed by workers who had not been dispatched from the union hiring hall. The agents met with the store manager and requested that Sears have the work performed by a contractor who employed dispatched carpenters. The manager stated that he would consider the request, but he never accepted or rejected it. Two days later the union set up picket lines on a private walkway and in a parking lot owned by Sears. The three sides of the store at which the union did not picket were adjacent to public sidewalks. The picketing was peaceful and orderly. Sears's manager demanded that the union remove the pickets from its property, but the union refused. Sears filed a complaint against the trespass in the Superior Court of California, and the court granted a temporary restraining order against the picketing on Sears property. The union removed the pickets, and the court entered a preliminary injunction, which was affirmed by the California Court of Appeals. The Supreme Court of California reversed, on the ground that the purpose of the picketing was arguably protected by Section 7 of the NLRA because it was intended to prevent the area standards of employment for carpenters from being undercut and was arguably prohibited by Section 8(b)(7)(C) of the NLRA because it was recognitional picketing which extended for more than 30 days without the union's petitioning for a representation election. Since the picketing was both arguably protected and arguably prohibited by the NLRA, the preemption doctrine applied, and the state court lacked jurisdiction to enjoin the peaceful picketing which was a trespass. The U.S. Supreme Court reversed the California Supreme Court, ruling that a state court has jurisdiction to enjoin peaceful picketing which violated a state's trespass laws. The Court held that the preemption doctrine should not be applied to oust the state court from jurisdiction to enjoin conduct arguably protected or prohibited by the NLRA when the state had a significant interest in regulating the challenged conduct and the exercise of state jurisdiction would entail little risk of interference with NLRB enforcement. According to the Court, the state had a significant interest in enjoining the union's trespass onto private property, and adjudication of the trespass claim would create no realistic risk of interference with the NLRB's jurisdiction to enforce the federal prohibition against unfair labor practices. Therefore, the state court had jurisdiction to enjoin peaceful picketing by the union which violated the state's trespass laws.[83]

Since most labor problems are governed by federal law, it might at first appear that the contractor should seek injunctive relief against union violence in a federal district court. However, the Norris–La Guardia Act, which restricts the issuance of injunctions by federal courts in cases arising out of labor disputes, has been interpreted by courts in such a way that injunctions in federal court against strike violence and mass picketing are very hard to obtain. A federal court will require a contractor to show that local police are unable or unwilling to provide adequate protection before it might enjoin the strike violence. Most police officers are reluctant to testify that they are unable effectively to perform their duties, and the courts are usually unwilling to find the police incapable to furnish adequate protection. There are other reasons why a federal court will probably not enjoin a union's misconduct, so the contractor should seek injunctive relief in a state court.

Sometimes a union which is faced with a possible state court injunction will remove the case to federal court, where the Norris–La Guardia restrictions apply, on the ground that there is a federal question in the controversy for the federal court to resolve. If the contractor's complaint only seeks an injunction against the union violence or mass picketing on the ground that state law has been violated, the suit will be remanded to state court, where the Norris–La Guardia restrictions do not apply, and the injunction may be more easily obtained. But if, in addition to seeking the

[83] *Sears, Roebuck & Co. v. San Diego County Dist. Council of Carpenters*, 98 S. Ct. 1745 (1978).

injunction, the contractor also brings a federal claim under Section 301 for breach of a no-strike promise or under Section 303 for damages from an illegal secondary boycott, then a federal question has been raised in the complaint, and the federal court may retain jurisdiction. It will therefore be more difficult for the contractor to get the strike violence and picket-line misconduct enjoined.

Under some circumstances a contractor may obtain an injunction in federal district court against strike violence without being subject to the Norris–La Guardia restrictions. If there is a no-strike clause and the union is required by its agreement with the contractor to arbitrate the dispute over which the strike arose, the contractor may obtain a *Boys Market* injunction in federal court to prohibit the strike pending arbitration of the dispute. Such an injunction may be obtained to attempt to end the strike violence within a few days after a complaint has been filed by the contractor's attorney, proceeding directly to federal court without going through the NLRB.

A contractor may recover in state court against a union on a common-law tort action for damages from strike violence. Even though substantial damages may be awarded, they rarely adequately compensate the contractor for all the injury caused by the union violence. Damages are recovered years after the violence has terminated, and there may be no recovery for damages caused by lawful, peaceful picketing. The contractor should pursue a damages suit and at the same time seek an injunction in state court as soon as possible after the violence begins.

Section 8(b)(1)(A) makes it an unfair labor practice for a union to restrain or coerce employees in their protected right to refrain from engaging in a strike or picketing. Many times picketers will make threats of physical attack against their replacements or members of other unions if they cross the picket line. This section makes unlawful acts or threats of violence against employees and mass picketing which prevents the free access of nonstrikers to the construction site. Contractors faced with strike violence or picket-line misconduct may file a Section 8(b)(1)(A) unfair-labor-practice charge with the NLRB regional director and, at the same time or earlier, file a complaint for an injunction in state court.

Contractors should not rely exclusively on the NLRB to obtain a quick halt to union violence and mass picketing. Although the Board is empowered to seek a Section 10(j) injunction in federal court to prohibit a Section 8(b)(1)(A) unfair labor practice, it takes a considerable time to obtain an NLRB injunction. The Board will not seek an injunction until it has made an investigation to determine whether there is reasonable cause to believe that the unfair labor practice has been committed. Also, the Board has discretion on whether to seek a Section 10(j) injunction at all, and contractors cannot obtain one themselves. Even if the Board decides to prosecute the Section 8(b)(1)(A) charge and wins, all the contractor will have is a cease-and-desist order against strike violence which probably has already ended.

There may still be some advantages to the filing of a Section 8(b)(1)(A) charge with the NLRB as long as the contractor also seeks an injunction in state court. Even if the union violence has ended when the cease-and-desist order is finally obtained, if the violence or unlawful picketing recur, the order may be enforced in federal court and the union may be cited for contempt of the court order. Also, if the contractor is charged with a Section 8(a)(1) unfair labor practice for illegally discharging a striker or picketer for engaging in a protected union activity, the NLRB's investigation of the unfair-labor-practice charge against the union may provide enough evidence for the contractor to justify the discharge.

The threat of discharge may discourage some union violence and picket-line misconduct. Section 10(C) of the NLRA provides that reinstatement of an employee shall not be required for an employee discharged "for cause." Only employees who actually commit serious acts of misconduct may be discharged. Employees who participate in the strike but do not themselves commit prohibited acts are engaged in a protected activity. A contractor who discharges or denies reinstatement to such an employee might be guilty of a Section 8(a)(1) unfair labor practice and be required to reinstate the employee with back pay. If an unlawful motivation for the discharge of an employee who has engaged in misconduct is claimed, the discharge might be an employer unfair labor practice. Therefore, the contractor should amass all available evidence to prove that the employee engaged in serious acts of misconduct. Evidence from the Board's investigation of the Section 8(b)(1)(A) charge will also aid in the contractor's defense.

Contractors who are faced with union violence and mass picketing which threatens violence must know how to stop it as quickly as possible if they want to keep the job running smoothly and not bow to the union's demands. To get any effective relief, evidence of the union's misconduct must be obtained. Injunctive relief is usually available most quickly in state court. Although the NLRB should not be relied upon for a speedy injunction, there are advantages to a contractor who files an unfair-labor-practice charge. Attempts to get assistance from the local police should be made, and appeals to the public's sense of justice might spur enforcement of criminal statutes applicable to much union violence. Damage suits seeking redress for the contractor should be pursued against the union and its international, if the international is involved.

5 BARGAINING OBLIGATIONS

The National Labor Relations Act (NLRA) requires both labor and management to bargain in good faith over wages, hours, and other terms and conditions of employment. This bargaining obligation may arise in a representation election conducted by the National Labor Relations Board (NLRB) in which a majority of the employees select a union as their exclusive bargaining representative. Often in the construction industry, however, management will voluntarily recognize a union because of benefits to the union employer, such as the availability of a trained workforce, or because employers believe that they will have more labor harmony on predominantly union jobs than if they were nonunion. This method of recognition results when management voluntarily bargains with a union and enters into a bargaining agreement.

Common voluntary recognition occurs when management enters into a collective bargaining agreement with a union prior to commencing operations at a jobsite. Prehire agreements are made lawful in the building and construction industry by Section (8)(f) of the NLRA (for a more detailed discussion of prehire agreements see Chapter 1, section "Prehire Agreements"). A previously unorganized contractor enters into an agreement covering existing employees as a result of union pressure, such as picketing at the jobsite. Also, as in other industries, an employer may voluntarily recognize a union if the union at that time is the designated representative of a majority of the employees in an appropriate bargaining unit.

Contractors in the construction industry will voluntarily bargain with the union either individually or, more commonly, with a group of other contractors on a multiemployer basis. Bargaining over issues common to contractors might be subject to joint negotiation, other issues being reserved for bargaining by individual contractors. Both the contractor and the union must demonstrate an unequivocal intent to bargain on a group basis to be bound by its results. A history of union agreements reached with a group of contractors negotiating jointly with the union or with an association representing the contractors will usually establish the duty of the union and contractors to bargain on a multiemployer basis.

The construction unions generally favor multiemployer bargaining because they can kill two birds with one stone by getting a group of contractors bound at the same time to a union agreement instead of negotiating separately with individual contractors. Contractors often prefer multiemployer bargaining in order to avoid a favorite union bargaining tactic, the "whipsaw strike," in which a union strikes some individual contractors and lets others alone. The union thus hopes to extract the greatest concessions from each contractor, since struck contractors see that their competitors are still working and believe that they will be allowed to work without a strike if they give in to the union. Since the craftsmen of the struck contractor can go to work for nonstruck contractors, there will be little pressure from union members to settle the strike except on the union's terms. Group bargaining will prevent the whipsaw strike. Once the union enters into negotiations on a multiemployer basis, it commits a Section 8(a)(5) unfair labor practice for not bargaining in good faith if it threatens to or actually strikes or pickets individual contractors to get them to negotiate apart from the group.

From an individual contractor's point of view, the duty to bargain on a multiemployer basis generally means that the contractor will be bound to a union agreement which is negotiated by the association or a group of other contractors with whom the contractor has participated in negotiations. The contractor may become bound to multiemployer bargaining either formally or informally. Bargaining in the construction industry is often conducted by employer trade associations which are authorized by their members to recognize and bargain with the unions. The association's constitution or bylaws may show whether the association has authority and cover the terms on which it is empowered to negotiate on behalf of its members. Or the contractors might sign letters of assent which make the association the agent for negotiating and signing a union contract. However, formal agreements are not essential to show a contractor's assent to group bargaining. The fact that a contractor has participated in joint negotiations with the union along with other contractors might require the contractor to adopt the terms of an agreement that the group concludes with the union.

The bargaining duty may be but rarely is established in the construction industry by a representation election conducted by the NLRB. A majority of voting employees in an appropriate bargaining unit must cast their ballots in favor of the union for the contractor or subcontractor to be required to bargain with the union. If the union prevails in the NLRB election, the contractor or subcontractor is obligated to bargain in good faith with the union for at least 1 year from the date on which the union is certified as the exclusive bargaining representative.

In addition to the election method of certification, a union may attempt to be recognized as the employees' representative by presenting cards to an employer. Under this method, the union presents cards signed by a majority of the employees which show that the employees favor union representation. Employers are under no obligation to examine these cards, and if they do not, they are not required to bargain with the union even if the cards are in fact signed by a majority of the employees. If an employer rejects bargaining on the basis of authorization cards, the burden is on the union to file a petition with the NLRB for a representation election.

It should be noted that a union may attempt to force recognition by illegal tactics. One illegal tactic is to use a secondary boycott to apply economic pressure to another company to force it to cease doing business with the employer unless the employer recognizes and bargains with the union. A secondary boycott results when a union strikes, pickets, or otherwise threatens another company to cease doing business with the employer in order to force the employer to recognize and bargain with the uncertified union. The purpose or effect of such activity is to have the other company sever business relations with the new employer unless the employer agrees to become a union employer. It is illegal for a union to put pressure on the other company to "kick the employer off the job or get him straightened up." The law provides for injunctive relief and recovery of monetary damages against a union to discourage secondary boycotts, and a company threatened with such a boycott should consult an attorney knowledgeable in labor law. (See Chapter 4, section "Secondary Boycotts.")

In another illegal tactic to force recognition, a union makes an agreement requiring an employer not to do business with any nonunion employer. The union's purpose is to induce the nonunion employer to sign a union contract, since otherwise it will be foreclosed from the other employer's business. The U.S. Supreme Court has ruled that the union and employers who agree to this illegal provision may be subject to liability under the antitrust laws, including treble-damage suits.[1] An employer who has been denied business with another employer because it has refused to recognize the union should by all means consult an attorney. (See Chapter 4, section "Restrictive Agreements," for a fuller discussion of the legal limits of such contracting agreements.)

Once a union has been certified or recognized, the bargaining process begins. There is no obligation that the bargaining result in an agreement, but if no agreement is reached, strikes and picketing usually ensue. Should no agreement be reached and no strike occur, it is reasonable to conclude that the union has lost its majority status or its interest in further bargaining for the employees of the company.

As discussed below, an employer may bargain directly with the union or through a multiemployer bargaining agent, which typically is a trade association. The method of preparation and bargaining is basically the same for both types of bargaining committees.

MULTIEMPLOYER BARGAINING

Over the years, individual contractors have increasingly joined together to bargain with the building trades unions on a group basis. This type of

[1] *Connell Constr. Co., Inc. v. Plumbers Local 100*, 421 U.S. 616 (1975).

bargaining possesses certain advantages over bargaining by contractors on an individual basis with a union.

Contractors may be most susceptible to union pressure tactics when they bargain individually. Since a craft union is often the sole, or at least the main, source of workers to fill construction jobs, a union that bargains with a single contractor may threaten to strike unless the contractor agrees to its proposals. An individual contractor faced with this type of selective strike will be under the greatest pressure to accede to the union's demands, since the contractors will be faced with a strike while other contractors are still permitted to work. Thus, a union that uses this tactic against each contractor individually may extract the greatest concessions from each, to the mutual disadvantage of all the contractors. In contrast, if the contractors join together to bargain with a union, the union is effectively prevented from playing off one contractor against the next to get the best bargain from each. Such multiemployer bargaining has enjoyed increasing popularity among contractors in the construction industry.

A prerequisite for multiemployer bargaining is that the union voluntarily consent to bargain on that basis. A contractor may not threaten to or actually lock out employees as an inducement to bargain with an association or an informal group of contractors. If the contractor locks out employees in this situation, it will be required to reimburse them for the wages and other benefits they would have received but for the improper lockout.[2]

Sometimes, however, individual contractors who have been members of a contractors' association or of an informal group of contractors who have bargained with a union wish to withdraw from multiemployer bargaining. Generally, the union must receive notice of withdrawal prior to the initiation of negotiations. If this notice is not timely, withdrawal will still be permitted with the union's consent or, if there is no consent, by unusual circumstances. In addition, notice of withdrawal to be effective must represent a clear and unequivocal desire to abandon multiemployer bargaining on a permanent basis. The consequences of an ineffective withdrawal may be that the contractor will actually be bound by the terms of the agreement reached through multiemployer bargaining despite a good-faith belief that the contractor had withdrawn. On the other hand, an effective withdrawal will mean that the union cannot lawfully compel the contractor, under the threat of economic reprisal, to reassign bargaining rights to an association.

Withdrawal by an individual contractor from multibargaining will be timely if written notice of intent to do so is given to the union before either the date set by the contract for such notices or the date set for the commencement of negotiations. When notice of withdrawal is timely, the contractor is not required to give any reason for wanting to withdraw. A request by the union for bargaining will not constitute the commencement

---

[2] *Siebler Heating & Air Conditioning, Inc. (Sheet Metal Workers Local 3)*, 219 NLRB No. 180 (1975).

of negotiations. Once the union has submitted its proposals to the contractor, negotiations have begun, so that any notice of intent to withdraw received after that time will not be timely.[3]

Nevertheless, even if a withdrawal is made before negotiations have commenced, it is still permitted if the union voluntarily consents to the withdrawal. However, the fact that the union may have consented to the withdrawal of one contractor from multiemployer bargaining does not necessarily mean that it also consents to other contractors' withdrawals. The union's consent to a late withdrawal may be manifested by its willingness to negotiate an individual contract with the contractor after an agreement with the association has already been reached as well as by its failure to present the association contract to the individual contractor for signature.[4]

If the union consents, the contractor need not also acquire the association's consent to effect a proper withdrawal. But under some agreements between the contractor and the association a contractor may still be liable in damages to an association for withdrawing without its consent. So the contractor should also look at the terms of any agreement the contractor may have with an association or the association's bylaws before seeking to bargain with the union independently of the association.[5]

A withdrawal that is not timely and is not consented to by the union may still be justified by "unusual circumstance." The mere fact that the contractor is dissatisfied with the terms of the contract which the association has negotiated will not justify the contractor's refusal to sign the contract. However, the U.S. Supreme Court has refused to review the ruling of a federal court of appeals which upheld the right of a contractor to decline to sign an association bargaining agreement when the association failed to represent fairly the contractor's interest and the terms of the agreement would severely disadvantage the contractor. The fact that the bargaining representatives for the association were familiar with a contractor's bargaining demands and made only feeble efforts to present them to the union will usually show the association's lack of fair representation to justify a late withdrawal.

Illustrative Case

Siebler Heating & Air Conditioning, Inc., and several other contractors were members of the Sheet Metal and Air Conditioning Contractors' National Association (SMACNA), which represented its members in collective bargaining with Sheet Metal Workers Local 3. Siebler and the others authorized SMACNA to negotiate an agreement for them and agreed to be bound by any contract resulting from such negotiations. Siebler was a residential contractor and a member of the negotiating committee, which consisted of commercial and industrial contractors. Because residential contractors were faced with severe competition from low-cost nonunion contractors for certain jobs, Siebler proposed that the committee seek

[3] *Carvel Co.*, 226 NLRB No. 18 (1976).

[4] *Atlas Sheet Metal Works, Inc.*, 148 NLRB No. 3 (1964).

[5] *Associated Gen. Contractors, N.Y. State Chapter v. Savin Bros.*, 356 N.Y.S.2d 374.

to have an existing agreement permitting payment of 75 percent of journeyman's rates on single-family dwellings to be extended to the construction of apartments and condominiums. The committee made this proposal to the union during the first bargaining session and did not even raise it in three subsequent sessions. The members of the committee representing commercial contractors agreed to settle for a wage increase on commercial work and decided not to press for the extension of the residential agreement as proposed by Siebler since they feared that the union might then reject the entire package and seek a greater wage increase. Siebler and the other residential contractors withdrew from SMACNA and refused to be bound by the agreement SMACNA signed with the union. The NLRB ruled that the contractors failed to bargain in good faith by withdrawing from SMACNA after negotiations had begun and that there were no unusual circumstances to justify the late withdrawal. The Eighth Circuit Court of Appeals, reversing, held that SMACNA's failure fairly to represent the contractor's interests constituted unusual circumstances to permit a late withdrawal from association bargaining. Although mere dissatisfaction with the results of group bargaining does not justify an untimely withdrawal, the court stated that an employer has a right to expect that its interests will be fairly represented by the association during negotiations and not be totally sacrificed in the interests of the majority in the group. The association made only a feeble effort to protect the residential contractors' interests and threw in the towel at the first sign of union opposition because the majority believed that their own interests would best be served by giving the wage increase accepted by the union and leaving the rest of the contract intact.[6]

Some federal courts of appeals have considered an impasse in bargaining an unusual circumstance that will permit an individual contractor to withdraw from group bargaining without the union's consent provided the contractor gives notice of withdrawal to the union.[7] The NLRB has continued to disallow late withdrawal in the face of an impasse, but the Board's order requiring an individual contractor to sign a group agreement will be ineffective if the court of appeals refuses to enforce it.

A further prerequisite for effective withdrawal from multiemployer bargaining is that it must be unequivocal. In other words, "the decision to withdraw must contemplate a sincere abandonment, with relative permanency, of the multiemployer unit and the embracement of a different course of bargaining on an individual employer basis."[8]

Therefore, a contractor who desires to abandon multiemployer bargaining should give the union written notice clearly stating that the contractor no longer desires to participate in multiemployer bargaining and wishes to negotiate with the union on an individual basis. A mere statement that the contractor is dissatisfied with the current association contract will not constitute an effective notice of withdrawal. As a result, the contractor will actually be bound by the terms of any multiemployer agreement ultimately reached.

Illustrative Case

When the contract was set for renegotiation, an individual contractor member of an association informed the union that he was dissatisfied with the current association contract. The individual contractor never notified the union that he desired to negotiate on an individual

[6] Sheet Metal Workers Local 3 v. Siebler Heating & Air Conditioning, Inc., 563 F.2d 366 (8th Cir. 1977).

[7] NLRB v. Independent Ass'n of Steel Fabricators, Inc.____F.2d____(2d Cir. 1978).

[8] Retail Associates, 120 NLRB No. 66 (1958).

basis, although that was the contractor's intent. The notice of withdrawal was held to be equivocal because it merely expressed the contractor's discontent with the current contract but not the intent to withdraw from multiemployer bargaining. Therefore, the contractor was required to make certain fringe-benefit payments pursuant to the terms of the multiemployer agreement.[9]

Contractor should avoid taking any action or making any statements that might be inconsistent with an intent to withdraw from multiemployer bargaining, for contractors who convey to the union "apparent acquiescence" to multiemployer bargaining will be bound by its results despite the fact that they intended to withdraw. So, besides dropping formal membership in an association, contractors should by all means refrain from participating in further negotiating sessions between the association and the union unless the contractors have also clearly stated to the union that they are acting on their own behalf and that the association no longer represents them.

Illustrative Case

Prior to the initiation of negotiations, the contractor notified the union of intent to withdraw from the association. Then, the contractor signed an interim agreement with the union, pending negotiations between the association and the union, under which the contractor was bound to execute the agreement subsequently reached between the association and the union. The union struck the contractor to protest refusal to make payments into the industry promotion fund, as required by the union's contract with the association. The NLRB held that the contractor was required to make payments into this fund even though it is not a mandatory subject of bargaining since he signed the interim agreement. "Although the contractor withdrew from the association, by signing the agreement, he in effect redelegated to the union and the association the power to bind him to any lawful agreement that they might negotiate."[10]

The fact that a contractor has effectively withdrawn from multiemployer bargaining does not mean that the union must then bargain with the contractor alone. The contractor will violate the NLRA by threatening to or actually retaliating against employees if the union refuses to bargain with the contractor individually.

The rules concerning effective contractor withdrawals from multiemployer bargaining apply equally to unions. Thus, a union that gives unequivocal notice of withdrawal before negotiations are initiated may lawfully refuse to bargain on a multiemployer basis. No reason for the withdrawal need be given. Once negotiations have begun, however, withdrawal by the union is permitted only with the association's consent or, if none, by "unusual circumstances."

So, if a union's withdrawal from multiemployer bargaining is ineffective for any of these reasons, a union cannot lawfully refuse to bargain with the association. Also, a union acts unlawfully if it threatens to or does

[9] *Interstate Constr. Co. v. IBEW Local 226*, 229 NLRB No. 37 (1977).

[10] *Sheet Metal Workers Local 270 (General Sheet Metal Co.)*, 144 NLRB No. 69 (1963).

picket individual contractors in an effort to get them to bargain with it apart from the association.[11]

A contractor violates the NLRA by refusing to bargain with a union that has effected a proper withdrawal unless the contractor agrees to continue to bargain on a multiemployer basis. Similarly, threats of or actual retaliation against employees for the union's refusal to bargain on that basis will be unlawful.[12]

UNION REPRESENTATION THROUGH AN ELECTION

A building trades union will sometimes attempt to organize a contractor's employees and then demand that a contractor recognize and bargain with it on the ground that a majority of the employees favor representation by the union. The safest course of a contractor faced with such a demand is to tell the union that the contractor has a good-faith doubt that the union represents a majority of the contractor's employees in an appropriate bargaining unit and that if the union wants to bargain with the contractor, it must petition the NLRB for a representation election.

Organizing the employees of a company is called "bottom-up organizing" (see Chapter 12 section "Bottom-Up Organizing"). An initial step normally taken by a union in a bottom-up organizing campaign is to appoint a field representative, a full-time employee of the union engaged in organizing activities, to be in charge of the organization of the company. The field representative who enjoys broad rights to visit and talk with employees, may visit employee entrances and other areas where outside solicitation is normally permitted by the company to distribute literature and to talk with employees unless the employer has already adopted and is enforcing a broad rule against solicitation on company property. The field representative may also visit employees at their homes, arrange meetings during nonworking hours, and solicit employees by mail.

Employees of the company who support the union organizing drive will also attempt to recruit additional support. Again, employees have the right to engage in this sort of activity, subject to certain restraints. They may solicit and freely discuss union organizing with other employees on company premises, but the employer may restrict such conversations to nonworking time, such as coffee breaks or lunch periods. An employee who is on break may not solicit another employee who is not on break. In general, employee solicitation is not protected activity if it unduly disrupts the normal working of a plant; however, an employer may commit an unfair labor practice by preventing employees from engaging in protected solicitation.

The objective of the union during the prepetition phase of the organizational campaign is to obtain authorization cards signed by the employees

[11] *Associated Plastering & Lathing Contractors*, 228 NLRB No. 179 (1977).

[12] *Evening News Ass'n*, 154 NLRB No. 121 (1965).

of the company. A union may demand that an employer recognize it as the bargaining representative of the employees once it has obtained authorization cards from more than one-half of all nonsupervisory employees in an appropriate bargaining unit. If the employer declines to recognize the union, the union may present the authorization cards to the NLRB and petition for an election to determine whether the union will be selected as the bargaining agent for the employees. To petition for an election before the NLRB, the union must submit authorization cards signed by at least 30 percent of the nonsupervisory employees in the bargaining unit that it wishes to represent.

A union is not required to demand recognition or to acquire more than a 30 percent showing of interest by authorization cards before submitting a petition for an election to the NLRB. However, in practice the union will normally wait until it has obtained signed authorization cards from at least half of the employees whom it wishes to represent and will begin by demanding recognition directly from the employer. In the usual situation, the field representative will arrive at the employer's office with the authorization cards in hand. The representative will show them to the employer, asking the employer to examine them so as to be satisfied that the union does indeed represent a majority of the contractor's employees.

Sometimes a union representative will send a letter or make a verbal request to the contractor claiming that it has majority status and stating that the contractor must bargain with it. Or a letter might include authorization cards or union membership cards that are purportedly signed by a majority of the employees along with a request that either the contractor or a third party count them. If the contractor examines the cards or allows a third party to count them and they demonstrate the union's majority status, the contractor will be required to recognize the union and will not be able to demand an election to determine the contractor's bargaining obligation. If the contractor refuses to examine the cards and commits no unfair labor practice, however, the contractor may legally refuse to bargain with the union unless the union petitions for and wins an NLRB election. The U.S. Supreme Court has held that a contractor who commits no unfair labor practice that will tend to prevent a fair election and who has a "good-faith doubt" concerning the union's majority status may lawfully refuse to negotiate with the union and may insist that the union petition for an election to demonstrate its majority support.[13] Even if the cards are actually signed by a majority of the employees, the contractor has a good-faith doubt that is sufficient for a refusal to bargain with the union pending a Board election if the contractor refuses to examine the cards or to permit another party to count them.

The contractor might be ordered by the NLRB to bargain with the union without an election if it engages in certain conduct in response to a request for recognition. A poll of employees concerning their union sympa-

[13]*Linden Lumber Div. v. NLRB (Summer & Co.)*, 419 U.S. 817 (1974).

thies by the contractor or a supervisor is especially dangerous and is unnecessary anyway, and the contractor should therefore refrain from questioning the employees in any manner. If the contractor's own poll of the employees shows that the union enjoys majority support, then the contractor will be bound by the results and must bargain with the union without an election.[14] The contractor might be required to bargain even though the poll showed that the union lacked majority status if the NLRB determined that the conduct of the polling was so "coercive" as to have destroyed the union's majority status, so that a bargaining order was warranted.[15] The NLRB has laid down guidelines concerning proper noncoercive polling of employees. Since the contractor might have to bargain whether or not the union wins the private poll and since a good-faith doubt to require a Board election can usually be shown by a mere refusal to examine to union's cards, the contractor should refrain from conducting any type of poll of the employees as to their union sympathies.

The U.S. Supreme Court has held that a contractor might be required to bargain with a union and would not be able to demand a representation election if it commited unfair labor practices serious enough to impede the conduct of a fair election.[16] Sometimes a contractor's unfair labor practices will require the contractor to recognize the union even though the union lost the election. In all the cases in which a *Gissel* bargaining order has been issued, the union had already demonstrated that it enjoyed majority status by a card check, but the Supreme Court suggested that if the unfair labor practice were very serious, a bargaining order might be warranted even if the union had never demonstrated majority support. The contractor should make sure that known union supporters are not threatened with discharges, actually discharged, or otherwise retaliated against pending a union's claim for recognition. Interrogation of employees concerning their attitude toward the union should be avoided. If the contractor offers employee benefits that are greatly out of line with prior practice pending an election, then a *Gissel* bargaining order might be forthcoming.

Illustrative Case

Food Store Employers Union Local 347 sought recognition by Gissel Packing Co. as the bargaining representative for its employees. The union waged an organizational campaign, obtained authorization cards from a majority of employees in the bargaining unit, and on the basis of the cards demanded recognition by the company. The company refused to bargain on the ground that the cards were unreliable indicators of employee desires. At the outset of the union's campaign, the company vice president informed two employees who were later discharged that if they were caught talking to "union men, you God-damned things will go." The company interrogated employees as to their union activities, had an agent present at a union meeting to report the identity of employees who attended, and promised the employees better benefits then the union could get. The union filed unfair-

---

[14] *Sullivan Elec. Co.*, 199 NLRB No. 97 (1972).

[15] *Struksnes Constr. Co.*, 165 NLRB No. 102 (1967).

[16] *NLRB v. Gissel Packing Co.*, 395 U.S. 575 (1969).

labor-practice charges with the NLRB against the company for unlawful discharge of union adherents and for illegal intimidation and coercion of employees in violation of Section 8(a)(1) and Section 8(a)(3). The NLRB ordered the company to bargain with the union without an election on the grounds that the union had obtained valid authorization cards from a majority of the bargaining-unit employees and that the conpany's unfair labor practices demonstrated that it did not have a good-faith doubt as to the union's majority status. The court of appeals refused to enforce the bargaining order, ruling that authorization cards are not reliable indicators of a union's majority status unless the employer has agreed that the cards are valid, so that a Board certification pursuant to a representation election is necessary to establish the bargaining obligation. The U.S. Supreme Court reversed the court of appeals, holding that a bargaining order by the NLRB without an election may be appropriate when the union demonstrated its majority status by valid authorization cards and the company committed unfair labor practices tending to undermine the union's majority and make a fair election unlikely.[17]

Both the officers of the company and the supervisory staff have certain rights and duties during the organizing campaign. Supervisors are employees who, under the terms of the NLRA, cannot be the subject of a union organizing campaign because they are too closely identified with management. Supervisors are defined in the NLRA as any individuals having the authority to do any of the following acts: "hire, transfer, suspend, lay off, recall, promote, discharge, assign, reward, or discipline other employees, or responsibly to direct them, or to adjust their grievances, or effectively to recommend such action," if the exercise of this authority is not routine but requires the use of independent judgment. Supervisors are excluded from the coverage of the NLRA and a union may not petition for an election seeking representation of a bargaining unit which includes supervisors.

Since supervisors are closely identified with management and are excluded from the bargaining unit, the actions of supervisors are attributed to the employer. This means that employees of a company who perform any of the functions listed above must observe the same rules in dealing with union organizing attempts as the officers of the company. A complete summary of supervisors' rights and responsibilities is beyond the scope of this chapter. (See Chapter 3 for an additional discussion of the rights and responsibilities of supervisors.) Like most areas of labor law, the permitted and prohibited actions of supervisors and company representatives are subject to change, so it is mandatory that a contractor consult a labor attorney for specific guidance in the face of an organizational campaign. However, the following is a general outline of the activities which supervisors are and are not permitted to engage in during the course of an organizing campaign:

Permitted Activities

1. Supervisors may continue the normal operations of the company, may direct the work of nonsupervisory staff, and need not tolerate insubordination or interference with work. They may continue to discipline and discharge employees in accordance with previously established company policy as long as these actions are taken for cause and as long as the discipline or discharge is not related to union activities of employees.

[17] Ibid.

2. Supervisors may continue to advise employees concerning the employer's personnel policies. However, they must be careful to avoid making any statements which could be interpreted to be threats of future punishment or promises of future reward in connection with the union campaign.

3. Supervisors may assist in campaigning against the union by distributing literature, speaking to employees individually or in groups on the premises, requesting employees to vote against the union, and asking them to support the company. However, threats or promises of benefits must be avoided, and supervisors must refrain from any interrogation or questioning of employees concerning their union activities or affiliations.

4. Supervisors may make certain statements to employees as long as these are consistent with the general guideline to avoid the promise of benefits or the threat of reprisals, including telling employees that the company neither wants nor needs a union; telling employees that they have the right not to join the union; telling employees that they need not be threatened or coerced into joining the union; informing employees of benefits which they enjoy presently with the company and comparing these benefits with those of unionized companies in similar situations; discussing the disadvantages of belonging to a union, such as dues, initiation fees, loss of income due to strikes, the possibility of picket-line duty, and union discipline in the form of fines and assessments; telling employees that if they engage in an economic strike they may be permanently replaced; telling employees that a union will always out-promise an employer but cannot guarantee any improvement in wages or working conditions; pointing out misstatements and falsehoods in union literature; criticizing union officials (provided the statements made are accurate); telling employees that they are not required to sign authorization cards and that signing an authorization card is a blank check giving the union the right to represent them; and informing employees that they have the right not to meet with or talk with the union organizer.

Prohibited Activities

1. Supervisors may not promise employees a reward of any sort, whether economic or otherwise, or give the impression that a reward would ensue in return for employees' express or implied promise or understanding to refuse to join the union or to campaign or vote against it.

2. Supervisors may not threaten employees, either economically or noneconomically, or use threatening or intimidating language calculated to influence employees in joining the union or voting.

3. Supervisors must not discriminate against employees who are taking part in union activities or make any adjustment in their work responsibilities or activities as a result of union activities.

4. Supervisors may not threaten to or actually discipline employees for soliciting other employees to join the union long as the solicitations are taking place during nonworking periods of the day, such as lunch periods and coffee breaks.

5. Supervisors may not under any circumstances question employees about their prior or present union affiliations, union activities, or union meetings or ask employees whether they have signed union cards or whether any other employees have signed authorization cards. (If employees volunteer such information, a supervisor does not commit an unfair labor practice merely by listening.)

6. Supervisors may not engage in surveillance of employees or give the impression that employees' activities are being watched.

7. Because of the appearance of coercion, supervisors may not call employees away from their places of work to an office or other isolated part of the premises to urge them to vote against the union or to discuss the union organizing campaign with them.

8. Supervisors may not ask employees questions concerning their personal opinions about the union or the feelings of employees in the plant in general.

9. Supervisors may not systematically visit the homes of employees to urge them to vote against the union.

10. Supervisors may not solicit or encourage employees to request the return of their authorization cards or assist them in returning or revoking their authorization cards.

These guidelines for supervisors apply equally to the officers and other representatives of the company. The company should be aware that this is an area in which there are many extremely technical rules and controlling decisions based upon particular fact situations. Therefore, although as a general rule employers would be safe as long as they conducted themselves so as to avoid any interrogation or intimidation concerning union activities, any reprisal or appearance of reprisal for union activities, and any promise of a benefit in connection with nonparticipation in union activities, the safest practice in this area is to plan carefully the company's responses and the actions of supervisors. Normally, this procedure would include meeting with all persons in the category of supervisors at the outset of any union organizing campaign to discuss with them in detail what they can and cannot do during the organizing drive. A second step would normally be to discuss in advance with competent labor relations counsel each planned response of the company and its supervisors, such as statements to be made to employees, policies to be enforced with regard to solicitations in working time, and the like.

NLRB Election Procedures

A labor organization may petition the NLRB to direct an election to settle the question of representation at any time after it accumulates signed authorization cards from more than 30 percent of the nonsupervisory employees. From that point forward the NLRB assumes an active role.

The employer need not contest the union's right to represent the employees by means of an election. Instead, the employer may voluntarily bargain with the union after the demand for recognition has been made. However, despite this voluntary recognition the union may seek an election to get the benefits of an NLRB certification order, which follows a successful election campaign. The NLRB certification order designates the union as the collective bargaining representative of a specified bargaining unit and ensures the union's status as collective bargaining representative for a period of at least 1 year.

A petition for an election will contain, in addition to the name and address of the union, a description of the bargaining unit for which the union seeks a certification order directing that it is the bargaining representative of the included employees. Thus, the union must at the outset designate the class of employees which it wishes to represent. The bargaining unit may not include supervisors defined under the NLRA, and ordinarily it may not contain office clerical personnel and security personnel.

As a first step, the NLRB makes an independent determination as to whether at least 30 percent of the employees in the bargaining unit designated by the union have signed authorization cards. If the NLRB determines that there has been a sufficient showing of interest to warrant an election, the employer may not contest this determination. In certain cases, an employer who suspects that authorization cards have been fraudulently or illegally obtained can submit evidence of this circumstance to the NLRB, which will then conduct a special investigation and hearing on the validity of the cards. However, lacking evidence which the employer can present of fraud, coercion, or the like, no party to a representation case is permitted to attack the petitioning union's showing of interest.

The NLRB's step will be to notify the parties of the petition for an election. The letter sent to the employer will contain the name of the Board agent, an employee of the Board in charge of handling such cases, who is assigned to the case. It will also request that the employer submit a payroll list of the employees in the requested bargaining unit and ask for information concerning the employer's business operation in order to determine whether the employer meets the jurisdictional standards of the act. The NLRB agent assigned to the case will investigate to determine whether the company's operations have a substantial enough effect upon interstate commerce to warrant the NLRB's exercise of jurisdiction, whether the union's showing of interest is sufficient, and whether the bargaining unit described by the union in its petition is appropriate under Section 9 of the NLRA.

An employer may contest each of these determinations at a representation hearing held by the NLRB or enter into a written stipulation with the union and the NLRB authorizing the election without a hearing. In most cases, the chief issue of any representation hearing is whether the unit described in the petition is appropriate for collective bargaining. Tests for appropriateness would include the question of whether supervisors are part of the unit and whether the employees described in the petition have a sufficient community interest to warrant their being placed in the same bargaining unit. The determination of an "appropriate bargaining unit" lies largely within the discretion of the NLRB.

The election will be conducted in an appropriate bargaining unit of the contractor's employees. After the petition has been filed, the Board will conduct a representation hearing to determine the scope of the appropriate unit. At this hearing both the contractor and the union may present arguments to support their views concerning the scope of the bargaining unit. On a construction project there may actually be several different appropriate units. The union will want as large a unit as it can reasonably expect to vote for the union. On the other hand, the contractor will want an election conducted among a group of employees that best favors the chance of a union defeat. The Board will generally consider the community of interest among the employees such as common craft skills, efficiency of operations, and prior bargaining history to determine the appropriate unit. The contractor should be prepared to present evidence to support the contractor's choice of the appropriate unit. In the construction industry the NLRB has found the following to be appropriate units: (1) separate units on the project according to separate trade or craft skills of the employees, (2) a single project-wide unit of all the contractor's construction employees, and (3) a unit of all or several of the contractor's projects consisting of all the construction employees on those projects.

Sometimes a union will file an election petition when the project work has just commenced. In this instance the contractor might be able to have the petition dismissed or held in abeyance pending the employment of a "substantial and representative complement" of employees in the bargaining unit. The theory is that an election does not properly reflect bargaining-unit sentiment concerning union representation until a representative workforce has been employed. In determining whether a representative workforce is currently employed, the NLRB will normally consider the anticipated number of employees whom the contractor will hire and the job classifications which will exist at peak employment in the bargaining unit. A contractor who seeks either to avoid an election or to delay it until a time when the union's support may have diminished should submit project plans to the Board which show that the project will be significantly expanded in the future, present employees are far fewer than the projected workforce, and a substantial number of new job classifications will be added. However, recent decisions suggest that the NLRB may give a loose interpretation to what is meant by a "substantial and representative complement" of employees. The Board has even ordered an election at a time when the construction contractor was employing only 40 out of an anticipated 190 workers and less than half the projected job classifications were in existence.[18]

The contractor may also be in a good position to obtain the dismissal of an election petition by a building trades union when the petition is filed toward the end of the construction project. For the collective bargaining process to work effectively, management and the union must have adequate time to narrow their differences and to find the bases upon which they can reach an agreement. The NLRB might not conduct an election that would serve no purpose because the project was about to end and the parties would not have sufficient time to negotiate an agreement. Construction projects are often of short duration. If the contractor is able to convince the NLRB that the job will be completed within a short time (for example, within a few months) and that there is little likelihood of the contractor's obtaining additional work in the area, then there is a good chance that the NLRB will not hold the election.[19]

[18] *NLRB v. Clement-Blythe Cos.*, 415 F.2d 78 (4th Cir. 1969).

[19] *Burns & Spangler, Inc. & Operating Engineers Local 470, Decision of Regional Director*, Case No. 11-RC-2561 (1967).

A contractor may also be able to dismiss an election petition if the contractor has a valid and current collective bargaining agreement with a union which will serve as a "contract bar." Under the NLRB's contract bar doctrine the Board will not normally conduct a representation election on behalf of a rival union if the contractor already has a current and valid agreement with a majority-status union which was executed when at least 30 percent of the total workforce was already employed and 50 percent of the job classifications were in existence. An agreement executed at that time will bar a rival union's election petition for the contract's duration up to a maximum of 3 years. A contract without a definite date of duration might not serve as a contract bar for any length of time at all.

A prehire agreement will not bar an election on behalf of another union if it was executed before a substantial and representative workforce had been employed. A contractor who desires to continue a relationship with the union with which it has a prehire agreement and to avoid the inconvenience of an election should execute another agreement with the union when it has majority support and 30 percent of the total workforce has been hired and half of the job classifications are in existence. A union's majority status may be shown by a card check of the employees in the bargaining unit.

Illustrative Case

On October 31 a representative of Carpenters Local 745 met with the president of Island Construction Co. and requested the negotiation of a collective bargaining agreement. The president replied that the company would not negotiate until Local 745 submitted proof of its majority status. The next day an official of ILWU Local 142 claimed that it represented a majority of the company's carpenters at its various jobsites in the area. The company refused to bargain with Local 142 at that time and notified the official that they might meet at some later time to discuss possible recognition of Local 142 as the carpenters' bargaining representative. On Novermber 8, Local 745 presented the company with authorization cards. The cards were checked against the payroll list, and since the president was satisfied that Local 745 had shown its majority status, he negotiated with the local a prehire agreement which required newly hired employees to join the union not later than the eighth day of their employment. ILWU Local 142 filed a petition for a representation election and contended that the prehire agreement with Local 745 could not serve as a contract bar to the election petition since Local 745 had not shown its majority status by NLRB certification as the exclusive bargaining representative. The NLRB held that the prehire agreement with Local 745 served as a contract bar to the election petition filed by Local 142. The Board ruled that a prehire agreement in the construction industry may not bar an election petition by another union unless the contracting union has demonstrated its majority status in the bargaining unit prior to the execution of the agreement. The union's majority status could be shown either by NLRB certification or by a voluntary method selected by the parties, such as a check of authorization cards signed by a majority of the bargaining-unit employees.[20]

There are various agreements and stipulations concerning the election into which an employer and a union can enter and which will affect the

[20]Island Constr. Co., 135 NLRB No. 1 (1962).

rights waived or maintained by either side. No agreements or stipulation should be entered into by any employer without weighing the advantages and disadvantages of each procedure with legal counsel familiar with the facts to be resolved at the particular stage. If no stipulation or agreement is entered into, the regional director of the NLRB will determine the bargaining unit, designate the union whose name is to appear on the ballot, specify the categories of employees eligible to vote in the election, and direct that an election be held within a certain time period. Either party may appeal from the regional director's decision by filing a request for review with the NLRB in Washington. The Board has discretion to grant or deny a request for an appeal.

Planning and conducting an election is the responsibility of the regional director. Normally an informal conference is arranged among the parties to settle the details of the election. The election will generally be held between the twenty-fifth and the thirtieth days after the regional director's decision or the consent or stipulation to an election.

As with organizing prior to the election petition, the employer must observe certain rules during the conduct of the NLRB election. Both the officers and the supervisors of the company must refrain from promises of benefits or threats of reprisal resulting from employees' activities during the election and voting. In a recent decision the NLRB indicated that it would no longer police union or employer campaign statements for truthfulness. Nevertheless, it is an unfair labor practice for an employer or a union deliberate to engage in the dissemination of false or misleading propaganda, threats of reprisal or promises of benefit, appeals to racial prejudice, or any other form of propaganda which because of its form or its timing interferes with the voters' free choice.

Conduct during an election is subject to a number of detailed rules. This is another subject which should be discussed in detail with labor relations counsel at the time to determine that each facet of a proposed plan will avoid unfair-labor-practice liability. If it is determined that unfair labor practices have been committed during the course of an election campaign and appropriate charges are filed, the NLRB may certify that the union is the bargaining representative of the unit involved even though it has lost the election.

The following is a list of certain types of conduct by employers or supervisors which create definite risks of unfair-labor-practice liability. It is certainly not meant to be conclusive, and as emphasized above, any plan should be reviewed in detail with labor relations counsel. Conduct to avoid includes:

1. Captive-audience speeches within 24 hours of scheduled voting.
2. Electioneering in and around the voting place.
3. Questioning, polling, or surveillance of employees concerning union activities or proposed voting.
4. Systematic preelection visits to employees' homes.

5. Reproduction of the NLRB's official ballots.

6. Granting or withholding benefits during an election campaign, including raising wages or adding fringe benefits, unless it is clear that these changes are made pursuant to *established* past practice, justifiable economic considerations, or independent industry or corporate policy. However, an employer who withholds normally scheduled benefits when an election is pendings may also commit an unfair labor practice. In both situations, the key question is whether circumstances make it clear that the employer's action has been prompted by normal and legitimate business consideration.

7. Indication by the company of favoritism to one union or another if two unions are competing for representation during the election. This is an unfair labor practice.

The election is conducted during working hours, normally at the employer's place of business, by an NLRB agent. Normally the parties will be entitled to observers whose function is to challenge the eligibility of voters, assist in the identification of voters, and act as checkers to see that election procedures are observed. Balloting by mail is normally used only when special situations require it, as when employees are scattered over a wide area.

There is a procedure for filing objections to an election. An election may be challenged in its entirely, or a challenge may be raised against one or more of the votes cast. Objections should be raised within 5 working days after the NLRB has tallied the ballots. After these objections have been heard, there is a further procedure for contesting the report on the objections. It is possible to have a hearing on exceptions to the report on objections either before an NLRB agent or before an administrative law judge.

After tallying the ballots and resolving any objections by the parties to the election, the regional director will issue a certification of the result of the election. In legal terms certification the determination that a majority of employees in the appropriate bargaining unit as defined by the NLRB's order directing the election have selected a particular labor organization as their collective bargaining representative. If the employer wins the election or prevails on objections to the votes cast in the election the employer is under no obligation to bargain with the union and all organizational efforts by the union will be stayed for 12 months.

However, if the union is successful in obtaining a majority of the votes, upon certification by the regional director the employer must assume the obligation to bargain in good faith with the union as the representative of all employees in the unit concerning wages, hours, and working conditions. This means only that if the union wins the election and is certified, the employer must bargain in good faith. It does not mean that the employer must agree to sign the area agreement negotiated by the union and the multiemployer bargaining association. Nor does it mean that the employer must agree to pay the scale. Construction unions will normally present the area agreement and demand that the employer sign it. The employer need not agree to any terms that do not accord with the employer's best business judgment, although the employer must negotiate in good faith, must meet at reasonable times and places, and should present proposals and counterproposals toward reaching an agreement. Construction unions will normally take a bottom-line stand that employers sign the area agreement and will not retreat from that position. In other words, in the typical construction situation the union will normally be the party that will not negotiate after winning the election. If the employer does not agree to the union's demands and an impasse is reached, the union's only choice will be to attempt to put pressure on the contractor by picketing or strikes. If the union strikes, the employer has the right to replace striking workers with permanent replacements. Because of the transient nature of the construction industry, it is normally easier to replace striking construction workers than it is in industrual union disputes. Therefore, it is possible that even if an employer loses the election and then bargains in good faith with the union and replaces strikers, the employer can still maintain nonunion status by replacing the strikers with a nonunion work force. After the 12-month period of bargaining obligation, the employees will be free to petition for decertification. It is the combination of the union's desire to present the area agreement as its bottom-line positions coupled with the relative ease with which a contractor can replace striking employees, that makes construction unions reluctant to engage in bottom-up organization.

GOOD-FAITH BARGAINING

It is important to realize that "good-faith bargaining" is basically a legal term. Section 8(d) of the NLRA defines good-faith bargaining in part as:

(d) For the purposes of this section, to bargain collectively is the performance of the mutual obligation of the employer and the representative of the employees to meet at reasonable times and confer in good faith with respect to wages, hours, and other terms and conditions of employment, or the negotiation of an agreement, or any question arising thereunder, and the execution of a written contract incorporating any agreement reached if requested by either party, but such obligation does not compel either party to agree to a proposal or require the making of a concession. . . .

Sections 8(a)(5) and 8(b)(3) make it unfair labor practice for employer and union, respectively, to fail to bargain in good faith over a mandatory subject of bargaining, which is one related to wages, hours, and other terms and conditions of employment. Other terms not directly related to wages, hours, and conditions of employment are known as permissive subjects. Neither party is required to bargain at all over permissive subjects, but they may be included in a contract if the parties agree. Either party's refusal to bargain over a mandatory subject unless the other party agrees to include a permissive term in the contract constitutes an unfair labor practice for failure to bargain in good faith. Other terms of employment are illegal, and management should not even consider a union's proposal that an agreement contain an illegal term.

In commonsense terms, good-faith bargaining requires a demonstrated active effort to reach a fair agreement concerning the terms and conditions of employment. The bargaining duty does not require an employer to agree to a particular proposal by the union or to grant a concession on one of its demands. Still, management must show a sincere desire to reach an equitable agreement. There are many considerations which go to show good or bad faith.

Appearances are often very important to show good-faith bargaining. The best way to ensure the demonstration of good faith is to be prepared to bargain. A willingness to bargain at reasonable times and places certainly goes to show good faith. When management has a strong desire to have a particular term included in or excluded from the agreement, it must be prepared to substantiate its position with reasons and proof, since an inflexible take-it-or-leave-it attitude may reflect bad faith. An employer who really wants a particular term included in a contract should present it in at least a general form early in negotiations, since a proposal made for the first time when an agreement is near might suggest that the employer unlawfully intended all along to frustrate the making of an agreement. Finally, to satisfy the bargaining obligation management must be prepared to execute a written contract once an oral agreement has been reached.

Illustrative Case

At the outset of negotiations B. F. Diamond Construction Co. and other contractors rejected the union's request for continuous meetings. After the first meeting the companies failed to get in touch with the union to schedule further bargaining sessions, as they had promised. Despite the union's requests for more frequent meetings, the employers never met with the union at less than 2-week intervals. On one occasion the companies refused to negotiate further until the union furnished them a new set of proposals, even though older proposals had been discussed 1 month earlier and the companies had never given any indication that they were unacceptable. At two meetings the parties agreed to a no-strike provision during arbitration of all disputes, but afterward the contractors reopened the strike issue in a proposal to ban all forms of work stoppages at all times. The NLRB held that the contractors committed a Section 8(a)(5) unfair labor practice. Their bad faith was shown by their intentional delays in meeting with the union and by their making proposals on strikes which undermined the no-strike agreement previously reached.[21]

MANDATORY SUBJECTS OF BARGAINING

An employer or the employer's multiemployer trade association is required to bargain with the certified or recognized union regarding "wages, hours, and other terms and conditions of employment." Likewise, the union must bargain in good faith with a contractor over these subjects. Either party may lawfully insist that a mandatory term be included in a contract as long as it demonstrates a sincere desire to reach an agreement. Among the mandatory subjects of bargaining are the following:

1. Duration of the agreement
2. Retroactivity of the agreement

[21]B. F. Diamond Constr. Co., 163 NLRB No. 25 (1967).

3. Pension, retirement, and group medical insurance

4. Layoffs

5. Seniority rights

6. Job classifications

7. Ratio of journeymen to apprentices

8. No-strike clause

9. Holiday and vacation pay

10. Hours of work including starting and quitting times

11. Union security

12. Grievance and arbitration procedure

13. Administration of collective bargaining contracts

14. Management rights

15. Discharge and discipline procedures

16. Hiring procedures

17. Wages and other rates of compensation including merit increases

18. Subcontracting out work of the bargaining unit

19. Changing worker classifications

Management must realize that it is obligated to bargain on these and any other mandatory subjects that are raised in bargaining sessions. The U.S. Supreme Court has held that an employer's unilateral changes in wages, hours, and conditions of employment without giving the union an opportunity to bargain over these changes is automatically a Section 8(a)(5) violation for refusal to bargain in good faith. Even if management had a sincere desire to bargain in good faith, the fact that the changes were made unilaterally is by definition inconsistent with a willingness to bargain over those conditions of employment.[22]

The obligation to bargain over mandatory subjects exists both during negotiations for a contract and during the term of an existing contract. Before instituting changes in wages, hours, and terms and conditions of employment, the employer must give the union a chance to bargain over the proposed changes. This bargaining obligation may apply even to mandatory subjects that were neither discussed during negotiations nor included in the contract. If management unlawfully makes a unilateral change in any of the mandatory subjects, the result likely will be a Section 8(a)(5) unfair-labor-practice charge. The NLRB has broad powers to force management to rescind the change and to make whole any employee who has suffered financial loss because of management's unilateral action. Therefore, it is important to give the union an opportunity to bargain over proposed changes in mandatory subjects of bargaining.

[22] NLRB v. Katz, 369 U.S. 736 (1962).

An employer will not be required to bargain over a particular mandatory subject if the union has clearly waived its right to bargain over it. The mere fact that the union raised a mandatory subject during negotiations but the subject was not included in the contract may not be enough to show that the union has surrendered its interest in bargaining over that term of employment. If the union has received notice of an employer's proposed change in a mandatory subject in time to bargain over the change but fails to request a chance to bargain, the employer might be permitted to institute the proposed change.

An employer might be able to include in the contract certain clauses which signify the union's waiver of certain bargaining subjects. The waiver must be in clear and unambiguous language. A management rights provision which states in detail the specific terms on which the employer reserves exclusive control will probably show the union's waiver of bargaining rights on those terms. But a management clause which generally states, for example, that management retains the right to take all measures necessary to run the job efficiently is probably not clear enough to establish a waiver of the union's right to bargain. A complete-agreement provision, or "zipper" clause, which states that the union has had an opportunity to bargain over all subjects, that the contract represents the parties' complete agreement, and that the union waives its right to bargain over all proper subjects of bargaining, might allow management to institute changes in mandatory subjects during the life of the contract without being required first to consult with the union.

Management may make unilateral changes in a particular mandatory subject if bargaining over that subject has reached an impasse. "Impasse" is a legal term which represents the stage in negotiations when the parties' positions have become fixed on an issue after all good-faith attempts to reach an agreement have been exhausted. It is often not easy to determine when an impasse has been reached. For example, an impasse will not have been reached despite little progress in negotiations if the parties have made counterproposals which show that each is still willing to bend a little. To reach an impasse there must have been good-faith bargaining. If the employer has committed unfair labor practices, the NLRB will be less likely to find that an impasse has occurred, so that a unilateral change in a mandatory subject will not be allowed. If an impasse is reached, the employer may unilaterally implement changes in the conditions of employment if the proposed change has been bargained for and the union has been given notice of the change. An impasse on one subject, however, does not excuse management from bargaining over other mandatory terms.

NONMANDATORY BARGAINING SUBJECTS

Contractors have all too often bargained away valuable rights in collective bargaining agreements by yielding on nonmandatory subjects of bargaining, upon which the union has no right to insist. If a particular item in the contract is not directly related to wages, hours, and other terms and conditions of employment, it is a nonmandatory, permissive, subject. A nonmandatory subject may lawfully be included in the contract if both parties agree, but either the employer or the union also may lawfully refuse even to consider a proposal that a nonmandatory subject be included in the contract.

A party fails to bargain in good faith and commits an unfair labor practice by insisting as a condition precedent to either bargaining or to final agreement that the other party agree to include a nonmandatory bargaining subject in the contract. The U.S. Supreme Court has considered whether an employer's insistence that the union agree to a permissive subject as a condition to final agreement on a proposed contract would alone constitute an unlawful refusal to bargain in good faith under Section 8(b)(3) of the NLRA.[23] The Court held that such conduct alone, without regard to whether the party might have intended to bargain in good faith, is an unfair labor practice. Therefore, a contractor who is faced with a union demand to include a permissive subject of bargaining in the contract as a precondition either to bargaining or to signing the contract should file unfair-labor-practices charges against the union for its failure to bargain in good faith. Likewise, the contractor should never condition further bargaining or final agreement upon the union's agreement to include a permissive subject in the contract.

This rule applies equally to "standard" or areawide multiemployer agreements and to an individual company's collective bargaining contracts. A contractor who is not a member of a multiemployer association can lawfully refuse to agree to the nonmandatory provisions of a standard agreement while accepting the wages, fringe benefits, and other mandatory items as long as the contractor has not assigned bargaining rights to the association in advance of negotiations. Although the notion may be difficult for some union business agents to accept, a union cannot lawfully insist that a nonmember contractor adopt every term and condition of a multiemployer agreement—only the mandatory bargaining items.

The fact that a contractor has once chosen to bargain over a permissive subject of bargaining does not convert it into a mandatory subject. Therefore, a contractor who has at one or more times included a permissive subject in a contract may thereafter refuse even to consider the subject without explanation during negotiations for a subsequent contract. Likewise, a contractor may legitimately bargain over a permissive subject and later, without giving any reason, decide no longer to consider its inclusion in the contract. The Supreme Court has ruled that a party who agrees to include a nonmandatory subject in a contract may unilaterally modify it during the contract term without committing an unfair labor practice.[24] However, a contractor who does this may still be liable to the union in an action for breach of contract.

[23] NLRB v. Wooster Div. of Borg-Warner, 356 U.S. 342 (1958).

[24] Chemical Workers v. Pittsburgh Plate Glass Co., 404 U.S. 157 (1971).

The following subsections illustrate some of the more important non-mandatory items which contractors should be wary of agreeing to include in their contracts.

Supervisors

The union cannot lawfully insist that the collective bargaining agreement set the wages, hours, and working conditions of supervisors. Even if supervisors are presently covered by an agreement, a contractor can lawfully refuse to consider having them covered in a renewal agreement when the present agreement expires, or decline to agree to portions of a "standard" multiemployer agreement covering supervisors so long as the contractor has not assigned bargaining rights to the association. (See Chapter 3, "Supervisors.")

Interest Arbitration Clauses

Interest arbitration is a collective bargaining procedure under which authority to determine the terms of a future contract is delegated by the contractor and the union to a third party. Such a procedure may provide for negotiations between the parties, and if unresolved issues remain after bargaining, then the procedure will provide for submission of these issues for resolution by a third party. In a recent case, the National Labor Relations Board held that an interest arbitration clause is a permissive subject of bargaining.[25] There, the existing collective bargaining agreement contained an interest arbitration clause under which deadlocked bargaining issues were to be resolved by an arbitrator. The Board ruled that since this clause did not vitally affect the terms or conditions of employment in the subsequent contract, but merely stated the procedures by which these contract terms would be determined, the clause was a permissive subject.

Some interest arbitration clauses provide for final resolution of the deadlocked issues by a panel with an equal number of management and union representatives. The fact that none of the management representatives are either chosen or designated by the contractor makes such a clause a permissive subject of bargaining. The Board reasoned that the contractor should not be required to designate a representative not of its own choosing as its bargaining representative. This is the result even if the arbitration panel's jurisdiction is limited to mandatory subjects of bargaining. Also, the fact that the contractor has agreed to an interest arbitration provision in the present agreement does not mean that the union may insist during bargaining for a new contract that the issue of whether to provide for interest arbitration in the new contract should be submitted to interest arbitration.

Illustrative Case

The existing collective bargaining agreement between the Employers Association of Roofers Local 59 of the Sheet Metal Workers provided that disputes concerning the terms of

[25] *Columbus Printing Pressmen*, 219 NLRB No. 54 (1975).

future agreements would ultimately be submitted for resolution to the National Joint Adjustment Board (NJAB). The NJAB is a panel consisting of representatives from the Sheet Metal Workers International and the Sheet Metal and Air-Conditioning Contractors' National Association (SMACNA). The employers association was not a member of SMACNA, and it had no representatives on the NJAB. During negotiations for a new agreement, the employers association notified Local 59 that it would not agree to any contract that would require it to submit unresolved bargaining issues to the NJAB. Local 59 thereafter ceased bargaining and unilaterally submitted the deadlocked issues to the NJAB. The NLRB held that the provision requiring disputes concerning the terms of future agreements to be submitted to a panel on which the employers association had no representation was a permissive subject of bargaining, since a contractor is never required to assign the right to bargain to a party not of the contractor's own choosing. Local 59 unlawfully refused to bargain when it submitted unresolved bargaining issues to the NJAB, since the effect of this action was to have these issues determined by a panel on which the association had no representation, "in patent derogation of its rights to bargain collectively through representatives of its own choosing." This is the result even though the association had previously contracted to submit unresolved bargaining issues to the NJAB, since "once having agreed to a nonmandatory term a party does not thereafter impliedly waive the right to insist that the term be removed from the bargaining table in any subsequent negotiations."[26]

Performance Bonds and Indemnity Clauses

Any provisions which would require indemnities or bonds to guarantee payment to the union upon a contractor's breach of any term of the collective bargaining agreement is a nonmandatory subject, since it is outside the scope of wages, hours, and conditions of employment. Therefore, a union's proposal that the contractor agree to post a bond to assure payment of wages and fringe benefits or to assure its performance of any other contract term can be rejected. Another type of performance bond which is a nonmandatory subject would require the contractor to reimburse the union for the loss of dues that it would have received but for the contractor's subcontracting work in violation of the agreement.

Illustrative Case

While negotiating with the Lathing Contracts Association of Southern California for a new contract, Lathers Local 42 stated that it would not sign any agreement unless the association agreed to an increase in the size of the performance bond to be posted by members of the association. The bond was to guarantee payment of wages and contributions to various employee benefit plans. Since a performance bond is not a mandatory subject of bargaining, the NLRB held that the union failed to bargain in good faith by conditioning agreement upon the association's agreement to increase the size of the bond.[27]

Along the same lines, any clause requiring a union to indemnify a contractor is a permissive subject of bargaining, since it is outside the scope of wages, hours, and conditions of employment. An example is a clause that would require a union to indemnify a contractor against any threats or intimidation against nonunion employees.

[26] *Sheet Metal Workers Local 59 (Employers Ass'n of Roofers)*, 227 NLRB No. 90 (1976).

[27] *Lathers Local 42 (Lathing Contractors Ass'n)*, 223 NLRB No. 8 (1976).

Industry Advancement Funds

Industry advancement funds (industry promotion funds) are trust funds established to promote the success of a segment of the construction industry or to finance employer association activities. Such a fund's purpose may be restricted to promoting, publicizing, and advancing the interest of the industry, or its purposes may extend, for example, to product research, education of employees, recruiting and training of minority employees, or promoting stable labor relations. Sometimes programs are funded by contractor contributions according to a predetermined formula, and sometimes contributions are voluntary. (See Chapter 9, "Industry Advancement Funds.")

Sometimes the contractor or the association will wish not to contribute to an industry advancement fund, because once the fund has developed, the contractor's negotiating power may be significantly eroded. A union's demand that the contractor contribute to an industry advancement fund is a nonmandatory subject of bargaining, even though the fund would be administered by the contractor. Although a fund that is successful may benefit the construction industry and the contractor so as to improve the employees' conditions of employment, the fund is still a nonmandatory subject since it is not directly concerned with relations between the contractor and the employees. Likewise, since the fund itself is a nonmandatory subject, so is a union's proposal that a contractor submit reports concerning the fund's financial status.

Illustrative Case

Local 264 of the Laborers had a contract with the Builders Association of Kansas City. The union presented this agreement to D. & G. Construction Co., a concrete subcontractor, for its signature. D. & G. objected to a provision which would require D. & G. to contribute $0.02 per hour for every hour worked by its employees who were members of Local 264 to an industry advancement fund. The stated purpose of the fund was to train and improve "the efficiency of workmen and to improve general conditions and relationship of the construction industry." Despite D. & G's objection, Local 264 insisted that D. & G. sign the entire contract including the provision concerning the industry advancement fund. The NLRB held, and the Eighth Circuit Court of Appeals affirmed, that an industry advancement fund is a nonmandatory subject of bargaining since it is not concerned with the contractor's relationship to the employees but relates to the contractor's relationship to the public.[28]

Contractor's Administrative Expense Account for Costs of Administering Employment Provisions of the Contract

A union might seek to have a contractor set up an administrative expense account to cover the costs of administering the contract's provisions relating to the terms and conditions of employment stated in the contract. Since such an arrangement is not a matter of contractor-employee relations but is more closely concerned with the contractor's financial arrangements

---

[28]*Laborers Local 264 (D. & G. Constr. Co.)*, 216 NLRB No. 4 (1975), *aff'd*, 529 F.2d 778 (8th Cir. 1976).

for compensating or reimbursing the contractor's bargaining representative, it is not a mandatory bargaining subject.[29]

General Business Practices

Certain business practices, such as decisions concerning products to be manufactured, financing, sales, and investment in laborsaving machinery, are normally nonmandatory subjects of bargaining. Although some of these decisions may have some effect on employees' conditions of employment, the Board will likely decide that such effects are too remote or speculative to make these decisions a mandatory subject of bargaining. Alternatively, the Board will reason that these decisions are basic to contractors' rights to run their own businesses, so that contractors should be able to make these decisions without union interference. The U.S. Supreme Court implied that in its ruling which made a decision to subcontract a mandatory subject of bargaining:

[T]his kind of subcontracting falls short of such larger entrepreneurial questions as what shall be produced, how capital shall be invested in fixed assets [laborsaving machinery], or what the basic scope of the enterprise shall be . . . [;] the court's decision has nothing to do with whether any aspect of those larger issues could under any circumstances be considered subjects of compulsive bargaining.[30]

One area that is unclear involves the question of whether a contractor has a duty to bargain concerning a decision to shut down business operations permanently for valid economic reasons. Although the contractor need not bargain with the union over this decision, since it is basic to the right to manage the contractor's own business, the contractor must still bargain over the effects that the decision will have on the employees' terms and conditions of employment.[31]

Strike Insurance

Contractors often find it advantageous to obtain strike insurance as a hedge against losses arising from a costly work stoppage. Strike insurance is a permissive subject of bargaining, since it is not a term or condition of employment and since it does not regulate the relation between contractor and employees. A contractor need not even consider a union proposal that the contractor abandon participation in a strike insurance plan, and the union acts unlawfully if it insists that the contractor abandon it as a condition of bargaining.[32]

[29] Ibid.

[30] Fibreboard Paper Products Corp. v. NLRB, 379 U.S. 203 (1964).

[31] NLRB v. Royal Plating and Polishing Co., 350 F.2d 191 (3d Cir. 1965).

[32] Operating Engineers Local 12 (Associated Gen. Contractors), 187 NLRB No. 50 (1970).

Abandonment of Litigation

A demand that a contractor abandon litigation against a union is a non-mandatory subject of bargaining, since it is not directly related to wages, hours, or terms and conditions of employment. Therefore, the union fails to bargain in good faith when it insists as a condition to bargaining that the contractor agree to withdraw unfair-labor-practice charges against the union. Similarly, the union may not insist that the contractor withdraw a suit against the union or that it withdraw a grievance against the union which it is seeking to have arbitrated under the contract's arbitration procedure.

Illustrative Case

Bay City Erection Co. had a hiring-hall agreement with Local 600 of the Ironworkers Union. The union operated the hiring hall in an unlawful manner by placing union members on the highest-priority list. The union placed Bay City on an "unfair" list, which meant that the union would refer no more employees to Bay City, because Bay City had hired six employees outside the unlawful hiring hall. Bay City filed unfair-labor-practice charges and a suit against the union, enjoining the union from maintaining Bay City on the unfair list. The union notified Bay City that it would not bargain until the injunctive suit and unfair-labor-practice charges were withdrawn. The NLRB held that the union unlawfully refused to bargain in good faith by conditioning bargaining upon Bay City's promise to abandon litigation against the union.[33]

Conditioning Agreement to a Mandatory Subject of Bargaining Upon the Contractor's Agreement to Nonmandatory Subjects

Although it is lawful for a union to bargain to an impasse concerning a mandatory subject of bargaining such as wages or fringe benefits, it is unlawful for the union to insist that a contractor agree to include a mandatory subject in the contract if agreement to the mandatory subject would also require the contractor to agree to a nonmandatory subject. The union fails to bargain in good faith since, by insisting that the contractor agree to a mandatory subject which in turn would also require the contractor to accept a nonmandatory subject, the union is in effect unlawfully conditioning its agreement to the contract upon the contractor's acquiescence to a nonmandatory subject, which is unlawful. For example, participation by the contractor in a pension plan for the contractor's employees is a condition of employment concerning which the contractor is required to bargain, and the union may insist upon it to impasse. But if participation in the pension plan is conditioned upon the contractor's agreement to a nonmandatory subject, the union fails to bargain in good faith.[34] Sometimes a union will insist that a contractor sign a standard agreement which contains both mandatory and nonmandatory subjects. In that situation, the contractor need not even consider signing the standard agreement, and the

[33] *Ironworkers Union (Bay City Erection Co.)*, 134 NLRB No. 20 (1961).
[34] *Sheet Metal Workers Local 59 (Employers Ass'n of Roofers)*, 227 NLRB No. 90 (1976).

union acts unlawfully by insisting that the contractor sign the entire standard agreement.

Illustrative Case

It was the practice of the union, Southern California Pipe Trades District Council No. 16, to contract with the Plumbing, Heating and Piping Employers Council of Southern California, a multiemployer association. Then the union would submit a similar contract called a standard agreement for signature to plumbing contractors who were not members of the association. The union requested that Aero Plumbing sign the standard agreement. Aero responded that it would agree to provisions in that agreement relating to wages, hours, and working conditions. But Aero was unwilling to agree to other provisions which would have required it to post a performance bond, to make payments into an industry promotion fund, to apply the contract to supervisors, and to appoint that it would not bargain any further unless Aero agreed to all the provisions of the standard agreement, and bargaining ceased thereafter. The NLRB held: "The union violated the LMRA by insisting upon the 'standard agreement' with the employer that contained nonmandatory subjects of bargaining that would have required the employer to select a different bargaining representative, post performance bond, contribute to an industry promotion fund, and to apply the contract to supervisors.[35]

Association Bargaining When a Union Seeks to Have a Contractor Designate an Association as Bargaining Agent

A contractor who is not a member of a multiemployer association need not even consider a union's proposal that the contractor designate the association as bargaining agent even for a limited purpose. This is true because Section 8(b)(1)(B) of the NLRA guarantees contractors' rights to select their own bargaining representatives. If the union insists during bargaining that the contractor appoint an association to represent the contractor or strikes for that purpose, it commits an unfair labor practice.

Illustrative Case

The union, Southern California Pipe Trades District Council No. 16, negotiated an agreement with a multiemployer association, the Plumbing, Heating and Piping Employers Council of Southern California. Then it submitted a similar though not identical contract called a standard agreement for signature to Aero Plumbing Co. Aero was not a member of the employers council. Aero made some concessions but notified the union that it could not agree to a provision in the standard agreement that would require it to designate the employers council as its bargaining representative. The union refused to bargain any further unless Aero agreed to all the provisions of the standard agreement.
The NLRB held that the union failed to bargain in good faith by insisting upon Aero's acceptance of the standard agreement that would have required Aero to select a different bargaining representative than it desired.[36]

---

[35] Southern California Pipe Trades Dist. Council (Aero Plumbing Co.), 167 NLRB No. 143 (1967).

[36] Ibid.

Association Bargaining When a Contractor That Is a Member of an Association Withdraws

A contractor who is a member of a multiemployer association is not fore-ever required to remain a member of the association. If the contractor gives timely and unequivocal notice of intent to withdraw from the association, then the contractor is no longer required to bargain with the union through the association. Insisting that the contractor continue to bargain through the association is an unfair labor practice. Conversely, the fact that the contractor has made an effective withdrawal does not require the union that has previously bargained with the association to negotiate with the contractor on an individual basis.

Illustrative Case

The Washington State Association of the Plumbers Union was certified by the Board to bargain on a statewide basis with the Washington State Employers Council for the Plumbing and Pipefitting Industry. Fourteen employers who were members of the state association made a timely and effective withdrawal. The association rejected these employers' requests to bargain with them individually on the ground that the only unit in which the employees wished to bargain was the multiemployer unit. The association sent letters to nine of the fourteen employers who had previously withdrawn from the employers council that they would be struck unless they signed a form agreeing to be bound by any agreement which might be reached between the council and the state association. Since the employees wished only to bargain on the established multiemployer basis and not on an individual basis, the union could lawfully refuse the request of the fourteen employers who had effectively withdrawn to bargain with them individually. However, the NLRB held that these employers had made an effective withdrawal from multiemployer bargaining and that they could lawfully resist the union's demand that they reassign bargaining authority to the multiemployer association.[37]

Demand to Submit Jurisdictional Disputes to a Board in Which None of the Members Are Chosen or Designated by the Contractor

Most collective bargaining agreements provide for an arbitration procedure for settling jurisdictional disputes (for a discussion of the Impartial Jurisdictional Disputes Board, see Chapter 4, section "Jurisdictional Disputes," and Chapter 6, subsection "Craft Jurisdiction"). If none of the members on the arbitration panel are chosen or designated by the contractor, the contractor need not even consider a union's proposal that jurisdictional disputes be submitted to such a panel. This is true because Section 8(b)(1)(B) of the act protects contractors' rights freely to select their own representatives for the purpose of adjusting grievances or resolving disputes. If a union strikes for the inclusion of this clause in a contract or insists that it be included as a condition to bargaining, the union commits an unfair labor practice.

[37] Plumbers Union (Arnold & Jeffers, Inc.), 195 NLRB No. 27 (1972).

Illustrative Case

The Evansville chapter of the Associated General Contractors Association had an agreement with Local 103 of the Ironworkers under which it agreed to submit jurisdictional disputes to the National Joint Board. During negotiations for a new contract, the union proposed that the association agree to participate in the Interim Joint Board or its successor, a new National Joint Board, since the old National Joint Board had been dissolved. At subsequent bargaining sessions, the union insisted on the association's submitting juridictional disputes to the Interim Joint Board or the new National Joint Board, but the association opposed such a provision since neither it nor its parent, the Associated General Contractors, had membership on either panel. Bargaining ceased, and a strike ensued. Since none of the members of the proposed panel for setting jurisdictional disputes were either chosen or designated by the association, the court held that the union unlawfully refused to bargain in good faith by insisting as a condition to final agreement that the association agree to submit disputes to the panel.[38]

Because of the likelihood of such subjects possibly being confused with mandatory subjects of bargaining, it is suggested that if a question arises as to whether a subject must be bargained for, an up-to-date opinion be obtained. Labor law is a dynamic area of the law which may change rapidly, particularly in the classification of mandatory versus permissive bargaining subjects. If there is any doubt, a legally safe approach is to bargain over the issue and decline to agree to it. If management declines to bargain over a subject which is mandatory rather than permissive, the union will have grounds for filing an unfair-labor-practice charge with the NLRB.

There are subjects which are not proper for bargaining even on a voluntary basis and should be avoided. Among them are:

1. Change in bargaining jurisdiction between two unions on a unilateral basis or by agreement with one union only

2. Inclusion of a subcontracting ban or a hot-cargo or secondary-boycott provision which does not come under the exceptions of the ally doctrine or the preservation-of-work doctrine and is not limited to the jobsite

3. Bargaining on issues beyond the appropriate bargaining unit

4. Any language which violates federal or state statutes such as validation of a closed-shop provision requiring union membership before or at the time of first employment

Renewal Contracts

Once the first bargaining agreement has been entered into, renewal agreements follow. It is customary in agreements to give either party the right to reopen the negotiations in order to change various aspects of the existing agreement. Regardless of whether or not the agreement contains a no-strike clause, the NLRA establishes a cooling-off period and requires four mandatory steps before the parties to a renewal collective bargaining agreement may resort to strikes or lockouts.

[38] *Associated Gen. Contractors v. NLRB,* 465 F.2d 327 (7th Cir. (1972).

First, 60 days prior to the expiration date of the contract the party desiring to initiate a change must give notice to the opposing party of a proposed termination or modification of the agreement. Second, the party must offer to meet and bargain with the opposing party during the 60-day notice period at reasonable times and places. Third, the party desiring to initiate a change must notify the Federal Mediation and Conciliation Services and any state mediation service of the existence of a labor dispute within 30 days after the initial notice has been given to the opposing party. Finally, neither party may strike or lock out employees for a period of 60 days after the initial notice has been given to the opposing party or until the termination date of the contract, whichever is later.

In this connection, the NLRB has held that the parties to the agreement may not strike or lock out employees until 30 days after the notice to the Federal Mediation and Conciliation Service and the state mediation agency. This is true even if more than 60 days have elapsed since the initial notice to the opposing parties.

It is suggested that whenever a modification or termination is in the offing by the union, the employer should also give the described notices. Failure to give such notices could result in unfair-labor-practice charges. In the case of a strike during the cooling-off period, the striking employees could lose their status as employees of the employer and could be discharged. The union might also be liable to the employer for damages caused by the illegal strike. If there was a lockout during the cooling-off period or if the notices were not timely given, the employer could be forced to make back payments of wages to employees for the duration of the illegal lockout. If a contract provides "that absent notice to the contrary the agreement is to remain in effect from year to year," a duty to bargain may not arise unless the 60-day notice to terminate or modify the contract is given by one of the parties. (See Chapter 6, section "Lockouts.")

6 COLLECTIVE BARGAINING

The construction industry in many areas of the United States is highly unionized. Even if a construction company is not unionized today, it is safe to assume that a union is now or soon will be attempting to organize it. If the number of union companies has increased, it is also certain that the legal and economic complexities surrounding labor-management relations have also increased. Despite the complexity and importance of collective bargaining, many contractors and subcontractors are only vaguely familiar with the bargaining process. Neither are the complexities of collective bargaining understood by the many multiemployer bargaining agents, usually employer trade associations, that do much of the bargaining in the construction industry. There are those who feel that the bargaining process begins only when the parties sit down at the bargaining table. On occasion, contractors or subcontractors may summarily execute a bargaining agreement proposed by a union although they have little understanding of its contents. Such uninformed attitudes concerning collective bargaining are invitations to financial ruin.

Accordingly, more and more contractors, subcontractors, and employer trade associations are coming to view more effective and informed collective bargaining as a necessity for efficient management and also for their survival. Certainly, labor agreements are among the most important contracts from a management and financial standpoint. They affect profits, bid quotations, personnel, hours of work, pensions, education and welfare plans, and other aspects of the work environment and work production. These agreements typically cover extended periods of time, and once an agreement has been entered into, an employer is usually locked in for years.

The purpose of this chapter is to point the way to more effective and informed collective bargaining by contractors, subcontractors, and their trade associations. It is intended to serve as a general guide to make lay negotiators aware of some of the intricacies of collective bargaining in the construction industry. Readers are cautioned that when they are faced with labor problems arising from specific facts, this book is no substitute for consultation with a specialist knowledgeable in labor law, nor is it a substitute for legal advice during labor negotiations.

PREPARING TO BARGAIN

There is no substitute for preparation in collective bargaining. Unions recognize this fact and are well armed with data and factual information with which to support their positions. Union negotiators are normally seasoned in the art of negotiation, and employers must prepare methodically for the bargaining encounter. The usual arrangement for bargaining in the construction industry is by multiemployer management trade associations represented by a management bargaining committee. The bargaining of a collective bargaining agreement is one of the most important functions of a management trade association, and one that usually affects all its members. Therefore, it is imperative that management trade association thoroughly prepare to bargain with a union.

The Negotiators

Without question, the most crucial step in preparing for collective bargaining is the selection of negotiators. These men and women must be intimately familiar with the operations of the employer or representative employees. Ideally they should be methodical and cool. Depending upon the size of the bargaining unit, most employer bargaining committees are composed of two to four persons. Usually the members are the labor committee of the management trade association.

The role of the association executive in bargaining varies widely in local management trade associations. The association executive may function as a member of the committee, serve as spokesman of the committee, or merely assist the committee without being an official member.

The union should not be permitted to bluff the management committee by refusing to negotiate with the association executive representative or a professional negotiator. The employer trade association has a legal right to appoint any representative it wishes.

The complexities and pitfalls of labor law have persuaded some employer associations to have an attorney aid the bargaining committee by advising the committee constantly before and after each meeting and assisting it legally. In some cases the attorney actually enters the bargaining directly.

Once the committee has been appointed, a spokesman should be selected. The spokesman will be the main representative for the committee, and he or she will also be the primary target for the union. Therefore, an ability to listen and to take abuse is as important as an ability to express the views of the employer. The spokesman is the quarterback for the committee and does most of the talking, although other members should be prepared to carry the ball when called upon. It is preferable that the spokesman decide when a committee member should speak; such a decision could easily be indicated by the spokesman's simply asking for a committeeman's opinion or knowledge on a given subject. If the spokesman has doubts about the committee's reactions on a certain matter, he or she should call a caucus. Caucuses should be called frequently, and members of the committee should exercise patience and realize that a point is never won in anger.

The spokesman should be a person of integrity, capable of presenting an offer and making the other side believe what he or she says. If the union believes that the spokesman is the type who says one thing and does another, little bargaining will take place. You must have a person whom people on the other side feel they can trust and rely on when a statement is made, whether it is a rejection of the union's offer or a demand by the company.

The spokesman should obviously be knowledgeable and have had some experience in negotiating labor agreements. It is also a good idea to have one or two inexperienced representatives on the committee in order to train experienced management negotiators for the future. The negotiators should also build their education and experience by attending educational seminars sponsored by national employer trade associations.

Notices and Demands

At the outset, the company should review the union's demand to reopen negotiations. Has the union given a 60-day notice prior to the termination of the old agreement? Has a 30-day notice of the existence of a labor dispute been furnished to the Federal Mediation and Conciliation Service and the state mediation association? If not, management may not be under an obligation to bargain. Similarly, if the former contract provides for a longer notice period, such as 90 or 100 days, management is under no obligation to bargain unless the notice required by the contract is furnished.

Notice requirements cut both ways. Because employers often find themselves in a defensive posture in bargaining with a union, they seem to forget that bargaining is a two-way street requiring both an offense and a defense. Far in advance of the reopening of the contract, management should review the contract for changes or additions which the employers wish to make and should serve on the unions a notice of modification or termination of the collective bargaining agreement. Certainly, the employers should not be trapped into a notice of modification of the agreement served by the union, which includes only a wage reopener and might foreclose bargaining on subjects which the employers might wish to change. Once faced with a notice of modification by the union, many employers also file a notice of termination of the entire agreement so that the entire contract is open for negotiation. A positive bargaining position by the employers is extremely helpful in aiding their defensive bargaining position in repelling the union's demands. If the employers propose changes in the agreement for their benefit, the proposed offensive changes may also be used as bargaining tradeoffs for the union's proposals. Therefore, the employers will have benefited by a positive bargaining stance even though the changes they propose may not ultimately be incorporated in the agreement.

If management wishes to open negotiations for its benefit, it should give a 60-day written notice (or for a longer period if required by the existing contract). However, if management slips up and does not give notice of termination, it may be able to rely on the union's notice of termination in order to leave the entire contract open for bargaining, since notification by either party terminates the contract. Also, the Federal Mediation and Conciliation Service and state mediation agencies must be notified of the existence of a labor dispute within 30 days of the 60-day notice, and in no event should either party resort to strikes or lockouts until after 60 days' notice to the opposite party, the expiration date of the contract, and the passage of 30 days after notice to the mediation services. Even after these notices, there can be no strike or no lockout if a no-strike, no-lockout agreement is in effect in a contract which prohibits such acts.

Once management is satisfied that the appropriate notices have been given, it should immediately review the union's demands and respond to the union. Management should furnish the union with its demands within a reasonable time. Once the union's demand list has been provided, the demands should be classified into mandatory and permissive subjects for bargaining. In preparation, mandatory subjects disagreeable to management should be listed and management's counterproposals also listed in writing. Some union and management negotiation committees have established a procedure which limits the subjects of bargaining to the initial list of demands exchanged by the parties in order to avoid last-minute demands that would complicate the subsequent bargaining.

Preparing to Answer Union Demands

Generally, management will have the union demands some time before bargaining begins or at the first meeting. It is very helpful to draft a list of the union demands and then, for each demand, to note whether it is acceptable to management. The union proposals should be evaluated and given priority. If a union demand is unacceptable, a detailed statement giving the reasons for the rejection should be written. Further, if any data form the basis for rejecting a union demand, they should be attached to the statement setting forth the reasons why the demand is unacceptable.

As a general rule, low profits should not be given as the basis for rejecting a union demand. To discuss profits is to open a Pandora's box of inquiry into employers' financing.

In gathering supporting data, management negotiators should obtain and review:

1. A list of all employees or classifications of employees, including hiring dates and rates of pay.
2. The turnover rate of employees for the past several years. The higher the employee turnover rate, the more likely that the union will claim that the company's wages are not

sufficient to keep employees with the company. On the other hand, the lower the turnover rate, the more reasonable is the company's claim that its employees are not entitled to higher wages.

3. The average number of weeks worked in the preceding several years.

4. The average hourly wage of such employees compared with the prevailing rate in the locality.

5. A list of all construction wages in the area for the other crafts and the dates and amounts of their contract increases. Employers should project the probable amount of increases that will be negotiated in collective bargaining agreements in the other construction crafts after consultation and coordination with the bargaining agents for those crafts. This information allows the negotiators to determine the degree to which the requested union wage is unreasonable. Further, it presents a comparison of the degree of experience and skill of the employees, which is a consideration for the appropriate rate of pay.

6. A list of competitors, both union and nonunion, including the number of employees, wage rates and fringe benefits. This list will allow management to urge an agreement in line with those of its competitors in the area. The growth of open-shop competitors should be emphasized particularly because a higher wage settlement or a continuation of restrictive bad practices will contribute to continuing open-shop growth.

7. A list of other contract settlements in other areas with the same union or with comparable trade unions.

8. Productivity analysis of employees. The ratio of labor costs to sales should be calculated over a period of at least 3 years. This figure will show whether the employees' productivity merits an increase or a decrease in wages.

9. Economic outlook. The construction industry rises and falls with the economy. With tight money, for example, it can be expected that construction will be adversely affected. Economic conditions should be a consideration in setting wages and employment policies.

10. Cost-of-living figures for the locality. These should be considered in wage and fringe-benefit changes.

Anticipating Union Tactics

The union spokesman will very probably be a skilled negotiator. Depending upon the nature of the union, the union bargaining committee may consist of local union representatives or national representatives. Employees may serve on the union committee. The demeanor of the union representatives will vary. Some representatives are threatening, noisy, and hard-nosed. Others may be gentle. No matter what the outward expressions or the language used, all union representatives have basically the same goal. That goal is to negotiate an agreement that allows the union maximum advantage over the employers and to obtain for employees maximum wages, benefits, and conditions of employment. Generally, the union will present a standard agreement. It will contend that the proposed agreement is the culmination of many hours of work and that it clearly is equitable to all parties. Union representatives will contend that they cannot delete or modify any aspect of the agreement, other employers have already signed the agreement, and uniformity of union agreements is a necessity. Finally, they will state that the national union has approved the standard agreement and that as the national union will allow no changes, the local union cannot make changes. In short, the union will say that it has no authority to negotiate, which, of course, is not true.

In spite of the adsurdity of this standard agreement stance, the union will very likely hold to its bottom-line position for as long as possible. Management should counter such union arguments by requesting factual data and information and should urge the union to dispense with the battle of words. If, in fact, the union is there to negotiate, it will retreat from its bottom-line stance. If, however, the union adheres to an inflexible position in the standard contract and refuses to consider management counteroffers, it is not bargaining in good faith and management should consider filing unfair-labor-practice charges with the National Labor Relations Board (NLRB).

Finally, management negotiators should anticipate the possibility of threats on the part of the union to strike, picket, or file unfair labor charges for various reasons. Generally, a union does not want to strike because employees and union lose money. However, a negotiator must realize when threats to strike are real. If a threat is not real but merely an attempt to soften management, it should be ignored. When an actual strike appears possible, management must reevaluate its position. This reconsideration is basically a business judgment concerning whether economic losses likely to result from a strike outweigh the potential injury done by yielding to the union demands.

If the union threatens to file unfair labor charges unless its demands are met, management negotiators should point out that the purpose of bargaining is to reach an agreement and that making threats can only taint the would-be good-faith atmosphere for bargaining. Furthermore, as union officials may well consider filing unfair labor charges during the crucial phase of bargaining, management should be extremely cautious in its activities regarding labor relations. No matter what the union demands or threatens, it cannot force an agreement under the law, but it can resort to strikes and picketing.

Some national specialty construction associations have established national joint management and labor councils which serve as arbitrators of bargaining issues that are not settled at the local bargaining level. Under this approach the local employer trade association and the local union have a clause in their collective bargaining agreement which prohibits strikes or other economic sanctions by the union or employers; in return, the dispute is submitted to the national arbitration panel of the national association and national union. These agreements, which are notably present in the electrical, mechanical, and sheet-metal industries, are growing in other specialty trades because they provide machinery to solve bargaining issues without resort to strikes. When an employer bargaining committee is faced with such a national arbitration clause, it must weigh its last offers against what might be imposed at the national level by the joint management-labor arbitration panel. It is therefore vital that the local negotiators compile economic data of recent economic wage settlements and other industry trends on contract clauses.

Developing Management Tactics

The ultimate management objectives at the bargaining table should be formulated well before the 60-day notice to modify or terminate the agreement and should be kept in constant focus in preparing to bargain as well as during bargaining. In addition, the members of the employer bargaining committee should map a strategy calculated to obtain their ultimate goals. The committee should formulate a strategy to attempt to restrict the union's demands during negotiations and also an offensive strategy to attempt to obtain benefits for the employers, such as better contract language, less restrictive work practices, or other changes in the agreement which will enable construction employers to manage their labor forces more efficiently and meet existing competition.

Unions learned long ago to ask for a number of items which they do not expect to get so that they can use items that they are not serious about in trade for items that they actually wish to obtain in the bargaining agreement. Employers should learn the same lesson and make demands on the unions not only for changes that management is serious about, but also for changes to which the employers do not realistically believe the union will agree but which can be valuable as tradeoff items. These items can be used effectively in bargaining to offset union demands.

In recent years, a number of employers in the construction industry have taken the offensive and successfully emerged with contract language and economic items more beneficial than those contained in the previous contract. These employers have basically regained the right to manage the workforce, eliminated all restrictive work practices, increased production, and obtained tight no-strike clauses, in addition to holding wage increases to a realistic level.

Employers who have previously bargained away to the unions much of their rights to manage their businesses now have a favorable climate to attempt to regain the rights that have been lost over the years. If management doesn't ask for these basic management rights, it certainly won't retrieve them from the unions.

Negotiators can count on the union's having well prepared its bargaining approach and tactics. Obviously, management should also methodically formulate its goals and tactics well before the first bargaining session. In addition, after each meeting management should review the session, plan the bargaining strategy for the next session, and also reaffirm and alter, if necessary, its long-range strategy. The strategy and objectives should be rated in the order of their importance. Decisions must be made as to which objectives cannot be compromised. Alternatives should be selected because of the likelihood of unexpected developments occurring at the bargaining table which will require changes in strategy and tactics. It is a good idea to sit down with a full committee for a review and planning discussion immediately before meeting with the union in addition to holding separate planning sessions between bargaining sessions.

Negotiations should be sure to appoint one member of the committee to take complete and extensive notes. This member should prepare a complete memorandum of each bargaining session and distribute copies to each member of the committee. Signing minutes by both union and management should also be considered. Notes and minutes should not be taken at the planning session. Also, the employer committee should keep a word-by-word record or history of all contract clauses involved: how they are worded; how they originated; how they have been interpreted, used, and arbitrated; and what changes in contract language have occurred during negotiations. And, obviously, the exact language as agreed upon should be reduced to writing immediately while it is fresh in the minds of all parties.

Management should make a sober determination of the economic and noneconomic gains that it is willing to give the union to avoid a strike. Such a determination should be tempered by the likelihood of a union strike. Needless to say, this analysis should be confidential and should be discussed only with management negotiators.

Establishing Liaison with Other Employer Bargaining Committees and Owners

History often repeats itself, and unions often use the same tactics with several employers simultaneously. Therefore, there should be close and regular communication with other employers dealing with the same union and with employer trade associations dealing with other local unions in the common industry. Such liaison will signal what is to be expected in bargaining and will provide a feeling for the union's tactics as well as coordinate a more solid front of employer bargaining in the industry. In addition to communications between individual employers, the various management trade organizations are excellent forums in which to discuss union strategies and past developments. Certainly, liaison between employer trade associations should include an exchange of bargaining agreements. This exchange will provide data to management negotiators which can be used to refute union claims regarding agreements with other employers. Also, it will go far to ensure that one employer or multiemployer bargaining group does not give up more than another and so does not accommodate a union's one-upmanship in its drive for higher wages and additional fringe benefits.

Historically, project owners have not been sympathetic to having their jobs stopped during an economic strike. However, there is presently a genuine recognition by many major industrial owners that an owner's policy of exerting pressure on a contractor to avoid strikes at any cost has contributed greatly to the inflationary spiral in the construction industry in both wage rates and restrictive work practices. It is wise for employer associations and even individual employers bargaining with a union to keep owners informed of the status of negotiations and to solicit their support for the contractor's position. Fully informed owners will be more likely to support the contractors' position when their jobs are shut down by an economic strike. The employer bargaining committee should also maintain liaison with owners and construction users' associations if there are any in the area, since the impact of owner support can be a material factor in adding clout to the employers' position at the bargaining table.

It cannot be overemphasized that a coordinated bargaining effort is a forward step in effective bargaining. Often employers in the construction trades must accept unfair bargaining agreements because owners or general contractors, in the case of subcontractors, demand that a job be completed without the delays which accompany strikes or other labor disputes.

Certainly, this problem is not easily resolved, but it is also certain that the affected parties should keep in touch with each other. The cooperation of owners and general contractors should be sought before labor disputes develop. Understanding between owners, general contactors, and subcontractors of the trials and tribulations of bargaining will strengthen the management bargaining position. Similarly, establishing relationships with management negotiators for other employer trades will be very valuable. Inasmuch as bargaining occurs only once in 1 to 3 years, it is important to learn from the experience of other management negotiators. The employers in an area should foster the exchange of ideas and the bargaining history of local unions. There is strength in numbers, and common goals can be more easily attained if employers present a unified front to the unions.

AT THE BARGAINING TABLE

Both management and unions should strive to establish procedural ground rules at the initial meeting. Some experienced negotiators suggest that management prepare an agenda to ensure that all the procedural items are discussed and agreed to at this meeting. The agenda could include the location of the meeting; the length of the meeting; sharing the cost of the meeting; the keeping of minutes, either one set agreed to by both parties or separate minutes kept by each side; a decision on whether there will be an alternating chairman of the meeting; the authority of the committees; and an agreement, if possible, to settle noneconomic items first.

Often the management and union bargaining committees will agree on a procedure whereby they will consider only those items on which change is requested in the initial exchange of demands. There should also be an understanding that any individual items, if agreed upon, are tentative agreements contingent upon reaching a full agreement on all items.

Site

Generally, bargaining sessions take place in the community in which the employers are located. There is clearly no obligation to meet at the union's headquarters, and it is urged that management not agree to meet at the union's office. There is truth to the adage that there is an advantage in playing on a home court. Therefore, the meeting should be arranged, if possible at a hotel or other neutral site. Management should always remember to provide its negotiators with a caucus room separate from the bargaining room. The caucus room will be used frequently for the regrouping of management forces. It will also, of course, be used to let off steam raised in the bargaining session. Never hold bargaining meetings where liquor is readily available.

The costs of the site of bargaining should be split or allocated alternately for each bargaining session. Bargaining is both union and management representation, so both sides should share the responsibility of paying for it.

Length of Session

Evening meetings should be avoided. Meetings should be held when the negotiators are fresh, and preferably enough time should be allowed to provide for several caucuses during each session. Sessions should be relatively short. Negotiators should avoid getting fatigued to the point that concessions are made just to end a meeting. Recesses should be frequent, and in such recesses the forces should be regrouped. It is difficult to state a generally applicable time span for sessions, but evening meetings particularly should be avoided if possible. In the evening, because most negotiators have worked all day, they are generally too tired to be capable of peak performance.

Conduct of Bargaining

At the initial meeting the employers should insist on a complete list of the union's demands and should also present the union with their demands soon after receiving those of the union. Employers should feel out the union's position during the opening rounds to determine which issues are serious for the union. Employer negotiators should not hesitate to reject each union demand, giving their reasons, even it they ultimately intend to agree with the union position.

The management spokesman should assume a position of leadership in the discussions. Personalities should not be allowed to enter into the bargaining, and the union negotiators should not be belittled. The chairman should call frequent caucuses, and other members may request a caucus by written note to the spokesman.

The management spokesman should use authority to concede items exceedingly sparingly and try to get the union rather than the employers to make the final acceptable offer. If the employers attempt to make the final acceptable offer, it is likely that management will be forced to compromise upward from its highest offer because of a strike or mediation. As a general rule, management negotiators should refrain from making an offer unless they have good reason to believe that it will be acceptable to the union or at least will produce a counterproposal. Rarely can anyone force acceptance of an offer that has already been rejected by the local union. Therefore, management negotiators should not lead off with their final offer and have it rejected by the union in the early stages of bargaining.

Negotiators should be firm but give the appearance of wanting to reach a satisfactory agreement. The union should be reminded at frequent intervals of management's demands. Management negotiators should not be dominated by discussing only the union's demands or be forced into fighting a defensive battle and bargaining only over those demands.

At the outset, management negotiators should state emphatically their opinion of conditions in the industry. Among the topics which may be raised are the volume of work on hand, work on the drawing board, non-union competition, and the inability of the market to absorb the increased prices which would result from increased wages and fringe benefits.

Management negotiators should learn a lesson from the unions by asking for more than they expect to get. The additional items may be used for trading purposes. In the compromising process management may even get more than expected. However, employers should not demand something of no value to them because the union may agree and demand something valuable in return. The management committee should always hesitate to concede anything without getting a concession in return. Management should never be unnecessarily candid at least until a crisis impends, and should never lay all its cards on the table early in negotiations. The employers should not make an offer on wages until the union comes in with a realistic figure. Since bargaining is give-and-take for both sides, negotiators should be flexible and prepared to shift their position a bit and never, even under the most trying circumstances, lose control. Emotional explosions merely lower management negotiators' prestige and usually make negotiations more difficult. Negotiators should not be frightened into making concessions by such common union tactics as walking out of the meeting or threatening to strike.

Gaining the Union's Respect

To negotiate successfully management negotiators must be credible. The union must believe what management says. When management proposes its bottom line, this must in fact be the bottom line. When management says no to a union proposal, the union must believe that management will not retreat from its position. This need for negotiators to gain respect is obvious. If management gains the reputation of a retreater the union will continue to pursue all its demands even to the point of calling a strike if it feels that management will continue to retreat under strike pressure.

On the other hand, if management consistently stands by its bottom-line proposals, it gains credibility, and the union will respect what management says. Further, a solid, immovable stand by management on bottom-line proposals once communicated to the union will cause the union to be more reluctant to call a strike. The union will seldom call a strike if it *believes* management when management says that it will not budge from a stated position. Not only must management be consistent, but the union must be made aware of management's consistency. Needless to say, this reading of management by the union may take several bargaining sessions or, more likely, several contracts. This circumstance reflects the advantage of using the same negotiators over a period of years.

Further, gaining the respect of the union involves a game. Management must condition the union to know when it reaches a bottom line. It may use key words or phrases which over time will convey to the union that management's position is not a bluff. The word *no*, directed to a union proposal, is a good word to signal a bottom-line stance. If *no* is never used except to communicate an absolutely steadfast refusal, the union will soon get its meaning.

In preliminary negotiations, management can refuse or invite compromises by words other than *no*. *No* should be used only when management is prepared to risk a strike to refuse a union proposal. After repetition, the union will realize that no means no. The result will be union respect and belief in management. A more important result will be the union's backing down unless it considers the disputed proposal an absolute necessity, in which event a strike is likely.

The upshot of this credibility game is to signal to the union how far management will go with or without a strike. Strikes will not be called simply to see if management will cave in.

Another important factor in gaining the union's confidence is never to mislead the union chief negotiator into shifting position by hitting reciprocity and then failing to deliver it. Above all, under no circumstances should a confidence be violated by using an off-the-record conversation held outside the bargaining room to undercut the business agent or union chief negotiator. Tough issues may be settled between the chief negotiators for management and union in meetings held off the record and not in the presence of other members of the committee. Management negotiators should always be alert for side discussions with union negotiators. Sometimes a chief employer negotiator establishes an understanding early with the chief union negotiators to attempt a side discussion before any real strike issues harden the bargaining positions at the table.

When a union is evidencing bad faith or stubbornness, management might suggest that the union call in an international union representative if the negotiations are bogged down.

Stating Authority of the Committees

The union committee should be required to state its authority as to whether it can give final acceptance to management or whether final ratification rests with the union's executive board or requires voting by its membership. Employer negotiators should be prepared to answer similar questions from the union as to their authority. It should be an almost ironclad rule that the management committee does not have full authority finally to bind the employer association; instead, it should have authority to negotiate an agreement subject to final approval by a full management representation such as the board of directors or the full membership of the employer trade association. This precaution mitigates against immediate beachhead concessions which could bind management at a bargaining session. It also allows the bargaining spokesman of the employers to bide time until the next meeting by stating that it is necessary to check with the full management authority before a complete answer can be given on a specific point. For these reasons, it is a good idea not to have the president do the bargaining, in the case of an individual employer, or the executive committee of an employer trade association.

Emphasizing Noneconomic Provisions

Often employer negotiators hit the economic provisions of an agreement hard to the neglect of the noneconomic aspects. Clauses pertaining to the method of hiring employees, restricting management's rights, or affecting the union's right to strike are extremely important. Though labeled "noneconomic," such provisions will certainly affect the productivity and profits of the employers, not to mention causing headaches for management. Among the more important noneconomic clauses are no-strike, management rights, arbitration, productivity, and union security clauses (these and other important clauses are discussed below in the section "Contract Clauses").

It is preferable that negotiators deal with the noneconomic items and contract language before negotiating the economic items. In other words, the contract language should be settled before any discussion of the money items. Management should not make any offer on wages or fringe benefits until the noneconomic subjects have been substantially settled. Changes in work rules which increase productivity often are not settled until the economic items have been discussed because it may be necessary to "buy" the productivity improvements.

Avoiding Contract Ambiguities

As in all contracts, the primary purpose is to make clear and understandable the parties' obligations. Negotiations should insist on clear language and reject union proposals which can be read in different ways. They should be sure that they understand the union proposals and have the union negotiators explain them.

Management should attempt to shift the negotiations to working from the management draft of a proposed clause. When an agreement has been reached on an item it should be expressed in exact and clear contract language before moving on to the next item.

Insisting upon an Entire Contract

Unions are known for requesting acceptance of certain proposals with the promise that if these are accepted, the union will soften its stand on other issues. Management should not fall for this tactic. Once management makes a concession, the concession is gone, and the union's promise to compromise on other issues vanishes. In short, management should agree that everything is tentative until there is complete agreement on the entire agreement. Negotiators should never make an unconditional concession but always state that the concession is conditioned on reaching a final agreement on all other matters in dispute.

Obligation to Produce Records

During collective bargaining, management is obligated to furnish certain data to the union upon request. The union must request specific information. General requests or fishing-trip inquiries may not require a response. Also, once information has been provided the union and it does not complain that the information is inadequate, it has no grounds for later complaints.

In general, the union is entitled to any specific data which is necessary (1) to prepare for contract negotiations; (2) to administer an existing agreement; or (3) to evaluate grievances. Failure to provide such information can result in a refusal-to-bargain charge. It is also important to realize that the union too is obligated to furnish specific data to management upon request. For example, the union is obligated to provide any and all wage surveys conducted by the union in the locality.

A union is entitled to records reflecting wage data, including job studies and evaluations. Other data that the union is entitled to receive include information concerning benefits, eligibility, and costs of group insurance and pension plans provided the employees. If management refuses to pay higher wages on the basis of an employer's past poor earning record, the union is entitled to seek profit and loss statements for the pertinent period. Therefore, an employer or an association negotiating for employers should not reject a union's wage proposal on the grounds of poor profits. Instead, the management committee should simply reject such proposals on the business judgment of management. Because of the confidential nature of financial records, it is suggested that legal authorities be consulted to review the specific facts and the specific requests made by the union before furnishing such financial data.

The management bargaining committee should anticipate the records and data likely to be requested by the union. This anticipation is necessary if management is to avoid possible inconsistencies in its discussions. For example, management would not want to reject the union's request for pay increases because of inability to pay if the profit and loss statement shows substantial increases in profits. A more prudent tactic would be to reject the wage increase on the basis of other wages in the area, inadequate productivity of the employees, or just the business judgment of management. In short, union data requests should be anticipated and management's arguments be made consistent with data which may be requested.

Mediation

The Federal Mediation and Conciliation Service will be apprised by the 30-day notice and will probably attend meetings during the final stages of negotiations if requested to do so by either party. However, it has the objective of getting a settlement, and the settlement may not necessarily represent the economic interest of the employers. Mediators are not concerned with employers, nor are they necessarily concerned with the industry's ability to pay. They have no authority to impose a settlement on any employer or union and may utilize only persuasive techniques and procedures with the objective of trying to reach a compromise settlement.

Management does not have to permit a mediator to enter negotiations, but a mediator can often be helpful in getting a deadlock off-center or putting a tough message across. Many government negotiators have received their training as labor officials. While they are not necessarily anti-employer, labor-oriented mediators may lean toward those with whom they identify in background and training. It is therefore prudent to check a mediator's background in deciding whether to permit the mediator to enter the negotiations.

If either the management committee or the union has requested the services of the mediator, the mediator can be expected to follow a pattern of (1) conferring separately with each party to understand the facts, issues, progress, and roadblocks; (2) scheduling a joint session and helping the bargaining committees substitute reason for emotion; (3) holding separate conferences to explore all issues raised in the joint conference; (4) making formal recommendations that both parties request; (5) attempting to find the cause for a deadlock and to straighten out any misunderstandings; and (6) perhaps suggesting compromises or alternative approaches.

Reducing a Contract to Writing

When a contract has finally been concluded, it should be set down on paper and signed no matter how tired the negotiators are. Management negotiators should put the agreement in writing, sign it, and make the union sign it. Too many times, following the heat of the battle, management and union negotiators embrace as long-lost friends and neglect to write down what they have agreed to. Such writing will avoid later disputes and confusion as to what was agreed. The contract should be in the clearest possible language and be signed by all members of the labor and management negotiating committees before the meeting is adjourned, and the committee members should agree on a meeting date to adopt the final formal agreement. If the agreement requires union ratification, each member of the union bargaining committee should be committed to obtaining union ratification. If the agreement requires ratification by the members of the trade association, such ratification by the association should come after the union ratifies the agreement. This procedure will avoid submitting the agreement to an association vote if the union fails to ratify the agreement. The final agreement should be carefully read to make sure that there are no inconsistencies, inadvertant or otherwise, with the negotiated terms.

The union should not be permitted to write the labor agreement. Management should take the initiative in typing the final agreement.

Impasse

"Impasse," as it pertains to collective bargaining agreements, is a legal term which signals the reaching of a crucial plateau in bargaining. In everyday terms it could be called a logjam which results when management and union negotiators bargain over a particular subject and both have taken inflexible and opposing positions concerning a proposal. Often, it is not easy to determine when an impasse is reached. For example, either party may offer counterproposals which would indicate flexibility and not cause an impasse despite the little progress being made.

Of particular importance is the fact that after an impasse has been reached, management may unilaterally implement a change in the conditions of employment if such a proposed change has been bargained for and notice of the change has been given to the union. The notice to the union should propose a meeting to bargain over the change. For example, in one case a company insisted upon a strong management rights clause which the union steadfastly rejected. After a series of sessions in which the clause was bargained for, both parties' positions became polarized on the issue. The company declared an impasse and unilaterally implemented the management rights clause bargained for. In a decision by the NLRB, it was held that if subjects are bargained for to an impasse, either party may unilaterally implement such proposed changes.

It is important to remember that to reach an impasse there must have been bargaining. In determining whether good-faith bargaining has occurred, the Board will consider the past history of the company in dealing with the union. If in the past the company has demonstrated a hostile attitude or been guilty of discriminatory acts toward the union, the Board may be more reluctant to find good-faith bargaining. Of course, if the Board fails to find good-faith bargaining, no real impasse has been reached, and consequently no unilateral change will be sustained. Thus, the impasse is a single route allowing companies unilaterally to implement changes concerning mandatory subjects of bargaining.

The impasse has been particularly effective when many competitive companies have signed the agreement proposed by the union. In such a situation, the union becomes quite inflexible and steadfastly insists upon uniformity of its agreements among competitor companies in a locality or even a region. Such a predicament for a weak union often gives rise to an impasse which allows company negotiators to implement unilateral changes. Needless to say, a contractor or subcontractor should not implement unilateral changes until (1) an impasse is reached and (2) possible alternative responses by the union have been evaluated.

The impasse is of particular significance when a multiemployer bargaining unit is involved. A favorite back-door union tactic designed to break up multiemployer bargaining strength is to attempt to reach agreements with individual companies within the group. Normally, such attempts to bargain with individual companies in the bargaining group are illegal; however, in the past, if an impasse was reached, the courts have held that the union could bargain directly with individual companies within the unit.

Obviously, this rule of law encourages unions to seek an impasse in order to break up a strong multiemployer group by dealing individually with its company members. Happily, this inequitable back-door tactic has recently been frowned on by some courts, and it is possible that the union tactic of pursuing individual members of the bargaining group can be an unfair labor practice.

Because of the legal complexities of the impasse, management would be well advised to consult a labor law specialist to determine the appropriateness of any proposed action stemming from an impasse.

STRIKES

There is always the possibility that negotiations may result in a strike, and there are some important considerations that management should consider if a strike should occur. Perhaps one of the most difficult problems facing an employer association during a strike is keeping its members in line and securing support from nonmember contractors. It is also necessary to gain the support of the owners and general contractors for the bargaining position when an employer association takes a strike, because owners and general contractors may attempt to put pressure on individual contractors to continue working on their job during the strike. The employer association should check jobsites to determine that none of the employees of the striking trade are employed and that other employers are not employing strikers in other areas. Management should seek lawful cooperation from employers in other areas.

To maintain the cooperation of the employers within the association there should be constant communication primarily over the telephone or in daily meetings. Independent contractors should be encouraged to support the position of the negotiating employers.

The union may attempt to get independents and even members of the bargaining group to sign short-form agreements in which the employers agree to the union's final demands. This tactic is designed to break multiemployer bargaining strength and may be illegal, even in strike situations. A strike is not synonymous with an impasse. Unless an impasse is reached, a union has no right to seek to negotiate with the employer members of the trade association individually but must continue to deal with the management bargaining committee. Any attempts by the unions to use the short-form agreement or to deal with the contractor members during a strike should be met with an unfair-labor-practice charge on behalf of the association.

Management negotiators should by all means continue to negotiate with the union. They should be ready to meet at any time during the strike, and the chief negotiators should be alert for any opportunities for sidebar discussions with union negotiators or possibly with international union officials. Frank outside discussions, which often increase the possibility of settling a strike, may be held.

During an economic strike an employer can replace the striking employees with new employees, or the employers might consider the feasibility of performing struck work with other trades. However, these options may rarely be feasible in a broadly based strike among all craft members in a particular locality. The alternative is riding out the strike. A strike not only interferes with the work of the contractors involved but also means that the union members are not employed. In addition, other union members will be unemployed if the striking craft pickets or interferes with the progress of the jobs.

If the striking employees continue to be unemployed and the employer association continues negotiating, a settlement normally will be reached in a reasonable time. A contractor who is on the verge of throwing in the towel and signing up because of financial or other pressures should be encouraged to hold out with an appeal to the contractor's sense of fair play. In particular, the employer association should attempt to ease the pressure if it is coming from an owner or a general contractor.

The management committee should check the legality of the strike. It should check to see if the union has complied with the provisions of Section 8(b) of the National Labor Relations Act (NLRA) and if the union has sent the required 60-day notice to management and the 30-day notice to the Federal Mediation and Conciliation Service. Obviously, a strike by a union during the 60-day period or the 30-day period is illegal, and injunctions should be sought immediately. Similarly, injunctions should be obtained against a union which strikes in violation of a no-strike clause during the term of an agreement or in violation of an agreement to arbitrate unsettled issues under the joint-council clauses which typically appear in the electrical, mechanical, and sheet-metal contracts. If the strike is illegal, the association should also consider filing damage suits against the union.

When the strike is settled, all parties concerned normally feel great relief, but no matter how tired both sides may be, the negotiators should not let down their guard until management and the union put the settlement down in writing.

The NLRA protects the interest of a contractor by allowing the contractor to replace striking employees and keep the business running during a lawful strike. On the other hand, the NLRA seeks to protect employees who engage in this form of protected concerted activity by proscribing certain illegal contractor responses to the strike. What the contractor does both before or during a lawful strike will have important legal and practical consequences. Thus, the contractor should be made aware of what actions may or may not be taken vis-à-vis the union or the employees, or both, before or during a lawful strike.

The actions that a contractor takes before or during a strike will make it either an economic or an unfair-labor-practice strike. An unfair-labor-practice strike is caused or prolonged in whole or in part in response to a contractor's unfair labor practices. In contrast, an economic strike results from the attempt of strikers to achieve economic objectives and is neither caused nor prolonged by a contractor's unfair labor practices. An economic strike may become an unfair-labor-practice strike if the contractor takes certain illegal actions during the strike. Unfair-labor-practice strikers are entitled to reinstatement in their former jobs even if reinstatement means that the contractor must discharge workers who were hired as replacements after the strike became an unfair-labor-practice strike. On the other hand, economic strikers may be permanently replaced, and are not automatically entitled to reinstatement if their jobs have been filled during an economic strike and no vacancies exist. So a contractor should refrain from taking certain actions which will turn an economic strike into an unfair-labor-practice strike.

A contractor may not condition bargaining with the striking union upon the termination of a lawful strike. A contractor's refusal to bargain while the strike is in progress will convert an economic strike into an unfair-labor-practice strike. The contractor therefore must reinstate the returning strikers even if reinstatement means that their permanent replacements must be discharged.

Illustrative Case

The employer, Pecheur Lozenge Co., insisted that the strike must be abandoned before the employer would resume any negotiations with the union. The court of appeals found that insistence by the employer that the strike must end before the employer would bargain with the union violated the employer's duty to bargain in good faith during a lawful strike. Therefore, economic strikers became unfair-labor-practice strikers when the employer conditioned resumption of negotiations upon the union's abandonment of the strike. The employer was required to reinstate strikers when they unconditionally applied for reinstatement even if that meant discharging all replacements hired after the employer committed the unfair labor practice.[1]

The fact that there is a lawful strike does not allow a contractor to institute changes in the terms and conditions of employment without first bargaining to an impasse with the union over these proposed changes. Sometimes, but not always, a strike is coincidental with a bargaining impasse. The contractor should check to see whether all good-faith attempts to bargain with the union have been exhausted before initiating any changes in the terms or conditions of employment. The contractor also must continue to process grievances in the same manner under an established grievance procedure unless the union is induced to agree to abandon or alter the grievance procedure.

Illustrative Case

Without bargaining with the union, the Bethlehem Steel Co. altered the grievance procedure. The Third Circuit Court of Appeals held that the employer committed an unfair labor practice for failure to bargain in good faith by altering the grievance procedure without first bargaining with the union, since the grievance procedure comes within terms or conditions of employment which are not subject to unilateral change by employer. If, on the other hand, the contract expires while the strike continues, the contractor may unilaterally cease giving effect to union security and a dues-checkoff provision even though they are both subjects over which the contractor is required to bargain, since these two terms automatically end with the expiration of the contract.[2]

A contractor may legitimately discontinue wages and related payments to strikers for the duration of a strike without first consulting the union. A contractor may also unilaterally discontinue group insurance contributions for employees on strike, since these contributions are analogous to wages. This rule is based on the reasoning that the contractor should not be required to pay employees for time not worked.

Illustrative Case

Philip Carey Manufacturing Company unilaterally discontinued group insurance contributions for strikers during a lawful economic strike. The NLRB found that the employer did not violate the NLRA by this action, since the employer has no duty to negotiate with unions about halting wage payments to strikers during the period of the strike, and because group insurance contributions are equivalent to wages, the employer was free to discontinue them without consulting the union.[3]

[1] *NLRB v. Pecheur Lozenge Co.*, 98 NLRB No. 84 (1952), *modified & enforced*, 209 F.2d 393 (2d Cir. 1953).

[2] *Bethlehem Steel Co.*, 136 NLRB No. 135 (1963), *aff'd*, 115 F. Supp. 231 (3d Cir. 1963).

[3] *Philip Carey Mfg. Co. v. NLRB*, 140 NLRB No.90 (1963).

However, a contractor may not impair the strikers' job tenure or conditions of employment during the strike. And a contractor may not deny the accumulation of seniority rights for strikers that it grants to nonstrikers and to strike replacements. Otherwise, the strikers' relative claims to jobs would be altered so that their job tenure would be illegally impaired.

Denial of credit during the strike period for vacation pay and pension benefits is lawful, since these benefits are analogous to wages and denial of these credits will not adversely affect the strikers' job tenure. The Supreme Court has ruled that a contractor may not deny paying vacation benefits to strikers that have accrued prior to the strike while paying vacation benefits to nonstrikers. Even a contractor's offer of legitimate economic reasons to justify this discriminatory treatment will have been an unfair labor practice.[4]

Particular promises of benefits to or threats of reprisal against employees to induce them not to strike are unlawful and will convert an economic strike into an unfair-labor-practice strike. This may be the result even if the contractor contends that the threats or promises were necessary to keep the business running, since the purpose of the NLRA is to protect employees against interference from the employer concerning their right to strike. The contractor should refrain from expressly or impliedly stating to the employees that they will be denied reinstatement for participating in the strike. Likewise, the contractor may not offer superseniority status to nonstrikers or to strikers who will agree to return to work. This mere offer, even if it is never actually instituted, is unlawful, so that an economic strike will become an unfair-labor-practice strike. The Supreme Court has held that extending superseniority credit to strike replacements or returning strikers is a discriminatory promise of benefits which violates the NLRA, since it has an inherently destructive impact upon the right to strike even if such offer is necessary for the employer to keep the business running.[5]

Contractors are entitled under the NLRA to hire permanent replacements during a lawful strike to keep the business running. Sometimes, however, the way in which a contractor replaces strikers will determine whether an economic strike is converted into an unfair-labor-practice strike. A contractor should refrain from making any statements or taking any acts that will suggest that employees will be denied reinstatement for participating in the strike.

Illustrative Case

During a carpenters' strike in Jacksonville, Florida, one of the employer's supervisors told a striker that the strikers would not be reinstated because they had engaged in the strike. The NLRB found that the employer violated the NLRA by informing the striker that he would

[4] NLRB v. Great Dane Trailers, Inc., 388 U.S. 26 (1967).

[5] NLRB v. Erie Resistor Corp., 373 U.S. 221 (1963).

not be reinstated because he had engaged in the strike, and this statement of the employer also made the strike an unfair-labor-practice strike.[6]

The contractor may lawfully replace economic strikers to make room for permanent replacements who are willing to perform the work. However, if no permanent replacements have already been hired, that fact will suggest that the strikers were unlawfully discharged for striking rather than lawfully replaced with people willing to do the work. In this way, an economic strike is converted to an unfair-labor-practice strike, and reinstatement of all the strikers may be the remedy.

Illustrative Case

The morning after three employees refused to cross a picket line, they received telegrams which read: "For failure to report to work as directed at 7 A.M. . . . , you are hereby being permanently replaced." At the time of this telegram, the employer had *not* hired any permanent replacements. The U.S. Supreme Court held that the three employees were entitled to reinstatement and back pay, either as discharged unfair-labor-practice strikers in a strike converted from an economic to an unfair-labor-practice strike or as victims of a Section 8(a)(3) unfair labor practice.[7]

A contractor is not under an obligation to reinstate economic strikers to their previous jobs if that would mean that permanent replacements must be discharged. Yet the contractor might still be required to offer to reinstate economic strikers who have offered to return to work whenever equivalent jobs become available even if no job opening existed when the strike ended or when the economic strikers offered to resume their jobs.

Illustrative Cases

An employer denied reinstatement to economic strikers because no job opening existed at the time of their unconditional offer for reinstatement, on the ground that their jobs had been filled by permanent replacements when the strike ended. When vacancies arose, the employer failed to notify the economic strikers of job vacancies and hired other applicants. The Seventh Circuit Court of Appeals held: "Economic strikers who unconditionally apply for reinstatement at a time when their positions are filled by permanent replacements . . . are entitled to full reinstatement upon the departure of replacements unless they have in the meantime acquired regular and substantially equivalent employment, or the employer can sustain his burden of proof that the failure to offer full reinstatement was for legitimate and substantial business reasons.[8]

Thus, when a strike ends, a contractor must first fill job openings as they become available with those economic strikers who have made uncon-

---

[6] *Carpenters District Council of Jacksonville, Fla., & Local 627,* 221 NLRB No. 118 (1975).

[7] *NLRB v. International Van Lines,* 409 U.S. 48 (1972).

[8] *Laidlaw Corp. v. NLRB,* 414 F.2d 99 (7th Cir. 1969).

ditional offers to return to work and who are able to perform the jobs. If the contractor fails to notify an economic striker of an equivalent job opening, this is an unfair labor practice, and even if the contractor had no antiunion motivation, the contractor may have to make to the economic strikers a back-pay award dating from the time when the jobs became available. Therefore, the contractor must notify economic strikers of available jobs rather than rely upon the union. The NLRB held that if an employer made the union its agent for the purpose of notifying employees of available job opportunities, the employer is liable for the union's failure to give notice to the employees, so that the employee violates the NLRA.[9]

A contractor does not fulfill obligations to economic strikers for whom jobs become available unless the offer to reinstate them is unconditional. Thus, the contractor must refrain from conditioning reinstatement upon the strikers' agreement not to strike again or to withdraw support from the union. Nor may the contractor offer to reinstate them on substantially less than the terms and conditions of employment that they enjoyed prior to the strike. So economic strikers must be given the same seniority status as they would have had if there had been no strike.

A contractor may not discriminate according to union membership considerations in offering reinstatement to returning strikers. If the contractor does so, this is an unfair labor practice.

Illustrative Case

Upon resumption of a construction job, the employer refused to retire six employees who were also union members. The NLRB found that the employer committed an unfair labor practice for failure to retire employees on the ground that they were union members since the employer had antiunion motivations and one employee was propositioned by the employer to return to work as a nonunion employee.[10]

But how long after a strike ends must a contractor continue to offer reinstatement to economic strikers? The Board has recognized the effectiveness of what are known as "strike settlement agreements" in some circumstances to limit the duration of a contractor's obligation to reinstate economic strikers.[11]

When a contractor has refrained from committing any unfair labor practices which might have caused the union's loss of majority status, then if enough permanent replacements have been hired after the certification year to raise a genuine doubt as to the union's majority status, the contractor may refuse to bargain with the union.

Illustrative Case

In the light of a large number of permanent replacements hired to replace economic strikers, the court of appeals held that there could be genuine doubt as to the union's majority

[9] Ernst Steel Corp., 217 NLRB No. 179 (1975).

[10] Torrington Constr. Co., 198 NLRB No 170 (1972).

[11] United Aircraft Corp., 192 NLRB No. 62 (1971).

status. Since the employer did not commit an unfair labor practice that could have been responsible for the union's loss of majority status and since it had a genuine doubt as to its continuing majority status, the employer could lawfully refuse to bargain with the union after 1 year from its certification by the Board.[12]

LOCKOUTS

While most people are familiar with strikes, the lockout is less frequently encountered. A lockout is the temporary laying off of employees to bring pressure to bear upon them in a labor dispute. The lockout has been defined by the Board and the courts as "the withholding of employment by an employer from his employees for the purpose of resisting their demands or gaining a concession from them."

An employer's right to lock out is not a corollary of employees' right to strike but is more closely restricted and legally treacherous. A contractor must know what is required to conduct a lockout in a lawful manner and should have knowledge of some of the things a contractor might say or do that would make a lockout illegal. If the lockout is illegal, the contractor will be liable for back pay to employees unlawfully deprived of work.

A lockout by an employer can deprive a union of the exclusive control of the timing and duration of work stoppages. A lockout may be an important economic weapon which an employer can use offensively or defensively when the employer cannot settle its differences with labor through collective bargaining.

An illegal lockout can result in back pay being awarded to the employees. It is imperative that the notices required by the NLRA have been timely given and that the employer does not lock out employees during the cooling off period.

It is usually preferable to goad a union into striking rather than to resort to lockout tactics if a cessation of work is inevitable. The usual use of lockouts in the construction industry is to prevent whipsaw tactics by the union; all employers in a multiemployer bargaining group will be shut down if the union singles out one employer to strike. Another use is to preempt the union from stalling until the employer is in a more vulnerable position. A lockout can prevent the union from delaying the real bargaining until summer, when the employer's work is at a maximum, on a contract expiring in winter, when the employer's work is slack and a strike would not have as great an effect.

The withholding of employment by a contractor is lawful when based on the grounds of "economic necessity." This type of lockout, which is used defensively, most frequently occurs in response to a union strike or threat of a strike by one craft of employees while other crafts are still willing to work. The justification is that the lockout is necessary to minimize financial losses to the contractor if the union did strike. Especially in the con-

---

[12]*Philip Carey Mfg. Co. v. NLRB*, 331 F.2d 720 (6th Cir. 1964), *cert. denied,* 379 U.S. 888 (1969).

struction industry, in which members of many different unions work alongside each other on the same project, there is an acute danger of economic loss if one of the unions carries out its threatened strike. A lockout of all the unions' employees in response to one union's threat to strike may be unlawful.

Illustrative Case

Contractors suspended operations on construction projects while negotiating with a union for a new contract covering operating engineers. The NLRB held that the lockout was motivated by lawful considerations, and was therefore lawful since

"(1). union had previously struck employers under similar circumstances, causing them to suffer financial losses;

"(2). statements made by union representatives during negotiations gave clear warning to employers that unless union's terms were met, union would strike again;

"(3). 'quickie strike' would have caused substantial losses to employers and created serious danger to health and safety of public; and,

"(4). union failed to give employers any assurance of continued work."[13]

A contractor should by all means avoid making any statements or taking any actions which might indicate that a lockout was motivated by unlawful considerations. A lockout motivated by a desire to discourage union membership will be unlawful, and the locked-out employees will be entitled to back pay. A lockout designed to discourage employees from engaging in protected concerted activities or in retaliation for their having engaged in protected activities will also be unlawful. Engaging in a lockout to avoid bargaining with a union or to force employees to bargain with the contractor directly rather than through the union will also be unlawful.

Over some circuit courts' disapproval, the Board has continued to rule that a lockout is unlawful if it is motivated even partially by prohibited reasons. But the court has denied enforcement of Board reinstatement orders unless there has been a finding that the primary motivation for the lockout was unlawful. Nevertheless, a contractor who wants to engage in a lockout takes the safest course by waiting for the union to strike.

A favorite device of some unions is presenting their contractual demands during negotiations with a multiemployer bargaining unit is to engage in a whipsaw strike, which is initiated against one contractor who seems particularly vulnerable to acceding to the union's bargaining demands. By engaging in a strike against an individual contractor, the union hopes that it will be able to force the contractor quickly to accede to the union's demands. Then it will direct strikes against other contractors, using threats of selective strikes to force them into acquiescence. The Supreme Court has ruled that to "preserve the integrity of the [multiemployer] bargaining unit," the other contractor member may use the lockout defen-

---

[13] *Building Construction Ass'n of Rockford, Inc.,* 138 NLRB No. 1405 (1962).

sively to lay off that union's members once the union strikes any one of the contractor members.

Illustrative Cases

During contract negotiations with a union, nonstruck members of a multiemployer bargaining association temporarily locked out their employees as a defense to a union strike against one of the members. The U.S. Supreme Court decision upheld the temporary lockout by other contractor members of a multiemployer bargaining unit to be lawfully used as a defense to a union strike against one of the contractor members in order to protect their legitimate interest in bargaining with the union on a group basis.[14]

Not only may the nonstruck contractor members of the association lay off the members of the striking union, but they may also close down their entire projects if continued operations without the striking union's members would be uneconomic. Because they are able to lay off these other union's members so that these unions will exert pressure upon the striking union to cease the strike and to make more reasonable bargaining demands, the other unions may feel that their members are being denied work because of the union's strike. Still, to avoid being liable for back pay to the other unions' laid-off members, contractors who close down their entire projects should make sure that continued operations without the striking union would be uneconomic.

Illustrative Cases

Nonstruck contractors who were members of a multiemployer association closed down their construction projects after being confronted with a union's refusal to continue negotiations and with an impending strike against one of the contractor members. The NLRB held that the lockouts by the nonstruck contractor members were lawful, since all were motivated by the desire "to minimize unusual economic and operational losses incident to uncoordinated construction jobs. . . ."[15]

The Supreme Court has ruled that a lockout may also be used by a contractor as an offensive tactic to induce a union to acquiesce to a contractor's bargaining demands. This type of lockout may not be initiated until an impasse in negotiations has been reached. Therefore, the contractor should first check to see whether all reasonable attempts have been made to bargain with the union over mandatory subjects and whether negotiations have reached the point where further bargaining would be fruitless. So under this rule a lockout may not be used to induce a union to agree to a contractor's proposal relating to a nonmandatory subject. Furthermore,

[14] NRLB v. Truck Drivers Local 449 (Buffalo Linen Supply Co.,), 353 U.S. 87 (1957).

[15] AGC, Ga. Branch, 138 NLRB No. 144 (1962).

the contractor should make sure that no possible unlawful motivation for
the lockout may be construed.

Illustrative Case

**After an impasse in bargaining over a mandatory subject had been reached with a union,
the employer temporarily shut down his plant for the purpose of placing economic pressure
on the union to accede to the employer's demands when the union was stalling around
until the employer had a fuller workload and the employer would be more vulnerable to a
strike. The Supreme Court held that the "employer does not violate [the Labor-Management Realtions Act] when, after bargaining impasse has been reached, the employer temporarily shuts down the plant and lays off employees for the *sole* purpose of bringing
economic pressure to bear in support of employer's legitimate bargaining position."[16]**

But the NLRA imposes a statutory requirement that may delay the
timing of a lockout in some circumstances. If the purpose of the lockout is
to put pressure on the union to modify or terminate an existing collective
bargaining agreement, certain notice requirements must first be met. Under the NLRA, the contractor must give written notice to the union of
intent to modify or terminate the contract at least 60 days before the
contract's expiration date. If the contract has no expiration date, similar
notice must be given to the union at least 60 days before the time at which
it is proposed to make the modification or termination.

Also, the NLRA requires that the contractor notify the Federal Mediation and Conciliation Service within 30 days "after such notice of the existence of a dispute," and at the same time notify any state or territorial
mediation and conciliation services in the locality where the dispute occurred, provided no agreement has been reached by that time.

Therefore, a contractor desiring to modify or terminate an agreement
with a union should check first to see whether these notice requirements
have been met before it locks out employees. If the contractor locks out
employees prematurely, the contractor will be committing an unfair labor
practice for not bargaining in good faith and will be required to reinstate
the laid-off employees with back pay.

Even if 60 days have passed since the contractor gave written notice to
the union of intent to modify or terminate an existing contract but 30 days
have not passed since notice was given to the appropriate mediation agencies, the contractor cannot engage in a lockout until 30 days since notice
was given to the mediation services have also passed.

On the other hand, if a union initially desiring to modify or terminate
an agreement gives a contractor the 60-day notice (or a longer notice set
forth in a collective bargaining agreement) but fails to abide by the 30-day
mediation notice requirements, does the contractor violate the NLRA by
locking out employees upon the union's misrepresentation that at least 30
days have passed since notice was given for mediation? One circuit court

[16]*American Shipbuilding Co.,* 380 U.S. 300 (1965).

refused to enforce a Board order that a contractor association committed an unfair labor practice under those conditions.

Illustrative Case

The union sent a 60-day written notice to a painting contractors' association that it was prepared to renegotiate an existing contract with an April 30 expiration date. The union notified the association that it had been in touch with state and federal mediation services, but these services did not receive written notice until April 11. On May 1, the association notified the union that it was immediately laying off its members because of the contract's unresolved status. The court of appeals held that the association's lockout was not unlawfully premature, since "once the non-initiating party [in this case, the association] has observed its duty to bargain collectively during the 60-day period, it has fulfilled its duty under §8(d) whether or not its obligation under §8(d)(3) to notify state and federal mediators."[17]

However, the Board has continued to rule that a contractor cannot rely upon a union's representation that appropriate notice has been given when the union is in the initiating party desiring to modify or terminate the contract. Under this NLRB rule, then, the burden is upon the contractor to satisfy the 30-day notice requirement which was originally placed on the union before it may lay off any employees.[18]

Since the rule as to notice requirements in this area is unclear, a contractor or multiemployer association faced with a union's demand to modify or terminate an existing contract should do the following before engaging in a lockout:

1. Avoid a lockout until the 60-day or longer period since the notice to terminate or modify the collective bargaining contract has passed or until the termination date of that collective bargaining contract expires, whichever is later.

2. Check to see that 30 days have passed since the notice of the dispute to the appropriate federal and state mediation service. Do not only ask the union whether it has given the 30-day notice but notify the mediation services directly.

A lockout which would be unlawful when used offensively, since, for example it was initiated prior to an impasse, may nonetheless be lawful if it would be justified on the ground of economic necessity and there is no evidence of unlawful motivation for the lockout.[19]

Often lawful offensive lockouts are imposed simultaneously by contractors who are all members of a formal multiemployer association for

---

[17] *Peoria Chapter, Painting & Decorating Contractors*, 204 NLRB No 66 (1973), *enforcement denied*, 500 F.2d 54 (7th Cir. 1974).

[18] *Hooker Chemical & Plastics Corp.*, 224 NLRB No. 203 (1976).

[19] *Lane v. NLRB*, 418 F.2d 1208 (D.C. Cir. 1969).

bargaining. Yet offensive lockouts may sometimes be lawfully imposed simultaneously by contractors who are not members of the same formal association. Such lockouts may be lawful if the contractors can show that they have a common interest in resisting a union's bargaining demands.

Illustrative Case

Twenty-seven area contractors who were members of three different associations all locked out members of several unions over those unions' bargaining demands for a shortened workday. The NLRB held that these lockouts were permissible even though there was no single multiemployer bargaining group, since variance in the length of the workday among the several crafts would be disruptive; and, the interest of the several groups of employers in the several crafts were sufficiently interwoven to justify their taking common action in their common interests."[20]

If a contractor who is a member of a formal contractors association resists a lockout order issued by the association, the association might be able to obtain an injunction requiring the contractor to abide by its lockout order.

Illustrative Case

Three multiemployer associations ordered one of their members to shut down his operation pursuant to a lockout order issued by the associations. The member refused, and the associations sought an injunction. The district court granted an injunction to compel the individual member to comply with the lawful lockout order since the assignment of bargaining rights by the individual member to the association precluded the member from resisting the lockout order issued by the association.[21]

A contractor's right to engage in a lockout may be and often is restricted by a no-lockout provision of a collective bargaining agreement. Therefore, a contractor who locks out employees in spite of a no-lockout obligation may be liable for the amount of back wages which the employees would have received during the unlawful lockout. Since most collective bargaining agreements also contain a provision for the arbitration of disputes covering the interpretation or application of an agreement, the court may defer to arbitration to let it decide whether the contractor has breached the contract by imposing the lockout. If the arbitrator determines that the contractor has violated the agreement, the court will likely uphold the arbitrator's decision and award damages to the union.

CONTRACT CLAUSES

If preparation for bargaining is important, knowing the meaning of clauses and being cautious of union traps is imperative if management negotiators

[20] *Capital District Contractors' Assn.*, 185 NLRB No. 90 (1970).

[21] *Construction Indus. Contractors v. Drake Co.*, 93 LRRM 2924 (W.D. Wash. 1976).

will be going to war without knowing the battlefield of the enemy. The following are comments and suggestions regarding various contract clauses.

Recognition of Union

The agreement should specifically define the employees covered by the agreement. If an NLRB election has occurred, the contract should indicate that recognition of the union extends to employees in the bargaining unit as determined by the Board. More typically, a union is recognized by the company's or the employer trade association's voluntarily recognizing the union. However, once the union gets in the door, the recognition clause should define the bargaining unit by craft and territory. Further, it should set out the classes of employees not covered by the agreement. In association bargaining the recognition clause should state that the union recognize the association as the multiemployer bargaining agent.

Union Security

Historically, building trades agreements have had the tightest union shop clauses found in any form of union contracts. Today such union shops are limited by the NLRA and state right-to-work laws. For building and construction trades the NLRA allows compulsory union membership after the seventh day of employment. However, many states have right-to-work laws which prohibit making union membership a condition of employment. Therefore, employers must determine the law applicable to the union security provisions in their state.

In support of union security, unions urge that everyone be required to join a union, as otherwise nonunion employees would be represented without paying dues for such representation. Such an inequity, they claim, would be unfair to the dues-paying employees. A union will further contend that requiring union membership will not hamper management in hiring new workers, as there is no requirement that employees join the union until several days after they begin work. Union tactics and claims regarding union security are many and varied. Negotiators should be aware that such provisions clearly coerce union membership and perpetually ensure a union majority and union bargaining strength. Management should repel the union's contentions and urge that employees be entitled to choose whether they wish to join the union. Of course, management negotiators may also have a legal argument against tight union security based upon state right-to-work laws and the NLRA.

Management negotiators should seriously consider hard bargaining tools of unions. Often a union may agree to modify a security clause for important concessions by the employer. Negotiators should avoid getting into give-and-take discussions on union security clauses. Management negotiators should emphasize the need for union security clauses that give employees the right to decide whether they wish to join the union. An example of a typical tight union security clause is as follows.

Illustrative Example

All present journeymen and apprentices covered by this agreement who are members of the union shall, as a condition of employment, maintain their membership in the union. All other journeymen covered by this agreement, excluding apprentices, shall, as a condition of employment, become members of the union seven days following the date this agreement is effective.

This provision guarantees a union majority and usurps the employees' right to decide whether they wish to join the union. On the other hand, the following union security clause allows employees to decide whether they wish to join the union.

Illustrative Example

All employees have the right to join or not join the union. Union membership is not a condition of employment and employees shall be retained on a nondiscriminatory basis, and the tenure of all employees shall not be based on, or in any way affected by, union membership, bylaws, rules, regulations, constitutional provisions, or any other aspect or obligation of union membership, policy, or requirements. The selection of applicants for jobs shall be on a nondiscriminatory basis and shall not be based on, or in any way affected by, union membership, bylaws, rules, regulations, constitutional provisions, or any other aspect or obligation of union membership, policies, or requirements.

Hiring Clauses

For many years unions have been the common source of workers in the construction industry. This condition is the result of hiring clauses in union agreements (see Chapter 1, "Hiring Halls"). Hiring clauses may vary considerably. Some agreements provide that management may hire new employees without going through the union. This method obviously has the advantage of permitting the contractor to select employees on the basis of their qualifications while giving the employer the option to obtain employees from the union. However, many contracts in the construction industry include hiring clauses requiring the exclusive use of hiring halls, or in actual practice, a method approaching the exclusive hiring-hall procedure. The hiring-hall arrangement is a work referral system for construction workers, sometimes even including supervisors, in which administrative control is delegated to union officials, to a joint labor-management committee, or occasionally to a third-party administrator. These referral systems are almost universally controlled by the union.

A pure hiring-hall arrangement would obligate a company to request workers from the union and to hire those workers referred by the union. In a variation of the hiring-hall procedure, the employer is granted the right to reject any applicants and the right to obtain employees from any source when the union is unable to provide qualified journeymen. Clearly, the more closely the provision approaches the pure hiring-hall procedure, the more control the union will exert over the makeup of the company workforce.

Taken as a whole, the hiring hall relieves the contractor of the difficulty and expense of operating a personnel department. That relief, however, is attained at the expense of creating a major base of union power and of severely handicapping the ability of a contractor to control the workforce. The primary problem is that the hiring hall creates a contractually limited source of labor. By using hiring halls, unions become the repository of virtually all available information on the quality and quantity of the pool of workers. The same information is inaccessable to contractors. This imbalance in the availability of information places a contractor at a severe disadvantage in performing as an employer. The hiring hall also provided a basis for union control of the apprenticeship program by which new workers are trained for eventual journeyman status.

Whatever the pros and cons for a union hiring hall or any other hiring procedure, management, through bargaining, has an opportunity to effect the best procedure. Management should study fully the effectiveness and possible disadvantages of the various hiring procedures for its locality and particular trade. An example of a clause providing for a strict hiring-hall arrangement is as follows:

Illustrative Example

The union agrees to furnish the competent journeymen selected for referral to jobs on a nondiscriminatory basis. The union agrees that it will maintain appropriate registration facilities in filling job vacancies on all projects; provided, however, the employer shall have the right to hire, fire, direct the working forces, and manage his business in accordance with his judgment. In the event that the registration facility maintained by the union is unable to fill requisitions for employees within a 48-hour period, the employer may employ applicants at the job site. In such an event, the employer will notify the union of the names and addresses of all individuals hired and the dates of such hirings.

Under such a provision, employers are provided a workforce by the union. Only if the union fails to provide qualified applicants within 48 hours of the request can the employers hire whom they please. Varying the number of hours in which the union may furnish employees will have little effect on the union's power under this clause because employers generally have not exercised the right to hire elsewhere for fear of reprisals by union officials or union membership.

A possible variation of this provision would make use of the hiring hall optional to employers. Such a modification would allow employers to seek employees from whatever source they desire and also to resort to the hiring hall.

It is also important for contractors and their collective bargaining representatives to press aggressively for amendments to existing agreements that would make the hiring hall less onerous. As one example among many, contract provisions that effectively reserve to employers the right to reject unqualified applicants without fear of some form of reprisal would give them a greater measure of control over the quality of their workforce.

The most important bargaining objective should be to eliminate any exclusivity features that tend to prevent contractors from utilizing an alternative or supplementary referral service, such as one operated by or for the employers themselves. A solution recommended by *The Business Roundtable Report of the Task Force on Hiring Halls in the Construction Industry* is a management-operated referral system including a contractor-supported data bank listing the availability and skill levels of craftsmen in a given labor market.

In an alternative or supplement to the hiring hall employers would engage directly in open advertising and other forms of communication of job openings and workforce needs. This process could parallel that practiced by typical employers in other industries. Whatever its practicality, the recruitment approach is another alternative to the hiring-hall system on which the organized segment of the construction industry depends so heavily at present.

Checkoff

The checkoff is a negotiated provision within a bargaining agreement by which an employer, upon written authorization of the employees, deducts from wages of the employees their initiation fees or dues and forwards them to the union. Such a provision typically accompanies the union security provision of an agreement. The dues checkoff is permitted by Section 302(c)(4) of the NLRA, which allows an employer to deduct membership dues from an employee's wages to pay such amount to the union provided:

That the employer has received from each employee, on whose account such deductions are made, a written assignment which shall not be irrevocable for a period of more than one year, or beyond the termination date of the applicable collective bargaining agreement, whichever occurs sooner. . . .

Still, many states, either by statute or by court decision, attempt to regulate or prohibit the checkoff. Thus, a contractor should check the applicable state law before agreeing to or enforcing checkoff provisions. But a federal court of appeals has held that states have been preempted by federal labor laws in regulating checkoff and that states' right-to-work laws validly apply to checkoffs.

The NLRA, in Section 302(d), provides for penalties of a $10,000 maximum fine or 1-year maximum imprisonment, or both, for willfully illegal payments by the employer to the union under the dues checkoff. Thus, the deductions are illegal if they are unauthorized, if the authorization has been revoked, or if the deductions are not "in payment of membership dues."

Enforcement of these criminal penalties is left to the Department of Justice, but there have been few prosecutions involving the dues checkoff. The Department has indicated that there may be deductions for payments of initiation fees and assessments, provided they are authorized. Also, although authorizations may not be irrevocable for more than 1 year, there is no criminal violation if an authorization with an automatic-renewal clause extends for more than one year, provided the employee is given an escape period within 1 year for revocation.

The checkoff is the union's main tool of financial support. If the checkoff is provided in the agreement, the union gains financial security, and its continued financial support is ensured. If the checkoff is not provided, the union has the problem of collecting its own dues. As this provision in no way benefits the employers, it should be hotly contested. The obvious basis for such opposition is that employers should not be required to be collection agents for the union.

Because of the importance of the checkoff to the union, the management committee should not consider conceding the checkoff for substantial concessions to the union. However, management must bargain with the union over the checkoff. Thus, an employer may not be bargaining in good faith if its refusal to consider the checkoff proposal is based solely on the ground that the employer is not going to do anything "to aid and comfort" the union. Still, even though management must bargain in good faith over the checkoff, it is not required to agree to it.

In fact, when a contractor appears readily to agree to the checkoff, that agreement may sometimes be evidence of an unfair labor practice for unlawful assistance to the domination of a union. Thus, an employer may be committing this unfair labor practice by agreeing to the checkoff without even bargaining, or by agreeing in the face of a rival union's claim of representation for the bargaining unit.

If management does concede a checkoff clause, the union should indemnify the employer for all claims resulting from the operations of the clause. The agreement should further provide that the employer will not be responsible for negligent inadvertence in failing to check off, in checking off the wrong amounts, or in failing to remit dues to the local union in accordance with the strict language of the clause.

Although an employer and a union may agree to the checkoff, individual employees are not required to authorize it. Moreover, the employer violates the NLRA by discriminating or threatening to discriminate against employees for their refusal to agree to the checkoff.

Illustrative Case

The employer, Adams Construction Company, threatened to discharge employees if they refused to sign checkoff authorization cards for the union. Two employees were subsequently discharged for failing to sign checkoff cards. The NLRB found that the employer violated Section 8(a)(1) of the NLRA through coercing employees who were justified in refraining from engaging in concerted activities by threatening to discharge employees if they refused to sign the checkoff authorization cards. Also, the employer violated Section 8(a)(3) of the NLRA through discriminating against employees to encourage union membership by discharging employees who refused to sign such cards.[22]

Similarly, threats to demote or transfer employees if they refuse to authorize the checkoff are unlawful. In fact, even requests for authorization by a supervisor during a private meeting with employees may support an unfair-labor-practice charge if all the circumstances suggest a reasonable fear in the employees that they would be adversely affected if they refused to make the authorization.

Although an employer and the union may agree to the dues checkoff, it is an unfair labor practice for the employer to check off dues for employees who have not authorized the checkoff. So, the employer violates the NLRA by deducting initiation fees and dues in anticipation of but prior to authorization or by making deductions after the expiration of the collective bargaining agreement. If one year has gone by since the authorization but the collective bargaining is in effect, continued deductions beyond the 1-year period are likewise unlawful. But if the contract contains an automatic-renewal clause and the employees are given an escape period within 1 year from the initial authorization by which they may revoke the authorization, checkoffs beyond the 1-year period are not unlawful.

An employer commits an unfair labor practice by failing to abide by a timely revocation of authorization. It is no defense for the employer to claim that employees failed to comply with a revised procedure for revocation if the employees did not consent to the new method.

Illustrative Case

Employees executed a dues-checkoff authorization in a procedure whereby revocation is effective upon written notice to the employer. The collective bargaining agreement had an automatic-renewal clause with an escape period at the end of each year for revocation. Later, in negotiating a new contract, the employer and the union agreed to modify the checkoff provision so that revocation was effective only upon written notice to the employer and the union. When two of the employees attempted to make revocations during the escape period, they were told that written notice must also be given to the union. However, the union never received notice from one of the employees, and the other did not even attempt to serve notice on the union. Upon the union's complaint that these employees' revocations were ineffective, the employer continued to make dues deductions from wages. The Board ruled that if an employer and a union are free to change the revocation procedure without the assent of the individual employee affected thereby, the terms of the written agreement by which the employee has authorized the dues deduction become meaningless, and the employee loses the protection intended by the requirement of a "written" assignment. Additionally, imposition of such changed revocation requirements undermines the prohibition of authorizations which are irrevocable for more than 1 year, because any attempted revocation not in compliance with the change procedure is ineffective, and the employee thus loses the opportunity to revoke for another year.[23]

[22]Adams Constr. Co., 220 NLRB No. 101 (1975).

[23]Cameron Iron Works, Inc., 227 NLRB No. 56 (1977).

Normally, an employee who authorizes the dues checkoff cannot revoke it within 1 year, provided that the collective bargaining agreement has not expired during that period. But what happens if the union security agreement has been nullified by a majority vote of the employees of the unit, pursuant to a deauthorization election? In that event, employees are entitled to revoke their checkoff authorizations. If the employer continues to deduct dues after the revocation, he must reimburse the employees. Nevertheless, the employer must continue to check off dues for those employees who desire to retain their union membership and to have their dues deducted from their pay.

On the other hand, when a representation election results in the certification of a rival union as the exclusive bargaining representative, the checkoff agreement is still valid until the expiration of the collective bargaining contract. Also, employees may not revoke their authorizations before the expiration of the contract.

The employer and the union are prohibited from using the dues checkoff to collect assessments unless the employees have also authorized a checkoff of assessments. Thus, an employer violates an employee's protected right to refrain from union activity by making an unauthorized deduction to pay a lawful union fine imposed against the employee without the employee's consent. Finally, if the checkoff is used in this manner to pay a fine without the employee's authorization, the employee cannot then be discharged for dues delinquency.

Craft Jurisdiction

Jurisdictional problems permeate many aspects of labor-management relations in the construction industry. Exclusive jurisdiction has been the cornerstone of the trade union movement in the construction industry. In the application of exclusive jurisdiction unions and their members attempt to achieve a form of property right in their craft jurisdiction and adopt an attitude that the unions and their members own the work. A craft union's claim to jurisdiction is a claim to exclusive control over the type of work performed by its members in a given territory, and it further implies that the union has the exclusive right to organize employees performing the work of that trade within a definite geographical area. It is important to understand that the essence of the union's jurisdiction is exclusiveness.

Craft jurisdiction is the emotional and cohesive force in a craft union. The diversity of specialty contractors is the direct result of the division of craft jurisdiction, and the several management sections of industry depend on their craft counterparts' retention of craft jurisdiction to ensure their own position within the industry. This is a *quid pro quo* relationship, with contractors agreeing to employ the crafts exclusively and the crafts agreeing to work only for the group of employers.

Competition is now entering the construction industry from industrial companies who actively seek and perform construction work. These companies are making substantial inroads into the union's historical role of exclusive jurisdiction. Many industrial companies are negotiating collective bargaining agreements which, instead of providing for exclusive jurisdiction, provide for the "primary duties of the craft employees." These agreements permit the craft employees to perform other work incidental to the primary duties of craftwork.

Management negotiators in the construction industry should not blindly agree to a union's exclusive jurisdiction but take a second look and attempt to expand their right to use employees as the economy and efficiency of the work may dictate. The negotiators should consider bargaining for a primary-duty definition of craftwork rather than an exclusive jurisdictional concept of the type of craft work.

Territorial jurisdiction is the other corollary of the claim to exclusivity of jurisdiction in which the union controls the work to be performed only by its members in a given territory. Management should insist upon free transportability of craftsmen in and out of the local union's territory. Unions continually attempt to limit the number of travelers brought in to perform work within their territory. Management should insist that there be no restriction on the number of travelers that an employer can bring into or out of the union's territory.

The NLRA declares that strikes and picketing or other disruptions of a job for jurisdictional purposes are unfair labor practices. It also sets up machinery for deciding jurisdictional disputes and provides for injunctions in federal court against any strikes, picketing, or other disruptions of the work caused by jurisdictional disputes. However, the NLRA will recognize any private settlement procedures for jurisdictional disputes in which all parties have an opportunity to participate and will not decide a jurisdictional dispute if the parties have established a private settlement procedure. (See Chapter 4 for a full discussion of jurisdictional disputes.)

The recently revised Plan for Settlement of Jurisdictional Disputes in the Construction Industry created the Impartial Jurisdictional Disputes Board (IJDB), in which practically all international unions and their locals are stipulated as parties. Contractors may be stipulated as parties by individual employers' signing a stipulation agreeing to be bound by IJDB procedures, by their associations' having authority to stipulate the employers to the board, or by negotiating a collective bargaining agreement providing that they are bound by IJDB procedures. The plan contains a no-strike clause in which all unions agree not to strike or picket pending a decision by the IJDB. In the event of picketing or strikes by a union, the employer who submits the dispute to the IJDB should seek a federal court injunction to enjoin all picketing and strikes.

A contractor who has not stipulated to the IJDB may pursue remedies through the procedures of the NLRB. The NLRB decides which union will be entitled to the work on the basis of the contractor's assignment, economy and efficiency, prior practice, area practice, special skills necessary for the performance of the work, and a number of other factors. By contract the IJDB decides disputes on the basis of trade practice, and union agreements, and, unfortunately, many times on the basis of union politics. The IJDB does not seriously consider contractors' assignments or economic realities when deciding which craft union is entitled to the work.

Time is normally important when strikes and picketing force a cessation of the work at a job because of a jurisdictional dispute. When a contractor files charges with the NLRB and follows its procedures, an injunction against picketing and striking can be obtained only by the NLRB, and this procedure takes approximately 1 week. However, to minimize the disruption of the work, the union will often cease picketing if the disputed work is discontinued. Under the Plan for Settlement of Jurisdictional Disputes in the Construction Industry an employer can directly obtain an injunction to enjoin picketing and strikes pending a decision by the IJDB. This type of injunction is called a *Boys Market* injunction after a 1970 U.S. Supreme court case. The procedure to obtain a *Boys Market* injunction to enforce a no-strike clause takes only a few days because the employer can go directly to federal court and seek a temporary restraining order without going through the NLRB.

If there is a no-strike clause in an agreement between the disputing union and the employer, the clause can quickly be enforced in federal court. A typical clause in a bargaining agreement might read:

The union agrees that there shall be no strikes, picketing, or other disruption of the work on account of jurisdictional disputes, which shall be settled through the rules and procedures of the Plan for Settlement of Jurisdictional Disputes in the Construction Industry.

A union which strikes, pickets or otherwise disrupts the work rather than following the established peaceable procedures of settling the dispute by either the NLRB or the IJDB will be liable for damage suits against unions that carry their jurisdictional disputes to the jobsite because the threat of a damage suit deters illegal union activity more than the threat of an injunction. Unions reason that they can picket or strike until an injunction has been obtained and that they can then cease the picketing or striking with impunity. However, damage suits cannot be turned off so easily. Employers should be keenly aware of their right not only to pursue injunctions in jurisdictional disputes under the procedures of both the IJDB and the NLRB but also to seek damage suits against unions that choose to disrupt the work rather than follow these peaceable procedures for settlement.

No-Strike, No-Lockout Clauses

In addition to establishing wages and other common bargaining subjects, an agreement has the further purpose of stabilizing, controlling, and monitoring union-management relations. No-strike, no-lockout clauses are vital to the settlement of disputes.

In the construction industry there are basically two types of no-strike clauses. One limits strikes, while the other totally prohibits them. Under the limited no-strike provision strikes and lockouts are prohibited in the event of a dispute arising out of the agreement. The unconditional no-strike, no-lockout clause prohibits strikes and lockouts for disputes under the agreement and for disputes not covered by the agreement. In either case, if at all possible, an employer should never agree to a no-strike clause that makes an exception of any provision of the agreement. If such exceptions are allowed, it is unlikely that the no-strike provision will be of real value in preventing strikes. The union will simply attempt to cause disputes in the excepted area if strike pressure is required for any desired concession. A good example of a tight no-strike provision is as follows:

Illustrative Example

Under no circumstances will the union cause or permit its members to cause, nor will any member of the union take part in any strike, sit-down, sympathy strike, or slow-down in any work or on any job of the employer or any curtailment of work or restriction of work or interference with the operations of the employer or any picketing or patrolling during the term of this agreement. In the event of a work stoppage, other curtailment of work, picketing, or patrolling, the employer shall not be required to negotiate on the merits of the dispute which gave rise to the stoppage or curtailment.

In the event of a work stoppage, picketing, or patrolling, or other curtailment, the union shall immediately instruct the involved employees in writing that their conduct is in violation of the contract and that they may be disciplined up to and including discharge and instruct all such persons to quit the offending conduct.

The employer shall have the right to discipline up to and including discharge any employee who instigates, participates in, or gives leadership to any activity herein prohibited.

The employer will not lock out any employees during the term of this agreement.

The union will undoubtedly resist such a provision. However, it is to management's advantage, as far as possible, to approach such a tight no-strike, no-lockout provision.

Once a no-strike clause has been incorporated in an agreement, the employer has a potent weapon. Should the union strike or carry on prohibited activities, the employer should not hesitate to seek the available legal remedies of an injunction and damages against the union for violations of the no-strike clause. (See Chapter 4, section "No-Strike Agreements.")

Another type of no-strike, no-lockout clause prohibits strikes after the expiration of the agreement and provides for arbitration of any unsettled issues by a third party. This clause typically appears in local agreements with the electrical, mechanical, and sheet-metal construction trades and provides that all unsettled issues will be submitted to a national joint council of management and union representatives. Some local agreements provide for settlement by arbitration. A typical no-strike clause providing for the settlement of negotiation issues is as follows:

There shall be no stoppage of work either by strike or lockout because of any proposed changes in the agreement or dispute over matters relating to this agreement. All such matters must be handled as stated herein.

There shall be a labor-management committee of three representing the union and three representing the employer. It shall meet regularly at such stated times as it may decide. However, it shall also meet within 48 hours when notice is given by either party. It shall select its own chairman and secretary.

All grievances or questions in dispute shall be adjusted by the duly authorized representatives of each of the parties to this agreement. In the event that these two are unable to adjust any matter within 48 hours, they shall refer the same to the labor-management committee.

All matters coming before the labor-management committee shall be decided by majority vote. Four members of the committee, two from each of the parties hereto, shall be a quorum for the transaction of business, but each party shall have the right to cast the full vote of its membership, and it shall be counted as though all were present and voting. Should the labor-management committee fail to agree or to adjust any matter, such shall then be referred to the National Joint Council for adjudication. The council's decisions shall be final and binding on both parties hereto.

For an employer to be able to seek an injunction enforcing a no-strike clause, the bargaining agreement must contain mandatory grievance and arbitration provisions. The U.S. Supreme Court has held that the existence of such mandatory grievance and arbitration procedures is a prerequisite for enforcing the no-strike clause by injunction. Therefore, the grievance and arbitration machinery should cover all disputes that arise during and under the terms of the collective bargaining agreement and should also apply expressly to any secondary boycotts or sympathy strikes.

Management Rights Clause

The bargaining agreement concerns union rights and benefits which restrict the employer, and it is important that the contract set forth a comprehensive management rights clause to preserve management rights to run the business. For example, the contract might include the following:

Illustrative Example

Nothing in this agreement shall be deemed to limit or restrict the employer in any way in the exercise of the customary functions of management, including the right to make such rules not inconsistent with the terms of this agreement relating to its operation as it shall deem advisable, and the right to hire, suspend, discharge, or otherwise discipline an employee for violation of such rules or for other proper and just cause.

The right to select and hire, to promote a better position, to discharge, demote, or discipline, and to maintain discipline and efficiency of employees, and to determine the schedules of work as recognized by both union and employer is the proper responsibility and perogative of management to be held and exercised by the company in a fair and just manner, and while it is agreed that an employee feeling himself to have been aggrieved by any decision of the employer in respect to such matters, or the union in his behalf, shall have the right to have such decision reviewed by top management officials of the employer under the grievance machinery herein set forth, it is further agreed that the final decision of the employer made by such top management officials shall not be further reviewable by arbitration.

Another example is the following:

Illustrative Example

It is agreed and understood that the employer has the sole and exclusive right to manage his business without limitation in any manner whatsoever unless, and only to the extent, expressly limited by a specific provision of this agreement. It is further agreed and understood that the employer has the sole right to determine the number of employees; make work assignments; direct the employees as to when, how, and where they will be employed; determine the methods, machines, processes, tools, laborsaving devices, and materials to be used; judge the satisfactory performance of work; and make and enforce reasonable rules for the maintenance of discipline, order, and efficiency. Failure of an employee to recognize, abide by, and cooperate with the employer when the above provisions are exercised shall be deemed just cause for disciplinary action.

A clause which is perhaps even stronger is:

Illustrative Example

The employer retains the sole right to manage his business, including but not limited to the right to decide the number and location of projects, the machines, tools, and equipment to be used, the type of construction to be done, the method, place, and company or individuals to conduct any and all prefabricating or subcontracting, the schedules of production, and the processes of assembling, together with all designing, engineering, and the control of semimanufactured and finished parts which may be incorporated into the finished construction; to hire, discharge, lay off, assign, transfer, and promote employees and to determine the starting and quitting time and the number of hours to be worked; and all other rights and perogatives including those exercised unilaterally in the past, subject only to such exercise of these rights as are expressly provided in this agreement.

It should be noted the last of those clauses incorporates an employer's right to subcontract. As a matter of tactics, incorporating a fabrication clause with a management rights clause is advisable. By integrating a fabrication clause with a management rights clause, the fabrication clause is less conspicuous and possibly less likely to be objected to by the union.

Admittedly, such provisions are strong, but it can be argued that if a company is to prosper, it must have the authority to make the best bargain it can for work and services. The company should insist that the primary consideration for its granting any contractual benefits to the union is the inclusion of a strong management rights clause. Such a provision is the foundation of agreement insofar as management is concerned. Furthermore, if an agreement is executed without a management rights clause, the union later will undoubtedly contend that by such an exclusion, management abrogated any of its historical rights which were not set out expressly in their agreement.

Management negotiators must strongly insist upon the inclusion of a definitive management rights clause. A union might argue that by insistence on a strong management rights provision the employer has failed to bargain in good faith over the terms and conditions of employment contained in the provision. However, the U.S. Supreme Court has held that an employer's insistence upon a management rights clause is not inconsistent with the duty to bargain in good faith on mandatory subjects.[24] If the employer is willing to negotiate at reasonable times and places and offers reasons and data to support the argument that a management rights clause in respect to certain employment conditions is necessary for the employer to run the business efficiently, the bargaining obligation is satisfied.

Subcontracting Clauses

This type of clause attempts to restrict management's right to manage. A typical clause preventing contracting work out might read:

Illustrative Example

The employer shall not contract, subcontract, or assign any of the usual work in the union's trade, craft, and geographical jurisdiction to any contractor, subcontractor, or employer who fails to provide for his employees the wages, hours, and economic benefits required by the union for such work, in prevailing collective bargaining contracts between the union and other employers existing at the time of the contracting, subcontracting, or assignment of the employer's work.

Certainly, management should oppose such a clause, as it restricts management's right to choose how and where it will do its work.

To ensure safely the legality of subcontracting to the firm of management's choice, management negotiators should attempt to include a provision specifically allowing the subcontracting of work to other companies, whether union or nonunion. This is particularly true if the contract contains a union membership requirement. In some jurisdictions federal courts have held that a clause making union membership compulsory impliedly includes a ban on subcontracting work out of the unit.

Construction companies often do considerable fabrication before the final work is installed. Prefabricated air conditioning and piping are typical examples. To facilitate the subcontracting of this work to another company and to guarantee the legality of such fabrication even by nonunion shop personnel, the following provision is suggested:

Illustrative Example

It is agreed and understood that the employer shall have the right to subcontract any aspect of the work, including the fabrication of work, to any company, and the employees

[24] *NLRB v. American Nat'l Ins. Co.*, 343 U.S. 495 (1952).

performing said work need not be covered by this agreement. The employees covered by this agreement shall install this material without objection or interruption.

In bargaining over such clauses, it should be remembered that the NLRB has held that unions have the right to bargain for a favorable subcontracting clause pursuant to their right to preserve bargaining-unit work and standards. Management negotiators should argue that subcontracting is exclusively a management decision and also should show that the proposed subcontracting clause is a necessary part of the employer's good business practice. Also, negotiators should present counterproposals to any subcontracting clauses offered by the union. Although management cannot in good faith refuse to bargain over the subcontracting clause, it is under no obligation to accept the union's proposal.

A union can violate the antitrust laws by insisting upon an unlimited clause which restricts subcontracting. The U.S. Supreme Court, in *Connell Construction Company, Inc. v. Plumbers Local Union 100*,[25] held that a union violated the antitrust laws when it picketed the jobsite of a general contractor with whom the union had no previous employer-employee bargaining relationship to force that general contractor to agree to cease subcontracting work to nonunion companies. The decision of the Supreme Court in *Connell* therefore establishes that an employer certainly should not agree to subcontracting restrictions at the request of a union which does not represent its employees. For example, it is possible that when an owner and contractors enter into project agreements which specify that all work will be done by union companies, the owner and contractors have violated the antitrust laws. (See Chapter 4, section "Restrictive Agreements.")

Even in an existing bargaining relationship between an employer and a union which represents its employees, restrictions on subcontracting should be resisted. In the *Connell* case, the Supreme Court also indicated that a ban on subcontracting be limited to a particular jobsite. Therefore, a subcontracting clause must contain language such as the following:

Illustrative Example

The employer shall not contract, subcontract, or assign any of the work *at the [name] jobsite* to any contractor, subcontractor, or employer who fails to provide for its employees the wages, hours, and economic benefits provided for in this agreement.

The *Connell* decision opens the door to future attacks upon subcontracting clauses based upon the antitrust laws. Management negotiators should explain to the union that subcontracting clauses carry with them a high risk of antitrust liability for both the employer and the union. In

[25]421 U.S. 616 (1975).

years to come, these clauses and the employers and unions who enter into them may become a primary target of open-shop companies, since subcontracting clauses force open-shop companies out of large segments of the construction industry. In addition, good business practice dictates that employees have the right to choose the firms with which they will do business. This precious management right should not be conceded by subcontracting clauses to the unions.

Restrictions on Tools, Equipment, and Productivity

Some unions often attempt to restrict the use of tools and equipment. To ensure unrestricted use of tools and modernization of equipment when desired, the following provisions should be considered:

Illustrative Example

The direction of the working force, the right to plan, control, and schedule all operations, in cooperation with other trades and the specified requirements of the user, shall be the responsibility of the employer, including the right to establish, eliminate, change, or introduce new or improved methods, machinery, or techniques to perform all tasks efficiently. There shall be no limitations on the productivity of workers or on full use of tools of the trade and construction of equipment.

These provisions will allow the unrestricted use of tools and will avoid union objections to the use of more modern and mechanized equipment.

The manufacturing industry learned that the best way to increase production was to set standards for employee work. Although the construction industry has generally not set production standards for its employees, many employers in the industry are beginning to learn the value of this technique to increase employee efficiency. Industrial engineering has developed various engineering methods for setting production schedules to increase production. The collective bargaining agreement should stipulate the employer's right to set reasonable production standards by the following clause:

Illustrative Example

The employer shall have the right to establish and enforce reasonable production standards for the work of his employees.

The following is a comprehensive memorandum of agreement negotiated between the building trades and employer associations in Atlanta, Georgia, which has virtually eliminated all restrictive work practices and increased the production of union employees significantly. This agreement to improve productivity has attempted to solve many of the problems that have long plagued the construction industry, including putting an end to jurisdictional strikes, ending all limitations on modern tools and work practices, ending organized coffee breaks and extended lunch periods, and eliminating the nonworking steward, and generally has provided for a full 8 hours of work for 8 hours' pay. Because of the comprehensive nature of this productivity agreement, it is set out in full as follows:

MEMORANDUM OF AGREEMENT
by and between
The North Georgia Building Trades Council, AFL-CIO
and
The Employing Construction Contractors
and Their Respective Associations

Whereas, it is the earnest desire of the parties to this Memorandum of Agreement to provide to the construction buyer who employs the services of the parties to this agreement the most economical construction installations consistent with desired quality and the highest quality of skilled construction craftsmanship, consistent with price, and

Whereas, any given project, be it large or small, must necessarily involve the skills of trained construction Craftsmen performing under the auspices and direction of responsible contractor management teams, and

Whereas, it is the avowed intent that the provisions of this Memorandum of Agreement shall apply to any job where the parties hereto are involved. Now, it is mutually agreed that:

1. There shall be no work stoppage due to unauthorized or illegal strikes, lockouts, disputes or grievances. In the event any jurisdictional or wildcat picketing occurs, the Unions and employees will refuse to honor any such action by continuing to work.

2. The contractor shall have the responsibility to efficiently manage his portion of the job including the supplying of sufficient tools and equipment with which to carry out the needed installation and the scheduling of an adequate number of workmen to meet job requirements and conditions. The direction of the working force, the right to hire, to plan, direct, control and schedule all operations, in cooperation with other trades and the specified requirements of the User, shall be the responsibility of the contractor, including the right to establish, eliminate, change or introduce new or improved methods, machinery or techniques to efficiently perform all tasks.

3. There shall be no limitations on the productivity of workmen or on full use of tools of the trade and construction equipment.

4. Every effort shall be made by the parties to insure the highest level of productivity and the expeditious performance of the work with the pledge of "eight hours work for eight hours pay."

5. All construction site crafts should have a common starting time. At the appointed starting time employees shall immediately proceed to work. There shall be no practices that result in starting work late in the morning or after lunch that result in stopping work early at lunch time or prior to the whistle at the end of the day.

6. There shall be no organized refreshment breaks. Employees will be permitted a break at the employee's immediate work station. The supervisor will designate someone to deliver refreshments but the employees will not leave their work stations for this purpose. There will be no lunch wagons, catering service, cafeteria or vending machine on the job site.

7. No rules, customs, or practices shall be permitted or observed which limit or restrict production or limit or restrict the joint or individual efforts of employees or full use of tools and equipment and it is understood that work productivity shall be maintained at a high level.

8. The unions should recognize the employer's right to establish reasonable company policies and these policies should be distributed, along with safety rules, to all unions and all employees, not to conflict with existing agreements.

9. To insure a sufficient number of skilled craftsmen to meet the needs of the industry, the Parties will continue to expand and improve their presently recognized apprenticeship and journeymen training programs.

10. Whenever possible, and for the best interest of the job, the employer will utilize apprentices to the fullest extent possible, if available.

11. Employees have a responsibility to take care of all tools and equipment on the job and will further make every effort to see that materials are not wasted, lost or damaged.

12. There shall be no non-working stewards.

13. The contractor will not discriminate against the steward in the proper performance of his union duties provided such duties do not interfere with his regular work or with the work of other employees. The union agrees that such duties shall be performed as expeditiously as possible and the contractor agrees to allow the steward a reasonable amount of time to perform during working hours such of his normal union duties as cannot be performed at other times. The steward's duties shall not include any matters relating to referral, hiring, termination or overtime of employees.

14. The employer retains the right to reject any job applicant referred by the union.

15. In the event any union, when requested, is unable to fill any requisitions for applicants within forty-eight (48) hours, the employer may employ applicants from any available source.

16. The employer shall be the sole judge of the employees' capabilities to perform the work in a workmanlike manner. Any violation of quality control standards or work rules established by the employer shall be grounds for discharge.

17. The selection of foremen and general foremen shall be entirely the responsibility of the employer. He shall take orders from individuals designated by the employer.

18. Slowdowns, standby crews and featherbedding practices will not be tolerated on the job.

19. It is agreed that overtime is undesirable and not in the best interest of the industry or the craftsman; therefore, except in unusual circumstances, overtime will not be worked. Where unusual circumstances demand overtime, such overtime will be kept at a minimum and the contractor shall have the right to determine when overtime will be worked and by whom. The steward or his designate will work when any work is performed.

20. The unions shall select and refer applicants to jobs on a non-discriminatory basis and referrals shall not be based on, or in any way affected by, union membership, bylaws, rules, regulations, constitutional provisions or any other aspect or obligation of union membership, race, color, sex, creed, policies, or requirements.

21. Employees must use diligent care to perform their work in a safe manner and to protect themselves and the property of the contractor and owner. Failure to do so may result in immediate dismissal.

22. The project safety rules and the rules and regulations of the Occupational Safety and Health Act shall apply and be abided by during the construction of a project. Each contractor and union shall be responsible for such rules insofar as they apply to their work.

23. Sufficient numbers of journeymen and apprentices will be made available for a project in order that working of overtime will be unnecessary except under extraordinary circumstances. Shift work may be utilized in order to expedite the job and meet completion schedules.

24. It is understood that the User of construction services is concerned with the total project being completed and delivered on time without unnecessary or undue delay created by the involved contractors. Full cooperation and coordination of the efforts of all contractors, their workmen and supervisory personnel is required. The parties hereto pledge to be responsible members of the construction team regardless of their affiliation or lack of affiliation with established trade unions or associations.

25. The requirements of the user with respect to security conditions, safety, maintenance of production, parking and use of vehicles and other regulations will be upheld. The contractor will inform himself of such requirements and, in turn, inform his work force.

26. It shall be the purpose and intent of the North Georgia Building and Construction Trades Council, and its affiliated craft unions to support in toto all existing Federal, State, County and City regulations in support of and directed toward Equal Employment Opportunity for blacks and other minorities, and not to exclude [persons because of] sex, creed [or] color.

27. Under no circumstances will there be a work stoppage or slow-down as a result of work assignment or jurisdictional dispute. Settlement of work assignment shall be as follows:

   a. Rules and procedures of the National Joint Board for the Settlement of Jurisdictional Disputes shall govern the parties to this agreement.

   b. Pre-Assignment Conferences with the contractors and Business Representatives of the Unions shall be held well in advance of actual work performance for the purpose of making a positive determination if there is thought to be a difference of opinion.
   Area practice, prior agreements and decisions of record shall be taken into account; however, in the event a unanimous agreement is not reached, the contractor who has responsibility for the performance and installation shall make specific assignment of the work in accordance with the procedural rules of the National Joint Board which shall be binding on all parties for the duration of the job in question.
   Any jurisdictional disputes occurring during the course of the job shall be handled in the same manner.

It is urged that all employer trade associations in a locality attempt to obtain a similar agreement with their local unions and insert these bargaining clauses into the next collective bargaining agreement.

Discipline of Employees

An agreement should contain a clause defining the basis for discharge or discipline. It is preferable that the employer have the sole right to discharge or discipline employees with a clause such as:

Illustrative Example

The employer retains the sole right to discipiine and discharge employees.

The union may insist that the right of the employer to discipline or discharge employees must be checked by a "just-cause standard." The following clause is an alternative:

Illustrative Example

The employer retains the sole right to discipline and discharge employees for just cause provided that in the exercise of this right he will not act in violation of the terms of this agreement. Complaints that the employer has violated this paragraph may be taken up through the grievance procedure.

Obviously, this provision should be amplified by a strong general management rights clause which would define certain misconduct amounting to cause for discharge.

Another and more detailed provision is:

Illustrative Example

The employer may discipline any employee for just cause. The employer shall have the right to post work rules defining what is expected of the employee, and the employer agrees that he will give written warnings prior to discharge if the misconduct is not so aggravated in the opinion of management as to call for immediate discharge. Grievances protesting disciplinary action must be filed within two working days after the action was taken. Failure to file a grievance within the said two days will result in a waiver of any protest by the employee.

It would be advantageous to management to omit the requirement that discharge be for just cause. "Just cause" invokes a standard which is determinable by the grievance procedure. The absence of just cause in the provision would allow for discharges without resort to the grievance procedure, but such unencumbered grounds for discharge are difficult to obtain. The second-best clause would allow for discharge for just cause. These clauses tie in with a strong general management clause to ensure that management maintains sufficient control to direct its operations. The management rights and disciplinary clauses are the source of strength for management. Therefore, management must insist upon strong provisions in these clauses.

Grievance Procedure

The grievance procedure is simply a process whereby employees' complaints are reviewed. A grievance should be defined clearly. A good example of an appropriate definition is as follows:

Illustrative Example

A grievance under this contract is a written dispute, claim, or complaint arising under and during the term of this labor contract and filed by either an authorized representative of or an employee in the bargaining unit. Grievances are limited to matters of interpretation or application of express provisions of this contract.

The union may complain that such a provision fails to allow grievances on matters not covered by contractual terminology. Management should respond that if there are any areas not covered, the union should mention them and propose their inclusion in the agreement. In short, the union should not be allowed to achieve a grievance adjustment when it has failed or neglected to include or raise such grievance possibilities during negotiations. Generally, the grievance procedure is outlined in step form, and the following clause provides for an equitable and organized manner of resolving grievances:

Illustrative Example

Step 1. The employee shall immediately, but in all cases within three working days of the occurrence of the grievance or dispute, discuss with the employer's representative on the job his grievance or dispute. If the grievance or dispute is not settled to the satisfaction of the employer,

Step 2. The employee shall within five days of the occurrence of the grievance reduce his grievance to writing, setting forth the date, time, and place and section of the agreement with which the grievance or dispute is concerned, and mail this to the office of the union and the employer. The representative of the union will contact the employer for the purpose of resolving this grievance or dispute.

Step 3. Should the parties be unable to resolve this grievance or dispute satisfactorily within ten working days of receipt of grievance, the union may demand arbitration to submit the grievance to an impartial arbitrator agreeable to and selected by the union and the company. If the parties are unable to agree upon an impartial arbitrator within a period of ten days, then either party may request the Federal Mediation and Conciliation Service to submit a list of seven names. After receipt of the names of the seven arbitrators, the parties shall meet and alternate in striking names from the list, with the first striking decided by the tossing of a coin. The remaining name, after each party has struck three names, shall be the impartial arbitrator. The decision of the arbitrator shall be final and binding on both parties. The costs and fees of an arbitrator shall be paid equally by the union and the employer.

Any grievance not carried to the next step by the union within the prescribed time limits or such extensions which may have been agreed to shall automatically be closed on the basis of the last disposition.

There are other possible provisions which can be included in the grievance procedure. One provision which would allow the bypassing of the union in the grievance procedure reads:

Illustrative Example

Provided that any individual employee or a group of employees shall have the right at any time to present grievances to their employer and to have such grievances adjusted, without the intervention of the bargaining representative, as long as the adjustment is not inconsistent with the terms of the collective bargaining contract or agreement then in effect; provided further, that the bargaining representative has been given the opportunity to be present at such adjustment.

Referral of grievances to a joint trade board composed half of union members and half of other employers should, if possible, be avoided, since such boards rarely are neutral. Joint trade boards typically reach a deadlock, with all the union members voting for the union position and all the management members voting for the employer's position. The union members nearly always will side with the union, while the competitor employers may also tend to side with the union. The employer board members gain a plus with the union by siding with the union while simultaneously injuring a competitor. These tendencies should be recognized in attempting to determine whether to submit to a joint trade board or a neutral arbitrator. The better approach is to have a dispute decided by a neutral arbitrator rather than by a joint trade board.

Grievance procedure language is closely related to that of the no-strike provisions previously discussed. Under the grievance and arbitration procedure, an attempt is made satisfactorily to resolve disputes that arise during the life of the contract while not interrupting the employer's work or affecting employees who are not involved in the dispute. In addition, when there is mandatory arbitration of unadjusted grievances, some courts have declared that this is tantamount to a no-strike, no-lockout promise by both parties. An agreement to arbitrate a grievance implies no strike with respect to that grievance. However, to be safe, the contract should include a strong no-strike clause.

Arbitration

Arbitration is basically the end of the grievance procedure. It may be permissive or mandatory. A permissive clause is as follows:

Illustrative Example

Either party may request arbitration of an unsettled grievance, but arbitration is not required unless the opposite party consents and a written submission agreement setting forth the dispute at issue is entered into.

Arbitrators may be selected by union and management from the list submitted by the Federal Mediation and Concilation Service, from the American Arbitration Association, or by some other method when a dispute arises for arbitration. The parties may also agree in their contract to name a permanent arbitrator who will serve throughout the life of the agreement. Such a permanent arbitrator may be needed if there are numerous grievances which typically arise in large industrial companies with many employees. Normally, arbitrators are chosen for a specific grievance, and the parties may agree to select an impartial arbitrator by any means.

Certainly, the choice is not limited to arbitrators named by the Federal Mediation and Conciliation Service or the American Arbitration Association.

If possible, management should attempt to strengthen the arbitration clause by including provisions such as:

Illustrative Example

Excluded from arbitration are disputes in unresolved grievances concerning the discipline or discharge of strikers who struck in violation of the no-strike pledge in this agreement. Excluded from arbitration are unadjusted grievances which question the use or application of any right over which the employer is given unilateral discretion in this agreement or over which the employer has exercised unilateral discretion in the past.

The powers of the arbitrator should be limited with the following clause so that the arbitrator cannot expand the terms of the contract:

Illustrative Example

The arbitrator shall have no power to add or subtract from or modify any of the terms of this agreement or any supplementary agreement or to rule on any matter except while this agreement is in full force and effect between the parties.
The arbitrator shall have no power to establish wage scales or rates on new or changed jobs or to change any wage rate.
The arbitrator shall have no power to rule on the proper assignment of work by the employer to members of various unions.
The arbitrator shall have no power to provide agreements for the parties in cases in which they have agreed in their contract that further negotiations should occur to cover the matters in dispute.
In the event that a case is appealed to an arbitrator and he finds that he has no power to rule on such case, the matter shall be referred back to the parties without decision or recommendation on the merits of the case.

Another important clause pertaining to arbitration is to provide specifically that both parties will bear the expense of the arbitrator. Finally, the contract should provide:

Illustrative Example

There shall be no appeal from an arbitrator's decision. It shall be final and binding on the union, on all bargaining-unit employees, and on the employer. The union will discourage any attempt by any bargaining-unit employee and will not encourage or cooperate with any bargaining-unit employee in any appeal to any court or labor board from a decision of the arbitrator.

The grievance and arbitration procedure is helpful to both employer and union. The employer benefits by avoiding the economic detriment of strikes, and the union benefits by having an organized procedure to file its complaints and to have such complaints ruled upon impartially. For both parties it provides a stabilized work environment, which is one of the principal goals of a bargaining agreement.

Hours of Work and Overtime

Most problems regarding hours of work and overtime arise as a result of ambiguities in or omissions from the bargaining agreement. Management negotiators should prepare a proposal for hours of work and overtime that is comprehensive and clear. It should take into account every conceivable possibility for dispute. For example, if in the type of construction work being done the employers prefer working evenings or shifts, the negotiating committee should be careful to avoid a provision which would require overtime premium pay for all work performed outside normal working hours or to provide for a differential in wages for different shifts.

The employers should strive to manage the workforce and retain the right to schedule employees' working hours. They should at least be able to require working shift time with only a minimum pay differential. The following is an example of a good shift clause:

Illustrative Example

Shift work shall be performed at the option of the employer. Employees working on the second or third shift shall receive the basic hourly rate of pay for the actual hours worked.

It is more usual that employers are required to concede to a shift differential; then the following language would be added:

Illustrative Example

The hourly rate for the men working on the second and third shift shall be _____ percent, respectively, over and above the basic hourly rate.

Probably no section in the contract provokes more numerous disputes in collective bargaining or throughout the life of the contract than that covering hours worked overtime. The provision covering hours of work and overtime should be clear to avoid disputes, as in the following clause:

Illustrative Example

Eight hours shall constitute a workday. The workday shall be scheduled from 8:00 A.M. to 4:30 P.M. for five (5) consecutive days. A half hour will be provided for lunch, normally scheduled between 12:00 noon and 1:00 P.M. An employer shall have the option to vary the starting time of the shift within one hour of 8:00 A.M.

It is important to avoid language which will entitle employees to overtime pay for all work performed outside normal or regular working hours unless the employee has already worked in excess of 8 hours, in the case of daily overtime, or in excess of 40 hours for weekly overtime contracts. The employer should make sure not to include a provision entitling employees to overtime for work performed outside regular working hours, since if the employer for some reason must make a temporary change in the work schedule, under such a provision employees would be entitled to overtime pay for work outside normal working hours even though they work 8 or fewer hours in the day.

Wage and Fringe Benefits

Most bargaining focuses on wages and fringe benefits. As a matter of tactics, it is essential that wages and fringe benefits be negotiated as a total package. Otherwise, if wages have been settled, the union will bend all efforts on the fringe benefits. Most data collected by the negotiating team will undoubtedly pertain to wages. Therefore, management generally should be well armed with data to repel union demands for higher wages. Tactically, it is best to avoid, if possible, committing management to a top wage offer. Instead, management should attempt to chip away at the union demands before committing itself to any figure. To avoid appearing thin on data as bargaining becomes serious, management negotiators should keep in reserve some data that support their offer on wages and fringe benefits. They should also avoid making final offers early, as early negotiations tend to be plagued by rejection of offers on both sides. Once an offer has been rejected by the union, it likely will never be accepted, so management's final offer should be held out until serious negotiations and concessions are being made by the union.

The wage clause should include:

1. The hourly rate and an overtime hourly rate
2. Frequency and dates of payment
3. Manner of payment (cash or check)
4. Number of days of wages held back upon initial employment
5. Payment upon layoff or discharge

The employer bargaining committee should insist upon the right of management to change the dates and manner of payments for business reasons. Payment in cash should be avoided since it is administratively cumbersome and very hazardous from a security standpoint. The contract should stipulate that overtime and other premium payments should not be pyramided; otherwise, an employee might claim a daily overtime premium on top of weekend or holiday premium pay.

A problem frequently arises when an employee who works on a holiday, vacation day or scheduled day of rest is covered by a contract which entitles the employee to pay for idle time on these days and premium pay for time worked on these days. The contract should be clear as to whether an employee who works on any of these days also has a right to idle-time pay.

The fringe-benefits clause should provide for joint administration of each fringe-benefit fund, and management should take steps to ensure that it is actively represented in the administration of the fund. (See Chapter 8 for a discussion of employee fringe-benefit plans.) To avoid making the fund a base of union control and thus of power for the union, it is imperative that management take advantage of its legal right to participate actively in the administration of the fund.

Management should always negotiate fringe benefits in dollars and cents, not in percentages. A percentage of fringe benefits which is fixed at a wage level will automatically increase in future years when wages are increased without the union having to negotiate for increased fringe benefits. It should not allow the union unilaterally to determine how much of any wage increase may be placed in the fringe benefits. Management should avoid agreeing to a union demand that "it is our money, and we will do what we want to do with it." Fringe benefits are subjects of bargaining and should be seriously bargained by the management committee.

Seniority

A number of possible seniority clauses may be placed in an agreement. In the construction industry, seniority clauses should be opposed. Employers should have the right to determine the competence of their employees, and seniority clauses usurp employers' rights to utilize and reward ability.

Employees with special or extraordinary ability may be needed out of line of seniority to facilitate certain work. Further, seniority clauses illogically reward time in a position while ignoring the ability of less senior employees. This frustrates the more capable but less senior employees and thereby adversely affects production.

The contract should stipulate that the employer has the right to reject any applicant, to determine the number and competence of employees, and to hire, transfer, promote, lay off, recall, and discharge employees. If the employer cannot avoid a seniority clause, the negotiating committee should carefully phrase the language so that length of service with the employer will prevail only if ability, experience, and training are equal. Particularly to be avoided is language that length of service shall govern if the senior employee can do the work satisfactorily. It may well be that the junior employee by ability and experience is able to do the work much more efficiently. Any seniority clause should apply only to layoff and recall of employees and should not permit bumping by a laid-off employee to another job.

Most-Favored-Nation Clause

Because of the competitive nature of the construction industry, it is vital that management ensure in its contract that other employers will not gain a competitive edge by obtaining more favorable terms from the union. The parties to a collective bargaining agreement can guard against one employer's obtaining such a competitive edge by inserting the most-favored-nation clause that typically appears in treaties between nations to guarantee that one nation will not be granted more favorable terms than another nation. Therefore, management should insert a clause to ensure that if more favorable terms are granted by the union to other employers, the present collective bargaining agreement will be automatically amended to incorporate the most favorable terms. A short most-favored-nation clause is as follows:

Illustrative Example

In the event that the union grants to any employer, orally or in writing, privileges, terms, or conditions of employment more advantageous than those contained in this agreement, then the employer shall have the immediate right to adopt, and the union will grant, the more favorable conditions to all employers doing the identical type of work.

An employer must be very careful in phrasing a most-favored-nation provision. According to the U.S. Supreme Court, an agreement that the union will not grant more favorable terms to any employer than those which are included in the employer's contract with the union will subject the union and the employer to antitrust liability.[26] Even though employer and union are permitted or even required to bargain over the conditions of employment included in a most-favored-nations clause, the clause violates the Sherman Antitrust Act as a conspiracy to restrain commerce if the parties agree to impose the same or more favorable terms on other employers.

Retroactivity

Often an old agreement expires before a new agreement is reached. In such cases the union will insist that the new agreement be effective retroactively from the date on which the former contract expired. Such clauses, if possible, should be rejected. Very likely the acceptance of such a clause will result in paying back fringe benefits and other personal problems. Moreover, even if retroactivity is to be agreed to, it is ill advised to make such an admission early in the bargaining. The concession will result in the union's holding out for more benefits as it knows that they will be paid retroactively no matter when an agreement is reached. On the other hand, to reject retroactivity immediately will cause the union to speed up bargaining: the earlier an agreement, the earlier it will reap the benefits of that agreement.

Complete-Agreement Clause

It is advisable to insert a wrap-up clause under which both parties agree that all matters not covered by the agreement, including matters negoti-

---

[26] *United Mine Workers v. Pennington*, 381 U.S. 657 (1965).

ated or discussed, are expressly waived and that the written agreement is an agreement by all parties which can be amended only in writing. A complete-agreement, or wrap-up clause, is as follows:

Illustrative Example

It is the intent of the parties hereto that the provisions of this Agreement, which supersede all prior agreements and understandings, oral or written, express or implied, between such parties, shall govern their entire relationship and shall be the sole source of any and all rights or claims which may be asserted in arbitration hereunder or otherwise.

The provisions of this agreement can be amended, supplemented, rescinded, or otherwise altered only by mutual agreement in writing hereafter signed by the parties hereto.

The parties hereto mutually agree not to seek during the term of this agreement to negotiate or bargain with respect to any matters pertaining to rates of pay, wages, hours of employment, or other conditions of employment, whether or not covered by this agreement or in the negotiations leading thereto, and any rights in that respect are hereby expressly waived.

7 SPECIAL AGREEMENTS[1]

Fragmentation has been cited repeatedly as a source of many of the problems of the construction industry. This fragmentation is particularly evident in the collective bargaining structure of the industry's unionized sector, with local contractor associations bargaining individually with the locals of eighteen international unions and generating about 10,000 local agreements. In addition, the industry has seen a proliferation of special agreements superimposed on the local agreements for individual jobs or particular types of work. Over several decades a wide variety of special agreements have been negotiated to cope with situations in which the local agreements have been perceived as inadequate for the work in question. Although the inadequacies vary as widely as the agreements, the most commonly cited reasons for special agreements are attempts to avoid work stoppages, to get greater assurance of adequate labor supplies, and to avoid the inefficient or inflationary provisions of local agreements.

Special agreements have evolved from attempts to correct one or more deficiencies in construction industry labor relations. For reasons including poor labor supply in remote regions, a lack of responsible local construction management, a multitude of short-term agreements expiring at different times, and the inclusion in local agreements of work practices and referral procedures not suited to large projects or specialty work, special agreements have become commonplace.

An owner has often faced the choice either of accepting what is in existence (and often is less than adequate) or of encouraging the contractor to negotiate a special agreement more responsive to the project in question. This situation has persisted because many local contractor associations have lacked both the time and the experience to arrive effectively at satisfactory agreements at the bargaining table, as well as the economic strength to withstand a prolonged strike, or simply have signed agreements detrimental to large projects because the work in question does not affect them. Unions, recognizing a competitive threat from open-shop construction or in-house forces, have frequently been receptive to special agree-

[1]Substantial portions of this chapter on special agreements have been reprinted from the report of the Business Roundtable Task Force on Special Building Trades Agreements.

ments to help union contractors improve their competitive position and thereby provide more jobs for union workers.

Some controversy has arisen among contractor associations and owners over these special agreements, the primary contention being that they undermine local bargaining. Local contractor negotiations are often conducted exclusively by local contractors. These contractors understandably are concerned primarily with the type of work which they perform, and the resulting contracts are often ill suited to efficient performance on large projects. Frequently, local contractor negotiators have been unreceptive to suggestions from owners or other affected contractors regarding contract provisions. National contractors are interested primarily in the timely completion of a particular project. Despite the impact of local negotiations on their future work, they sometimes offer little input to local bargaining and have often seemed oblivious to the impact of their activities on local management's bargaining position.

There is little question that firm no-strike, no-lock-out clauses in special agreements weaken local contractor groups at the bargaining table, particularly if a strike occurs and the project in question becomes a haven for strikers. This situation is detrimental not only to the local contractors but also to the owners, who must absorb the costs of excessive wage increases and inefficient work practices which result from the disadvantaged position of the local management negotiating group.

Project agreements have been the most controversial of the special agreements. Some view them as an anachronism, a temporary expedient which exists only because of the inadequacies of local construction bargaining and one which will disappear if and when construction collective bargaining responds in some other way to industry needs. Others view them as a beneficial means of gaining contract improvements for a specific project, in situations in which local unions recognize the threat of other labor sources and are willing to include in a project agreement features which for political reasons they are unwilling to incorporate across the board in local agreements. A project agreement can be a constructive influence on local bargaining if local-contractor input is obtained in negotiating the agreement, a clause permitting the contractor to support local contractors during an economic strike is included, and local bargainers later seek to incorporate in their local agreements any more favorable work practices that have been included in the project agreement.

National construction agreements negotiated by the National Constructors Association (NCA) and the Building and Construction Trades Department of the AFL-CIO on a national level are considered by most owners to have been beneficial on larger projects. As in the case of project agreements, the primary objection to national agreements has been the undermining of local bargaining by the continuation of work through economic strikes. This issue has been diminished by the inclusion in some national agreements of a "5-day clause" which permits support of local contractors, and by better understanding among owners of the impact of lack of support of local bargaining groups. More recently, dissatisfaction with locally negotiated wages, fringe benefits, and work practices has spurred interest in industry-sector multicraft national agreements that include rates for wages and fringe benefits.

National specialty agreements have generally been effective in providing skilled labor on specialized work and in many cases have been extremely advantageous by allowing an influx of skilled craftsmen from outside the local area when labor shortages exist and by providing temporary intercraft flexibility. Such agreements have covered many employees in pipeline, tank, and elevator construction. National specialty associations have also negotiated agency-type national specialty agreements such as the agreements covering interior construction between the Wall and Ceiling Contractors Association International and the Carpenters, Plasterers, Lathers, Laborers, Bricklayers, and Painters.

In-house and open-shop maintenance pose an ever-increasing competitive threat to the construction trades. To combat this threat there have evolved maintenance agreements permitting greater flexibility among the crafts and eliminating many costly work practices, such as double time for overtime, shift differentials, coffee breaks, and so on. These agreements have become a significant benefit to both the large industrial user and the local unions. In practice, however, they have not generally yielded the potentially available efficiencies because of reluctance on the part of both union members and contractor supervision to depart from construction work practices. Greater acceptance of maintenance agreement hinges upon the development of an effective mechanism for changing construction work rules and wage rates.

Overall no single clear path to solve the problems of construction collective bargaining has evolved. Each of the types of special agreements examined appears to have filled a constructive role in some circumstances. Each can be beneficial to owners by reducing labor costs and construction delays and often can contribute to longer-term improvements. The key importance of negotiating and implementing these agreements so that they are not detrimental to local bargaining and, when possible, support and contribute to it must not be overlooked. The greatest need is for improved openness and meaningful communication among contractor bargaining groups whose actions affect one another. Secrecy and isolation in construction collective bargaining have been a divisive element and the root of many animosities.

Many owners and contractors are generally in agreement in endorsing the following general recommendations:

1. Owners should urge national contractors on major work to maintain communication with local contract bargainers, seriously consider their views, and seek ways of supporting local bargaining most effectively.

2. Owners should urge local contract bargainers to communicate their bargaining goals to both the local owners and the national contractors in the area and to invite input and dialogue.

3. Contractors should seek provisions in national and project agreements to allow suspension of work in support of local bargaining in the event of a local economic strike.

4. Owners should recognize the independent employer status of their contractors and not attempt to usurp the contractors' prerogatives in their labor relations with their employees. They should strive to understand construction labor problems which can affect their businesses and effectively make their views known to their contractors (especially regarding the provisions of any project agreement which might be negotiated for their facilities) but should avoid direct participation in negotiations or becoming signatories to an agreement.

5. Efficiencies gained at the negotiating table can be quickly lost by poor administration in the field. Owners should develop an understanding of the provisions of agreements applicable to their work and strongly encourage their contractors to implement the agreements fully so as to realize all potentially available efficiencies.

6. Contractors foreign to an area should consult local contracting groups or associations regarding local work practices and jurisdictional precedents. They should avoid arbitrary departures from local practices in ways which decrease efficiency or set undesirable precedents for the local contractors.

7. In the event of a local economic strike, owners and their special-agreement contractors should each consider how they can appropriately support local bargainers. Among the options are suspension of work, suspension of hiring, and reduction in the workforce of the striking craft.

8. Agreements in advance to pay retroactively any negotiated wage increases to employees who work through a local strike tend further to undermine local bargaining and should be avoided. Owners should urge their contractors to make wage increases effective on the date of the new agreement or the date of return to work after a strike, whichever is later.

NO-STRIKE, NO-LOCKOUT PROVISIONS

Owners and investors involved in construction projects have a natural concern about the effect of work stoppages on their project costs and schedules. There have been numerous examples of costly delays on large projects because of strikes and slowdowns resulting from jurisdictional disputes or bargaining at the expiration of local contracts. Many owners and contractors have attempted to avoid these delays by the simplistic approach of a no-strike, no-lockout clause in project and national agreements. (See Chapter 4, section "No-strike Agreements.")

Of course, the theory behind the no-strike, no-lockout clause is to spare the owner and the contractors, by virtue of their special agreements, the threat of a strike every time that one of the more than eighteen individual unions reaches an impasse with a local bargaining group. Building trades unions have usually been eager to offer a no-strike pledge in return for a no-lockout agreement by the contractors, especially if it is accompanied by a guarantee of retroactive payment of any locally negotiated wage settlement.

No-strike clauses have been the most controversial feature in special agreements because of their effect on the local labor relations situation when an agreement provides the opportunity for a contractor to continue working through a local economic strike. When local-contractor bargainers find major portions of the union membership able to continue working through a local strike because of such a clause, the strike becomes a single-edged weapon, directed only against the contractor bargainers. Thus, the owner and the special-agreement contractor, by virtue of the fact that they employed a significant number of members of a striking craft or crafts, can weaken the bargaining strength of the local contractors, thereby increasing the possibility of a poor settlement. Since most special agreements automatically incorporate locally negotiated wages and working conditions, such inflationary settlements are quickly felt by the owners.

More specifically, concern about no-strike clauses has arisen from the following sequential effects:

1. When work continues through a local strike on a project with labor requirements which constitute a substantial portion of the local-union membership, the union can provide work for most of its active voting members on the project. Working members contribute to strike funds which help support the minority who are on strike and unable to find other employment. This makes the strike a single-edged economic weapon, putting pressure only on the contractor management side of the bargaining table. Settlements arrived at under these circumstances have included highly inflationary wage and fringe benefit increases and efficiency-stifling work practices.

2. Union leaders, recognizing their position of strength in such circumstances, press for exorbitant demands and call strikes in situations in which peaceful settlements could otherwise be reached.

3. Smaller construction jobs on offices, schools, hospitals, sewer plants, and so on that are not covered by special agreements suffer costly work stoppages.

4. Animosities develop among contractors and owners because of these effects. These have sometimes resulted in the introduction into local agreements of costly provisions which impinge only on local industrial projects.

5. The cost of all future construction soars because of inflated settlements, and thus the entire community must pay the bill.

These undesirable and divisive effects can be avoided without sacrificing most of the benefits of special agreements. Many project and national agreements today include a 5-day notice-of-contract-termination clause. This clause allows a contractor the option of shutting down work requiring the use of employees represented by a union on strike against the local employer bargaining group. It sacrifices none of the protection against strikes over jurisdictional or other disputes while the local contracts are in effect. There is a widespread view that the 5-day option clause is an essential element of national or project agreements. It preserves all the options for a review in the light of conditions at the time the decision must be made instead of "giving away the store" well in advance.

It is true, of course, that at least a portion of the economic costs of exercising the 5-day clause must be borne by the owner, as is also true of the longer-term costs of not exercising it if an inflationary settlement results. The owner always bears the cost of delayed completion which results from the increase in the time during which the owner's investment is non-productive. In many cases the owner also reimburses the contractor for continuing overhead and other expenses during the shutdown, but this reimbursement is dependent on either prior agreement or subsequent negotiation. In each instance, the owner must assess the likely long-term costs of undermining local bargaining versus the short-term economic impact of shutting down the work. An owner should consider the following in deciding whether to encourage a contractor to give a 5-day notice of intent to shut down the work:

1. The economic impact on the owner's business of delay in the project (this is often overestimated.)

2. The compensating higher costs of the remaining work on the current project and of all future construction work which could result from a higher-than-otherwise settlement if the work is not shut down. Added to this is the ultimate impact of a higher construction settlement on wage levels and work practices of industrial plant employees.

3. The fact that experience has shown that construction work on a no-strike job is often less efficient during an area strike. Union efforts to distribute unemployment result in high turnover and sometimes in overstaffing. Productivity and work quality decline.

4. The fact that after settlement of an area economic strike some of the card-carrying union members who shifted to the no-strike project during the strike will return to their preferred positions with a local contractor. This turnover has a detrimental effect on productivity which may continue for several weeks after the strike settlement.

5. The possibility that a strike will not occur when notice of intent to shut down is filed. Giving a 5-day notice is often sufficient stimulus to serious bargaining that a strike is averted. The strikes which do occur tend to be shorter when there is unified contractor support.

Contractors must recognize, however, that sometimes an owner will determine that the short-term economic impact on business of shutting down a project is too high to afford. In such cases, contractors and owners have found the following considerations helpful in reducing the impact on local bargaining of continuing the work and lowering the total cost to the owner.

1. When shutting down is anticipated well in advance, it is sometimes possible to reprogram the project so as to shift some of the work of the affected craft ahead of the contract expiration date or to defer it until later.

2. On some occasions, the union may shift men in advance of contract expiration so as to replace travelers or permit men on the no-strike job with local card carriers. If this is happening, hiring can sometimes be suspended a few weeks in advance of contract expiration.

3. During a strike contractors can reduce crews as much as possible and can sometimes suspend hiring of the striking craft.

4. It is generally recognized that an agreement to pay retroactively a yet-to-be-negotiated increase is detrimental to local bargaining.

In summary, the inclusion of a firm no-strike, no-lockout clause in special agreements can have a seriously unfavorable impact on construction costs and efficiency. The short-term benefits of such a clause are highly questionable, particularly when compared with potential long-term costs.

PROJECT AGREEMENTS

Project agreements are ad hoc in nature, apply only to specific projects, and exist only for the duration of those projects. They are multicraft agreements, generally signed by the local building trades council or all local unions involved, or both, and by the prime contractors on the project. Provisions supersede those in applicable local agreements, but project agreements rely on local agreements for wage and fringe-benefit rates and for any other provisions which they do not specifically address.

When project agreements were first developed, they were sought by contractors. Today, owners often provide the driving force to negotiate a project agreement; sometimes an owner is a signatory and "imposes" the agreement on contractors who desire to work on the project.

Management's objectives for project agreements include (1) securing more advantageous terms and conditions from management's point of view than are contained in the local agreements; (2) stabilizing the cost of the project as much as possible; (3) involving international union officials in the staffing of large projects, at times in remote areas; (4) easing contractor management of a large project by bringing all unions under a single stable agreement; and (5) decreasing exposure to work stoppages.

Today union leaders see project agreements as a means of assuring the use of union employees in the face of open-shop competition and as a stabilizing influence when the high employment levels of a large project might otherwise encourage activist members to press for unreasonable work practices. These considerations sometimes make possible the exclusion of the productivity-stifling provisions of local agreements at a time when removal of these provisions from local agreements would be politically unacceptable to the union leadership.

Project agreements existed as far back as the 1930s when they were used on large jobs to pin down labor costs in the face of obvious unionization. For instance, in 1937–1938 a portion of Grand Coulee Dam was built under a project agreement between the Washington State Building Trades Department and a joint venture headed by Guy F. Atkinson Company. In 1940 the Shasta Dam in California was built under a project agreement between the building trades and a ten-company contractor group.

The practice of such agreements was continued during World War II for atomic energy installations and other government war production enterprises. After the war the use of project agreements was continued for certain large projects. Most major dams built with union labor on rivers west of the Mississippi after 1945 for instance, were built under project agreements. Contractors for these jobs wanted to eliminate uncertainties about labor costs for firm unit-price bidding, and they obtained assurances of no strikes in their project agreements. In some instances, they referred to local agreements for their wages; in others, wages for a period of several years were included. If wages were included, the local-contractor bargaining representatives were sometimes consulted before the project agreement was reached or were invited to be present at the bargaining.

In the 1950s project agreements continued to be used for other large projects such as the atomic energy plants at Paducah, Kentucky, and Portsmouth, Ohio, and the expansions at Washington, Hanford, and Oak Ridge, Tennessee. Multiple sites for a single large project also were covered, as in the St. Lawrence Seaway Agreement, which was really a loose series of addenda to local agreements for the geographically spread-out project. The Missile Sites Agreement, in the early 1960s, was another example of a multiple-site agreement.

Public-type projects like the New York World's Fair and major amusement centers also were covered under project agreements in the 1960s. An example from that era, the Disneyworld Agreement (1968), included a no-strike clause and a settlement procedure for jurisdictional disputes. It also provided for shift work, a flexible day-shift schedule, the elimination of travel and subsistence pay, a grievance procedure, and a contractor management rights clause. In addition, local contractor groups and unions renegotiated their contracts to carry the same expiration date as that of the project agreement.

In the mid-1960s construction unions began to capitalize on their greater power at the bargaining table over local contractors. The result was an accelerated rate of construction wage inflation, an increase in restrictive and costly work practices, and an erosion of contractor management rights. Many national contractors, who did not participate in local bargaining, and their industrial owner clients believed that this imbalance of power was not their problem. By ignoring it, by emphasizing project completion, and by working during pivotal local strikes, they enhanced the power of the unions. Gradually owners realized that construction bargaining was sharply increasing their field costs, was affecting their own in-plant wage costs, and in many other ways was increasing the cost of doing business. Lower-cost open-shop construction, when feasible, became one of the owners' options.

Project agreements proliferated in the late 1960s and the 1970s, stimulated by this rapid increase in competitive open-shop construction, the dismay of owners over their inflated union construction labor costs, and the recognition by unions, in varying degrees and in varying areas, of the undesirability of pricing themselves out of work by high wage costs and restrictive work practices. This acclerating proliferation of project agreements has been a source of concern, especially to building trades leadership and to some elements of contractor management. Some fear that the system is out of control and may be proceeding in directions contrary to the long-term best interests of the industry.

The provisions of these agreements have ranged from little more than a no-strike clause and hiring procedures in some early arrangements to very detailed conditions under which the workforce is to be managed. Today project agreements generally are becoming more specific in delineating contractor management rights and eliminating costly work practices. In many agreements the no-strike provision has been modified so that with a 5-day notice either the contractor or the union may support local bargaining (stop work or withdraw workers). Since these agreements have been developed in most instances for very large projects, the contractor signatory is usually a large national contractor. In a few instances the owner becomes a signatory to the agreement along with the contractor and the unions.

The use of project agreements has been a source of irritation between national contractors and local contractors responsible for local bargaining. The national contractors have blamed the local contractors for the provisions of local labor agreements which cause inefficiency or are slanted against visiting contractors on large projects, while the local contractors have accused the national contractors of agreeing to undesirable provisions which had been kept out of local agreements by local contractors and of undermining local bargaining by working during strikes. These attitudes are less prevalent today. There is greater recognition by each group of the different conditions and pressures to which they are exposed and increasing acceptance of the need for national and local contractors to coordinate their bargaining activities in order to improve their mutual positions without detriment to each other.

Not all owners press for project agreements. Many feel that an experienced and well-managed contractor working under local or national agreements can be at least as efficient overall as one working under a project agreement. In a recent survey of user groups, owners who have employed project agreements expressed general satisfaction with the performance of their contractors but would like to see stronger implementation of the terms of the agreements. When difficulties were encountered, they seemed to stem from contractor supervisors who found it difficult to change their own habitual ways of running a job, particularly in the face of resistance to any innovative project agreement terms at the worker-steward level.

Owners also believe that there has been a limited incorporation of some of the gains made in project agreements into local agreements in later negotiations, but not as yet to a very significant extent. Certain provisions may not be relevant to the work of local contractors. Project agreements are only one of many influences, including the coordination of contractor bargaining, the upgrading of contractor bargaining, and an attitudinal change by the building trades unions, which can produce lasting improvements in local agreements. Project agreements can make a contribution only in combination with some of these other forces, and when improvements are made in local agreements, assessment of the relative influence of each force is virtually impossible. Nevertheless, it is felt that properly developed and administered project agreements can be a constructive influence on local bargaining.

In a few recent instances owners have become party to a project agreement in addition to the contractor and the building trades unions. Owners have cited a number of reasons for this participation: concern over construction labor costs, need for assurance before contractor selection that efficient work rules will apply on the project, anxiety to follow the negotiations more intimately and exercise greater control by being closer to the action, and a desire to lend their weight and support to the contractor position.

In addition, there is increasing union awareness of freedom of choice for owners, who are paying the bill, and a desire by the unions to discuss construction problems directly with owners to convince them that they should remain with union construction. The complexity and critical nature of a project might also prompt an owner to become directly involved. The Alaska Pipeline provides an example of this: a consortium of oil companies negotiated with the Building and Construction Trades Department the agreement under which their contractors subsequently worked.

An owner should exercise extreme legal caution before becoming a signatory to a project agreement which limits the work to union contractors. Because the owner may not be in the construction industry, the agreement may be an illegal "hot-cargo agreement," and the effect of the owner's agreement with the unions may also be illegal restraint of trade in violation of the antitrust laws. (See Chapter 4, section "Restrictive Agreements.")

Before undertaking a signatory role, owners are also urged to give serious consideration to the following possible effects:

1. The contractor's responsibility as employer for the management of the work may be undermined by owner participation in project agreement negotiations.

2. It is possible that an owner might be viewed as a coemployer under labor law if the owner either participates directly in project agreement bargaining or becomes a signatory to the agreement.

3. From an overall point of view, there is a danger of further fragmenting the construction industry by adding one more participant, the owner, in the collective bargaining process and of doing serious harm to the position of the contractor.

In general, contractors strongly object to the direct involvement of an owner in negotiating project agreements. Contractors feel that they are better equipped to evaluate the tradeoffs which arise in negotiations and believe that owners can make their influence felt more effectively through contractors.

Project agreements have existed in one shape or another for a long time in construction. In the unique environment of this industry, it is safe to assume that in the foreseeable future project agreements will continue because there will be instances in which they will be in the interest of all of the three parties concerned: contractor, owner, and union. Perhaps the growth will not be as extensive as it was in the early 1970s because the building trades unions are disturbed by the competition among contractors to win additional concessions with each new agreement. On the other hand, there will always be a unique project of such complexity, duration, technical difficulty, area, size, or critical nature that a conventional labor agreement will not cover it adequately. The optimum approach appears to be not to deny the parties access to a project agreement but to encourage them to fashion an agreement that meshes with the surrounding collective bargaining environment.

There are several ways to facilitate such an agreement:

1. A contractor seeking a project agreement may find it useful to consult local-contractor bargaining groups as a resource in negotiations. They can provide information on bargaining history, agreement provisions, union leadership, and so on in the locality. The representative of a local contractor sitting in the negotiations as an observer-adviser might also be helpful.

2. It is poor strategy and a divisive practice for contractor groups not to review with each other their negotiations with the same union workforce. Project agreements may provide the owners with an opportunity to encourage multiple-contractor groups to work together harmoniously.

3. An owner can encourage a contractor to include a 5-day notice of termination clause to allow the contractor to support local bargaining when local agreements are being renegotiated. The owner can also impress on the contractor the importance of contractor unity in local bargaining. (This subject is discussed in greater detail in the preceding section, "No-Strike, No-Lockout Provisions.")

4. Local-contractor bargaining groups can in turn invite the project agreement contractor into their local prenegotiation discussions and possibly into actual union negotiation meetings as an observer-adviser. The rationale is the same as for coordination in negotiating the project agreement.

5. Project agreement terms should be adhered to by both sides. It makes no sense to win concessions at the bargaining table and give them away in the field. Owners should understand the special provisions of any project agreements applicable to their work and should monitor the performance of their contractors in implementing them.

Local contractors will always be a major factor in unionized construction because of the local nature of the construction industry. Even when project and other special agreements are employed on major projects, local contractors will continue to handle other portions of the industrial owner's work and often will act as subcontractors on the larger projects.

A local contractor who believes that local agreements should serve all of an owner's requirements faces a twofold challenge: (1) to reorganize bargaining to eliminate the local fragmentation that so weakens the contractor's strength and (2) to incorporate in the agreements the modifications and flexibility required to serve the owner's needs. Sometimes a local contractor may have the opportunity to accelerate the improvement of local agreements by pressing for incorporation of those elements of a project agreement which have proved beneficial.

National contractors can contribute to this process by inviting local-contractor input into project agreement negotiations and by contributing to local negotiations in areas where they are working. With the cooperation of local and project agreement contractors, project agreements can be supportive and not disruptive of local bargaining.

NATIONAL CONSTRUCTION AGREEMENTS

Most labor contracts governing construction wages and working conditions are negotiated by local unions and contractor associations, usually on a single-craft basis, in thousands of locations across the United States. A substantial volume of work in the industry, however, is performed by large contractors, operating around the country, who do not participate in such local bargaining. The existence of such national contractors has led to the development of national construction agreements.

National construction agreements have been a significant element in collective bargaining in the construction industry for the last 30 years or so, but their history is more than twice that long. They existed even before World War I, when a few large contractors found them to be useful. Among the first of these contractors was Stone & Webster Engineering Corporation of Boston, which signed a national agreement with the Bricklayers International Union on September 1, 1911. Stone & Webster was already designing and building power plants, which in those days were monuments to the arts of stone masonry and bricklaying. The company was also active in institutional and large-scale commercial construction, and it included masonry supervisors on its permanent management staff.

The United Brotherhood of Carpenters and Joiners of America was also an early participant in national agreements. Among the first companies to sign agreements with this union were Raymond Concrete Pile Company (now Raymond International), in 1919, and Leonard Construction, on August 27, 1920. The Carpenters' agreement, in those pre-Taft-Hartley Act days, was a closed-shop contract, the employer agreeing to hire union members only. The union pledged itself to make no changes in hours and wages in any locality and to "impose no conditions other than are enforced on all local firms." The union also agreed not to strike "pending any dispute being investigated and all peaceable means taken to bring about a settlement."

At that time a national agreement was little more than a "hunting license," a document that permitted a contractor to obtain workers from a local union when operating in areas outside a company's home territory. A major *quid pro quo* was that the contractor recognize the union's jurisdictional claims, pay the locally established or claimed wage rate, and comply with local working rules. For the national or international union, a national agreement was doubtless an organizing tool in areas in which the national contractor had large projects and no local union existed. It also enabled the building trades to penetrate large industrial complexes such as steel mills whose operating forces at that time were unorganized. Agreements such as these were aimed at organizing contractors who, as the industry grew, were beginning to undertake larger projects in parts of the country distant from their home bases. In return for their agreement to use union labor and pay union wages, contractors building projects in unfamiliar locations were provided with a source of skilled workers and the assistance of the national union in settling disputes that might arise on the projects.

During the 1920s and particularly in the Depression years of the 1930s, national general or industrial contractors pursued labor policies which can only be described as flexible. Many firms which operated as union contractors in the industrialized cities of the North and had national agreements with some crafts often assumed a different pose in carrying out projects in the largely rural and open-shop areas of the South. The policy was catch-as-catch-can: union when necessary, open-shop when possible.

In this early period, national agreements were not bargained collectively. The agreement form in most cases contained standardized wording developed by the union. A builder who had outgrown the label of local contractor and was actively seeking contracts on larger projects in a wider geographic area could apply, more or less hat in hand, to the union headquarters for a national agreement. If the contractor's request was approved, an agreement form was usually presented on a take-it-or-leave-it basis. Some unions, such as the Electrical Workers and the Pipefitters, were particularly reluctant to enter into national agreements with general contractors. In some instances these unions, after signing a national agreement, were unable or unwilling to force some of their larger local unions to accept its provisions. Local 597 of the United Association of Plumbers and Pipefitters in Chicago was a prime example of this resistance. For many years it flatly refused to supply men directly to holders of national agreements, insisting that these firms engage Chicago-based local piping subcontractors.

Meanwhile, the value of national agreements as sales tools began to increase as large engineering-construction firms, in their approaches to clients, began to push the single-contract–single-responsibility concept for carrying out big projects, particularly in the process plant field. This concept encompassed not only combining engineering design and construction in a single contract but also performing field work on a direct-hire basis without subcontracting. Although both union and contractor sought and obtained mutual benefits, the agreements were offered unilaterally by the national union. It was in the periods of heavy industrial expansion before, during, and after World War II that groups of national contractors in various branches of the industry began to involve themselves more deeply in negotiations with national unions and that more explicit national agreements emerged.

The first organized step by management to convert national agreements into documents that were in fact collectively bargained came in the late 1940s, following the founding of the National Constructors Association in 1947. Initially composed of fourteen companies, all of which designed and built industrial plants on a national scale, the NCA opened talks with several national and international building trades unions which led to the revision of existing agreements or to the signing of new ones.

The timing was propitious. The recent end of the war had brought a tide of new work in the industrial plant field. The existence of the Tennessee Valley Authority (TVA) promised a dramatic industrialization of much of the South, and the passage of the Labor-Management Relations Act (Taft-Hartley Act) set up new rules to govern labor-management relations. The early talks on national agreements by NCA representatives were held with the Pipefitters, Ironworkers, and Carpenters, with which many member companies already had some form of agreement. Discussions also were begun with the Operating Engineers.

The association's initial objectives were to obtain improvements, particularly in hiring practices, management rights, and grievance procedures. In the years that followed, the NCA negotiated national agreements with a total of nine crafts. In addition to those mentioned above, these agreements were with the Cement Masons, Bricklayers, Laborers, Painters, and Sheet Metal Workers. A number of companies had individual national agreements with the International Brotherhood of Electrical Workers (IBEW), but that union rejected proposals for substantive collective bargaining with the NCA on behalf of its member companies. It should be noted that the national agreements also were developed with the Boilermakers and the Teamsters. Although the NCA was active in promoting these negotiations and representatives of member companies composed almost all the negotiating teams, the association was not an official participant.

In the late 1950s and 1960s management efforts were directed toward strengthening national agreements vis-á-vis local agreements, that is, toward making national agreements more self-contained and more fully operative.

All the national construction agreements in use today provide for the exclusive use of union labor. Most of them briefly describe the conditions that apply to the use of that labor, requiring a contractor to meet the wages, fringe benefits, and working conditions contained in locally negotiated agreements and to use the local union as the sole source of labor. The national agreements serving special branches of the industry, such as pipeline, tank, building, and elevator construction, go further, in that they spell out the wages and fringe benefits to be paid and allow the use of other than solely local union labor.

Most national construction agreements contain no-strike, no-lockout provisions. The application of these provisions commonly involves working during local economic strikes. When an impasse in local collective bargaining results in a strike against local contractors, national contractors have been able to keep their projects open, and the local union has an obligation to supply them with workers. This aspect of both project agreements and national agreements and its effect on the balance of local bargaining are a subject of serious discussion within the industry.

During the late 1960s, national agreements came under increasing attack by local contractors and their associations, and to some extent by owners, because of the effect of their no-strike provisions on local wage bargaining. Local contractors complained loudly that their resistance to excessive wage demands by local unions was undermined whenever one or more large projects were being carried out in the locality under national agreements, thus permitting many union members to continue working on those projects while maintaining a strike against local employers.

In partial recognition of this problem, the NCA has always insisted on a nonautomatic-retroactivity clause in all national agreements. Under this clause, in the event of a local strike over wages and subsequent agreement on a contract, any wage increase would not be automatically retroactive to the start of the strike but rather would apply to the effective date of the new agreement. In recent national agreements the NCA has also been successful in obtaining a 5-day clause as an amendment to the no-strike, no-lockout provision. Under this arrangement a contractor, on 5-day notice, can shut down operations in support of local contractors who are affected by an economic strike. The union has been given a corresponding right to refuse to furnish workers.

Opinions as to the effectiveness of national agreements vary widely. Their usefulness can sometimes depend on which union, which contractor, which owner, or even which part of the country is involved in their implementation. Several representative national agreements are discussed individually below.

NCA National Construction Agreements

National agreements are particularly prevalent in the industrial construction sector, in which much of the work is done by contractor members of the NCA. As a result, the NCA has been involved, directly or indirectly, in most national agreements. Organized in 1947, the NCA now comprises more than fifty major engineering and construction companies, plus a number of national electrical and mechanical contractors, who build facilities primarily in the oil, chemical, metals, and utilities industries. Over the years it has negotiated agreements with many of the building trades national unions. In recent years, several of these have been agency agreements, binding all NCA members. Today the NCA has agreements with the Boilermakers, Carpenters, Ironworkers, Pipefitters, Cement Masons, Sheet Metal Workers, and Teamsters. Many but not all NCA contractors have national agreements with the Electrical Workers.

Given the competitive nature of the industry, particularly the pressures of open-shop construction, it is not surprising that almost all NCA agreements are being regarded today with a view to improving them. Reflecting the growing volume of industrial work performed by open-shop competitors, the NCA is attempting to include in national agreements conditions that it hopes will increase production and efficiency. These attempts involve such things as more efficient work rules, standard shift and overtime provisions, worker-recruiting provisions to supplement local-union referral systems, the expediting of grievance and arbitration procedures, and greater involvement of the national union in the application of the agreement.

There are other recent developments regarding NCA national construction agreements that are indicative of this trend. One is the announcement by the NCA that it will no longer negotiate on any agency basis that binds all its members to a single agreement. The NCA national agreements have been renegotiated recently without an agency clause. This move away from agency agreements would appear, at least technically, to allow individual NCA member companies the option either to utilize the national agreements with building trades unions or to seek an alternative to the use of building trades labor.

Another development within the NCA has been a movement toward agreements which specify wages rather than requiring the payment of wage rates provided for in local agreements. For example, the NCA Tri-State Agreement with the Laborers (discussed below in the section on "Regional Construction Agreements") sets wage and benefit rates within zones in the states of Texas, New Mexico, and Oklahoma. Another NCA agreement, though it appears to be an expedient resulting from unusual local bargaining difficulties, sets wage and benefit rates for its members working in the state of Washington. Given these precedents, it would not be surprising to see the development of NCA agreements that include wage scales in other parts of the country.

A third development in NCA national construction agreements is the National Industrial Construction Agreement. Committees representing the NCA and the AFL-CIO Building and Construction Trades Department have negotiated a single national agreement to cover all the building trades unions involved in industrial construction. In response once again to the growth of open-shop construction, the NCA has sought an agreement that would depend less on the terms of local agreements and instead would provide uniform national terms and conditions applicable to all the construction unions which its members employ.

The greatest success in this direction was with the United Association of Plumbers and Pipefitters. The United Association (UA) agreement contains a standard, or uniform, shift clause; it limits overtime premiums and bans special premiums (for high work and the like); it establishes a national training fund to which signatory contractors contribute in lieu of local funds; and it makes travel expense a matter of negotiation with the international union. It leaves little to local agreements except the establishment of hourly wage rates. In recent years even this has been limited by a provision authorizing the UA and a contractor to set up new conditions, including wages, if prevailing local conditions are against the best interest of the industry.

The UA agreement, in addition to being operative, was also for many years an agency agreement. Under this concept, the agreement was negotiated by a team appointed by the NCA as its agent and, upon approval by the Association, became binding on all member companies. This is no longer the case with the NCA-UA national agreement.

National Plans for Settlement of Jurisdictional Disputes

The national agreements described thus far are single-union contracts; that is, each document is an understanding entered into by an individual international union with one or more contractors. In all cases they relate to the work of a single craft. One rather notable exception to the general run of national agreements should be mentioned. Although not generally thought of as a national agreement, the Plan for Settlement of Jurisdictional Disputes in the Construction Industry, first negotiated in 1947, is in fact a national industry-wide labor-management contract. It was signed on the labor side by the Building and Construction Trades Department of the AFL-CIO on behalf of all affiliated unions and, on behalf of management, by various national employer associations. The plan, referred to in the industry as the Green Book, addressed only the problem of jurisdictional disputes, setting up machinery for the settlement of these disputes without work stoppages. For many years the mechanism was a joint labor-management board with a neutral chairman which received and heard cases and issued decisions. In recent years the board has consisted of three neutral members.

Aside from the area of work jurisdiction, national agreements remained in the single-craft category until 1970, when the Building and Construction Trades Department and the NCA negotiated and signed the Work Rules Agreement. It contained a set of commonsense working rules intended for application on all NCA projects throughout the United States. The agreement was the first contract of its kind that recognized the growing competition of the open shop on a national scale and the urgent need to eliminate unnecessary field labor costs. It provided for a ban on slowdowns, standby crews, and featherbedding and on illegal strikes, work stoppages, and lockouts. (See Chapter 4, section "Jurisdictional Disputes.") It declared that there would be no limit on production by workers or restrictions on the full use of tools and equipment.

Also signed was a companion agreement (later discarded as unworkable) to enforce decisions of the National Joint Board for Settlement of Jurisdictional Disputes by a system of financial penalties on violations. The Work Rules Agreement was revised and strengthened in 1973.

Nuclear Power Construction Stabilization Agreement

A significant example of the new breed of multicraft national agreements is the Nuclear Power Construction Stabilization Agreement, concluded in early 1978 by the Building and Construction Trades Department and four large engineering and construction companies which have designed and built a preponderant number of the nuclear power plants in the United States. The nuclear pact was the result of nearly 2 years of negotiations carried out under the guidance of Dr. John T. Dunlop, Harvard economist and former Secretary of Labor, serving in the role of mediator. It was tailored to meet the specific and somewhat unique requirements of nuclear plant construction, involving projects of huge size, immense capital investment, long completion schedules, and often remote locations.

The agreement is unusual because it is completely self-contained and fully operative. It is administered by a joint administrative committee which has the authority to set wage rates independent of local bargaining and settle jurisdictional disputes independent of the National Joint Board of Settlement of Jurisdictional Disputes. Among its major features are:

- A flat, unconditional ban on strikes and lockouts

- A standardized shift arrangement

- Overtime limited to time and one-half for the first 2 hours and on Saturday

- A provision permitting a work schedule of 7 consecutive days of alternating 10-hour shifts

In announcing the agreement, the parties indicated their belief that it would substantially lower construction costs through more efficient operations and capital costs through shorter periods of construction. It was to be applied initially to new nuclear projects started by the four companies that participated in the negotiations: Bechtel Corporation, Ebasco Services, Incorporated, Stone & Webster Engineering Corporation, and United Engineers & Constructors, Inc. The agreement can also be applied to new projects of other contractors.

The effectiveness of the nuclear agreement remains to be seen, but it appears to be in the mainstream of change in the industry. It moves away from the "pea patch" syndrome under which the wage rates and working conditions for a given craft for commercial and residential work in a small town must be recognized as controlling for huge industrial projects in the area.

Some observers have raised some questions about the nuclear agreement, particularly with reference to possible operational difficulties. To these observers the agreement appears to be largely an agreement to agree, leaving a large bundle of specific issues on wages and other items to be settled by the administrative committee for each project within its coverage.

National Industrial Construction Agreement

Soon after the nuclear agreement had been developed, another and equally significant entry in the new breed of national agreements in the construction industry was announced. This pact, the National Industrial Construction Agreement (NICA), was negotiated at about the same time between the NCA and eight of the major national and international unions.

NICA is openly and frankly a response by the unionized sector of the industry to open-shop advances in the area of industrial plant construction. Its principal features include:

■ *Scope and participants.* Although entitled a national agreement, the agreement was made applicable initially to eleven states: Alabama, Georgia, Florida, Mississippi, North and South Carolina, Arkansas, Louisiana, Oklahoma, Texas, and all of Virginia except for an area immediately adjoining the District of Columbia. The eight signatory international unions were the Carpenters, Ironworkers, Boilermakers, Laborers, Plumbers and Pipefitters, Operating Engineers, Asbestos Workers, and Cement Masons.

■ *Standard shifts.* The agreement provides for a 10 percent premium for the second shift and 20 percent for the third shift, which will be 7 hours long and will include a paid lunch period.

■ *Overtime limitations.* Time and one-half is provided for the first 2 hours Monday through Friday and on Saturday.

■ *Semiskilled workers.* Subjourneymen at 60 percent of the journeyman rate can be employed in numbers up to one-third of the force of each craft.

■ *Fringe Benefits.* There will be no payments into promotion or administrative funds.

■ *Production; use of tools.* There is no limit on production or restrictions on the full use of tools.

■ *Portable equipment.* In accordance with the currently recognized craft jurisdiction, employees will start, stop, and maintain all small portable construction equipment, but such employees will be utilized on other work of their craft. Only one employee is required on hydraulic equipment of 20 tons or under.

■ *Work breaks.* There will be no organized coffee breaks or other non-working time.

■ *Slowdowns, standby crews and featherbedding.* There will be none.

■ *Wages.* Basic rates are as in local arrangements, but there are no premiums for high work, special skills and so on.

■ *Strikes and lockouts.* These are prohibited. An exception involves an area strike over renegotiation of a local collective bargaining agreement. In such an event the union may refuse to furnish men, provided it gives 5-days' notice prior to the expiration of the local contract or at any time during the course of the area strike. A corresponding right is accorded the employer to shut down the project under the same terms.

■ *Grievances.* Except for jurisdictional disputes, grievances will be resolved through a standard three-step procedure, with provision at Step 4 for mandatory and binding arbitration.

■ *Travel and subsistence.* None will be provided unless approved by the joint administrative committee.

■ *Administrative committee.* It is composed of eight members each from labor and management and has wide-ranging authority under the agreement. The committee can extend the agreement to other new projects and apply it to other states and areas.

It is apparent that a change is taking place in national agreements. The old one-on-one type of contract which has been around for nearly three-quarters of a century is on its way out. The new national agreements are multicraft and multiemployer and are custom-tailored to meet problems in specific areas of construction such as nuclear plants or heavy industrial work.

NATIONAL SPECIALTY AGREEMENTS

The preceding description of national construction agreements has pointed out that most of those agreements refer to local contracts for their explicit wages and working conditions and depend on local unions for their labor. There are also national construction agreements in special branches of the industry that include specific wage rates or allow the use of other than local-union labor. In general, these specialty agreements seem to be well suited to the unique kinds of construction that they encompass. They have enabled unionized contractors to be reasonably competitive and have received little criticism from local contractors. Brief descriptions of several national specialty agreements follow.

National Pipeline Agreements

Prior to World War II most pipeline work was handled on an open-shop basis. As the industry expanded, however, the growing length and numbers of pipeline projects put economic pressure on open-shop contractors and brought them increasingly into unionized areas. An extensive organizing campaign by building trades unions brought about the signing of the first national pipeline agreement in 1949. It is estimated that by 1952 more than 90 percent of the industry was unionized. In recent years, with the growth of open-shop work, this percentage has declined somewhat, but unionized pipeline contractors continue to be competitive in many areas.

Negotiated today by the Pipeline Contractors Association, the pipeline agreement consists of four separate collective bargaining agreements, with the Laborers, Operating Engineers, Pipefitters, and Teamsters national unions. Each of these agreements provides working conditions uniformly applicable anywhere in the United States, no-strike no-lockout clauses, and grievance and arbitration procedures. Jurisdictional disputes are handled by a special committee and appear to be a minimal problem.

One of the more notable features of the pipeline agreement is its staffing provision, which provides that pipeline contractors may hire up to 50 percent of their labor directly and the remaining 50 percent from the local union. The exact formula for the alternate hiring of contractor and local-union employees varies with the particular craft. The Pipefitters, for instance, have a central union that has jurisdiction in thirty states. While in practice the final composition of the workforce sometimes depends on the ability or willingness of a local union to comply with the terms of the national agreement, pipeline contractors can develop and maintain productive work crews which they may use along the length of a project and from project to project. The use of such directly hired key employees is a genuine advantage for pipeline contractors.

Specific hourly wage rates and fringe benefits covering various worker classifications are negotiated by the Pipeline Contractors Association on a location, zone, or statewide basis. In the case of the Laborers, Operating Engineers, and Teamsters, much of the rate structure is based on area heavy and highway rates. In 1977 these three crafts agreed to a wage reduction for work performed on pipelines 16 inches and less in diameter, but the contractors were unable to negotiate similar concessions with the Pipefitters. The contractors had proposed the wage reduction for all crafts in an attempt to protect their smaller-diameter pipeline work from increasing open-shop competition.

National Tank Construction Agreement

The contemporary version of the National Transient Members (NTM) was first signed in 1947. Negotiated between the Boilermakers national union and contractors who build boilers, tower tanks, storage tanks, nuclear vessels, and other pressure vessels, the agreement covers their work in forty-one states. (Similar work in eight Western states and Hawaii is performed under a separate agreement.)

The agreement depends on local agreements for most of its terms and working conditions. In particular, it calls for the payment of wages and fringe benefits as established in the agreement for the locality or area in which the work is performed. There are, however, a number of provisions in the NTM Agreement that apply in any part of the country in which the work is performed. It contains, for instance, grievance and arbitration procedures, a no-strike no-lockout clause, reporting and travel pay provisions, a wage incentive provision, and a procedure for the referral of workers. The last two items, the wage incentive provision and the referral procedure are among the more notable features of the NTM Agreement. Like many other branches of the construction industry, tank building originally was handled on an open-shop basis, and there evolved a pool of transient workers who followed a contractor from project to project. Even though the industry is extensively unionized today, the wage incentives and referral practices pertaining to these transient workers have been carried over to the national agreement.

The essence of these provisions is that they enable a tank-building contractor to maintain a cadre of key employees and pay them production incentives. The ratio of contractor employees to those hired from a local union varies with the kind of work being performed. For example, on water tower tanks, contractors may use their own employees exclusively; and on storage tanks, 50 percent of their own and 50 percent of local-union employees. On nuclear vessels and other pressure vessels, the ratio is two contractor employees for every local-union employee. Wage incentives are computed by a mutually agreed method with each individual contractor. The net result of these procedures is to provide tank-building contractors with genuine advantages in productivity.

National Elevator Construction Agreement

A national agreement covering elevator construction was first developed in the 1920s. It has since evolved into a detailed labor contract that today is negotiated between a national multiemployer association and the Elevator Constructors' national union. Except for New York City, which has a separate agreement, there is little local bargaining in this branch of the construction industry. Instead, the national agreement governs almost all the terms and conditions of employment. It includes, for instance, a no-strike, no-lockout clause, grievance and arbitration provisions, specific work rules, a vacation plan, a wage formula, and pension, health, and educational funds. A few provisions, such as travel and subsistence allowances are negotiated locally, and a local-option clause allows local parties to alter the hours of work and shift schedules of the national agreement.

The national agreement depends in the main on local unions to supply the workforce needed by contractors working in a particular area. There is a restricted allowance for contractors to bring certain key employees into a local union's jurisdiction, but this provision is narrowly interpreted and allows only the temporary transfer of such employees.

The most notable feature of the National Elevator Construction Agreement is that it does not leave the determination of wage rates to local bargaining. Rather, the agreement provides for an involved formula that, in effect, relates the wages of elevator constructors to the average of the four highest wage rates among seven building trades unions. A new 5-year agreement, liberalizing the use of prefabricated units, mobile lift equipment, and shift schedules, was agreed to in August 1977. It covers 20,000 members in 100 locals.

REGIONAL CONSTRUCTION AGREEMENTS

Unions and contractors have worked out on a multicraft and multiemployer basis special agreements which have been limited to a regional area. These agreements typically are limited to specified industries such as industrial work, offshore construction, iron mining, or boilermaking.

Houston Industrial Agreement

The Houston Industrial Agreement (HIA) was negotiated between the NCA and the Houston Building and Construction Trades Council in November 1973. The steady growth of open-shop contractors in the Gulf Coast area around Houston was the primary stimulus for this multicraft, multiemployer negotiation. Union contractors and union members had recognized that work was going to open-shop contractors because "working conditions spelled out in local-union agreements were resulting in costs well in excess of those incurred by open-shop competitors; and jurisdictional and other labor disputes, with strikes and other disruptions, were the source of additional costs for union contractors."

The resulting agreement addressed itself to industrial construction with a project cost of $2 million or more in the twenty-county jurisdiction of the Houston-Gulf Coast Building Trades Council. The agreement was unique in that it was multicraft and multiemployer, covered a specific type of work in a relatively small area, and applied to work above a minimum sum. Thus, the stage was set for two or more unions and industrial contractors to work on the same project under different labor agreements.

The Houston Industrial Agreement included provisions similar to those in some of the NCA national agreements, such as the industry fund exemption, a grievance procedure, the 5-day clause. In addition, it provided for a series of work rules aimed at promoting increased efficiency, the right to use apprentices or trainees in ratios of 20 to 30 percent of the workforce of each craft, and a strengthened management rights clause.

On reexamining the situation 3 years after the HIA was negotiated, the majority of the industrial owners felt that few of its provisions which differed from local practice had been put into effect. Both management and labor were responsible for failure to implement the agreement. On the one hand, stewards insisted upon conditions and practices prevalent in local agreements which contravened the HIA, and on the other hand, jobsite foremen and superintendents who were accustomed to working under other conditions and who did not fully understand the provisions of the HIA were not insisting on compliance. Business agents and contractors compounded the problem by not printing and distributing copies of the agreement or properly educating stewards and foremen and by not using all practical means at their disposal to obtain cooperation and compliance. Overall, except for the shift clause, which has been very helpful on some jobs, it appears that the terms of the HIA have been largely cosmetic in application and have done little to improve productivity and correct inefficient work practices, high turnover, absenteeism, and other artificial cost factors.

The original HIA expired in February 1977 but continued to apply to covered projects then under way. A 2-year extension of the agreement, incorporating further improvements, was agreed to verbally by the parties on January 18, 1977, but the Operating Engineers, Electrical Workers,

Teamsters, and Boilermakers declined to sign the new agreement. An effort to enforce the agreement reached by the negotiating teams failed when the federal district court ruled that the agreement was invalid insofar as the nonsignatory unions were concerned. It now appears that no further attempts wil be made to negotiate a new HIA.

Owners generally view the HIA as a commendable effort on the part of union contractors and most of the local unions to improve the competitiveness of union construction in the Houston area. If it had been extended as proposed and if the provisions to improve productivity had been more effectively implemented, it could have significantly aided unionized contractors in recovering a share of industrial construction in the Houston area.

General Presidents' Offshore Agreements

The West Coast Offshore Construction Agreement is a contract between offshore construction firms, seven building trades unions (Electrical workers, Carpenters, Operating Engineers, Painters, United Association of Plumbers and Pipefitters, Ironworkers, and Boilermakers) and the Seafarers. The work covered by the agreement is limited to offshore construction and related work for exploration and drilling facilities for oil, natural gas, and other natural resources. The geographical boundaries of the agreement include all United States West Coast territorial waters from the Mexican boundary north, including Alaska. Pipeline and onshore work is excluded.

The West Coast Offshore Construction Agreement evolved from a 1965 understanding between the United Brotherhood of Carpenters and the International Association of Bridge, Structural, and Ornamental Ironworkers to eliminate jurisdictional disputes between the two crafts on construction work on offshore drilling platforms. Essentially, the two groups agreed that all construction of platforms in the area would be done under a fifty-fifty composite-crew arrangement.

Because of the unique requirements of offshore work, the need for uniformity of contract provisions across numerous local jurisdictions, and the desire for immunity from local strikes, by 1969 the understanding had developed into a full-fledged areawide contract agreement between the seven building trades unions, the Seafarers, and the offshore contractors (initially, only Kaiser Steel and J. R. McDermott). In 1971 the agreement was renegotiated effective in 1972, and in December 1976 negotiations for a new 3-year agreement effective on January 1, 1977 were concluded.

The agreement includes a number of clauses commonly found in national and project agreements, in addition to more distinctive provisions providing for the following:

1. A uniform journeyman wage for all crafts is specified, along with a formula for annual updating, based on the average of prevailing construction rates in specified nearby metropolitan areas. (Seafarers' rates are excluded from this determination and presumably conform to local agreements.)

2. A travel and subsistence standby clause provides payments in recognition of the unique requirements of offshore work. In addition to a conventional shift clause, there is a provision for 12-hour shifts.

3. Provision is made for composite crews and for the relaxation of craft jurisdictions in emergencies and when appropriate crafts are not available on the job.

4. A firm no-strike, no-lockout clause is included, except for the proviso that employees may honor "any properly authorized picket line."

Contractors who have erected offshore structures under this agreement have generally been satisfied with its provisions and implementation.

In June 1976 an offshore construction agreement for the East Coast was proposed by the unions signatory to the West Coast agreement, in anticipation of offshore work on the East Coast. To date no work has been performed under this agreement, and no employers have signed it. The agreement essentially duplicates the 1971 version of the West Coast agreement, with the following exceptions:

1. The geographical boundaries include all United States East Coast territorial waters from the Canadian boundary south to the southern tip of Florida.

2. Certain flexibilities available to the contractors were deleted from the referral clause.

3. Double-edged most-favored-nation clauses were added.

4. The reference to composite crews is not included.

Taconite Agreement

During the initial development of facilities on the Mesabi Range in Minnesota, the owners believed that a standard contractual arrangement would benefit the owners, contractors, and union employees. Several owner-operators established the Taconite Contracting Corporation, which negotiated the Taconite Agreement. The initial agreement was negotiated with international representatives of the craft unions and the Teamsters and was signed by the local unions in November 1953. There have been several negotiated extensions.

The contract covers all work relative to "the construction of facilities for the converting of Taconite into iron ore pellets in the State of Minnesota, the construction of facilities for the transportation of such pellets to a shipping point on Lake Superior, the construction of dock and loading facilities and power plant at that point, and necessary housing facilities. . . ." The intent of the agreement was to provide a vehicle that would standardize contract terms, contain a common expiration date, and otherwise minimize the likelihood of work stoppages through the incorporation of a no-strike provision.

While the Taconite Agreement does give owners and their contractors the right to work through a strike, the *quid pro quo* is that most work rules and all wage rates and fringe benefits are taken from local agreements. In effect, since the taconite contractors employ a significant portion of the area's labor, the unions are able to play off Mesabi Range owners and contractors against contractors negotiating in the local area by finding employment on the taconite project for members on strike against local contractors. This, of course, weakens the bargaining position of local contractors for the unions can hold out longer for higher wages and benefits and more restrictive contract language, knowing that they will be under minimum pressure from the membership to settle and that all improvements will be recognized retroactively under the terms of the Taconite Agreement.

On analysis, there appears to no significant advantage to contractors in using the Taconite Agreement rather than local agreements. Several of the NCA national construction agreements and some recently negotiated project agreements contain more favorable terms and conditions. Moreover, the Taconite Agreement has made more difficult the hiring of construction labor for other work in the area and has undermined the efforts of the Regional Congress of Construction Employers (RCCE) to coordinate construction bargaining and remove restrictive and nonproductive work rules from local contracts.

NCA Tri-State Agreement

The Tri-State Agreement was negotiated in 1977 between the NCA and the Laborers International Union of North America and its affiliated district councils within the three-state area of Texas, New Mexico, and Oklahoma. Since it is not an agency agreement, it becomes effective for each NCA contractor only if and when the contractor signs it.

This single-craft regional agreement is a departure from prior NCA reliance on national agreements and seems in conflict with current efforts to negotiate industry-wide multicraft agreements. Local contractor associations have been invited to sign the agreement. Once signed, it supersedes, for work by signatory contractors within the tri-state area, both the NCA national Laborers' agreement and local Laborers' agreements.

Proponents have cited as beneficial the provision for the transfer of employees from one job to another by a single contractor without union approval, the exclusion of employees above the foreman level from the agreement, all Monday–Saturday overtime at time and one-half, decreased exposure to leapfrogging in future wage negotiations, and ease of administration as a result of the uniformity of terms throughout the three-state region. Critics have expressed the following concerns:

1. Checkoffs for dues and initiation fees and the use of the hiring hall are prescribed. These procedures previously had not been in effect in many of the areas involved.

2. The reason for the departure from the usual 5-day clause in other NCA agreements, by requiring written direction from the owner, is not apparent. Some view this as an abrogation by the signatory contractors of any responsibility for local bargaining. Some owners may be concerned that the written notice would directly involve them in a contractor's

labor dispute, causing them to incur coemployer risks. In any event, it seems inappropriate to address the relationship between contractor and client in an agreement between contractor and employees.

3. There appears to be no logic for the geographic scope of the agreement other than its correspondence to the area serviced by a Laborers international representative. Some portions of the area have a high volume of open-shop activity, while others have virtually none. Much of central and west Texas and New Mexico is remote, with a low, primarily commercial construction volume. The Texas Gulf Coast is primarily industrial, with a high construction volume, and in construction labor relations has more in common with the Louisiana-Mississippi Gulf Coast than with the remaining area of the Tri-State Agreement.

4. Because of this situation, the coordination between the regional or national wage negotiating committees, or both, and the various local-contractor bargaining groups will be difficult, with leapfrogging pressures in many areas. Future settlements appropriate for both booming industrial areas and remote low-activity areas will be difficult to achieve.

5. The likely acceptance of this agreement by only a portion of the employers working in a given area will further divide and weaken, rather than strengthen and unify, the area. In the Houston area the possibility exists that a single jobsite could include different contractors working under the Tri-State Agreement, the NCA national Laborers' agreement, and the local Laborers' agreement, all with varying work rules.

It is too early to assess accurately the impact of the Tri-State Agreement. However, it poses potentially serious long-range problems, and contractors should carefully analyze its potential long-range impact.

Boilermakers' Agreements

Various local and regional construction agreements have been drawn up between different employer groups and the International Brotherhood of Boilermakers, Iron Ship Builders, Blacksmiths, Forgers, and Helpers. They cover all field construction work within the geographic scope of the contract and also contain supplemental provisions applicable to maintenance work. Management's bargaining committee is usually composed of representatives of local contractor groups, national contractors, and tank manufacturers. The actual makeup of the committee depends on the geographic coverage of the agreement and the presence of one or more strong local industrial contractor groups.

Controversy surrounds several of the key aspects of these agreements. Proponents of this type of agreement point to the following provisions:

1. Uniformity of terms and a common expiration date over a broad area (generally statewide or multistate)

2. A uniform wage and benefit package for all locals within the jurisdiction of the agreement

3. A functional hiring-hall arrangement that can supply adequate labor when necessary, recognizing the need for a mix of local craftsmen and experienced longer-term employees from outside the local area

4. Provision for either management or labor to shut down a project in support of local bargaining that has reached a strike, provided a 5-day notice has been delivered.

However, critics argue:

1. The geographical area covered by an agreement includes areas with varying economic interests and therefore does not correspond to local bargaining or regional bargaining processes.

2. Uniform terms are established but, again, often are in conflict with the terms in other craft local agreements, thus leading to craft-by-craft whipsawing.

3. The common expiration date generally does not correspond to those of local bargaining groups, thus frustrating local efforts to achieve uniform multicraft expiration dates.

The negotiating structure involved in the Boilermakers agreement has an important feature worthy of comment. At least in some instances, local industrial contractors have sat and bargained with national contractors and tank manufacturers to consummate agreements with the union that have been considered acceptable to both local and national groups. A fair exchange of ideas and bargaining strategy has taken place in various Boilermakers negotiations. It appears that there has been greater cooperation among affected contractor groups in these negotiations than in other regional construction negotiations.

MAINTENANCE AGREEMENTS

In some areas, total employment under maintenance agreements (General Presidents', National Erectors, and local maintenance agreements) has reached a significant percentage of the local building trades workforce. These agreements generally include a no-strike, no-lockout clause without provision for shutdown of the work in support of local bargaining. Owners tend to regard their contract maintenance activity as unrelated to construction activity or to building trades bargaining.

When the total employment under these agreements is large, however, they do risk undermining contractor management strength in local bargaining by providing a haven for striking workers. Because much of the work performed under these agreements, once started, is very costly to interrupt and because some is of an emergency nature, the introduction of a 5-day clause into the contracts would not, in most cases, be helpful in avoiding the problem. Many owners are sensitive to these relationships, however, and believe that the following steps can be used to minimize the impact on local bargaining:

1. Maintenance managers in their advance planning should be aware of the expiration or wage reopener dates in local contracts with the crafts employed. Scheduled turnarounds or renovation work can often be programmed to be completed before, or start after, these dates.

2. With preplanning it is often possible to avoid buildups in the employment of a craft just prior to and during its contract negotiations and especially during a period when the craft is on strike against local contractors. This may require deferral of desirable but nonemergency work.

Blue Book Agreement

In 1956 the General Presidents of the unions comprising the Building and Construction Trades Department of the AFL-CIO developed with the Catalytic Construction Company an agreement for performing maintenance work by contract for the Tidewater Oil Company's new refinery in Delaware. The result was called the General Presidents' Project Maintenance Agreement by Contract, but because it was initially printed on blue paper it has come to be more commonly known as the Blue Book. This agreement is generally available to responsible contractors on a nationwide basis. There have been four revisions of the Blue Book, in September 1960, June 1970, November 1972, and 1975. Today there are more than 150 Blue Book agreements in effect in thirty states.

Each of these agreements is limited to work at a particular plant. These are multicraft agreements, signed by international unions representing all crafts to be used. Although the owner is not a signatory, before authorizing an agreement the General Presidents seek some indication that the owner intends continuously to engage a contract maintenance crew from the signatory contractor. Crew sizes may be increased to accommodate major overhauls and emergencies, but the agreements are not intended for the intermittent or infrequent use of contract employees.

In summary, the agreement reached in 1956 eliminated many of the restrictive provisions contained in local construction trade agreements and gave the employers latitude to assign work in a more economical manner. A grievance procedure terminating binding arbitration and a no-strike provision were included. The agreement also excluded subsistence, travel allowance, mileage, and travel time pay. Shift work was permitted at a shift premium rather than at overtime rates, and overtime rates themselves were reduced to time and one-half for all hours worked during the week and on Saturday. Basic wage and fringe-benefit rates were not covered; the rates in the local building trades agreements for each craft apply.

Agreements entered into more recently include a strengthened management rights clause and, in some cases, wage rates less than prevailing area construction rates (commonly 80 to 90 percent of the construction rate). The reduced rates recognize the fact that many employees are attracted to maintenance work because of increased job security, continuing work at the same location, and greater availability of overtime work.

Orange Book Agreement

In March 1972, a special revision to the General Presidents' Project Maintenance Agreement was developed for the Baton Rouge, Louisiana, area as the result of an effort by local building trades unions to compete with an independent union organized to provide employees with maintenance work. The revised agreement is referred to as the Orange Book, again deriving the name from the color of the paper used initially.

Some of the more notable improvements in the Orange Book over the Blue Book are included in provisions related to the following:

1. *Wages.* This agreement set common area rates for certain specialized crafts and lower common rates for other crafts. In addition, all future wages and benefit increases were to escalate by the same percentage as the national average for manufacturing industries.

2. *Management rights.* There were explicit major improvements in field practices involving hiring, firing, work assignment, and other facets of field flexibility. These management rights improvements were later incorporated in the Blue Book, and the two agreements now are essentially the same in this regard.

3. *Jurisdiction.* There was a significant reduction of craft lines, and one jobsite union representative, who must be a qualified working craftsman, replaced the individual craft shop stewards. The uniform wage rate for related crafts provided in the Orange Book has contributed to the avoidance of jurisdictional problems.

Although the General Presidents have recently agreed to extend the use of the Orange Book throughout Louisiana, the wage rates established for the Baton Rouge area do not apply to other locations where the Orange Book is utilized for maintenance work. Use of the Orange Book must be negotiated on a plant-by-plant basis, but "wage rates may be established by the General Presidents' Maintenance Committee" in Washington. This, of course, means that maintenance wage rates vary for each area, and although the agreement indicates that wage rates are also to be established by the General Presidents' Committee on Contract Maintenance, in practice the rate for each craft and area, as well as for the "mechanic classification," must be agreed upon by the building trades local unions.

Although both the Blue Book and the Orange Book were developed by the General Presidents' Committee on Contract Maintenance of the Building and Construction Trades Department and signed by the General Presidents, implementation of the agreements is strongly influenced by local business agents and the existing labor climate:

1. A particular craft local or business agent can decide not to furnish workers for maintenance at rates below existing construction rates. The contractor, after a 48-hour waiting period, contractually has the option to fill labor requirements from any other source. However, picketing and a work stoppage, though in violation of the agreement, may result from such action by the contractor, and this option has seldom if ever been exercised.
   The contractor may have difficulty in retaining or, more likely, in increasing craft skills to a level necessary for maintenance work at the lower wage rates when higher-paying construction jobs become plentiful.
   The mechanic A, B, C, and D classifications for the Orange Book may be unobtainable in areas where wide wage differences exist between crafts in each mechanic group. The higher-paid crafts may be unwilling to take a larger cut in pay than the other crafts working in the same mechanic classification in order to achieve the uniform rate groupings.
   While the contract language provides certain flexibilities in work assignments aimed at the more efficient performance of maintenance work, these flexibilities usually have not been vigorously exercised. This is true because (a) contractor supervision tends to follow the rigid craft distinctions to which it has been accustomed in construction work; (b) business

agents and stewards are generally resistant to departure from construction work rules; and (c) contractor management, recognizing its dependence on the unions for its labor supply, is reluctant to ruffle any feathers.

Contractors signatory to General Presidents' maintenance agreements have formed the Maintenance Contractors Association, which provides a forum for discussion of experience with the agreements. Although this association does not bargain formally with the General Presidents, it has contributed to improvements in the agreements.

The General Presidents of twelve building trades international unions and the Teamsters are signatory to the agreements, and each has a representative on the General Presidents' Committee on Contract Maintenance. The committee meets monthly to resolve grievances and to authorize new agreements. It employs a full-time administrator to assist in the prompt resolution of any problem.

In 1975 it was reported that about 6000 craftsmen were working under General Presidents' maintenance agreements nationwide, mainly in oil refineries and chemical plants, with about half of these in the Baton Rouge area. A Building and Construction Trades Department spokesman stated that 15 million hours were worked under these agreements in 1976; the 1977 total was expected to approach 20 million.

National Erectors Association National Maintenance Agreement

In June 1970 the National Erectors Association (NEA) appointed a National Maintenance Agreement Committee to explore, with several international building trades unions, the feasibility of negotiating national maintenance agreements. This step was prompted by a situation in which building trades contractors were continually losing repair and rehabilitation work because of their inability to control the workforce and because of contract terms which generally made them less competitive in the industrial maintenance field. By April 1972 four national maintenance agreements had been established; the first work under these agreements began that year. As of last count, ten international unions were signatory to individual National Erectors Association maintenance agreements.

The national maintenance agreements are administered by a National Maintenance Agreements Policy Committee, which meets quarterly and consists of ten contractors and ten international union representatives who are jointly empowered to interpret the agreements. NEA agreements are applicable nationally, but they are individual agreements with selected crafts rather than single-location multicraft agreements. In practice, while this type of agreement eliminates the requirement for a separate contract at each site, it also tends to reduce craft flexibility by reinforcing individual craft lines. In contrast to the General Presidents' maintenance agreements, NEA agreements have found their application mainly in intermittent requirements for major repair or rehabilitation work rather than in the provision of continuous maintenance crews. Their greatest use has been in metals-processing industries.

FEATURES OF SPECIAL BUILDING TRADES AGREEMENTS

As might be expected, the language of individual special agreements varies widely, but recurring examples of clauses aimed at basic deficiencies in local agreements can be found. The more prevalent of these clauses will be discussed below individually. In most cases, illustrative clauses from actual contracts are quoted.

Management Rights

Special agreements commonly include language aimed at reserving to management an unencumbered right to take certain actions which may otherwise be limited by local agreements or area practice. The following actions are sometimes addressed:

- Right to reject persons referred by unions
- Right to select and hire supervisors and to determine the number required
- Right to assign work and to determine crew sizes and schedules
- Right to employ efficient work methods, tools, or prefabricated items
- Right to determine when overtime shall be worked and by whom
- Right to subcontract
- Right to establish safety rules and other work rules

Older special agreements generally addressed only a few of these items, which were often scattered piecemeal among articles devoted to other subjects. Later agreements tend to group them in a separate article entitled "Management Rights."

Illustrative Example

1. The Contractors retain full and exclusive authority for the management of their operations.

2. The Contractors shall have the unqualified right to select and hire directly all supervisors they consider necessary, without such persons being referred by the Union.

3. The Contractor shall have the responsibility and shall be the sole judge of the selection and number of all Foremen and General Foremen for all classifications and for employees required for the project.

4. No rules, customs or practices shall be permitted or observed which in any way restrict production, or limit, or restrict the working efforts of employees as deter-

mined by the Contractor. The Contractor shall have the right to utilize any efficient work methods, procedures or techniques of construction, and select and use any type of materials, apparatus or equipment. There shall be no refusal of any kind, concerning the use of machinery, equipment, or materials, tool or other labor-saving devices, nor shall there be any limitation whatsoever upon choice of materials or design. The contractors at their sole discretion shall assign and schedule work and shall determine when overtime will be worked and by whom. The Contractor shall have the right to subcontract all or any part of such work or services, including the maintenance of machinery or equipment. This shall apply to warranty service, crane and vehicle repair, etc.

5. The on-site installation, fabrication, assembly or application of materials generally shall be performed by the craft traditionally and customarily having jurisdiction over such work; provided, however, it is recognized that in some cases personnel having special training, skills, experience or qualifications not employed under this Agreement, or other collective bargaining agreements, may install, apply, set up, test items or perform other work as determined and directed by the Contractor. There shall not be any restriction on the size or type of pre-fabrication or pre-assembly of process equipment shipped to the site for erection and installation by the craft having jurisdiction.

6. The furnishing of materials, supplies, or equipment and the delivery thereof shall in no case be considered as subcontracting. Equipment purchased by or at the discretion of the Owner shall not be subject to any restrictive provision.

7. It will be the Contractor's right to establish project rules, including safety, for all work on this project that are within the purpose and the scope of this Agreement. These rules will be presented at the pre-job meeting.

8. The parties agree that the foregoing enumeration of the Contractor's rights shall not exclude other functions not specifically set forth. Therefore, they shall retain all rights not otherwise specifically covered by this agreement.

While management rights clauses are sometimes helpful in correcting abuses, they are no panacea. Actual exercise of agreed management rights has been spotty at best. Contractors have generally been reluctant to take action at variance with well-established area practices.

No-Strike, No-Lockout Clauses

The obvious aim of these clauses is to eliminate or minimize work stoppages. Older agreements usually contain an unqualified prohibition of "strikes, work stoppages, picketing, or slowdowns by the unions or employees . . . or lockout . . . (see above, section "No-Strike, No-Lockout Provisions"). More recent agreements attempt to provide for a possible shutdown of the job in support of local bargaining while retaining the prohibition of strikes or lockouts for any other purpose.

Illustrative Example

The Council agrees that there will be no strike or other collective action which will interfere with, or stop, the efficient operation of construction work of the Employer. Participation by an employee, or group of employees, in an act violating the above provision may be cause for discharge by the Employer. If there is a strike, work stoppage or picket line in violation of the Agreement by any craft, it is agreed that the other crafts will be bound to ignore such action and continue to man the project without interruption. The Council will support the Employer in maintaining operations in every way during such a work stoppage.

The Employer may suspend a portion of the work or shut down a project in the event of a slowdown by one or more Unions or a partial or complete work stoppage by one or more Unions.

In the event of an area strike over local contract negotiations, it will not be considered a violation of this agreement for the Employer to stop work covered by this agreement for the duration of the strike. The Employer is required to give notification to the Council for five (5) working days prior to taking such action.

In the event of an area strike over local negotiations, it will not be considered a violation of this agreement for the Council to refuse to furnish men to the Employer for the duration of the strike. The Council is required to give notification to the Employer five (5) working days prior to taking such action.

Nothing in this agreement shall be construed to limit or restrict the right of the union or the Employer to pursue fully any and all remedies available under the law in the event of a violation of this article.

Overtime

Local agreements generally require double-time payment for all overtime. Clauses limiting double-time payment to Sundays and holidays are found in most special agreements.

Illustrative Example

All hours worked in excess of the regular working hours Monday through Friday, excepting shift work, and all hours worked on Saturday shall be at time and one-half. On Sunday and holidays employees shall be paid for hours worked in accordance with the provisions established in locally negotiated agreements. There will be no duplication of or pyramiding of overtime pay.

Some more recent project agreements also provide for working on Saturday at straight time when the work is undertaken to make up for work cancelled because of unfavorable weather conditions earlier in the week.

Shift Work

Many local agreements have no provision for shift work, requiring overtime payment for all work outside the normal Monday–Friday day shift. Others pyramid a shift differential on top of the common provision of 8 hours' pay for 7 or 7½ hours' work. Special agreements provide for shift work with clauses like that in the following example.

Illustrative Example

Shift work may be performed at the option of the contractors; however, when shift work is performed, it must continue for a period of not less than three (3) consecutive days. The

Contractors shall have the sole right to designate the craft or crafts on the project, or any portion thereof, who shall work on a multiple shift basis. When two or three shifts are worked, the first, or day shift, shall work a regular eight (8) hour shift with no shift differential. The second shift shall be established on a seven and one-half (7½) hour basis, for which each employee shall receive eight (8) hours pay at the regular straight time rate. The third shift shall work seven (7) hours and be paid eight (8) hours at the regular straight time rate. No shift premium shall be paid where overtime premium rates are paid for the same hours.

Referral Procedures

Local agreements commonly designate the union as the sole and exclusive source of referrals for employment. Some bind the union to referral only of union members. Special agreements generally refer to or duplicate established local referral procedures, with the following exception:

1. There is a requirement that the unions "accept for registration and referral all applicants for employment without discrimination against any applicant by reason of membership or non-membership in the Union. . . ."

2. The employer is free to employ applicants directly at the jobsite if the union is unable to fill requests within 48 hours.

3. Most special agreements emphasize the employer's right to select foremen and general foremen, and some provide the right to hire directly for those positions.

The Distribution Pipeline Agreement provides additional flexibility:

Illustrative Example

The Employer shall have the right to bring directly into the job journeymen who are considered by the Employer to have special knowledge and experience in gas distribution pipeline work and shall have the right to keep such journeymen on all work throughout the territory covered by the pre-job conference.
It is agreed that the Employer may bring directly into the job 50% of the number of employees required for such job. For purposes of this provision, it is understood that the Union shall refer the first employee required; the Employer shall bring the second one; the Union shall refer the third one; the Employer shall bring the fourth one; the Union shall refer the fifth one; and so on, in accordance with this procedure.

Specialty contractors generally seem to exercise the flexibilities to depart from local referral procedures provided in their agreements in order to retain an experienced and loyal cadre of employees, who move with the contractor from job to job. This is especially true of highly mobile contractors, such as those who construct pipelines, tanks, and chimneys. On project agreement work, on the other hand, there has been little discernible departure from the normal referral procedures of local unions.

Travel and Subsistence Pay

Travel and subsistence pay for work outside urban areas is common in local contracts, some of which even require expense payments to employees who use contractor vehicles. Most project and special agreements prohibit travel and subsistence pay.

It should be noted that the absence of provisions for travel or subsistence pay, or both is not necessarily advantageous. When employees are drawn from a union whose jurisdiction includes both an urban area and distant rural areas, it may be very difficult to attract sufficient numbers of skilled craftsmen in the more distant areas without travel and subsistence pay. Such pay provisions also provide an additional inducement to attract travelers from other areas.

Show-Up Time

Employees reporting for work under local contracts may get from 2 to 4 hours' pay when no work is available or when inclement weather prevents work. Provisions for show-up time often vary from craft to craft within the same area. Some special agreements merely adopt the provisions for show-up time of applicable local agreements, while others attempt to achieve consistency from craft to craft and to avoid abuses by the inclusion of more restrictive clauses.

Illustrative Example

Reporting time. Any employee who reports for work and for whom no work is provided shall receive two hours pay provided he remains available for work. Any employee who reports for work and for whom work is provided shall be paid for actual time worked, but not less than two hours provided he remains available for work. However, no such payment shall be paid when an employee leaves work of his own accord.

No Formal Coffee Breaks

Most local contracts do not address the issue of employee coffee breaks, but these are accepted local practice in many areas. Most special agreements specifically prohibit coffee breaks and other scheduled nonworking periods. Some recognize the use of personal thermos jugs on the job in lieu of organized breaks.

Illustrative Example

There shall be no organized coffee, coffee pot, or rest breaks on the project. The employer has no objection to employees taking their thermoses to a point adjacent to their place of work.

Grievance Procedure

Local agreements generally provide a grievance procedure including specified steps and time limits, with final resort to binding arbitration. Some local IBEW contracts call for submission of unresolved disputes to the

Council of Industrial Relations (a permanent board of National Electrical Contractors Association and IBEW representatives in Washington) for final resolution.

Grievance procedures in special agreements follow a similar pattern. A uniform procedure is provided for all crafts and additional intermediate reconciliation steps are sometimes specified. Time limits for each step tend to be shorter. The final step in most agreements is binding arbitration (there is a consensus that the threat of binding arbitration contributes to the early resolution of disputes). Special agreements normally include a proviso that work continue without interruption or interference during the operation of the grievance machinery.

Activities of Stewards

Most local agreements provide for a working steward for each craft on each shift. The steward is to perform journeyman work but is to be excused to perform necessary union work, such as the investigation of grievances. Abuse of these provisions has been a pervasive problem. Stewards have been given preferential treatment and have been allowed to collect dues and to participate in referral, indoctrination of new employees, and so on. Practices of this sort are sometimes contended to be "area practice" despite limiting language in local contracts. In an effort to avoid these abuses, special agreements sometimes discuss at some length the duties of stewards as well as what stewards are prohibited from doing.

Illustrative Example

The Union shall have the right to designate one (1) working steward on each shift who will be recognized as the Union's representative on the project.

The steward designated by the Union shall be a qualified workman assigned to a crew, and shall perform the assigned work of his craft.

There will be no non-working stewards on the project. The steward shall be paid at the applicable wage rate for the job classification in which he is employed.

In the case of overtime, in order for the steward to work such overtime, he must be qualified to perform the work being undertaken during the overtime period.

The steward shall, in addition to his work as a journeyman, be permitted to perform, during working hours, such of his normal union duties as cannot be performed at other times. The Union agrees that such duties shall be performed as expeditiously as possible and the Contractors agree to allow the steward a reasonable amount of time for the performance of such duties. The Contractors shall not discriminate against the steward in the proper performance of his Union duties, provided such duties do not interfere with his regular work or with the work of employees, and he shall not leave his work area without first notifying his appropriate supervisor as to his intent, the reason thereof, where he can be reached and the estimated time he will be gone.

The steward's duties shall not include any matters related to referral, hiring, assignment, overtime, termination or discipline of employees. Nor shall the steward be authorized to halt any work or otherwise interfere with work progress.

The steward shall only represent those employees of his craft employed by his employer/contractor, and not employees of other Contractors working at the project site.

The steward shall not be entitled to any preferential treatment by the Contractors, and will be subject to disciplinary action (up to, and including discharge) to the same extent that other employees are. The Contractors shall notify the Union prior to the discharge of any steward.

Exclusion of Industry Fund Payments

Most current project agreements and other special agreements provide for the payment of all local wages and benefits but exclude industry fund payments. A recent project agreement contains language restricting payment of industry funds:

Illustrative Example

The Contractors shall pay only fringe benefits for employees that have been legally negotiated and established by a bona fide collective bargaining agreement. Industry promotion funds and similar funds which are not of direct benefit to the employee shall not be paid by the Contractors.

Resolution of Jurisdictional Disputes

While jurisdictional disputes have declined steadily in recent years (recorded work stoppages over jurisdictional matters declined from 845 in 1968 to 222 in 1976), they nonetheless deserve continued attention in an effort at further reduction.

Many local and national agreements prohibit strikes over jurisdictional disputes and prescribe settlement in accordance with the Plan for Settlement of Jurisdictional Disputes in the Construction Industry or with "the procedure established by the National Joint Board for the Settlement of Jurisdictional Disputes or any successor agency. . . ." Problems most often stem from situations, in which one of the crafts involved (most notably the Teamsters) or a contractor association (for example, the Sheet Metal and Air-Conditioning Contractors' National Association) does not participate in the Impartial Jurisdictional Disputes Board. Project agreements commonly address this problem with language like the following:

Illustrative Example

There will be no strikes, no work stoppages or slowdowns, or other interference with the work because of jurisdictional disputes.

Work shall be assigned by the employer in accordance with the procedural rules of the Impartial Jurisdictional Disputes Board, and jurisdictional disputes will be settled in accordance with the procedural rules and decisions of such board or successor agency. If the work in dispute can be delayed pending settlement, the employer shall so delay it. If the employer undertakes to execute the work, all unions shall respect the assignment unless and until changed by the IJDB.

When a jurisdictional dispute involves any union or employer not a party to the procedures established by the Impartial Jurisdictional Disputes Board and is not resolved between the unions, it shall be referred for resolution to the international unions with which the disputing unions are affiliated. The resolution of the dispute shall be reduced to writing signed by representatives of the international unions and the employer.

If the unions cannot reach agreement, the employer will make his assignment, which will be respected by all unions.

Use of Apprentices and Trainees

Local contracts commonly provide for the use of apprentices and specify a ratio of apprentices to journeymen, usually in the range of lesser numbers of apprentices. If apprentices are available, they usually are not allowed to work alone. This practice results in inefficient use of apprentices and in considerable unskilled and semiskilled work performed by journeymen.

Efforts to rectify this situation have resulted in provisions in special agreements which decrease the limitations imposed on the use of apprentices and which in some instances add a new classification of "trainee" in the skilled crafts. The following extract from the Houston Industrial Agreement is similar to clauses in a few recent project agreements:

Illustrative Example

(4) Trainee classifications should be included in all skilled crafts. Such classifications shall be considered a training classification and the rate of pay will be at the equivalent apprentice rate of pay. The trainee may be overaged for apprentice training, but will have the necessary qualifications to become skilled craftsman.

Training period will be at least the length same as the apprentice. The trainee will be assigned by the Employer to perform any work which is within the capability of the trainee. The trainee will remain in training until qualified to become a journeyman. Trainees and/or apprentices shall comprise from 20 to 30 percent of each craft's work force at any time and the composition of this ratio shall be at the craft's discretion.

(5) Journeymen will have the necessary skills required to perform all work within their jurisdiction. Wage premiums such as those based on height of work, type of work or material, special skill, etc., shall not be paid.

(6) Recognizing the need to maintain continuing support of apprenticeship and similar training programs in the construction industry, the Employer will, to the extent permitted by job conditions, employ apprentices to perform work which is performed by his craft and which is within his capability.

Trainees, however, have generally been unavailable from union halls, and contractors do not seem to have exercised their right to hire them directly. Union business agents find it politically unacceptable to accept trainees as long as only journeymen are seeking employment, and contractors are reluctant to rock the boat. This situation continues to represent a major competitive disadvantage to union contractors vis-á-vis open-shop contractors.

Craft Flexibility Clauses

There have been some attempts, especially in maintenance contract agreements, to decrease the use of rigid jurisdictional lines when these result in inefficiencies or delays. The following extract from the Baton Rouge Orange Book agreement is an example:

Illustrative Example

The Contractor may, if he desires, maintain a variety of skills within his group of employees to be prepared to have skills and/or leadership for any type of work that may arise.

It is understood that all employees will work together harmoniously as a group and as directed by the Contractor. Employees will also cooperate with and follow directions of Owner Representatives as required.

The Unions understand the extreme importance of keeping operating equipment and units running at all times. The Unions also understand that the loss of production and the cost of repairs together create a great loss to the Owner. Therefore, the Unions will encourage and advise the employees to exhaust every effort and ways and means to perform work of good quality and quantity. The Contractor and the Unions recognize the necessity for eliminating restrictions and promoting efficiency and agree that no rules, customs or practices shall be permitted that limit production or increase the time required to do the work, and no limitation shall be placed upon the amount of work which an employee shall perform, nor shall there be any restrictions against the use of any kinds of machinery, tools, or labor-saving devices.

It is understood by the Contractor and agreed to by the Unions that any employee will accept any work order, pertaining to any type of work, and perform the work to the best of his ability.

It is understood by the Contractor and agreed to by the Unions, that the employees of this Contractor will perform the work requested by the Employer without having any concern or interference with any other work performed by any employees who are not covered by this Agreement.

The signatories to this Agreement agree to the concept that work assignments cannot and shall not interfere with the efficient and continuous operations required in the successful application of the intent of this Agreement.

It appears that except in emergencies these provisions have not resulted in appreciable economies through the avoidance of the use of redundant labor because of jurisdictional lines. In the General Presidents' West Coast Offshore Construction Agreement, the following clauses are aimed at this same objective:

Illustrative Example

In the event that an emergency arises which would not warrant the "call in" of other men or others could not be reached, the Employer shall have the right to assign those on the shift to such emergency work as is necessary. The Employer agrees that in such cases it will have due regard where practicable to craft jurisdiction.

In the event qualified craftsmen are not immediately available and referral requests have been on file for at least forty-eight (48) hours, excluding Saturday, Sunday, and Holidays, with the appropriate Union, the Employer is free to assign such employees as are available on the job to perform work of any nature until qualified craftsmen can be referred by the appropriate Union.

In the interest of promoting harmony and efficient operations throughout the Industry, the parties agree to the concept that composite crews can often satisfy that interest.

When agreement can be reached on the manning requirements of a project, or series of projects, between the Employer and two or more of the Unions directly involved, then the

Employer can make work assignments to the employees affiliated with the agreeing Unions on any work falling within the joint jurisdiction of the agreeing Unions.

The Distribution Pipeline Agreement includes a similar clause:

Illustrative Example

Employer may establish for a project or job a crew or crews, known as a "Composite Crew," which shall consist of the required crafts in such proportions as are respective to the type of work to be performed, subject to provisions of Article IV, Section L.
In performing its work, the "Composite Crew" shall be allowed relaxation from strict craft jurisdiction, provided the employees from each craft are assigned to their craft's jurisdiction as far as practicable and possible but not inconsistent with the provisions of this Agreement.

Subcontracting

The building trades unions have traditionally sought restrictive language in subcontracting clauses so as to give themselves exclusive rights to construction work by excluding open-shop and independent-union employees. (For a detailed discussion of the legal limits of subcontracting clauses, see Chapter 4, section "Restrictive Agreements.") An example follows:

Illustrative Example

The Unions and Employers agree to be bound by the terms of this Agreement; however, nothing in this Agreement shall be construed to limit the Employer from selecting the most competitive bidder for the award of any work, provided such bidder has contractual relationships with the appropriate Unions or International Unions affiliated with the Northern Michigan Building and Construction Trades Council and signatory to this Agreement.

The Supreme Court in *Connell* ruled that for such agreements to escape antitrust vulnerability and be lawful under Section 8(e) of the National Labor Relations Act three ingredients must be present:

1. A collective bargaining relationship between the union and the employer.
2. Limitation to a particular jobsite.
3. Congruency with the basic purpose of the Section 8(e) proviso, which is to protect union employees from working alongside nonunion employees. Thus, a requirement that subcontractors have contractual relationships with a particular union or group of unions does not qualify.

Most-Favored-Nation Clauses

The term "most-favored-nations" has been applied to clauses the objective of which is to protect an employer from a competitive disadvantage which might result from later negotiation by a union of more favorable terms with another employer. Examples of these clauses are found infrequently in construction collective bargaining agreements, in both ordinary local agreements and some of the special agreements being considered here.

The U.S. Supreme Court in *Pennington*[2] found that any such clauses which prohibit a union from negotiating more favorable terms with other employers do not have the shelter of the labor exemption to the antitrust laws. Parties to such agreements could be found in violation of antitrust laws if the intent or effect of the agreement were an unreasonable restraint of trade. On the other hand, the type of most-favored-nation clause which makes automatically available to an employer more favorable terms subsequently agreed to by a union with other employers does not fall within the *Pennington* rationale of antitrust vulnerability.

Illustrative Example

More favorable terms. If, during the life of this agreement, the union grants any more favorable terms or conditions than are contained in this agreement, the union shall promptly notify the contractor in writing of any such concession, and the contractor may adopt such more favorable terms or conditions.

Apart from the matter of antitrust vulnerability, in considering the use of most-favored-nation clauses, the long-term effect of their widespread use must be taken into account. In many situations, special agreements have provided an opportunity to negotiate more favorable conditions than unions at that time could accept for all work in the area. If, however, most-favored-nation clauses become commonplace, the knowledge that any more favorable terms obtained in a special agreement would apply to all area work would deter unions from making concessions in special agreements. One might thereby conclude that these clauses would tend to lock in inefficient practices to a greater degree and that consequently they are not in the industry's best interest.

[2] *United Mine Workers v. Pennington*, 381 U.S. 657 (1965).

8 EMPLOYEE BENEFIT PLANS

Employer contributions to union pension and welfare funds have become an extremely important issue in collective bargaining. National labor laws have affected the bargaining and nature of employer contributions in two significant aspects. Initially, there is the question of whether employers must bargain collectively with respect to contributions to employee benefit plans. Second, if employers are assumed to be obligated to contribute to union-negotiated employee benefit plans, restrictions imposed by law on the nature and extent of employer contributions must be considered. In addition, recent legislation governing virtually all types of employee benefit plans has had a significant impact on the establishment, negotiation, and administration of these plans. It is therefore imperative that employers understand the effect of these various laws on their businesses and labor–management relations to avoid problems in this area.

Because of the nature of the construction industry, employers may be faced with decisions on employee benefit plans in the context of both salaried personnel and employees covered by collective bargaining agreements. While the legal aspects of employee benefit plans for both types of employees are similar, the approach to dealing with the questions can be very different. Particularly when collectively bargained employee benefits are concerned, employers' prerogatives can be severely curtailed; it is thus particularly important to be aware of the legal and economic consequences of decisions. Once employers are aware of the obligations imposed by the applicable laws, an approach to negotiations can be formulated.

EFFECTS OF NATIONAL LABOR LAWS

Employer contributions to employee retirement and welfare plans are included in the terms "wages" and "other conditions of employment" as defined in the National Labor Relations Act (NLRA).[1] As such, employer contributions to employee benefit funds (with the exception of scholarship funds for employees and their dependents and the provision of day care centers) are mandatory subjects of collective bargaining.

[1] 29 U.S.C. § 151, *et seq.*.

The NLRA makes it an unfair labor practice for employers to refuse to bargain collectively with employee representatives respecting "rates of pay, wages, hours of employment, or other conditions of employment."[2] The National Labor Relations Board (NLRB) has ruled that these terms of the NLRA oblige employers to bargain collectively with employee representatives regarding contributions to pension and profit-sharing plans and other employee welfare and insurance plans.[3] Even though employee benefit plans may have been established by a company prior to the unionization of its employees, the union, once entrenched, has the right to negotiate the terms of what were previously company-sponsored plans.

Thus, under the NLRA an employee must bargain with respect to employee benefit plans if collective bargaining is requested by the proper union representatives. The employer's duty is subject to all conditions relative to collective bargaining set forth in the NLRA, and the employer is not excused by any complexities which bargaining might involve. The requirement of collective bargaining does not mean, of course, that the employer must agree to any union proposal but merely that the employer bargain in "good faith."[4] (See Chapter 5, "Good Faith Bargaining.")

National Labor Relations Act Section 302

Section 302(a), the operative provision in the statute, provides that it is illegal for an employer or an employer association or their labor relations consultant to pay or lend money or anything of value to:

1. A union or an agent of a union which represents the employer's employees or which may potentially represent them or admit them to membership

2. Any employee or employee group for the purpose of causing them to influence other employees in exercising their right to organize and bargain collectively

3. Any union officer or employee for the purpose of influencing that person's actions as a representative of employees

Section 302(b) of the NLRA also prohibits the acceptance of any prohibited employer payments by the above-specified groups of employees or their representatives. Section 302(d) provides further that any violation of Section 302(a) or 302(b) is a misdemeanor and can be punished by a fine of up to $10,000 or imprisonment of up to 1 year, or both.

While the following discussion will focus on the requirements of the NLRA regarding the nature and administration of employee benefit plans, the scope of the NLRA is not limited to trust funds for these plans. Nor is the effect of the law manifested only in the form of civil actions by employers against unions and vice versa, as the following illustrative cases will

[2] 29 U.S.C. § 158.
[3] *Inland Steel Co. v. NLRB*, 170 F.2d 247 (7th Cir. 1948).
[4] *NLRA* §8(a)(5) and §8(d).

seem to indicate. As noted above, the statute makes the payments themselves and the acceptance of the payments a misdemeanor punishable by a prison term and a fine. Criminal prosecutions for violation of the NLRA are numerous. The following examples should be of particular interest to members of the construction industry.

Illustrative Cases

Arthur Fisher was employed as a master mechanic by Camarco Contractors, Inc. Aside from his employment with Camarco, Fisher was also building a new home for himself. During the process of building the home, Camarco gave Fisher quantities of sand, gravel, cement, and concrete to aid in its construction. Unfortunately for Fisher, in the same period he was also the financial secretary of Local 137, International Union of Operating Engineers, which represented a group of Camarco employees. After investigation of the gifts of construction materials to Fisher, the government charged Fisher with violating Section 302 of the NLRA by accepting payments from an employer while serving as an officer of the union. Upon trial, Fisher was convicted of a misdemeanor. Fortunately for Fisher, the court suspended the imposition of sentence and only placed him on probation for 1 year.[5]

A business manager of a local union was honored by a testimonial dinner for his involvement in the labor movement. The proceeds of the dinner came from the sale of tickets to the dinner and from advertisements in a souvenir program, some of which were purchased by employers who employed members of the business manager's local. The proceeds were used to pay the expenses of the dinner, to purchase a new car and a color television set for the business manager, and, finally, to make a lump-sum cash payment of more than $25,000 to the business manager. Aa a result, the business manager was indicted for violating Section 302(b) of the NLRA.[6]

Exceptions are, of course, specified in the law; otherwise there would be no permissible financial interaction between employers and unions. Section 302(c) of the NLRA exempts from the prohibition of Section 302(a) payments by employers to employees whose duties include acting openly for the employer in the labor relations area, compensation to a union agent for services rendered as an employee, satisfaction of a judgment or award or the settlement of a claim, payments that relate to the purchase or sale of a product for business purposes, and the properly authorized deduction of union dues from employees' pay (the checkoff exception).

With respect to employee benefits, Section 302(c) of the NLRA exempts employer payments to certain trust funds established for the sole and exclusive benefit of the employees (and their families and dependents) of the employers who contribute to the fund. Section 302(c) specifies that the payments received from the employers must be held for the purpose of providing one or more of the following employee benefits:

1. Medical or hospital care

2. Pension benefits

[5] United States v. Fisher, 387 F.2d 165 (2d Cir. 1967.)
[6] United States v. Pecora, 484 F.2d 1289 (1973).

3. Compensation for illness or injury resulting from occupational activity

4. Unemployment benefits

5. Life insurance

6. Disability and sickness insurance

7. Accident insurance

8. Vacation, holiday, severance, or similar benefits

9. Apprenticeship or other training programs

10. Scholarships

11. Day care centers

12. Prepaid legal services

Illustrative Case

The South Louisiana Chapter of the National Electrical Contractors Association (NECA) entered into a trust agreement with Local 130 of the International Brotherhood of Electrical Workers, which provided for the establishment of a fund for the training of apprentices in the electrical industry and the improvement of the skills of journeymen. The fund was to be supported by contributions of 1½ cents per hour worked for all employer members of the local NECA chapter. Two years after the trust agreement was effected, the collective bargaining agreement regulating working conditions for union employees expired. The collective bargaining agreement was not renewed because the local NECA chapter refused to accede to the union's new demands. A strike resulted. In a move which was directed ostensibly at testing the validity of the apprenticeship trust fund under Section 302 of the NLRA but more likely was a device intended to break the strike, the NECA chapter filed suit to have the apprenticeship trust fund agreement declared void. The court held that the apprenticeship fund was designed to promote harmony in an industry and benefited employer and employee alike. Thus payments by employers to the fund were exempt from the prohibition of Section 302(a) of the NLRA.[7]

This case illustrates one type of employee benefit trust which is maintained for a single exempt purpose specified in the statute. While many trust funds established by employers and unions for the benefit of employees are created to serve exempt purposes, payments to these trust funds may yet run afoul of the prohibition of NLRA Section 302(a) if a trust's assets are employed for purposes in addition to those specified in the statute.

Illustrative Case

In 1952 the Northern California Conference of the Plumbing and Heating Industry, Inc., entered into a collective bargaining agreement on behalf of the Associated Plumbing Contractors of Central California, Inc., with Local 246 of the United Association of Plumbers and Pipefitters. In 1954 the union negotiated an amendment to the 1952 agreement which

[7] *South Louisiana Chapter, Inc., National Electrical Contractors Ass'n v. Local 130, International Bhd. of Electrical Workers, AFL-CIO,* 177 F. Supp. 432 (E.D. La. 1959).

provided for the establishment of an employees' pension trust, an employees' health and welfare trust, and "any labor-management setup." Shortly after the amendment was negotiated, the Associated Plumbing Contractors entered into a trust agreement with Local 246 for the purpose of establishing the Plumbing and Pipe-Fitting Labor-Management Relations Foundation, which encompassed a pension fund, a health and welfare fund, and what was effectively an agency for the protection of wages, rates of pay, hours of labor, and other conditions of employment in the plumbing and pipe-fitting industry. The following year, 1955, the union again attempted to negotiate an amendment to the 1952 collective bargaining agreement which would have required employer payments to the foundation in addition to those already being remitted to the pension fund. The Associated Plumbing Contractors acceded to the union's demands, but several of its members refused to abide by or execute the agreement. The union threatened to strike the recalcitrant employers. In retaliation, the employers sued to have the foundation enjoined from receiving any payments from employers on the ground that such payments would violate Section 302 of the NLRA. The court agreed with the employers, holding that the payments were not to a trust established solely for the purpose or purposes of providing the employee benefits enumerated in Section 302(c) of the NLRA and thus were prohibited under Section 302(a) of the NLRA.[8]

In addition to the requirement that the trust fund receiving employer contributions be established for the purpose of financing one of the employee benefit plans noted above, Section 302 of the NLRA provides certain additional requirements concerning the administration of the trust. The first such requirement noted in the statute is that a detailed plan of distribution for the employee benefits must be set forth in a written agreement with the employer.

Illustrative Case

An electrical contractors association in Southern California negotiated a collective bargaining agreement, on behalf of its employer members, with Local 11 of the International Brotherhood of Electrical Workers. The agreement provided for the establishment of two separate trust funds, one a pension trust fund and the other an apprenticeship trust fund. It further provided for employer contributions to the two trust funds of 20 cents per man-hour worked. Several members of the contractors association refused to make the required payments on the ground that "the detailed basis on which the payments . . . [were] to be made" was not specified in the collective bargaining or trust agreements.[9] The employers specifically attacked the provision of the collective bargaining agreement concerning the apprenticeship fund, conceding that there were sufficient details with respect to the pension fund. The employers then filed suit to enjoin collection and receipt of payments by the union. The union contended that the statutory requirement of a written agreement setting forth a detailed basis for making payments referred to the manner in which employer payments to the trust funds were to be made. The employers contended that the statute referred to the manner in which benefits were to be distributed ultimately to employees and that the collective bargaining agreement establishing the apprenticeship fund failed to provide sufficiently detailed distribution terms. The court agreed with the employers' interpretation of the detailed-basis requirement but found that the collective bargaining agreement met the statutory requirement. It stated that Congress had intended such specificity as would guarantee the proper use of the funds. The funds held by the apprenticeship trust

[8]*Conditioned Air and Refrigeration Co. v. Plumbing and Pipe-Fitting Labor-Foundation Management Relations,* 159 F. Supp. 887 (N.D. Cal. 1956).

[9]NLRA § 302(c)(5)(B).

could be spent only for education and training, and no money payments could be made to any of the beneficiaries of the trust. The court further stated that if persons who are entitled to the benefits of the trust can be determined with reasonable certainty and the general form and nature of the benefits are clear, Section 302(c)(5)(B) of the NLRA is satisfied.[10]

An additional statutory requirement imposed upon trust administration provides that employees and employers must be represented equally in the administration of the trust fund. Given that qualifying funds take the form of trusts, the equal-representation requirement is generally fulfilled by a joint board of trustees composed of an equal number of employer and union representatives. As a result of the equal-representation provision, Section 302(c) of the NLRA also allows the selection of neutral persons as agreed upon by the employers and the union to participate in the administration of the trust fund. If there is a deadlock in the trust administration decision-making process and there are no neutral persons involved in the trust administration who are empowered to break the deadlock, the trust or collective bargaining agreement must provide for the selection of an impartial umpire by employer and union representatives to decide the dispute. The relevant agreement must further provide that if the two groups fail to select an impartial umpire within a reasonable time, a federal district court may appoint such an umpire upon petition of either group.

Not only must employers and union be represented equally at the trustee level, but the trustees must have equal access to competent professional advice.

Illustrative Case

A union welfare fund, otherwise qualifying under the NLRA Section 302, was administered by three trustees representing employers and three representing the union. The benefits provided by the trust, principally through the medical and hospitalization benefits, were funded through insurance selected by the trustees. The insurance adviser to the trustees initially had been selected by the union trustees and considered himself to owe primary allegiance to the union. Upon recognition of this situation, the employer trustees attempted to employ an impartial insurance adviser to aid them in the appraisal of differing insurance alternatives. The union trustees objected, and a deadlock ensued. After the trustees failed to reach agreement on a disinterested party to settle the dispute, the employer trustees petitioned a federal district court for the appointment of an impartial umpire to resolve it. The court-appointed umpire decided in favor of the employer trustees. The umpire stated that while the mandate of the stature had been carried out respecting an equal number of representatives, it was essential that each group of trustees have equal facilities for obtaining advice and counsel with respect to matters involved in the administration of the trust. The umpire further stated that the adviser selected by each group of trustees would be subject to removal and replacement by the particular group and that each adviser would possess the same authority and receive the same compensation.[11]

[10] Floyd Auten et al. v. Local 11, International Bhd. of Electrical Workers et al., 51 LC ¶19,552 (S.D. Cal. 1965).

[11] Ware v. Swan, 38 LC ¶ 65,727 (S.D. Cal. 1959).

As noted above and in the preceding examples, the administration of qualifying funds normally lies in the hands of a joint board of trustees. A person assuming a position on such a board must realize that he or she is assuming more than a title. As trustees, the persons administering a trust fund must exercise the care and judgment which persons of prudence, discretion, and intelligence would exercise, under the particular circumstances, in the management of their own affairs. When dealing with trust property, trustees are bound to exercise reasonable diligence in the preservation and protection of it. It is also the duty of trustees not to accept any position or enter into any relation or do any act inconsistent with the interest of a trust beneficiary.[12] If trustees breach any of the foregoing duties, they may be personally liable for any loss or damage, pecuniary or otherwise, to the trust or trust beneficiaries.

Illustrative Case

An employee welfare fund was established by a trust agreement entered into by the Employing Bricklayers Association of Philadelphia and Bricklayers Local 1 of Pennsylvania. The trust agreement was drawn to bring the operation of the trust fund within the exceptions provided by Section 302 of the NLRA. It contained a provision specifying that the trustees of the fund would be limited to investments permitted to trustees under Pennsylvania law. Pursuant to the applicable Pennsylvania statute, the trustees petitioned a Pennsylvania state court for permission to invest trust funds in the purchase of a building to house the offices of the fund. Several employees opposed the petition on the ground, among others, that investment in an office building was a violation of Pennsylvania law governing investments by fiduciaries, which provided that investment of trust funds should be made with "that degree of judgment and care, under the circumstances then prevailing, which men of prudence, discretion and intelligence exercise in the management of their own affairs. . . ." In deciding the issue, the court stated that it was clear that the fund required office space and that evidence adduced at the trial left no doubt that the space then available was inadequate. The court also pointed to the fact that during the first several years of ownership by the trust, when the entire building would not be required for office purposes, a large portion of the building could be rented, producing a positive income stream from the investment. In addition, the price of the building was set at only $45,000, while two independent appraisers fixed its value at $50,000 and $52,000 respectively. On the basis of the combination of the foregoing factors, the court held the investment to be within the permissible discretion of the trustees.[13]

There is an additional requirement concerning the administration of trust funds seeking to qualify under NLRA Section 302(c). The trust agreement must also provide for an annual audit of the trust fund, a statement of the results of which must be available for inspection by interested persons at the principal office of the trust fund and at such other places as may be designated in the trust agreement. This requirement of the statute is intended to provide interested persons with access to accurate information concerning the financial status of the trust fund, and its effect may not be

[12] See, e.g., D. H. REDFEARN, WILLS AND ADMINISTRATION IN GEORGIA (3d ed. 1964), § 210, citing Perdue v. McKenzie, 194 Ga. 356 (1942).

[13] In re Bricklayers Local 1 of Pa. Welfare Fund, 159 F. Supp. 37 (E.D. Pa. 1958).

avoided through union or employee pressure on persons seeking to exercise the right of inspection.

Illustrative Case

Local 138 of the International Union of Operating Engineers was involved in the establishment of an employee welfare fund qualifying under Section 302(c) of the NLRA. In accordance with the terms of the trust agreement, the trustees caused to be produced a document which purported to be the result of an annual audit. A union member named Wilkens, who received a copy of the financial report, presented the document to his attorney to inquire into the legal sufficiency of the financial statement. Upon learning of this action, several members of Local 138 filed formal charges against Wilkens, pursuant to the union disciplinary procedure, citing, among other things, that Wilkens's disclosure of the welfare fund audit report to his attorney violated his duty as a union member. The union notified Wilkens that he would be tried on that charge at an upcoming union meeting and could be expelled from the union if the charge was upheld. To avoid trial by the union, Wilkens filed a motion for a temporary injunction to stop the union from trying him on the charge. Wilkens claimed that charges were instigated by the union to preclude him and other welfare fund beneficiaries from investigating the finances of the fund. The court granted Wilkens's motion, stating that his examination of the financial report and consulting his attorney about it constituted the exercise of a right granted by Congress and that it could not be tortured into a violation of Wilkens's duty as a member of the union.[14]

There is one final requirement specified in Section 302(c) of the NLRA that is applicable only to pension funds. When employer payments are to be used for pensions and annuities, they must be segregated in a separate trust which provides that the funds held therein cannot be used for any purpose other than paying such pensions or annuities.

In addition to the NLRA, other federal laws have an impact on employee benefit plans. Perhaps the greatest impact in recent years has been made by the Employee Retirement Income Security Act of 1974 (ERISA).

EMPLOYEE RETIREMENT INCOME SECURITY ACT OF 1974

Deferred-compensation and welfare plans have flourished in recent years for a number of reasons, many of which are related to tax savings. The popularity of employee benefit plans is illustrated by the number of employees covered and the total assets of these plans. Rapid growth of the private pension system from 1960 to 1970 resulted in approximately 30 million workers, comprising 48 percent of the workforce, being covered by private pension plans in 1970. Plan assets in 1970 totaled $138 billion and were increasing by $12 billion to $15 billion a year. Benefits paid by private pension plans totalled $7.4 billion in 1970. It has been estimated that there are 350,000 pension plans and 1,800,000 million pension and welfare plans in operation in the United States.

This rapid growth of the pension system was accompanied by prob-

---

[14] *Wilkens v. De Koning*, 152 F. Supp. 306 (E.D.N.Y. 1957).

lems. Many workers, even after long service, ultimately lost their benefits because they had left their jobs. Other workers were denied benefits when companies ceased operation with insufficient funds in a pension plan with which to pay promised pensions. Some pension funds were invested primarily for the benefit of the company or the plan administrators rather than for the workers.

The growth of the plans and the accompanying problems led to the enactment of the Employee Retirement Income Security Act of 1974. For the employer, ERISA carries both benefits and burdens; the law imposed some new responsibilities and liabilities upon employers and those who operate pension and welfare plans, including, of course, collectively bargained employee benefit plans.

Effect of ERISA

Almost without exception, any pension and profit-sharing plan in existence in 1974 required amending to comply with ERISA. With the exception of governmental and church plans, it is not the party who operates the plan but the type of plan operated that is important. Thus, jointly administered plans, found throughout the construction industry, are subject to ERISA if the type of plan in operation is covered by all or part of the act. Although the law placed the most stringent rules upon "defined-benefit plans" (normal pension plans that promise a specific benefit to an employee after a certain period of time), ERISA also put new requirements on "defined-contribution plans" (plans that provide for individual accounts for participants and benefits based solely on contributions, gains, and losses, a category that includes profit-sharing plans, money-purchase pension plans, thrift and savings plans, and stock bonus plans). For the first time, "employee welfare benefit plans" (plans providing benefits for medical, surgical, or hospital care; accident, sickness, disability, or death; unemployment or vacation; scholarship, apprenticeship, or training; day care centers; prepaid legal services; or stock purchase, savings, or other plans, except pension plans, described in Section 302(c) of the NLRA) were also regulated to some extent.

Thus, virtually all employers who maintain any retirement or welfare benefit plans were affected by ERISA to some extent. Further, heavy penalties and liabilities were imposed for failure to comply with ERISA's requirements.

In addition to affecting employer-maintained benefit plans directly, ERISA affected employer financial statements and company operations. The balance sheet and income statement reflected the increased costs of administration and changes made in a plan's funding policy or other necessary disclosures. The provisions of ERISA that permit an employee to transfer vested benefits from one qualified plan to another increased the likelihood of employee turnover. The new disclosure requirements gave employees more information about their benefits, thus increasing or decreasing employee morale and satisfaction. Moreover, the new funding requirements for defined-benefit plans increased the annual contributions required of employers, thus hindering cash flow. The law also mandated insurance coverage for the termination of defined-benefit plans and required the contribution of a portion of the employer's assets to plan benefits if a defined-benefit plan should terminate with insufficient assets.

The picture, however, was not entirely bleak for the employer. ERISA permitted an employer to exclude employees from a plan and still satisfy the coverage and antidiscrimination tax rules if the excluded employees were covered by a collective bargaining agreement and there was evidence that retirement benefits were the subject of good-faith bargaining. This provision gave greater freedom to construction industry employers in particular in adopting salaried-only plans.

ERISA contains provisions that are enforced by the Internal Revenue Service (IRS) and the Department of Labor. Violations of ERISA can result not only in the loss of tax benefits or the imposition of penalty taxes but also in criminal penalties. Thus, it is important for employers to be aware of the law's requirements for both salaried-only plans and collectively bargained plans.

There are five essential parts to ERISA, all aimed toward the goal of providing new protections and guarantees for employees covered by private pension and welfare plans. In the area of *participation* in plans, ERISA extended the coverage of private retirement plans to greater numbers of workers by requiring earlier participation. In the area of *vesting,* standards were established to assure that a worker who participates in a plan actually receives benefits and does not lose them because of unreasonable forfeiture provisions or inadequate fund resources. ERISA also established *fiduciary standards* that require those controlling a benefit fund to act as reasonable and prudent persons, discharging their duties solely in the interest of protecting the beneficiaries. Tough *reporting and disclosure standards* were imposed, making full disclosure to participants and the government of all information concerning the operation of a plan mandatory. Finally, a federally sponsored, privately financed Pension Benefit Guaranty Corporation (PBGC) was established to ensure the payment of adequate retirement benefit to employees whose private pension plans have *terminated* with assets insufficient to meet obligations.

What Plans Are Covered

ERISA does not apply only to pension plans. It is for this reason that the acronym ERISA, which stands for Employee Retirement Income Security Act, has become the standard rather than Pension Reform Act, which has been used by some people.

There are *three basic types* of plans that are covered by ERISA:

1. *Defined-contribution plans.* Also referred to as individual-account plans, they provide for individual accounts for participants and for benefits based solely on contributions and on

gains, losses, and expenses related to the contributions. These plans include profit-sharing plans, money-purchase pension plans, thrift and savings plans, and stock bonus plans.

2. *Defined-benefit plans.* These plans, which are the usual "pension" plans, promise to an employee a fixed dollar benefit, usually based on the number of years of service. For example, a plan may provide that an employee upon retirement is to receive a certain number of dollars for every year of service. ERISA defines these plans to include pension plans other than defined-contribution plans.

3. *Employee welfare benefit plans.* These are defined as plans, funds, or programs established or maintained to provide, through insurance or otherwise, benefits for medical, surgical, or hospital care; accident, sickness, disability, or death; unemployment; vacation; scholarship, apprenticeship, or other training programs; day care centers; prepaid legal services; and stock purchase, savings, or other plans (other than pension plans) described in Section 302(c) of the NLRA.

In addition to these three types, which were already well known and had been in existence, ERISA created a new type of retirement plan, known as the "individual retirement account (IRA)," to be utilized by any individual not covered by a private or public retirement plan. The IRA can be established by the employee, the employer, or the employee's union.

Not all of ERISA's requirements apply to each of the above plans. Employee welfare benefit plans are not covered by plan termination insurance and are not subject to the participation, vesting, and funding provisions of ERISA. However, these plans must meet certain reporting and disclosure requirements and are subject to the fiduciary standards. Defined-benefit plans are the most strongly affected by ERISA. They are subject to the requirements for plan termination insurance, as well as the participation, vesting, funding, reporting, and disclosure requirements and the fiduciary standards. Defined-contribution Plans fall in between; they are not covered by the requirements for plan termination insurance but must comply with the participation and vesting rules. If these plans are money-purchase pension plans or target benefit plans, they must meet the funding requirements also. Generally, however, defined-contribution plans are exempt from ERISA's funding provisions. These plans are also covered by the reporting and disclosure requirements and the fiduciary standards. Finally, it is most important to note that the fiduciary responsibility standards apply to practically all plans.

Employee Eligibility and Participation

As a condition of tax qualification, the prior law required that plans generally be nondiscriminatory. Certain mathematical tests were devised to ensure that employers benefited their employees as well as themselves.

Under ERISA, statutory limits were established for both service requirements and age limitations. However, other than the age, length-of-services, and antidiscrimination rules, there are no specific limitations for the participation of classes of employees. ERISA generally requires plans that do not confer immediate vesting upon participation to admit to participation each employee who has either (1) achieved a "year of service" or

(2) reached age 25, whichever occurs later. Further, maximum-age provisions are permitted for only certain types of plans. Employees who start employment at an age that is within 5 years of the normal retirement age set by the plan can be completely excluded from participation in a defined-benefit plan or a target benefit plan, but a plan may not otherwise exclude employees because they are too old. This rule was designed to avoid discouraging the hiring of older employees.

Many of ERISA's eligibility and participation rules are subject to time limitations based on years of service. A "year of service" is any 12-month period (to be specified in the plan) during which the employee puts in at least 1000 hours of service. An "hour of service" has been defined by Department of Labor regulations. If an otherwise eligible employee is on the payroll on the anniversary of the starting employment date and has worked 1000 hours during that 12-month period, the employees participation must begin on or before the earlier of (1) the first day of the next plan year after the employment anniversary or (2) 6 months after the first employment anniversary.

Under prior law, if union employees bargained for and were covered by a qualified plan, a salaried-only plan could generally be established. Otherwise, however, an employer was often unable to set up a management-only plan because the IRS insisted on counting the union employees for the purposes of nondiscrimination and eligibility percentage tests. ERISA remedied this situation by providing that if retirement benefits have been the subject of good-faith bargaining, union employees can be excluded for purposes of satisfying the coverage and antidiscrimination rules of the tax law. It has been suggested that the test of good-faith bargaining will be that adopted in NLRA cases; therefore, the issue should be raised at the bargaining table at the very least. Although it is probable that the collective bargaining agreement need not state specifically that employees either have elected out of an employer's plan or have elected to take a lesser benefit, an employer should amass some evidence of good-faith bargaining. The IRS does request that evidence regarding retirement benefits for these excluded employees be submitted when an employer requests approval for a plan excluding union employees.

Vesting

Although an employee may be eligible to participate in a plan, this does not mean that benefits which may be accruing for that employee are vested. A benefit is vested, or nonforfeitable, when a participant or the participant's beneficiary has a legally enforceable claim to receive the benefit, either immediately or at some time in the future. The new vesting standards of ERISA were designed to assure that a worker who participates in a plan actually receives some benefits from the plan and does not lose them because of forfeiture provisions.

The vesting standards apply to both employee and employer contributions. Accrued benefits from employee contributions are required to be fully and immediately vested. For accrued benefits from employer contributions, there are three statutory minimum vesting schedules. Of course, more liberal vesting schedules can be utilized. The IRS has the authority to impose more liberal vesting schedules when a history of rapid turnover among employees makes discriminatory a threat. The following are the minimum statutory vesting schedules.

1. *Ten-year 100 percent vesting.* A participant's accrued benefit must be 100 percent vested by the time that the participant completes 10 years of service. This method has been described as a "cliff" rule; that is, the employee goes along for 9 years with no vesting and in the tenth year becomes 100 percent vested. However, if the IRS finds that this or any of the other vesting schedules, despite their being specified by ERISA, will result in abuse in favor of highly paid employees, it may not accept the vesting schedule and may disqualify the plan or may withhold qualification until a vesting schedule satisfactory to the IRS is adopted.

2. *Gradual vesting.* Under this rule an employee must be at least 25 percent vested in the employee's accrued benefit after 5 years of service. The percentage is increased by 5 percent for each of the next 5 years of service, resulting in 50 percent vesting after 10 years. Finally, an additional 10 percent vesting is required for the next 5 years, resulting in 100 percent vesting after 15 years of service.

3. *The "rule of 45".* A participant's accrued benefit must be at least 50 percent vested when the sum of the participant's age and years of service equals 45. Then 10 percent additional vesting is required for each year of service thereafter, so that the accrued benefit must be 100 percent vested by the time the sum of the participant's age and years of service equals 55. However, a participant's accrued benefit must be at least 50 percent vested after 10 years of service regardless of age, and there must be an additional 10 percent for each year of service thereafter, resulting in 100 percent vesting after 15 years of service.

Regardless of which vesting scheduled is adopted, ERISA requires full vesting at the normal retirement age specified under the plan, but no later than a participant's sixty-fifth birthday or the tenth anniversary of commencement of participation in the plan, whichever is later. ERISA specifies rules applicable to employees who return to work for an employer after a break in their period of service with that employer. No break occurs unless 500 hours or less were worked in the course of 1 year.

As a general rule, once an employee's rights are vested, they are not forfeitable. Thus, if a plan changes its vesting schedule, the vesting percentage of each participant's accrued benefit from employer contributions cannot be reduced as a result of the amendment. And all accrued benefits in a qualified plan must become fully vested, to the extent then funded, in the event of the plan's termination or partial termination (for example, a large reduction in the number of participants in a plan or in the level of funding). However, a plan amendment may retroactively reduce vested accrued benefits derived from employer contributions if the Secretary of Labor approves the amendment on the basis that substantial business hardship threatens the existence of the plan.

As can be seen, the question of the vesting schedule is important and can have a significant inpact on the economic cost of an employer's plan.

Fiduciary Responsibilities and Liabilities

The requirements of ERISA that place responsibilities and liabilities upon fiduciaries have aroused the greatest apprehension among all persons dealing with any type of plan—pension, profit-sharing, or welfare. In addition, those who act as trustees on collectively bargained plans must be aware of ERISA's requirements.

ERISA places burdens on a large number of people who are connected with a plan. In particular, certain standards of conduct and other requirements are placed on fiduciaries. A "fiduciary" is any person who

1. Exercises discretionary authority or discretionary control respecting the management of a plan.
2. Exercises any authority or control respecting the management or disposition of plan assets.
3. Renders investment advice for compensation with respect to money or other property of a plan or who has any authority or responsibility to do so.
4. Has any discretionary authority or responsibility in the administration of a plan.

If any individual's association or dealings with a plan fall within these categories, that person is a fiduciary and must comply with the provisions applicable to fiduciaries. Persons occupying the following positions especially should examine their activities to determine whether they are fiduciaries: plan administrator, plan sponsor (employer or employee organization), plan trustee, plan administrative committee member, plan consultant employee of the plan, and the plan's or the plan sponsor's accountant. This list is not inclusive; it is the relationship to the plan and the powers of the individuals, and not the title they carry, that will determine their status as fiduciaries.

With certain very limited exceptions, the fiduciary provisions of ERISA apply to all plans. In general the provisions can be grouped into four main categories:

1. *Standards of conduct.* Persons dealing with plans and plan assets must perform their duties solely in the interest of plan participants and must act in accordance with the "prudent-man rule." This rule, which has also been called the "prudent-expert rule," provides that duties be discharged "with the care, skill, prudence, and diligence under the circumstances then prevailing that a prudent man acting in a like capacity and familiar with such matters would use. . . ."

2. *Prohibited acts.* Persons dealing with plans and plan assets are prohibited from engaging in certain types of conduct and certain transactions. They may not deal with the plan assets for their own account or benefit personally from any transaction involving these assets. With certain exceptions, transactions with certain "parties in interest" (such as the employer, a fiduciary of the plan, other parties who have an interest in or a relationship with the plan, or a union whose members are covered by the plan) are prohibited. In addition, for certain plans the acquisition and holding of employer stock or real property is severely curtailed.

3. *Required acts.* The act requires that plans be maintained pursuant to a written document; that certain funding policies and allocations of responsibility be specified in the document; that assets be held in trust; that investments be diversified to minimize the risk of large losses, unless diversification is imprudent under the circumstances; and that extensive reporting and disclosure of information about employee pension, profit-sharing, and welfare plans, their operations, and financial condition be made to the Department of Labor and to plan participants and beneficiaries.

4. *Liability and penalties.* For breaches of the above duties and responsibilities, the act provides for a number of remedies and penalties. For willful violations of the reporting and disclosure requirements, criminal penalties of up to 1 year in jail or $5000 in fines, or both, for an individual, and up to $100,000 in fines for a defendant who is not an individual (for example, a corporation) are provided. For cases involving embezzlement, kickbacks, or related violations, prosecution by the Justice Department under the U.S. Criminal Code is possible.

In addition to mandating and prohibiting certain actions by fiduciaries, ERISA provides methods for enforcing participants' rights. A participant or a beneficiary may bring a civil action against a plan administrator who refuses to respond to certain requests. For failure to suppy a participant or a beneficiary with a copy of the items that are required to be furnished within 30 days of a request (certain reports and plan description), the plan administrator can be held personally liable to the requesting party for $100 a day for each day that the failure continues. If a participant or a beneficiary has been denied benefits due or other rights under a plan or has been unable to ascertain future benefit rights, that person may sue the plan for relief. Also, participants, beneficiaries, fiduciaries, or the Secretary of Labor may sue for breaches of fiduciary responsibility. Any fiduciaries who improperly handle plan assets entrusted to them or who in any other way breach their responsibility are personally liable to make up any losses to the plan resulting from their breach and must also restore any profits that may have been made through the use of plan assets. The fiduciaries may also be removed from their posts. Civil penalties are authorized against parties in interest who engage in prohibited transactions with a plan. These penalties can be as much as 100 percent of the amount involved in the transaction. The Court, in any of these suits, may allow reasonable attorney fees to the suing party.

A fiduciary of a plan may also be liable for a breach of fiduciary responsibility of another fiduciary. This cofiduciary liability, however, arises only if (1) the fiduciary knowingly participates in or undertakes to conceal another fiduciary's act or omission when it is known that a breach has been committed, (2) the other fiduciary's breach was enabled by the failure of this fiduciary to comply with fiduciary standards; or (3) the fiduciary knows of another fiduciary's breach and makes no reasonable effort to remedy the breach. However, ERISA also permits allocation of fiduciary responsibility by proper plan provisions.

Trustees of collectively bargained plans and employers contributing to these plans must also be aware of the problems of employers failing to make required contributions to multiemployer plans. Under ERISA, unless the plan makes the proper efforts to collect delinquent contributions, both the employer and the plan fiduciaries, generally the trustees, can violate the law. The trustees run the risk of personal liability for plan losses resulting from this breach of responsibility.

The question of the extent of fiduciary liability is one that will take some time to develop through court cases. In the meantime, however, all fiduciaries must be aware of their responsibilities in order to avoid legal action and potential personal liability.

Reporting and Disclosure

The reporting and disclosure requirements of ERISA are in some ways similar to those under prior law and are in many ways different and generally administratively more burdensome and expensive. The drafters of ERISA were deeply concerned with protecting as well as possible the rights of employees and beneficiaries. Thus, reports must be provided to them as well as to the government.

While the Secretary of Labor has the authority to modify or eliminate some requirements for certain plans, the reporting and disclosure requirements apply to all pension, profit-sharing, and welfare plans regardless of size. Certain regulations exempting some plans from certain requirements and other regulations modifying the impact of the requirements on specific plans have and will continue to be issued, and all plan administrators and employers should keep abreast of developments in this area.

There are several principal informational requirements. A detailed plan description and a summary plan description must be published, as must an annual report. The summary plan description must be written in language that can be understood by the average plan participant and must be furnished to plan participants and, in most cases, to the Secretary of Labor. Technical terms should be avoided, and the summary should be easily understandable. The test is not whether the executive or high-level participant can understand the summary but whether the average participant can do so. The annual report requires much more detail than the summary plan description. If the plan is a pension plan (and not a profit-sharing, savings, or other individual-account plan), the annual report will include, in addition to the information required in the summary plan description, a detailed audited financial statement and opinion, certified in most instances by a certified public accountant, and, for the first plan year to which the funding requirements apply and for each third plan year thereafter, an actuarial statement and opinion, certified by an enrolled actuary. Information that must also be provided includes the number of employees covered by the plan; the name and address of each fiduciary; the name of each person receiving compensation, directly or indirectly, for services to the plan or its participants; the nature of such services; the relationship, if any, of the person with the plan sponsor; and any other office, position, or employment which that person holds with any party in interest. An explanation of any change in an insurance carrier, trustee, accountant, enrolled actuary, administrator, investment manager, or custodian must also be included. In addition, if participants or beneficiaries receiving benefits make requests in writing, they must be provided with a statement of total benefits accrued to them and nonforfeitable benefits, if any, or the earliest date on which such benefits will become vested. Finally, when a plan is terminated, a report must be filed with the Secretary of Labor and the Pension Benefit Guaranty Corporation. Trustees of defined-benefit plans must notify the Pension Benefit Guaranty Corporation at least 10 days before they terminate.

ERISA's reporting and disclosure requirements are an added administrative burden and expense to virtually all employers. However, this burden can be converted into an excellent employee relations tool. The increased contact that employers will have with employees can benefit employer-employee relations. In addition, employers, instead of waiting for employees to request personal benefit statements, could provide such statements automatically. It is up to employers to utilize these additional employee contacts to their and their employees' advantage.

Insurance

ERISA's new responsibilities and liabilities can be devastating if an employer does not properly take advantage of shifting certains risks to insurance companies. The act allows fiduciaries to obtain certain types of insurance and requires bonding of all fiduciaries. Sound business practice mandates that employers obtain certain insurance coverages if they are not already in force.

With regard to the liabilities imposed by ERISA it is important to note that, with the exception of cofiduciary breach and the appointment of investment managers, any provision of a plan that relieves fiduciaries from liability is void. The previously used exculpatory provisions are no longer permitted. Current Labor Department interpretations have, however, approved the use of certain forms of indemnification agreements which the plan sponsor assumes the responsibility to pay claims against individual fiduciaries.

ERISA contains only two explicit provisions with respect to insurance. The law provides specific permission for the purchase of malpractice insurance covering fiduciaries and allows three alternative purchasing methods:

1. The plan itself may purchase the coverage for its own protection. However, this coverage must permit the insurer to have recourse against the individual fiduciary. This choice is not recommended unless some effort is made to protect the individual against loss due to recourse.

2. Fiduciaries may buy the coverage and pay the premiums.

3. The employer or employee organization may purchase insurance for the fiduciaries.

The act does not address the question of purchasing insurance to protect parties in interest from losses resulting from this relationship. It has been suggested that this silence may indicate that such insurance may be procured. However, currently available errors-and-omissions coverage most likely will not include this coverage.

Directors-and-officers coverage that is currently available generally will not cover all fiduciaries adequately. And the normally high deductibles on such coverage may expose a fiduciary's personal assets to a major loss. The employer or fiduciary should obtain, in writing, the position of the insurer regarding the extent of coverage of present policies.

There are other insurance considerations. If a plan owns real or personal property, or both, coverage against loss should be obtained. Employees of a plan may require separate workmen's compensation insurance. Conflicts of interest in obtaining coverage for a plan and its sponsor should be avoided.

Another coverage available is employee benefits liability coverage, which normally will protect against claims brought by employees, former employees, beneficiaries, and legal representatives arising from negligent acts, errors, or omissions by employers, their executives, directors, and stockholders in administering employee benefit programs. However, depending on how "administering" is defined, this coverage may or may not provide a fiduciary with protection for all of ERISA's responsibilities. It has been suggested that for full protection of a fiduciary's potential exposure to loss, both fiduciary liability coverage (errors-and-omissions coverage) and employee benefits liability coverage will be required. However, it is highly unlikely that any policy can or will provide protection for the civil or criminal fines or penalties that can be imposed under the act.

Since the employer corporation or employer association is both a fiduciary and a party in interest with respect to its employee benefit plans, it is important that it too be covered as an insured party. In addition, if a plan is covered by plan termination insurance, some protection should be provided for the employer's exposure to a lien on assets in the event of the failure or termination of a plan (see below, subsection "Plan Termination and Plan Termination Insurance").

Bonding

Certain provisions of ERISA require bonding of fiduciaries and persons who handle funds or other property of any employee benefit plan (including pension, profit-sharing, and welfare plans) unless the only assets from which benefits are paid are the general assets of an employer or a union. The required bonds must be in an amount not less than 10 percent of the amount of funds handled and, in any event, not less than $1000 or normally more than $500,000. The bond must provide protection to the plan against loss by reason of acts of fraud or dishonesty. The bond surety must be a corporate surety company that is an acceptable surety on federal bonds, and the surety must not be connected with the plan. The act states that it is unlawful for persons who should be bonded, but who are not, to handle or control the funds of a plan. It is also unlawful for persons who have the authority to direct these functions to allow unbonded persons to carry out such duties.

The requirements of ERISA and the potential for personal liability of fiduciaries makes it mandatory that competent insurance counsel be consulted on insurance and bonding matters.

Funding

Funding is the process by which employers contribute to retirement plans in order to assure that sufficient funds are available to pay employees their earned benefits upon retirement. In the past, many plans were unfunded or underfunded. Funding deficiencies occurred because of inflated benefits, poor investments, large benefits based on past service, or high unemployment which resulted in inadequate employer contributions. Consequently, many employees received little or no benefits when the employer or the plan could not pay at retirement.

Under both prior law and ERISA, employers are required to fund costs attributable to current service. However, ERISA requires that employers fund the total cost of pension credits for prior service (unfunded past-service liabilities) over a specified period of time in accordance with mandatory formulas. The funding rules generally apply to defined-benefit (pension) plans and not to defined-contribution (profit-sharing) plans, and contributions in general must cover the normal (current-service) cost of a pension plan; past-service costs must be amortized over 30 years by level annual contributions. Plans in existence on January 1, 1974, and multiemployer plans have a 40-year amortization period. The gains or losses that a plan experiences must be amortized over not more than 15 years (20 years for multiemployer plans). Under the "full-funding limitation," if in a given year comparison of total plan liabilities (the present value of all accrued benefits) with the total value of the plan assets results in a lesser amount than the minimum funding requirements previously discussed, the amount to be contributed need not be more than the difference between plan liabilities and assets. The Secretary of Labor, upon application, may extend the amortization periods or waive the funding standard in a given year.

For tax-qualified plans that fail to comply with the funding requirements, a 5 percent nondeductible excise tax is imposed on the accumulated funding deficiency annually. Unless relief is obtained by the plan sponsor, failure to correct the deficiency after notice has been received from the IRS may result in a 100 percent additional tax. In the case of a collectively bargained multiemployer plan, each contributing employer's liability for excise taxes is determinated by IRS regulations.

Limitations on Contributions and Benefits

Although the tax laws have generally governed the amount of money that can be deducted and contributed to plans, ERISA amended and expanded the rules to provide for more nearly equal treatment for different kinds of plans. Specific rules limit the amounts that can be contributed for any participant under a defined-contribution (profit-sharing) plan and the amount of benefits that a participant may receive upon retirement under a defined-benefit (pension) plan. If more than one plan is maintained, the total limitations of prior law have been changed to a minor extent. There are now two limitations on contributions. The first regulates the amount deductible by the employer. This limitation does not prevent employees and employers from making excess, nondeductible contributions; such amounts would be taxable to the employee and fall outside the structure of the qualified plan. The second limitation regulates the maximum annual contribution (or benefit in the case of pension plans) that may be made on behalf of any individual participant. Violation of the latter limitation will disqualify the plan. There are also other rules to cover self-employed (Keogh) plans, individual retirement accounts (IRAs), and plans of Subchapter S corporations. Accordingly, an employer must pay very careful attention to the limitations to avoid very costly mistakes.

Plan Termination and Plan Termination Insurance

In the past, participants in defined-benefit (pension) plans sometimes lost accrued and even vested benefits because the employer maintaining the plan went bankrupt or the assets of the plan were insufficient to pay the benefits. For example, in 1972 there were about 1200 plan terminations with 19,500 participants in 546 plans not receiving benefits that were due.

Under ERISA, the Pension Benefit Guaranty Corporation has been established to insure against these contingencies. About 23 million of the 30 million workers who participate in pension plans are covered by the PBGC's insurance. Generally, defined-benefit plans are now covered by plan termination insurance. This insurance is intended to provide some benefits to participants if such a plan terminates without sufficient assets to pay promised benefits. Although plans subject to PBGC insurance requirements have been required to pay premiums, multiemployer plans that terminated before July 1, 1979, are not covered by plan termination insurance. The PBGC, however, in its discretion, can cover benefits for such a plan if it was in substantial compliance with the funding requirements of the Internal Revenue Code and the employer had no other recourse other than plan termination.

Under ERISA, employers are liable to reimburse the PBGC for the full amount of insurance benefits paid to plan participants upon termination of the plan. For a multiemployer pension plan, liability that arises due to failure of the plan to pay promised benefits is imposed on *all* employers who contributed to the plan within 5 years of its termination. The PBGC is empowered to allocate liability among the employers on an "equitable" basis. One such basis suggested in ERISA is that the allocation be made in accordance with the amounts required to be contributed to the plan by each employer in the 5 years preceding termination of the plan.

Once the deficiencies in benefits have been determined, ERISA limits the individual employer's liability for guaranteed benefits to 30 percent of the employer's net worth. In the case of the multiemployer plan, the limitation of liability to 30 percent of net worth is applied separately to each employer.

A question that remains unsettled under ERISA is whether the rule of 30 percent of net worth is to be applied as an absolute limitation on employer liability, regardless of the number of plans to which the employer contributes, or whether an employer will be liable for up to 30 percent of net worth *for each plan* to which the employer contributes. The latter interpretation, of course, could have disastrous consequences for an employer who contributes to many plans. The PBGC's general counsel has said that if two terminations are widely spaced, the obligation may be to 30 percent of net worth for each plan (that is, 60 percent of net worth), but if the two terminations occur on the same day, the obligation would be 30 percent of the worth for the combined terminations. Thus far no regulations have been issued on this point. It is hoped that when final regulations are issued, they will be more favorable to the contributing employer than the position of PBGC's general counsel. There is also a move to amend the ERISA law to eliminate the 30 percent contingent liability on multiemployer plans when the employer has made the required contribution.

There are a high number of underfunded multiemployer plans in existence. A report recently issued by the PBGC indicated that if all the financially shaky plans became insolvent, the PBGC would have a staggering $8.3 billion liability, which would in turn be passed on to contributing employers under ERISA. The potential for a catastrophe in the private pension plan industry brought about by the contingent employer liability provisions of ERISA is a great concern to PBGC and employers, and it is quite possible that legislative action will be forthcoming in the near future to modify this aspect of ERISA.

Of the approximately 350,000 employee retirement plans of all kinds covered by ERISA, some 100,000 will be covered by PBGC plan termination insurance. Profit-sharing, stock bonus, money-purchase, and other types of defined-contribution plans, although covered by ERISA, do not qualify for PBGC insurance. However, a cents-per-hour collectively bargained plan is not exempt if the plan promises a defined benefit.

As can be seen, ERISA is a complex and comprehensive piece of legislation. The IRS and the Department of Labor continue to issue regulations interpreting the act. All employers must keep abreast of new developments and consult professional counsel regarding compliance with this law. The cost of noncompliance may be too great to management, companies, and employees.

A Practical Approach to Retirement Plan Negotiations

Once an employer is familiar with the requirements of the laws applicable to retirement plans, an approach to labor negotiations on these issues can be developed. Prior to the commencement of negotiations, an employer must study trends and developments in the particular industry and geographical area regarding every aspect of a potential benefit plan. In addition, the employer must anticipate union demands and prepare alternatives to these demands. The employer must evaluate the cost of the anticipated union demands and the alternatives which the employer intends to propose. The management group preparing for the negotiations should consist of at least an attorney, a labor relations specialist, and a person experienced with employee benefit plans.

If the employer has not previously established a retirement benefit plan for the employees represented by the union with which negotiations are about to commence, the employer must consider two primary issues. First, the desirability of increasing the current wages of employees must be weighted against the desirability of installing a retirement benefit plan. If a decision is made to establish a retirement benefit plan, the employer must decide upon the type of plan to be negotiated with the union.

Whether the employer already maintains a collectively bargained pension plan or is on the verge of negotiating a new plan, the employer must consider and confront certain goals of labor unions concerning various aspects of retirement plans. Labor representatives will nearly always propose that the plan provide for early vesting of retirement benefits or otherwise permit employees to take their accrued retirement credits with them from company to company. With respect to funding the plan, union negotiators will seek to avoid mandatory contributions by employees, if at all possible. A plan provision allowing older employees to continue at work as long as they so desire and are able to do so is another union objective. Union representatives will also want to avoid plans which contain integrated and offset formulas and will favor those which provide for widow's benefits.

Any employer entering into union negotiations who does not have in effect some sort of retirement plan should expect that labor representatives will demand the establishment of such a plan. An employer who already is maintaining a plan should expect a demand for more liberalized benefits or, at the very least, a reduction in mandatory employee contributions if these exist.

Whether an employer favors increasing the current wages of employees or increasing other payments which result in deferred compensation for them, labor costs will rise. The choice will, of course, depend upon the employer's business decision as to which mode of compensation is more likely to serve to attract and retain key personnel, improve employer-employee relations, increase employee efficiency, and promote the employer's competitive posture. Many employers voluntarily offer older employees retirement benefits as an incentive for retirement even without establishing a formal plan. An employer should take into account the effect of retirement plans on older employees, since it has been found that a formal retirement plan properly funded in advance does not substantially increase labor costs above those of voluntary programs used as retirement incentives. Labor organizations generally adhere to the principle that employers are obligated to provide their employees with reasonable economic support after retirement as well as during employment, often admitting that the employees are unable to save and invest for their own retirement. Thus, union proposals during the negotiations will generally entail increases in both current- and deferred-compensation costs to the employer.

An additional factor which the employer must consider prior to entering into union negotiations is the average age of the union employees who may be covered by a particular retirement plan. A younger worker to whom retirement may seem very remote is generally not agreeable to giving up current compensation for the assurance of a retirement benefit to augment social security retirement age. Such a worker's concern is current cash compensation to cover daily family living expenses. However, older employees have a greater interest in the establishment and liberalization of retirement plan benefits.

An employer who has decided to establish a retirement plan must then decide whether a pension plan or a profit-sharing plan will be most beneficial. The union representative will generally demand a pension plan, with guaranteed benefits, but for economic and administrative reasons there is a trend toward collectively bargained profit-sharing plans. Once the decision respecting the type of retirement plan has been made, an employer with an existing plan may extend that plan to cover employees who are members of the union with which the employer is bargaining. If this will be an initial retirement plan, the employer may negotiate a plan to include all the covered craft employees. In the construction industry employer associations will typically negotiate a plan to make contributions to a jointly administered retirement plan.

An employer with an existing retirement plan is likely to favor an extension of the present plan rather than negotiating a new plan or making contributions to a union retirement fund. Such an employer may feel that different pension plans would result in discrimination in favor of one group of employees over another, not to mention the resulting duplication of bookkeeping and administration expenses. Also, an employer who is dealing with more than one union will generally want to have all union employees under one retirement plan. Unfortunately, as a matter of practice, the employer will likely be forced to negotiate a distinct retirement plan with each union bargaining unit. There are, of course, many instances in which an employer will be encouraged to negotiate the establishment or the joining of a multiemployer or industry-wide retirement plan.

In some instances, instead of establishing their own retirement plans, employers will find it advantageous to make contributions to a multiemployer retirement fund. In the construction industry a multiemployer retirement fund is the only practical way of ensuring retirement benefits for employees, since the nature of the industry is such that the labor force is extremely mobile. In many construction trades there is a heavy turnover, with few employees remaining with a single employer long enough to accumulate a reasonable amount of retirement benefits.

With the advent of ERISA, one of the principal obstacles to successfully negotiating a retirement plan has been removed. ERISA has had a tremendous impact in the area of plan funding. Prior to ERISA, the funding of a retirement plan was a controversial issue, with labor, of course, demanding that the plan be fully funded. As noted earlier, ERISA requires that defined-benefit pension plans, that is, those guaranteeing a specific benefit upon retirement, be fully funded.

Another critical issue involved in retirement plan negotiations was affected by the enactment of ERISA. Union representatives would uniformly demand that retirement plans provide for full, immediate vesting of retirement benefits so that the union members' retirement benefits did not depend on employment by a single employer until retirement. Union representatives will consistently demand "portable pensions," retirement plans under which employees can "carry" accumulated retirement benefits when changing their employment to another company. This type of arrangement has become characteristic of collectively bargained multiemployer pension plans. ERISA has been at least partially responsive to the idea of portable pensions. Under ERISA, retirement benefits must be vested according to the minimum specified limits. While ERISA does not require full, immedate vesting, nothing in the law would prevent union representatives from demanding such vesting of retirement benefits.

Labor's position with respect to portable pensions is very likely due to a view that pension benefits are earned rather than being a gift from employers. When workers change employment, labor representatives reason that they should have as much right to transfer accumulated pension credits as they do to receive back pay when they terminate their employment. There is an assumption that employees have agreed to serve a particular employer for less current cash compensation in return for deferred-compensation benefits and that if the retirement plan had not been in effect, they would have received a greater amount of current cash compensation. Labor also believes that without portable pensions the mobility of union employees is decreased. While this may be beneficial for a particular employer, labor believes that it is detrimental for union employees because it will ultimately result in depressing wage levels.

There are several ways in which a union may approach the issue of portable pensions. In negotiations for a single-employer plan, labor representatives may demand full and immediate vesting, in the form of a paid-up annuity that an employee will receive on attaining retirement age under the plan or a credit to an individual account in a retirement trust fund from which the employee will be entitled to a retirement benefit in relation to length of service with the employer, again upon attaining retirement age. If the union finds it necessary to compromise on the vesting issue, it should be possible to negotiate a graduated vesting schedule. The employer must be cognizant, as labor representatives will be, of the most implications of the vesting arrangement. The longer vesting is deferred and the greater the employee turnover, the less the retirement benefits will cost the employer.

There is a trend among labor unions to attempt to negotiate multiemployer retirement plans. This type of retirement plan is very attractive in trades in which there is a high degree of interemployer mobility but, in which relatively few employees leave the particular trade. The typical multiemployer plan provides that all employers who are parties to the collectively bargained agreement with the union will make contributions to a central retirement fund. An employee's service with any of the contributing employers will count toward the accumulation of pension benefits. Another feature which is becoming increasingly popular with unions that negotiate retirement plans in more than one geographical area is that of reciprocity provisions in the different local plans. These reciprocity provisions provide for the shifting of accumulated retirement benefits from one retirement trust fund to another. In this situation, an employee who has moved from one area to another will not sacrifice the accumulated retirement credits to which the employer became entitled by reason of employment at the first location. These provisions may expand the portability provisions of ERISA.

On the issue of employee contributions to retirement plans, labor representatives are generally extremely reluctant to concede that union members should be required to make contributions. Again, the view of labor is that since the employees are foregoing current cash compensation in favor of payments which ultimately will result in deferred compensation, the employees are already contributing to the retirement plan, albeit indirectly. Labor representatives also argue that mandatory employee contributions are inadvertently burdensome to employees from a tax standpoint, in that employees must contribute to the plan with aftertax dollars. The employer, however, can take a tax deduction for contributions to a tax-qualified retirement plan. Thus, the employer need not bear the entire burden of the contributions, as the government will be paying for a portion of the plan through decreased tax payments, while employees would have to bear the entire cost of their contributions.

Unions will generally oppose a plan that is integrated with social security, that is, a plan in which all or part of an employee's social security benefits are deducted from the pension benefit ceiling established by the plan and in which the company's contributions are intended to provide only for the differences between the plan level of benefits and the worker's social security. Of course, any increase in social security benefits enacted by Congress would decrease the retirement benefits payable under the negotiated plan as well as the employer's costs of providing them. Since social security payments have now been tied to cost-of-living increases, an integrated plan may result in an automatic decrease in the dollar cost of plan benefits as inflation continues. However, as social security benefits rise, the employer can be sure that union demands for higher levels of retirement plan benefits will be quick to follow. Integrated plans have been, and still are, quite common, but there appears to be a trend away from this type of plan. This trend may be furthered by the ERISA provision which states that when a plan participant is receiving pension benefits or has terminated employment with a particular employer leaving behind vested benefits in the plan, social security increases will not result in any forfeiture of vested plan benefits.

Construction employer associations should always attempt to negotiate contribution levels to retirement plans in cents per hour worked by employees. Negotiating a contribution to a retirement plan based upon a percentage of the employees wages is a trap to be avoided. Under a percentage of wages contribution, the funding contribution level will automatically increase when the employees' base wages increase. (See Chapter 6, section "Wages and Fringe Benefits.")

As can be seen, employers must be well prepared for negotiations on retirement programs just as on other economic issues. They must know the cost of funding a particular plan prior to entering the negotiations. Plan costs can be estimated by an actuary or an insurance company as long as they are supplied with the necessary information, such as pay rates, past service, age, and sex of the employees. Employers can be sure that union representatives will be prepared with all the necessary cost information when they arrive at the bargaining table. Only if employers are equally well informed, can they negotiate effectively. Also, knowledge of legal responsibilities will help employers defeat proposals that may give rise to fiduciary liability or are economically unsound for employees. Just as in business matters generally, the party who is best prepared is often the most effective.

9 INDUSTRY ADVANCEMENT FUNDS

Industry advancement funds, often known also as Industry promotion funds or simply as industry funds, are trust funds which are established with the basic goal of promoting the success of an industry, or, in some cases, of financing an association's activities. Construction employers as well as their employees can benefit from the activities of an industry fund which advances the interest of their specific segment of the industry. Many employer associations and unions have therefore included in their collective bargaining agreements a clause providing that contractors who use union labor contribute to an industry fund. Industry funds may be administered by trusts or by corporations.

The purposes for which such funds are established vary greatly. A fund may be restricted to use for promoting, publicizing, and advancing the interest of the industry, or its purposes may extend to product research, the education of employees, the recruiting and training of minority employees, the promotion of stable relations between labor and management, the payment of management's collective bargaining expenses on an industry-wise basis, the payment of certain expenses of running an employer association, or administering the arbitration of disputes and the adjustment of grievances.

The attractiveness to construction management and labor of an industry fund financed through collective bargaining will vary with the fund's purposes and the amount of control each of the parties has over the fund. Employer associations may desire funding through collective bargaining agreements because they are likely to obtain contributions from a larger number of employers. However, many employer associations have preferred to adopt a voluntary dues structure rather than a dues structure based on enforced contributions to an industry fund through a collective bargaining agreement. These associations argue that they have a greater incentive to perform substantial and beneficial services for their members than an association whose continued existence depends upon enforced contributions. Further, some individual employers may be opposed to the payment of industry fund contributions because they lack effective control over how the funds are spent, while others may simply not want to have to pay money into an industry fund.

Construction unions have an interest in obtaining employer contributions to industry advancement funds in collective bargaining agreements because such funds increase an employer's share of the construction industry and, therefore, employment opportunities for the union's members.

Despite the potential advantages of industry funds, there are potential disadvantages as well. Some trade associations which have taken a hard look at the results of cooperating with a union to obtain income for their industry funds have found that once enforced funding has been used to build up a staff and expensive programs, employers' negotiating power is severely diluted. The continued high level of industry fund income depends entirely upon the outcome of collective bargaining with the union and tends to result in large concessions in wages and fringe benefits. For example, the Building Contractors Association of New Jersey refused to bargain on industry funds because, according to association officials, "certain parasitic groups in New Jersey, through a desire and need for IAFP income, have prostituted the entire collective bargaining process and virtually signed any type of agreement to gain their objectives."[1] Funding industry advancement programs through a collective bargaining agreement has advantages, but contractors' associations should take care to avoid becoming dependent upon the unions and sacrificing basic bargaining power.

The Business Roundtable "Report on Contractor Association Financing" cautioned against an association's becoming dependent upon industry advancement funds which are enforced by union agreements. The report further reaffirmed that "unions have been granted concessions by contractors in order for them to maintain the association financing clause in the union agreement. In addition, where paid contractor association staff positions become dependent upon industry fund payments, the staff personnel have become vulnerable to union pressure." The Roundtable report suggests that the following alternatives be made available to contractors so that they need not depend upon the union agreement for collecting money to finance the association:

One such alternative is a 100% dues system, which is in force among a large number of local contractor associations. In view of the emphasis by some on the importance of industry funds to support contractor associations, it is surprising to note that a number of local associations still rely on dues. It appears to be the best alternative for most situations. Those associations that now rely on industry funds could wean themselves away from dependence on the funds over a period of time. During this change period, the objective would be to finance vital association functions through dues and allow industry funds to support other functions which could be eliminated without severely handicapping the association.

Another approach has been to combine contractor association labor relations functions into a single area association supported by voluntary contractor dues and contributions from users as subscribers for construction data information. Along with this type of area association, there is an increased willingness to use dues payments for the individual local contractor association support.

A voluntary charge on a cents-per-hour basis might be substituted for dues payments from contractors.

[1]Constr. Lab. News & Opinion (July 1975).

CONTROL

A group of employers may legally form and operate an industry advancement fund for the purpose of promoting their industry if there is no union control, but it is a violation of Section 302 of the National Labor Relations Act (NLRA) for the union to participate directly in the joint control of the fund. The situation becomes more complicated when an element of indirect union control is introduced into the administration of the fund.

Employer Control

The National Labor Relations Board (NLRB) has indicated that including a provision in a collective bargaining agreement for an industry fund controlled by employers is legal. In one case, the Board dealt with a fund of which all the trustees were selected by the employer and activities were restricted to promoting, publicizing, and advancing the interest of the floor-covering industry. After holding that a provision in the collective bargaining agreement for contributions to such a fund was a permissive rather than a mandatory subject of bargaining, the Board stated:

Nothing prevents an employer and a union from joining voluntarily in a mutual effort to attempt to influence their industry's course of development, provided, of course, that other legislative enactments do not prohibit such activities. . . . [O]ur finding herein does not imply in any way that parties are not free to include provisions of this type in collective bargaining agreements.[2]

Joint Control: The Industry Fund as an Employee Representative

Several cases have involved the joint control of industry funds in which a union participates in control by appointing some of the fund's trustees.

These cases have turned upon the issue of whether or not the industry fund is a "representative" of a labor organization under Section 302 of the NLRA. Pertinent parts of that section provide:

(a) It shall be unlawful for any employer or association of employers or any person who acts as a labor relations expert, adviser, or consultant to an employer or who acts in the interest of an employer to pay, lend, or deliver or agree to pay, lend, or deliver, any money or other thing of value

    1. to any representative of any of his employees who are employed in an industry affecting commerce; or

    2. to any labor organization, or any officer or employee thereof, which represents, seeks to represent, or would admit to membership, any of the employees of such employer who are employed in an industry affecting commerce. . . .

[2] *Detroit Resilient Floor Decorators Local 2265, Carpenters, AFL-CIO,* 136 NLRB No. 76 (1962); *Window-cleaners Local 139,* 126 NLRB No. 8 (1960).

(c) The provisions of this section shall not be applicable . . .

    (5) with respect to money or other thing of value paid to a trust fund established by such representative, for the sole and exclusive benefit of the employees of such employer, and their families and dependents . . . provided (A) that such payments are held in trust for the purpose of paying, either from principle or income or both, for the benefit of employees, . . . for medical or hospital care, pensions or retirement or death of employees, compensation for injuries or illness resulting from occupational activity or insurance to provide any of the foregoing . . .; (B) the detailed basis on which such payments are to be made is specified in a written agreement with the employer, and employees and empoyers are equally represented in the administration of such fund, together with such neutral persons as the representatives of the employers and the representatives of the employees may agree upon . . . and shall also contain provisions for an annual audit of the trust fund, a statement of the results of which shall be available for inspection by interested persons. . . .

It should be noted that the industry funds are *not* included in the specific exceptions to the general prohibition of any payment of money or other thing of value by an employer to a representative of the employees.

A Section 302 "representative" has been defined as any person authorized by the employees to act for them in dealing with their employer.[3] A factor to be given heavy weight in determining whether the payments are made to an employee representative is whether the parties are attempting to avoid the narrowly restricted exceptions to Section 302(c)(5).[4]

The majority of cases involving a joint industry fund have resulted in the finding that the fund *is* a representative under Section 302. In one case, employers made contributions to a fund which was jointly managed by union and employer trustees. The employers agreed to pay 19 cents for each hour worked by each employee. Authorized fund activities included paying the operating costs of the fund, such as expenses for conducting public relations, for the promotion of stability in labor-management relations, for the employer's cost of collective bargaining, and for maintaining facilities for arbitration and adjustment of grievances. The court held that the trustees were persons authorized by the employees to act for them in dealing with the employers and, therefore, that they were employee representatives under Section 302.[5]

---

[3] *Mechanical Contractors Ass'n v. United Ass'n of Journeymen & Apprentices of the Plumbing and Pipefitting Indus.*, 167 F. Supp. 35, *aff'd*, 265 F.2d 607 (1959).

[4] *United States v. Ryan*, 350 U.S. 299 (1956).

[5] *Mechanical Contractors Ass'n v. United Ass'n of Journeymen & Apprentices of the Plumbing and Pipefitting Industry*, 167 F. Supp. 35, *aff'd*, 265 F.2d 607 (1959); *accord, Sheet Metal Contractors Ass'n v. Sheet Metal Workers Int'l Ass'n*, 248 F.2d 307 (9th Cir. 1957), *cert. denied*, 355 U.S. 924 (1957); *Conditioned Air & Refrigeration Co. v. Plumbing and Pipefitting Labor Management Relations Trust*, 159 F. Supp. 887 (D.C. Cal. 1956), *aff'd*, 253F.2d 427 (9th Cir. 1956); *Operative Plasters and Cement Masons aff'd, Int'l Ass'n v. Paramount Plastering, Inc.*, 310 F.2d 179 (9th Cir. 1962), *cert. denied*, 372 U.S. 944 (1962).

Only one court has adopted the minority view that joint trusteeship does not necessarily mean that the trustees are employee representatives. The court stated:

> . . . that the term representative would necessarily have to vary in construction according to the purpose of the fund and the particular circumstances of each case. A broad construction of the term is both necessary and proper where employee welfare fund administration is concerned. *Here the only fund in question is a promotional fund* which is stated to be for the joint benefit of employer and union. To adopt the theory of the plaintiff would in effect destroy many present and future joint management-union cooperative efforts, which theory is expressly contrary to the congressional history of Section 302 and the philosophy of the Taft-Hartley Act.[6]

In the Ninetieth Congress there was introduced a bill which would have added two specific exceptions to Section 302; jointly administered product promotion programs and jointly administered committees for the interpretation of collective bargaining agreements. The bill was opposed by contractor associations and was not enacted. The associations argued that joint control would allow union intrusion into management prerogatives, lead to union harassment of employers who refused to contribute, and prevent industry funds from spending money to develop new laborsaving construction methods.[7]

Indirect Union Control

A union may attempt to assert indirect control over an industry fund without appointing trustees or sharing in the actual administration of the fund. For instance, a union may negotiate a clause in the industry fund provision of the collective bargaining agreement which states that the fund may not participate in any antilabor lobbying, may not subsidize a local employer during a strike, may not oppose express union policy or union interests, or must have advisory union trustees.

Employers may oppose any union control of an industry fund because they want to direct expenditures into such areas as employers' collective bargaining expenses, antilabor lobbying, research on methods of construction that use less labor, or perhaps even aiding employers to operate an open shop. Even if labor has no control over the administration of the fund, it may use the threat to eliminate the fund from the collective bargaining agreement as a bargaining tactic once the fund has come to depend upon enforced contributions. Employer associations which benefit from the fund

[6]*Employing Plasterers Ass'n v. Journeymen Plasterers Protective & Benevolent Soc'y,* 186 F. Supp. 91 (N.D. Ill. 1960).

[7]*See Hearings on S. 3149 before the Senate Subcomm. on Labor of the Senate Comm. on Labor and Public Welfare,* 90th Cong., 2d Sess. (1968).

may then be more willing to trade higher wages and fringe benefits to encourage the union to bargain with local employers for the continued presence of the industry fund contribution in the collective bargaining agreement. The unions, of course, favor joint control of industry funds so that they may prevent antiunion expenditures and negotiate for a clause which prohibits any fund activities contrary to union policy.

Actual indirect control can arise by inserting a provision in the industry fund that the fund may not adopt a policy contrary to the union's policy or interest. The requirement that the industry fund conform to union policy constitutes indirect control by the union, which may also be tantamount to direct control and violative of Section 302.

A provision stating that the industry fund shall not oppose union policy may also violate Section 101(a)(2) of the Labor-Management Reporting and Disclosure Act, which guarantees that "[e]very member of any labor organization shall have the right . . . to express any views, arguments, or opinions. . . ." Section 101(a)(2) was intended to allow union members to voice opposition to a union's policy. A union may not stifle the democratic and free expression of opinion on union policy granted by Section 101(a)(2) by removing a union member from office and punishing the member with a 5-year ban of silence.[8]

Similarly, when industry fund policy makers may not adopt any policy contrary to the union's expressed policy, they are foreclosed from considering any union member's views which may be contrary to union policy. Thus, it may be argued that the union member's free expression is stifled. But if the industry fund's activities are limited, as in the case when it may only promote and advertise the industry, it may be concluded that the union members have no interest in the industry fund and no right to contribute to its policy-making function.[9]

To avoid the prohibition of jointly controlled industry funds and to attempt to gain the safe status of an employer-controlled fund, the employers and the union may provide that the employers appoint all the voting trustees but that the union appoint advisory trustees without apparent power. The union would hope to assert the same amount of influence over the expenditures of the fund as it would have by appointing joint trustees and at the same time avoid violation of Section 302. For example, it could threaten to be generally uncooperative if the "advisory" trustees' recommendations were not followed.

Thus, actual control exerted by the union, when its advisory trustees had no apparent control would vary according to the particular situation, ranging from no actual control to joint control as a practical matter. Although no reported cases have dealt with an industry fund which includes advisory trustees, it seems likely that if actual joint control were established, a court could find a violation of Section 302. Furthermore, when a

[8] *Salzhandler v. Caputo,* 316 F.2d 445 (2d Cir. 1963).

[9] *Wagor v. Cal Kovens Constr. Corp.,* 382 F.2d 813 (5th Cir. 1967).

court applies the definition of an "employee representative" (someone authorized by the employees to act for them in dealing with their employer), it might find that activities of advisory trustees short of joint control, such as advising how funds should be used to affect labor-management relations, are sufficient to make the fund an employee representative.

To summarize, it appears that an industry advancement fund totally controlled by employers may be legally financed by providing for employer contributions in local collective bargaining agreements. At the other extreme, an industry fund controlled by joint union and employer trustees will be struck down as a violation of Section 302 of the NLRA. Intermediate situations, in which the union exerts indirect control over the fund, have not yet been directly considered by the courts.

USES

No reported cases which set outside limits for prohibited industry fund activities or purposes have been found. In practice, industry funds have been used for a myriad of purposes including publicity and advertising, public service projects, product development, labor-management relations, and administration of employer associations.

For example, the Sheet Metal and Air-Conditioning Contractors National Association Industry Promotion Fund has been used to:

- Conduct project research
- Establish industry standards
- Educate employers and employees
- Recruit and train minority employees

The Industry Advancement Program of the Florida West Coast Chapter of the Associated General Contractors (AGC) was established to:

- Promote stable labor-management relations
- Establish a public relations program
- Pay management's collective bargaining expenses
- Maintain facilities for the arbitration of disputes and the adjustment of grievances
- Administer health, welfare, and pension funds
- Promote relations between architects and contractors
- Promote safety programs
- Maintain apprenticeship programs

The Laborers' Industry Advancement Fund was created generally to:

- Train and improve the efficiency of workers

- Improve general conditions in the construction industry as a whole, including industrial relations, public relations, labor relations, and safety

- Advance and promote the general interests of the building industry

Industry funds have been used to interpret and administer collective bargaining agreements, work with architects and engineers toward improving and standardizing plans and specifications for the construction industry, pursue the construction industry's collective interests in the courts or public service commissions, and even sponsor public service television broadcasts. Specific expenditures from the AGC Florida West Coast Chapter's industry fund were for:

1. Seminars for management personnel on taxation and accounting; the critical-path method as a scheduling technique to improve the coordinating and planning of the parts and components associated with modern structures; the use of computers; insurance and bonding; provisions of a new state licensing law for general contractors and requirements for the competency examination provided for therein.

2. Publication of an area industry dictionary listing, for the twelve-county area covered by the chapter, building officials, architects and engineers, and labor unions and representatives and containing licensing requirements, collective bargaining agreements, and wage scales for the area.

3. Work with building departments of cities and counties within the chapter area on evaluation of the departments, building codes, and qualifications for contractors doing public work.

4. A 30-week foreman training program. This program, though obviously of interest and value to both employer and employees, has required the organizing and administrative experience of management to be put into effect. To plan the content of the course, attendance record keeping, and so on and to provide suitable speakers for many sessions of the program have been management's responsibility.[10]

Industry funds are sometimes used to run recruiting and training programs, and it has been suggested that industry promotion funds represent a tool, perhaps the only tool for the construction industry in the private sector with sufficient cutting edge in the way of money, to create a dynamic process for participation in construction by underpriviledged minorities.[11]

Since there are as yet no legislative or judicial guidelines for which uses are proper, the only restraints at present are the terms of the trust documents or corporate charter. Most states allow corporations to be formed for any lawful purpose not specifically prohibited to corporations under the other laws of the state.

It probably may be assumed that when the use of an industry fund is restricted to the area of promotion of the industry, consumer relations, product research, and other traditional management functions, such use will be proper. The situation becomes complicated when a fund is used in

[10] *Hearings on S. 3149, supra* at 98.

[11] *Hearings on S. 3149, supra* at 96.

areas which involve wages, hours, or working conditions, such as interpretation of a collective bargaining agreement. However, at this time there appears to be no legal reason for avoiding such uses.

There is one use which would be clearly illegal. If the industry fund were to transfer any part of its revenues to another fund administered by the union or jointly by the union and management, it would violate Section 302 of the NLRA unless the other fund was permitted by Section 302(c)(5).

EMPLOYER CONTRIBUTIONS

It has become very common for a collective bargaining agreement to include a promise by the employer to contribute to an industry advancement fund. The agreement includes a clause requiring that each employer who employs labor under the agreement contribute to the fund. This is usually stated in cents per hour worked but may be stated as a percentage of the employer's total payroll. Payments made to an industry fund established in accordance with the provisions of a negotiated labor agreement to be used for the common good of all employers covering matters of safety, education, and relations with labor, industry, and the public at large are ordinary and necessary business expenses and are deductible under the Internal Revenue Code.[12]

Some employers may not wish to participate in the industry advancement program or contribute to the fund. Normally, employers will not want to contribute to an industry fund established for the benefit of an association of which they are not members. An employer may lawfully refuse to bargain on the subject of contributions to an industry fund, and a union may commit an unfair labor practice if it insists that an individual employer sign a collective bargaining agreement containing a provision requiring contributions to an industry fund. In an NLRB case [13] the subject of industry funds was held to be a permissive rather than a mandatory subject of collective bargaining. The industry fund was strictly a promotional fund:

The employers agree as of the effective date of this agreement to establish a floor covering industry association promotional fund, which shall be used exclusively for the purpose of promoting, publicizing, and advancing the interest of the floor covering industry.

Each employer agrees to contribute $.01 per hour for each hour worked by each employee covered by this agreement to said promotional fund in addition to the other funds paid under this agreement. Said promotional funds shall be administered under the direction of four trustees selected by all the employers signatory to an agreement identical to this agreement . . . ratified by a majority of such employers.

[12]Rev. Rul. 63-137, 1963-2 CB 84.

[13]*Detroit Resilient Floor Decorators Local 2265, Carpenters AFL-CIO,* 136 NLRB No. 76 (1962), *enforced,* 317 F.2d 269 (1963).

The board held that this promotion fund was outside the employment relationship and concerned only the relationship of employers to one another or the relationship of an employer to the consuming public. Therefore, it was not a mandatory subject of bargaining.

In subsequent decisions, the NLRB has upheld the right of an employer to refuse to agree to a provision in a collective bargaining agreement requiring payments into an industry fund.

Illustrative Cases

The Board found that the Carpenters local union, the Metropolitan District Council of Philadelphia, committed an unfair labor practice when it insisted, as a condition of entering into a bargaining agreement with McCloskey & Company that the company agree to be bound by the terms of an industry advancement fund. McCloskey & Company was a large general construction contractor. When it undertook a construction project in Philadelphia, it attempted to obtain carpenters from the Metropolitan District Council. The council asked McCloskey to sign the area agreement which the Carpenters had entered into with the General Building Contractors Association (GBCA), an employer association. McCloskey had resigned from the GBCA about 10 years earlier and was not a party to the GBCA negotiations. The GBCA agreement involved a provision for contributions to the Industry Advancement Program, an industry fund with broad public relations and industry advancement purposes. When McCloskey objected to including the industry fund provision in the agreement, the council struck and picketed McCloskey's jobsite. To end the strike, McCloskey signed the entire GBCA agreement, including the industry fund provision, under protest and then filed an unfair-labor-practice charge with the NLRB. The Board held that the council had committed two unfair labor practices: (1) By conditioning the signing of a final contract with McCloskey upon McCloskey's agreeing to the industry fund, which was not a mandatory subject of bargaining, the union had refused to bargain under Section 8(b)(3) of the NLRA. (2) By striking and picketing McCloskey to force agreement to the industry fund, the union coerced and restrained McCloskey in the selection of its collective bargaining representative in violation of Section 8(b)(1)(B) of the act. The Board ordered that the council cease and desist from demanding that McCloskey agree to contribute to the Industry Advancement Program and notify McCloskey in writing that it would not insist upon contributions to the fund.[14]

The NLRB held that an employer could not be forced to pay into an industry fund if agreement to the fund was obtained in the manner found unlawful in the *McCloskey* case. The employer, Turner-Brooks, Inc., was a construction subcontractor who had signed an employer association's bargaining agreement with Local 80, Sheet Metal Workers. When the employer association and Local 80 amended their agreement to include an industry promotion fund, Local 80 demanded that Turner-Brooks also agree to be bound by the industry fund modification. Turner-Brooks objected, but when Local 80 threatened to call a strike, Turner-Brooks agreed to the industry fund provision under protest. Afterward it made no payments into the fund. The NLRB ruled that the union could not enforce Turner-Brooks to pay into the fund and that since agreement to the fund had been obtained in an illegal manner by insisting upon the provision over objection, despite the fact that it was a nonmandatory subject of bargaining, the industry fund provision in the Turner-Brooks contract with Local 80 was invalid and inoperative as a matter of law. The NLRB ordered Local 80 to

---

[14] *Metropolitan Dist. Council of Philadelphia (McCloskey & Co.)*, 137 NLRB No. 176 (1962).

cease and desist from enforcing the industry fund provision of the collective bargaining agreement with Turner-Brooks and to reimburse Turner-Brooks for all contributions made into the Industry Promotion Fund, plus interest.[15]

The U.S. Court of Appeals for the Eighth Circuit has affirmed the principles of NLRB decisions that an employer cannot be forced to bargain over an industry fund. The employer D. & G. Construction Company was the concrete construction subcontractor for a project in Kansas City, Missouri. D. & G. Construction hired four laborers who were members of Local 264 to work on the project. On the same day the field representative of Local 264 asked D. & G. Construction to sign a contract stipulation agreeing to all provisions of Local 264's bargaining agreement with a multiemployer bargaining group known simply as the Association. When D. & G. objected to certain provisions in the agreement requiring a contribution of 3 cents per hour to the Laborers' Industry Advancement Fund and the Laborers' Administrative Expense Account, it was told by the field representative that the contract stipulation must be signed without deletion of the contribution to the funds; otherwise Local 264 would picket the project. The general contractor, Price Brothers, also threatened to terminate D. & G.'s subcontract if the dispute with Local 264 was not resolved. As a result of this pressure, D. & G. signed a contract stipulation under protest. Later it filed a timely unfair-labor-practice charge against Local 264 within 6 months. The NLRB held that by insisting upon D. & G.'s participation in the Laborers' Administrative Expense Account, Local 264 violated Section 8(b)(3) of the act, since the funds were a nonmandatory subject of bargaining. The NLRB, reversing the trial examiner's decision, also held that Local 264 had coerced and restrained D. & G. in its selection of a bargaining representative in violation of Section 8(b)(1)(B) of the act by threatening to picket D. & G.'s jobsite to force it to accept the funds. The court of appeals affirmed both rulings and granted enforcement of the NLRB's cease-and-desist order.[16]

There have been attempts by employer associations which control industry advancement funds to force employers who are not members of the associations to make contributions to an industry fund. The issue of whether a nonmember must contribute to such a fund is analogous to the question of whether a nonmember is bound by collective bargaining agreements negotiated by a multiemployer bargaining unit. An individual employer may be held to belong to the multiemployer unit and to be bound by its agreement with the union when the individual employer has not formally joined the multiemployer unit. However, it must be shown by the individual employer's actions that the employer intended to belong and to be bound. For example, one court concluded that when five companies jointly solicited authorization cards on behalf of a particular union local, the companies were part of a multiemployer bargaining unit and intended to be bound by group action even though there was no formal membership.[17] Such participation must be wholly voluntary. By analogy a nonmember of an industry fund may not be forced to contribute to the fund unless the nonmember's actions indicate an intention to participate.

[15] Local 80, Sheet Metal Workers (Turner-Brooks, Inc.), 161 NLRB No. 7 (1966).

[16] NLRB v. Local 264, Laborers' International Union, 529 F.2d 778 (8th Cir. 1976), enforcing, 216 NLRB No. 4 (1975).

[17] NLRB v. Jan Power, Inc., 421 F.2d 1058 (9th Cir. 1970).

While it may be argued that a nonmember participates without taking any personal action because of benefits from the activities of the fund, an employer's actions may demonstrate a clear wish not to participate. In *Wagor v. Cal Kovens Construction Corporation,*[18] the South Florida Chapter of the Association of General Contractors (AGC) attempted to enforce contributions to its industry fund by a local nonmember. The nonmember employer negotiated independently a contract with the union which was very similar to that negotiated by the AGC except that the industry fund contribution clause was excluded. The court held that the local contractor was not a member of the employers' association, had never designated it as its bargaining representative, did not participate in the association's agreement with the union, and did not adopt the contract negotiated by the association. The court stated that nothing in the national labor laws prevented a nonmember employer from chosing to go it alone in negotiating with a labor union. The AGC also argued that it should be clothed with quasi-legislative authority over local contractors to further industrial stability achieved through employer associations. The court held that authority for employer associations to impose their collective bargaining agreement upon nonconsenting employees within the industry must come from Congress.

When an employer assigns bargaining rights to an employer association, however, and the association and the union agree to establish an industry fund, the employer may be bound to contribute to the industry fund.

Illustrative Case

A contractor had bargained as a member of a multiemployer association, withdrew from the association prior to the expiration of its current union agreement, but executed an interim union contract which stated that it would be superseded by an agreement to be negotiated by the association. The association and the union adopted an industry fund in the new bargaining agreement. When the contractor refused to execute this agreement and pay into the industry fund, the trustees of the fund sued the contractor, and the union called a strike. The NLRB ruled that the union had the right to strike to enforce the industry fund payments, since by signing the interim agreement the contractor had accepted whatever contract the association would negotiate even if it included nonmandatory subjects of bargaining such as industry funds.[19]

An employer who is a member of a multiemployer bargaining unit might avoid being bound to an industry fund by stipulating in the multiemployer bargaining authorization that the employer does not give the multiemployer bargaining agent the authority to negotiate contributions to an industry fund. The general rule of multiemployer bargaining is that

---

[18]382 F.2d 813 (5th Cir. 1967).

[19]*Sheet Metal Workers Local 270 (General Sheet Metal Co.),* 144 NLRB No. 69 (1963).

one who seeks its benefits must accept the burdens of the resulting collective bargaining agreement.

The NLRB, however, has determined that when it was the practice of a group of employers to negotiate with the union as a group but then to sign separate collective bargaining agreements which often contained special modifications, particular employers could indicate at the start of negotiations that they would not be bound by any agreement on a particular issue without violating the NLRA.[20] This case involved a mandatory bargaining subject, a pension plan, and so the same result should certainly apply to a permissive subject such as industry fund contributions. The key to withdrawing the industry fund issue from multiemployer bargaining is to notify the union, prior to the negotiations, that the issue is reserved for separate bargaining.[21]

Some contractors sign a national union's collective bargaining agreement which may require them to accept the wages, fringe benefits, and conditions established in a collective bargaining agreement between the local union and the local employers' association. These national agreements, however, often do not expressly require contributions to an industry fund established at the local level. In a case in which an industry fund tried to enforce contributions, the defending contractor was not a member of the local construction advancement program or of the contractors' association, nor had the contrractors signed the local collective bargaining agreement, which required contributions to the construction advancement program. The contractor did, however, sign agreements with two international unions. Under these agreements, the contractor was required to pay the fringe benefits and meet the working conditions agreed upon in the contracts between the local unions and the local contractors. The contractor paid into the various fringe-benefit funds but refused to contribute to the industry fund. The court held that the industry fund was not a fringe benefit or a working condition within the meaning of those terms as contained in the contractor's agreement with the international union. The contractor's right to refuse to make contributions to the local industry fund was upheld.[22]

An employer who is not bound as a member of a multiemployer bargaining unit can legally insist that any industry fund contribution requirements be deleted from a collective bargaining agreement negotiated by a union and an employer association. A union commits an unfair labor practice if it attempts to force the employer to sign the collective bargaining

[20] Retail Clerks' Union No. 1550, AFL-CIO v. NLRB, 141 NLRB No. 40 (1963), 330 F.2d 210 (D.C. Cir. 1964).

[21] International Bhd. of Electrical Workers Local 68, AFL-CIO v. NLRB, 178 NLRB No. 108, aff'd, 448 F.2d 1127, 1237 (D.C. Cir. 1971).

[22] Construction Advancement Program v. A. Bently and Sons Co., CA No. 7784 (Lucas Co., Ohio, Court of Appeals, Mar. 7, 1975).

agreement containing requirements for contributions to an industry fund by a nonmember employer.

The net result of the cases indicate that careful contractors who are not members of a multiemployer bargaining unit can avoid paying contributions to an industry fund while they enjoy any accomplishments of such a fund along with its members. Contractors who demonstrate their intention to remain independent of an industry advancement fund may not be forced to contribute to it.

10 ADMINISTERING THE AGREEMENT

Successful labor relations are more than negotiating a favorable labor agreement. The real test starts after an agreement has been signed. The presence of the union and the temperament and background of the union business agents, coupled with any political pressures they face from the membership, combine to complicate the problem of employers in managing their own businesses. The basis of employers' day-to-day living with a union is a consistent labor relations policy. If employers wish to maintain good labor relations, it is important that management establish a reputation for truthfulness, predictability, and fairness with employees and unions. The contractors who are most respected by labor unions are those who resist expedient solutions and operate on a fixed policy so that recurring problems and situations will be handled consistently. Good labor relations start with basic courtesy and good human relations.

A primary concern of contractors must be to improve the productivity of their employees. Contractors who recognize this necessity can increase their profits by working at improving labor production to control their labor costs so that they may more successfully bid on jobs and complete them at a lower cost than the job estimate. Unions are not responsible for improving productivity; it is incumbent upon contractors to initiate necessary improvements in this area. Often contractors will state, "The union men won't work." The answer is, "Then you should go to work and get them to work. That's your job."

The major thing employers must do to establish their labor relations policy and improve productivity is to manage their businesses. Management should proceed to act and assume its rightful leadership role unless in managing its business or in dealing with a specific situation there is an express prohibition in the agreement against the action of management. In other words, management should act and let the union react to grieve or complain. Management should not seek advance permission from the union to do something that is not covered by the contract. The union will not give employers advance permission for something that is not in the union's interest.

Management can be a leader and at the same time consult with the union. Disputes often arise as to whether a certain work practice is permitted or required under the contract, and meetings between a supervisor and a business agent will sometimes result in a quick resolution satisfactory to both sides. But the supervisor must run the job as the supervisor sees fit and let the union bring a grievance if the dispute cannot be settled in management's favor. It should be kept in mind that if the labor agreement has a provision for mandatory arbitration of the dispute, the contractor may get an injunction against a union work stoppage and have the dispute settled by the arbitrator. The contractor stands a better chance of victory at arbitration when business economy and efficiency are on the contractor's side.

A union operates as a political organization. Union officials must be reelected preiodically, and the employee members of the union are their political constituents. This may explain the reason why some meritless complaints and grievances are presented to management by a business agent, who may be responding to members' wishes rather than exercising independent judgment. Even though the grievance may not be won, the business agent fulfills a role by taking it up with management; if the business agent does not win, the employees can blame management and not the business agent.

The job steward or the business agent cannot serve as a second boss. The employer and the employer's supervisors alone must run the job, and it is the function of a union to protect employees from management and not to join with management in managing the employees. Employers should not abdicate authority to union stewards or union business agents by allowing them to dictate how a job should be done. Management should also encourage shop employees who are long-term union employees to stay with one employer and attend union meetings. In this way union meetings will have meaningful input from loyal company employees as opposed to being run by hotheads who float from employer to employer.

It is essential that employer and supervisors read and become familiar with the provisions in the labor agreement in order to administer it properly. Many employer bargaining committees have won a point at the bargaining table and then lost it because the contractors in the area have allowed to develop a practice which was not clearly set forth in the labor agreement. Employers should be alert to dangers inherent in establishing past practices which add to or subtract from the contract and do not allow compromise. Management must not fall into the trap of permitting a union to demand organized coffee breaks when coffee breaks are not provided for in the agreement. It should insist upon 8 hours' work for 8 hours' pay. Late arrivals, tardiness, or extended lunch hours should not be tolerated. Management negotiators may have fought very hard for an issue which the union may try to avoid by various excuses. The collective bargaining agreement itself already is a package of compromises for which the management negotiating committee may have paid dearly in the course of negotiations.

ROLE OF ASSOCIATIONS

Contractor associations can play a key role in helping individual employers administer a contract. Regular meetings between the association bargaining committee and contractors and their supervisors should be held to discuss the meaning of the various contract terms. It has often been found that when experienced superintendents meet to discuss various parts of a labor agreement, not one of them has understood the agreement to mean the same thing. An association meeting should be held once the contract has been signed so that the negotiating committee can explain the exact results of bargaining to the contractors and their supervisors. The revisions in the new agreement and what they will mean in conducting daily job operations should be carefully examined. Members must be thoroughly informed as to what the contract says, what it requires them to do, and what it does not require them to do. Contractors and their supervisors should be encouraged to telephone the association's manager or labor law attorney to resolve every question of contract interpretation as soon as it arises. Otherwise, the union will be permitted to gain the upper hand in administering the contract.

Local associations and the union often schedule regular meetings on a set day each month so that labor relations committee members and an equal number of union representatives can deal with disputes and other problems that may arise under the collective bargaining agreement. Even if there are no specific matters on the agenda, it is a good idea to hold regularly scheduled meetings to build rapport between the sides. Just as in bargaining, the meeting sites of the labor relations committee during the administration of the contract should be rotated between management and labor sites. Each meeting should work from an agenda which is prepared by each side's notifying the other, several days before the meeting and in writing, of those matters which it wishes to put on the agenda.

The association manager and the union business agent should maintain open communications at all times. This practice will prevent surprise actions, and both parties can operate in good faith. Very often the association manager and the business agent can settle grievances before a formal meeting. In most areas where good labor relations exist, there will be a strong union and an equally strong management organization. Both sides should make an effort to support each other. Labor harmony and productivity will increase when both sides are led by strong leaders. There may be many areas in which both sides are interested in the same objective.

An electrical contractors' association instituted a concerted effort to put management back into the business of running its day-to-day work force through fair and consistent enforcement of the work rules, and both the employers and the unions were happy with the results. Production increased significantly, and management ran its workforce on a more businesslike basis, thus making life a lot easier for management and for the union.

It is vital that management become involved in all phases of the administration of the contract, particularly apprenticeship. Although management will have equal trustees on the apprenticeship committee, it is important that they function with an equal voice. The association manager must be strong enough to tell the members when they are in violation of the agreement before a grievance is filed. This can be done if there are good relations between the management association and its members. The association must represent its members' interests if it is to handle labor relations on a multiemployer basis.

The association can serve as an excellent device for members to exchange information on union attempts to avoid the labor agreement and add costly work practices to it. Contractors and their supervisors must promptly report unwanted union practices on their jobs so that other members will be prepared to handle the problem if it arises on their projects. In this manner the union will be prevented from establishing wasteful practices that might erode the terms of the current contract and be used by the union to set the terms of a subsequent contract. Also, the negotiating committee will be made aware of union practices to attack in order to make sure that they are not included and are clearly prohibited in a new contract.

HIRING AND FIRING

Employers must retain and exercise authority to hire qualified applicants and to reject applicants and terminate employees who do not measure up. It is a basic fact that good productivity begins with hiring a labor force that possesses the necessary skills and attitudes to achieve maximum production. Employers should spend a great deal of time in getting the maximum amount of information on applicants referred by the union before hiring them. They should screen each applicant through an appropriate application form in an effort to obtain as much information as possible regarding the applicant's skill, experience, and employment history. Each applicant should be interviewed by personnel who are familiar with the particular skills claimed by the applicant. The applicant should fill out an application form with the names of the immediate past employer and several previous employers so that the prospective employer can check with them for references and determine the applicant's work habits before hiring. The accompanying application form might be used as a guide.

When an employee has consistently disregarded company policies or work rules or commits a serious breach of conduct which cannot be tolerated, such as gambling or drinking on the job, the employer should be quick to terminate the employee. It is a good idea to get witnesses and statements from those who have knowledge that an employee has violated a company rule. Work rules must be written in company policies and should be fairly and consistently enforced. To keep an employee who con-

EMPLOYMENT APPLICATION

Full name	Date of birth

Present address	Zip code

Permanent address	Zip code

	Social Security No.	No. of dependents

Phone no. In case of emergency notify	Name	Address	Phone	Business Phone
	Name	Address	Phone	Business Phone

Do you have a disability that will prevent you from accepting any particular work assignment: Yes _____ No _____

If answer is "yes" describe _____

_____

Past employer _____

Former employers _____

_____

Signature	Date

sistently does not measure up or to enforce rules sporadically will have a devastating effect on the morale of other employees. Except in the case of a flagrant violation of company rules, no employee should be discharged until a supervisor has counseled the employee in an effort to correct a work habit or an attitude. The result of such a discussion should be noted in the employee's records for future reference.

Should it become necessary to discharge an employee, the termination notice should show the reason why such action has been taken. If the employee had been previously warned by a supervisor, the date of the warning should also be shown on termination notice. The employee should get a copy, and so should the union local. The employer should list the exact cause of termination on a termination report and not equivocate as to the reason. Of course, the employee should be interviewed by the supervisor prior to termination so that the supervisor can perform a thorough investigation. The supervisor should be patient, honest, and fair in dealing with the employee. The notice should list the exact reason for termination, such as nonproduction, tardiness, irregular attendance, drinking, use of drugs, gambling, disregard of safety rules, abuse of company tools, theft, horseplay, physical incapacity to perform the job, leaving the jobsite without permission, or violation of coffee or lunch break rules. An example of company policy is as follows:

COMPANY POLICY

1. All applicants for employment shall report to the office for an interview between the hours of 8 and 10 A.M.

2. All applicants shall complete the standard company application. All questions must be answered.

3. As part of the employment procedure, applicants shall be told of the following company rules and must agree to abide by them before they can become company employees:

    a. The employee must be at a designated work station at a preagreed starting hour. Should the employee be tardy, the following shall be observed: If the starting time is 8 A.M. and the employee arrives at 8:07, the employee must wait until 8:15 A.M. to start work. If the employee arrives at 8:35, the employee cannot start work until 8:45, etc. The supervisor must record this as lost time, and the employee shall be paid accordingly.

    b. There shall be no organized sit-down refreshment breaks. The supervisor may permit a break, but it shall be at the employee's work station.

    c. The lunch hour is 30 minutes, as specified in the labor agreement. If the employee takes more than 30 minutes, the supervisor will enforce this provision on the same basis as is outlined in Section 3, Paragraph a.

    d. The company will permit the employee sufficient time to put away tools and materials at the end of the workday.

    e. The employee must agree to observe all safety conditions and wear such protective equipment as may be required by job, contract, or project conditions.

    f. Use of alcoholic beverages or illegal drugs will not be permitted. The employee shall be subject to immediate termination if the employee is at any time found to be using alcoholic beverages or illegal drugs on the job.

    g. The company cannot operate unless it can depend upon its employees to be on the job when needed. Should the employee be unable to come to work, the employee should give the supervisor or a company representative as much notice as possible so that a suitable replacement can be obtained or the work reassigned.
        Additionally, if employee knows that there will be delay in arriving at the work station, the supervisor or a company representative must be so informed. The company does not feel that this is an unreasonable request, and unless the employee can furnish a legitimate reason, the employee will be subject to termination for failure to comply with this rule.

    h. The employee must have permission from the supervisor before removing company tools or material from the jobsite.

    i. The company tries to schedule all jobs for a 40-hour workweek, but on some jobs spot overtime may be necessary. To be eligible to work this overtime, the employee shall have worked 8 hours per day, Monday through Friday, preceding.
        Exceptions to this rule are sickness (in this case a doctor's certificate is required) and jury duty, a death in the immediate family, or prearranged absence with the approval of the job supervisor.

j. The company will not pay off an employee at the office without the approval of the supervisor.

k. The employee will not abuse the company's tools while they are in the employee's custody.

l. The employee shall immediately advise the supervisor of any injury or illness suffered on the job, regardless of its severity.

PLANNING AND COORDINATION

Initially, one of the most important decisions affecting productivity which a contractor must make is whether to bid on a particular job. In most trades there are contractors whose organizations are much better suited to one type of work than to another. Choices include renovation work versus new construction, one-story buildings versus high-rise, heavy industrial versus light commercial work, plan-and-specification versus negotiated or design-and-build work, and so on. The successful contractor can rarely be all things to all people. As long as an adequate supply of the type of work which a given contracting firm can do best is available, the beneficial effect on productivity of working within the firm's area of expertise can be very rewarding. Conversely, venturing into unknown territory can prove to be devastating.

The quality and completeness of plans and specifications has an important effect on productivity. Even the best of these documents available today require a significant degree of study, interpretation, coordination with other trades, and careful dimensioning to ensure that the worker in the field gets it right the first time without a lot of discussion with other workers on the jobsite as to location, routing, and so on. Very few things have as demoralizing an effect as having to take down and reinstall good-quality work which has been installed in conflict with the work of other trades.

A contractor must remain constantly aware of areas in which productivity may be improved and of feasible methods for implementing these improvements. This will require the contractor to remain in close contact with supervisors and experienced employees to obtain their advice on the most efficient handling of an aspect of a job. Close contact with employees serves another valuable purpose. A contractor seeking advice from supervisor and experienced employees gives employees a feeling of involvement in the contractor's business, and this feeling alone is likely to contribute to their efforts to work more efficiently. Another potential source for suggesting needed improvements and implementing them is other construction contractors. Contractors should examine other contractors' methods for improving labor productivity and determine whether those methods may be feasibly employed in their own businesses.

Often a contractor will work out a new method for improving productivity on a jobsite, but because of the fractionated nature of the construction industry the method will probably not be communicated to other contractors and will shortly be forgotten or recontracted anew by some other contractor. Contractors who are serious about improving productivity should make a concerted effort to communicate with other contractors in order to seek out new methods to improve productivity. Attending national conventions is a good way to maintain communications with contractors in the industry in other sections of the county. Reading construction trade journals such as *Engineering News-Record* and *Construction Contracting* (published by the McGraw-Hill Publications Company) and other specialty trade publications is a means of discovering new productivity standards.

A starting point for increasing productivity is to identify areas in which improvements might be made. Recent productivity sampling techniques have sought to determine how much of an employee's workday is spent in productive activity. A recent study revealed that up to 5 hours per worker per day on construction jobs are wasted in nonproductive activities. This breakdown revealed that two-thirds of a construction worker's scheduled hours consist of late starts and early quits, personal breaks, traveling, and waiting for tools, equipment, and instruction. Once the employee's unproductive activities have been identified, the next step is to devise reasonable means of reducing or eliminating the time spent in these activities.

Productivity can be improved by more thorough planning and coordination of the steps necessary to complete the job in the least time and at the lowest cost. The contractor must learn the requirements for the projects in hand and determine which crafts and methods will be necessary to complete particular portions of the work. An obvious consequence of poor planning is wasted effort, with some employees being paid for remaining idle or at least for inefficient work. In agreements with craft unions, a contractor should reserve the exclusive right to plan, control, and schedule all operations and to establish, eliminate, change, or introduce new or improved methods, machinery, or techniques to perform all tasks efficiently. Such a clause will allow the contractor to adjust to changed conditions and improved technology by permitting the introduction of new methods or equipment to promote efficiency.

Careful planning and coordination of a construction job will require that all necessary tools, equipment, and materials be readily available. Obviously a job cannot proceed if employees are delayed by lack of tools or materials. If there is a lack of materials because of a contractor's oversight, some employees will undoubtedly be paid for remaining idle. One union official, in response to a contractor's complaint that too many employees were not productive, retorted that the bricklayers would have been quite willing and able to lay more bricks if only the company had supplied them with more hod carriers. A contractor must identify what materials are required at each step of the job and should make sure that these materials will be readily available when needed.

The importance of accurate and thorough preplanning cannot be over-emphasized. Today many contractors are going a step beyond careful coordination to standardization and shop fabrication. The careful detailing and organization of material required successfully to prefabricate assemblies off the jobsite together with the careful selection of rigging and material-handling methods for each specific job pay off by leveling productivity at the jobsite. For example, if instead of being supplied with a stack of pipe, a box of fittings, and the necessary tools and miscellaneous materials to rough in the plumbing on the tenth floor of a multistory building, a plumbing crew is supplied with completely prefabricated assemblies, properly tagged and referenced to an accurate shop drawing and, especially, if all the material for the floor arrives together in one basket so that it may be unloaded directly from the crane onto the floor and set in place, then most of the negative variables associated with building height, remote storage, bad weather, large crews and work congestion are minimized.

Illustrative Example

A medium size mechanical contractor in Atlanta, Georgia, obtained a contract to perform the plumbing, heating, and air-conditioning work on a very large federal building. A slight loss of productivity could have meant a severe financial loss to this company. It invested a great deal of time and money in preplanning and organizing the job so that the men in the field would always have a clear sense of direction as to the productivity expected of them. The company limited the crew size to an optimum number of men to do the job efficiently within the time constraints of the project. A system of productivity measurement resulted in rapid and accurate measurement of the productivity of the new men who were hired because a substantial increase in the labor force. By using one man who had been with the company for enough time to be considered dependable as a "lead mule," it was possible to integrate two or three new men in a small crew and isolate them so that their productivity could be measured directly. Troublemakers, who are unproductive workers, could be isolated and spotted easily and corrective measure's taken without great delay.

A contractor who pursues this type of detailed advance planning must also be prepared to make an investment in the training of both the engineering and detailing staff and field crews. The contractor must be prepared to define objectives carefully, to develop and communicate standards, and train field crews to adopt streamlined methods to produce jobsite savings. Once these savings have been accomplished, the far smaller number of man-hours required on the jobsite will allow subcontractors to schedule their work more efficiently and will minimize the negative impact of the stacking of trades which results from poor contractor planning.

SUPERVISION

Not too many years have passed since almost every construction contractor brought a key foreman into the office, briefly reviewed the plans and specifications for a job on which work was about to begin, tried to impress the foreman with the importance of this job to the company, and then sent him to the field with an armload of plans and specifications and the contractor's best wishes to build the job. The tightening competitive situation, combined with the usual lack of predictability of this method of job management, has made contractors realize increasingly that to be really effective management must get involved in the detailed planning of a project. Modern management techniques, long standard in other industries, have begun to find their way into construction contracting. However, the transition from traditional field control to professional project management has not been easy. Some contractors have tried to professionalize field supervision while others have tried to teach professional engineers field supervision. Still others have split the job of project supervisor by combining a field supervisor with a project engineer. The concept of a young engineer telling a journeyman with 20 or 25 years' field experience how to do his job better has gone down extremely hard in some quarters.

The effectiveness of any effort to improve job productivity will ultimately depend upon the control that the contractor retains over the supervisors. It is through the supervisor that management instructions are transmitted and work rules enforced. It is likely that the union will seek a provision in the collective bargaining agreement that supervisors be union members. By requiring supervisors to be union members, a union seeks to influence them to act on behalf of the union in doubtful situations. A contractor may lawfully insist that the authority to hire, discharge, discipline, and control the working conditions of supervisors remains exclusively with the contractor (see Chapter 3, "Supervision"). If the supervisors are already union members, a contractor should resist illegal union efforts to influence supervisor-members in the performance of their supervisory tasks. A contractor should always emphasize to the supervisors that whether or not they are union members, their loyalty is always owed to the contractor.

Illustrative Example

A large international electrical contracting firm places primary emphasis on its first-line supervisors to improve and maintain productivity. The company has an effective program to change the attitude of supervisors who move up from jobs as union journeymen so that they are loyal to the company rather than to the union. It promotes journeymen to be supervisors with favorable attitudes toward the company. Supervisors' attitudes toward the company are further enhanced by assuring them that they will have steady employment and by increasing their wages and other fringe benefits above those paid under a collective bargaining agreement. This policy of turning union journeymen into loyal company supervisors and then vesting them with primary authority for controlling the productivity of the workers has been a successful company formula for more than 65 years.

Contractors should look for particular leadership when they choose their supervisors. Supervisors must first have a thorough knowledge and mastery of all the job skills, tools, and equipment used by their crews. A good record by a supervisor in handling a job will give a crew confidence that the supervisor knows the job and "can talk shop." A good supervisor leads by example: the supervisor who practices good work habits and is respected is more likely to instill these admirable qualities in the crew. Supervisors must be able to organize: they must be able to anticipate problems, adjust to change, and give comprehensible instructions to employees before their job assignments commence. They must exercise consideration, thinking of themselves as assistants to help workers get the job done, to smooth the way, see that they have what they need, make suggestions, and give support.

Contractors must instruct and control their supervisors concerning their responsibilities. Supervisors should normally be the first to enter and the last to leave the jobsite. They should arrive in advance of their crews to coordinate the work for the day, anticipate potential problems before they arise, and assign work to individual crew members. Supervisors must know their crews so that they can allocate the various jobs to the workers who are best able to perform them. They must also train new crew members, ascertaining their special qualifications and making sure that they know all the particular aspects of their new jobs. Supervisors must be available if an unforeseen problem occurs so that it may be resolved expeditiously. They must also make certain that all materials and equipment are readily available.

In addition, it is the supervisors' responsibility to enforce work rules. They should keep record of crew members' attendance, work habits, and work progress. Supervisors should consult with affected employees when problems arise. Sometimes there is a good reason for the employees' problems, so that compassion and assistance to the employees to rectify the problems will be the best solution. Harsh and inflexible enforcement of work rules sometimes leads to diminished employee morale and lower productivity. On the other hand, inexcusable absences from work, late starts and early quits, insubordination, and shoddy workmanship should never be tolerated. The failure to enforce these rules in a strict and evenhanded manner, when appropriate, will erode employee effectiveness and consequently lessen productivity.

Supervisors must be able to motivate their crews to work more efficiently. Increased wages are not the answer: they diminish dissatisfaction but do not necessarily lead to better work efforts. Motivation to work efficiently is built in part by giving employees a feeling of involvement in the company. Supervisors should state the reasons for their plans and also seek suggestions concerning possible alternatives. Work motivation is also strengthened by giving employees responsibilities they can handle, results they can show, and recognition for what they accomplish. One supervisor had this explanation for his success: "I try to put everybody in business for himself. Each one of my people is in charge of some part of the job. I just hang around to keep them out of trouble. When the work gets done, they get the credit. When it doesn't, they get the blame, and they know it. Mostly they blame themselves."

PRODUCTIVITY GOALS AND MEASUREMENT

Incentives for increasing productivity are also enhanced by setting goals. These goals must be understood by the crew and be reasonably attainable for each job function. Productivity standards will vary with the job, but the goals should emphasize both quantity and quality. They should be set high enough so that crews will have something to aim for, but not so high that they will adversely affect employee morale and have no meaning for the contractor when they are not attained. Supervisors should be told that they are responsible for improving their crews' work performance and that their own performance will be evaluated in terms of how close their crews are to attaining their goals. In collective bargaining agreements with unions the employers should exercise their right to set reasonable minimum production standards and to discharge or denote supervisors or employees who do not satisfy them.

Illustrative Example

The second-generation president of an interior contractor in Detroit who was trained as an industrial engineer instituted productivity standard for plasters, latherers, laborers, carpenters, and dry-wall finishers. The union complained to him, but it backed down when he pointed out that there was nothing in the collective bargaining agreement to prevent him from setting productivity standards. He estimated that his productivity increased between 15 and 20 percent because of these standards and that his employees were better satisfied by continually attaining realistic goals.

Employees who regularly fail to meet realistic productivity standards should be discharged. A company cannot afford to keep unproductive employees who constantly do not measure up because they will have the adverse effect of dragging down the other employees. The threat of discharge is often a positive influence. When a supervisor was asked how long he had been working for his company, he replied, "Since they threatened to fire me."

To improve and control productivity, contractors should establish a "feedback loop," a control system that measures productive output, compares it with an established production standard, and makes the necessary adjustments if productive output does not meet the established productivity standard. "Feedback" is the engineering term for the automatic measuring of output and the measuring of output against a predetermined standard so that input may be adjusted to maintain the quality and quantity of output. It is accomplished by furnishing continual, automatic data on output to a control device so that errors may be corrected immediately.

The essence of automatic control, feedback is particularly well suited to the control of the productive output of employees. A production standard should be established and actual production output measured continuously against the standard. Contractors should take steps to ensure that production standards are maintained through their supervisors, who should be responsible for correcting production deficiencies.

While many construction contractors have recognized the need for improving productivity, few have adopted methods for measuring productivity. The development of meaningful productivity measurements is important so that periodic reports of labor productivity can be compared with predetermined goals. Measurements will also provide meaningful feedback for the contractor, the supervisors, and their respective crews, who will all know whether the goal is attainable with current working methods. If it is not, the contractor can initiate adjustments to make the crews more productive. The contractor can predict whether the job will be completed in the time and at the cost that were preset. Productivity measurement allows the contractor to determine whether labor costs will exceed the job estimate, so that the contractor may consider either altering construction methods or adjusting estimates on future projects.

The work should be divided into easily identifiable small segments whenever possible. Attempting to use broader classifications generally results in a loss of contact with the estimate and a loss of employees' ability to keep track of how they are doing. If a mistake is found in the estimate, whether high or low, it should be corrected before it is used as a performance objective. For example, using an unreasonably low estimate for a task will probably result in more man-hours being spent on the job than if the contractor admitted the erroneous estimate and used a corrected estimate as the goal. No one likes to be measured against impossible criteria, and even the best field supervision will write off an entire work segment unless a realistic objective is established.

One of the most important factors in achieving good productivity is the establishment of realistic objectives for field foremen. The simplest and most direct way is to use the estimate for a particular clearly defined task as a yardstick and to share the estimated man-hours required with the foreman in charge of the installation. Of course, there has traditionally been much hesitancy to share this information with field installation personnel because of the fear that if a given work segment is too fat, the crew will take the maximum number of hours anyway, and if another estimate is too tight and cannot be accomplished, the crew will run over the allotted time and feel no responsibility for the overrun. Another cause for hesitancy is possible mutual suspicion between contractor management and field personnel. Management may be tempted to reduce the number of man-hours in an attempt to pick up labor on the job. Whether management does or not, the field foreman might well suspect that management does. In any event, this feeling of doubt will wreck any effort to gain an accurate measure of productivity by using the estimate. The only way to overcome this problem is to be completely honest about the number of man-hours in the estimate. Instead of loafing on loosely estimated segments of work, the foreman and the crew will take great pride in beating the estimate if possible, and certainly the fact that they are able to do so lends a great deal of credibility to a very tight estimate on another segment of work and generally results in a much greater effort to achieve a tightly estimated labor goal.

Illustrative Example

An interior contractor with offices throughout Virginia, Maryland, and the District of Columbia spent 4 years in developing a productivity feedback system that communicates the actual job estimate to the responsible supervisors in units that are meaningful to the employees in the field. If the original estimate is incorrect, a corrected estimate is communicated to the field to avoid employee and supervisor frustration in attempting to attain an unrealistic goal. Weekly reports are communicated back to the office to measure accurately the work units performed by the crews of each supervisor. Once a month the president of the contracting firm calls all his supervisors in to compare how well they have done with the productivity goals. Productivity has increased substantially, and the information has disclosed that the productivity of some crews varies by as much as 100 percent. The company then sets about adjusting low-productivity areas to increase their productivity. The company has utilized data processing equipment to provide very fast feedback to measure productivity weekly as a basis for corrective action and to establish more accurate estimates. This approach to the control of labor is the most effective way of refining estimating techniques. It also provides a rapid and accurate measurement of the productivity of new workers.

Current data processing techniques have developed inexpensive, readily available, and meaningful methods of measuring productivity. For such a system to be of the greatest utility to contractors, a weekly production report should be made of job progress according to a specific job function or job crew. Field report worksheets are distributed each day to the supervisor of a specific job function. Quantities of work whose measurements have meaning to supervisor and crews are filled out.

The field report worksheets are returned and compared with the productivity goals, which can be obtained from the contractor's estimate. Then a projection can be made from current work to show whether the total job estimate will be met if current productivity remains stable. If this projection shows that the cost of the work, when completed, will exceed the job estimate, the contractor will become aware of areas, in which productivity can be improved. The contractor may then alter existing work methods, and the measurement system will enable contractor, supervisor, and crews to determine whether the new methods have improved productivity. If new methods do not appear to be more useful, this measurement might suggest to the contractor that the goals should be lowered and future job estimates increased.

By following these relatively simple, perhaps obvious, but surprisingly often neglected techniques, a construction contractor can effectively minimize downside risk and maximize profit potential through much-improved labor productivity.

11 DUAL SHOP

The term "dual shop" is misleading. The ultimate legal goal in converting to dual shops is for the established company and the new company to attain the status of *separate employers* under Section 2(2) of the National Labor Relations Act (NLRA).[1] A contractor who wishes to establish and maintain a nonunion operation as well as a union operation must set up *two distinct companies.*

To "go dual shop" is a perfectly legitimate goal. In the usual but most difficult situation a contractor presently operating a unionized company desires to begin a nonunion operation in the same or a similar line of business, either to take advantage of business opportunities or to become more competitive and flexible. Often, the contractor will decide that it makes good business sense to try to capture that part of the construction market which is primarily available to contractors not bound to pay high union-scale wages and fringe benefits, and provide union working conditions. On occasion, however, a nonunion contractor may wish to start a union shop on either a temporary or a permanent basis to obtain work available only to union companies.

Although establishing and maintaining dual-shop operations in the construction industry has been done successfully, it is no easy matter. Both the strict requirements of the national labor laws and the practical realities of the industry contain traps for the unwary.

Establishing a dual shop is a matter of degree. On the one hand, two companies which are independently owned, are independently operated, and are engaged in different businesses are, of course, separate employers. On the other hand, two companies owned and operated on a day-to-day basis by the same person, engaged in the same type of work, and sharing employees, office space, and funds would undoubtedly not be considered separate employers. Between these two extremes lies a gray area composed of companies which have separate-employer status and others which do not. The most that can be said with certainty is that the more independent two companies are in every aspect of their operations, particularly their labor relations, the more likely it is that they will be found to be separate employers within the meaning of the NLRA.

---

[1] As discussed below, separate-employer status is not absolutely necessary, since it might still be determined that a bargaining unit composed of both companies is not appropriate under Section 9 of the act. Nevertheless, separate-employer status is the key to a successful dual-shop arrangement.

Careful planning is a prerequisite to going dual shop. The decision should be made only after serious consideration of the economic and possible legal consequences. The discussion which follows will point out some of the factors which are considered by the courts and by the National Labor Relations Board (NLRB) in determining whether or not dual-shop operations are separate employers. The consequences of success or failure in achieving a legally unassailable dual-shop arrangement will also be discussed.

In addition to the legal guidelines which can be followed in conversion to a dual shop, in the end the decision must also consider the practical and economic realities. The contractor must be able to foot the bill for establishing a separate operation and for defending the conversion from the union's attack. Practically, open-shop work must be available. The difficulty encountered in conversion will depend upon the militancy of the union and the general public attitude in the area. The dual shop had been found to work better in areas where there is a fairly strong open shop.

Once a dual shop has been established, constant vigilance is required to maintain a stable situation. This is best accomplished by drafting a plan which meets applicable labor law standards and sticking to it.

The procedure by which an owner of a union shop construction company may successfully establish a dual-shop operation requires patience, steadfastness, and experienced legal assistance. The job cannot be done overnight. It requires planning to establish and maintain separate-employer status and the persistence of both employers to preserve their position regardless of union pressure.

SEPARATE-EMPLOYER STATUS

The primary benefit of separate-employer status is that the new nonunion company need not deal with the union which represents the employees of the predecessor union company (or if the predecessor company is a nonunion employer, the new company's union agreements will not apply to it). The union involved will not be recognized as the representative of the employees of the nonunion company. The collective bargaining agreements between the contractor and the union will not extend to cover the employees of the nonunion company. The nonunion company need not meet the wage, fringe-benefit, and work rule requirements of the union company's bargaining contracts.

Of course, the union which represents the employees of the predecessor company may attempt to attack the new arrangement. There are several fronts on which this battle can be fought.

The union may contend that the new employees are an accretion to the original bargaining unit and seek to have itself declared their representative. If the companies are found to have separate-employer status, this request will be denied.

If the new nonunion company has purchased assets or business from the predecessor union company, the union may contend that the new company is a successor employer to the old and demand to bargain with it. If the new company continues to operate substantially the same business, employs a substantial number of the old employees, and uses the same equipment, this request may be granted.

When the union which represents the predecessor company's employees strikes or refuses to bargain with the old employer in retaliation for setting up the new company, the union may have committed an unfair labor practice under Section 8(b)(3) and an illegal secondary boycott under Section 8(b)(4)(B) of the NLRA if the new company has separate-employer status.

Another issue which must be faced is the possibility of sympathy strikes by the union against the unionized company in retaliation for the formation of the nonunion company. The union seeking to organize the nonunion company may attempt to picket the union company's job. There are two basic routes for ending such activities.

A sympathy strike can be attacked by filing a charge of illegal secondary boycott with the NLRB under Section 8(b)(4)(B) of the NLRA. A private employer cannot go directly to court to obtain an injunction against a secondary-boycott strike or picketing but must convince the NLRB to seek one on the employer's behalf. The NLRB must investigate the facts before an injunction ending the strike can be obtained, a procedure which may delay matters from about 1 week to 10 days. (See Chapter 4, section "Secondary Boycotts.")

The quickest route to relief is to enforce no-strike clauses in the union company's bargaining agreements by seeking an injunction in federal or state court. If the company's agreement with the union contains a no-strike clause whose terms apply to sympathy strikes and a mandatory-arbitration clause, getting an immediate injunction is one possible route. However, the U.S. Supreme Court had ruled that a federal court may not issue an injunction to enforce a no-strike clause against a sympathy strike.[2] (See Chapter 4, section "No-Strike Agreements.") This means that an injunction would have to be sought in state court, and at present there is a possibility that such an action could be removed from state court to federal court by the union, which the union has the right to do.[3] If the action is removed to federal court, that court could not grant an injunction.

Whether or not an injunction can be obtained, the union company will be able to sue the union for damages suffered as a consequence of the secondary boycott or breach of the no-strike clause. The prospect of such damage suits has a strong effect in deterring or stopping a union's illegal strike. Damage suits should be filed concurrently with seeking injunctive relief.

[2] *Buffalo Forge Co. v. United Steelworkers,* 428 U.S. 397 (1976).

[3] *AVCO Corp. v. Aero Lodge No. 735,* 390 U.S. 557 (1968).

As can be seen, once separate-employer status has been obtained, each company has labor law shields available to protect it against union retaliation. However, failure to attain separate-employer status has serious consequences for the established employer, who will probably have committed an unfair labor practice for failing to bargain with the union representatives of his employees. The union company may be subject to a lawsuit by the union for breach of the existing collective bargaining contract under Section 301 of the NLRA. The NLRB may order the accretion of the employees of the new company to the established company's bargaining unit and direct that these employees receive back pay consisting of the difference between the union scale and the wage rate paid by the new company. Other damages such as "delinquent" payments to union health and welfare funds or pension funds could also be sought by the union. In short, the difference between the union contract and the nonunion wage and fringe-benefit payments must be paid by the contractor.

If a union contractor goes dual shop but fails to gain separate-employer status, it still must be determined that the two companies are an *appropriate bargaining unit* under Section 9 of the NLRA before the employer is required to include the employees of the new company within the employer's collective bargaining obligations to the union.

In a significant decision, the NLRB held that a finding that two companies "[c]onstitute a single employer . . . does not necessarily establish that the employerwide unit is the appropriate bargaining unit."[4] This decision may allow some dual shops to be saved, even if they are found to be a single employer, by a finding that the union and nonunion employees lack sufficient community of interest to be lumped together in a single bargaining unit. However, the selection of an appropriate bargaining unit lies almost entirely within the discretion of the NLRB. In addition, two companies which are the same employer but different bargaining units may not enjoy the secondary-boycott protections accorded to separate-employer status as discussed above.

A decision of the U.S. Supreme Court known as the *Higdon* case should also be of significant benefit to a union contractor who goes dual shop but fails to attain separate-employer status.[5] In this case, the Higdon Construction Company entered into a contract with an owner for the construction of a distillery in Kentucky. The owner required that the distillery be constructed with union labor, and after initial reluctance Higdon Construction entered into a prehire agreement with Ironworkers Local 103 for the purpose of acquiring labor for the project. Higdon Construction's agreement with the Ironworkers, however, was not merely a single-project agreement but covered all labor employed within the union's jurisdiction. After the completion of the distillery project, the sole stockholder of Hig-

[4] *Peter Kiewit Son's Co. & South Prairie Constr. Co.*, 231 NLRB No. 13 (1977), aff'd. F.2d (D.C. Cir., Case No. 77–2031, 1979).

[5] *NLRB v. Local 103, Int'l Ass'n* of Bridge, Structural, and Ornamental Ironworkers, 434 U.S. 335 (1978).

don Construction formed a new company, Higdon Contracting Company, to perform open-shop work. While Higdon Construction's prehire agreement with Ironworkers Local 103 was still in effect, Higdon Contracting started open-shop work on two projects within the union's jurisdiction. Local 103 protested, claiming that Higdon Construction and Higdon Contracting were one and the same employer company and that Higdon Construction's prehire agreement should also bind Higdon Contracting. However, Higdon Contracting refused to honor the prehire agreement and Local 103 began picketing. After the union had picketed for more than 30 days, Higdon Contracting filed unfair-labor-practice charges against the union under Section 8(b)(7)(C) of the NLRA, contending that the union was engaging in recognitional picketing beyond a reasonable time without filing a petition for an NLRB election. The Ironworkers asserted that Higdon Contracting was merely the alter ego of Higdon Construction and that it was picketing not for recognition but to protest Higdon Contracting's failure to honor the prehire agreement.

The NLRB agreed with the union that the two Higdon companies should be treated as a single employer. However, despite this finding the Board held that since the Ironworkers did not represent a majority of the employees of Higdon Contracting at the two projects within the union's jurisdiction, the prehire agreement was not binding on the open-shop company and that the union was necessarily engaged in recognitional picketing. Although prehire agreements are permissible under Section 8(f) of the NLRA, the Board stated that these agreements are voidable unless the union can establish that it represents a majority of the employees in the relevant bargaining unit. The U.S. Supreme Court subsequently adopted the Board's view of prehire agreements in the construction industry. This decision should benefit contractors subjected to union attacks in the course of conducting dual-shop operations. If a union does not represent a majority of the contractor's employees at an open-shop project and it has not been certified as the collective bargaining representative of contractor's employees, it may not be able to extend collective bargaining agreements with the contractor's closed-shop company to the open-shop project.

In determining whether a union has attained majority status, it is necessary to determine the relevant bargaining unit. If the revelant unit is held to be all employees of a contractor, the union may well be the majority representative of all employees, even open-shop employees. However, the Supreme Court *Higdon* decision indicates that each project site may be treated as a separate bargaining unit. If the project site is used to determine the relevant bargaining unit, union agreements will be binding only on jobsites, at which the union represents a majority of the employees.

Even in light of the *Higdon* decision, the key to successful dual-shop operations is to maintain separate-employer status and not to rely on last-ditch defenses after the union has filed an unfair-labor-practice charge or a suit alleging breach of a collective bargaining agreement.

If companies are found not to be separate employers and a single bargaining unit with majority union representation is appropriate, the contractor's labor relations will revert to the starting point, while at the same time the contractor will have incurred legal fees and possibly also damages for back pay, fringe benefits, and breach of the bargaining agreement. An important practical consequence is that the contractor may find that a contract undertaken on the assumption of using nonunion labor must be completed under union pay scales and working conditions, or else that the contractor will intentionally walk away from the contract and suffer the resulting legal consequences for its breach.

Although adding a union company to an existing nonunion construction operation presents fewer risks, there are still some important pitfalls to watch out for. It is possible that the union will refuse to enter into an agreement with the new company unless the employees of the old company are also included.

If the new company succeeds in obtaining a bargaining agreement with the union on either a temporary or a permanent basis, it may find that it cannot close up the union shop when it desires. Attempting to terminate the new union employer may be a breach of the terms of the bargaining agreement entitling the union to sue for damages under Section 301 of the NLRA, and it may also constitute the unfair labor practice of refusing to bargain collectively with the union and discriminating with regard to tenure of employment on the grounds of union membership, in violation of Section 8(a)(5) and Section 8(a)(3) of the NLRA.

Despite the sharp differences in result, there are no sharp lines to guide the contractor in setting up dual shops. The next section will discuss the characteristics considered by the NLRB and the courts in deciding the separate-employer question.

CHARACTERISTICS OF THE IDEAL DUAL SHOP

To decide whether there is a single- or a dual-employer relationship, the NLRB and the courts consider several factors which will indicate that the employers are either independent or allied. The courts and the NLRB balance all the indicators to see which group outweighs the other.

The most important guidelines for the determination of separate-employer status were summarized by the U.S. Supreme Court in *Radio and Television Broadcast Local 1264 v Broadcast Service of Mobile, Inc.*[6] These criteria are (1) common management and supervision of operation, (2) common control of personnel policies and labor relations, (3) interrelation of operations, and (4) common ownership or financial control. No one of these factors is decisive, although the presence or absence of common control of labor relations, common supervision and management of operations, and interchange of employees between companies are particularly important.

[6]380 U.S. 255 (1965).

Common ownership is normally not in itself an obstacle to separate-employer status.

A recent federal court case in the construction industry,[7] which ultimately went to the U.S. Supreme Court and is known as the *Peter Kiewit* decision, has added two important criteria. The first is that all dealings between the two companies must be on an arm's-length basis. The second is that the federal courts will be inclined to find that the companies are not separate employers when the evidence shows that the new company will tend to siphon away business from the predecessor company and its union employees. While this decision signifies that contractors must be more careful than ever in establishing a dual shop, both the United States court of appeals and the Supreme Court approved of the operation in the *Smith Associates* and *Gerace Construction* cases as models for lawful dual-shop operations (these two cases are discussed below in the subsection "Illustrative Cases: Successes").

The following discussion will outline the requirements of separate-employer status in greater detail.

Independent Control of Labor Relations

Establishing a legally sound dual shop requires that different persons have independent control over each company's dealings with its employees. This independence must be maintained both at the executive policy-making level and at the level of day-to-day supervisory personnel decisions. If the companies are commonly owned, the owner must turn control of labor relations or one company over to someone else and not continue to direct that person's handling of labor problems.

Before the *Peter Kiewit* decision, the NLRB examined this factor by focusing on the labor relations decisions made within the established open-shop framework of the new company. This may no longer be the approach, because the Court in *Peter Kiewit* stated that the decision by the owners of the predecessor company that the new company should operate as an open shop *in itself* indicated a very substantial degree of centralized control of labor relations. In the future, the mere fact that the owners choose to operate the new company as an open shop may establish that there is common control of labor relations, and this decision may be persuasive on the issue of separate-employer status. This implies that the safest course is not to decide the basic labor question of open shop versus closed shop for the new company in advance. Once the new company has been established, those persons who are operating it and making independent decisions on labor policies should make an independent decision on whether or not to sign a contract with the union. There should be a business justification for each decision.

[7]*Local 627, Int'l Union of Operating Eng'rs v. NLRB,* 518 F.2d 1040 (D.C. Cir. 1975), *aff'd in part per curiam,* 425 U.S. 800 (1976).

Active Management

Just as labor relations must be divided, so must active day-to-day control of the companies' operations. Again the separation must be strictly maintained if the common owner has the potential power to control the management of both companies. The companies should have separate chief executives and separate supervisors and foremen. They should keep separate offices, separate payroll accounts and bookkeeping systems, and separate telephones and should advertise separately.

Employees should not be interchanged, nor should those of one company do work for the other, on either a temporary or a permanent basis. It is also desirable for each company to have different legal counsel, particularly in labor relations. The common owner should try to avoid taking part in the affairs of the new company despite the natural tendency to do so.

A construction contractor trying to establish a dual shop faces an inevitable tension between the necessity of maintaining independent management for separate-employer status and the temptation and, occasionally, the need commonly to supervise and manage both operations. A successful dual-shop arrangement therefore requires constant vigilance and avoidance of acts which would break down the independence of the two companies. Directing the nonunion company's managers on business matters may be enough to show lack of separate-employer status.[8]

Interrelation of Operations

The new company should normally be formed as a distinct legal entity under state law. For large, diversified national corporations, separate subsidiaries may be enough.[9] In most cases, the new company should not be a wholly owned subsidiary of the other company.[10] However, in some instances this arrangement has worked out, particularly if the subsidiary is purchased as a going concern rather than divided away from the original company.[11] There are several traps to avoid:

Operational dependence. The new company should not depend on the established company in obtaining work. It should bid separately and work under separate contracts. The established company should not subcontract work to the new company. The new company should not take work away from the original company or take over contracts that originally had been let to the established company.

Type of work. The new company should not compete directly with the union company, since such a situation makes the contractor appear to be

---

[8] *Central N.M. Chapter, NECA,* 152 NLRB No. 145 (1965).

[9] *Teamsters Local 391 v. NLRB (Vulcan Materials Co.),* 78 Lab. Cas. ¶ 11,475 (D.C. Cir. 1976).

[10] *Milwaukee Plywood Co., v. NLRB,* 285 F.2d 325 (7th Cir. 1960); *Madden v. Teamsters Local 743* (E.D. Wis. 1959).

[11] *Hershey Foods Corp.* 208 NLRB No. 70 (1974); *Packing House Employees & Warehousemen's Local 616,* 203 NLRB No. 113 (1973).

trying to deprive union members of work. A better approach is to keep both union and open-shop employees supplied with steady work. The new company is more likely to be accepted as a separate employer if it was formed to seek business for which the established company was not able to bid competitively. Similarly, the new company should not simply be the successor to a continuing aspect of the business of the established company which the latter no longer pursues.

Financial dependence. The new company should not rely on the established company in obtaining credit, nor should its loans be guaranteed by the established company.

Common equipment and facilities. The new company should have separate offices and separate equipment. However, if the two companies use the same office or construction equipment, the new company should pay a fair rent for their use.

Geographical location of work. Operating the two companies in different areas or different union local jurisdictions helps to show that there is a lack of competition between them and that the contractor is not trying to harm the union which represents the established company's employees.

Interchange of the workforce. It may be possible for the new company to hire workers who once worked for the established company because all construction workers commonly change jobs, but it is safer to staff the new company with new employees. In this area the employer is vulnerable to charges of refusal to bargain or discrimination in employment on the basis of union membership. Staffing the administrative positions of the new company with employees of the company in a wholesale manner may be dangerous.

Employees must not routinely switch from one company to the other. If the wages, working conditions, and rules on crossing craft lines differ in each company, the two groups of employees are less likely to fit together in a single bargaining unit.

Common Ownership

The courts consider whether there is *actual* exercise of the power of common ownership or financial control. The standard for measuring the actual exercise of control is whether there is an arm's-length relationship between the companies like that typically found between unintegrated companies.

When only common ownership is shown, the NLRB normally will not find single-employer status.[12] The absence of common ownership, however, may lead to a finding of dual employers even if other factors indicate a single employer. In one case four companies shared office space, equipment and supplies, and working personnel. The NLRB held that two of the

---

[12] *E.g., International Bhd. of Boilermakers, Iron Ship Builders, Blacksmiths, Forgers, and Helpers (Bigge Drayage Co.,),* 197 NLRB No. 34 (1972); *Bachman Machine Co. v. NLRB,* 266 F.2d 599 (8th Cir. 1959); *J.G. Roy & Sons Co. v. NLRB,* 251 F.2d 771 (1st Cir. 1958).

companies owned by the same person were a single employer but that the other two were separate employers by virtue of their separate ownership.[13]

In the usual dual-shop conversion, the owner of the established company normally wishes to hold controlling stock in the new company. Although this factor weighs against the owner, it can be overcome by adhering to the safest position with respect to the other factors. It may help to have different members on each board of directors. Putting the ownership of the new company in the hands of another person, such as a relative, weighs in favor of a finding of dual employers.

Appropriate Bargaining Unit

When the *Peter Kiewit* case was remanded to the NLRB by the U.S. Supreme Court for a determination of the appropriateness of a single bargaining unit, the NLRB salvaged the dual shop by finding that a single bargaining unit was not appropriate. To make such a finding, the NLRB must determine that union and nonunion employees do not have the same community of interests. In its decision the Board stated that the following factors are to be considered as bearing upon the community-of-interest question:

- Bargaining history of each company

- Functional integration of operations among the companies

- Differences in types of work and skills of employees

- Extent of centralization of management and supervision, particularly with regard to labor relations, hiring, and discipline of employees

- Control of day-to-day operations

- Extent of interchange and contact between the groups of employees

Each of these factors overlaps with the criteria of separate-employer status discussed above. Therefore, the guidelines for separate-employer status are equally applicable here. Since the factors do overlap and since the NLRB's discretion as to the appropriate scope of a bargaining unit will only rarely be disturbed by the federal appeals courts, the practical consequence of *Peter Kiewit* is that the courts will find it difficult to overrule a Board finding that two companies are separate employers. In effect, the NLRB will have the last word in cases in which it decides to uphold a dual shop.

The following illustrative cases show how all the factors considered by the NLRB and the courts interrelate and lead to a determination of whether the dual-shop operation is a single employer or separate employ-

---

[13] *Coast Delivery Serv.* 198 NLRB No. 146 (1972) 538.

ers. The first and second cases were expressly approved as proper dual-shop operations by the court in *Peter Kiewit* and in other cases by the NLRB.[14]

Illustrative Cases: Successes

Smith Associates
A construction contractor, Smith Associates, formed a new open-shop company, Keuka, to bid on jobs that Smith Associates did not bid on because of its high labor costs for union carpenters. The same stockholders owned both companies, but neither was a subsidiary of the other. Two separate stockholders handled labor relations policy for each company, and daily labor problems were handled by the respective job superintendents. Keuka paid a fair rent for the office space shared by the companies. None of the owners participated in the active management of the two companies on a daily basis. There was no interchange of employees, and there were no common work facilities since the projects were geographically separated. Associates did not bid on the same jobs that Keuka bid on. If one company used the equipment of the other company, a fair rental was paid. There was no subcontracting between them. Smith Associates always worked on significantly larger projects than Keuka did. The employees never reported to the same place, and Keuka had no craft divisions, so that accretion of these workers into the Smith Associates bargaining unit would have been inappropriate. The NLRB applied the four principal separate-employer criteria to this dual-shop operation and determined that the companies were separate employers.[15]

Gerace Construction Company, Inc.
A contractor, Gerace Construction, normally worked on jobs in excess of $100,000 and found itself unable to bid competitively on smaller jobs. Therefore, Helger Construction Co. was organized by the owners of Gerace to operate as an open shop. The day-to-day management of Helger was entrusted to another person, who acted independently of Gerace's management. This person bought controlling stock in Helger so that he had actual ownership and control of Helger, and the principal shareholder of Gerace was no longer a shareholder or a director of Helger. Separate bank accounts and bookkeeping were maintained. The firms relied on their own capital to guarantee job performance. There was no interchange of employees. Although the manager of Helger had previously worked for Gerace and sometimes consulted with Gerace's management, although they hired a common bookkeeper, and although rent was not always paid for common facilities, the NLRB pointed especially to the independent control of labor policies and held that the employers were separate. Since there was no evidence that Helger had been set up to discourage unionism or discriminate against unions, no unfair labor practice was established on that ground.[16]

Peter Kiewit
A parent company owned two subsidiaries, Kiewit and South Prairie. Kiewit was engaged in highway construction work and also in heavy construction work, including airport, mill, and railroad bridge construction in Oklahoma, and had signed an agreement with the Operating Engineers union under which it was obligated to pay higher wages than those of

[14] *See, e.g., Western Union Corp.*, 224 NLRB No. 25 (1976). Other dual-shop successes in the construction industry include *Universal Elec. Co.*, 227 NLRB No. 259 (1977); *Carvel Co.*, 226 NLRB No. 18 (1976); *Vulcan Materials Co.*, 208 NLRB No. 81 (1974); *J.G. Roy & Sons Co. v. NLRB*, 251 F.2d 771 (1st Cir. 1958).

[15] *Smith Assoc.* 194 NLRB No. 34 (1972).

[16] *Gerace Constr., Inc.*, 193 NLRB No. 91 (1971).

its nonunion competitors. South Prairie was a nonunion contractor engaged in highway construction work outside Oklahoma. To be more competitive, the board of directors of the parent company decided that South Prairie should be activated in Oklahoma. When this was done, the Operating Engineers union charged that the two subsidiaries were a single employer that had committed an unfair labor practice by refusing to bargain with the union representing the employees of South Prairie. The two subsidiaries were separately incorporated and had operated as independent enterprises for years. Each company submitted separate and independent bids and was precluded by state law from bidding against the other. Each had a different dollar maximum for the work that it could undertake. Neither company subcontracted work to the other, and the companies did not work together on common projects. Each company used its own tools and raw materials. The companies leased heavy equipment from each other under signed agreements at the going rental rate. South Prairie's labor policies were set by its president, and Kiewit's were set by an official of the parent corporation. The two subsidiaries had different officers, and separate accounting records, bank accounts, office telephone numbers, supervisors, and office staffs. However, the board of directors of the two companies shared offices in Omaha, South Prairie took over Kiewit's Oklahoma City office and storage yard, an employee who worked for South Prairie was paid by Kiewit on one occasion, and a batch plant crew from a Kiewit job was switched to a South Prairie job. There was also interchange in key personnel: Kiewit's Oklahoma area manager became the president of South Prairie, South Prairie's president went to Kiewit as controller, and the majority of the South Prairie supervisory staff had formerly worked for Kiewit. Although the accounting records were separate, the parent company performed accounting services for both subsidiaries and made out all their paychecks in Omaha.

After an unfair-labor-practice charge had been filed by the Operating Engineers, the NLRB found that Kiewit and South Prairie were separate employers. The Court of Appeals for the District of Columbia reversed the Board, holding that the decision by the parent company to impose an open-shop framework on South Prairie constituted a substantial degree of centralized control of labor relations. The court of appeals also found that there was a substantial degree of interrelation of operations and common management resulting from the interchange in key personnel. A final factor which weighed heavily in the court's decision was that the evidence showed a likelihood that Kiewit's union employees would lose job opportunities as a result of the presence of South Prairie in Oklahoma.

The U.S. Supreme Court affirmed the judgment of the court of appeals that Kiewit and South Prairie were a single employer, but it also ruled that it still must be determined that the two companies were an appropriate bargaining unit and that only the NLRB could decide that issue.

After the case was returned to the NLRB to determine the appropriate bargaining unit, the NLRB held that although Kiewit and South Prairie were a single employer, nevertheless their employees did not have a sufficient community of interest to warrant their being placed in a single bargaining unit. The NLRB noted that Kiewit and South Prairie retained separate coporate identities and had operated as separate enterprises in different geographical areas for years. The NLRB also noted that although the skills of Kiewit's South Prairie's employees were similar, Kiewit was engaged in a wider variety of construction work than South Prairie and that therefore the interests of South Prairie's employees were narrower than those of Kiewit's employees. The Board also stated that the fact that the parent company set up South Prairie to be a nonunion employer was outweighed by the fact that the day-to-day operations and labor relations policies of Kiewit and South Prairie were conducted independently by separate individuals. The NLRB noted that day-to-day control of South Prairie ultimately rested with its president, who had control over hiring, disciplining, firing, and establishing wages and conditions of employment. The Board weighed the various factors and found that the operations of South Prairie and Kiewit were not so closely intertwined in all respects that their projects were indistinguishable or their employees equally under the jurisdiction of both firms. The Board ruled that the operating engineers employed by Kiewit and those employed by South Prairie constituted distinct and separate bargaining units and that it would be inappropriate to impose Kiewit's collective bargaining agreement upon the employees of South Prairie.[17]

Baxter Construction Company

A long-established general contractor in Houston, Baxter Construction Company, employed carpenters, masons, laborers, ironworkers, operating engineers, and cement finishers under union agreements and hired from union halls. The president and 95 percent owner of Baxter organized another company, Basic Constructors, to operate as a general contractor. Basic, which was wholly owned by Baxter's president and his family, did not sign any union agreements, and no union was certified to represent its employees.

The NLRB held that Baxter and Basic were separate employers, despite common ownership by the same individual, because the actual day-to-day control of Basic was exercised by a different person from the owner and president of Baxter, whose control over Basic was merely potential and not actually exercised. The Board found that picketing of Baxter's jobsites was an illegal secondary boycott.[18]

Joe Robertson & Son, Inc.

The owner of a lathing and plastering contracting firm which did a small amount of dry-wall installation discontinued his dry-wall operations and set up another firm, under the management of his son, to do dry-wall business on a much larger scale. The goal was to avoid the jurisdictional strife between lathers and carpenters. Neither firm participated in controlling the other's labor relations or day-to-day operations. There was no common ownership or sharing of profits, the only connection between the companies being an initial loan to the new firm. Although the type of business was similar, it was not found to be identical. The NLRB held that there was no improper refusal to bargain with the Lathers union.[19]

In the following cases the dual employers were held to be allied and not separate. These cases show the mistakes which can be made in attempting to establish and operate a dual shop.[20]

Illustrative Cases: Failures

P. A. Hayes, Inc.

A heating and air-conditioning contractor operated for several years under various names from a building in Boston. Under the name P. A. Hayes, Inc., the company had a collective bargaining agreement with Local 537 of the Plumbers and Pipefitters. The owner of Hayes, Inc., formed a new company known as Hayes Mechanical, appointed a black employee of Hayes, Inc., to be president of the new company, and gave him a 23 percent stock interest in the new company. The employee never paid for his stock interest and continued as an employee of Hayes, Inc. The owner of Hayes, Inc., also announced his intentions to the local business manager by stating to him that it was easy to beat the union agreement by forming another company. Hayes, Inc., and Hayes Mechanical operated from adjacent buildings connected by open passageways. The owner and principal officer of Hayes, Inc., was in full charge of all business operations of Hayes Mechanical and signed all checks for both companies. Neither corporation paid anything to the other for the use of office facili-

[17] Local 627, Int'l Union of Operating Engineers v. NLRB, 518 F.2d 1040 (D.C. Cir. 1975), aff'd in part per curiam, 425 U.S. 800 (1976), on remand, 231 NLRB No. 13 (1977).

[18] Carpenters Dist. Council v. Baxter Constr. Co., 201 NLRB No. 16 (1973).

[19] Joe Robertson & Son, Inc., 174 NLRB No. 160 (1969).

[20] Other unsuccessful dual-shop attempts in the construction industry include Crawford Door Sales Co., 226 NLRB No. 174 (1976); Mackies Roofing & Sheet Metal Co., 221 NLRB No. 51 (1975); Local 519 v. Service Plumbing Co., 401 F. Supp. 1008 (D. Fla. 1975); Edward E. Schultz a/b/a Schultz Painting & Decorating, 202 NLRB No. 23 (1973).

ties or equipment even though business records, office equipment, tools, and other equipment of Hayes, Inc., were acquired by Hayes Mechanical. Customers of Hayes, Inc., were taken over by Hayes Mechanical without any formal arrangements. Ultimately, Hayes Inc., defaulted in its payment of wages and fringe benefits under its union agreement and executed an assignment of accounts receivable for the benefit of creditors. Its remaining accounts were simply taken over by Hayes Mechanical. Of the eleven employees of Hayes Mechanical, five were former employees of Hayes, Inc. Approximately 80 percent of the accounts of Hayes Mechanical were former customers of Hayes, Inc. The administrative law judge found, and the NLRB affirmed, that Hayes Mechanical was the alter ego of P. A. Hayes, Inc., and was bound to P. A. Hayes, Inc.'s collective bargaining agreement and its recognitional, bargaining, and other obligations.[21]

Glendora Plumbing

A plumbing contractor, Glendora Plumbing, did both service and new construction work. The owner of Glendora formed a new company, Service Company, which did the same type of service work and used the same offices, telephone, and equipment as Glendora Plumbing. There was a substantial interchange of employees. Glendora Plumbing made the estimates for some jobs for Service Company and supervised the jobs. Service Company signed a contract with a different union from the one that represented Glendora's employees, and Glendora Plumbing urged its employees to join the new union. The workforce of Glendora was substantially reduced and not recalled to do work for Service. The NLRB held that the two firms were a single employer and were guilty of unfair labor practices in trying to withdraw from collective bargaining agreements with the first union, in interfering with the employees' choice of bargaining representatives, and in discriminating against the members of the first union in their layoff and recall policy.[22]

Don Burgess Construction

The majority stockholder and president of a construction company which employed union carpenters entered into an oral partnership agreement with the foreman of a carpentry crew to go into the contracting business under the name V. & B. Builders. His original company, Burgess Construction, transferred its carpenter employees from its payroll to that of V. & B. Builders; the employees were not aware of the change until they received their paychecks following the transfer. V. & B. Builders continued to make payments into health and welfare funds provided for in Burgess Construction's bargaining agreement for several months. When the partnership was formed, the owners contributed only $500 in initial capital, an amount which was clearly insufficient to meet the financial needs of the business. To pay wages and fringe benefits, funds were transferred from Burgess Construction to V. & B. Builders, and Burgess Construction purchased several hundred dollars' worth of power tools which were used by V. & B. Builders. V. & B. Builders and Burgess Construction submitted separate income tax returns and withholding reports. They operated from separate offices with separate telephone numbers. Burgess Construction, but not V. & B. Builders, advertised in the Yellow Pages of the telephone directory. Burgess Construction and V. & B. Builders each purchased its own construction materials and office supplies. Each company had its own workmen's compensation insurance. The president of Burgess Construction remained as general manager of that company, and his partner in V. & B. Builders was in charge of hiring, firing, and supervising the V. & B. employees without the intervention of the president of Burgess. However, V. & B. obtained all its contracts for construction work from Burgess Construction. In most cases, the subcontracts were awarded to V. & B. Builders without competitive bids from other contractors. Neither company bid on jobs in competition with the other company.

After V. & B. Builders had been in operation for several months, Burgess Construction ceased employing union carpenters entirely. V. & B. Builders utilized the state contractor's license held by the president of Burgess Construction. At times, the president of Burgess Construction personally supervised the work of carpenters employed by V. & B. After trans-

[21] *P.A. Hayes, Inc., and P.A. Mechanical Corp.*, 226 NLRB No. 39 (1976).

[22] *J. Howard Jenks, d/b/a Glendora Plumbing*, 165 NLRB No. 1 (1967).

ferring or discharging all its union carpenter employees, Burgess Construction began to hire nonunion carpenters. When the business representative of the local Carpenters union discovered that nonunion carpenters were working on Burgess Construction's projects, the union instituted grievance proceedings against Burgess Construction under the terms of the collective bargaining agreement and ultimately filed charges with the NLRB. The NLRB concluded that Burgess Construction and V. & B. Builders constituted a single employer. The NLRB found that Burgess Construction had deliberately shifted work from union employees to nonunion employees and ordered it to reinstate its former employees, to give retroactive effect to the collective bargaining agreement, and to bargain with the Carpenters union. The NLRB also concluded that since all the employees possessed the same skills, performed the same functions, shared the same general working conditions, and usually worked at the same situs, the employees of Burgess Construction and V. & B. Builders constituted a single bargaining unit.[23]

RESTRICTIVE CLAUSES IN COLLECTIVE BARGAINING AGREEMENTS

Certain types of clauses in existing collective bargaining agreements attempt to restrict conversion to a dual shop. Section 8(f) of the NLRA, an amendment added by the Taft-Hartley Act, allows construction unions to sign collective bargaining agreements with contractors before any employees are hired, that is, before the employees can have any say as to who will be their bargaining representative. A contractor may enter into a collective bargaining agreement and subsequently attempt to convert to a dual-shop operation. If the contractor has agreed to a clause providing that the collective bargaining agreement apply to any similar company that the contractor establishes, Section 8(f) allows it to apply to the new company even though it was made before the new company had any employees. An example of such a clause reads as follows:

Illustrative Example

This agreement shall be binding upon the employer and heirs, successors, and assigns of the employer. If the employer's business is purchased, assumed and/or continued by any corporation, partnership, or proprietorship, then this agreement shall continue in full force and effect and be binding upon such successors and assigns with the same effect as if it had originally been signed by the successor or assignee.

This clause was held not to bind a second company owned by a member of the employer's family since the new company was a nonsignatory and an independent entrepreneur.[24] "Employer" in such a clause may be defined by the agreement to include all business entities owned or operated by members, stockholders, or officers of the primary company which signed the collective bargaining agreement. While it is uncertain whether a newly formed company would be bound by this type of clause, the union may argue that if the same person owned both companies and refused to recog-

[23] *Don Burgess Constr. Corp. d/b/a Burgess Constr.* 227 NLRB No. 119 (1977).
[24] Joe Robertson & Son, Inc., 174 NLRB No. 160 (1969).

nize the union as the representative of the second company's employees, that person might be liable to the union for damages for breach of contract.

Some bargaining agreements contain language like the following:

Illustrative Example

This agreement shall be binding on all business entities owned or financially controlled by the employer.

The objective of such a clause is to prevent dual-shop operations owned or controlled by the unionized employer. If a contractor's agreement with a union contains such a clause, setting up a dual-shop arrangement in which the nonunion employer is "owned or financially controlled" by the original employer may be a breach of contract.

While the limits and applications of these types of restrictive clauses have yet to be specifically tested in the courts, the enforceability of these clauses must be viewed in light of the *Higdon* decision.[25] In *Higdon,* the Supreme Court held that while Section 8(f) of the NLRA permits a contractor to enter into a prehire agreement, if the union does not prove that it represents a majority of the employees in the relevant bargaining unit, the prehire agreement is not enforceable. If a union attempts to bind a contractor's open-shop company to the terms of a collective bargaining agreement in force with the contractor's union company on the basis of one of these types of restrictive agreements, the *Higdon* decision indicates that the union company's collective bargaining agreement would not be binding upon the open-shop company unless the union could attain majority status in the open-shop company.

Some bargaining agreements contain clauses restricting joint ventures with nonunion employers or subcontracts with nonunion employers. Such provisions could be the basis of a breach-of-contract attack by the union if dual-shop operations cooperate in performing work or have business dealings with each other. However, the legality of unlimited subcontracting clauses is questionable, since the U.S. Supreme Court has held subcontracting agreements to be a violation of the antitrust laws when there is no employer-employee relationship or when the subcontracting ban is not limited to the jobsite.[26] (See Chapter 4, section "Restrictive Agreements.") The NLRB has interpreted the *Connell* decision as requiring an employer-employee relationship but has not adopted the Supreme Court's "particular jobsite" suggestion in several cases decided in 1978.[27] However, an appeal of these NLRB decisions is in progress.

[25] See section "Separate-Employer Status" *supra for a detailed discussion of the Higdon* case, NLRB v. *Local 103, Ironworkers,* 434 U.S. 335 (1978).

[26] *Connell Constr. Co. v. Plumbers Local 100,* 421 U.S. 616 (1975).

[27] *Carpenters Local 944 (Woelke & Romero Framing, Inc.),* 239 NLRB No. 40 (1978); *Colorado Bldg. & Constr. Trades Council (Util. Serv. Eng'ring, Inc.),* 239 NLRB No. 41 (1978); *Los Angeles Bldg. and Constr. Trades Council (Sullivan-Kelley & Assoc.),* 239 NLRB No. 42 (1978); *International Union of Operating Engineers, Local 701 (Pacific Northwest Chapter of Assoc. Builders & Contractors, Inc.),* 239 NLRB No. 43 (1978).

12 MERIT SHOP

The rise of merit shop, or open-shop, construction has been an important factor in the construction industry during the past two decades. It is estimated that the volume of this comparatively new way of doing business now comprises a substantial portion of the total construction market, which is constantly growing. By its very definition, merit shop construction makes statistical analysis difficult. It is a method of construction which finds both union and nonunion firms engaged on the jobsite with the ratio of union to nonunion firms varying considerably. Ordinarily the general contractor on a merit shop job has no direct collective bargaining relationship with unions. On a so-called 100 percent union jobsite, the general contractor is usually union but may engage some nonunion subcontractors, particularly small specialty contractors; in a sense, this practice converts the job to merit shop as well. The jobsite preparation for a union contractor may be done by a nonunion firm, and finishing touches such as landscaping and fencing and certain interior work may often be handled by nonunion firms.

Understanding the penetration of the construction market by the merit shop is also complicated by the public impression that union construction is dominant. This impression derives from the high visibility of union projects, which include high-rise apartments and office buildings, large manufacturing plants, and more spectacular jobs such as bridges, dams, airports, and public utility plants. However, it is generally recognized that, except for larger projects, the housing industry in the United States is essentially merit shop or nonunion. Large commercial, institutional, and industrial work is commonly union, but the merit shop has made rapid inroads in this area in the last 20 years. In some sections of the country, especially the South and Southwest, the heavier construction field is predominantly open-shop. Even larger industrial projects are no longer exclusively a union domain. The merit shop contractor competes with union rivals and has created an industry based upon economic efficiency that is proving increasingly acceptable to the owner and user.

The merit shop has prospered because it has developed new methods in manpower recruitment and training, legal defensive tactics, flexibility of operation, and introduction of laborsaving devices in construction materials and, especially, because it has traditional union bonds. It has emphasized continuity of maximum employment of the workforce. Merit shop operations have eliminated the problems of jurisdictional disputes, economic work stoppages, featherbedding, and make-work practices of all kinds which have proved costly in time and money to union contracting. Users have observed that merit shop contractors often have a driving zeal to get a job, finish it as quickly and as economically as possible, and discard outmoded methods of construction that traditionally linger in the industry.

The focal point of the merit shop is Associated Builders and Contractors, Inc., a construction industry trade association organized in 1950 in Baltimore as a proponent of the merit shop. The first trade association to undertake the organization of nonunion firms willing to work with union firms in any phase of construction, it has grown into a nationwide association, recognized as the spokesman for the merit shop movement. The association was set up in Maryland in response to union efforts to force union contractors into working only with union shops and to eliminate merit shop operations or to force them back to the union shop.

For a company to operate on a merit shop basis, its management must have a clear concept of its rights under the law. Merit shop contractors must understand the legal underpinnings of the structure of federal, state, and local laws directly affecting the construction industry which guarantee certain employer rights and place important restrictions upon operations.

Taking advantage of management rights enunciated in the Labor-Management Relations Act (Taft-Hartley Act) in 1947, merit shop contractors have succeeded in establishing the right of any firm to do business with any other firm in the construction industry. Through a series of important court cases, the groundwork established under the act was confirmed, and the door was opened to the merit shop.

One of the remarkable changes related to the merit shop during this period has been the establishment of dual shops, as discussed in Chapter 11. This procedure involves the operation of a union, firm and a merit shop firm. In some cases, the union firm is phased out, and the dual shop becomes a step on the road to complete merit shop operation. In others, the union shop is continued but works in different areas from those of the merit shop sister firm. In attempting to establish a balance between the competing powers of unions and management, Congress in 1947 forbade union pressure to force or require one firm to stop doing business with another. The merit shop continued to operate and grow to its present strength because the unions were denied their traditional method of organizing from the top down, particularly with the use of the illegal secondary boycott. Direct methods of organization from the bottom up likewise produced few results because the nature of the construction industry does not lend itself to traditional union organization.

The success of the merit shop concept has been due in large degree to a continuing program of management education with respect to employer rights. Among important management rights are the right to contract, guaranteed to all business enterprises; the right to hire and fire; the right to set work standards; the right to use any kind of construction equipment that will increase productivity; and the right to use the entire range of technological improvements in construction materials with such variants as preglazed windows, precut doors, prefitted boilers, and many other products whose introduction and use have been opposed by building trades unions intent on preserving their traditional work on the jobsite. Employer rights are the guarantee of the merit shop freedom to choose, and since they are reinforced with prohibition of the secondary-boycott weapon, unions can do little in the face of a determined merit shop operation that has won the acceptance of the user.

OBTAINING WORK

Many persons who are presently connected with union contracting or who are just considering entering the merit shop field are baffled by the question of how to obtain jobs. It is this problem which tests the mettle of an enterprising firm that must be able to sell its services. Essentially, there is no difference between the merit shop and the union shop when it comes to getting business. In many locales, the merit shop contractor begins with a handicap because of a prounion attitude on the part of owners, abetted by the sly suggestions of unions and union contractors that merit shops lack quality. Individual owners must be convinced one by one to overcome their prejudices against merit shop firms. As the merit shop gains in experience, it can introduce innovations in time-saving on the job without the inhibitions of union tradition. This freedom to improvise and innovate is a strong stimulus to improving productivity.

Consideration to pleasing architects and engineers also plays a role in the progress of merit shop firms. Success on one job leads to another. In particular, proving that merit shop subcontractors are dependable is important, for often their knowledge of management practices needs upgrading. Since many subcontractors come up through the trades rather than enter the business at staff levels or after formal business education, they must compensate for a lack of formal managerial education. Yet it is recognized that the merit shop contractors of the type who work their way up to establishing their own businesses frequently have the qualities necessary to succeed on higher levels once they have the advantage of managerial training and experience.

Merit shop contractors find in their trade association not only the opportunity to learn new techniques but the protection afforded by numbers. When labor relations problems occur on a jobsite, merit shop contractors receive from the association practical assistance with manpower, equipment, and material that is often far more decisive than the legal aspects.

The merit shop has made increasing inroads in the public works area. Despite the problem of dealing with fixed wage rates required by government contractors, more and more merit shop contractors have succeeded in getting a share of this work. Merit shop firms have the same obligations under federal standards as union firms have. Problems of wage and hour laws, compliance with the Davis-Bacon Act, affirmative action, and the Occupational Safety and Health Administration (OSHA) are all subjects about which a merit shop contractor must become knowledgeable. Legal counsel and association assistance can help overcome these difficulties.

Occasionally, because of union talk of trouble or a mass visit by union delegates, owners announce that the only bidders eligible for a job will be union contractors. If an argument based on the principle that the greatest competition produces the best price proves unpersuasive, a merit shop contractor may turn to consideration of legal recourse. There may be recourse under the National Labor Relations Act (NLRA) or the antitrust laws. If the owner is a public authority, there is considerable legal authority that nonunion bidders may not be eliminated from bidding under state "low and responsible bidder" statutes. Also, letting contracts only to those who employ union labor or nonunion labor may create unlawful class discrimination or restrain trade and competition. (See Chapter 4, section "Restrictive Agreements.")

RECRUITMENT OF WORKERS

Merit shop firms must be careful not to make mistakes in labor relations which would tend to drive their employees toward seeing the necessity of joining a union. Because merit shop firms control recruiting, assigning, and directing employees on the jobsite, they must assume a posture that will lead to satisfactory job experiences and relations between employees and supervisors and among fellow workers. Union exclusivity in the building trades, which is based upon the concept of creating an artificial scarcity of labor, has been called the seedbed of the merit shop workforce. When the building trades unions excluded outsiders from their ranks, many persons who had sought unsuccessfully to enter the construction industry via the union route turned to merit shop firms for employment. As merit shop operations began in many sections of the United States, they welcomed employees who were able to upgrade their skills though ability and ambition. At the same time, merit shop contractors were keenly aware of the need to eliminate the irregularity of employment which in the union sector was a constant source of dissatisfaction among workers. For years before the troughs of recession became deep, merit shops were able to maintain large and steady crews at work. Many times this meant taking jobs at little or no profit to ride out a lean period, but contractors were rewarded in employee loyalty and willingness and in such simple but important factors as lower unemployment compensation rates resulting from a firm's experience rating. In recent years, as union construction was pricing itself out of many markets, longtime union workers opted for the continuous employment of merit shops.

The positive side of merit shop operations is focused on accenting education and on recognizing employees as individuals. The common adversary relationship between unions and management is eliminated. Also eliminated is the common union conviction that the benefits of employment come from the union and not from the employer.

Trained workers are usually recruited within the industry, and often they include union members who are looking for work with a minimum of layoffs. Recruiting methods include word-of-mouth information, recommendations of existing workers and supervisors, community organizations, news media, and posters. The primary method probably is training people, either formally or on the job. Most merit shop contractors use journeymen to teach unskilled workers. Some journeymen are better teachers than others, who merely watch what unskilled workers do and fail to supply the reasons behind complex questions. On-the-job education therefore may not prepare unskilled workers for other work, leaving them skilled only for the particular job which they did under a supervisor's eye. Proper on-the-job training may be geared to improve workers for other assignments. Thus, some workers may become helpers and others trainees. The contractor should know the difference and develop skilled workers.

The best of the merit shop labor force typically is trained in more than one job classification. The workers may be trained as cement masons, carpenters, or laborers and perform some sheet-metal and minor electrical tasks. Later, they may read blueprints, perform more difficult tasks, and assume greater responsibility such as anticipating material needs. The ultimate goal for a merit shop employer is to train crews of all-around skilled journeymen who enjoy what they do. The competitive edge in performance by teams is important to productivity. New workers should receive training even if it is on a one-job-only basis in which fundamentals are offered. Merit shop contractors can train and use workers so that they overlap traditional jurisdictions, thus maximizing the use of specialists while minimizing overall hourly labor costs.

The utilization of helpers to perform menial chores while all the journeymen handle skilled or semi-skilled work often makes merit shop construction more economical than union construction, which almost always must use skilled journeymen or apprentices to perform helper work.

Upward mobility is apparent in merit shop construction. A laborer moves into cement masonry, into brick or block work, and then into rough carpentry. Workers' incomes improve, and line-of-work changes motivate and encourage the workers. Such movement is less likely to occur in the mechanical trades, which typically are subcontracted. In these crafts onsite work is often supplemented with institutional training.

TRAINING

Dependence upon an available or floating workforce was insufficient for merit shop labor needs, and it was recognized that the merit shop must create its own skilled workforce. Training in the merit shop is normally task-oriented; union crafts are broken down into modules, and craft jurisdiction lines are disregarded. Task training has become an extremely important feature of merit shop operations. Some of the most successful firms have set up intensive training programs in special aspects of the various trades and provided for the enhancement of employees' ability in several areas. Not only does the possibility of growth offer an opportunity to increase earnings, but the learning of additional skills increases the opportunity for regular work. Task training can also bring into the construction industry disadvantaged youths who are having great difficulty in finding jobs.

Proponents of the merit shop complain that wage laws such as the Davis-Bacon Act (see Chapter 13, section "Davis-Bacon Act") inhibit task training on government work. The Department of Labor, through formulas weighted toward protecting the building trades unions, generally finds the union wage rate to be the prevailing rate. Under Department regulations union craft jurisdictions are usually recognized, and union jobsite practices are required of contractors even though they may have no collective bargaining relationships. It is a rule of thumb that any worker picking up a tool of the trade and using it becomes *ipso facto* a journeyman in that trade according to the union classification and must be paid the specified rate for it. With few exceptions, this rule leads to the elimination of helpers and to the employment of apprentices to perform the elementary tasks of a trade for reasons of economy. In practice, a merit shop contractor must have certified apprentices at work or be forced to pay top journeymen's rates for the simpler tasks.

As a result of these requirements, the ABC, Association of Independent Electrical Contractors (AIECA), and other merit shop contractor associations began formal apprentice courses like those of the unions under the supervision of the Bureau of Apprenticeship and Training (BAT) of the U.S. Department of Labor or state apprenticeship councils that govern activities in particular states. While some contractors feel that this requirement is long outmoded, serving to increase costs and placing upon apprentices the burden of a long-term curriculum, others see that the thorough training of the apprenticeship courses does give employees a head start to becoming foremen and jobsite superintendents.

Setting up apprenticeship courses has often been a political problem for merit shop contractors, and it was not until 1971 that ABC finally succeeded in gaining federal approval for its apprenticeship standards. Nonunion contractors desiring to set up certified apprenticeship programs have often found the road blocked because in the great majority of states, apprenticeship councils are dominated by the building trades unions. In an extreme case, the Sheet Metal Workers union brought suit to prevent the establishment of an open-shop apprenticeship course. In other cases, regional directors of the BAT have interpreted Department of Labor rules in a way that makes matters difficult outside the union sector. The BAT requires approval by state-approved training agencies, but in the state of Washington it recently approved a program for AIECA despite the refusal of the union-dominated state agency.

"Indentured apprenticeship" is a schedule of work progression over a given time, beginning with simple tasks and ending with the most complex ones. The agreement to indenture, or train, for a time period is signed by the apprentice, the employer (or the organization with responsibility and capability), and the state agency or the BAT. "Preapprenticeship" is a brief indoctrination period for persons who need such basic skills as reading, mathematics, and knowledge of tools, materials, and equipment. The use of preapprenticeship training has grown with the need to fulfill affirmative-action plans and goals in construction contracts with governments.

Apprenticeship rules contain stringent requirements for the opening of opportunities for minorities and for hiring women on the jobsite. These requirements obligate a contractor or any group to maintain an apprenticeship program. The in-house problems attendant upon administering apprenticeship programs require expertise and expense that management must be prepared to furnish. While the road is often hard there is agreement that in the end there is economic reward in having a certified apprenticeship program. If a firm wants to perform government work, such a program is well worth the trouble.

COMPENSATION

Many union contractors find it difficult to set wage rates in the nonunion field. They are so well accustomed to having wage rates and fringe benefits bargained collectively that they do not realize that they can adopt the pay practices of other industries and still enjoy satisfactory employee relations. It may not be necessary for them to equal or top union wage scales, which often are predicated upon substantial periods of unemployment. There is often a differential between nonunion, merit shop wage rates and union wage rates. The merit shop concept involves the reward of performance, so that in a specific trade there may be two or three rates. This does not mean that labor costs for skilled craftsmen in a merit shop necessarily are going to be substantially less than union journeyman rates for unskilled work. Construction unions normally require union contractors to pay such rates for all work unless it is performed by an apprentice. Unions typically allow a ratio of only about 1 apprentice to 4 journeymen, and average apprentice pay is about 75 percent of the journeyman's rate. Merit shop contractors may well have a ration of one skilled craftsman to 4 relatively unskilled employees. The rate of the less skilled employees may average 50 percent of the skilled craftsman's rate or less often a substantial amount of merit shop construction is performed with a few skilled craftsmen supervising and working with relatively unskilled employees, and merit shop contractors therefore have lower labor costs than union contractors.

Merit shop contractors are required by competition to have acceptable fringe-benefit programs. ABC's fringe-benefit plans include a health and welfare program with broad benefits called the Security Plan which is available to its members. The program covers such areas as life insurance, sickness indemnity, medical and surgical benefits, major medical insurance income continuance, dental insurance, and accidental death and dismemberment features. It had a 30-day portability feature for employees who move from one association member to another.

Many merit shop firms also have pension programs, often of the profit-sharing type. In addition, numerous firms grant regular paid vacations, depending upon length of service, and observe the usual holidays embodied in collective bargaining agreements. Another feature that finds great favor with employees is the establishment of credit unions, which are helpful in saving and in group purchasing at special discounts.

Open-shop contractors have a morale problem with their jobsite workforce on Davis-Bacon jobs when they are required to pay higher than usual rates in the open market. However, the fact that merit shop contractors increasingly are engaged in government work proves that this problem can be satisfactorily solved. Ordinarily, scheduling workers according to seniority and skills and equalizing opportunities for higher rates, along with a careful explanation of what is necessary in the particular situation, will clear up the matter. Moreover, when employees understand that continuity of employment with a contractor is far more important than a temporary advantage or disadvantage, they will usually appreciate the realities involved.

Differentials in wage rates and fringe benefits between firms do not necessarily coincide with costs. For example, merit shop fringe programs may provide equal or superior benefits but cost substantially less per hour since union program premiums frequently are predicated on the fact that union employees are more subject to spells of unemployment.

As a general rule, administrators of prevailing wage statutes permit the transfer of fringe-benefit payments between varying types of programs within the fringe package. If a contractor does not make irrevocable payments to a third party for benefits to employees in the area of typical construction industry fringe benefits, the contractor must pay the differential in cash to the employees. Often nonunion employees who receive higher wage rates on government work, with fringe benefits paid in cash while they enjoy employment with fewer interruptions are better off financially than typical union workers on such projects.

JOBSITE MANAGEMENT

Each of the eighteen AFL-CIO building trades unions has laid down an absolute right of to claim work within its trade jurisdiction, as well as a "duty" to refuse to work shoulder to shoulder with any nonunion workers. When unions adamantly take these positions, the effect is to limit union contractors in contracting with nonunion firms. To organize or to halt work labor unions will often risk violation of boycott laws and antitrust statutes. Since 1952 the building trades have tried unsuccessfully to change the boycott laws and legalize common-situs picketing to rid themselves of the reserved-gate system (see Chapter 4). They want to involve neutrals in a controversy to stop work. Their strategy is to induce neutral workers and employers to refuse to work or do business on the common site while nonunion workers are there. Resort to top-down organization rather than employee persuasion seems the common tactic of unions in their attempts to organize merit shop contractors. Therefore, merit shop contractors not only should review boycott and antitrust laws and each participant at a prejob conference but consider practical strategies to anticipate the problems that may occur when nonunion workers are employed and time is valuable.

Evaluation of owners' and the design professionals' attitudes is an important part of planning. If their attitude is known to be semisoft, unions are likely to risk the use of pressure tactics to intimidate them into ceasing business dealings with nonunion contractors, subcontractors, and suppliers. Owners should be informed of their contract rights, the procedures of a boycott situation, and the use of techniques like reserved gates to isolate disputants, as well as other legal relief.

A jobsite security plan should be initiated and planned at the beginning of the project. Theft, sabotage, vandalism, or damage directed against nonunion jobs can cause escalated labor costs, the loss of key workers, increased bond and insurance rates, and material and equipment charges. The parties should decide who should have access to the jobsite. If the teamsters union has organized the local police, it may be advisable to see if they can be expected to be objective. If not, this eventuality should be discussed with the elected officials of the governmental entity. If assurances are not given for equal law enforcement, the contractors may want to petition the state authorities and have a discussion of law enforcement procedures and policies. The local community's attitude can help, as can the local press, radio, and television. Their attitudes are worth assessing in light of the enthusiasm for economic and commercial improvement of the community.

A site map and a road map should be used in on-site analysis. Roadways should be viewed as points of authorized and unauthorized access. Other considerations are the possible need for chain link, snow, or other fencing; the temporary lighting to be established at the start; the availability of water for fire protection by pumping or hydrant; and the route to the site from fire protection services and from the site to a hospital or aid facility.

After the site, attitudes, and so on have been evaluated, a preliminary decision should be made on whether the facts justify high-risk, low-risk, or ordinary-risk security. While the answer isn't clearly predictable in all situations, doubts should be resolved conservatively so that all the risks are considered. If savings in security investments are salvageable or unused, they can be transferred to the next jobsite. If the general contractor is unionized and the subcontractor is not, the subcontractor may have a high-risk classification but can expect little assistance. This important point should be considered in bidding and planning.

Many security methods are available to protect sites from sabotage. Various types of fencing, lighting, guard service, and guard dogs are worth considering; their cost should be included in the bidding price. Contractors should consider whether the job is high-risk or low-risk, and appropriate preventive techniques implemented at the beginning. Sabotage stops because of public pressure and concern. The press, television, and radio become involved. The elected leaders of the community and state should be shown pictures and told of evidence of any threats or intimidation. Public knowledge is necessary in achieving law and order. What contractors say is important and show how strongly they feel about it. Insurance investigators are usually able and persistent. The state bureau of investigations or another group may supply undercover agents.

The federal government is ordinarily difficult to move, even when contractors start at the top; it is easier to obtain local and state law enforcement. Contractors should see the local district attorney and have crimes such as arson given high priority. They should know the state laws on arson, firearms, bombings, assault, mass sabotage, mass vandalism, and the like. Crimes should be reported so that elected officials are not able to say that "it's only a labor dispute." The fact that people are being put out of business and jobs should be pointed out.

Some self-help devices to discuss and adopt are no-admittance, no-solicitation signs. Depending on state law, they may be better than no-trespassing signs. Supervisors should be informed of all facts and encouraged to supply all facts. They are the frontline of management. Handouts, letters to homes, payroll stuffers, and other means should be used to communicate management's view on any sabotage and what is being done about it. Employees respect bold management.

TOP-DOWN ORGANIZING

Pressure or persuasion on the contractor is the method that unions use in "top-down" organizing. If a strike or picketing occurs at a construction site gate where deliveries may be cut off or workers walk off because of the pickets and where those affected are neutrals in the labor controversy, the National Labor Relations Board (NLRB) may find a secondary boycott under Section 8(b)(4)(B) of the NLRA. (See Chapter 4 for a more detailed discussion of secondary boycotts.)

Nonunion contractors realize that the possibility of pickets during construction can result in less confusion and lost time if a separate-gate, or reserved-gate, system is ready before the job starts. In a separate-gate system job access at one gate is reserved by list exclusively to the contractor and the contractor's suppliers targeted by the union picketing. Other neutral contractors and suppliers should have their own similarly designated separate gate, which should be as far as practicable from the targeted employer-employees gate. The picketing union should be notified of the existence and location of the gates and asked to refrain from affecting neutrals by picketing at the gate reserved for the party with which they have a controversy.

All contractors should know which gate they and their suppliers and all their employees should use. No deviation is allowable because if a neutral gate is used by the targeted employer or suppliers in arriving or leaving, the pickets can move to that gate. An advance contractor's conference is recommended so that everyone understands the gates and the reasons for them. It is mandatory that gates be monitored to ensure that proper parties enter and leave by their designated gates. The names of parties should be on both sides of signs. Signs stating "No Admittance without Permission or [Name of responsible person]" signs should be posted intermittently at fences. Credentials such as driver's licenses and business cards of all visitors should be checked. Any authorized persons should be permitted to enter, and unauthorized ones should be asked to leave immediately. There should be a daily log which includes visitors, license numbers, number of pickets, wording on signs, time of picketing, occurrences or events involved in picketing, and witnesses.

When union business agents get in touch with the contractor, their names and positions should be ascertained. If possible, a business card should be obtained. The meeting should be held in a neutral place with a witness from the company present; the witness's position and responsibilities should be stated. The business agents should be asked to state why they are visiting. They should do the talking without argument from the contractor. The meeting should be short and to the point. Immediately after the event, an account of who was there and exactly what was said, including whether threats were made, should be dictated or noted. If asked to sign a labor agreement, the contractor should accept but not sign it and should state that it will have to be studied. A contractor who receives a letter from the union should talk to an attorney but not refuse delivery. A contractor who is told to leave a construction project because of union pressure should find out who gave the order, request, or demand, and make a record of the information. (Strikes, picketing, and boycotts are more fully discussed in Chapter 4.)

BOTTOM-UP ORGANIZING

When union representatives get in touch with a contractor's employees to persuade them to assign bargaining authority to the union, this is sometimes called "grass roots" or "bottom-up" organizing. Generally, workers are asked to sign bargaining authorization papers or cards which simply require a signature on the bottom of a preprinted statement to the effect that the employee says he or she wants the union to be his or her agent in bargaining for a contract. There are few surprises in the merit shop contractor's life to equal the shock of discovering that at least 30 percent of the contractor's employees have signed union authorization cards seeking a federally supervised election to select a collective bargaining agent.

If the union induces 30 percent or more of the contractor's workers to sign cards or papers, it can petition to the NLRB for an election. If the union gets 51 percent or more of cards or papers signed, it will write or call asking the employer to start bargaining without an election. When union organizers show up, they should be treated professionally. Supervisors are to report their presence directly to management, and if an interview is requested, the contractor should see the organizers after arranging to have a witness present. Supervisors should not discuss anything with the organizers.

Since the contractor has a good-faith doubt, the contractor need not and should not verify the cards or signatures by looking at the cards. The contractor should return the cards if they have been mailed and refuse to look at them if they are presented in person. To do otherwise may constitute acquiescence and verification of majority status. If there is a good-faith doubt that a majority have assigned their rights, the employer should *not* compare signatures with payroll records, acquiesce in a third party's verifying the cards, discuss the cards or how they were signed, or poll employees. This is true because if contractor analysis shows that the union does not have a majority, union representatives will simply return later with additional cards. If the union has a majority of employees, the NLRB, because of the de facto recognition, may order the employer to bargain without an election. (See Chapter 4, "Bargaining Obligations.")

Upon being presented with authorization cards or a petition, the contractor should simply state that a secret ballot is the best way to determine whether a union has majority support. A mechanical quick look at signatures in no way resolves the question of whether an employee has been coerced into signing a card or of whether it was signed as a result of misrepresentation as to its purpose (as, for example, that it was a "petition for an election"). At this point, legal counsel should be brought in, if not already involved, and the contractor should work closely with the attorney.

The union usually files a petition with the regional director of the NLRB for certification (see Chapter 5, subsection "Union Representation through an Election"). The regional director's office staff then investigates and determines whether the employer's business is in commerce (most contractors are) or whether a bargaining agreement is already in effect. Then, in a usual case, the petition is processed. The director notifies the employer that a petition has been filed, requests a list of employees' names and job classifications (to see who is eligible to vote and if 30 percent or more of the employees have signed the union's cards), and may schedule a conference. At the conference, the NLRB representative will attempt to effect a "consent agreement" for an election. The agreement is to cover details of the forthcoming election. The employer should sign the consent agreement only when the employer is satisfied with the unit, the specific employees eligible to vote, and the election date.

After a list of current employees has been furnished the Board for eligibility and the Board has furnished a copy to the union, the organizer begins a program of extensive house calls, phone contacts, visits, mailings, and mass meetings. The employer must undertake the same kind of persuasive effort. An effective way consists at group meetings of which employees listen to top company executives give a carefully prepared factual presentation. Some pointers are:

■ People vote against a candidate. Ask the employees to vote "no" to the union.

■ Neither side may threaten or coerce the employees. The union may promise certain wages or benefits; the employer cannot promise anything if the workers do not certify the union.

■ The employer should plan and execute a calendar of election events, which should include supervisor and employee meetings, posters, home mailings, and so on.

■ Time should be spent writing speeches, drafting mailings and handouts, and so on.

■ Available information about the union, its reputation, financial status, strikes, and so on should be sought for inclusion in the campaign.

PREVENTIVE LABOR RELATIONS

Open-shop contractors should be practical. They have an advantage in offering year-round employment. Their employees have a choice under the law to join or not join a union. There are broad rights of free speech, including expressing opinions in meetings, letters, poster, and so on, so that employees have the facts about the terms and conditions of their employment. Some questions that a merit shop contractor should consider are:

■ Are employees' wages and fringe benefits keeping up with inflation and competitors for their services?

■ Are supervisors trained and performing well?

■ Are legitimate grievances being processed and settled fairly?

■ Is the contractor dealing individually and personally with employees?

■ Is the contractor dealing impartially, candidly, and without emotion with employees?

A merit shop contractor who can answer an objective "yes" to these questions is a long way down the road in preventing a union from being selected by the workers to represent their interests.

Most contractors choose to keep an open-shop operation because they feel that they can run the company without the union as a business partner. They can hire people whom they want and need, and there are no unnecessary restrictions on work assignments, pace of production, and other vital matters. Employees work as a team, they start and complete the job, and they take satisfaction in their job and their work. They feel closer to the company than to their union.

One of the most important areas of employee relations is the attitude and performance of foremen and supervisors. It is commonplace that one of the sorest points of employee dissatisfaction is unequal treatment or favoritism shown by foremen or supervisors to individual employees. There is no one management mistake that can lead more quickly to a dissatisfied workforce and possible union organization efforts than a crude, unfair supervisor on the jobsite. Frequently top management may not be aware of the attitudes and performance of such supervisors. It is vital that procedures be developed to assure that employee grievances are dealt with in a fair manner and that not only are jobsite conditions safe and in compliance with the law but normal conveniences for employees are satisfactorily provided.

Every merit shop contractor should have some means of auditing employee relations periodically. Some labor-wise attorneys suggest that such an audit, covering wages, fringe benefits, jobsite conditions, supervisors, and generally, privileges for employees as keys to morale, be made every 6 months. A definite plan to correct deficiencies should be laid out and steps taken to see that it works.

A good labor relations program is founded on the solid philosophy of the Golden Rule, to do unto your employees as you would have them do unto you.

13 FEDERAL EMPLOYMENT STANDARDS

Federal laws impose employment standards with which a contractor must comply. Practically all contractors are covered by the Fair Standards Act (FLSA), requires that contractors pay their nonexempt employees at least the minimum wage for compensable working time and time and one-half of the employees' regular rate of pay for all compensable hours worked in excess of 40 hours in any week. For contractors engaged in federal or federally assisted construction work, the Davis-Bacon Act imposes the requirement that they pay the prevailing wages which are set in each area for each craft by the Department of Labor. Federal contractors must also comply with the craft by the Contract Work Hours and Safety Standards Act, which requires the payment of time and one-half as the basic overtime premium for all hours worked in excess of 8 hours in 1 day or 40 hours in 1 week. The Copeland Anti-Kickback Act stipulates that only certain deductions may legally be made from an employee's paycheck on a federally funded project and that it is illegal for an employee to kick back to a contractor certain unpermitted payments. There may also be state and local employment standards acts and laws with which the contractor must comply. States and localities typically have little Davis-Bacon acts which require that the prevailing wage be paid on state or locally funded projects.

FAIR LABOR STANDARDS ACT

The Fair Labor Standards Act requires employers to pay their employees at least the minimum wage rate for compensable working time specified by the act and premium pay for overtime work over 40 hours in a week. In addition, child labor restrictions prohibit employers from using workers under certain ages on particular job assignments. Payroll records with certain required information must be retained to show compliance with FLSA requirements. Failure to comply with the minimum wage, overtime pay, and record-keeping requirements and the child labor prohibitions may subject employers to back-pay suits, liquidated damages, injunctions, and even criminal penalties. The FLSA merely sets the minimum standards for compensation, and employers may be legally bound to pay higher wages and overtime pay under collective bargaining or individual employment contracts. In some cases an agreement to pay for particular times when no work is done will determine whether or how much an employer must pay for overtime work under the FLSA. Or an agreement to pay extra for work during certain times of the day or in excess of a certain number of hours may either increase or decrease the amount of overtime pay owed under the FLSA. Therefore, an employer must consider the effect that agreement to particular terms of compensation will have on overtime obligations under the FLSA before signing a contract.

Contractors and subcontractors in the business of construction or reconstruction, including remodeling and repair work, are covered by the FLSA if they have two or more employees who handle goods that have moved in interstate commerce. A minimum dollar volume of business is not necessary to bring such contractor within coverage. Since almost all contractors employ at least two workers who handle nails, tools, materials, or even equipment materials, that at some point has moved through interstate commerce, these workers and all the contractors' employees unless specifically exempt are protected by the minimum wage and overtime pay requirements.

Employees or Independent Contractors

Independent contractors who are not employees under the FLSA are not subject to its requirements. This is a very important distinction since improper characterization of an employee as an independent contractor may subject an employer to penalties for unintentional violations of the overtime pay and record-keeping requirements of the FLSA, as well as liability for back pay and penalties, social security payments, Internal Revenue Service (IRS) withholding requirements, state and federal unemployment taxes, and noncompliance with workmen's compensation laws. For example, an employer who has paid a sum to a craftsman to perform a particular job in whatever time it takes to complete the job may sometimes discover that the worker must be paid an additional amount for overtime work on the ground that the craftsman is an employee and not an independent contractor.

Illustrative Case

Sidney Vihlen, an electrical subcontractor, hired a licensed electrician to do electrical wiring in connection with the construction of a post office building since Vihlen did not have a license to operate in the area. The electrician used his own tools but furnished no materials or supplies for the work. Also, he operated under general instructions from Vihlen in regard to the type of work performed, and his work was at times supervised and directed by Vihlen. The electrician was paid at an hourly rate of $3 regardless of the number of hours worked and was not conpensated at an overtime rate for hours worked in excess of 40 per week. In a back-pay suit it was held that Vihlen violated the FLSA by failing to pay the electrician the required overtime since he was an employee, not an independent contractor.[1]

[1] *Wintz v. Sidney Vihlen, d/b/a Randall Elec. Co.,* 59 LC ¶ 32, 140 (M.D. Fla. 1969).

Although there is no absolute rule for determining whether a worker is an independent contractor or an employee, there are a number of factors to consider even though the presence of one or more of them in a case is not necessarily conclusive. Such factors are important as guides to the broader question of whether the worker is in fact independent or subject to the control of the employer in performing the work. It has generally been held that the test of what constitutes independent service lies in the control exercised, the decisive question being who has the right to *direct what shall be done and how it shall be done*. Other commonly recognized tests of the independent-contractor relationship are the existence of a contract for the performance by a person of a certain piece of work at a fixed price, the independent nature of the business, the employment of assistants with the right to supervise and control the progress of their work except as to final results, the time for which the worker is employed, the method of payment (whether by time or by job), and whether the work is part of the regular business of the employer.

Right to control work. The most important test in determining whether a person is an independent contractor or an employee is the control reserved by the employer. Independent-contractor status depends upon the extent to which the person is in fact independent in performing the work. Broadly stated, a person under the direct control of the employer is an employee; a person not under such control is an independent contractor.

The control of the work reserved in the employer which affects an employer-employee relationship is the control of the *means and manner of performance* of the work as well as of the result. An independent-contractor relationship exists when the person doing the work is subject to the will of the employer only as to the *result* and not as to the means or manner of accomplishment. Also, it is not the fact of actual interference or exercise of control by the employer but the existence of the right or authority to interfere or control which renders a person an employee rather than an independent contractor.

Furnishing of labor and materials. Whether a contractor or an employer furnishes the workers, material, tools, and equipment is a factor to be considered in determining whether the contractor is independent, since as a rule employees generally use the means provided by the employer, while independent contractors furnish the labor and materials for doing the work. Thus, evidence that all the labor required for the performance of the stipulated work was furnished by the contractor, that the contractor hired the persons who helped perform the work, and that the contractor agreed to furnish all or a portion of the materials required for the performance of the work is considered indicative of independent-contractor status.

Right to inspect work. Retention by the employer of the right to supervise or inspect work as it progresses, for the purpose of determining whether it is being completed according to plans and specifications, does not in itself operate to create the relation of employer and employee between the employer and those engaged in the work. Thus, an employer of an independent contractor may retain a broad general power of supervision and control as to the *result* of the work so as to ensure satisfactory performance of the contract, including the right to inspect, to stop the work, to make suggestions or recommendations as to the details of the work, or to prescribe alterations or deviations in the work, without changing the relationship from that of employer and independent contractor or the duties arising from that relationship.

Control of premises. Whether the employer or the person employed to do the work has control of the premises on which the work is to be performed is a factor to be considered in determining whether the latter is an independent contractor or an employee, as this factor itself goes to the question of right of control over the work. If the premises on which the work is performed is placed under the control of the person employed, this tends to show he is an independent contractor.

Compensation. The measure of compensation for work to be done is sometimes an important element to be considered, but it is not in itself controlling. Thus, the fact that the compensation of a contractor is by the day, in a lump sum, or on a commission basis is not a compelling factor. However, an independent-contractor relationship is probable when the person employed undertakes to perform the work as a whole for a *specific sum,* when the compensation to the person employed is computed with reference to the *quantity* of work performed, and when compensation is computed with reference to the amount which that person is to pay others for performing the work. Also, it has been held that remuneration computed with reference to the time during which a person is engaged in the performance of the work tends to prove that the person is not an independent contractor.

Nature of business. The nature of the business or occupation in which a person is engaged may be an important factor to be considered with others. Work to be done that requires special skill for its proper performance tends to show that the relation between the employer and the person employed is an independent one. However, the fact that a person is given employment by reason of special skill does not fix the person's status as an independent contractor rather than as an employee if the employer retains the right to control work, as discussed above.

Power to terminate relationship. The power of an employer to terminate a contract or to discharge the person employed at any time, irrespective of whether there is or is not a good cause for so doing, strongly tends to show that the person employed is not an independent contractor but an employee. The relation between the parties is, however, to be determined from all the surrounding factors of contol, and the sole circumstance that the employer has reserved the right to terminate the work and discharge the contractor does not necessarily make the contractor a mere employee. On the other hand, the fact that the employer cannot terminate the employment strongly tends to show that the contractor is independent.

The factors discussed above are those most often addressed when the question of status as an independent contractor or employee arises. It is not always easy to distinguish between an independent contractor and an employee, and there is no uniform criterion by which they may be differentiated. However, distinctions do exist between the duties, rights, and obligations arising in connection with these different relationships, and all factors must be considered in making a final determination of a person's status.

Exempt Employees

There are white-collar exemptions from the minimum wage and overtime pay requirements for workers who meet the act's definitions of executive, administrative, or professional employees, or outside salesmen. Whether the exemption applies to a particular employee will not necessarily depend upon the job title but is determined by the nature of the employee's duties and whether the employee is employed on a salary basis. Employees are paid on a salary basis if they receive a predetermined amount each week or longer which is not subject to reduction because of a lesser number of hours worked unless the employees work fewer hours because they are absent from work for personal reasons. A record must be kept of salaried employees' total compensation in the week to assure that the employees have received the minimum salary which is a prerequisite for the white-collar exemption.

Executives. Employees who receive a minimum weekly salary of $155 and whose primary duties consist of managing an enterprise, department, or subdivision and supervision of at least two other workers are exempt executives as long as they do not spend more than 20 percent of their working time performing routine nonexempt work. Executives must have the authority to hire and fire employees and to recommend changes in workers' job status and they must regularly exercise discretionary powers. For employees who manage an enterprise, department, or subdivision and who supervise at least two other workers and receive a salary of at least $250, the requirements to qualify as an executive are less stringent. Officers of the construction firm are exempt executives. Field superintendents on the worksite are normally executives since most of their time is spent performing managerial duties which require the exercise of discretion such as planning the work and determining the techniques to be used, ordering the tools and materials, apportioning the work among workers, and hiring and firing employees or recommending changes in their job status, and handling employee grievances. The fact skilled craftsmen are paid more than $250 in weekly salary does not make them exempt executives because they regularly perform production work which at best is related only remotely to any supervisory functions they might perform. It may be difficult to bring working foremen within the white-collar exemption if their primary duties consist of performing the same routine construction work that is done by covered employees.

John Land was a warehouse foreman working for Bellhouse Aluminum Windows in Deca-
tur, Georgia. He had the authority to hire and fire employees as necessary. In addition, he
directed a work crew which varied in number from three to eight men. Although he had
supervisory duties, Land worked along with the men whom he was supervising. Approximately half of his time was spent in supervisory activity and half in physical or manual
work. The district court held that he was not an exempt executive employee under the
FLSA because he consistently was engaged in manual or other nonexempt duties far in
excess of the 20 percent tolerance which is permitted by the regulations at 29 CFR Section
541.1, which apply to the FLSA.[2]

Administrative employees. Administrative employees are exempt from
FLSA coverage if they receive a minimum salary or fee of $155 and their
primary duties require the exercise of independent judgment in the performance of office work or nonmanual work which relates to management
policies and general business operations. They must regularly and directly
assist a proprietor, or administrative employee, or work under only general
supervision along specialized or technical lines, requiring special training,
experience, or knowledge, or execute special assignments and tasks under
only general supervision. They must not spend more than 20 percent of
their working hours on nonexempt work which is not directly and closely
related to their exempt administrative functions. There is a shorter test for
administrative employees: they are so considered if they are paid a salary
or fee in excess of $250 per week and if their primary duty requires the
exercise of discretion and independent judgment in the performance of
office or nonmanual fieldwork relating to the management policies or general business operations of their employers or their employers' customers.

Professional employees. Office clerical workers and lower-level secre-
taries may not be administrative employees since their regular duties do
not require independent judgment. A worker whose primary duties are to
keep payroll records or to distribute paychecks will not be exempt from
coverage since the employee's normal duties are of a routine nature. Executive assistants to the contractor, tax and insurance experts, wage rate ana-
lysts, accountants, and safety and personnel directors may be exempt since
they normally must exercise independent judgment to help plan business
operations and effectuate management policies. Draftsmen help contractors plan their business operations, and whether they are exempt administrative employees may depend upon how much independent judgment
they are required to utilize. The fact that a draftsman is given a general
plan and then is required to utilize specialized training and skills to trans-
late the plan into a detailed blueprint may make such an employee exempt
from FLSA coverage.

White Construction Co., a contractor building a naval air station, employed a draftsman
named Mertens. The major duty of Mertens as an architectural draftsman was to prepare

---

[2] *Wintz v. Bellhouse Aluminum Windows of Ga. Inc.,* 16 W.H. Cas. 653 (N.D. Ga. 1964).

plans to scale for the buildings to be constructed. In addition, he had other men working under his supervision, and he was designated the supervisor of his department. The testimony of White Construction's chief engineer revealed that Mertens's supervisory work involved the exercise of discretion and independent judgment. When all these job characteristics were taken into account, Mertens was held to be an administrative employee and exempt from the coverage of the FLSA.[3]

To qualify as exempt professional employees, employees must regularly exercise independent judgment and perform work requiring scientific or specialized study, as distinguished from apprentice training or training for routine work; or perform original and creative work in a recognized artistic endeavor, depending primarily on their invention, imagination, or talent; or be teachers or tutors who instruct or lecture in the activity of imparting knowledge and are employed and engaged in this activity as teachers certified or recognized as such in the school system or educational establishment by which they are employed. The work must be predominantly intellectual and varied (not routine) and work which cannot be standardized in point of time. Professional employees must receive a salary or fee of $170 per week; there is a shorter test for professional employees who earn $250 or more per week. Lawyers, accountant, architects, and engineers with graduate degrees who perform work that is predominantly intellectual and varied and not routine in nature are exempt professionals. Apprenticeship training is not considered academic study, so skilled craftsmen who have successfully completed an apprenticeship program are not professionals.

Illustrative Case

J. J. Rausch, a certified public accountant worked for the accounting firm of Wolf and Company, the defendant in his action to recover overtime compensation allegedly due him. Rausch's recovery of the overtime pay hinged upon his status under the FLSA. If he were found to be a nonprofessional employee, he would be entitled to recover. The court looked at Rausch's job duties and found them to include the following: (1) auditing the employer's clients' books, (2) determining whether the clients had complied with all applicable state and federal laws, (3) preparing federal and state tax returns and Securities and Exchange Commission reports for clients, (4) handling accounting matters connected with recapitalization of corporate clients, and (5) preparing balance sheets and other financial documents for clients. Rausch was found to have a guaranteed salary which exceeded the amount specified by federal regulations as indicating a professional status. Because of these facts, Rausch was held to be a bona fide professional employee for purposes of the FLSA. He was unable to recover any overtime pay.[4]

Outside sales representatives. Outside sales representatives are also exempt from the minimum wage and overtime requirements of the FLSA. To qualify for this exemption, they must customarily and regularly make sales and obtain orders or contracts for services while away from the employer's place of business. Selling or soliciting business at the customer's place of business qualifies for the exemption, but to do the same either at

---

[3]*Landadio v. White Constr. Co.,* 163 F.2 383 (2d Cir. 1947).

[4]*Rausch v. Wolf,* 72 F. Supp. 654 (N.D. Ill. 1947).

the employer's premises or at any fixed site used by the sales representative, such as the sales representative's home, does not qualify for the exemption. If outside sales representatives spend more than 20 percent of nonexempt employees' weekly hours worked on nonexempt activities, except for time incidental to their sales, such as clerical duties, deliveries, collections, travel, or attending sales conferences, they are no longer exempt from the minimum wage and overtime requirements for the workweek.

There are many other employee exemptions from coverage by the FLSA, but they are far too numerous to describe here in their entirety. The foregoing discussion is not intended to be anything but a brief sample of exemptions under the FLSA. Any employer with serious questions as to whether employees are exempt should refer to Section 13 of the FLSA, in which all FLSA exemptions are set forth in considerable detail.

Compensable Working Time

It is essential that contractors understand what is meant by the FLSA's definition of "compensable working time" or its related meaning, "hours worked." Compensable working time will determine the hours for which minimum wages must be paid and the hours for overtime compensation. Contractors must pay careful attention to the interpretation of compensable working time made by the Wage and Hour Administrator; otherwise they may be liable in large amounts for unpaid wages and perhaps liquidated damages.

The hours worked by an employee must be determined for each workweek, which is a fixed and regularly recurring period of seven consecutive 24-hour periods. The workweek may vary for different employees and need not coincide with the payroll period, but once it is set for an employee, it cannot be changed unless the change is permanent and is not designed to evade the contractor's overtime obligations. The workweek may be set in such a manner that work on a shift may begin in one workweek and end in the next and that no overtime is worked in either week. Hours worked in 2 workweeks may not be averaged together to determine if overtime is owed. For example, if an employee works 35 hours in the first week and 45 hours in the second, overtime pay is owed for the 5 hours worked in the second week, even though the employee has worked an average of 40 hours for each of the weeks.

Under the *de minimis* rule, employers need not record insubstantial periods of working time which occur only infrequently if there is no practical way to keep a record of those times. If the work is scheduled or lasts more than a few minutes, that time must be recorded. The Wage and Hour Administrator will accept an employer's established practice of rounding off to the nearest tenth or quarter of an hour employees' starting and quitting times on the ground that employees will likely be paid for all hours worked if this practice is followed for a long period of time.

What is hours worked, or compensable time, is determined by two statutes, the Fair Labor Standards Act and the Portal-to-Portal Act. Time spent by employees during their workday performing work for the employer and time spent before or after the workday performing part of their principal duties is generally compensable working time under the FLSA. The Portal-to-Portal Act controls nonproductive activities before or after employees have engaged in part of their principal duties and makes such time not hours worked unless there is a contrary contract, custom, or practice not inconsistent with the contract to make such time hours worked. Contractors have a choice as to whether these incidental activities will be considered compensable working time. The Wage and Hour Administrator will determine that an agreement to pay for the time spent on the incidental activity is a decision to include it in hours worked unless the contract expressly states that such time spent should not be considered hours worked, or compensable working time. Therefore, if a contractor agrees to pay for time spent on a noncompensable activity but does not want such payment to increase the number of hours worked so as possibly to trigger an obligation to pay for overtime work, the contractor should make sure that the contract expressly states that such time will not be compensable working time.

Work which is not requested from an employee but which is "suffered or permitted" is hours worked. For example, an employee may stay after scheduled workhours to finish an assignment or to perform another task for the contractor's benefit. If the contractor or one of the foremen knew or had reason to know that the employee was working, the hours worked are compensable. The contractor may not rely on a management rule forbidding such work if the contractor or one of the foremen had reason to know that the employee was performing it. The employee might even have to be discharged to avoid having to pay for those hours the employee continued to perform unauthorized work.

An employee who voluntarily arrives at the job before scheduled workhours and who was neither requested nor expected to arrive at that time is not engaged in hours worked. That waiting time is not compensable hours worked since the employee was not there for the employer's benefit during that time. Time spent waiting to punch a time clock or to receive paychecks after the workday is over is not compensable working time.

Activities which are an indispensable part of an employee's principal duties are compensable hours worked under the FLSA even if they are performed before or after scheduled working hours. For example, an employee who operates a piece of equipment might normally oil, grease, or clean the machine before work commences. Or a worker may be assigned to transport tools and supplies from one location to another either before the workshift had begun or after it has ended. Foremen might be required to arrive before their shift or remain afterward to discuss problems with foremen on other shifts. Time spent on all these activities is compensable hours worked no matter when such work is performed, since these activities are integrated with the employees' regular duties.

When an employee arrives at a particular location as requested by the contractor and is ready to work, but for some reason beyond the employee's control there is not enough work to do, the time spent there is hours worked. The employee is there at the employer's request and for the employer's benefit, so the waiting time is compensable working time under the FLSA. A lesser amount of time spent waiting for work need not be counted as hours worked because of the *de minimis* rule.

Sometimes there is a temporary work stoppage because of weather conditions or defective machinery. Workers who are required to remain at their job posts until the work starts up again must be compensated under the FLSA since the waiting is an integral part of the job. Even if employees are allowed to leave the jobsite, the waiting time in compensable if the work stoppage is of short duration or if the employees cannot reasonably predict when the work will commence again. The waiting is an integral part of the employees' jobs, since they cannot effectively use the waiting time for their own purposes but must spend it primarily for the employer's benefit.

Periods during which workers are completely relieved from duty and which are long enough to permit them to use the time for their own purposes are not hours worked. Employees are off duty and need not be compensated if the employer tells them in advance that they may leave the job and need not return until a specified hour, provided that time is long enough to permit the employees to use it effectively for their own benefit. The time will not be compensable just because the employees are required to leave a telephone number or address where they may be located, but the waiting time will be compensable if they are required to remain at a particular location, since the employees in that case will not be able to use the time effectively for their own purposes.

Meal periods. A meal period of 30 minutes or longer need not be included in hours worked if an employee is completely relieved from all duties during that time. A worker who is given 30 minutes for lunch but is required to remain at the workbench while eating must be compensated for that time since the worker has not been completely freed from all duties. However, an employee may be required to remain on the jobsite during meals and that time will not be hours worked if the employee is not restricted to the workbench and is relieved of all duties during that time. If the employer knows or has reason to know that an employee is working during the meal break, that work time is compensable.

Rest Periods. Rest periods and coffee breaks are not required by the FLSA, but if they are provided and last less than 20 minutes, they are compensable hours worked under the FLSA. Whether longer rest periods are hours worked might depend on whether the employees are relieved of all their duties during that time. Off-duty principles apply to rest periods of more than 20 minutes. Although rest periods are not mandatory under the FLSA, they may still be required by local, state, or another federal law.

Grievance time. The time that an employee spends adjusting grievances with management either during workhours or after hours if the employee is required to be on the employer's premises is compensable. However, the time that an employee spends discussing grievances with other employees alone is not compensable. Time spent in grievance adjustment will not be included in hours worked if a valid collective bargaining agreement or a custom or practice under the agreement treats that time as not compensable. Whether or not an agreement exists, the time that an employee spends in a union meeting handling internal union affairs is not compensable.

Training time. Attendance at employer-sponsored training programs, lectures, and meetings need not be considered working time if (1) attendance is outside the employee's regular working hours, (2) attendance is voluntary, (3) the employee does no productive work while attending, and (4) the course or lecture is not directly related to the employee's job. Attendance is not voluntary if it is required by the contractor or if a worker is led to believe that failure to attend will adversely affect present working conditions or continuance of employment. Training is directly related to workers' jobs, so that time spent at the program is counted as hours worked, if it is designed to enable them to perform their present jobs more effectively but not if it trains them to hold other jobs or to learn a new or additional skill. If the training program's purpose is to prepare employees for advancement by teaching higher skills, the training is not directly related to their jobs even though it coincidentally improves their skills in performing their present jobs.

If employees voluntarily attend an independent training program or participate in a correspondence course outside regular working hours, attendance or time spent studying for the course is not working time even if the course is job-related. Voluntary attendance outside regular hours of work at an instructional program established by an employer is not compensable if it corresponds to courses offered by an independent institution of learning. Attendance at such a program need not be counted as working time even if the employer pays for the course or they are related to the employees' present jobs.

Time spent by apprentices in classroom instruction under an apprenticeship program need not be counted as hours worked if the apprentices are employed under a written apprenticeship program approved by the Bureau of Apprenticeship and Training (BAT) of the U.S. Department of Labor or a state agency recognized by the BAT and if such time is not spent doing productive work in the performance of the apprentices' regular duties. If the agreement requires the training time to be counted as working time, the time is hours worked, but the mere agreement to pay for the training time does not make it hours worked. Time spent studying outside the classroom is not working time even if outside study is required for continued enrollment in the program.

Travel time. To determine whether travel time is compensable hours worked, contractors must consider the FLSA, the Portal-to-Portal Act, and the employment contract. The Portal-to-Portal Act makes travel by an employee between home and worksite noncompensable in the absence of a contrary contract, custom, or practice. The FLSA determines whether travel which is undertaken during the workday or which is part of the employee's regular duty is compensable working time. If such travel time were never considered working time under the FLSA, it need not be counted as hours worked even though compensation is required by a contract or practice.

Ordinary travel from an employee's home to work before the workday begins and back after work is ended is not compensable working time even if the employee must travel to an outlying worksite. If the time is treated as compensable hours worked by the contract or a custom or practice not inconsistent with the contract, then the travel time might not be compensable hours worked for the FLSA, especially if there is no correlation between the amount of allowance and the time spent traveling.

Illustrative Case

Tidewater Construction Corporation was the contractor for the construction of a bridge-tunnel across Chesapeake Bay. The workers had to have transportation from the shore to their places of work on the bay, and travel time between these locations ranged from 15 minutes to 1 hour. Tidewater and Local 79 of the Ironworkers reached an agreement under which each employee would receive a $2.50 daily travel allowance. The agreement specified that "time spent by employees riding in boats to and from work will not be considered working time for any purpose." The agreement with Local 147 of the Operating Engineers gave a $2.50 travel allowance and stated that "this allowance shall fully compensate the employee for any time spent riding to and from work." The workers agreed that riding time must be counted as hours worked so they were entitled to overtime compensation since the time spent traveling made their hours worked in excess of 40 for the week. The United States court of appeals held that the riding time was not compensable working time, since ordinary travel from home to work and back was governed by the Portal-to-Portal Act. The fact that these two agreements awarded travel allowances did not constitute contracts making such travel time compensable hours worked.[5]

The time that an employee spends on the construction site before scheduled workhours is governed by the Portal-to-Portal Act and is not compensable working time, absent a contract or practice to the contrary. The time that an employee spends going from the project entrance to a time clock or from there to the job post or both, need not be counted as working time since the employee's regular duties have not yet commenced, unless the contract states that an employee's work schedule starts when the employee arrives at the time clock or any location other than the job post.

If an employee is required by the contractor to arrive at a preliminary meeting place, for example, to receive work instructions or to pick up tools and supplies, then work duties commence when the employee arrives there and travel time afterward is hours worked under the FLSA. If employees meet there for their own convenience and not because they are required to

---

[5] *Ralph v. Tidewater Constr. Corp.,* 361 F.2d 806 (4th Cir. 1966).

do so by the contractor, travel time from there is not hours worked because they are not there for the contractor's benefit. An employee who is required to pick up a truck at the job yard to carry equipment or workers to the construction site commences duties there, and travel time to the project site is working time for the employee under the FLSA. The same reasoning obviously applies if the employee must deliver the truck from the jobsite to the job yard after the workday is over. Employees who are transported by the driver to and from the job yard or other location are not engaged in compensable hours worked under the FLSA unless they are required by the employer to use that mode of transportation or to perform work along the way or before beginning the trip or after ending it. This is so because travel time before or after the employees' principal activity is held to be noncompensable. If the transportation service is furnished by the contractor as a convenience for the employees which they are free to accept or reject, the travel time for the riders is not hours worked.

Illustrative Case

Audet was a master electrician for E. R. Field, Inc., a contractor on various jobsites for the construction of hospitals, schools, and so on. He reported each morning at 7:30 at Field's shop to drive a truck to the jobsites. Although Audet derived some benefit from use of the truck to get to the job, the primary purpose of the truck was to transport tools and supplies to the jobsite. Other employees rode in the truck, which Audet was required to drive. After work at 4:00 in the afternoon, Audet was required to drive the truck back to Field's shop and leave it there. Audet claimed that the return trip was compensable hours worked and that he was entitled to time and one-half of his hourly rate because all time after 4:00 was overtime. The United States court of appeals held that the time spent traveling on the return trip was compensable hours worked. The activity was employment under the FLSA since it was done at least in part for Field's benefit, even though it may also have been beneficial to the employee. It was irrelevant that Audet and the employee might have reached the job by other means or that Field could have stocked the jobsite without the use of the truck, since the truck was utilized primarily as an integral function of Field's business.[6]

There are some instances in which travel from home to work must be counted as working time. If an employee after returning home from a day's work is called out to travel a substantial distance to perform emergency work at a customer's premises, the travel time is hours worked. The Wage and Hour Administrator has taken no position as to whether travel from home to work to perform emergency work at the employee's regular place of business is hours worked.

Time spent traveling during the workday from one jobsite to another must be counted as hours worked since the travel is part of the worker's principal duty. If an employee normally finishes work at 5:00 P.M. and is then sent to another job which the employee finishes at 8:00 and is required to return to the job yard at 9:00 before going home, all the time is working time. But if the employee goes home after 8:00 instead of returning to the job yard, the time after 8:00 is ordinary work-to-home travel and is not compensable hours worked.

[6]*Department of Labor v. E.R. Field, Inc.*, 495 F.2d 749 (1st Cir. 1974).

Minimum Wages

Contractors must pay all their employees not exempt from FLSA coverage at least the minimum wage rate in any workweek. Subminimum wage rates set by law may be paid to learners and apprentices if special certificates which will be granted under certain conditions are obtained, but these are rare in the construction industry. The FLSA does not excuse the failure to pay a higher wage rate that is required by contract, local or state law, or another federal law, such as the Davis-Bacon Act. On the other hand, a union contract which pays less than the minimum rate will not protect contractors from liability to pay the difference, since employees are not permitted to waive their rights concerning minimum wage and overtime compensation under the FLSA. The fact that the minimum rate is raised will not require contractors to increase other rates in a contract in order to preserve traditional wage differentials between laborers and skilled tradesmen. Whether the minimum rate has been paid must be determined for each workweek. Wages paid for 2 weeks may not be averaged together to satisfy the minimum wage requirement. The minimum wage requirement is satisfied if for each workweek the total compensation less premium pay for overtime work, divided by the total compensable hours worked, is at least equal to the minimum rate. Although the minimum wage rate is set on an hourly basis, employees may be paid on an hourly, weekly, piece-rate, or any other basis, provided the minimum rate requirement is met for that workweek.

Employees paid solely on an hourly basis must be paid at least the minimum rate for each hour worked. They may not be paid at less than the minimum rate for some hours and higher rate for others even if the average equals the minimum rate. If an employee works at two different tasks in the week at two different hourly rates, the hourly rate for each task must be as high as the FLSA rate, and the two may not be averaged together. For employees who receive a fixed weekly salary, the salary divided by the number of hours worked in the week must equal or be higher than the minimum rate.

For workers hired solely on a piece-rate basis, their total compensation excluding overtime pay for the week, divided by the number of hours worked, must at least equal the minimum wage rate. It is no excuse for a contractor who pays less than the minimum rate to a piece-worker to claim that some workers are not as efficient as others. Even though the contractor may lawfully not credit the piece-worker with pay for faulty work or may deduct the sum if it has already been credited, the contractor may not reduce the piece-worker's pay for the workweek below the FLSA minimum. A piece-worker is entitled to the minimum wage for the number of hours worked in the week even though not a single piece which has been produced passes inspection. Piece-workers must be paid at least the statutory minimum for each workweek. The difference between piece-rate earnings and the minimum rate in one week cannot be made up in another week.

Under some employment contracts employees work on both a piece-rate and an hourly basis in the same week. If the worker is paid a combination of a piece-rate and an hourly rate for the same hours worked, the earnings from each rate in the workweek may be totaled and divided by the number of hours worked to determine whether or not the statutory minimum had been paid. But if the employee is compensated on an hourly rate for some hours and on a piece-rate for others, then the hourly rate and the piece-rate earnings, divided by the hours worked on the piece basis, must each be at least as high as the minimum rate. If the hourly rate is less than the minimum and there is an understanding between the contractor and employees that the piece-rate also includes compensation for nonproductive time which is compensable working time for piece-workers, such as waiting time and washup time, then the piece-rate and hourly rate earnings for the week may be averaged. Without such an understanding, averaging is not permitted to meet the minimum wage requirements.

The FLSA generally requires that covered employees be paid at least the minimum wage rate on the regular payday for the payroll period in which each workweek ends. Some deductions which reduce a worker's pay below the minimum rate are allowed under particular conditions. Union dues are deductible if the checkoff had been authorized by the employee under a valid union security agreement. If the agreement is illegal or if the checkoff had not been properly authorized, the contractor violates the FLSA if the deduction reduces the worker's pay below the minimum rate in the week. Taxes which workers are legally required to pay, such as social security and income taxes, are also deductible. Other deductions are permitted if employees voluntarily assent and the contractor derives no profit or benefit from the deductions. For example, deductions for employee contributions to pension, health, and welfare plans are allowed if the plans are administered in such a manner that the contractor has no control over the funds and the employees assent to the deductions. Since it is not clear under the FLSA whether a union agreement authorizing such deductions constitutes voluntary assent by nonunion members, contractors should get written authorizations for the deductions from these employees, especially since a state law might impose that requirement anyway. Any deductions from the employees' paychecks from which a contractor derives a benefit and which reduces the employees' pay below the minimum wage for straight time or cuts into the required time and one-half of the regular rate for overtime hours are a violation of the FLSA. Contractors should be aware of applicable state laws, since some of them may bar certain deductions allowed by the FLSA.

Overtime

The requirement of the FLSA concerning premium pay for overtime work is that employees must be paid time and one-half of their "regular rate" for hours worked in excess of 40 in a workweek. Whether more than 40 hours have been worked must be determined for each week. An employee who works 35 hours in one week and 45 hours in the next must be paid time and one-half for the 5 hour's overtime work in the second week. Premium pay for daily overtime work, for work on holidays, vacations, and the like, or for work in excess of less than 40 hours' work in the week is not required by the FLSA, but the contractor must give extra pay for such work if the employment agreement or another law so requires. Under certain conditions, the contractor may credit some of these premium payments to offset the overtime pay obligation under the FLSA.

The regular rate of pay on which premium pay for overtime work is calculated is expressed as an hourly rate. It is computed by dividing a worker's total compensation for employment in the workweek, except for certain exclusions listed in the statute by the total number of compensable hours worked in the week. The employee's total compensation is figured before allowable deductions for taxes, union dues, contributions to pension plans, and so on are made. The FLSA contains a list of premium payments for certain types of work which may be excluded from the employee's compensation and which perhaps will also be creditable toward the contractor's overtime liability under the FLSA. In addition, there are some payments to employees which are not considered compensation and are not included in figuring the regular rate.

If the regular rate is computed to be lower than the FLSA minimum, overtime work must be paid for on the basis of the FLSA minimum. Of course, if the regular rate is higher than the minimum rate, overtime pay will be based on the higher regular rate. An employee who is paid solely on the basis of one hourly rate for all work in the week has a regular rate for up to 40 hours' work and must be paid time and one-half of the hourly rate for work in excess of 40 hours in the week.

Sometimes an employee works on different tasks or different at times of the day during the week which pay different hourly rates. For example, the employee may work both the day and the night shift, which pays a higher rate, or during part or the week may perform hazardous work that pays a higher rate. There are several ways in which the regular rate for overtime compensation may be set. Under the weighted-average method, the total compensation less premium pay for weekly overtime and other exclusions listed in the FLSA is divided by the total number of hours worked. For each hour worked in excess of 40 in the week only one-half of this rate must be paid, since the straight-time rate for over 40 hours worked was already paid the employee.

The regular rate for overtime in excess of 40 hours instead may be set as the hourly rate in effect during the overtime hours, provided the contractor, either with the individual or through the union, agrees to use that rate before overtime work is performed. In no event may this rate be lower than the FLSA minimum. The contractor may not avoid the FLSA overtime pay requirements by arbitrarily setting a lower rate for the overtime work. Such a rate may not be lower than the rate which would apply to the same work had it been done during nonovertime hours. A record which shows the terms of the agreement and the period for which it applies must be kept. The employee must be paid time and one-half of the hourly rate applicable to the work performed during the overtime hours.

The contractor and employees either individually or through the union are permitted to set a basic rate for overtime work, provided the agreement is made before such work is done. The basic rate must be at least as high as the FLSA minimum and must also be about the same as the employee's average hourly earnings over a representative period of time for the particular work. A record of the basic-rate agreement and the period it covers must be retained. Overtime is paid at time and one-half of the basic rather than the regular rate of pay.

Fixed pay–fluctuating hours. A common plan for weekly-salaried employees who work varying numbers of hours in a week is to have them agree that the salary is compensation for all hours worked in a week. Under this fixed-pay–fluctuating-hours plan a worker who is employed at a fixed salary under an agreement to work whatever number of hours is necessary to complete the duties has agreed to be paid on a fluctuating-workweek basis. Under this method, there will be no fixed regular rate for calculating overtime pay since the rate will vary with the actual number of working hours in a week. As the number of hours worked increases, the regular rate will decrease, but in no event may the regular rate be lower than the FLSA minimum. Only one-half of the regular rate must be paid for more than 40 hours' work, since the weekly salary includes straight-time compensation for the overtime hours. Deductions from earnings for figuring the regular rate which are otherwise permitted for paid-for occasional absences are not allowed under this procedure, since the fixed salary is meant to cover long and short workweeks. An employee who had been paid a fixed salary for a fixed number of weekly workhours may not be paid for overtime work according to the lower regular rate figured on the fluctuating-workweek basis unless the employee agreed to the change before the overtime work was performed.

Weekly-salaried employees might instead have a regular rate which will not fluctuate with the number of hours worked in a week, on the ground that the salary represents compensation for a workweek with a fixed number of hours, which may be fewer or greater than 40 hours. The regular rate need not be computed because of an employee's occasional absences, but the regular rate must be figured anew and increased if the employee's weekly hours are permanently reduced while the salary remains the same.

Piecework. One of the biggest traps for construction contractors under the overtime provisions of the FLSA is that relating to piecework. It is not unusual for contractors to have employees working on a piecework compensation basis. If an employee working on piecework works more than 40 hours in any one week, then the employee must be compensated at time and one-half of the employee's regular rate of pay for all hours worked in excess of 40 hours. The regular rate may be determined by dividing the total weekly earnings by the total weekly hours worked, then multiplying the regular rate by one-half for the appropriate additional overtime compensation for all hours in excess of 40 hours, or the straight-time piece-rate, or the overtime rate may also be determined by multiplying the straight-time piece-rate by 1½ for all piecework performed during the overtime period, provided the employee agrees to the arrangement. This means that if an employee is on a piecework rate of $1 for a unit of work and then works more than 40 hours, the employee must receive $1.50 for the *same* units of work performed in excess of 40 hours.

Another important requirement for an employer is to keep accurate records including time records on piece-workers. Many employers must enforce a 40-hour limit on their employees because of their employees' desire to earn more money and therefore work longer than 40 hours. The employer must enforce the limit or pay 1½ times the basic piecework rate or additional half-time premium during the overtime period. Of course, if an employee does not produce enough piecework to earn the minimum wage, the employee must be paid the minimum wage. Employer and employee may agree that downtime and faulty piecework will not be credited toward an employee's compensation to prevent inefficient piecework practices. But the employee must be paid at least the minimum wage and time and one-half for work in excess of 40 hours, or 1½ times the piecework rate for all piecework performed after 40 hours.

Bonuses and premium pay. Contractors may make certain payments to workers apart from straight-time wages which must be included in the total compensation of employees and will increase the regular rate of pay and the contractor's overtime liability. Bonuses which are promised to employees to induce them to work harder or more efficiently are like wages and are part of their earnings for computing the regular rate. Attendance bonuses, length-of-service bonuses, and bonuses for the greatest number of hours of overtime worked are also includable in the regular rate. Such bonuses not promised to employees are discretionary and are excludable from the regular rate since the employees have expended no additional effort in justifiable reliance that the bonus will be paid. A decision to reward an employee for past services is a discretionary bonus. Christmas bonuses or other small gifts are not part of the regular rate even though regularly paid, unless they are promised in a contract or the amount of the bonus depends upon the number of hours worked. However, the size of the bonus may vary with employees' hourly rates or length of service and still be excluded from the regular rate.

Sometimes there is temporarily no work for employees to do because of events beyond a contractor's control, such as a machinery breakdown, adverse weather conditions, or failure of ordered supplies to arrive, but the contractor elects to pay the worker for the idle time. If the employees are allowed to leave the jobsite for a long enough period that they may spend it for their own benefit, then the idle time is not hours worked, and payment for the idleness may be excluded from earnings. But if the employees are not told that they may leave work or if the length of time that they are permitted to go elsewhere is not long enough for them to spend for their personal benefit, then the idle time is hours worked, and the payment must be included in the employees' earnings for calculating the regular rate.

Under some employment contracts workers are paid "show-up" pay for a minimum number of hours worked at the straight-time or premium rate when they arrive on time for work but there is not enough work for them to perform. Or a provision might provide for "call-back" pay which guarantees straight-time or premium pay for a minimum number of hours worked for infrequent occasions when employees are called back to perform work outside scheduled workhours. In either case the pay which represents straight-time compensation for actual hours worked is part of earnings for computing the regular rate, and the portion which represents premium pay for actual hours worked is excludable from earnings and may be credited against the contractor's FLSA overtime obligation. That portion of the show-up and call-back pay which is not compensation for actual hours worked is not part of earnings for figuring the regular rate, nor is any part creditable against any overtime obligation.

As an illustration, let us suppose that a worker is paid $5 an hour and that the contract requires show-up pay for 4 hours worked. The worker arrives on Monday and is sent home after 2 hours' work and works 8 hours per day Tuesday through Saturday. The employee will have worked 42 weekly hours and received $210 for actual work and $10 show-up pay which was not actual hours worked. The earnings for figuring the regular rate will be $210, not $220, since the $10 show-up pay was not for actual hours worked. The regular rate, then, is $210 divided by 42 hours worked, or $5. The FLSA overtime pay requirement is satisfied if the employee is paid $210 straight-time wages, plus $5 premium pay for 2 hours' overtime work, and $20 show-up pay for 4 hours worked as required by the contract.

Other provisions in a contract may permit compensation for time not worked due to occasional absences caused by holidays, vacations, personal or family illness, attendance at the funeral of a family member, inability to reach work because of adverse weather, and so on. Payments for these occasional absences which are about the same as the employee's straight-time rate are not included in earnings for computing the regular rate. Occasional absences must be infrequent, so that pay for regularly scheduled lunch breaks or for scheduled days of rest must be included in earnings for purposes of computing and employee's regular rate of pay, even though the FLSA does not consider these paid absences as compensable working time.

When contractors reimburse workers for expenses that they incurred for the contractor's benefit and the amount of the reimbursements reasonably approximates their expenses, these payments are excluded from the regular rate. If a reimbursement is for expenses normally incurred by the employees for their own benefit, such as a travel allowance for ordinary home-to-work travel, the payment is like wages and must be included in the regular rate. A travel allowance for employees' travel during the workday between jobsites may be excluded from the regular rate, since these expenses are incurred for the contractor's benefit. Travel and subsistence allowances for employees who must travel round-trip distances of 130 to

200 miles between their homes and jobsites because either there are no living quarters at the site or the job is temporary, so that it is not reasonable to expect the employees to move there for a short time, are not included in the regular rate. Employees who are repaid for the cost of tools, supplies or equipment will not have these reimbursements included in their regular rates since those expenses were incurred on behalf of the contractor's business. That portion of an allowance beyond the amount reasonably necessary to compensate workers for expenses incurred for the contractor are earnings and are includable in the regular rate.

Contractors often agree to make premium payments which are not required under the FLSA. Premium payments for daily overtime work, for work done on special days, and for work outside an employee's shift are not mandated by the FLSA, but contractors must make these payments if that is what the contract requires. To prevent the injustice in making a employer pay overtime on overtime, under certain conditions some of the premium payments may be excluded from earnings for computing the regular rate and then credited against the FLSA overtime obligation. A decision to make premium payments in other situations will cause these payments to be included in earnings and will increase the regular rate and the amount of overtime pay owed, unless the payment can be fitted into one of the categories which exclude the extra pay from the computation of the regular rate. The contractor must make sure that a premium payment can be excluded from earnings before agreeing to it; otherwise the contractor will inadvertently increase overtime liability under the FLSA.

Union contracts often require extra pay for hours worked over 8 hours in the day even though the FLSA does not require it. Premium pay for such work is excluded from the regular rate and is creditable toward an employer's overtime liability. The premium pay may be less or greater than 150 percent of the straight-time or base rate. Some contracts require premium pay for work in excess of fewer than 8 hours worked in the day. For example, a contract may call for a higher pay rate for over 7 hours worked in the day. The contractor must make sure that the 7-hour workday is normal; if it is not, premium pay for the eighth hour of work will be considered straight-time earnings and be included in the regular rate even if it is over 150 percent of the straight-time rate. In effect, management will be forced to pay overtime on overtime by agreeing to pay extra for an amount of work under 8 hours in the day which is less than the standard workday. As the workday falls farther below 8 hours, it will be harder to convince the Wage and Hour Administrator that the shorter workday is normal and that premium pay for work in excess of those hours should be excluded from the regular rate. Premium pay for over 8 hours should be excluded from the regular rate and is creditable against overtime liability since any workday of at least 8 hours is always considered to be of normal duration.

Although the minimum workweek under the FLSA is 40 hours, some contracts provide for premium pay of less than 40 hours worked in the week. If the contractor can establish the lesser number of hours as the standard workweek, premium pay for hours worked over that amount may be excluded from the regular rate and credited toward overtime owed under the FLSA whether the premium pay is less or greater than time and one-half of the straight-time or base rate. As with premium pay for daily overtime the contractor should make sure that the workweek of less than 40 hours is normal and regular; otherwise premium pay for those hours must be included in straight-time earnings and the regular rate.

Some contracts contain preshift or postshift premium clauses requiring a higher pay rate for work done outside an employee's shift. Payments in excess of the straight-time rate for such work are excludable from earnings and the regular rate and creditable toward overtime liability under the FLSA only if such work is in excess of 8 hours' work in the day or a lesser amount established as the standard workday, whichever is smaller. If not, the premium pay is considered extra pay for undesirable working hours, which under the FLSA is included in earnings and will raise the FLSA obligation for overtime work. If employees are paid during occasional absences or while they remain idle because of a temporary lack of available work, the contractor may, but is not required to, count the paid-for nonproductive time as hours worked. In that manner, the extra pay for work outside the employee's shift may be excluded from earnings and allowed to offset the FLSA overtime obligation if the hours worked are increased over 8 hours or the lesser amount which is the normal workday.

Extra pay for a worker who is asked to perform work on a scheduled day off without sufficient notice is held to be the same as premium pay for working during undesirable hours. Therefore, the entire payment for such work must be included in earnings for calculating the regular rate, so that liability overtime work under the FLSA will be increased.

Another provision often requires premium pay for night-shift work. The clause may mandate a higher pay rate for the night shift as opposed to day-shift work, mention a shift differential which is stated as a percentage of the daily or base pay rate, or allow 6½ or 7 hours' work on the night shift to be paid for in the same amount as is 8 hours' work on the day shift. Premium pay for night-shift work is treated in the same way as extra pay for undesirable working hours, so that the entire amount is includable in earnings and the regular rate. The only way that the amount above the straight-time rate may be excluded from earnings and used to offset the FLSA overtime obligation is if the extra work on the night-shift, along with the work already done on the same day on the day shift, is over 8 daily hours or the lesser standard workday. For an employee who works an 8 hour night shift and does no other work in the day, the entire payment is part of earnings, and the regular rate will be increased. If the employee has already worked the day shift and then performs night-shift work, premium pay for the latter is considered true overtime pay and is excluded from the regular rate and may be used to offset overtime due under the FLSA for those hours worked on the night shift in excess of 8 or fewer daily hours which is the normal workday.

The FLSA does not require premium pay for Saturday or Sunday work or for work on the sixth or seventh day or the scheduled day of rest, unless work during those times extends the hours worked in the week to over 40. If work on any of those days is part of the 40-hour workweek, premium pay must be at least 150 percent of straight-time rate to be excluded from earnings; otherwise it will all be considered straight-time earnings and be included in figuring the regular rate. The premium pay for work on any of those days may be less than 150 percent of the straight-time rate and be excluded from earnings and used to offset overtime owed under the FLSA only if more than 40 hours are worked in the week. A contractor is permitted to count paid-for nonproductive time because of occasional absences or temporary lack of work as hours worked, so that extra pay for work on those special days at less than 150 percent of the straight-time rate may be excluded from earnings and creditable toward FLSA overtime liability if more than 40 hours are worked in the week.

Union contracts may require pay for unworked holidays or vacations or premium pay for work on holidays or vacations even though the FLSA does not require it. A holiday under the statute is defined as a day normally observed in the community for the celebration of historic or religious occasion. Sundays, scheduled days of rest, and days when there is no work to do are not holidays. Premium pay of less than 150 percent of the straight-time or base rate for holiday work is part of an employee's straight-time earnings and must be included in the regular rate even if work on the holiday is more than the standard or 40-hour workweek, since the Wage and Hour Administrator considers pay for work on holidays to be the same as pay for undesirable work, for which premium pay is not creditable. Premium pay for holiday work must be at least 150 percent of the straight-time rate for it to be excluded from the regular rate and offset against overtime due under the FLSA.

Contractors should make sure that holiday pay is only for holiday work and not for idle time during the holiday; otherwise employees may have to be paid double-time for holiday work. If the contract provides pay for idle time on a holiday, the contractor should make sure that employees who work during the holiday understand that they have waived their right to idle-time pay. In that event, the premium pay for the holiday work must be still at least 150 percent of the straight-time base to be excluded from the regular rate and creditable toward overtime liability under the FLSA.

Child Labor

The FLSA contains provisions which restrict the employment of children, including summer employment of children. An employer may be guilty of unlawfully employing a child even if the employer does not directly supervise the child and the child receives no compensation. The child will be employed if the employer knows that one of the employees is using the services of a child as a helper or to do the work for the employee. The FLSA contains no special minimum wage requirement for children, but it does control the minimum ages for various occupations.

The following occupations, which are particularly applicable to construction, have been found to be hazardous by the Secretary of Labor and are prohibited to children below 18 years of age. Employment by a parent in these occupations is just as unlawful as if the child were employed by other employers.

1. Occupations involving the operation of power-driven woodworking machines

2. Occupations of motor vehicle drivers and outside helpers except that 16- and 17-year-old children are permitted to work as helpers on motor vehicles as long as they ride inside the vehicle cab

3. Occupations involving the operation of or riding on power-driven elevators and other hoisting apparatus, except that 16- and 17-year-old children are permitted to operate and ride on automatic enclosed elevators meeting certain safety requirements

4. Occupations involving the operation of power driven farming, pushing, and shearing machinery

5. Occupations involving the operation of circular saws, band saws, and guillotine shears, with the exception of machines equipped with fully automated feed and ejection

6. Occupations in roofing operations

7. Occupations in excavation operations

8. Occupations involved in the wrecking and demolition of buildings

Children who are 16 or 17 years old may be lawfully employed in the following hazardous occupations as apprentices or student-learners after apprentice certificates or student-learner certificates have been obtained:

1. Occupations involving the operation of power-driven woodworking machines

2. Occupations involving the operation of circular saws, band saws, and guillotine shears

3. Occupations in roofing operations

4. Occupations involving excavation operations

For an apprentice certificate to be obtained, the child must be registered as an apprentice by BAT or a state apprenticeship agency, the hazardous work must be incidental to training, and such work must be for intermittent and short periods of time under the direct supervision of a journeyman. A student-learner certificate may be obtained if the child is enrolled in a vocational training program and employed under a written agreement which provides that the hazardous work is incidental to training, the work will be for short lengths of time and under the close supervision of a journeyman, and a schedule of progressive work processes to be performed on the job will be followed.

Children who are 16 or 17 years old may be employed in any nonfarm occupation other than the hazardous occupations listed above for which the minimum age of 18 is required. Children who are 14 or 15 years old may be employed in some nonhazardous occupations normally prohibited to children under 16 years of age if they are employed exclusively by a parent. Even the employment of a child by a parent who is a corporate official is not exempt when the child is employed by the corporation unless the child's mother and father own all the stock of the corporation.

Employers will be protected against *unintentional* violations of the FLSA if they have on file an unexpired age certificate issued pursuant to the regulations of the Secretary of Labor. An age certificate is an official statement of the child's age based on the best available documentary evidence of age and signed by the child and the issuing officer. If there is a possibility that a job applicant is under age for the contemplated work, an age certificate should be obtained for the applicant. The certificate should be retained until termination of employment. Many states issue employment certificates which list the child's age and the hazardous occupation in which the child is to be employed. The employment certificate will serve as a defense to a child labor violation only if it shows the child's age to be above the minimum age requirement for that occupation under the FLSA. If state law sets a higher age requirement than does the FLSA, the employer must comply with state law.

For an employer who violates the child labor laws there are civil penalties of up to $1,000 in fines as well as criminal penalties. Usually the employer is enjoined from continuing to violate the child labor laws.

Record-Keeping Requirements

The FLSA imposes particular record-keeping requirements on construction contractors. These requirements are enforceable by injunction suits instituted by the Wage and Hour Division and by Criminal penalties in the case of willful violations. A contractor may be criminally liable for coercion of employees by a foreman to falsify time records. Records also benefit contractors since they often serve as good defense to back-pay suits.

Payroll records must be clearly and accurately recorded and kept for 3 years, while supporting records such as time cards showing starting and stopping times must be kept for 2 years. Records may be microfilmed if they accurately and clearly reflect the original records which were required to be kept. Since the required records are usually subject to inspection by Wage and Hour Division investigators upon request at reasonable times, it is important always to have the records up to date and readily available. The Secretary of Labor and the Wage and Hour Administrator may issue a subpoena to compel production of the payroll records for inspection, and the subpoena is enforceable by court order. Contractors should consult with their accountants or attorneys before making their books immediately available.

Contractors must keep for 3 years records which accurately and intelligibly contain the following information for each covered employee:

1. Name, home address, and birth date if under 19
2. Sex and occupation

3. Hour and day on which the employee's workweek begins

4. Regular hourly rate of pay, the basis on which wages are paid, and regular-rate exclusions for any week when overtime is worked

5. Hours worked each workday and total hours worked each workweek

6. Total daily or weekly straight-time earnings

7. Total overtime pay for the workweek

8. Deductions from or additions to wages

9. Total wages paid each pay period

10. Date of payment and pay period covered by the payment

11. Retroactive wage payments under government supervision

The FLSA requires contractors to display in conspicuous places at the worksite posters which specify the minimum wage rate, overtime pay requirements, and the right to equal pay regardless of sex. The poster also informs employees that it is illegal for contractors to discriminate against them for pursuing their rights under the FLSA. Copies of the poster are available at regional offices of the Wage and Hour Division.

Enforcement Remedies

Enforcement of the FLSA requirements for minimum wages and overtime pay and the use of child labor is carried out in a variety of ways. Investigations are carried out by the Wage and Hour Division in response to complaints of violations from employees and competing employers. The division will also reinspect contractors who have previously violated the FLSA to assure compliance and will make spot checks of contractors in areas where there have been high rates of violations in the past. State and local agencies frequently aid in the investigations of violations. Payroll records must usually be opened for inspection at reasonable times after sufficient notice, and the Wage and Hour Administrator is authorized to subpoena records. Contractors who violate the FLSA may be met with injunctions and the recovery of unpaid wages and liquidated damages by the government and back-pay suits by employees with the recovery or liquidated damages, attorneys' fees, and court costs. Some contractors have been fined substantially and have even gone to prison for willful and repeated violations of the FLSA. Contractors should make sure that they understand how to comply with all the FLSA requirements and that their supervisors and bookkeepers have complied, since contractors might be liable for violations by their employees.

Injunctions may be obtained by the Secretary of Labor to restrain future violations of the FLSA and also to obtain a back-pay order. Or the Secretary may institute a wage suit to recover unpaid wages under the FLSA on behalf of the affected employees. An injunction for a back-pay order may be sought without the employee's consent and terminates the employee's right to sue individually for back pay. Liquidated damages are not recoverable in the injunction suit but may be recovered in the wage suit. Contractors may be also required to pay court costs and prejudgment interest on the unpaid wages but are not liable for attorneys' fees. The money recovered in a government wage suit is held in a special deposit and paid to the affected employees on the government's order. Normally the government will attempt to supervise voluntary payment by the contractor before it will institute a suit. Good-faith reliance on a written administrative regulation, ruling, interpretation, or enforcement policy may serve as a complete defense to a back-pay suit.

Employees may sue contractors in state or federal court for unpaid wages and liquidated damages unless the government has already filed suit for a back-pay order pursuant to an injunction. Employees are entitled to reasonable attorney fees and court costs if they win. It is also possible in a wage suit to recover liquidated damages equal in amount to the unpaid wages recovered. Contractors who can establish a good-faith defense or reason to believe that they were not violating the FLSA may get liquidated damages reduced or eliminated. For example, relief has been given to a contractor who relied upon the erroneous advice of his attorney. Good-faith reliance upon a written agency regulation, ruling, interpretation, or enforcement practice or policy may serve as a defense not only to liquidated damages but also to any back-pay liability. A contractor may not justify reliance on a general-information pamphlet on working time.

The federal statute of limitations for government wage suits and back-pay orders sought in an injunction and employees' suits is 2 years, but the period is 3 years for willful violations. The fact that the contractor knew or had a strong reason to believe that FLSA pay requirements had been violated may constitute a willful violation. A separate cause of action accrues each payday for unpaid wages, so the statute bars suits only for wages still due for which the limitations period has run.

If employees voluntarily agree to accept full payment under government supervision of the unpaid wages, the employees' suit is barred. It is to the advantage of a contractor who feels that he probably will lose a back-pay suit to pursue this mode of settlement, since he need pay only the amount of wages due and not risk liability for liquidated damages and attorney's fees in an employees' suit. A back-pay request by the government in an injunction suit will waive the employees' right to sue for back pay, even though the employees did not consent to the suit and no damages were recovered in it. Employees waive the right to sue if they consent to a wage suit by the government in their behalf and the government loses. A compromise settlement between contractor and employees for less than the entire amount of wages due under the FLSA will not constitute a defense to an employees' suit.

Criminal prosecutions for willful and repeated violations of the FLSA requirements are sometimes instituted by the Department of Justice. First offenders may be fined up to $10,000, while second offenders may be subject to both fine and imprisonment for up to 6 months. The Secretary of

Labor's practice is to recommend criminal suits only for serious and repeated violations and to seek injunctions for lesser violations. Repeated and willful falsifications of payroll records are a type of offense which may lead to a substantial fine and jail term.

It is illegal for contractors or supervisors to threaten to or actually retaliate against or discharge an employee for filing a complaint or for testifying concerning an FLSA violation. An employee who furnishes information to a Wage and Hours Division investigator concerning an alleged violation is also protected against reprisal by the employer. It makes no difference that the employee is exempt from coverage under the FLSA. A contractor who acts unlawfully in this area might be faced with criminal prosecution.

A contractor may face an injunction or criminal prosecution for purchasing goods which were produced in an establishment that violated the FLSA provisions concerning minimum wages, overtime, and child labor unless the contractor purchased the goods for value without notice of the violations. The contractor should require the seller of the goods to furnish a written assurance that the specific goods were produced in compliance with all the FLSA requirements before accepting them.

DAVIS-BACON ACT

Under national laws and many state and local laws, construction performed and paid for by tax funds is to be paid at the "prevailing" wages and fringe-benefit levels in each area. The federal statute, the Davis-Bacon Act, was enacted to "protect local standards," which during the Depression of the 1930s may have been hard won. Today, however, these prevailing wages are used to keep wages high and are highly inflationary.

The Davis-Bacon Act[7] requires contractors and subcontractors to pay prevailing wage rates and fringe benefits to laborers and mechanics on federal or federal-aid construction contracts in excess of $2,000. The purpose of the act as originally passed was to prevent the depression of local wage rates by competition paying lower wages on government projects. However, the act is often criticized as being administered to keep wages on government contracts unrealistically higher than actual competitive wages paid on private construction projects. The act requires contractors and subcontractors to pay the prevailing wage rates in general for similar construction in the area of the federal project to various classes of laborers and mechanics who work on federal projects. Determination of the prevailing wage, which is made by the Secretary of Labor, must be included in the advertised specifications by the contracting agency. Employees protected by the act must be paid at least once a week. Because failure to comply with the Davis-Bacon requirements can result in severe penalties, such as back-pay liability, termination of the contract, and debarment from other

[7]40 U.S.C. §276(a) *et seq.*

federal contracts, contractors and subcontractors must learn how to comply with the Davis-Bacon provisions and become familiar with the steps that they may take to alleviate the harshness of the requirements.

Work Covered by the Davis-Bacon Act

The Davis-Bacon provisions must be included in the specifications of a contract in excess of $2,000 for the construction, repair, or alteration of public works and public buildings of the United States. The regulations define the terms "building" and "work" to include without limitation buildings, structures, and improvements of all types, such as bridges, dams, plants, highways, streets, subways, tunnels, sewers, mains, power lines, pumping stations, railways, airports, terminals, docks, piers, wharves, lighthouses, breakwaters, jetties, levees, canals, dredging, rehabilitation and reactivation of plants, scaffolding, drilling, blasting, excavating, clearing, and landscaping.[8] A manufactured object may become a public work once it had been installed at a location to serve a public use, so that substantial repair or alteration of the object with the use of federal funds may be subject to the Davis-Bacon requirements.[9]

A federal contract in excess of $2,000 for the painting or decorating of a public building or work is considered within Davis-Bacon coverage whether it is performed as part of the original construction or as regular maintenance. However, contracts for routine maintenance, including touch-up painting, of public works may be exempt from Davis-Bacon requirements.

Contracts for the supply and installation of prefabricated materials often contain a warranty that the equipment is in good condition and will function as promised. Minor repair work on the previously installed equipment is incidental to performance of the original warranty and is not governed by the Davis-Bacon Act. Substantial repair work which is done at the site where the equipment was installed is, however, subject to the Davis-Bacon requirements, and workers must be paid at the prevailing wage rate for the classifications of work which they perform.

Illustrative Case

Alcoa Construction Systems, Inc., requested review of a Davis-Bacon compliance decision concerning the repair and replacement of kitchen and bath modules on site at a Housing and Urban Development project. Alcoa argued that the repairing and replacing of the modules were not covered by Davis-Bacon requirements because the work was incidental to supply contracts and part of the warranty that was pursuant to those contracts. The Wage Appeals Board (WAB) upheld the decision against Alcoa on the ground that the adjustment, alignment, and plumbing work on the modules was substantial construction and repair work. It held that substantial construction and repair work on prefabricated materials

---

[8]29 CFR §5.2(f).

[9]Memorandum No. 95, Workplace Standards Adm'r (Apr. 30, 1971).

which were installed either in parts or as a whole and which subsequently become damaged or defective is on-site construction work subject to the Davis-Bacon requirements.[10]

Many contracts for the supply and installation of materials and equipment also require some work of the construction type. The Davis-Bacon Act does not apply unless a substantial amount of construction activity accompanies the installation of the equipment. The Comptroller General held that Davis-Bacon requirements did not apply to an installation contract for which 13 percent of the work was construction-related.[11] On the other hand, the Solicitor of Labor has ruled that Davis-Bacon applies to an installation contract when construction work is the major cost of the installation job or when the installation work requires the performance of complex construction tasks.[12] Often the construction portion of the work under a supply and installation contract will be subcontracted. If such subcontracted work is in excess of $2,000 and is of more than incidental nature, Davis-Bacon requirements will apply.[13]

The Davis-Bacon requirements apply only to contractors and subcontractors who employ laborers and mechanics "on the site of the work." Employees of a contractor or subcontractor generally need not be paid Davis-Bacon rates for work that they perform off the site, even if the product of their work will become part of the project, because the act's requirements only apply to on-site work. Thus, employees who mix concrete for use on the project at an off-site commercial plant need not be paid Davis-Bacon wages.

The site of the work includes the physical place where the contract construction will remain when the work has been completed and areas adjacent to it. For example, in the construction of a small office building the worksite will probably include the building and its grounds and other land or structures across the street or down the block which contractor and subcontractors use to perform the contract.

Contractors on Davis-Bacon construction projects frequently utilize the services of facilities that are located farther than across the street from the construction site and may even be miles away. For example, borrow pits, tool yards, mobile factories, and fabrication plants may be used to provide necessary materials for a Davis-Bacon project many miles away. The Solictor of Labor and the Comptroller General have issued conflicting rulings concerning coverage of these off-site facilities.

The Solicitor of Labor has held that off-site facilities established and operated especially to service a Davis-Bacon project several miles away are considered on-site, so that laborers and mechanics at these facilities must be paid Davis-Bacon wages.[14] The Comptroller General has taken a much

---

[10]WAB 75-6 (Sept. 11, 1975).

[11]Op. Comp. Gen., B-150318 (June 8, 1963).

[12]Op. Solic. Lab. (Nov. 6 and 30, 1961).

[13]*Sec, e.g.,* Op. Solic. Lab. (Mar. 25, 1964).

[14]*Sec, e.g.,* WAB 75-1, 75-2 (Aug. 14, 1975), involving W.D. Mayo Lock and Dam, Arkansas River, Oklahoma.

more limited view of the scope of the worksite. For example, he has held that quarries ranging from ¼ mile to 6 miles from a construction project which were established solely to service the federal project were not considered on-site. Thus, quarry employees were not entitled to Davis-Bacon coverage. The Comptroller's definition of on-site work on these projects is particularly significant when the work is contracted directly by a federal agency, because the Comptroller has the power to decide whether expenditures are unauthorized and whether federal funds should be disbursed to the contractor. In contrast, on federal-aid construction contracts the Comptroller has no direct authority to withhold funds, although state agencies could adopt his rulings. The Comptroller's opinions are actually reports to Congress concerning waste of federal funds, so eventually Congress may adopt the Comptroller's view and amend the Davis-Bacon Act to give a more restrictive meaning to on-site work.

Illustrative Case

Employees of Sweet Home Stone Company Company were engaged in quarrying, loading, and transporting stone from various quarry sites to certain Davis-Bacon jobsites. The distance from the quarries to the Davis-Bacon jobsites ranged from ¼ mile to 6 miles. Sweet Home had made no sales to the general public but only to Davis-Bacon contractors. There was no indication that Sweet Home intended to continue quarry operations after its commitments to the contractors were fulfilled. The Wage Appeals Board agreed with the contracting officer that because the quarries were operated exclusively for use in connection with government contracts and were located in reasonable proximity to the construction sites, the quarry operations were considered on-site and quarry employees were covered by Davis-Bacon. The Comptroller General held to the contrary on the ground that the act was not intended to provide coverage for off-site work whether by contractors, subcontractors, or materialmen even though performed in the immediate vicinity. The Comptroller held that he had authority to decide whether to withhold payments of federal funds to contractors, and because the quarry employees were exempt from Davis-Bacon coverage, the Comptroller directed that steps be taken to effect the release of money withheld from the contractor.[15]

Both the Solicitor of Labor and the Comptroller General agree that employees of a commercial supplier (bona fide materialmen) are not laborers and mechanics entitled to Davis-Bacon protection, because the materialmen's work is not an integral part of the construction activity. There is often a question of whether a prefabrication firm or a quarry operator who provides materials and equipment for a Davis-Bacon project is a covered subcontractor or an exempt materialman. To be exempt as a bona fide materialman, the firm must make sales to the general public, and the plant or operators must not be set up exclusively to service the Davis-Bacon project. A company which has a contract with a Davis-Bacon contractor to produce certain prefabricated materials but manufactures more than enough to fill the purchase order is more likely to be an exempt materialman.[16] If a firm sets up a plant or quarry pit and intends or continues to

[15]Comp. Gen. B-185020 (Dec. 27, 1976).

[16]WAB 73-7 (Sept. 14, 1973), involving Navajo Indian Reservation Irrigation Project, New Mexico.

operate it after it has supplied the contractor for a Davis-Bacon project, the firm probably is an exempt materialman. Likewise, production of materials for use on a Davis-Bacon contract that can also be used to fill orders to the general public is probably part of a larger commercial operation not subject to the Davis-Bacon requirements.[17]

A company that uses an existing quarry to fill a contractor's purchase order for sand fill or concrete on a Davis-Bacon project is probably an exempt materialman unless it opens a new pit solely to service the project. In that case the company is more likely to be regarded as a Davis-Bacon subcontractor.[18] Often a quarry operator has contracts with several contractors to fill orders on a series of contracts associated with a single Davis-Bacon project, such as an interstate highway project. If the quarry is established and operated for the several Davis-Bacon contractors, the operator is probably a Davis-Bacon subcontractor. It is unclear whether a company is considered a covered subcontractor or an exempt materialman when it opens an operation to serve a wide range of Davis-Bacon contracts of various types and in different areas.

While the employees of a bona fide materialman generally are not covered by the Davis-Bacon Act, employees who spend a substantial amount of their working time on the site of a Davis-Bacon project performing construction or repair work are covered. For example, an employee of a supplier who sells to the general public and who spends a substantial amount of time performing complex construction tasks while installing the equipment at the jobsite probably is covered by the Davis-Bacon Act. An equipment rental dealer who sells to the general public is generally considered an exempt materialman. If the dealer rents equipment to a contractor for use on a Davis-Bacon project site, however, employees of the dealer who spend more than 20 percent of their working time on the site making repairs to the equipment are laborers or mechanics who must be paid Davis-Bacon wages.[19]

A typical compliance problem for a contractor concerns failure to pay Davis-Bacon minimum wage rates for truck drivers who haul materials to the construction site. Employees of a Davis-Bacon contractor or subcontractor who transport materials or supplies to or from the construction project from any source are considered laborers and mechanics protected by the act.

Whether employees of an independent trucking firm must be paid Davis-Bacon wages will depend upon the source from which they haul the materials and supplies. The drivers are covered if they haul materials between locations that are considered part of the construction site, as in delivery of materials to the project from an adjacent site established solely

[17]WAB 65-2 (Apr. 12, 1965), involving Stanford Linear Accelerator Center, Palo Alto, Cal.

[18]See, e.g., WAB 69-2 (Aug. 11, 1969), involving interstate highway project, Lafayette Parish, La.

[19]See WAB 64-3 (July 21, 1965), Griffith Co., 17 W.H. Cav. 49 (1965).

to service the project.[20] But drivers are exempt from Davis-Bacon coverage if they transport material to the jobsite from an off-site supplier who sells to the general public.[21]

Drivers who transport supplies from an off-site operation which is established especially for the project and which does not sell to the general public will be within Davis-Bacon coverage only if the off-site location is considered to be "on the site of construction." The department of Labor and the Comptroller General have conflicting views concerning Davis-Bacon coverage of these off-site operations, so the respective decisions on this issue will determine the drivers' coverage in that situation.

There is sometimes a question of whether a trucking firm is truly independent of the contractor so that its drivers are exempt from Davis-Bacon requirements if they make deliveries from a noncovered off-site source. If the trucking company and the contractor have a common ownership and an integrated operation with an interchange of employees, the truck drivers will be considered employees of the contractor and be covered under the Davis-Bacon Act regardless of the place from which the supplies are transported. A contractor who effectively sets up a double-breasted operation with separate labor relations and no interchange of employees might be able to exempt from coverage drivers employed by the wholly owned trucking company who haul from an off-site commercial source.

Illustrative Case

Cox Construction Company performed three Utah highway construction projects that were federally funded and subject to the Davis-Bacon requirements. Cox sought review of an enforcement action by the Utah State Highway Department, the Federal Highway Administrator, and the U.S. Department of Labor to compel payment of Davis-Bacon rates for twenty-seven truck drivers. Cox contended that the drivers were employed by an independent hauling firm, Cox Enterprises, Inc. and were not covered because they made deliveries from a commercial source. The Wage Appeals Board affirmed the enforcement against Cox. The Board held that the two companies were actually one for Davis-Bacon purposes because they were owned and controlled by the same management and that even though separate payroll records were kept, the operations were integrated and employees were interchanged as needed. The Board held that the Davis-Bacon Act applied to the hauling of materials to the project by employees of a covered contractor, and that because the twenty-seven truck drivers delivered supplies to the covered projects and were employed by a wholly owned and controlled subsidiary of a covered contractor, they were subject to the Davis-Bacon requirements.[22]

Truck drivers employed by an independent firm to make deliveries from a commercial source might still be covered as laborers or mechanics if they spend more than 20 percent of their working time performing construction or repair work on the project site. Drivers employed by independent firms who drive through the construction site while concrete is

[20] O.G. Sansone Co. v. Department of Transportation, 22 W.H. Cas. 1008 (Cal. 1976).

[21] H.B. Zachry Co. v. United States, 344 F.2d 352 (Ct. Cl. 1965).

[22] WAB 72-10 (Jan. 29, 1973).

automatically unloaded from the truck are exempt from Davis-Bacon requirements because their work is considered part of the delivery process and not on-site construction work.[23]

Bona fide owner-operators of trucks enjoy a unique status because they are not required to be paid Davis-Bacon wages. Although owner-operators are laborers or mechanics, there are practical difficulties in enforcing a required wage rate for them because payment for their services covers both truck rental and wages. At present, the payroll records required for other laborers and mechanics need not be kept for owner-operators of trucks who are truly independent contractors. To satisfy Davis-Bacon record-keeping requirements, the notation "truck owner-operator-independent contractor" is all that is needed on the payroll.

A contractor violates the Davis-Bacon Act by failing to pay Davis-Bacon wages to an owner-operator who is not a bona fide independent contractor. The mere fact that an owner-operator is listed on the payroll as an independent contractor may not be determinative. A proposed addition to the Davis-Bacon regulations lists the following factors to determine whether an owner-operator is an independent contractor:

1. Amount of investment by the owner-operator in facilities and equipment and whether the contractor shares a financial interest with the owner-operator in the truck or incurs some or all of the truck's operating expenses

2. Whether the services are an integral part of the contractor's business

3. Nature and degree of control exercised by the contractor over the owner-operator

4. Whether the owner-operator presents the trucking business to the general public as being for the owner-operator's account

5. Whether there are clear opportunities for profit and loss to the owner-operator

Determining Prevailing Wage Rates

The responsibility for determining whether the Davis-Bacon requirements should apply to a particular contract rests primarily with the contracting agency. The Davis-Bacon provisions are binding on contractor and subcontractors only if they are included in the contract. The agency will request a prevailing-wage determination from the Secretary of Labor, who is required to find the wage rates and fringe benefits prevailing in the area for the various classes of laborers and mechanics on similar construction. This determination must be included by the agency in the advertisement for bids and in the contract, whereupon the requirement to pay prevailing wages and to keep accurate payroll records becomes binding upon the contractor. In addition, the contractor is required to include these Davis-Bacon provisions in all subcontracts entered into for work on the project and will be liable for violations committed by the project subcontractors.

The Department of Labor makes known its findings concerning the

[23]Op. Solic. Lab. DB-14 (Oct.11, 1961).

prevailing wage rates in either a general area determination or a project determination. The list contains a schedule of the various types of construction in the area or for the specific project (buildings, residential, heavy, highway, and so on) as well as the classifications of laborers and mechanics with their prevailing wage rates. The contracting agency will decide what type of construction and job classifications will be required for the project and include the wage schedules for these categories in the advertisement for bids.

A general area determination is normally made for an area which has settled wage patterns and in which considerable construction activity of a particular type is anticipated. Area determinations are published weekly in the *Federal Register;* each applies to all projects in the area. A project determination applies to a specific project and is effective for 120 days from it issuance. This determination is issued by the Employment Standards Administration (ESA). Project and area determinations are normally made several weeks prior to advertisements for bids. Area contractors should examine prevailing-wage determinations as soon as they are made, because most erroneous wage determinations cannot be corrected once bidding on the contract has begun.

A project determination that expires after bids have been advertised can cause problems. At one time it was the rule that once a wage determination expired, cancellation and readvertisement of bids were required. Therefore, the contracting agency was permitted to include a clause in the invitation for bids which permitted a new determination to be made and included if an old one expired before the contract was awarded. However, this procedure was unfair to the contractor, who sometimes was bound by a higher wage determination than had been considered in preparing the bid. At present the Department of Labor is permitted in its discretion, to grant a request from the contracting agency to extend an expired wage determination which was included in the advertisement for bids if the extension is "in the public interest to prevent injustice, undue hardship, or serious impairment of the conduct of Government business."

The major source of information from which the Secretary of Labor makes a prevailing-wage determination is the Department of Labor construction payroll records. The Division of Construction Wage Determination of the ESA maintains files of data which break down wages and fringe benefits according to the various classifications of laborers and mechanics, the type of construction, and the geographic area. Information regarding prevailing wages is also received by the Davis-Bacon staff word of mouth, letters from unions and contractors, copies of recently negotiated union agreements, and the staff's own field investigations.

Open-shop contractors have a vital interest in promptly submitting their payroll records to members of the Davis-Bacon staff, who have a tendency to assume that negotiated union rates which have been used in past wage determinations without protest continue to prevail in the area. If these union rates are increased in a new collective bargaining agreement, the staff might even include those rates in a new wage determination without determining that these rates have actually been paid. Open-shop contractors should not let the building trades unions dictate the wage rates that they must pay on government projects. Only if enough open-shop contractors submit their payrolls to show that the union rates no longer prevail will these rates likely be changed.

Contractors and the building trades unions will be informed of a pending wage determination by a survey notification letter, which generally specifies the area, the type of construction to be surveyed, and the time period during which payroll data may be submitted. The notification is often accompanied by Form WD-10, "Contractor's Report of Construction Wage Rates." Contractors should promptly submit Form WD-10 or a similar record to the Davis-Bacon staff upon the completion of each project. It is more difficult to convince the staff that an error in the wage determination has been made than it is to supply information for an original accurate determination.

In making a prevailing-wage determination, the Davis-Bacon staff utilizes current payroll data for similar construction from the county in which the proposed project is to be located. If there is no similar construction in that county, the staff might consider payroll data from an adjacent county even if that county is in a different state.[24] Preferred payroll data are based on similar construction that either has been completed within the previous 12 months or is in the construction process. If there is no recent similar construction in the county or an adjacent county, the staff might use older payrolls for similar construction.

For each category of construction which is similar, the Davis-Bacon investigators will break down their payroll information according to the various classifications of laborers and mechanics being utilized in the area of the proposed project. For each project and each worker classification reviewed, the staff will ordinarily examine data from the peak payroll period, which is the one week in the life of each project in which the greatest number of employees in each classification were employed. The peak payroll period will not be used, however, if higher rates are paid after the peak period has passed and enough workers are still employed to give an accurate picture of prevailing wages.[25]

The Department of Labor has defined the prevailing wage as that single rate which is paid to a majority of workers in the classification of work in the area on similar construction. If no single rate is paid to more than 50 percent of the employees, the Department will consider the prevailing wage to be that single rate which is paid to at least 30 percent of the employees on similar construction in that area. If less than 30 percent of the employees receive the same wage, then the prevailing wage is calculated by a weighted-average method. The following examples illustrate a prevailing-wage determination under each of these formulas.

[24]WAB 72-6 (June 14, 1972).

[25]WAB 65-1 (Mar. 1, 1965), involving Carters Dam, Murray County, Georgia.

Illustrative Example

Majority rule

Number of carpenters	Hourly rate
20	$7.00
12	8.50
50	7.60
16	5.90
98	

Since a majority (more than 50 percent) of the carpenters are paid $7.60 per hour, it is the prevailing wage rate.

30 percent rule

Number of carpenters	Hourly rate
20	$7.00
12	8.00
8	6.50
18	6.75
58	

Since a majority of the carpenters are not paid the same hourly rate, but more than 30 percent are paid $7.00 per hour, it is the prevailing wage rate.

Weighted-average rule

Number of carpenters	Hourly rate
6	$7.00
6	6.50
4	7.50
4	8.00

Neither a majority nor 30 percent of the carpenters are paid the same rate. Therefore, the prevailing wage rate is a weighted average.

Number of carpenters	
6 at $7.00/per hour =	$ 42.00
6 at $6.50/per hour =	39.00
4 at $7.50/per hour =	30.00
4 at $8.00/per hour =	32.00
20	$143.00

The prevailing wage rate is 143/20 = $7.15 per hour.

The majority and 30 percent rules have been widely criticized by the Comptroller General and open-shop contractors because they fail to take into account the wage rates of 50 percent and 70 percent respectively of the employees and often lead to inflated wage rates. Congress has had numerous opportunities to require the Department of Labor to adopt new rules but has failed to do so. Contractors should therefore learn how to use the rules of the game to their best advantage.

The rates that open-shop contractors pay now may help to establish future minimum rates on federal projects. Contractors who commence work on a government job may also be protesting a Davis-Bacon rate which is the same as the union rate. If the contractors pay the same rate, their payroll will be counted along with those of union contractors, resulting in perpetuation of the union rate on future projects. The contractors may avoid adding their required pay rate to the union group by paying a few cents more or less than the Davis-Bacon rate. In that event, the negotiated union rate would be less likely to become the prevailing wage rate on future Davis-Bacon projects in the area.

Contractors covered by negotiated union contracts will pay precisely the same wage rates in the area for similar work, while nonunion rates may differ by a few cents per hour. Under existing rules, if the rates differ by even a penny, the rate is not a single rate. Open-shop contractors who pay the same single rate will be able to have this rate used on future federal projects instead of higher union rates if the open-shop rate is paid to a majority or 30 percent of the employees in the area. They should arrive at paying the same rate by a voluntary, informal procedure and not by actual or implied agreements between nonunion contractors.

The Davis-Bacon staff is required to find the wage rates prevailing in the area on similar construction for the various classifications of laborers and mechanics. This means that the prevailing wage rate must be determined for each type of work. To make this determination the staff must decide which craft normally performs a particular type of work and which wage rate prevails for that craft. However, a decision that a particular craft performs a particular type of work does not necessarily mean that a contractor must award the job assignment to that craft. The contractor may assign the work to any desired group of employees and still comply with the Davis-Bacon requirements, provided the employees who perform that work are paid Davis-Bacon wages.

A list of different wage determinations in a contract will not answer a contractor's questions concerning the rate that must be paid for a particular type of work, because it is often unclear which job classification is included in a specific job task. Under the present "substantial area practice" rule, a contractor may pay a wage rate for a particular type of work and comply with the Davis-Bacon prevailing-wage provisions if the contractor can show that a substantial number of employees in the area on similar construction are paid at the same rate for that work. A contractor who desires to pay a lower wage rate for a specific job assignment must first make sure that there are other contractors in the area performing the same type of construction who are paying the same wages for that work assignment. If 25 to 30 percent of the employees involved in similar construction in the area are paid the same wages to perform a particular job task, this probably constitutes a substantial area practice. The contractor could therefore pay that amount to the employees and comply with the Davis-Bacon Act.

Illustrative Case

The work involved the installation of underground ducts to carry electrical wiring. The Electrical Workers brought a Davis-Bacon enforcement action to force the contractors to pay the electricians' rate rather than the lower pipelayers' rate. In some parts of the United States installation work was done by laborers, and in others by electricians or by both. The Comptroller General rejected the Department of labor's ruling that the electricians' rate had to be paid. The Comptroller held that there was a substantial but not preponderant practice of installing similar ducts in the area with the use of laborers and pipelayers. If a local-area practice concerning the classification for the job task is exclusive, it must be followed. However, if the area practice is prevailing, but not exclusive and different, area practices exist, the contractor may pay the employees in accordance with either practice.[26]

[26] *T.L. James Constr.Co.*, Comp. Gen. B-147602 (Jan. 23, 1963).

Union contracts normally contain a uniform wage rate for each journeyman's classification and do not attempt to adjust the rate schedule according to the skills and experience of individuals. On the other hand, open-shop contractors frequently pay their workers according to qualifications and experience, so that within each general job classification there may be a helper or other worker in a subclassification with a lower wage rate. The Davis-Bacon staff will not include a helper subclassification if its records show that building trades craft classifications have prevailed in the past. The Department of Labor has stated, however, that it will include a helper or other subclassifications in its wage determination if it receives information to show that such subclassifications prevail in the area. Therefore, open-shop contractors should promptly submit their payrolls to the regional Davis-Bacon staff, so that a helper or other subclassifications with a wage rate lower than the union journeyman rate can be included in a wage determination. The Department has stated that it will not include such a helper category if this classification in local usage is actually an informal trainee position, which is not included in a wage determination. Open-shop contractors should include a definition of a helper in their payroll data, showing that the classification is not the same as a laborer or an informal trainee.[27] If the Davis-Bacon staff receives enough information to show that the category of a helper or other subclassification is prevalent in the area, it will be included in a subsequent wage determination. In this manner, the open-shop contractor may be able to pay a lower wage rate on government construction than would otherwise have been possible.[28]

There has been much confusion among contracting agencies, contractors, and the building trades concerning the classification of particular types of construction. The Department of Labor has generally classified construction projects as building, heavy, highway, or residential. Below is a definition of each of these types of construction and the kinds of projects which are normally included within each:

1. *Building construction.* This type includes the construction of sheltered enclosures with walk-in access for the purpose of housing persons, machinery, equipment, or supplies. It includes all construction of such structures and the installation of utilities and equipment, both above and below grade level, as well as incidental grading, utilities, and paving. The installation of heavy machinery or equipment, or both, does not generally change the project's character as a building.

    Examples. Alteration and additions to buildings; apartment building (five stories and more); commercial buildings; industrial buildings; power plants; prefabricated buildings; remodeling, renovating, and repairing buildings; restaurants; shopping centers; stores; subway stations; warehouses; and water and sewage treatment plants (buildings only).

2. *Residential construction.* This type includes the construction, alteration, or repair of single-family houses or apartment buildings of no more than four stories in height, including all incidental items such as site work, parking areas, utilities, streets, and sidewalks.

    Examples. Town or row houses; apartment buildings (four stories or less); single-family houses; mobil-home developments; and multifamily houses.

[27] WAGE-HOUR OP. LETTER No. 1254 (W.H. 202), Mar. 1, 1973.

[28] *See* Comp. Gen. B-147847 (Feb. 7, 1967).

3. *Highway construction.* This type includes the construction, alteration, or repair of roads, streets, highways, runways, taxiways, alleys, trails, paths, parking areas, and similar projects which are not incidental to building or heavy construction.

    Examples. Alleys; base courses; bituminous treatments; concrete pavement; curbs, excavation, and embankments (for road construction); highway fencing; highway guardrails; highway signs; highway overpasses, underpasses, and medians; parking lots; parkways; roadbeds; roadways; runways; storm sewers incidental to road construction; and street paving and resurfacing of streets and highways.

4. *Heavy construction.* This type includes projects not properly classified in the first three categories. Projects within the heavy classification may sometimes be distinguished on the basis of their peculiar project characteristics, and separate schedules will be issued for each. For example, separate schedules may be issued for dredging projects, water and sewer line projects, dams, major bridges, and flood control projects.

    Examples. Antenna towers; bridges (major bridges contain elements of both heavy and highway construction); breakwaters; canals; channels; chemical complexes or facilities (other than buildings); dams; dikes; docks; drainage and dredging projects; flood control projects; irrigation projects; industrial incinerators (other than buildings); oil refineries (other than buildings); pipelines; railroad construction; reservoirs; sewage collection and disposal lines; sanitary, storm, and other kinds of sewers; storage tanks; outdoor swimming pools; subways (other than buildings); tunnels; viaducts (other than highway viaducts); water mains; waterway construction; water supply lines (not incidental to buildings); water and sewage treatment plants (other than buildings); and wells.

    Contracting agencies are directed to use these descriptions and illustrations in including the appropriate wage schedules for the various facets of work on Davis-Bacon projects. In the past contractors were often unsure as to which schedule to apply to various portions of construction work. At present, agencies will break the project into segments and define the appropriate wage schedule for each segment in the advertised bid and contract specifications. Certain projects may comprise substantial construction of one type along with incidental construction which falls in another category. For example, water or sewer line work which is part of an overall building project will generally not be classified separately as heavy construction. Construction work is usually considered to be incidental if it is less than 20 percent of the total project cost. On the other hand, on large building projects for which segments of the contract involve more than incidental construction, separate schedules should be issued for these segments. On these projects contractors need not pay the higher building rates for the entire project but may pay the lower highway rates for particular segments.

    The Davis-Bacon staff is required to determine what is "similar construction" according to area practice. In some areas there may be a close question whether a particular project or a portion of it should be one category or another. Contractors who want a project classified contrary to the Department of Labor's general guidelines must show that the construction techniques, materials, equipment, and types of skills called for on the project are more similar to another rate classification in that area. A comparison of the wages on this project with wages on projects in the favored classification may also be utilized. For example, under the general guidelines discussed above, construction of apartment buildings over five stories high is classified as building construction. Building projects usually pay high union rates, whereas residential construction may be governed by lower open-shop rates. Contractors desiring to pay the lower residential rates should demonstrate that the wages, construction methods, materials, equipment, and skills required of employees in that area are similar to those used in area residential construction and unlike those in area building construction. The wages, construction methods, and employee skills used by open-shop contractors will help dictate the wage schedules to which they will be bound in the future; so when contractors have a choice concerning those matters, they should keep these effects in mind.

Illustrative Cases

Mattapony Towers Apartments requested review of a wage determination for Prince George County, Maryland, that included high-rise residential construction in the commercial building category. The Wage Appeals Board rejected Mattapony's request that high-rise residential construction be included in the lower-rate residential construction category, on the ground that the construction of a six-story high-rise apartment building retained much more of the characteristics of a high-rise commercial building than of a garden-type residential building. In WAB 70-7 (January 14, 1971), the Board affirmed the WAB 64-2 ruling that high-rise residential construction be included in the commercial building category. But the Board implied that it would have made a separate determination for high-rise residential construction had the contractors submitted facts to show that the construction industry in the area had "accepted the exclusion of high-rise residential construction from the general building construction category for wage rate purposes."[29]

Subsequently in a case involving the Edgewood Terrace high-rise apartment project in Washington, D.C., the Board stated that high-rise residential construction is closer to commercial building construction than to any other category. The Board stated, however, that a separate determination would have been made if enough facts had been submitted to show that "the industry has, in recognition of a local situation, carved such projects out of general building construction for wage rate purposes."[30]

All contractors should have an interest in ascertaining whether or not accurate wage determinations are being made, because inaccurate determinations may inflate local wage rates and provide a basis for higher rates on future projects for which the contractors may wish to bid. Area and project determinations should be examined as soon as they are issued, because many erroneous determinations cannot be corrected once bidding on a contract has commenced. For example, a project determination for building construction may be applied to a facet of the work which contractors believe should be governed by the lower-rate residential schedule. Or the determination may fail to include a work classification which prevails in the area and pays the lower nonunion rate. These errors usually cannot be corrected once the project work has commenced unless the contract is canceled and bids are readvertised, which is unlikely. Contractors should therefore examine all wage determinations as soon as they are issued to be

[29] WAB 64-2 (June 29, 1965).
[30] WAB 73-2 (April 4, 1973).

certain that they are correct. They should also constantly update this wage information. Otherwise, contractors may find themselves bound to pay higher wage rates, avoidable had they taken adequate precautions.

Any wage determination protest should be directed to the regional administrator of the ESA. Copies of each protest should be sent to the director of the Construction Wage Determinations Division, Employment Standards Administration, U.S. Department of Labor, 200 Constitution Avenue, N.W., Washington, D.C. 20010. The protest should be in writing, state the reasons why the determination is wrong, and include survey data to support contentions regarding what the contractor alleges to be the correct wage rate. If the Davis-Bacon regional staff refuses to make the recommended changes, an in-depth field investigation should be requested. A meeting with the national staff during which the contractor's supporting data are presented may help to resolve the problem or at least prompt the national staff to order a field investigation by the regional staff. If the initial protest to the ESA is unsuccessful, an appeal may be made to the Wage Appeals Board (WAB) to review the correctness of a wage determination as well as other controversies. For example, the WAB decides appeals concerning debarments of contractors from federal construction jobs, controversies involving prevailing job classifications and whether employees performing particular work are paid under the correct classification, and the assessment of liquidated damages against a contractor for alleged violations of overtime requirements under the Contract Work Hours and Safety Act.

A review by the WAB may be obtained by filing a written petition for review, which is signed by the contractor or the contractor's representative. The petition must clearly identify the adverse decision from which the contractor is appealing, the project location, and the agency involved, and it should state that an initial review with ESA was requested and describe the action that was taken on that request. A concise statement of the grounds for review should also be included accompanied by supporting data (payroll records and the like) and views or arguments which support the contractor's contentions. A petition for review should be directed to the Wage Appeals Board, U.S. Department of Labor, 200 Constitution Avenue, N.W., Washington, D.C. 20010.

The WAB's normal procedure is to conduct a hearing based solely on the written record which it has before it, so the contractor should be sure to present all available data supporting the contractor's position to the Davis-Bacon administrators and to the agency. In some cases the WAB will permit witnesses to testify and new evidence to be introduced, or it may remand the case to the ESA for it to gather the necessary information. It had been held that the WAB may lawfully deny the contractor the opportunity to introduce evidence and to cross-examine witnesses if the contractor had declined such an opportunity before the contracting agency.[31]

[31] *Framulau Corp. v. Dembling,* 360 F. Supp. 806 (E.D. Pa. 1973).

Time is of the essence for a contractor who seeks to have a modified wage determination or classification decision apply to a proposed Davis-Bacon contract. The contracting agency must receive timely notice of a modification prior to bid opening before that agency will be required to use it in its invitation for bids. Modifications to project wage determinations will not apply to contracts when the agency receives notice of the new determination less than 10 days before the bid-opening date. A new area determination must be published in the *Federal Register* more than 10 days before bid opening for the agency to be required to include it in the invitation for bids. A modified area determination that is published within the 10 day period should be applicable if the agency has a reasonable opportunity to notify bidders of the change. The agency is required to make a good-faith effort to notify bidders of the modification.

If the contractor is able to convince the contracting agency to postpone the bid-opening date, any modifications can be included in the contract. The contractor must appeal directly to the agency to extend the bid-opening date, however, because the WAB has no authority over the agency in that regard. A contractor who discovers an error in a wage determination should promptly check with the agency to ascertain how much time is available to correct the error before bid opening. An argument that the WAB has decided to review the wage determination and that the probable modification will result in lower wages and a lower contract price might be persuasive in convincing the contracting agency to postpone the bid-opening date.

On the other hand, a union may argue to the contracting agency that bidding should be postponed so that a higher negotiated rate which is soon to take effect may apply to the contract. The Comptroller General has ruled that a contracting agency properly refused an extension of a bid opening at the union's request, the effect of which would have permitted a union agreement with higher wage rates to take effect 5 days after the scheduled bid opening.[32]

After bid opening and either before or after the contract is awarded, changes in the wages which contractors must pay are harder to obtain. If an inadvertent clerical error is made in the wage determination, the Secretary of Labor will issue a "letter of inadvertence" to notify the contracting agency that the error has been made and providing it with the correct rate. The Comptroller General has defined a clerical error as "the failure to correctly reflect the wage information in Davis-Bacon files at the time the wage determination was issued." A mistake in the transcription or computation of the prevailing wage rate when all the data were on file is a clerical error for which a letter of inadvertence will be issued. It is discretionary with the contracting agency whether or not it chooses to adopt a formal wage change in the contract. Therefore, it is better for contractors to dis-

[32]47 Comp. Gen. 754 (1968).

cover errors in a wage determination and get them corrected before bidding on the contract has begun.

A letter of inadvertence will not be issued to get a nonclerical error in a wage determination corrected. A redetermination that a building construction schedule should apply to a portion of the work instead of a heavy-highway schedule, for example, represents a judgmental as opposed to a clerical change, so a letter of inadvertence will not be issued.[33] The proper procedure to correct a judgmental order is to have the contract canceled and bids readvertised with the correct wage determination, but this is rarely done.

Sometimes contractors discover after work has begun that a project determination fails to include a particular job classification or that such work is included in the wrong classification. For example, the contract may require certain work to be done at the mechanics' rate but the contractor will feel that there is other work within that category for which it is the prevailing area practice to pay the lower laborers' rate. In that event, the contractor should try to persuade the contracting agency to amend the contract to include the lower rate for that work. If the agency does not agree, the contractor should seek a reclassification from the Davis-Bacon staff. In either case, the contractor may not pay the lower wage rate until the staff agrees to the reclassification. It is preferable, however, for contractors to make certain that accurate wage determinations have been included in the project documents before bidding begins, because it is often hard to convince the Davis-Bacon administrators that they have made an error which requires a reclassification.

It is essential that contractors make certain that the wage rates contained in the schedule in the advertisement for bids are actually prevailing. In some instances contractors may bid on a job in reliance upon a rate schedule which is lower than the wages which actually prevail in the area. As a result, the contractors will discover that they must pay higher wages than they anticipated when they bid on the job in order to attract a sufficient number of workers to complete the project. The U.S. Supreme Court has held that contractors need not be reimbursed for their higher labor costs in this type of situation because the purpose of the minimum rate schedule is to benefit employees. The schedule does not warrant to contractors that the published rate will be the prevailing rate.[34]

Sometimes, however, the contracting agency will know certain facts of which the contractor is unaware and which will cause the area wages to be higher than the published rates. In that event, the contractor might be reimbursed in a Court of Claims suit for excess labor costs on the ground that the agency failed to disclose certain facts of which only it had knowledge and which would likely increase the area wage rates. For example the

[33] Comp. Gen. B-150293 (Feb. 13, 1963).

[34] *United States v. Binghamton Constr. Co.*, 347 U.S. 171 (1954).

agency may have had plans for increased construction in the area which would cause a labor shortage and require the contractor to pay higher wages to attract a sufficient labor force. For a contractor to be reimbursed for premium wages in such a situation, the contracting agency must have known of the planned construction and its probable consequences when the contract was awarded, the contractor must not have known or had reason to know those facts, and the agency must have known or should have known that the contractor was unaware of those facts and yet failed to disclose the relevant information.[35]

Changes in the wage rate because of a clerical error will not necessarily result in a change in the contract price. Whether the contract price will be raised or lowered will depend upon principles of equitable adjustment. A contractor may be entitled to a price increase if an upward change in the wage rate increased the cost of performance. However, the burden of proof is upon the contractor to show increased costs from the higher wage rate before reimbursement will be allowed. A contractor who had been paying the higher rate all along would not be entitled to a price increase because the change order would not increase the contractor's labor costs.[36] If the change will require the contractor actually to pay a higher rate than the contractor had been paying, an upward adjustment of the contract price will normally be allowed.[37]

If issuance of a change because of a clerical error results in a downward adjustment to a wage rate it has been held that a price increase to reimburse the contractor for the amount of wages that the contractor should not have had to pay prior to the correction is justified. The rationale for this decision is that the Secretary of Labor's determination of the prevailing wage rate is not subject to judicial review, so the Court of Claims will not reimburse the contractor for excess costs. However, it has been argued that the contractor is not attacking the Secretary's determination but instead is attempting to enforce it because the letter of inadvertence admits that a mistake in the determination was made, so that the contractor should be permitted an equitable adjustment for increased costs as a result of the government's admitted mistake.[38] This argument appears to be sound and should be raised again by a contractor in a similar situation, even though it has not yet been accepted.

Sometimes an agency will seek a price adjustment downward on the ground that a change order has lowered the contractor's labor costs. It has been held that if the contractor had knowledge of the lower prevailing wages and submitted the bid in reliance on the lower rate, the agency is not entitled to a downward adjustment of the contract price.[39]

[35] See, e.g., J.A. Jones Constr. Co. v. United States, 390 F.2d 886 (Ct. Cl. 1968).

[36] 43 Comp. Gen. 623 (1964).

[37] Sunswick Corp. of Del. v. United States, 75 F. Supp. (Ct. Cl. 1948); 37 Comp. Gen. 326 (1957).

[38] 11 Gov't Contractor ¶ 306.

[39] Burnett Constr. Co. v. United States, 413 F.2d 563 (Ct. Cl. 1969).

Payment of Wages and Fringe Benefits

The 1964 amendments to the Davis-Bacon Act[40] require, among other things, that the prevailing wage determined for federal and federally assisted construction include (1) the basic hourly rate of pay and (2) the amount contributed by the contractor or subcontractor for certain fringe benefits (or the cost to them of such benefits). The wage determination should contain the prevailing rate of contribution or cost of the fringe benefits. If no type of fringe benefits is prevailing, the wage determination will contain only the base hourly rate of pay. Among fringe benefits which are common to the construction industry and which might be included in a wage determination are:

- Medical or hospital care

- Pensions on retirement or death

- Insurance

- Unemployment benefits

- Vacation and holiday pay

- Costs of apprenticeship training

- Other bona fide fringe benefits (new fringe benefits may be recognized by the Secretary as they become prevailing)[41]

For a contractor to meet an obligation to pay a prevailing fringe benefit the payment must be "bona fide." This means that the contribution must be made to a trustee or a third party in such a manner that in no event will the contractor be able to recapture or divert any of the funds for personal benefit or profit. Payment of a fringe benefit into a fund, plan, or insurance program that is common in the constrution industry is usually bona fide. The contractor may take credit for contributions to such a conventional fund without prior approval of the Secretary of Labor. Most fringe-benefit programs established by a valid agreement with a union do not require prior approval.

A contractor may also take credit for contributions to an unconventional, unfunded plan. Such plans are normally set up by a contractor or an employer association, and the union does not participate. A contractor must make a written request to the Secretary of Labor for approval of an unfunded plan before credit may be taken for contractor payments to the plan. For an unfunded plan to be approved it must:

1. Be reasonably anticipated to provide benefits described in the act
2. Represent a legally enforceable commitment
3. Be carried out under a financially responsible plan or program
4. Be communicated in writing to the affected employees

[40]Pub. L. No. 88-349.

[41]29 CFR §5.23.

A contractor who does not wish to participate in a union fringe-benefit plan may also take credit for the obligation to pay the fringe benefit by making a direct cash payment to the employees in lieu of the fringe benefit. The contractor and the agency must be able to agree on an hourly cash equivalent to the fringe-benefit payment; normally it is permissable to use a percentage of the basic hourly rate. If the parties cannot agree on a conversion formula, the dispute must be submitted to the Secretary of Labor.[42]

The contractor is not permitted to take credit for fringe benefits that the contractor is obligated to provide under federal, state, or local law. Payment for workmen's compensation insurance which is required under either a compulsory or an elective statute is not creditable. Administrative expenses that are incurred pursuant to either a funded or an unfunded plan are not considered part of the contractor's contribution for fringe benefits. Payments made to travel, subsistence, or industry advancement funds are normally not considered payments for fringe benefits.[43]

A contractor performing work subject to a Davis-Bacon Act wage determination may discharge minimum wage obligations for the payment of both straight-time wages and fringe benefits by paying in cash, by making payments or incurring costs for bona fide fringe benefits of the types listed in the applicable wage determination or otherwise found to be prevailing by the Secretary of Labor, or by a combination thereof. Examples are:

1. Paying not less than the basic hourly rate to the laborers or mechanics and making the contributions for fringe benefits in the wage determinations as specified therein

2. Paying not less than the basic hourly rate to the laborers or mechanics and making contributions for bona fide fringe benefits in a total amount not less than the total of the fringe benefits required by the wage determination

3. Paying in cash directly to laborers or mechanics for the basic hourly rate and making an additional cash payment in lieu of the required benefits

4. Using a combination of these methods[44]

A contractor who has employees working on a federal project subject to the Davis-Bacon and related acts is entitled to segregate job classifications and wages, provided the following procedure is followed:

1. An accurate record must be kept of the *actual* hours that an employee works in each job classification

2. The actual hours worked in each job classification each workday on the certified payroll must be recorded

A contractor who has an employee who performs work in several job classifications, but for whom accurate records are not kept, must pay the employee as though that employee worked in the highest job classification

[42]OP. SOLIC. LAB. DB-43 (Apr. 28, 1965).

[43]29 CFR §5.29(f).

[44]29 CFR Subtit. A, Pt. 5, §5.31.

for all hours worked. The contractor cannot estimate the hours worked in a particular job classification; records must reflect the actual hours.

Apprentices and Trainees

There is no longer a Davis-Bacon wage determination for apprentices and trainees, although contractors may still pay them lower wages if certain conditions are met. A contractor must furnish written evidence to the contracting agency of employees' enrollment in an apprenticeship program registered with either the BAT or a state apprenticeship agency recognized by the BAT, as well as the appropriate ratios and wage rates for the area of construction, prior to using any apprentices on the contract work. The allowable ratio of apprentices to journeymen in any craft classification cannot be greater than the ratio permitted to the contractor as to the contractor's entire workforce under the registered program.

If a contractor employs an apprentice who is enrolled in a registered program outside the project area, the minimum wage rate applicable to that apprentice is based on the rate in the registered program for the area where the apprentice is working.

Illustrative Case

Jack Picoult was the contractor on a Davis-Bacon project for a post office in New Jersey. The contractor sought review of a Davis-Bacon compliance action which cited him for failing to pay his apprentices the rate set for apprentices registered in New York. The contractor argued that he had complied with the act by paying the rates set in the apprenticeship program registered in New Jersey, where the apprentices were working. The Wage Appeals Board ruled that the apprentices were required to be paid at the rates set in the New Jersey program. Apprentices are laborers and mechanics under the act and must be paid the rates prevailing for apprentices in the area of the construction project.[45]

Approval is normally granted by the BAT or a state apprenticeship council to programs administered under agreement with building trades. Registration of open-shop programs is often more difficult. If there already is a union program in the area, the state council might refuse to approve another program, or the BAT or the state agency might require the open-shop program to meet the standards of the union program. Some of these requirements, such as a minimum number of hours of classroom training, are difficult for individual open-shop firms to match; so they may have problems in getting their programs approved. Open-shop contractors may be better able to obtain approval of their programs by pooling their resources and making the necessary investment. (See Chapter 12, section "Training" for a discussion of open-shop apprentice programs.)

Contractors who seek to pay lower apprentice and trainee rates to some of their workers must make sure that each of them is currently enrolled in a program registered with either the BAT or a state apprenticeship council; otherwise the contractor will be liable to pay the higher rate

[45]WAB 68-9 (Dec. 19. 1968).

which prevails for the classification of work that the employee has been performing. If such a employee has also worked overtime, the contractor's liability will be even greater, because the contractor must also pay time and one-half of the higher rate, plus possible liquidated damages of $10 per employee for each day on which the employee was erroneously paid at the apprentice or trainee rate.

Enforcement

A contractor subject to the Davis-Bacon provision must submit payroll records to the contracting agency each week, along with a statement of compliance that is signed by the contractor or an employee in charge of administering the payroll. The records must include the name and address of each laborer and mechanic and their correct classification, rate of pay, daily and weekly number of hours worked, deductions made, and actual wages paid. A contractor may submit to the agency Form WH-347, which lists the required payroll data and also contains a statement of compliance, or Form WH-348, which is the compliance statement plus the weekly payroll with the required information. Under the law the contractor must retain all payroll records for 3 years from completion of the project and allow them to be inspected by the contracting agency of the Davis-Bacon staff.

The general contractor is also responsible for subcontractors' full compliance with these record-keeping requirements. The contracting agency and the Davis-Bacon staff will examine the records to make sure that the prevailing wages and benefits have been properly paid to all the employees for the classification of work they performed and that not impermissible deductions have been made. The contractor should examine the payrolls of all subcontractors before paying the subcontractors, because the contractor can be held liable for their violations. The agency may also withhold from the general contractor amounts owed by a subcontractor to laborers and mechanics. The Comptroller General is then empowered to pay the amount withheld directly to the affected employees. Employees in charge of record keeping should certainly be instructed not to falsify the payroll records, because the contractor may be debarred from government contracts for up to 3 years for employees' failure to keep accurate records.

The contracting agency will examine the contractor's weekly payroll records to determine whether the laborers and mechanics of contractor and his subcontractors are being paid the wages that the Department of Labor has determined are prevailing in the area for the type of work they are performing. If underpayments are found to exist, then upon written notice to the contractor the agency may terminate the contract and hold the contractor and the contractor's sureties liable for the excess costs to complete the contract.

If the amount withheld from the contractor under a contract is not sufficient to reimburse the laborers and mechanics for the entire amount of wage underpayments the difference may be withheld from the contractor under another government contract that the contractor is performing. This will be the rule if the contractor has paid either less than the prevailing wages or no wages at all for the work on the project.[46] Although a general contractor may be liable for a subcontractor's underpayments under the same contract, a federal district court has held that the government may not withhold from a contractor amounts owed by the subcontractor to the subcontractor's employees on another contract.[47]

A contracting agency's case against a contractor usually begins with a notice of noncompliance and an informal effort to resolve the problem. The agency is entitled only to withhold from the contractor amounts reasonably necessary to cover the alleged underpayments. A contractor who believes that either an excessive sum has been withheld or that no violation at all has been committed should request from the agency a written statement of the facts and the reasons for the charge of noncompliance. If the dispute cannot be resolved after meetings with the regional and national offices of the agency, an appeal may be made to the Davis-Bacon administrative staff. The Davis-Bacon Administrator is required to issue a written decision stating the reasons for the noncompliance charge, so that an appeal record is available to the WAB.

An appeal to the WAB is initiated by filing a timely petition which identifies the project and agency involved, the grounds for review, and the contractor's data and arguments. It is important that the contractor and subcontractors keep accurate payroll records, because the WAB has held that it is the contractor's responsibility to prove, if asked to do so, compliance with the Davis-Bacon requirements.[48] The WAB will schedule a date for an informal hearing and afterward issue a written decision setting forth the reasons for its decision.

Appeal from an adverse WAB ruling may be made to the Comptroller General with respect to federal contracts, since the Comptroller General has authority on those contracts to determine whether to disburse federal funds to the contractor and the contractor's employees. An appeal to that office must concern the Davis-Bacon staff's authority to enforce certain standards, because the Comptroller General will not review Davis-Bacon determinations concerning prevailing wages and classifications unless they are arbitrary or ar not supported by substantial evidence.[49] Routine enforcement decisions are left for the Davis-Bacon administrator to resolve, and the Comptroller General will normally not intervene unless the case concerns a basic policy issue such as the question of coverage of off-site operations.

If a contractor on a federal contract believes that all obligations under a Davis-Bacon contract have been performed and that the Comptroller

---

[46]Comp. Gen. B-123227 (Sept. 14, 1955).

[47]*Whitney Bros. Plumbing & Heating v. United States*, 224 F. Supp. 860 (D. Alas. 1968).

[48]22 W.H. Cas. 1115 (1976).

[49]50 Comp. Gen. 103 (Aug. 19, 1970).

General has improperly withheld funds, the contractor may bring suit in the U.S. Court of Claims. Under certain circumstance suit may be brought in an appropriate federal district court.

If the sums withheld from a contractor by the Comptroller General are insufficient to reimburse the employees, the employees may sue the contractor directly in an appropriate federal district court. It is no defense to the employees' suit for the contractor to claim that such employees accepted or agreed to accept less than the required rate of wages or voluntarily refunded wages to the contractor. The contractor may raise a statute-of-limitations defense to an employee suit if a 2 year period has elapsed since an unintentional violation or if 3 years have elapsed since a willful violation. Therefore, it is wise as well as necessary that contractors keep their payroll records and those of their subcontractors for at least 3 years from completion of the project.

A contractor who fails to comply with the Davis-Bacon provisions may be debarred for a 3 year period from future government contracts. Upon finding that there is reasonable cause to believe that the contractor has committed violations of the Davis-Bacon Act which constitute a disregard of the contractor's obligations to employees or subcontractors, the Deputy Administrator of the Wage and Hour and Public Contracts Divisions of the Department of Labor is to notify the contractor promptly by registered or certified mail of the finding and afford the contractor an opportunity to present such reasons or considerations as can be offered as to why debarment action should not be taken. In the notification letter the Deputy Administrator is to furnish the contractor with a summary of the investigative findings and make available any information disclosed by the investigation which is not privileged or confidential. If the contractor desires, an informal proceeding shall be held before an assistant regional administrator for the Wage and Hour, Employment Standards Administration or any other departmental officer of appropriate ability. At the conclusion of the informal proceeding, the hearing officer shall issue a written decision. The hearing officer's decision can be appealed to the Solicitor of Labor, U.S. Department of Labor. The decision of the Solicitor is final except in cases accepted for review by the WAB.

Any person who has been debarred may request in writing removal from the debarment list. As with the debarment procedure set forth above, an informal hearing is held, giving the contractor an opportunity to demonstrate a current responsibility to comply with the Davis-Bacon labor requirements. This responsibility can be shown through such means as voluntary submittal of payrolls on federal projects since the alleged violations.

CONTRACT WORK HOURS AND SAFETY STANDARDS ACT

The Contract Work Hours and Safety Standards Act[50] regulates the payment of overtime and requires the observance of health and safety stan-

[50] 40 U.S.C. §327–332.

dards on federal and federally financed construction, repair, and alteration of public works projects in excess of $2,000. The act will apply whenever the Davis-Bacon Act applies and protects not only labors and mechanics but also watchmen and guards on covered projects. Off-site employers who specifically service a covered construction project are covered by the act. Contractors must know their obligations under the act, because violations may result in back-pay suits, assessment of liquidated damages, debarment from government contracts, and criminal penalties and fines for intentional violations.

The Contract Work Hours portion of the act does not prohibit overtime work, but it does require the payment of time and one-half of the basic rate of pay for hours worked in excess of 8 hours per day or 40 hours per week. No premium pay is required for weekend work as such, except to the extent that work on a Saturday or Sunday is in excess of 8 hours per day or 40 hours per week. An employee who works both daily and weekly overtime need not be paid time and one-half for both but must be paid time and one-half for the daily or the weekly hours, whichever is greater.

To be covered by the act an employee must devote more than 8 hours per day or 40 hours per week to actual performance of work covered by the Davis-Bacon contract. Hours worked under the act are governed by the same standards as under the FLSA. Time spent in the classroom under a government-sponsored program which includes on-the-job training is not included in hours worked. An employee who, in a given day, works 8 hours on a Davis-Bacon project and 2 hours on a non-federal project need not be paid time and one-half for the two hours, because only 8 hours have been spent working on the covered project. The contractor's payroll records should show, however, that 2 of the hours worked were on an uncovered project; otherwise it might be assumed that all the hours worked were covered by Davis-Bacon, and the contractor would have to pay time and one-half for the 2 hours. If an employee works more than 8 hours per day or 40 hours per week on two or more projects covered by the Davis-Bacon Act, all the hours worked on the covered projects must be added together to determine if overtime must be paid.

The basic rate of pay on which time and one-half is computed for overtime work on a Davis-Bacon project can be no less than the basic hourly rate of pay listed in the contract as prevailing for the classification or work performance by the employee. Contractors may meet their Davis-Bacon obligations to pay prevailing wages and fringe benefits by paying less than the basic hourly rate provided the difference is paid for prevailing fringe benefits. Premium pay for overtime, however, is calculated according to the prevailing basic hourly rate. For example, if the wage determination provides for $6 per hour and $1 in fringe benefits, the contractor may pay $5.50 per hour and $1.50 in fringe benefits, but time and one-half is still based on the $6 basic hourly rate.

Amounts paid by a contractor for fringe benefits are excluded in the computation of overtime as long as the basic rate of pay is not less than the prevailing basic hourly rate. Employee contributions to fringe benefits which are deducted from the paycheck are not excluded in determining the basic rate of pay, but employer contributions for fringe benefits are excluded as long as the basic rate of pay remains as high as the prevailing wage rate.

A contractor who pays a cash wage rate that is higher than the prevailing basic hourly rate and a fringe benefit smaller than the prevailing must pay time and one-half for overtime based on the higher cash wage rate. For example, if the prevailing wage determination requires $6 in wages and $1 in fringe benefits and the contractor pays $6.50 in wages and 50 cents in fringe benefits, then time and one-half for overtime is calculated according to the cash wage rate of $6.50. Premium pay for hazardous work is included in the basic rate for computing overtime pay. The Solicitor of Labor held that under the expired Eight-Hour law a differential for hazardous work was not premium pay for overtime work, so that it was fair to include it in the regular rate for calculating overtime.[51] Because the Contract Work Hours and Safety Standards Act replaced or adopted many of the older law's requirements in 1962, this is probably still the rule today.

Contractors may pay a cash equivalent for any prevailing fringe benefit which will be excluded from the basic rate of pay for overtime provided the basic rate remains as high as the prevailing wage rate. For example, if the prevailing wage determination lists $6 in wages and $1 in fringe benefits, a contractor may pay $6 in wages and $1 in cash in lieu of paying into the fringe-benefit plan, and the basic rate of pay for overtime will still be the prevailing wage rate of $6. If the cash payment is not in lieu of a fringe benefit but is part of an employee's straight-time cash wages, it is not excludable in computing overtime. For example, if a contractor had been paying $6 in wages and 50 cents in fringe benefits and the prevailing wage determination includes $5.50 in wages and $1 in fringe benefits, time and one-half is computed on the $6 cash wage rate that the contractor had been paying. However, if the contractor had been paying $5.50 in wages and $1 in fringe benefits and decided to pay $1 in cash directly to the employee instead of into the benefit plan, then under the prevailing wage determination the basic rate of pay for overtime purposes would still be $5.50 in wages, since the $1 cash payment was in lieu of a fringe-benefit payment. The contactor must first get the contracting agency to agree that a cash payment is a proper equivalent to the contribution or cost for the prevailing fringe benefit before it will be excluded in calculating overtime compensation.

Contractors who fail to pay a time-and-one-half wage rate to employees who work more than 8 hours per day or 40 hours per week are liable to the employees for the amount of underpayments and to the government for liquidated damages. Since contractors may be liable for the violations of subcontractors, they should be instructed as to their overtime obligations,

[51] Op. Solic. Lab., Nov. 3, 1961.

and their payroll records should be examined to determine that there has been full compliance. The contracting agency is authorized to withhold from amounts due a contractor the amount owed for underpayments and liquidated damages. The Comptroller General will pay directly to the employees from the sums withheld amounts necessary to reimburse them for the underpayments, and the difference, if any will be held as liquidated damages for the benefit of the government. If the sums withheld are insufficient to reimburse all the affected employees for the underpayments and the government for liquidated damages, the amounts available are first used to compensate fully all the employees. The remainder, if any, shall be used for liquidated damages. An equitable distribution is made among the affected employees if not enough can be withheld to reimburse all of them fully.

The Comptroller General has held that it is improper to withhold from the sums due a contractor the amounts necessary to reimburse the employees of the contractor for underpayments outstanding on another contract. However, liquidated damages outstanding on an earlier contract may be withheld from the contractor on another contract.[52]

Employees may sue contractors and their subcontractors and their sureties if the sums withheld by the government are insufficient to reimburse them fully for underpayments. It shall be no defense against an employee suit for the contractor to claim that the employees voluntarily accepted less than was owed them or that they voluntarily refunded any wages they received.

Liquidated damages are assessed at $10 per worker for each calendar day in which the employee was required or permitted to work more than 8 hours per day or 40 hours per week on a covered project or projects without full overtime compensation. So if an employee works in excess of 8 hours on 2 days but the total number of hours worked in the week is less than 40, liquidated damages will be $20. If an employee works more than 8 hours in any one day and also works in excess of 40 hours in that workweek, the amount of liquidated damages is computed by totaling the daily overtime hours and comparing that sum with the weekly overtime hours. If the daily overtime hours equal the weekly overtime hours, liquidated damages are computed for the days in which overtime was worked. If the daily overtime hours exceed the weekly overtime hours, liquidated damages are assessed for the days when the employee worked more than 8 hours. On the other hand, if the weekly overtime hours exceed the daily overtime hours, liquidated damages are computed at $10 per day for each day on which the weekly overtime hours were worked.

Sometimes contractors pay for overtime in excess or 40 hours per week but fail to pay daily overtime. If the daily overtime hours equal or exceed the weekly overtime hours, the weekly overtime hours for which payment has been made may offset the daily hours as they accrue. But if the weekly

[52]Comp. Gen. B-123227 (Dec. 9, 1968).

overtime hours exceed the daily overtime hours, liquidated damages are assessed for the days on which weekly overtime hours were worked and not paid for at time and one-half.

A contractor who wishes to appeal to withholding of payments for liquidated damages must appeal to the head of the contracting agency within 60 days after the withholding. The agency head can issue a final order affirming the assessment of liquidated damages. Or if the head finds that either the computation was incorrect or that the contractor violated the overtime provisions inadvertently despite the exercise of due care, the head can recommend to the Secretary of Labor that either an appropriate adjustment of liquidated damages be made or that damages not be assessed at all. The Secretary will conduct an investgation of all the facts, and the Secretary's decision is a final order. The agency head may reduce or eliminate an assessment of less than $100 if the computation is incorrect or if the violation was inadvertent. Either a decision of the agency head affirming the assessment of liquidated damages or the Secretary's decision is a final order. Appeal of a final order must be made within 60 days by filing a claim in the U.S. Court of Claims. The Court of Claims will not question findings of facts made by the agency head and the Secretary which are supported by substantial evidence.

Although the act does not specifically so provide, a United States court of appeals has held that the Department of Labor may debar contractors and subcontractors from government contracts for aggravated or willful violations of the overtime requirement. The name of the contractor or subcontractor is placed on an ineligibility list which is distributed to the contracting agencies by the Comptroller General, and the contractor may be debarred from government contracts for up to 3 years from the date on which the list is published. The contractor must demonstrate a current responsibility to comply with the overtime provisions in order to be removed from the blacklist. Intentional violations of the overtime provisions are misdemeanors, punishable by fines of up to $1000 and imprisonment for up to 6 months.

A 1969 amendment to the overtime provisions in the act requires contractors and subcontractors on government construction projects to provide safe working conditions for laborers and mechanics. Every contract must contain a provision which assures that contractors will not require their employees to work in surroundings or under working conditions which are unsanitary, hazardous, or dangerous to the workers' health and safety. Minimum health and safety standards for construction projects are promulgated by the Assistant Secretary of Labor for Occupational Safety and Health after formal hearings and consultation with the Advisory Committee on Construction Safety and Health. These standards are published in the *Federal Register* and become binding on contractors and their subcontractors on Davis-Bacon projects.

The Secretary of Labor is authorized to make inspections of the workplace to determine whether minimum safety standards are being met. An injunction may be obtained in a federal district court to require compliance with the standards if a violation is found. Failure to remedy the violation will constitute contempt of the court's order. In addition, if there is probable cause to believe that safety standards are not being met, a notice of noncompliance will be sent to the contractor. There will be a formal hearing at which the contractor may offer evidence and present arguments. If the Secretary determines that the contractor has violated the minimum health and safety requirements, the contracting agency is entitled to terminate the contract and assess the costs of completion against the contractor. Contractors may appeal such an adverse decision to a United States court of appeals within 60 days of the district court order.

Contractors who commit repeated willful or grossly negligent violations of the safety provisions may be debarred from government contracts for up to 3 years. The Secretary of Labor will conduct a hearing to determine whether the contractor has intentionally disregarded the obligation to provide safe working conditions. If the Secretary finds that to be the case, the Comptroller General will include the contractor's name on an ineligibility list which is circulated to the various contracting agencies and which debars the contractor from all government contracts for up to 3 years. Contractors may appeal to a United States court of appeals within 60 days after receiving notice of the listing. It is unlikely, however, that an appeal will result in the contractor's name being removed, because the court's review of the facts is limited. Contractors who wish to be struck from the debarred list should request a hearing with the Secretary, at which time they must show willingness to and capability to comply with the minimum health and safety standards.

Contractors and subcontractors on Davis-Bacon projects must remain aware of their obligations to pay for overtime work and to provide healthy and safe working conditions. Contractors must remember that on Davis-Bacon projects, unlike private construction work, time and one-half must be paid for daily as well as weekly overtime work. In addition, in deciding the type of payments to make to meet their obligations to pay prevailing wage and fringe benefits, contractors must always consider the effects which those decisions will have on their liabilities for overtime work. Harsh sanctions sometimes attend violations of the act's overtime and safety standards provisions, so it is essential that contractors monitor not only their own but also their subcontractors' operations to assure full compliance with the act's requirements.

COPELAND ANTI-KICKBACK ACT

The Copeland Anti-Kickback Act[53] makes it a federal crime to engage in kickbacks on federal and federally funded construction projects. A "kickback" is an unauthorized refund to the contractor from the wages and

---

[53] 18 U.S.C. §874.

fringe benefits that the contractor is required to pay under the Davis-Bacon Act and related federal laws. The penalty for violation of the act may be indictment and trial in federal court; a conviction may result in a fine up to $5000 or 5 years in jail, or both. There have been few if any convictions. Administrative rulings under the act may be appealed to the WAB.

The act allows certain deductions to be made from employees' paychecks. Some of these deductions do not require the prior approval of the Secretary of Labor, while others may lawfully be made only after the Secretary's approval has been given. The following deductions may be made automatically without prior approval:

1. Withholding social security taxes and federal or state income taxes

2. Deductions in payment of advances without interest to employees

3. Deductions required by court order unless they are in favor of the contractor or subcontractor

4. Deductions to pay premiums on fringe-benefit programs established by the contractor or the union, or both. For such a deduction to be permitted, it must either be consented to voluntarily in writing by the employee prior to the payroll period in which the work is to be done or be provided for in a valid collective bargaining agreement. The consent must not be a condition for obtaining or continuing employment. No benefit or profit may flow directly or indirectly to the contractor or subcontractor, and the deduction must serve the convenience and interest of the employee

5. Deductions for the purchase of United States savings bonds when voluntarily authorized by the employee

6. Deductions requested by the employee to repay loans or to purchase shares in credit unions operated in accordance with law

7. Deductions voluntarily authorized for contributions to the Red Cross, Community Chest, United Givers Fund, and similar organizations

8. Deductions to pay regular union initiation fees and membership dues, not including fines and assessments, provided a valid collective bargaining agreement provides for such deductions and the employee has voluntarily consented in writing to the deductions

9. Deductions for reasonable costs of board, lodging, or other facilities when the requirements of Section 3(m) of the FLSA are met

10. Deductions for the cost of safety equipment of nominal value which the contractor or subcontractor is not legally required to furnish. If the equipment is purchased from the contractor, the deduction cannot exceed the cost of the equipment to the contractor. The deduction must either be authorized voluntarily in writing by the employee or be provided for in the collective bargaining agreement.

Approval must be given by the Secretary of Labor for other deductions before the contractor may legally make them. The Secretary is authorized to permit such deductions upon receipt of a written application from the contractor if the following conditions are found to exist:

1. The contractor derives no benefit or profit directly or indirectly from the deduction

2. The deduction is not prohibited by law

3. The deduction is either authorized voluntarily by the employee in writing prior to the payroll period in which the work is done and the consent is not a condition for obtaining or continuing employment or the deduction is provided for in a valid collective bargaining agreement

4. The deduction serves the employee's interest and convenience.

14 EMPLOYMENT DISCRIMINATION

It is an understatement to assert that the law of employment discrimination has been in a state of flux for the past two decades. The entire field of equal-employment-opportunity law and the principle of affirmative action are creations of the 1960s and 1970s. Rapid change is understandable as courts and society come to grips with an increasing plethora of statutes, regulations, and court decisions. It is not the purpose of this chapter to focus on minute particulars of employment discrimination law and affirmative-action requirements; rather, this chapter is in the nature of an introductory survey of points which may be helpful to contractors who find themselves confronted with seemingly impenetrable problems in the employment discrimination context. While this discussion may provide general answers to certain recurring questions, there is no substitute for the advice of legal counsel in specific cases.

The most fundamental protection which the United States affords all persons is in the Constitution itself. The Fifth Amendment provides that no person shall be deprived of life, liberty, or property without due process of law. Its applicability is to the federal government and not to the states. The Fourteenth Amendment was enacted in the aftermath of the Civil War to extend the scope of the Fifth Amendment to the individual states. In addition to reiterating the Fifth Amendment's due-process guarantee, the Fourteenth Amendment forbids a state to deny "equal protection of the laws" to any persons within its jurisdiction.

To implement the concepts of due process and equal protection promulgated by the Fourteenth Amendment, Congress enacted several statutes during the Reconstruction era. These statutes, the Civil Rights Acts of 1866 and 1871,[1] were originally intended as a means by which blacks could enforce the constitutional rights which had previously been denied them. These postwar Civil Rights Acts lay buried until the middle of the twentieth century, when they were exhumed by the growing civil rights movement. Increasingly they have been employed in ways broader than had been originally contemplated by Congress. Ultimately, however, it became apparent that further legislation would be needed to deal with the specific problems involved in the area of employment discrimination, for the law as

---

[1] 42 U.S.C. §§1981 *et seq.*

it stood in the early 1960s was capable of dealing with these problems only indirectly. Title VII of the Civil Rights Act of 1964[2] was Congress's first comprehensive law of employment discrimination. Typical of first attempts in most fields of endeavor, it has occasioned much disagreement, and it has spawned an immense amount of ancillary legislation and regulations. Nonetheless, it remains the basis of the law of employment discrimination. As such, Title VII is the logical point of departure for this chapter's treatment of equal employment opportunity and affirmative action as applicable to contractors.

TITLE VII OF THE CIVIL RIGHTS ACT OF 1964

Small contractors may not be subject to the coverage of Title VII. The statute applies to employers in general, but it defines an "employer" as "a person engaged in an industry affecting commerce who has fifteen or more employees for each working day in each of twenty or more calendar weeks in the current or preceding calendar year, and any agent of such a person. . .."[3] The word *person* is defined by Title VII as "including one or more individuals, . . . partnerships, associations, corporations,"[4] and numerous other political and commercial entities. From the statutory scheme, it is clear that most contractors of substantial size will fall within the purview of Title VII. Contractors not employing fifteen or more employees for 20 or more calendar weeks or the year, while not subject to the provisions of Title VII, may still fall within the ambit of one or more of the federal laws regulating contractors as employers (for example, Executive Order No. 11246). A contractor must not assume that not being subject to Title VII will obviate the need to comply with other equal-employment-opportunity regulations or to formulate affirmative-action plans.

There are several enumerated exceptions to Title VII's coverage of employers, but only two are likely to be applicable to contractors. First, Section 702 of Title VII provides an exemption for employers "with respect to employment of aliens outside of any state." Only contractors using aliens as employees outside the United States will be able to avail themselves of this provision. Second, a contractor does not fall within the coverage of Title VII as to persons whom the contractor hires as independent contractors. Not specifically mentioned in Title VII, this exception is one which the courts have formulated.[5] Its practical import is that if all other prerequisites are assumed to have been met, a contractor will not be covered by Title VII as to the subcontractors with whom the contractor deals.

The courts have generally held that the absence of an employer-employee relationship does not preclude an individual from gaining a remedy

[2] 42 U.S.C. §§2000 *et seq.*

[3] 42 U.S.C §20002e(b).

[4] 42 U.S.C. §2000e(a).

[5] *Mathis v. Standard Brands Chem. Indus.*, 10 FEP 295 (N.D. Ga. 1975).

against an employer under Title VII. Thus, Title VII's protection extends not merely to individuals who are actually employees of a covered contractor but, in certain cases, to prospective employees and to former employees as well. Title VII protects current employees, applicants for employment, former employees, and even discharged employees. The implication is that a contractor must use discretion not only in relations with employees but also in hiring, recruitment, and pension programs. Title VII's protection extends not only to individuals but to classes of individuals, and a contractor under attack for allegedly unlawful employment practices may face either a class action or an individual suit.

The mere fact that an employee had been unsuccessful in a proceeding before a state fair-employment-practice agency does not preclude the employee from filing a new federal Title VII action. The rationale that there is a paramount federal policy of antidiscrimination concern means that the federal government has a right to an ultimate federal determination even if an employee has already gone to a state agency.[6] Whether an employee who loses a Title VII action may turn around and bring a state fair-employment-practice action has not yet been settled.

Prohibited Discrimination

Title VII expressly forbids discrimination by employers with regard to an individual's race, color, religion, sex, or national origin. The statute enumerates the following specific instances of unlawful discriminatory conduct on the part of an employer:

Section 703
(a) It shall be an unlawful employment practice for an employer: (1) to fail or refuse to hire or to discharge any individual, or otherwise to discriminate against any individual with respect to his compensation, terms, conditions, or privileges of employment, because of such individual's race, color, religion, sex, or national origin; or, (2) to limit, segregate, or classify his employees or applicant for employment in any way which would deprive or tend to deprive any individual of employment opportunities or otherwise adversely affect his status as an employee, because of such individual's race, color, religion, sex, or national origin.
(b) It shall be an unlawful employment practice for any employer, labor organization, or joint labor-management committee controlling apprenticeship or other training or retraining, including on-the-job training programs, to discriminate against any individual because of his race, color, religion, sex, or national origin in admission to, or employment in, any program established to provide apprenticeship or other training.

Because these provisions are applicable to hiring, firing, employer-employee relations, and apprenticeship or other training programs, there is virtually no phase of a contractor's operations which will fall outside the areas sought to be regulated by Title VII. There are only extremely limited exceptions to the general rule, and a contractor is best advised to refrain from any actions or practices, intentional or unintentional, which directly

[6]*Alexander v. Gardner-Denver*, 415 U.S. 36 (1973).

or even indirectly operate in a discriminatory manner against individuals on the basis of race, color, religion, sex, or national origin. Best intentions may not be sufficient to exonerate a contractor if the ultimate effect of the contractor's conduct is held to be discrimination made unlawful by Title VII.

A union that participates in discrimination may also be liable under Title VII. The union may be solely liable for discrimination that it causes or may be jointly and severally liable with an employer for discriminatory practices that it negotiated in a collective bargaining agreement or for discrimination caused by both union and employer. Title VII has been amended to prohibit discrimination also on the basis of pregnancy; therefore if an employer gives a disability plan for disabled workers, it must include pregnancy within the definition of disability in addition to providing medical benefits to pregnant women.

The most obvious form of unlawful employment discrimination is that labeled "disparate treatment." Disparate treatment is discrimination against an individual or individuals based entirely upon race, color, religion, sex, or national origin. It generally appears when an employer uses one or more of these characteristics as the basis upon which to discriminate between individuals who are otherwise similarly situated. A typical example of disparate treatment is the situation in which two employees, one white and one black, commit some act forbidden by the employer. The employer merely places the white worker on disciplinary probation but fires the black worker. The safest course for a contractor in a similar situation is to treat all the parties involved with absolute equality. If disciplinary measures are called for, all employees involved should be disciplined according to a uniform standard. Care should be taken to keep complete records of all disciplinary warnings or reprimands to prevent an employee with a poor record from successfully claiming that discrimination has occurred if he or she is later discharged.

Disparate treatment can occur in all phases of a contractor's operations, and the contractor should establish uniform standards for dealing with applicants for employment and present employees. Quite simply, a contractor who deals with all employees and applicants for employment according to a guideline of absolute equality will normally avoid Title VII violations based upon disparate treatment.

Title VII extends its coverage to protection of an individual's religious beliefs and practices in the employment context. Section 701(j) establishes an affirmative duty reasonably to accommodate "all aspects of religious observance and practice, as well as belief, unless an employer demonstrates that he is unable to reasonably accommodate to an employee's or prospective employee's religious observance or practice without undue hardship on the conduct of the employer's business." In other words, an individual's religious beliefs and practices enjoy protection except to the extent to which an employer cannot reasonably accommodate to them without undue hardship. The most typical example of the kind of accommodation contemplated would involve the case of an employee whose religion forbids its adherents to work on specific days such as the Sabbath. Such cases present the problem of juggling the employee's work schedule so as to compromise between the employee's beliefs and the employer's work needs. Less simple would be the case of a religion requiring its members to dress in a certain style when an employer's job requirements are that employees wear standard attire. In any event, a contractor presented with an apparent conflict between an employee's religious beliefs and the contractor's own needs should first attempt to resolve the problem by accommodation. If such a compromise is truly impossible, however, the contractor should stand firm in insistence on business needs.[7]

There are extremely limited instances in which it is permissible for an employer to discriminate for or against classes of individuals including Communists and for national security. A contractor engaged in a project on or near an Indian reservation may accord preferential treatment to Indians if preference is a publicly announced employment practice of the contractor.

Title VII will allow differential treatment of individuals on basis of religion, sex, or national origin if there is a bona fide occupational qualification. This is permissible under Section 703(e) "where religion, sex, or national origin is a bona fide occupational qualification reasonably necessary to the normal operation" of the particular business or enterprise involved. It is to be emphasized that the courts will look quite carefully at an employer's assertion that disparate treatment of individuals is related to a bona fide occupational qualification, and the exception is a narrow one. In the case of an allegation of sex-based discrimination, for example, a bona fide occupational qualification will be found only if being a particular sex goes to the essence of the job (for example, actors and actresses) or relates to the privacy concerns of customers.

As long as a contractor's motives are nondiscriminatory, the contractor may deal with employees by differing standards if those standards are related to differences in the quality of the employees' job performance or to differences in the type of job categories. Section 703(h) allows "an employer to apply different standards of compensation, or different terms, conditions, or privileges of employment pursuant to a bona fide seniority or merit system, or a system which measures earnings by quantity or quality of production or to employees who work in different locations, provided that such differences are not the result of an intention to discriminate because of race, color, religion, sex, or national origin." However, even a facially neutral seniority or job-ranking practice which has a disparate impact upon protected individuals would be interpreted as intentional in nature for the purposes of Title VII. For a contractor's seniority or merit

[7] *TWA v. Hardison*, 432 U.S. 63 (1977).

system to be bona fide, it must discriminate neither intentionally nor by its impact upon employees according to their race, color, religion, sex, or national origin.

Illustrative Case

Crown Zellerbach, a huge paper-manufacturing company with numerous federal contracts, had formerly discriminated between black and white employees in its Bogalusa, Alabama, plant, employing whites in its more desirable jobs while allowing blacks to work only in its lower-paying, less responsible positions. By the mid 1960s, Crown had ceased direct discrimination and merged its plants jobs into a single line of progression, all the formerly black jobs being arbitrarily ranked below what was formerly the lowest-ranking white job. Blacks were no longer overtly precluded from working in any of the jobs of the employer. However, a worker could bid for a higher job only by using the amount of time spent working in the job slot just below the position that the worker was seeking. Although the seniority system seemed facially neutral, it made it virtually impossible for a black employee to get a formerly white position because the time that a black employee had worked in an all-black job counted for nothing in bidding for any of the formerly white jobs except those which had once been entry-level positions. Taken as a whole, the system had the effect of so limiting black employees' upward job mobility that it preserved the past system of segregation at the plant. Crown was ordered to institute a new bidding system based entirely upon the amount of time that an employee had spent in Crown's employ.[8]

The case of *Quarles v. Phillip Morris, Inc.*[9] was the first to propound the legal theory that a present employment practice which perpetuates the effects of past intentional discrimination violates Title VII even if the present system is not directly intended to discriminate. The court held that a seniority system which had its genesis in pre-Title VII intentional racial discrimination could not be termed a valid seniority system even though it was facially nondiscriminatory. Although under Section 703(h) an employer may differentiate between employees' terms, conditions, and privileges of employment pursuant to a bona fide seniority system when this differentiation is not the result of an intention to discriminate, the fact that the seemingly nondiscriminatory seniority system in *Quarles* was actually derived from a past system of direct racial discrimination was sufficient to make the present seniority system unlawful. It should be mentioned that only contractors who discriminated in the pre-Title VII era would have cause to examine their present seniority and departmental transfer provisions to ascertain whether their present practices perpetuate past unlawful conduct. For such contractors, the best way to avoid Title VII problems is to make certain that, regardless of past conduct, present policies allow all persons equal opportunity for advancement, security, and transfer. Security clauses should be avoided if possible in construction labor agreements not only because they might perpetuate past discrimination practices but also because they restrict management's right to manage its workforce efficiently.

[8] *Local 189, Papermakers v. United States,* 416 F.2d 980 (5th Cir. 1969), *cert. denied,* 397 U.S. 919 (1970).
[9] 279 F. Supp. (E.D. Va. 1968).

Selection Criteria

A very common method for screening out prospective applicants involves the use of scored tests. Section 703(h) provides that it is not an unlawful employment practice "for an employer to give and to act upon the results of any professionally developed ability test provided that such test, its administration or action upon the results is not designed, intended or used to discriminate because of race, color, religion, sex, or natural origin."

It is not uncommon for an employer to select or judge employees by using criteria such as an individual's education, experience, or lack of a criminal record. If a selection criterion operates to exclude a protected class of individuals and cannot be shown to be directly related to successful job performance, the criterion may not be used. For example, if a contractor were to require that all its employees have a high school diploma, and if this requirement eliminated more blacks than whites from job consideration without its being a true measure of their ability to perform the jobs in question, the requirement could not stand. Similarly, a contractor's absolute refusal to hire persons with criminal records, a policy which often excludes more blacks than whites, might not hold up unless it could be shown that the job sought was one requiring an individual whose record for honesty was impeccable.

Illustrative Case

Duke Power Company, an employer, required a high school education or the passing of a standardized general intelligence test as a condition of employment in or transfer to its job openings. The jobs in question had formerly been filled by whites only, but no overt discrimination now existed. Nonetheless, neither of Duke's requirements was demonstrably related to successful job performance. Indeed, the requirements, though seemingly impartial, operated to disqualify black applicants at a higher rate than white applicants. The U.S. Supreme Court held this to be prohibited by Title VII.[10]

The *Griggs* case and others which have followed relate to the idea that employers violate Title VII when they use screening devices which operate to discriminate against individuals even if this disparate impact upon such protected individuals is not directly discriminatory in nature. Thus, in the absence of mitigating factors, scored employment tests and other job requirements, such as a high school education, prior experience, and a record free from arrests, convictions, or garnishments, can run afoul of Title VII if they operate to discriminate against individuals on the basis or race, color, religion, sex, or national origin. The Supreme Court has held in *Griggs,* and it has reiterated as recently as in *Furnco Construction Corp. v. Waters et al.,*[11] that when there has been a showing of substantial adverse impact, the defendant employer must rebut this showing with evidence that the practice in question is related to business necessity. In short, the practice must be related to successful job performance. In the *Furnco* case, three black applicants suing a contractor for alleged employment discrimination were

[10]*Griggs v. Duke Power Co.,* 401 U.S. 424 (1971).

[11]438 U.S. 567 (1978).

able to make a prima facie case that the contractor's hiring policies had an adverse impact upon blacks. The Supreme Court held that at that point the burden shifted to the employer to prove that the employment decision was based on a legitimate consideration and not on an illegitimate one such as race. To prove this, employers need not prove that they pursued a course which would both enable them to achieve their business goals and allow them to consider the greatest number of employment applications.

Whenever a contractor sets up any form of screening mechanism for applicants or present employees, the contractor should ask the following question: Does this requirement exclude persons of a certain race, color, religion, sex, or national origin more often than others? The answer should be "no" unless the contractor is prepared to prove, by statistics or job studies, that the requirement at issue is truly job-related.

The U.S. Supreme Court stated in the *Griggs* case that when a showing had been that an employer had engaged in practices which had a disparate impact upon individuals protected by Title VII, the employer must come forward with proof that the discriminatory practices were related to job performance. According to *Griggs*, "the touchstone is business necessity." From this has evolved what is known as the business necessity defense. It is important to recall that in cases involving disparate treatment an employer must defend on the basis of the discriminatory treatment's being founded upon a bona fide occupational qualification. However, when disparate-impact cases are concerned, the business necessity defense is appropriate. It becomes operative when there has been a showing that an employer's practices have had a disparate impact. Business necessity seems to be somewhat synonymous with job relatedness, for if an employer can show that the requirements or screening standards that the employer has used are job-related, this can be a basis of a successful defense against charges of an unlawful disparate impact.

The *Griggs* case established the requirement that a job requirement must bear a demonstrable relationship to successful job performance. The Supreme Court in the *Griggs* case stated that in demonstrating job relatedness, the Equal Employment Opportunity Commission (EEOC) Guidelines[12] are entitled to "great deference." Section 1607.4 of the guidelines mandates that an employer who uses tests to select or screen applicants must have available for inspection evidence that the tests are not being used in a manner which leads to prohibited discrimination. Specifically, the employer should have "empirical data demonstrating that the test is predictive of or significantly correlated with important elements or work behavior which comprise or are relevant to the job or jobs for which candidates are being evaluated."[13] The EEOC Guidelines require a very high degree of statistical validation (a 95 percent correlation coefficient). The Uniform Guidelines on Employee Selection Procedures,[14] a new set of

[12] 29 CFR 1600 *et seq.*
[13] 29 CFR 1607.4(c).
[14] 29 CFR 1607.

guidelines proposed for use by the Civil Service Commission, the EEOC, the Department of Justice, and the Department of Labor will also exact a very high differential validity of employer testing. Any contractor feeling compelled to select applicants or evaluate employees by testing should consult the guidelines closely and design the testing to be as fully in harmony with its standards as possible.

The EEOC Guidelines indicate that a bottom-line approach will be used in the future to evaluate job selection procedures. Under this system a contractor could conceivably use any criteria to screen out applicants as long as the ultimate result, or bottom line, is that there is no discriminatory impact. This seems to liberalize the evaluation procedures available to employers. Nonetheless, it is still wise for contractors wishing to use screening criteria to utilize only criteria which can be shown to be dictated by business necessity.

Reverse Discrimination

One of the most controversial sections of Title VII is Section 703(j), which deals with reverse discrimination. It states:

Nothing contained in [Title VII] shall be interpreted to require any employer . . . to grant preferential treatment to any individual or to any group because of the race, color, religion, sex, or national origin of such individual or group on account of an imbalance which may exist with respect to the total number or percentage of persons of any race, color, religion, sex, or national origin employed by any employer . . . in comparison with the total number or percentage of persons of such race, color, religion, sex, or national origin in any community, State, section, or other area, or in the available work force in any community, State, section, or other area.

On its face, this section would seem to forbid all forms of reverse discrimination, including affirmative action, in cases involving employer subject to Title VII. In reality, the section is not as broad as it seems. Under Section 706(g), the federal courts are empowered, upon finding unlawful employment practices, to enjoin the employer from engaging in such unlawful practices. They may "order such affirmative action as may be appropriate." Thus, section 703(j)'s prohibition of reverse discrimination will apply except in cases in which a court has found unlawful employment discrimination. In such cases, affirmative action is a legitimate Title VII remedy.

There has been some controversy as to whether Section 703(j) precludes all affirmative-action plans by employers when there has been no showing of unlawful employment discrimination. The consensus seems to be that an affirmative plan based solely upon Title VII must be a remedy for unlawful employment discrimination, while affirmative-action plans may be formulated pursuant to other statutes or regulations without there having been a judicial finding of unlawful employment practices. *Contractors Association of Eastern Pennsylvania v. Secretary of Labor*[15] involved a

---

[15]442 F.2d 159 (3d Cir. 1971), *cert. denied*, 404 U.S. 854 (1971).

challenge to the Philadelphia Plan, an area-wide affirmative-action plan imposed by the Secretary of Labor upon bidders as a precondition for bidding on federal or federally assisted construction contracts for projects in a five-county area around Philadelphia. The court of appeals upheld the plan, although it stated that it probably could not have done so under Title VII without running afoul of Section 703(j). However, because the Philadelphia Plan was promulgated pursuant to Executive Order No. 11246, it could stand.

Retaliation against Complaining Employees

Employers are restrained from retaliating against employees or applicants who complain of unlawful employment practices or file charges or testify in an action arising under Title VII. Section 704(a) protects an employee who has sought the protection of Title VII from employer retaliation.

It shall be unlawful employment practice for an employer to discriminate against any of his employees or applicants for employment . . . because he has opposed any practice made an unlawful employment practice by this title, or because he has made a charge, testified, assisted, or participated in any manner in an investigation, proceeding, or hearing under [Title VII].

This section's protection extends to an individual who has "opposed any practice made an unlawful employment practice" by Title VII. There is a division of opinion as to whether the practice opposed by the employee must actually be an unlawful employment practice or whether an individual's good-faith belief that he or she is opposing an unlawful employment practice will suffice. The EEOC argues the latter position, while most employers would argue the former. The section also protects individuals who have participated in any manner under Title VII. This provision is broadly interpreted by the courts and by the EEOC. An employer is forbidden from taking any retaliatory measures against an individual who avails himself or herself of the protection of Title VII. This includes actual participation in Title VII or EEOC procedures as well as informal invocation of Title VII's protection, such as in the case of an employee who was unlawfully discharged for writing a letter to the EEOC complaining about his or her employer. The mere writing of the letter was deemed participation for the purposes of the statute. A contractor who is faced with opposition to alleged unlawful employment practices or with an individual who has participated in protected Title VII activities should let the law run its course rather than taking action of a retaliatory nature. While firing an "offending" employee may seem to be an immediate solution, it may well result in later liabilities.

Advertisements

A contractor must not discriminate in the placing of advertisements seeking employees. Section 704(b) forbids an employer's advertising from "indicating any preference, limitation, specification, or discrimination, based on race, color, religion, sex, or national origin." It allows such preferences, limitations, or specifications only when religion, sex, or national origin is a bona fide occupational qualification for employment. A contractor's advertisements should therefore omit any reference to a preference for persons of a particular race, color, religion, sex, or national origin. For practical purposes, race or color can never be bona fide occupational qualifications. It would be rare, in the construction industry, that an individual's religion, sex, or national origin could be considered a bona fide occupational qualification and thus lawfully includable in employment advertising. Even when a contractor's business involves heavy or arduous physical work for which most women, for example, would be unsuited, a court would probably require that a contractor allow applicants of both sexes to answer job advertisements. In addition, a court could require that all applicants be afforded the opportunity to demonstrate their employment capabilities under work simulation tests. Thus, a woman would be able to prove or disprove her ability to work in jobs which, like many construction or contractor jobs, have traditionally been male-dominated. In summary, a contractor is best advised to direct employment advertising to all potentially interested persons without regard for personal characteristics such as religion, sex, or national origin. The final hiring decision can then be made from the entire applicant pool without fear of incurring liability for unlawful advertising.

Record Keeping

Conformity with the provisions of Title VII involves not only substantive compliance, but record keeping, reporting, and notice compliance as well. Section 709(c) sets up the record-keeping standards expected of all employers subject to Title VII coverage:

Every employer . . . subject to [Title VII] shall:
(1) make and keep such records relevant to the determination of whether unlawful employment practices have been or are being committed.;
(2) preserve such records for such periods; and
(3) make such reports therefrom as the Commission shall prescribe by regulation or order.. . .

Similar record keeping is required of joint labor-management committees controlling apprenticeship or training programs. Pursuant to this section, the EEOC has formulated more specific record-keeping and reporting requirements. All employers subject to Title VII who have 100 or more employees must file an annual employer information report EEOC-1 with the Commission.[16] A copy of the most recent report filed must be retained by the employer and be available to the EEOC if it so requests. Employers making false statements in EEOC-1 reports violate 18 U.S.C. Section 1001 and are subject to fine or impi ,onment. The EEOC may obtain a court

[16]29 CFR §16-2.7.

order compelling a recalcitrant employer to file. In addition, the EEOC can require other nonstandard reports whenever it deems them necessary to accomplish the purpose of Title VII.

Although the EEOC does not have any specific requirements as to what records all employers must keep, it does have the right to set up such requirements for individual employers or groups of employers when it deems it necessary to accomplishing the purposes of Title VII. The EEOC Regulations and Guidelines require any personnel or employment records made or kept by an employer to be kept for 2 years from the date of the making of the record or the taking of the personnel action involved, whichever occurs later. When a charge of discrimination is filed against an employer under Title VII, the employer must preserve all records relevant to the charge until the matter reaches a final disposition.

Section 711(a) of Title VII provides that every employer "shall post and keep posted in conspicuous places upon its premises where notices to employees [and] applicants for employment . . . are customarily posted a notice to be prepared or approved by the Commission setting forth excerpts from or, summaries of, the pertinent provisions of [Title VII] and information pertinent to the filing of a complaint." The EEOC has prepared a standard notice for posting. Those failing to post it are punishable by a fine of not more than $100 for each separate offense.

EXECUTIVE ORDER NO. 11246

The executive branch of the federal government has sought to extend equal-employment-opportunity coverage to an increasing number of contractors. Executive Order No. 11246[17] establishes equal-employment-opportunity requirements applicable to most contractors entering into contracts with the federal government or performing under federally assisted construction contracts. Most government contracts which are in excess of $10,000 are to include special provisions, which include the equal-employment-opportunity clause:

(1) The contractor will not discriminate against any employee or applicant for employment because of race, color, religion, sex, or national origin. The contractor will take affirmative action to ensure the applicants are employed, and that employees are treated during employment, without regard to their race, color, religion, sex, national origin.
(2) The contractor will, in its solicitation of applicants for employment, state that all qualified applicants will receive consideration for employment without regard to race, color, religion, sex, or national origin.
(3) The contractor will send notice of its commitments under Executive Order No. 11246 to any union or representative or workers with which it has a collective bargaining contract, other contract or understanding.
(4) The contractor will comply with all provisions of Executive Order No. 11246 and with the ancillary rules, regulations, and relevant orders of the Secretary of Labor.

[17]30 F.R. 12319.

(5) In the event of the contractor's noncompliance with the nondiscrimination clauses of the contract or with any of the ancillary rules, regulations, or orders, the contract may be cancelled, terminated, or suspended, in whole or in part, and the contractor may be declared ineligible for further government contracts.

(6) The contractor will include all of the contractual provisions in every subcontract or purchase order so that the provisions will be binding upon each subcontractor or vendor.

Even if the requirements of this executive order are omitted from a construction contract, the equal-employment-opportunity clause will be deemed to be included by operation of law.

The terms of Executive Order No. 11246 charge the Secretary of Labor with its enforcement and administration. The actual administration of the order has been delegated to the Office of Federal Contract Compliance Programs (OFCCP), an administrative agency established within the Department of Labor.

Compliance with Executive Order No. 11246 involves more than the mere inclusion of equal-employment-opportunity clauses in appropriate federal contracts. For most contractors and subcontractors it involves taking the required affirmative action and reporting requirements. The OFCCP conducts compliance reviews to determine whether contractors or subcontractors are actually honoring their obligations under the order. Contractors and subcontractors are required to develop written affirmative-action programs to be in compliance with the order.

The OFCCP regulations require that every nonexempt prime contractor or subcontractor file an EEO-1 report on or before March 31 of each year. Specifically, a contractor must file if the contractor is subject to the requirements of Executive Order No. 11246, has fifty or more employees, is a prime contractor or a first-tier subcontractor, and has a contract, subcontract, or purchase order amounting to $50,000 or more. A contractor receiving an award of a contract must file an EEO-1 report within 30 days of the award of the contract unless the contractor has already submitted such a report within 12 months preceding the date of the award. Subsequent reports are to be submitted annually on or before March 31. Failure to file timely, complete, and accurate reports is deemed to be noncompliance with Executive Order No. 11246 and may make the contractor subject to sanctions.

Additional reporting requirements apply to bidders or prospective prime contractors or subcontractors. All such bidders or contractors must state, if applicable, whether they have developed and have on file an affirmative-action program, whether they have participated in any previous contract or subcontract subject to Executive Order No. 11246, and whether they have filed all required reports with all applicable agencies. It is important to stress that bidders or prospective prime contractors can be required to submit whatever information the OFCCP requests both prior to and after the award of the contract.

The OFCCP regulations prohibit segregated facilities of any type in contractors' operations, and the regulations require that prior to the award of a contract all nonexempt contractors must submit a certification that they do not and will not maintain any facilities for their employees in a segregated manner. In addition, all contractors must certify that none of their employees will be permitted to work in locations under their control where segregated facilities are maintained. A similar certification must be filed prior to the award of any nonexempt subcontract.

A compliance review is a comprehensive analysis of many aspects of a contractor's employment practices, policies, and conditions to determine whether the contractor maintains nondiscriminatory hiring and employment practices and is taking affirmative action to ensure that applicants and employees are not discriminated against on the basis of race, color, religion, sex, or national origin. If the award of the contract is equal to or more than $1 million, the contractor and the known first-tier subcontractor with subcontracts of $1 million or more will be subject to a compliance review prior to the award of the contract. No contract of $1 million or more may be awarded unless a preaward compliance review has been conducted within 12 months prior to the award.

Executive Order No. 11246 does not create a private cause of action whereby individuals may sue and obtain relief from unlawful employment practices. It does provide for the imposition of sanctions by the OFCCP when a contractor fails or refuses to comply with the order. These sanctions include cancellation, termination, or suspension of the contract or even complete debarment of the contractor from eligibility for future federal contracts. In addition, judicial proceedings may be instituted by the Department of Justice to obtain injunctive relief against noncomplying contractors. The OFCCP takes the position that back pay may be awarded to applicants denied employment in violation of the order. It is not certain whether this position will be accepted by the courts as a remedy authorized by Executive Order No. 11246.

AFFIRMATIVE-ACTION PLANS

Perhaps the most important and complex phase of compliance with Executive Order No. 11246 is the development and implementation of affirmative-action plans. Each contractor or subcontractor with fifty or more employees and a contract of $50,000 or more must develop a written affirmative-action program. A contractor must, within 120 days of the beginning of a contract, maintain a copy of separate affirmative-action plans for each of the contractor's establishments at each local office responsible for personnel matters. Very general requirements for the affirmative-action plans of construction contractors are set forth at 41 CFR Section 60-1.40. Construction contractors may also be subject to compliance with area plans or bid conditions. Nonconstruction contractors are subject to quite specific affirmative-action plan standards set forth at 41 CFR Section 60-2, which is also known as Revised Order No. 4.

An affirmative-action plan under Executive Order No. 11246 is a written program whereby a contractor provides in detail specific steps to guarantee equal employment opportunity. If the problems and needs of minority groups or women are involved, the plan must develop specific goals and timetables for the prompt achievement of full and equal employment opportunity. The plan may also integrate the affirmative-action requirements to achieve equal employment opportunity of handicapped individuals and employment of Vietnam era veterans. Each affirmative-action plan must include a table of the contractor's job classifications, including job titles, principal duties, and rates of pay. The plan must be signed by an executive of the contractor. In formulating the plan, the contractor must evaluate the utilization of minority groups and women in all job categories. The contractor's hiring, transfer, and promotion practices over the preceding year must be analyzed to determine whether equal employment opportunity is actually being afforded. In other words, the plan must include an analysis of areas in which the contractor is deficient in the utilization of minority groups and women. If a deficiency exists, the contractor must develop remedial goals and timetables to which good-faith efforts must be directed.

The following is an outline of suggested procedures to follow in developing an affirmative-action program which specifies the requirements of Executive Order 11246. Construction contractors affected by area plans or bid conditions must also comply with any requirements they impose. An *affirmative*-action program must be actively enforced. An affirmative-action plan that is passively enforced or administered does not comply with the law.

Contractors should start a file labeled "Equal Employment Opportunities" and maintain in it copies of all the information and materials which they have obtained concerning equal employment. Any additional information that relates to equal-opportunity employment should be placed in the file. A written "employment affirmative action commitment" should be made. The chief executive officer of the company should issue a policy statement indicating that it is the company's policy to hire qualified, reliable, and productive employees without regard to race, color, religion, sex, or national origin. While Executive Order No. 11141 requires contractors not to discriminate on the basis of age, there is no affirmative-action requirement. The company's commitment to a policy of compliance with equal-opportunity laws should be clearly stated. Specific items to be mentioned should include:

1. Recruiting, hiring, training, and promoting persons in all job classifications, without regard to race, color, religion, sex, age, or national origin except when sex is a bona fide occupational qualification

2. Basing decisions on employment so as to further the principle of equal employment opportunity

3. Ensuring that promotion decisions are in accord with the principle of equal employment opportunity and placing only valid neutral requirements on promotional opportunities

4. Ensuring that all personnel actions, such as compensation, benefits, transfers, layoffs, company-sponsored training, education, tuition assistance, and social and recreational programs, will be administered without regard to race, color, religion, sex, age, or national origin

The company policy statement should be publicized. Foremen, managers, and supervisors may be informed by written communication from the chief executive. All employees should be informed of the company policy through such means as posting the statement on bulletin boards, in areas near time clocks, at or near work areas, and in hiring offices or by providing copies of the affirmative-action policy statement directly to the employees, or both. Copies of the policy statement may also be sent to general contractors, subcontractors, vendors, and suppliers with which the company does business in order to inform them of its equal-employment policy.

An affirmative-action officer should be appointed as director or manager of the affirmative-action program to be responsible for the equal-employment-opportunities files, the affirmative-action program, and any matters involving equal-employment problems that may arise. A comprehensive job description should be drafted for this officer making it clear that he or she is more than just a token or a figurehead. The affirmative-action officer's responsibility should include developing the policy statement and a written affirmative-action program; assisting management in collecting and analyzing employment data, identifying problem areas, and setting goals and timetables; implementing reporting systems to measure the effectiveness of the affirmative-action program; and distributing current legal information on equal employment to responsible company officials.

All announcements, advertisments, or other company-related correspondence should indicate that the company is an equal-opportunity employer. It would be a good idea to indicate this on letterheads and other company designations. The company should draft a form letter which can be sent to any persons with whom it may negotiate or enter into a contract, informing them that the company is an equal-opportunity employer. A copy of this letter should be placed in the equal-opportunity file. The fact that the company is an equal-opportunity employer should be indicated in all advertisments for recruiting employees and in all contracts and correspondence with employment agencies.

Above all, the company should follow the affirmative-action program that has been adopted to show that it is an equal-opportunity employer. In essence, an affirmative-action program is a set of specific result-oriented procedures under which a contractor is committed to apply every good-faith effort. An acceptable affirmative-action program must include an analysis of areas in which the contractor is deficient in the utilization of minority groups and women as well as goals and timetables designed to correct the deficiencies and thus to increase materially the utilization of minorities and women at all levels and in all segments of the workforce.

IMPOSED PLANS

The requirements enumerated in Executive Order No. 11246 and its regulations are not the only affirmative-action measures required of contractors dealing with the federal government. Pursuant to the implied authority granted it by Executive Order No. 11246, the Department of Labor has imposed, in certain metropolitan areas, areawide affirmative-action plans applicable to bidders on federal or federally assisted contracts. As an example, the first imposed area plan was the Philadelphia Plan, which imposed upon bidders in a five-county Philadelphia area on federal or federally assisted projects in excess of $500,000 the requirement to submit an affirmative-action program with their bids. The plan submitted commits the bidder to the achievement of specific goals of minority labor utilization by taking affirmative action to reach annual numerical goals. These goals must be in conformity with the areawide goals set for the area by the OFCCP. The Philadelphia Plan also set a requirement that a contractor who agrees to the achievement of employment goals must use "every good-faith effort" to attain those goals. The Philadelphia Plan listed examples of minimum good-faith efforts. Such steps include the notification of community organizations which have agreed to refer minority applicants to opportunities for employment and the contractor's utilization of training programs of craftsmen in the trades involved. The terms of the Philadelphia Plan indicate that a contractor who has made good-faith efforts to meet the requisite hiring goals is in compliance with the plan even if no minority employees have been hired. This, however, does not mean that token recruitment efforts resulting in no minority hiring would suffice for compliance. The key is the employer's good faith.

There have been other imposed areawide plans since the Philadelphia Plan. Most of the subsequent plans have been quite similar to the Philadelphia Plan, applying to contracts on projects the estimated cost of which exceeds $500,000. The plans have generally tightened the hiring steps to be taken by contractors for them to be acting in good faith. As a result of the furor which accompanied the imposition of the Philadelphia Plan, the Department of Labor imposed other areawide plans only when the appropriate parties have failed to formulate a voluntary hometown affirmative-action program. Thus, the number of imposed plans was small, and such plans were of practical importance only to contractors within an area to which such a plan was applicable.

In the years since the promulgation of the Philadelphia Plan, the alternative to an imposed plan was the hometown plan. Affirmative-action plans of this type were developed as agreements between area unionized contractors, local unions, and the ostensible representative of the local minority community. Hometown plans were approved by the OFCCP and contained employment goals negotiated by the signatories. The goals set were tradewide goals for percentages of minority and women employees and were not formulated as requirements that individual contractors achieve set percentages of minority or women employees. Thus, a contractor who signed the agreement met only its reasonable portion of the plan's overall areawide goals. In 1978 the OFCCP promulgated new regulations[18] which completely restructured preexisting affirmative-action requirements for contractors holding federal construction contracts and which included for the first time affirmative-action requirements and goals for employment of women by construction contractors. These regulations abolished the system of using imposed plans for certain geographical areas, such as Philadelphia, Atlanta, and Washington, and special bid conditions for substantial projects in areas not covered by imposed plans or hometown plans, and substituted a uniform system of solicitation notices and specifications to govern affirmative-action requirements in every locality that is not covered by an approved hometown plan.

In addition, these regulations apply to the entire workforce of all contractors or subcontractors who hold a federal or federally assisted construction contract in excess of $10,000 rather than simply to projects on which the total exceeds $500,000, as was the case with the prior regulations. The regulations set goals for the employment of females as well as racial minorities and provide that efforts must be made to meet goals for each particular group, for example, females and all minorities. The regulations provide for debarment of contractors who are found in violation and provide that no contractor covered by the regulations may enter into any contract with a debarred contractor. These regulations took effect on May 8, 1978, and set a goal of 3.1 percent employment of women in construction after 1 year, 5 percent after 2 years, and 6.9 percent after the third year.

Other than the inclusion of female affirmative-action requirements, the most sweeping change was that these regulations apply to every contractor or subcontractor holding a contract or subcontract for federal work or federally assisted work, which contract is in excess of $10,000, including construction contracts entered into between a construction contractor and a federal nonconstruction contractor when the construction work is necessary in whole or in part to the performance of that nonconstruction contractor. Once a contractor is covered by the regulations, they apply to all the contractors's employees actually engaged in on-site construction, and part of the affirmative-action requirements are that the minority and female employees of the contractor must be spread out over all the projects on which the contractor is engaged, both federal and nonfederal.

A notice setting forth the requirements of regulations and specific standard federal equal-employment-opportunity construction contract specifications must be included in any solicitation for bids put out by federal contracting officers, applicants for federal funds, and federal nonconstruction contractors soliciting bids. The OFCCP must be notified within 10 days of the specifics of any contract awarded subject to these regulations. In addition, the notice provides that all contractors holding a con-

[18]41 CFR Pt. 60-4.

tract subject to the regulations must notify the OFCCP within 10 working days of the award of any subcontract in excess of $10,000 resulting from the same solicitation. To enforce the regulations, there is provision for an administrative show-cause procedure to call the accused contractor before the OFCCP. As an alternative, the Department of Justice may proceed against the contractor under the enforcement provisions of Section 209(a)(2) of Executive Order 11246, upon which the regulations are based.

The regulations specifically provide that the provisions of a collective bargaining agreement or failure by a union to refer either minorities or women is no defense to the contractor in an enforcement action and add that the contractor has the affirmative duty to provide immediate written notification to the OFCCP when the union has not referred to the contractor a minority person or a woman sent by the contractor or when the contractor "has other information that the union referral process has impeded the contractor's efforts to meet the obligations" under the regulations. This introduces an area of great danger to the contractor, both in determining whether to "report" the union to the OFCCP and in calculating how hard the contractor should push with the union itself to provide women and minorities. The employer is thrust in the middle between the union and the OFCCP and required to make very difficult practical decisions.

The regulations also provide that the contractor must "insure and maintain a working environment free of harrassment, intimidation and coercion at all sites," including assigning two or more women to each project. This requirement sets no standard of conduct which can be measured in the field, only good faith. Another tremendous burden created by these new regulations is in record keeping, although the preamble to the regulations professes that no specific record-keeping formats are established. Nevertheless, the contractor must (1) establish and maintain a list of minority and female recruitment sources; (2) provide written notification to the sources when any employment opportunities are available; (3) maintain a record of the responses from such organizations to such notices; (4) maintain a file of each minority and female off-the-street applicant; (5) maintain a written record of each minority or female referral from a union or recruitment source and of what action was taken with respect to each such individual; (6) as stated previously, provide written notification to the OFCCP when the contractor believes that the union is failing to refer minorities or females or is otherwise impeding the contractor's obligations in that regard; (7) document its development or participation in on-the-job or other training programs which expressly include minorities and women; (8) include the contractor's equal-employment-opportunity policy in notices to unions and recruitment sources, policy manual, collective bargaining agreement, company newspaper, and annual report, and on the company's bulletin boards; (9) document meetings in which equal-employment-opportunity policies are reviewed at least annually with each of the employees who have any responsibilities concerning employment; (10) document dissemination of the company's equal-employment-opportunity policy externally in the news media; (11) document the notice, no later than 30 days before the beginning of any training program, to female and community organizations and schools and other minority and female recruitment organizations; (12) document an annual examination of all minority and female personnel for promotion; (13) document and maintain a record of all solicitations of offers for subcontracts from minority and female construction contractors and suppliers; and (14) document an annual review of all supervisors' adherence to the requirements of the company's equal-employment-opportunity policy and these regulations.

The regulations specifically provide that contractor trade associations may substitute their efforts for those of individual contractors in meeting the affirmative-action requirements but that each contractor in such associations is still individually responsible for the contractor's own affirmative-action requirements should the association's efforts fail to comply fully.

The regulations are very specific in providing that a contractor must take affirmative action for each specific minority group, both female and male, or for women, both minority and nonminority. Consequently, the contractor may have achieved its goals or otherwise acted in good faith regarding women and a particular minority group but may still be in violation of the regulations for not having achieved the requirements of the regulations concerning another minority group which is employed in a substantially disparate manner.

HANDICAP DISCRIMINATION

The Rehabilitation Act of 1973[19] is of importance to almost all contractors doing work or providing services pursuant to federal contracts. The act protects persons against employment discrimination in federally funded programs on the basis of handicaps. It also requires that any federal contract or subcontract in excess of $2500 contain a provision that, in employing persons to carry out the contract, the contractor will take affirmative action to employ and advance in employment qualified handicapped individuals.[20] Federal contractors and subcontractors to whom the act applies must not discriminate against applicants for employment or employees on the basis of a handicap.

The Rehabilitation Act of 1973 requires federal contractors and subcontractors to develop affirmative-action programs aimed at the achievement of equal employment opportunity for handicapped individuals. This requirement is applicable to every government contractor or subcontractor holding a contract of $50,000 or more and having fifty or more employees. An affirmative-action plan pursuant to the act may be integrated into or kept separate from other affirmative-action plans of the contractor. Be-

[19]29 U.S.C. §701 *et seq.*
[20]29 U.S.C. §793(a).

cause the type of plan to be developed for compliance with the Rehabilitation Act will be similar to other affirmative-action plans required of federal contractors, integration of plans is advisable. The format for the type of plan needed under the act is basically the same as that of an affirmative-action plan for compliance with Executive Order No. 11246, except that there are no goals.

The basic components of a contractor's affirmative-action obligation under the act are set forth in an OFCCP regulation.[21] The following list illustrates some of the most important steps required.

1. Review personnel processes to determine whether present procedures assure proper consideration of all applicants. Take steps to assure that this will be done.

2. Develop and adhere to a schedule for reviewing all physical or mental job requirements. Make certain that if such qualification requirements exclude handicapped individuals, they are job-related and are consistent with business necessity and the safe performance of the job.

3. Make reasonable accommodations to the physical and mental limitations of handicapped employees or applicants unless it can be demonstrated that this would impose an undue hardship on the business.

4. Take active steps to recruit handicapped individuals from the local community.

The Rehabilitation Act of 1973 does not give an aggrieved individual the right to sue a contractor directly. The act does provide that any handicapped individual believing that a contractor has failed or is refusing to comply with contractual obligations relating to the employment of handicapped individuals may file a complaint with the Director of the OFCCP.[22] When a complaint is filed, the OFCCP will investigate, and if the charges are deemed to be well founded, it will attempt to secure compliance through conciliation and persuasion. If this attempt is unsuccessful, the Director of the OFCCP may seek judicial action, either to enforce the contractual clause proscribing handicap discrimination or to enjoin the contractor from violating the clause. The OFCCP may also attempt to secure compliance by withholding progress payments on contracts, and it may cancel a contract in whole or in part. As an ultimate sanction, recalcitrant contractors may be debarred from receiving future contracts for failure to comply with their affirmative-action obligations.

Many states also have laws protecting the handicapped in the employment context. All contractors should take steps to ascertain whether any state laws are applicable to their operations.

EMPLOYMENT OF VETERANS

The 1974 amendments to the Vietnam Era Veteran's Readjustment Assistance Act of 1972[23] impose duties upon federal contractors and subcontrac-

[21]41 CFR §60-741.

[22]29 U.S.C. §733(b).

[23]38 U.S.C. §2011 et seq.

tors with regard to the employment of disabled veterans and Vietnam era veterans. Every federal contract of $10,000 or more must contain provisions that the contractor will not discriminate against any employee or applicant for employment because he or she is a disabled veteran or veteran of the Vietnam era and that the contractor will take "affirmative action to employ and advance in employment qualified disabled veterans and veterans of the Vietnam era."[24] This provision is also applicable to any subcontract entered into by a prime contractor subject to the requirements of the act.

The affirmative-action obligations of contractors under the Vietnam Era Veterans' Readjustment Assistance Act are contained in the regulations of the OFCCP.[25] All federal contractors or subcontractors holding a contract of $50,000 or more and having fifty or more employees are required to develop and maintain affirmative-action plans at each of their establishments. As with affirmative-action plans under the Rehabilitation Act or 1973, an affirmative-action plan for Vietnam veterans may be incorporated into a contractor's other affirmative-action plans. The OFCCP regulations[26] will be helpful in showing the structure of a basic affirmative-action plan which may be adapted so as to conform to the requirements of the act. Some of the most important steps of an affirmative action plan under the Vietnam Era Veterans' Readjustment Assistance Act which the contractor must undertake are:

1. Take affirmative action to employ and advance in employment qualified disabled veterans and veterans of the Vietnam era at all levels of employment and in all phases of employment operations.

2. Review personnel processes to determine whether they assure careful, thorough, and systematic consideration of the job qualifications of known disabled veteran applicants and Vietnam era applicants for job vacancies filled by either hiring or promoting.

3. Develop and adhere to a schedule for reviewing all physical or mental job requirements. Make certain that such qualification requirements exclude qualified disabled veterans, they are job-related and are consistent with business necessity and the safe performance of the job.

4. Make a reasonable accommodation to the physical and mental limitations of a disabled veteran unless the contractor can demonstrate that such an accommodation would impose an undue hardship on the conduct of the contractor's business.

5. Undertake appropriate outreach and positive recruitment activities in the community.

6. Adopt, implement, and disseminate company policy internally so as to make supervisors and employees aware that such a program is in effect.

The Vietnam Era Veterans' Readjustment Assistance Act states that any disabled veteran or veteran of the Vietnam era who believes that a contractor has failed or is refusing to comply with contractual affirmative-

[24] 38 U.S.C. §2012(a).
[25] At 41 CFR §60-250.
[26] At 41 CFR §60-250.

action duties may file a complaint with the Veterans Employment Service of the Department of Labor.[27] The complaint will be referred to the contractor if the contractor has an internal-review procedure. If no internal resolution is reached, the complaint will be referred to the OFCCP, which will attempt to secure compliance through conciliation and persuasion within a reasonable time. If these informal settlement procedures fail, the Director of the OFCCP is empowered to seek appropriate judicial action to force the contractor to adhere to affirmative-action obligations. The Director may also withhold progress payments to the contractor, terminate the contract in whole or in part, or debar the contractor from receiving future federal contracts for failure to comply with the provisions of the affirmative-action clause. Like the Rehabilitation Act, the Vietnam Era Veterans' Readjustment Assistance Act does not provide a private cause of action to permit an aggrieved individual to sue an offending employer.

AGE DISCRIMINATION

The past few years have seen a growing movement and concern for protecting older persons from employment discrimination based upon age. The Age Discrimination in Employment Act of 1967[28] (ADEA) provides a statutory basis for the prevention and remedying of cases of age discrimination. It is applicable to all employers engaged in an industry affecting commerce and having twenty or more employees for each working day in each of 20 or more calendar weeks in the current or preceding calendar year. Many contractors fall within its scope. Section 623 of the ADEA makes it unlawful for an employer:

(1) to fail or refuse to hire or to discharge any individual or otherwise discriminate against any individual with respect to his compensation, terms, conditions, or privileges of employment, because of such individual's age;
(2) to limit, segregate, or classify his employees in any way which would deprive or tend to deprive any individual of employment opportunities or otherwise adversely affect his status as an employee, because of such individual's age; or
(3) to reduce the wage rate of any employee in order to comply with [the ADEA].

These general prohibitions mean that virtually all forms of employment discrimination against individuals based upon age are forbidden. It is also unlawful for an employer to discriminate or retaliate against employees or applicants for employment who have opposed unlawful age discrimination by the employer or who have participated in any way in investigations, proceedings, or litigation under the ADEA. Finally, the ADEA proscribes employer job advertising which indicates any preference, limitation, specification, or discrimination, based on age.

The ADEA was formerly applicable to age discrimination involving employees at least 40 years of age but less than 65. Congress amended the

[27]28 U.S.C. §2012(b).
[28]29U.S.C. § 621 *et seq.*

ADEA in April 1978, and the act now prohibits age discrimination against individuals who are at least 40 years of age but less than 70 years old. It should be noted that the ADEA applies to age discrimination between individuals even if all the individuals involved are within the age bracket of 40 to 70. Thus, it is unlawful for an employer to give an age-based preference to a 30-year-old individual over an individual from 40 to 70 years old, and it is equally unlawful to give such an age preference to an individual within the age bracket from 40 to 70 years over another individual within the same protected age bracket.[29]

The ADEA is quite similar to Title VII in what it permits as lawful differentiation between individuals even when age is involved as a determining factor. Section 623(f) allows an employer to take action based upon the age of individuals if this is a bona fide occupational qualification reasonably necessary to the normal operation of the particular business. It also permits differentiation between employees according to the terms of a bona fide seniority system or employee benefit plan, as long as such a plan is not a subterfuge designed to evade the ADEA. No employee benefit plan will be an excuse for failing to hire an individual because of that individual's age.

In addition to changing the age bracket to which the ADEA applies, the 1978 amendments to the act added a proviso that no seniority system or employee benefit plan may lawfully require or permit the involuntary retirement of any individual because of age prior to the age of 70. The amendments do permit the compulsory retirement of employees who are at least 65 but not 70 and who, for the 2 years immediately before retirement, have been employed as bona fide executives or in high policy-making positions and entitled to pension benefits of at least $27,000.

The ADEA creates a private cause of action for individuals who are discriminated against in the employment context on the basis of age. An aggrieved individual may sue for monetary damages, including back pay, or for injunctive relief. Prior to filing suit, a person alleging that he or she has been discriminated against on the basis of age must file a charge within 180 days of the alleged discrimination. The Secretary of Labor will seek to resolve the dispute by mediation and conciliation. If this fails, the individual has recourse to the courts. The Secretary may also institute legal proceedings seeking injunctive relief for age discrimination. When this occurs, the individual's right to sue ends. In any event, employers violating the ADEA may face liability for monetary relief as well as injunctive measures.

EQUAL PAY ACT

The Equal Pay Act of 1963[30] is an amendment to the Fair Labor Standards Act of 1938 (FLSA).[31] It provides protection against cases of sex-based

[29] 29 CFR §890.91.
[30] 29 R.S.C. §206(d).
[31] 29 U.S.C. §201 et seq.

discrimination in which an employer pays lower wages to employees of one sex when the work done by employees of both sexes is the same. The act makes it unlawful for an employer whose employees are subject to the FLSA to discriminate "between employees on the basis of sex by paying wages to employees . . . at a rate less than the rate at which he pays wages to employees of the opposite sex [in the same place of work] for equal work on jobs the performance of which requires equal skill, effort, and responsibility, and which are performed under similar working conditions.. . .[32] The act allows a payment differential if it is based upon a seniority system, a merit system, or a system measuring earnings by quantity or quality of production or if it is based upon any factor other than sex. An employer faced with a suit under the Equal Pay Act may successfully defend if the employer can prove the allegedly unlawful wage differential falls within one of these four exceptions. When an employer is violating the act by paying an unlawful sex-based wage rate differential, the employer may not reduce the wage rate of any employee to achieve compliance.

Because the Equal Pay Act is part of the FLSA, it deals only with sex-based wage rate discrimination. Protection against other forms of sex-based employment discrimination is found in Title VII and in Executive Order No. 11246, as amended by Executive Order No. 11375. As part of the FLSA, the Equal Pay Act applies to all employees and enterprises subject to the minimum wage provisions of the FLSA. Thus, a contractor whose employees are covered by the FLSA as to minimum wages will also be required to comply with the Equal Pay Act's proscription of sex-based wage discrimination. It should be mentioned that the Equal Pay Act applies to bona fide executive, administrative, professional, and outside sales employees even though such employees are otherwise exempted from coverage under the FLSA. Therefore, as a practical matter few employees of a contractor will be exempted from the provisions of the Equal Pay Act.

The FLSA gives a private cause of action to aggrieved individuals. This cause of action is applicable to persons or classes of persons alleging a violation of the Equal Pay Act. A plaintiff may sue and recover unpaid wages or overtime compensation. If the employer is shown to have acted in bad faith, the plaintiff can recover an additional amount equal to the amount otherwise recoverable. An employer found to be violating the Equal Pay Act may also be subject to injunctive relief in suits brought by individuals, classes, or the Secretary of Labor. The Secretary is also empowered to sue on behalf of individuals for monetary relief. When this occurs, an individual's right to sue is preempted. In addition to the civil sanctions, there is a criminal penalty for violation of the Equal Pay Act. Any person convicted of a willful violation is subject to a fine of not more than $10,000 or imprisonment for not more than 6 months, or both. Imposition of these penalties is extremely rare.

---

[32] 29 U.S.C. §206(d)(1).

15 OCCUPATIONAL SAFETY AND HEALTH ACT

The Occupational Safety and Health Act (OSHA) of 1970 was passed by Congress for the declared purpose of "assur[ing] so far as possible every working man and woman in the Nation safe and healthful working conditions and to preserve our human resources." Because the provisions of this law and its implementing regulations are so broad and complex, this chapter will not cover all provisions of the the law, such as record-keeping requirements and variance procedures. Rather, the citation and enforcement procedures will be emphasized.

The OSHA applies to all employers in a business affecting commerce, which encompasses essentially every employer in the United States. The United States, individual states, and political subdivisions of a state are excluded from the coverage of the act, and certain other limited exclusions apply to employers who are already covered by extensive federal safety laws and regulations, such as the Atomic Energy Act and the Federal Coal Mine Health and Safety Act.

Although the "employer" subject to the requirements of the act usually encompasses only the corporation, partnership, or proprietorship which actually employs the workers involved, there is some authority for also holding corporate officers and stockholders liable for violations. Thus far such liability has been found only in limited circumstances, but every partner, corporate officer, director, and stockholder should be aware of the potential for personal liability. If a death has occurred, this liability could even reach down to lower-level supervisors and foremen responsible for the working conditions of the fatally injured worker.

The administration and enforcement of the act have been delegated to the Secretary of Labor and a new administrative agency, the Occupational Safety and Health Administration. The administration and enforcement scheme is without parallel in the history of the United States.

The OSHA undoubtedly has a widening effect on most businesses. Each employer must educate both its supervisors and labor in the requirements of the regulations, institute and enforce by discipline company safety rules, and review citations while weighing the amount of penalties, the possibility of repeat conditions, the feasibility of abating the conditions, the availability of defenses, and the possibility of a civil suit growing out of the same conditions. The OSHA is a legal and regulatory thicket into which no employer should venture without reliable, up-to-date advice and guidance.

RULE MAKING

The act empowers the Secretary of Labor to make regulations having the force of law, with which employers are thereby required strictly to comply. Such regulations, called by the act "occupational safety and health standards," are defined as standards requiring "*conditions,* or the adoption or use of one or more *practices, means, methods, operations,* or *processes, reasonably necessary* or appropriate to provide safe or healthful employment and places of employment" (emphasis added). This definition is very broad but also is severely limited by the "reasonably necessary" clause; however, no court has yet interpreted the meaning of that clause or struck down any regulation in violation of it. There have been a few cases in which the Secretary's interpretation of a regulation was rejected because it was found that the standard would not be reasonable if it were interpreted and applied to working conditions in the manner urged by the OSHA.

Illustrative Case

A roofing manufacturer was cited for violation of the health standard on coal tar pitch volatiles by reason of excessive asphalt fumes in its plant. A regulation defines "coal tar pitch volatiles" as including the derivatives of petroleum as well as coal. On the basis of evidence that asphalt and coal tar pitch are completely different substances chemically and that their effects on the health of animals and humans are completely different, it was found that the regulation was unreasonable, and the citation was vacated.[1]

In making a new regulation, the Occupational Health and Safety Administration (OSHA) must first publish a proposal in the *Federal Register* and afford a period for public comments on it. If a public hearing is requested within the comment period, OSHA must hold such a hearing to receive comments. In addition, OSHA may appoint any advisory committee to review the proposal, whose recommendation may or may not be followed.

The last step is the publication of the standard itself, which may or may not become effective on the date of its publication. Together with this publication, OSHA must explain its reasons for publishing the standard, as well as its reasoning on decisions on significant issues raised either by commentators or by OSHA in its own proposal. Failure to explain the reasons adequately could be grounds for setting aside the regulation if an employer contests the regulation in court.

Illustrative Case

OSHA promulgated a regulation limiting exposures to 14 chemicals claimed to be cancer-causing, which was contested in court by several employers and trade associations. The

[1] *GAF Corp.,* Case No. W6259-003-77 (Maryland Dept. of Licensing and Regulation, Hearing Examiner Dec. Oct. 26, 1977).

regulation was vacated and sent back to OSHA for additional work, because OSHA failed to state what evidence it relied upon in finding the chemicals to be carcinogens, and it also failed to state the reasons why the protective measures required by the regulation were necessary to protect employees from the harmful effects of the chemicals.[2]

Even if a full statement of reasons is included in the publication, the regulation may still be invalid if it is found that there is no substantial evidence in the record of the rule-making proceeding to support either the conclusions and findings of OSHA or the requirements of the standard. "Substantial evidence" basically means that there must be enough evidence to reach an objective conclusion that OSHA carried out its essential legislative rule-making function in a reasonable manner, considering the evidence actually before it.

Illustrative Case

OSHA adopted an emergency standard on certain pesticides, which was challenged in court by both employers and unions representing their employees. Even though the record consisted of transcripts, articles, and various other documents comprising approximately 2½ feet of shelf space, the regulation was set aside because there was not substantial evidence to prove a "grave danger" to employees, one of the conditions for adopting an emergency standard. Evidence of the inherent toxicity of the pesticides and of statistics indicating illnesses and deaths attributed to these substances was found insufficient, because this evidence did not prove that the pesticides were dangers in the *manner* in which they were *used* by the employers and employees affected by the standard.[3]

STANDARDS OF CONDUCT WITH WHICH EMPLOYERS MUST COMPLY

The act imposes the general duty on each employer to "furnish to each of his employees employment and place or employment which are free from recognized hazards that are causing or likely to cause death or serious physical harm to his employee." This is commonly called the "general-duty clause," and this vague and ambiguous language has become a catchall requirement upon which OSHA inspectors base violations when they cannot find that the employer has violated any specific standard applicable to the particular hazard involved. Regulations provide that an employer who is in compliance with specific safety and health standards shall be deemed to be in compliance with the general-duty clause insofar as it applies to hazards covered by specific standards. However, any recognized hazard created in part by conditions not covered by a standard may be the basis for a citation under the general-duty clause.

For OSHA to prove a violation of the general-duty clause, a "recognized hazard" must be shown. What is a recognized hazard is measured by the common knowledge of safety experts who are familiar with the circumstances of the industry or activity in question.

[2] *Dry Color Mfrs. Ass'n, Inc. v. Department of Labor et al.*, 486 F.2d 99 (3d Cir. 1973).
[3] *Florida Peach Growers Ass'n, Inc. v. Brennan et al.*, 489 F.2d 120 (5th Cir. 1974).

Illustrative Case

After an inspection revealed three employees disassembling an oil rig, working off steel beams 125 feet high, OSHA issued the employer a citation for exposing the employees to the "recognized hazard" of a fall from the drilling rig. The employer contested, and the evidence showed that derrick men working with both hands for extended periods of time on the rig were tied off with safety belts, while employees rigging down an oil derrick did not customarily wear tied-off safety belts, because they could hang on with a free hand and were aloft for only short periods of time. On the basis of the fact that the latter work was not considered hazardous in the industry, for the above reasons as well as others, it was found that OSHA failed to prove that the practice at issue was recognized as hazardous.[4]

Further, OSHA must prove that the recognized hazard could be eliminated from the workplace by specified means of protection. Again, the standard of proof is whether the precaution specified by OSHA is recognized as feasible by safety experts familiar with the industry.

Illustrative Case

An employer was charged with a violation of the general-duty clause after a foreman was killed while riding on the running board of a piece of heavy construction equipment. It was found that, while this practice was a recognized hazard, the employer had a safety policy which prohibited it, and OSHA did not show what else the employer could feasibly have done that would have been practical and would have helped to prevent the practice. The citation was accordingly vacated.[5]

Because of this often torturous requirement of proof to uphold a violation of the general-duty clause, a question has been raised about its constitutionality. To date, only California has declared its own general-duty clause in its state code unconstitutional.

There are two types of express standards with which employers must comply: "general standards," which are applicable to all employers, contained in Title 29, Code of Federal Regulations, Part 1910; and "particular standards," applicable to specific industries, such as the Safety and Health Regulation for Construction contained in Title 29, Code of Federal Regulations, Part 1926. An employer in the construction or maritime industry or other industry for which particular standards may be promulgated must comply with the general standards in areas in which no particular safety standards are applicable to the condition. If a particular standard for a specific industry is applicable to a safety condition, that particular standard prevails over another standard which might otherwise be applicable under the general industry standards. Also, even within a set of specific industry standards, such as the construction industry standards, a specific standard applicable to a condition or part of a workplace will prevail over a more general construction standard which would otherwise be applicable to the same condition or workplace. To eliminate some of the confusion over which general standards may apply to construction sites, OSHA has pub-

[4] *Penrod Drilling Co.*, OSHRC Docket No. 5991, 4 BNA OSHC 1654 (1976).

[5] *National Realty & Constr. Co., v. OSHRC et al.*, 489 F.2d 1257 (D.C. Cir. 1973).

lished a "vertical" set of construction standards to encompass all standards applicable to construction.[6]

Illustrative Case

A steel erection contractor was erecting the structural steel of a penthouse type of structure on top of a high-rise building. Its employees were working on open steel 11 feet and 22 feet above the uppermost completed floor of the building without using tied-off safety belts. OSHA cited the contractor for a violation of Section 1926.28(a), a construction industry standard generally requiring the use of safety belts in "hazardous conditions." It was determined that there were a separate set of specific standards within the construction standards applicable only to steel erection work and that the employer was in compliance with all the fall protection requirements of these standards because of the heights at which the employees were working. Accordingly, the application of these specific standards was held to prevail over Section 1926.28(a), and the citation was vacated.[7]

There are severe penalties for failure to comply with each standard, and a violation of a subsection of the standards constitutes a separate violation for which an employer can be cited. For example, an employer can be cited for each condition of a scaffolding that does not comply with the subsection of a particular standard. Specifically, scaffolding more than 10 feet aboveground without a midrail on its platform is a violation for which an employer may be cited, and if scaffolding planks do not extend over the edge supports by more than 6 inches and less than 18 inches the scaffolding also violates another subsection. There may be dozens of other ways in which scaffolding may not comply with subsections of particular standards applicable to scaffolding, and an employer may receive a citation for each subsection violated, with total penalties from one inspection of nonconforming scaffolding amounting to substantial sums of money.

Two very similar "personal protective equipment" standards, one in the general OSHA standards and one in the construction industry standards, also raise severe compliance problems for employers because they constitute "little general-duty clauses" which offer little guidance to employers. However, the courts have ruled, as in the case of the general-duty clause, that these standards can be construed to prohibit only conduct which reasonably falls within the common understanding and practices of those working in the industry and against which, therefore, a reasonably prudent person familiar with the circumstances of the industry would have used protective measures.

Illustrative Case

An electric power company was cited by OSHA for failure to require its employees to use proper personal protective equipment when one of its linemen did not completely cover high-voltage lines close to him and was electrocuted by one of those lines. The reviewing court, recognizing that OSHA proved that an accident *did* occur, that more protective

[6]44 Fed. Reg 8577 (Feb. 9, 1979).

[7]*Williams Enterprises of Ga., Inc.*, OSHRC Docket No. 13063, 5 BNA OSHC 2040 (1977).

covering *could* have been used, and that more protective covering *might* have prevented the accident, nevertheless vacated the citation on the ground that OSHA did not produce evidence from witnesses familiar with the industry to show that the lineman did not act prudently in the circumstances. On the contrary, the employer's evidence established that the type of work which the lineman was doing did not require him to come into close proximity with the wires and that further protection was therefore unnecessary.[8]

Again, as with the general-duty clause, for OSHA to prove a violation of the personal protective equipment standard, it must show what specific measures an employer should have taken and the feasibility and utility of those measures. On these questions, the customs and practices of the industry are extremely pertinent, if not controlling.

Illustrative Case

An employer was cited for failure to require employees working on a flat roof to use tied-off safety belts. On evidence that it was not customary in the industry to use safety belts in those circumstances and that employees considered such use not practical, the citation was vacated.[9]

PENALTIES

The law provides for both civil and criminal penalties for various kinds of conduct, including violations of the standards or the general-duty clause. For a willful violation causing the death of an employee, the act provides for a criminal fine of not more than $10,000 or imprisonment of up to 6 months, or both. Upon a second conviction for a willful violation, involving a death, an employer may be fined up to $20,000 or imprisoned up to 1 year, or both. A civil penalty of not more than $10,000 is authorized for an employer who willfully or repeatedly violates the act or standards.

A "willful" violation is defined by the courts as conduct which is an intentional, knowing, or voluntary violation, as distinguished from accidental conduct, and may even result from careless disregard for whether or not the conduct violates the act. A malicious intent or a "flaunting" of the act is not required for a willful violation to exist.

Illustrative Case

An employer was cited for piling loose dirt too close to the edge of a trench. The employer defended on the ground that the soil had to be kept at that location so as not to interfere with nearby traffic and that the soil at the edge acted as a barricade against bad drivers and water entering the trench. The employer admitted knowledge of the standard and of the fact that the employer's conduct violated the express terms of the standard. On this basis, the employer's conduct, although it did not constitute an obstinate refusal to comply with the standard or a flaunting of the standard, was found to be a willful violation.[10]

[8] *Cape 2 Vineyard Div. of New Bedford Gas and Edison Light Co. v. OSHRC et al.*, 512 F.2d 1148 (1st Cir. 1975).

[9] *Croom Constr. Co.*, OSHRC Docket No. 12686, 5 BNA OSHC 1145 (1977).

[10] *Kent Nowlin Constr., Inc.*, OSHRC Docket Nos. 9483, 9485, and 9522, 5 BNA OSHC 1051 (1977).

However, if there is a mere difference in opinion between an employer and an OSHA inspector as to whether a violation exists and the employer proceeds on the basis of the employer's own opinion the employer's conduct does not constitute a willful violation even though it may later be determined to be in violation of the act or a standard.

Illustrative Case

An employer digging a trench without complete shoring on the bottom was inspected by OSHA. OSHA cited the employer for lack of shoring because its inspector believed the soil at the bottom to be soft and unstable, and its inspector so informed the employer's representatives on the worksite. The employer believed the soil to be hardpan, in which case no shoring would be required by the applicable regulations. When the OSHA inspector returned several days later and found essentially the same conditions, he cited the employer for a willful violation of the shoring requirements. The employer contested, and the violation was found not to be willful, because an employer is entitled to hold his own good-faith opinion that he is in compliance even after being informed by OSHA that OSHA feels otherwise.[11]

A "repeated" violation differs from a failure to abate in that the repeated violation exists when the employer has abated an earlier violation and, upon later inspection, is found to have committed a new violation of the same standard. What is repeated is still uncertain after almost 7 years under the act. One court to consider the question ruled that it applied to the conduct of an employer who violated a standard more than twice and whose conduct flaunted the standard's requirements. A second court disagreed with both prongs of the first court's test. The Occupational Safety and Health Review Commission (OSHRC) has not yet been able to get a majority to agee on whether flaunting conduct is part of a repeated violation.

Illustrative Case

An employer was cited for failure to keep aisles and passageways clear on a worksite, and the citation was not contested. Later, on an inspection of a similar worksite of the same employer, the same condition was found, and OSHA cited a repeated violation. It was determined by the reviewing court that the second violation was not repeated because the word *repeatedly* means many times, not just twice, and because the legislative history of the act shows that Congress meant to penalize only flagrant flaunting violations of the act with the penalties assigned to repeated violations.[12]

A civil penalty of up to $1000 may be assessed for each serious violation. Under the terms of the act a "serious violation" is deemed to exist in a place of employment if there is a substantial probability that death or serious physical harm could result from a condition which exists there or from one or more practices, means, methods, operations, or processes which have been adopted or are in use in such place of employment unless the

[11] *Northeastern Contracting Co.*, OSHRC Docket No. 1409, 2 BNA OSHC 1539 (1975).

[12] *Bethlehem Steel Corp. v. OSHRC et al.*, 540 F.2d 157 (3rd Cir. 1976).

employer did not and could not with the exercise of reasonable diligence know of the presence of the violation. What all that means is that there are two elements that an inspector must consider in determining whether or not a violation is a serious violation: First, is there "a substantial probability that death or serious physical harm" will result? Second, did the employer know or with "reasonable diligence" should have known of the hazard?

As to the first element, if the more likely consequence is that an injury less than death or serious physical harm will result, the violation is not serious. However, the term "likely" used in this element is slightly misleading, because the rule developed by the courts is that no matter how improbable it is that an injury would occur at all, if that injury would most likely be a serious one, then the violation is serious.

Illustrative Case

An employer unloading cargo from ships was cited for leaving a hatch beam in place and unsecured while unloading through the hatch, exposing its employees to the danger of the beam's dislodging and falling. Although the evidence showed that the chances that the beam would dislodge were remote, it was just as clear that if the beam did dislodge, it would cause death or serious physical harm to the employees affected. This was determined to be sufficient evidence to prove a serious violation.[13]

To determine whether the employer "knew or should have known of the hazard," the test in general is that standard of diligence of a reasonable and prudent employer who is safety conscious and who possesses the technical expertise which would normally be expected of an employer engaged in that particular business. Thus, if a reasonably prudent employer took all steps and precautions which were reasonably possible to eliminate hazards in the workplace and yet a hazard or hazards remained because of a breakdown by the employees in effectuating the safety program and policies of the employer, the employer would not be liable for such violations because of a lack of knowledge.

Illustrative Case

An employer, a sole proprietor, left a construction worksite under the control of two employees who had foreman qualifications, both being very experienced in the industry. The employer also left sufficient material at the site to shore a trench at the site, and he specifically instructed the employees to construct the shoring in the trench. The same employees had received the same instructions on prior jobs, and they had always obeyed the instructions and constructed the shoring. On this day, they did not construct the shoring before starting work in the trench, and OSHA cited the employer for failing to use shoring. The employer contested, and it was found that under the circumstances the employer could not be said to have known or had reason to know of the violation, because he had taken all precautions that a reasonably diligent person would have taken in the same circumstances. Reasonable diligence did not require his constant supervision of such experienced employees.[14]

[13] *California Stevedore and Ballast Co. v. OSHRC et al.*, 517 F.2d 986 (9th Cir. 1975).

[14] *Horne Plumbing and Heating Co. v. OSHRC et al.*, 528 F.2d 564 (5th Cir. 1976).

The act provides that any employer may be assessed a civil penalty of up to $1000 for *each day* during which an employer fails to correct a violation for which a citation has been issued within the period allowed for abatement. However, the period for abatement will not begin to run until the date of the final order of OSHRC in case of any contest proceedings initiated by the employer in good faith and not solely for delay or avoidance of penalities. Also, the merits of an earlier *uncontested* citation can be contested in a later proceeding on a contest of a citation for failure to abate the earlier alleged violation. Nevertheless, it is always best to contest an improper citation promptly, for even a citation with a very small proposed penalty can amount to a very large liability when a penalty of $1000 per day is imposed on an employer for failure to abate a condition set forth in a citation.

Illustrative Case

An employer on a construction site was cited for a number of minor, nonserious violations, with penalties of approximately $600. Several months later, the same worksite was reinspected, and when the same violations were found, OSHA cited the employer for failing to abate the first group of violations, imposing daily penalties from the date of the first citations to the date of the subsequent inspection totaling $31,744 which were subsequently substantially eliminated when contested before the OSHRC.[15]

INSPECTIONS

The primary responsibility of an inspector in conducting a inspection is to determine whether the employer is complying with the safety and health standards promulgated under the act and whether the employer is furnishing a place of employment free from recognized hazards prohibited by the general-duty clause. The act contains a general prohibition against giving advance notice of inspection except in limited circumstances. This prohibition is intended to avoid giving an employer the opportunity to make adjustments in an attempt to create a misleading impression of the safety conditions at an establishment.

The act authorizes inspectors to enter without delay at reasonable times places where work is performed by employees or an employer covered by the act and to conduct investigations during regular working hours and at other reasonable times within reasonable limits and in a reasonable manner. The act also authorizes the inspection of all pertinent conditions on the worksites, including structures, machines, apparatuses, devices, equipment, and materials therein, and to question privately any employer, owner, operator, agent, or employee. The time of inspection will usually be during normal working hours except in very special circumstances. Inspectors are instructed not to make any inspections during strikes or labor disputes except with the express approval of the area director.

15 *Beall Constr. Co.*, OSHRC Docket No. 557, 1 BNA OSHC 1559 (1974).

The act purports to give the Secretary of Labor and the inspectors almost unlimited powers to make investigations on the employer's private premises without search warrants. The Supreme Court has ruled that part of the act unconstitutional but has left open for future decisions what showing of "probable cause" OSHA must make to obtain a search warrant. OSHA has determined to seek consent from employers for all inspections and to seek warrants only when consent is expressly refused.

After the inspector presents credentials to the employer, the normal procedure is to conduct an opening conference. In the opening conference the inspector informs the employer that the purpose of the visit is to make an inspection to ascertain whether the employer is in compliance with the act. The inspector outlines the general terms and scope of the inspection, including any records or employee interviews that may be desired and physical inspection of the applicable worksites or workplaces. The inspector gives the employer copies of the laws, standards, regulations, or promotional materials which are applicable to the employer's business and informs the employer how to obtain additional copies of the appropriate materials. The employer is furnished with a copy of the complaint or complaints if the inspection is conducted on the basis of a complaint.

If the employer does not object to the inspection and ask for a warrant, the inspector will continue the opening conference by discussing the "walk-around" provisions of the act, which require that a representative of the employer and a representative of the employees accompany the inspector during the physical inspection of the workplace for the purpose of aiding in the inspection. The employer will then be asked to designate the employer representative. Ordinarily, the selection of the employer representative will cause no difficulty, since the representative could be owner, officer, manager, supervisor, or other employee of the company. If the employees are represented by a certified or recognized bargaining agent, the union ordinarily will be asked to designate the employee representative, who generally should be an employee of the establishment being inspected.

However, the courts have held that even when an inspector conducts an inspection without either an employer or an employee representative, the inspection is still valid unless the employer can show that the right to defend against any citation issued as a result of the inspection was prejudiced. In effect, the ruling is that OSHA will not be restrained because of technicalities even though such technicalities are clearly mandatory in the language of the act.

Illustrative Case

OSHA inspectors investigating a fatal fall arrived at the worksite for the purpose of inspecting scaffolding involved in the accident. No representative of the employer was on the premises, but the inspectors conducted an inspection of the premises after they had the building manager try to reach the employer by telephone. OSHRC held the inspection and resulting citation invalid because the employer was not afforded the opportunity to be present for the inspection. The reviewing court reinstated the citation on the ground that the employer was not shown to have been prejudiced in a defense of the citation. The court said that vacating the citation was too drastic a remedy for the violation of the employer's walk-around rights.[16]

During the first inspection the employer should always remain objective and should not be abusive or antagonistic to the inspector, which would tend to cause overinspection. An employer should never forcibly interfere with the conduct of an inspector. The act makes it a federal criminal offense forcibly to assault, resist, oppose, impede, intimidate, or interfere with employees of the Department of Labor while they are engaged in their official duty. In addition, the employer representative should duplicate the acts of the inspector, taking the same photographs, running the same tests as soon thereafter as possible, and making copious notes of everything that the inspector says or notes.

Follow-up inspections are usually conducted if any citation is issued in order to ensure the abatement requirements in such citations are enforced. These follow-up inspections are mandatory for serious, willful, or repeated violations and in imminent-danger situations. The primary purpose of a follow-up inspection is to determine if the hazard has been abated within the abatement period. Follow-up inspections will be held as soon as possible after the expiration of the abatement period.

CITATIONS

When an inspection reveals that the employer has violated the general-duty clause or one or more of the regulations, the Secretary of Labor through an authorized designee, the area director, will issue to the employer a citation and proposed penalty. Each citation will be in writing and must describe with particularity the nature of the violation, including reference to the provisions of the act, standard, rule, regulation, or order which have been violated. In addition, the citation must fix a reasonable time for the abatement of the violation. No citation may be issued after 6 months following the occurrence of any violation. This provision is a complete bar to a citation's being issued more than 6 months following any alleged violation.

Upon receipt of any citation under the act, the employer is required immediately to post the citation or a copy of it at or near the place where the alleged violation occurred. If because of the nature of the employer's operation it is impossible to post the citation at or near the place where the alleged violation occurred, the citation may be posted in a prominent place where it is readily observable by all affected employees. Each citation must remain posted until the violation has been abated or for 3 working days, whichever is later. If an employer files a notice of contest the citation must remain posted until the OSHRC issues a final order vacating the citation.

---

[16]*Marshall v. Western Waterproofing Co. et al.*, 560 F.2d 947 (8th Cir. 1977).

CONTEST OF CITATIONS

An employer who receives a citation becomes subject to innumerable risks whether or not the employer contests the citation and proposed penalty. If the employer does not contest the citation and attempts to abate, the employer can, at the discretion of the Department of Labor inspector, be fined additional daily penalties if the inspector believes that the employer has not abated according to the standards or regulations.

If the employer contests the citation and proposed penalties through the administrative procedure, the employer runs additional risks. An employer who desires to contest the amount of the penalty proposed in the citation is liable to daily penalties if the violation is not immediately abated. These penalties can become quite substantial, even at only $100 per day, since administrative procedures can take years before the OSHRC's final order is issued.

An employer who decides not to abate and contests the citation as well as the proposed penalty runs the risk that the area director will make a subjective decision that the contest is solely for delay or avoidance of the penalties, in which case the employer runs the risk of being assessed daily penalties.

After an employer has run the risks of contesting the citation through the administrative channels and the OSHRC has issued its order, the employer runs additional risks in appealing the order to the court of appeals. An employer who appeals the OSHRC's order continues to carry the burden of being assessed daily discretionary penalties by the Department of Labor. As a protection against the OSHRC's order to abate by the specified date, the employer must obtain from the court of appeals a stay of the OSHRC's order of abatement. An employer who is not granted a stay of the order for abatement must abate even though the employer may eventually win the appeal. In the latter case, the employer has no recourse to recover any expenses or losses incurred as a result of complying with the abatement order.

There are numerous other factors to consider when deciding whether or not to contest, including whether abatement is possible or feasible within either the time limits, or the methods prescribed in the citation; whether abatement will be so economically depressing over the long run as not to be a feasible alternative; whether the employer has a solid defense based on OSHA case law (which is discussed in depth below in the section "Defenses to a Citation"); whether the defense would be procedural or on the substance of the alleged violation; and whether the penalty is unreasonable.

Obviously, the employer must also weigh the costs of a contest against its advantage but must always keep in mind that a repeated, willful, or failure-to-abate citation can easily grow out of an innocuous citation which carried a penalty so small that the cost of a contest initially made a contest seem unwise. Also, the costs of abatement over the long run, not just the initial abatement cost, must be weighed against the costs of a contest.

Finally, in cases of a serious injury or death, the employer must weigh the possibility of a civil suit in determining whether or not to contest, for an uncontested citation may be admitted into evidence in a civil suit as an admission of an OSHA violation. As discussed below in greater depth in the section "Liability to Injured Employees," this may be evidence of negligence per se in a civil suit. On the other hand, if the likelihood of a civil suit is low and the likelihood of losing an OSHA contest is great, the employer must consider the risk of increasing visibility to a potential civil plaintiff by exercising the "right" to have OSHA prove the employer's guilt in a public trial, the record of which is readily accessible to the public at large.

An employer who wishes to contest a citation or proposed penalties before the OSHRC must initiate the contest procedure, and the rules for filing a notice of contest are very tricky to comply with. Within 15 working days (Monday through Friday, excluding federal holidays) from receipt of a citation and proposed penalty, an employer who wishes to contest must file with the area director of the OSHA a "notice of contest." It should be noted that, unlike the filing of pleadings with the OSHRC or with most courts in civil cases, filing of a notice of contest to OSHA is *not* complete simply with the act of mailing. Strictly construed, the notice must be *received* within 15 days to be timely. However, in practice, OSHA and the OSHRC appear to concede timeliness if the notice is mailed within the 15 days. In addition, there is some authority for the position that a timely oral notice of the contest is effective if it is followed up with something in writing confirming the employer's intention to contest.

The notice of contest may be a letter or a formal legal pleading which states which of the citations and proposed penalties the employer is contesting, or the notice of contest should state that the employer is contesting each and every citation and proposed penalty. If the employer fails to file the notice of contest, the citation and proposed penalty become the final order of the OSHRC and cannot be contested or reviewed by any agency or court.

However, there is now ample authority that if an employer filed a timely notice which did not on its face appear to contest the citation, the OSHRC has jurisdiction to receive evidence and rule on whether the employer intended to contest the citation, thus relieving the employer of the technical error. Obviously, better practice is to make clear what is being contested in the notice.

Illustrative Case

A small employer, a sole proprietorship, received a citation from OSHA and within the 15-day contest period wrote to OSHA "to notify you that I desire to contest the proposed penalty of $500.00 (five hundred dollars) levied against my firm.. . ." Several months later, he wrote to the OSHRC, stating that "I now realize that my first letter . . . did not meet all the requirements of the Commission as I did not state therein my reasons for contesting the penalty" and setting out his reasons why he thought abatement was impractical and unsafe. The OSHRC concluded that his second letter showed his intent to contest the citation as well as the amount of the penalty and granted a hearing on whether the employer had committed the violation alleged in the citation.[17]

The OSHRC has even decided that there may be justifiable reasons for an employer's failure to contest within 15 days a citation technically "received" by personnel of the employer more than 15 days before the notice of contest was mailed.

Illustrative Case

OSHA issued a citation to a construction employer but sent it to a supervisor on the construction site rather than to the corporate headquarters of the employer. When the representatives at the corporate office first learned of the citation, the 15-day contest period had expired. Nevertheless, it was found that the notice of contest filed thereafter was timely, because OSHA should have sent the citation to the corporate office in the first place, and the 15-day contest period did not begin until the corporate office had notice of the citation.[18]

By comparison, however, if a citation is sent to the proper office, the fact that it is misplaced is no excuse for filing a late notice of contest.

Once the employer has mailed the notice of contest to the area director, a quasi-legal proceeding is initiated. Within 7 days of the reciept of the notice of contest, the area director will file with the OSHRC the notice of contest and all citations. Within 20 days of the receipt of the notice of contest, the Secretary of Labor will file with the OSHRC a complaint against the employer. The employer will receive a copy of the complaint, as will any representative of employees who have filed with the OSHRC or OSHA a notice requesting to become a party to the contest proceedings.

The employer *must* file an answer within 15 calendar days after receipt of the complaint. The answer should contain the employer's reply to each of the allegations of the complaint to which the employer elects to respond, denying those allegations in the complaint which the employer intends to contest. Any allegation not denied is deemed to be admitted. The employer must serve each party with a copy of the answer and attach a certificate of service.

After the OSHRC has received the employer's notice of contest from the area director, it appoints an administrative law judge (formerly called a hearing examiner) to conduct the hearing. The judge has control over all proceedings, discovery, depositions, and production of documents in the case. The parties are notified by the judge of the time, place, and nature of the hearing, and the employer is required to post the notice of hearing if the affected employees are unrepresented. The hearing is conducted ac-

---

[17] *Turnbull Millwork Co.*, OSHRC Docket No. 7413, 3 BNA OSHC 1781 (1975).

[18] *Buckley & Co. v. Secretary of Labor*, 507 F.2d 78 3d Cir. (1975).

cording to the rules of evidence, and each party has the right to subpoena witnesses and produce relevant books, records, and documents.

During the hearing the Secretary of Labor has the burden of proof to sustain the allegations contained in the citation. At the hearing each party has the right to cross-examine witnesses and present evidence in its own behalf. The proceedings at the hearing are recorded, and the employer or any interested person may purchase a copy of the transcript. Within a reasonable time after the hearing and the submission of briefs, proposed findings of fact and conclusions of law, the judge will prepare his or her decision upoon the basis of the evidence received and will file the decision with the executive secretary of the OSHRC.

The judge's decision will become final unless the employer files a petition for discretionary review with the OSHRC not later than 25 days after receipt by the OSHRC of the judge's decision. The OSHRC does not have to review the report, and it will become the final order of the OSHRC at the end of 30 days, unless within the 30-day period a member of the OSHRC grants discretionary review.

If the OSHRC does not grant review, the employer or other party that receives an adverse order from it has the right to have the order reviewed by the court of appeals. The review by the court of appeals is limited to the questions of law or objections raised before the OSHRC. The court will not review questions of fact on which there is merely a dispute in the evidence.

DEFENSES TO A CITATION

The OSHRC and the courts have created a number of recognized defenses which employers may assert and prove in a contest proceeding. Those discussed here include matters on which the employer has the burden of proof, such as impossibility of compliance; matters on which OSHA has the burden of proof but which employers may want to raise and present evidence thereon, such as infeasibility of compliance; and matters on which the employer has not only the burden of proof but also the obligation to raise the defense at the first available opportunity or it will be considered waived, such as that employee conduct was an "isolated occurrence" of disobedience of a company rule.

Perhaps the first defense that should be examined in any case is whether the standard applies to the alleged hazard and the circumstances in which the hazard is found. In addition to the cases in which a standard is found to be per se unreasonable and therefore inapplicable or in which one standard prevails over a more general standard, which have been previously discussed, an employer may defend on the ground that the standard was not intended to apply to the circumstances at the worksite, relying either on the language of the standard or on the history of its adoption by OSHA or other standard-making bodies, or both.

A roofing contractor was cited for violating the construction standard, Section 1926.500(d)(1), which requires guardrails around the edges of "open-sided floors." The employer contested on the ground that its worksite was a flat roof, which was functionally different from a floor, and that its workers were specially trained regarding the hazards of the open sides of the roofs while doing roofing work. Relying on these arguments as well as the history of the adoption of this standard by the private American National Standards Institute and the specific language of the regulation, the reviewing court found that this regulation did not apply at all to flat roofs.[19]

Another defense often cited by the OSHRC is that the conduct of the employee who committed the violation was so unforeseeable and idiosyncratic that the employer could not have been expected to guard against it.

Illustrative Case

An employer was in the business of processing railroad ties. The ordinary method in which it unloaded truckloads of the ties held together by large steel bands was to move a forklift under a package of the ties and then cut the band. During this process, which was repeated several times until the truck was empty, all other employees remained a safe distance away. On one particular day, however, an employee whose duties did not require him to be in the unloading area unaccountably walked up to the truck and cut one of the steel bands, fatally injuring himself when the ties fell on him. The reviewing court vacated an OSHA citation issued to the employer on the ground that this conduct was entirely unforeseeable and held that the fact that the deceased employee had not been trained in the unloading procedure was irrelevant, since he was not expected or instructed to take in the unloading.[20]

A similar defense is that an employee who committed a violation did so by disobeying an express company policy which had been communicated to all employees. However, an employer relying on this defense must be careful to prove that all employees had been thoroughly trained in this policy and that the safety policies were enforced with appropriate disciplinary measures.

Illustrative Case

An electrical contractor was cited for a violation caused by an action taken by one of the contractor's employees, a foreman, which was in violation of an OSHA standard. The employer defended on the ground that the employee had been trained in his work and was experienced enough to know not to do what he had done in violation of OSHA standards. The citation was upheld, and the defense rejected, because no specific company work rule was proven, the specific nature of the training was not proven, and the specific nature of the enforcement of work rules not proven.[21]

[19] *Diamond Roofing Co. v. OSHRC at el.*, 528 F.2d 645 (5th Circ. 1976).

[20] *Brennan v. OSHRC and Republic Creosoting Co.*, 501 F.2d 1196 (7th Cir. 1974).

[21] *Ocean Electric Corp.*, OSHRC Docket No. 5811, 3 BNA OSHC 1705 (1975).

A defense which is generally applicable only to alleged violations of noise standards, the general-duty clause, and personal protective equipment standards is the lack of a feasible means of abatement.

Illustrative Case

An employer was cited for failure to use engineering controls to correct a noise level above the permissible limits of the standard. The employees exposed wore custom-fitted ear protectors which reduced the noise level far below the maximum permissible levels, and the evidence showed that the engineering controls which were technologically possible to install would cost $30,000. It was held by the reviewing court that the OSHRC must determine whether or not the benefits to be gained from installing the engineering controls, if any, outweighed the $30,000 cost in determining whether engineering controls were feasible.[22]

As discussed previously, OSHA has the burden of proving a feasible means of abatement, but employers usually must defend on this ground as well, because OSHA almost always will present some evidence of feasibility, which will sustain the citation if the employer does not attack OSHA's evidence with the employer's evidence.

Illustrative Case

An employer engaged in laying planks to make up a flat roof was cited for failing to use tied-off safety belts in this operation. When the employer contested, OSHA presented testimony that the employees could have worn safety belts tied off to a lifeline attached to the walls of the building or a structure bolted to the wall. The employer presented testimony that the constant crisscross movement of the employees in the performance of the work would render the lifelines a great hindrance and danger because of the entanglements which would result. The OSHRC held that the use of safety belts was not shown to be feasible, particularly in light of the fact that OSHA's witness had no expertise in the industry or activity involved and had never been on this particular roof.[23]

A related defense, applicable to any type of violation, is that abatement or compliance with the terms of the standard is impossible.

Illustrative Case

An employer constructing a log deck for a paper mill was cited for failure to use safety belts on employees working on structural framing above water. Upon evidence that the only employee exposed was working at the very top of an A-frame structure, it was held that the citation was invalid, because compliance with the standard's requirement that the safety belts be tied off overhead was impossible in these circumstances.[24]

A similar defense is that compliance with the standard cited would expose employees to a "greater hazard" than that to which they were exposed without compliance with the standard.

[22] *Turner Co. v. Secretary of Labor et al.*, 561 F.2d 82 (7th Cir. 1977).

[23] *M.K. Binkley Constr. Co.*, OSHRC Docket No. 12876, 5 BNA OSHC 1411 (1977).

[24] *Isaacson Structural Steel Co.*, OSHRC Docket No. 1731, 3 BNA OSHC 1138 (1975).

Illustrative Case

An employer was cited for lack of safety belts on ironworkers who were connecting large steel beams suspended from a crane. Upon evidence that it would be more dangerous to restrict the freedom of movement of the workers to escape a wayward-swinging steel beam, the citation was vacated.[25]

However, to prove this defense, an employer must also prove that a variance from the standard had been requested or that the variance procedure was inappropriate and that there were no alternative means or methods of protection which the employer failed to afford the worker.

Employers on multiemployer worksite may defend a citation on the ground that even though their employees are exposed to a violation, they did not create or cause the violation, they do not control the site of the violation in such a manner as to have the power to abate the violation, and they afforded their employees whatever alternative methods or means of protection were available, or if none were available, that they took all possible steps to assure that the responsible employer abated the violation.

Illustrative Case

A subcontractor on a construction site was cited for improperly constructed and guarded stairwells. He contested and proved that neither was he responsible for the construction of the stairwells nor was it possible to correct the conditions, since he employed only union electricians and correction work would be the work of other trades. The subcontractor further proved that he had complained repeatedly to the general contractor to correct the conditions and had scheduled most of the work in other buildings on the site while he attempted to get the general contractor to abate. The citation was vacated.[26]

EMPLOYEE DISCRIMINATION

OSHA has specific provisions forbidding employers to discriminate in any way against their employees because of such employees' filing a complaint, instituting a proceeding, or testifying in any proceeding "under or related to the Act," or because such employees have exercised any other right afforded by the act. If any employees are discriminated against, they may file a complaint with the Department of Labor, as in a case of race, sex, or age discrimination, and the government will file a suit in their behalf seeking their reinstatement and payment of back wages, plus interest.

Under the interpretations of the courts, the actions protected by this provision of the act include making a complaint to a federal or state OSHA official about a safety matter, making a safety complaint directly to the employer, contesting the abatement times proposed by OSHA in a citation, testifying in a contested citation hearing, talking to OSHA officials, and accompanying an inspection.

[25] *Industrial Steel Erectors, Inc.*, OSHRC Docket No. 703, 1 BNA OSHC 1497 (1974).
[26] *Howard P. Foley Co.*, OSHC Docket NO. 14634, 5 BNA OSHC 1071 (1976).

However, there is some authority that an employee has no right guaranteed by OSHA to refuse to work in allegedly dangerous conditions. The employee's is to get in touch with OSHA and ask for an immediate, or imminent-danger, inspection. There is also authority than an employee accompanying an inspector on an inspection has no right to be paid for this time, although OSHA takes a contrary view and at the date of publication is fighting this issue in cases in the courts.

It should be noted that the employee cannot file a suit under the act's antidiscrimination provision (the suit must be filed by the Department of Labor), and the government must prove that the employee's discharge or harassment, or other discriminatory treatment was directly related to a "protected activity." Therefore, even if an employee was engaged in protected activity, if the discharge was for other, proper job-related reasons, the employer will not be found in violation of the act. However, overlapping jurisdiction of the National Labor Relations Act and the Occupational Safety and Health Act is recognized in this area. Thus, employees who walk off an allegedly unsafe jobsite may not be protected by OSHA, but it may be an unfair labor practice under the NLRA to fire employees engaged in this concerted activity. Also, on the other side of the jurisdictional overlap, it has been found that the failure of an arbitrator to uphold an unfair-labor-practice charge or grievance growing out of a safety complaint is no bar to a discrimination complaint under OSHA for the same conduct.

LIABILITY TO INJURED EMPLOYEES

One of the extreme liabilities of the act can be the cost of suits brought by injured employees against third parties who are responsible for the injury. Although most workman's compensation laws do not permit personal-injury suits by injured employees, directly against their employer, these laws have no prohibition against employees' suits against other parties who are solely or jointly responsible for the injury. Therefore, an injured employee of a construction subcontractor could file suit against a general contractor, an architect, or other subcontractors who were solely or jointly responsible for the injury. The regulations for construction provide that the prime contractor will not be relieved of overall responsibility for compliance with the safety standards for all work performed under the general contract. Under court decisions interpreting the act, the general contractor and subcontractors performing the affected portion of the work are deemed to have a joint responsibility for compliance with the provisions of the act.

In the event that a subcontractor's employee is injured, the injured employee would be entitled to file suit for personal injuries against the general contractor, architect or other subcontractor as third parties responsible for the injury. An injured employee could contend in such a suit that a violation of one of the standards or a violation of the general-duty clause is per se negligence, fixing liability as a matter of law upon the parties responsible. Negligence is normally a question of fact of whether the party who caused the injury did what a reasonable person would have done in the same or similar circumstances. However, if a governmental regulation or law has been broken, the law implies that the culpable party is negligent as a matter of law, without resorting to the factual question of negligence. Practically all that is left for the jury to determine in such a case is the amount of damages.

To make matters worse, a subcontractor who has signed a "hold-harmless clause" may be responsible to the general contractor for any liability to the injured employee and for the general contractor's attorney's fees as well. In other words, under the hold-harmless clause the subcontractor would have to assume the ultimate cost and responsibility of an employee's suit against the general contractor. The subcontractor would be in the position of having to pay workman's compensation to the employee and then would have to pay under the hold-harmless clause any judgments incurred by the general contractor.

Thus, unless an employer is adequately insured and contractually protected as well as possible from employee damage suits, the employer must beware of OSHA violations and, most particularly, must contest unwarranted violations, which can become evidence of negligence per se if they go uncontested.

TABLE OF CASES

No. 76 (1962); *Windowcleaners Local 139,* 126 NLRB No. 8 (1960), 259, 265

Diamond Roofing Co. v. OSHRC et al. 538 F.2d 645 (5th Cir. 1976), 414

Don Burgess Constr. Corp., d/b/a Burgess Constr., 227 NLRB No. 119 (1977), 299

Dorchy v. Kan., 272 U.S. 306 (1926), 39

Dry Color Mfrs. Ass'n, Inc. v. Department of Labor et al., 486 F.2d 99 (3d Cir. 1973), 401

Eazor Express, Inc. v. IBT, 357 F.Supp. 158 (W.D. Pa. 1973), 43

Edward E. Schultz, d/b/a Schultz Painting & Decorating, 202 NLRB No. 23 (1973), 297

Electrical Workers Local 501 v. NLRB, 566 F.2d 348 (D.C. Cir. 1977), 76

Employing Plasterers Ass'n v. Journeymen Plasterers Protective Benevolent Soc'y, 186 F.Supp. 91 (N.D. Ill. 1960), 261

Emporium Capwell Co. v. Western Community Addition Organ., 420 U.S. 50 (1975), 20, 47

Ernst Steel Corp., 217 NLRB No. 179 (1975), 155

Evening News Ass'n, 154 NLRB No. 121 (1965), 108

Fibreboard Paper Products Corp. v. NLRB, 379 U.S. 203 (1964), 127

Florida Peach Growers Ass'n, Inc. v. Brennan et al., 489 F.2d 120 (5th Cir. 1974), 401

Florida Power & Light Co. v. Electrical Workers Local 641, 417 U.S. 790 (1974), 34

Floyd Auten et al. v. Local 11, International Bhd. of Electrical Workers et al., 51 LC Par. 19,552 (S.D. Cal. 1965), 236

Framulau Corp. v. Dembling, 360 F.Supp. 806 (E.D. Pa. 1973), 355

GAF Corp., Case No. W6259-003-77 (Maryland Dept. of Licensing and Regulation, Hearing Examiner Dec. Oct. 26, 1977), 400

Gateway Coal Co. v. Mineworkers, 414 U.S. 368 (1974), 48

Gerace Constr., Inc., 193 NLRB No. 91 (1971), 295

Glaziers Local 558 v. NLRB, 408 F.2d 197 (1969), 62

Granny Goose Foods, Inc. v. Teamsters, 415 U.S. 423 (1974), 52

H.B. Zachry Co. v. United States, 344 F.2d 352 (Ct. Cl. 1965), 346

Harnischfeger Corp. v. Sheet Metal Workers Int'l Ass'n & Local 94, 436 F.2d 351 (6th Cir. 1970), 91

Hershey Foods Corp., 208 NLRB No. 70 (1974); *Packing House Employees & Warehousemen's Local 616,* 203 NLRB No. 113 (1973), 292

Hod Carriers Union (Calumet Contractors Ass'n), 133 NLRB No. 57 (1961), 84

Hooker Chemical & Plastics Corp., 224 NLRB No. 203 (1976), 159

Horne Plumbing and Heating Co. v. OSHRC et al., 528 F.2d 564 (5th Cir. 1976), 406

Howard P. Foley Co., OSHC Docket No. 14634, 5 BNA OSHC 1071 (1976), 416

IBEW Local 3 (Gessin Electrical Contractors), 224 NLRB No. 195 (1976), 80

IBEW Local 25 (S. & M. Electric Co.), 223 NLRB No. 223 (1976), 7

IBEW Local 437 (National Electrical Contractors Ass'n), 180 NLRB No. 32 (1969), 77

IBEW Local 441 (Jones & Jones, Inc.), 158 NLRB No. 57 (1976), 57

IBEW Local 441 (Robbins Communications), 222 NLRB No. 24 (1976), 64

IBEW Local 592, 223 NLRB No. 139 (1976), 6

Industrial Steel Erectors, Inc., OSHRC Docket No. 703, 1 BNA OSHC 1497 (1974), 415

Inland Steel Co. v. NLRB, 170 F.2d 247 (7th Cir. 1948), 232

International Brotherhood of Boilermakers, Iron Ship Builders, Blacksmiths, Forgers, and Helpers (Bigge Drayage Co.), 197 NLRB No. 34 (1972), 293

International Brotherhood of Electrical Workers Local 68, AFL-CIO v. NLRB, 178 NLRB No. 108, aff'd, 448 F.2d 1127, 1237 (D.C. Cir. 1971), 269

International Union of Operating Engineers, Local 701 (Pacific Northwest Chapter of Assoc. Builders & Contractors, Inc.), 239 NLRB No. 43 (1978), 300

Interstate Constr. Co. v. IBEW Local 226, 229 NLRB No. 37 (1977), 107

Ironworkers Local 21 (Weder Constr. Co.), 233 NLRB No. 158 (1978), 89

Ironworkers Local 433 (AGC of California), 228 NLRB No. 181 (1977), 7

Ironworkers Local 597 v. Linbeck Constr. Co., 434 U.S. 955 (1977), 66

SUBJECT INDEX